2015

CHILDREN'S WRITER'S & ILLUSTRATOR'S MARKET

includes a 1-year online subscription to **Children's Writer's & Illustrator's Market** on

Where & How to Sell What You Write

THE ULTIMATE MARKET RESEARCH TOOL FOR WRITERS

To register your *2015 Children's Writer's & Illustrator's Market* book and **start your 1-year online genre-only subscription**, scratch off the block below to reveal your activation code, then go to www.WritersMarket.com. Find the box that says "Have an Activation Code?" then click on "Sign Up Now" and enter your contact information and activation code. It's that easy!

UPDATED MARKET LISTINGS FOR YOUR INTEREST AREA
EASY-TO-USE SEARCHABLE DATABASE • RECORD-KEEPING TOOLS
PROFESSIONAL TIPS & ADVICE • INDUSTRY NEWS

Your purchase of *Children's Writer's & Illustrator's Market* gives you access to updated listings related to this genre of writing (valid through 12/31/15). For just $9.99, you can upgrade your subscription and get access to listings from all of our best-selling Market Books. Visit **www.WritersMarket.com** for more information.

WritersMarket.com
Where & How to Sell What You Write

Activate your WritersMarket.com subscription to get instant access to:

- **UPDATED LISTINGS IN YOUR WRITING GENRE:** Find additional listings that didn't make it into the book, updated contact information, and more. WritersMarket.com provides the most comprehensive database of verified markets available anywhere.

- **EASY-TO-USE SEARCHABLE DATABASE:** Looking for a specific magazine or book publisher? Just type in its name. Or widen your prospects with the Advanced Search. You can also search for listings that have been recently updated!

- **PERSONALIZED TOOLS:** Store your best-bet markets, and use our popular recording-keeping tools to track your submissions. Plus, get new and updated market listings, query reminders, and more—every time you log in!

- **PROFESSIONAL TIPS & ADVICE:** From pay-rate charts to sample query letters, and from how-to articles to Q&A's with literary agents, we have the resources writers need.

27TH ANNUAL EDITION

2015

CHILDREN'S WRITER'S & ILLUSTRATOR'S MARKET

Chuck Sambuchino, Editor

Harold Underdown, Contributing Editor

WRITER'S DIGEST
BOOKS

WritersDigest.com
Cincinnati, Ohio

Publisher & Editorial Director, Writing Community: Phil Sexton

Writer's Market website: www.writersmarket.com
Writer's Digest website: www.writersdigest.com
Writer's Digest Bookstore: www.writersdigestshop.com
Guide to Literary Agents Blog: www.guidetoliteraryagents.com/blog

Distributed in Canada by Fraser Direct
100 Armstrong Avenue
Georgetown, Ontario, Canada L7G 5S4
Tel: (905) 877-4411

Distributed in the U.K. and Europe by F+W Media International
Brunel House, Newton Abbot, Devon, TQ12 4PU, England
Tel: (+44) 1626-323200, Fax: (+44) 1626-323319
E-mail: postmaster@davidandcharles.co.uk

Distributed in Australia by Capricorn Link
P.O. Box 704, Windsor, NSW 2756 Australia
Tel: (02) 4577-3555

ISSN: 0897-9790
ISBN-13: 978-1-59963-846-1

Attention Booksellers: This is an annual directory of F+W Media, Inc. Return deadline for this edition is December 31, 2015.

Edited by: Chuck Sambuchino
Cover designed by: Claudean Wheeler
Interior designed by: Claudean Wheeler
Page layout by: Geoff Raker
Production coordinated by: Greg Nock and Debbie Thomas

CONTENTS

FROM THE EDITOR 1

GETTING STARTED

HOW TO USE *CWIM* 2

QUICK TIPS FOR WRITERS & ILLUSTRATORS 6

BEFORE YOUR FIRST SALE 9

RUNNING YOUR BUSINESS 16

ARTICLES

MIDDLE GRADE VS. YOUNG ADULT
    by Marie Lamba 26

SELL YOUR PICTURE BOOK
    by Lara Perkins 30

SERIES CHARACTERS FOR YOUNG READERS
    by Jacqueline Mitchard 34

WRITING ABOUT SENSITIVE TOPICS
    by Kerrie Flanagan 39

CRAFTING A QUERY
    by Kara Gebhart Uhl 46

WRITING FOR BOYS (AND OTHER "RELUCTANT READERS")
    by Carmela A. Martino 55

TALKING CRAFT IN YOUNG ADULT
    by Ricki Schultz 65

YOUR WEB PRESENCE
    by Lee Wind 75

NOTHING BUT THE TRUTH: WRITING & SELLING NONFICTION
    by Suzanne Morgan Williams & Jenny MacKay 81

MAKE THEM CARE ABOUT CHARACTER
    by Mary Kole 88

INTERVIEWS

KATHY APPELT
by Michele Corriel 93

LOREN LONG
by Kara Gebhart Uhl 97

JAMES DASHNER
by Donna Gambale Kuzma 104

RED FOX ROUNDUP
by Kara Gebhart Uhl 109

LAUREN DESTEFANO
by Ricki Schultz 123

JANE YOLEN
by Nancy Parish 128

SHERRI DUSKEY RINKER
by Kara Gebhart Uhl 133

ANNIE BARROWS
by Kara Gebhart Uhl 140

CINDA WILLIAMS CHIMA
by Victoria A. Selvaggio 148

DEBBIE DADEY
by Kerrie Flanagan 156

LAURA RESAU
by Kerrie Flanagan 161

FIRST BOOKS: DEBUT AUTHORS
by Chuck Sambuchino 168

DEBUT ILLUSTRATORS
by Jodell Sadler 182

RESOURCES

NEW AGENT SPOTLIGHTS
by Chuck Sambuchino 193

GLOSSARY OF INDUSTRY TERMS 196

MARKETS AND MORE

BOOK PUBLISHERS 202

CANADIAN & INTERNATIONAL BOOK PUBLISHERS...........................253

MAGAZINES..265

AGENTS & ART REPS..295

CLUBS & ORGANIZATIONS...347

CONFERENCES & WORKSHOPS...355

CONTESTS, AWARDS & GRANTS..379

INDEXES

SUBJECT INDEX..407

EDITOR AND AGENT NAMES INDEX..420

AGE-LEVEL INDEX 429

PHOTOGRAPHY INDEX 431

ILLUSTRATION INDEX..433

GENERAL INDEX 435

PHOTO: Al Parrish

FROM THE EDITOR

As I write this editor's letter, my daughter just passed 18 months of age. And every time she walks over to me with a book in her hand, as if begging me to read to her, I count my blessings and fulfill her request. There is something extraordinarily magical about reading to your children. Isn't that why we want to write and illustrate for kids—to continue that magic? Creating books for the young is an honorable and wonderful thing.

Mushy parent stuff aside, welcome to the 27th annual editon of the *Children's Writer's & Illustrator's Market*. The big news this year is that Harold Underdown, editor of the fantastic website The Purple Crown, has come onboard as a contributing editor. Between he and I, we'll show you oodles of markets for your work, no matter if you're creating content for readers of picture books, early readers, middle grade, young adult or magazines.

For instance, this year's literary agent listings section is bigger than ever. As fewer book publishers welcome direct, unsolicited submissions from writers, getting an agent provides an avenue to get your stuff read by editors everywhere. Besides the agent listings, we've got plenty of publishers, international publishers, contests, conferences and more for you to enjoy. And, of course, check out all our interviews—especially our all-new "Debut Illustrators" article, where nine first-time illustrators explain their path to success.

Please stay in touch with me at guidetoliteraryagents.com/blog and on Twitter (@chucksambuchino). I love hearing feedback and success stories. (And don't forget to download your free supplemental webinar at www.writersmarket.com/cwim15-webinar.)

Chuck Sambuchino
literaryagent@fwmedia.com; chucksambuchino.com
Editor, *Guide to Literary Agents* / *Children's Writer's & Illustrator's Market*
Author, *How to Survive a Garden Gnome Attack* (2010); *Red Dog* / *Blue Dog* (2012); *Create Your Writer Platform* (2012)

HOW TO USE
CWIM

As a writer, illustrator or photographer first picking up *Children's Writer's & Illustrator's Market*, you may not know quite how to start using the book. Your impulse may be to flip through the book and quickly make a mailing list, then submit to everyone in hopes that someone will take interest in your work. Well, there's more to it. Finding the right market takes time and research. The more you know about a market that interests you, the better chance you have of getting work accepted. We've made your job a little easier by putting a wealth of information at your fingertips. Besides providing listings, this directory includes a number of tools to help you determine which markets are the best ones for your work. By using these tools, as well as researching on your own, you raise your odds of being published.

USING THE INDEXES

This book lists hundreds of potential buyers of freelance material. To learn which companies want the type of material you're interested in submitting, start with the indexes.

Editor and Agent Names Index

This index lists book and magazine editors and art directors as well as agents and art reps, indicating the companies they work for. Use this index to find company and contact information for individual publishing professionals.

Age-Level Index

Age groups are broken down into these categories in the Age-Level Index:

- **PICTURE BOOKS OR PICTURE-ORIENTED MATERIAL** are written and illustrated for preschoolers to 8-year-olds.

- **YOUNG READERS** are for 5- to 8-year-olds.
- **MIDDLE READERS** are for 9- to 11-year-olds.
- **YOUNG ADULT** is for ages 12 and up.

Age breakdowns may vary slightly from publisher to publisher, but using them as general guidelines will help you target appropriate markets. For example, if you've written an article about trends in teen fashion, check the Magazines Age-Level Index under the Young Adult subheading. Using this list, you'll quickly find the listings for young adult magazines.

Subject Index

But let's narrow the search further. Take your list of young adult magazines, turn to the Subject Index, and find the Fashion subheading. Then highlight the names that appear on both lists (Young Adult and Fashion). Now you have a smaller list of all the magazines that would be interested in your teen fashion article. Read through those listings and decide which ones sound best for your work.

Illustrators and photographers can use the Subject Index as well. If you specialize in painting animals, for instance, consider sending samples to book and magazine publishers listed under Animals and, perhaps, Nature/Environment. Because illustrators can simply send general examples of their style to art directors to keep on file, the indexes may be more helpful to artists sending manuscript/illustration packages who need to search for a specific subject. Always read the listings for the potential markets to see the type of work art directors prefer and what type of samples they'll keep on file, and obtain art or photo guidelines if they're available online.

Photography Index

In this index, you'll find lists of book and magazine publishers that buy photos from free-lancers. Refer to the list and read the listings for companies' specific photography needs. Obtain photo guidelines if they're offered online.

USING THE LISTINGS

Many listings begin with symbols. Refer to the pull-out bookmark (shown later in this article).

Many listings indicate whether submission guidelines are indeed available. If a publisher you're interested in offers guidelines, get them and read them. The same is true with catalogs. Sending for and reading catalogs or browsing them online gives you a better idea of whether your work would fit in with the books a publisher produces. (You should also look at a few of the books in the catalog at a library or bookstore to get a feel for the publisher's material.)

➕ market new to this edition

Ⓐ market accepts agented submissions only

◍ award-winning market

◍ Canadian market

◓ market located outside of the U.S. and Canada

◐ online opportunity

◒ comment from the editor of *Children's Writer's & Illustrator's Market*

◔ publisher producing educational material

◒ book packager/producer

ms, mss manuscript(s)

SCBWI Society of Children's Book Writers and Illustrators

SASE self-addressed, stamped envelope

IRC International Reply Coupon, for use in countries other than your own

b&w black & white (photo)

(For definitions of unfamiliar words and expressions relating to writing, illustration and publishing, see the Glossary.)

Especially for artists & photographers

Along with information for writers, listings provide information for illustrators and photographers. Illustrators will find numerous markets that maintain files of samples for possible future assignments. If you're both a writer and an illustrator, look for markets that accept manuscript/illustration packages and read the information offered under the **Illustration** subhead within the listings.

If you're a photographer, after consulting the Photography Index, read the information under the **Photography** subhead within listings to see what format buyers prefer. For example, some want the highest resolution .jpg available of an image. Note the type of photos a buyer wants to purchase and the procedures for submitting. It's not uncommon for a market to want a résumé and promotional literature, as well as sample URLS linking to previous work. Listings also note whether model releases and/or captions are required.

⊕ MERIT PRESS

A DIVISION OF ADAMS MEDIA (PART OF F+W MEDIA), 57 LITTLEFIELD ST, AVON, MA 02322. (508)427-7100. **E-MAIL:** MERITPRESS@FWMEDIA.COM. **WEBSITE:** WWW.AD AMSMEDIA.COM/MERIT-PRESS-BOOKS. **CONTACT:** JACQUELYN MITCHARD, EDITOR-IN-CHIEF.

○ Focuses on contemporary YA, usually based in reality.

FICTION "Natural is good; a little bit of supernatural (as in, perhaps foreseeing the future) is okay, too. Normal is great (at least until something happens) but not paranormal. What we are not seeking right now is tryphids, blood drinkers, flesh eaters and even yetis (much though we love them)."

HOW TO CONTACT "We do accept direct submissions as well as submissions from literary agents. We don't accept submissions in hard copy. Send full or partial manuscripts and queries to meritpress@fwmedia.com."

TIPS "I want to publish the next *Carrie, The Book Thief, National Velvet, Tuck Everlasting, Mr. and Mrs. Bo Jo Jones,* and *The Outsiders.* These will be the classics for a new generation, and they're being written right now. Since suspense (noir or pastel, comic or macabre) is my love, I hope I have a sense for finding those stories. As it turns out, a big part of my vocation, at this point in my career, is the desire to discover and nurture great new writers, and to put great books in the hands of great readers."

ADDRESSES AND WEBSITES

SPECIFIC CONTACT NAMES

INFO ON WHAT A PUBLISHER HANDLES

SUBMISSION TIPS

QUICK TIPS FOR WRITERS & ILLUSTRATORS

If you're new to the world of children's publishing, buying *Children's Writer's & Illustrator's Market* may have been one of the first steps in your journey to publication. What follows is a list of suggestions and resources that can help make that journey a smooth and swift one:

1. MAKE THE MOST OF *CHILDREN'S WRITER'S & ILLUSTRATOR'S MARKET.* Be sure to take advantage of the articles and interviews in the book. The insights of the authors, illustrators, editors and agents we've interviewed will inform and inspire you.

2. JOIN THE SOCIETY OF CHILDREN'S BOOK WRITERS AND ILLUSTRATORS. SCBWI, more than 22,000 members strong, is an organization for both beginners and professionals interested in writing and illustrating for children, with more than 70 active regional chapters worldwide. It offers members a slew of information and support through publications, a website, and a host of Regional Advisors overseeing chapters in almost every state in the U.S. and a growing number of locations around the globe. SCBWI puts on a number of conferences, workshops, and events on the regional and national levels (many listed in the Conferences & Workshops section of this book). For more information, visit scbwi.org.

3. READ NEWSLETTERS. Newsletters, such as *Children's Book Insider, Children's Writer* and the *SCBWI Bulletin,* offer updates and new information about publishers on a timely basis and are relatively inexpensive. Many local chapters of SCBWI offer regional newsletters as well.

4. READ TRADE AND REVIEW PUBLICATIONS. Magazines like *Publishers Weekly* (which offers two special issues each year devoted to children's publishing and is available on newsstands as well as through a digital subscription) offer news, articles, reviews of newly published titles and ads featuring upcoming and current releases. Referring to them will help you get a feel for what's happening in children's publishing.

5. READ GUIDELINES. Most publishers and magazines offer writers' and artists' guidelines that provide detailed information on needs and submission requirements, and some magazines offer theme lists for upcoming issues. Many publishers and magazines state the availability of guidelines within their listings. You'll often find submission information on publishers' and magazines' websites.

6. LOOK AT PUBLISHERS' CATALOGS. Perusing publishers' catalogs can give you a feel for their line of books and help you decide where your work might fit in. If catalogs are available (often stated within listings), visit publishers' websites, which often contain their full catalogs. You can also ask librarians to look at catalogs they have on hand. You can even search Amazon.com by publisher and year. (Click on "book search" then "publisher, date" and plug in, for example, "Lee & Low" under "publisher" and "2014" under year. You'll get a list of Lee & Low titles published in 2013, which you can peruse.)

7. VISIT BOOKSTORES. It's not only informative to spend time in bookstores—it's fun, too! Frequently visit the children's section of your local bookstore (whether a chain or an independent) to see the latest from a variety of publishers and the most current issues of children's magazines. Look for books in the genre you're writing or with illustrations similar in style to yours, and spend some time studying them. It's also wise to get to know your local booksellers; they can tell you what's new in the store and provide insight into what kids and adults are buying.

8. READ, READ, READ! While you're at that bookstore, pick up a few things, or keep a list of the books that interest you and check them out of your library. Read and study the latest releases, the award winners and the classics. You'll learn from other writers, get ideas and get a feel for what's being published. Think about what works and doesn't work in a story. Pay attention to how plots are constructed and how characters are developed, or the rhythm and pacing of picture book text. It's certainly enjoyable research!

9. TAKE ADVANTAGE OF INTERNET RESOURCES. There are innumerable sources of information available online about writing for children (and anything else you could possibly think of). It's also a great resource for getting (and staying) in touch with other writers and illustrators through listservs, blogs, social networking sites and e-mail, and it can serve as a vehicle for self-promotion.

10. CONSIDER ATTENDING A CONFERENCE. If time and finances allow, attending a conference is a great way to meet peers and network with professionals in the field of children's publishing. As mentioned earlier, SCBWI offers conferences in various locations year round. (See scbwi.org and click on "Events" for a full conference calendar.) General writers' conferences often offer specialized sessions just for those interested in children's writing. Many conferences offer optional manuscript and portfolio critiques as well, giving you a chance for feedback from seasoned professionals. See the Conferences section of this book for information on conferences.

11. NETWORK, NETWORK, NETWORK! Don't work in a vacuum. You can meet other writers and illustrators through a number of the things listed earlier—SCBWI, conferences, online. Attend local meetings for writers and illustrators whenever you can. Befriend other writers in your area (SCBWI offers members a roster broken down by state)—share guidelines, share subscriptions, be conference buddies and roommates, join a critique group or writing group, exchange information and offer support. Get online—sign on to listservs, post on message boards and blogs, visit social networking sites and chatrooms. Exchange addresses, phone numbers and e-mail addresses with writers or illustrators you meet at events. And at conferences, don't be afraid to talk to people, ask strangers to join you for lunch, approach speakers and introduce yourself, or chat in elevators and hallways.

12. PERFECT YOUR CRAFT AND DON'T SUBMIT UNTIL YOUR WORK IS ITS BEST. It's often been said that a writer should try to write every day. Great manuscripts don't happen overnight; there's time, research and revision involved. As you visit bookstores and study what others have written and illustrated, really step back and look at your own work and ask yourself—honestly—*How does my work measure up? Is it ready for editors or art directors to see?* If it's not, keep working. Join a critique group or get a professional manuscript or portfolio critique.

13. BE PATIENT, LEARN FROM REJECTION, AND DON'T GIVE UP! Thousands of manuscripts land on editors' desks; thousands of illustration samples line art directors' file drawers. There are so many factors that come into play when evaluating submissions. Keep in mind that you might not hear back from publishers promptly. Persistence and patience are important qualities in writers and illustrators working toward publication. Keep at it—it will come. It can take a while, but when you get that first book contract or first assignment, you'll know it was worth the wait. (For proof, read the "First Books" article later in this book!)

BEFORE YOUR FIRST SALE

If you're just beginning to pursue your career as a children's book writer or illustrator, it's important to learn the proper procedures, formats and protocol for the publishing industry. This article outlines the basics you need to know before you submit your work to a market.

FINDING THE BEST MARKETS FOR YOUR WORK

Researching markets thoroughly is a basic element of submitting your work successfully. Editors and art directors hate to receive inappropriate submissions; handling them wastes a lot of their time, not to mention your time and money, and they are the main reason some publishers have chosen not to accept material over the transom. By randomly sending out material without knowing a company's needs, you're sure to meet with rejection.

If you're interested in submitting to a particular magazine, see if it's available in your local library or bookstore, or read past articles online. For a book publisher, obtain a book catalog and check a library or bookstore for titles produced by that publisher. Most publishers and magazines have websites that include catalogs or sample articles (websites are given within the listings). Studying such materials carefully will better acquaint you with a publisher's or magazine's writing, illustration and photography styles and formats.

Many of the book publishers and magazines listed in this book offer some sort of writers', artists' or photographers' guidelines on their websites. It's important to read and study guidelines before submitting work. You'll get a better understanding of what a particular publisher wants. You may even decide, after reading the submission guidelines, that your work isn't right for a company you considered.

SUBMITTING YOUR WORK

Throughout the listings, you'll read requests for particular elements to include when contacting markets. Here are explanations of some of these important submission components.

Queries, cover letters & proposals

A query is a no-more-than-one-page, well-written letter meant to arouse an editor's interest in your work. Query letters briefly outline the work you're proposing and include facts, anecdotes, interviews or other pertinent information that give the editor a feel for the manuscript's premise—enticing her to want to know more. End your letter with a straightforward request to submit the work, and include information on its approximate length, date it could be completed, and whether accompanying photos or artwork are available.

In a query letter, think about presenting your book as a publisher's catalog would present it. Read through a good catalog and examine how the publishers give enticing summaries of their books in a spare amount of words. It's also important that query letters give editors a taste of your writing style. For good advice and samples of queries, cover letters and other correspondence, consult the article "Crafting a Query" in this book, as well as *Formatting & Submitting Your Manuscript, 3rd Ed.* and *The Writer's Digest Guide to Query Letters* (both Writer's Digest Books).

- **QUERY LETTERS FOR NONFICTION.** Queries are usually required when submitting nonfiction material to a publisher. The goal of a nonfiction query is to convince the editor your idea is perfect for her readership and that you're qualified to do the job. Note any previous writing experience and include published samples to prove your credentials, especially samples related to the subject matter you're querying about.
- **QUERY LETTERS FOR FICTION.** For a fiction query, explain the story's plot, main characters, conflict and resolution. Just as in nonfiction queries, make the editor eager to see more.
- **COVER LETTERS FOR WRITERS.** Some editors prefer to review complete manuscripts, especially for picture books or fiction. In such cases, the cover letter (which should be no longer than one page) serves as your introduction, establishes your credentials as a writer, and gives the editor an overview of the manuscript. If the editor asked for the manuscript because of a query, note this in your cover letter.
- **COVER LETTERS FOR ILLUSTRATORS AND PHOTOGRAPHERS.** For an illustrator or photographer, the cover letter serves as an introduction to the art director and establishes professional credentials when submitting samples. Explain what services you can provide as well as what type of follow-up contact you plan to make, if any. Be sure to include the URL of your online portfolio if you have one.

- **RÉSUMÉS.** Often writers, illustrators and photographers are asked to submit résumés with cover letters and samples. They can be created in a variety of formats, from a single-page listing information to color brochures featuring your work. Keep your résumé brief, and focus on your achievements, including your clients and the work you've done for them, as well as your educational background and any awards you've received. Do not use the same résumé you'd use for a typical job application.
- **BOOK PROPOSALS.** Throughout the listings in the Book Publishers section, publishers refer to submitting a synopsis, outline and sample chapters. Depending on an editor's preference, some or all of these components, along with a cover letter, make up a book proposal.

A *synopsis* summarizes the book, covering the basic plot (including the ending). It should be easy to read and flow well. The gold standard for synopsis length is one page, single-spaced.

An *outline* covers your book chapter by chapter and provides highlights of each. If you're developing an outline for fiction, include major characters, plots and subplots, and book length. Requesting an outline is uncommon, and the word is somewhat interchangeable with "synopsis."

Sample chapters give a more comprehensive idea of your writing skill. Some editors may request the first two or three chapters to determine if they're interested in seeing the whole book. Some may request a set number of pages.

Manuscript formats

When submitting a complete manuscript, follow some basic guidelines. In the upper-left corner of your title page, type your legal name (not pseudonym), address and phone number. In the upper-right corner, type the approximate word count. All material in the upper corners should be single-spaced. Then type the title (centered) almost halfway down that page, the word "by" two spaces under that, and your name or pseudonym two spaces under "by."

The first page should also include the title (centered) one-third of the way down. Two spaces under that, type "by" and your name or pseudonym. To begin the body of your manuscript, drop down two double spaces and indent five spaces for each new paragraph. There should be one-inch margins around all sides of a full typewritten page. (Manuscripts with wide margins are more readable and easier to edit.)

Set your computer to double-space the manuscript body. From page two to the end of the manuscript, include your last name followed by a comma and the title (or key words of the title) in the upper-left corner. The page number should go in the top right corner. Drop down two double spaces to begin the body of each page. If you're submitting a novel, type each chapter title one-third of the way down the page. For more information on manuscript formats, read *Formatting & Submitting Your Manuscript, 3rd Ed.* (Writer's Digest Books).

Picture book formats

The majority of editors prefer to see complete manuscripts for picture books. When typing the text of a picture book, don't indicate page breaks and don't type each page of text on a new sheet of paper. And unless you are an illustrator, don't worry about supplying art. Editors will find their own illustrators for picture books. Most of the time, a writer and an illustrator who work on the same book never meet or interact. The editor acts as a go-between and works with the writer and illustrator throughout the publishing process. *How to Write and Sell Children's Picture Books*, by Jean E. Karl (Writer's Digest Books), offers advice on preparing text and marketing your work.

If you're an illustrator who has written your own book, consider creating a dummy or storyboard containing both art and text, and then submit it along with your complete manuscript and sample pieces of final art (hi-res PDFs or .jpgs—never originals). Publishers interested in picture books specify in their listings what should be submitted. For tips on creating a dummy, refer to *How to Write and Illustrate Children's Books and Get Them Published*, edited by Treld Pelkey Bicknell and Felicity Trotman (North Light Books), or Frieda Gates' book, *How to Write, Illustrate, and Design Children's Books* (Lloyd-Simone Publishing Company).

Writers may also want to learn the art of dummy-making to help them through their writing process with things like pacing, rhythm and length. For a great explanation and helpful hints, see *You Can Write Children's Books*, by Tracey E. Dils (Writer's Digest Books).

Mailing submissions

Your main concern when packaging material is to be sure it arrives undamaged. If your manuscript is fewer than six pages, simply fold it in thirds and send it in a #10 (business-size) envelope. For a SASE, either fold another #10 envelope in thirds or insert a #9 (reply) envelope, which fits in a #10 neatly without folding.

Another option is folding your manuscript in half in a 6x9 envelope, with a #9 or #10 SASE enclosed. For larger manuscripts, use a 9x12 envelope both for mailing the submission and as a SASE (which can be folded in half). Book manuscripts require sturdy packaging for mailing. Include a self-addressed mailing label and return postage. If asked to send artwork and photographs, remember they require a bit more care in packaging to guarantee they arrive in good condition. Sandwich illustrations and photos between heavy cardboard that is slightly larger than the work. The cardboard can be secured by rubber bands or with tape. If you tape the cardboard together, check that the artwork doesn't stick to the tape. Be sure your name and address appear on the back of each piece of art or each photo in case the material becomes separated. For the packaging, use either a manila envelope, a foam-padded envelope, or a mailer lined with plastic air bubbles. Bind nonjoined edges with reinforced mailing tape and affix a typed mailing label or clearly write your address.

Mailing material first class ensures quick delivery. Also, first-class mail is forwarded for one year if the addressee has moved, and it can be returned if undeliverable. If you're concerned about your original material safely reaching its destination, consider other mailing options such as UPS. No matter which way you send material, never send it where it requires a signature. Agents and editors are too busy to sign for packages.

Remember, companies outside your own country can't use your country's postage when returning a manuscript to you. When mailing a submission to another country, include a self-addressed envelope and International Reply Coupons, or IRCs. (You'll see this term in many listings in the Canadian & International Book Publishers section.) Your postmaster can tell you, based on a package's weight, the correct number of IRCs to include to ensure its return. If it's not necessary for an editor to return your work (such as with photocopies), don't include return postage.

Unless requested, it's never a good idea to use a company's fax number to send manuscript submissions. This can disrupt a company's internal business. Study the listings for specifics and visit publishers' and market websites for more information.

E-Mailing submissions

Most correspondence with editors today is handled over e-mail. This type of communication is usually preferred by publishing professionals because it is easier to deal with as well as free. When sending an e-mailed submission, make sure to follow submission guidelines. Double-check the recipient's e-mail address. Make sure your subject line has the proper wording, if specific wording was asked for. Keep your introduction letter short and sweet. Also, editors and agents usually do not like opening unsolicited attachments, which makes for an awkward situation for illustrators who want to attach .jpgs. One easy way around this is to post some sample illustrations on your website. That way, you can simply paste URL hyperlinks to your work. Editors can click through to look over your illustration samples, and there is no way your submission will get accidentally deleted because of attachments. That said, if editors are asking for illustration samples, they are most likely used to receiving unsolicited attachments.

Keeping submission records

It's important to keep track of the material you submit. When recording each submission, include the date it was sent, the business and contact name, and any enclosures (such as samples of writing, artwork or photography). You can create a record-keeping system of your own or look for record-keeping software in your area computer store.

Keep copies of articles or manuscripts you send together with related correspondence to make follow-up easier. When you sell rights to a manuscript, artwork or photos, you can "close" your file on a particular submission by noting the date the material was accepted, what rights were purchased, the publication date and payment.

Often writers, illustrators and photographers fail to follow up on overdue responses. If you don't hear from a publisher within their stated response time, wait another month or so and follow up with an e-mail asking about the status of your submission. Include the title or description, date sent and a SASE (if applicable) for response. Ask the contact person when she anticipates making a decision. You may refresh the memory of a buyer who temporarily forgot about your submission. At the very least, you'll receive a definite "no" and free yourself to send the material to another publisher.

Simultaneous submissions

Writers and illustrators are encouraged to simultaneously submit—sending the same material to several markets at the same time. Almost all markets are open to this type of communication; those that do not take simultaneous submissions will directly say so in their submission guidelines.

It's especially important to keep track of simultaneous submissions, so if you get an offer on a manuscript sent to more than one publisher, you can instruct other publishers to withdraw your work from consideration. (Or, you can always use the initial offer as a way to ignite interest from other agents and editors. It's very possible to procure multiple offers on your book using this technique.)

AGENTS & ART REPS

Most children's writers, illustrators and photographers, especially those just beginning, are confused about whether to enlist the services of an agent or representative. The decision is strictly one that each writer, illustrator or photographer must make for herself. Some are confident with their own negotiation skills and believe acquiring an agent or rep is not in their best interest. Others feel uncomfortable in the business arena or are not willing to sacrifice valuable creative time for marketing.

About half of children's publishers accept unagented work, so it's possible to break into children's publishing without an agent. Writers targeting magazine markets don't need the services of an agent. In fact, it's practically impossible to find an agent interested in marketing articles and short stories—there simply isn't enough financial incentive.

One benefit of having an agent, though, is it may speed up the process of getting your work reviewed, especially by publishers who don't accept unagented submissions. If an agent has a good reputation and submits your manuscript to an editor, that manuscript will likely bypass the first-read stage (which is generally done by editorial assistants and junior editors) and end up on the editor's desk sooner.

When agreeing to have a reputable agent represent you, remember that she should be familiar with the needs of the current market and evaluate your manuscript/artwork/photos accordingly. She should also determine the quality of your piece and whether it is saleable. When your manuscript sells, your agent should negotiate a favorable contract and clear up any questions you have about payments.

Keep in mind that however reputable the agent or rep is, she has limitations.

Representation does not guarantee sale of your work. It just means an agent or rep sees potential in your writing, art or photos. Though an agent or rep may offer criticism or advice on how to improve your work, she cannot make you a better writer, artist or photographer.

Literary agents typically charge a 15 percent commission from the sale of writing; art and photo representatives usually charge a 25–30 percent commission. Such fees are taken from advances and royalty earnings. If your agent sells foreign rights or film rights to your work, she will deduct a higher percentage because she will most likely be dealing with an overseas agent with whom she must split the fee.

Be advised that not every agent is open to representing a writer, artist or photographer who lacks an established track record. Just as when approaching a publisher, the manuscript, artwork or photos, and query or cover letter you submit to a potential agent must be attractive and professional looking. Your first impression must be as an organized, articulate person. For listings of agents and reps, turn to the Agents & Art Reps section.

For additional listings of art reps, consult *Artist's & Graphic Designer's Market*; for photo reps, see *Photographer's Market*; for more information and additional listings of literary agents, see *Guide to Literary Agents* (all Writer's Digest Books).

RUNNING YOUR BUSINESS

The basics for writers & illustrators.

A career in children's publishing involves more than just writing skills or artistic talent. Successful authors and illustrators must be able to hold their own in negotiations, keep records, understand contract language, grasp copyright law, pay taxes and take care of a number of other business concerns. Although agents and reps, accountants and lawyers, and writers' organizations offer help in sorting out such business issues, it's wise to have a basic understanding of them going in. This article offers just that—basic information. For a more in-depth look at the subjects covered here, check your library or bookstore for books and magazines to help you. We also tell you how to get information on issues like taxes and copyright from the federal government.

CONTRACTS & NEGOTIATION

Before you see your work in print or begin working with an editor or art director on a project, there is negotiation. And whether negotiating a book contract, a magazine article assignment, or an illustration or photo assignment, there are a few things to keep in mind. First, if you find any clauses vague or confusing in a contract, get legal or professional advice. The time and money invested in counseling up front could protect you from problems later. If you have an agent or rep, she will review any contract.

A contract is an agreement between two or more parties that specifies the fees to be paid, services rendered, deadlines, rights purchased, and, for artists and photographers, whether original work is returned. Most companies have standard contracts for writers, illustrators and photographers. The specifics (such as royalty rates, advances, delivery dates, etc.) are typed in after negotiations.

Though it's OK to conduct negotiations over the phone or via e-mail, get a written contract once both parties have agreed on terms. Never depend on oral stipulations; written contracts protect both parties from misunderstandings. Watch for clauses that may not be in your best interest, such as "work-for-hire." When you do work-for-hire, you give up all rights to your creations.

When negotiating a book deal, find out whether your contract contains an option clause. This clause requires the author to give the publisher a first look at her next work before offering it to other publishers. Though it's editorial etiquette to give the publisher the first chance at publishing your next work, be wary of statements in the contract that could trap you. Don't allow the publisher to consider the next project for more than 30 days and be specific about what type of work should actually be considered "next work." (For example, if the book under contract is a young adult novel, specify that the publisher will receive an exclusive look at *only* your next young adult novel.)

Book publishers' payment methods

Book publishers pay authors and artists in *royalties*, a percentage of either the wholesale or retail price of each book sold. From large publishing houses, the author usually receives an advance issued against future royalties before the book is published.

After your book has sold enough copies to earn back your advance, you'll start to get royalty checks. Some publishers hold a reserve against returns, which means a percentage of royalties is held back in case books are returned from bookstores. If you have a reserve clause in your contract, find out the exact percentage of total sales that will be withheld and the time period the publisher will hold this money. You should be reimbursed this amount after a reasonable time period, such as a year. Royalty percentages vary with each publisher, but there are standard ranges.

Book publishers' rates

First-time picture book authors can expect advances of $500–20,000; first-time picture book illustrators' advances range from $2,000–15,000. Rates can go up for subsequent books. Experienced authors can expect higher advances. Royalties for picture books are generally about five percent (split between the author and illustrator) but can go as high as 10 percent. Those who both write and illustrate a book, of course, receive the full royalty. Advances for novels can fetch advances of $1,000–100,000 and 10 percent royalties.

As you might expect, advance and royalty figures vary from house to house and are affected by the time of year, the state of the economy and other factors. Some smaller houses may not even pay royalties, just *flat fees*. Educational houses may not offer advances or may offer smaller amounts. Religious publishers tend to offer smaller advances than trade publishers. First-time writers and illustrators generally start on the low end of the scale, while established and high-profile writers are paid more. For more information, SCBWI members can request or download SCBWI publication "Answer to Some Questions About Contracts." (Visit scbwi.org.)

Pay rates for magazines

For writers, fee structures for magazines are based on a per-word rate or range for a specific article length. Artists and photographers have a few more variables to contend with before contracting their services.

Payment for illustrations and photos can be set by such factors as whether the piece(s) will be black and white or four-color, how many are to be purchased, where the work appears (cover or inside), circulation, and the artist's or photographer's prior experience.

Remaindering

When a book goes out of print, a publisher will sell any existing copies to a wholesaler who, in turn, sells the copies to stores at a discount. When the books are "remaindered" to a wholesaler, they are usually sold at a price just above the cost of printing. When negotiating a contract with a publisher, you may want to discuss the possibility of purchasing the remaindered copies before they are sold to a wholesaler, then you can market the copies you purchased and still make a profit.

KNOW YOUR RIGHTS

A copyright is a form of protection provided to creators of original works, published or unpublished. In general, copyright protection ensures the writer, illustrator or photographer the power to decide how her work is used and allows her to receive payment for each use.

Essentially, copyright also encourages the creation of new works by guaranteeing the creator power to sell rights to the work in the marketplace. The copyright holder can print, reprint or copy her work; sell or distribute copies of her work; post her work online; or prepare derivative works such as plays, collages or recordings. The Copyright Law is designed to protect work (created on or after January 1, 1978) for her lifetime plus 70 years. If you collaborate with someone else on a written or artistic project, the copyright will last for the lifetime of the last survivor plus 70 years. The creators' heirs may hold a copyright for an additional 70 years. After that, the work becomes public domain. Works created anonymously or under a pseudonym are protected for 120 years, or 95 years after publication. Under work-for-hire agreements, you relinquish your copyright to your employer.

Copyright notice & registration

Although it's not necessary to include a copyright notice on unregistered work, if you don't feel your work is safe without the notice (especially if posting work online), it is your right to include one. Including a copyright notice—(©) (year of work, your name)—should help safeguard against plagiarism.

Registration is a legal formality intended to make copyright public record, and it can help you win more money in a court case. By registering work within three months of publication or before an infringement occurs, you are eligible to collect statutory damages and attorney's fees. If you register later than three months after publication, you will qualify only for actual damages and profits.

Ideas and concepts are not copyrightable, only expressions of those ideas and concepts can be protected. A character type or basic plot outline, for example, is not subject to a copyright infringement lawsuit. Also, titles, names, short phrases or slogans, and lists of contents are not subject to copyright protection, though titles and names may be protected through the Trademark Office.

You can register a group of articles, illustrations or photos if it meets these criteria:
- the group is assembled in order, such as in a notebook
- the works bear a single title, such as "Works by (your name)"
- it is the work of one writer, artist or photographer
- the material is the subject of a single claim to copyright

It's a publisher's responsibility to register your book for copyright. If you've previously registered the same material, you must inform your editor and supply the previous copyright information; otherwise, the publisher can't register the book in its published form.

For more information about the proper way to register works and to order the correct forms, contact the U.S. Copyright Office, (202)707-3000. For information about how to use the copyright forms, request a copy of Circular I on Copyright Basics. All of the forms and circulars are free. Send the completed registration form along with the stated fee and a copy of the work to the Copyright Office.

For specific answers to questions about copyright (but not legal advice), call the Copyright Public Information Office at (202)707-3000 weekdays between 8:30 a.m. and 5 p.m. EST. Forms can also be downloaded from the Library of Congress website: copyright. gov. The site also includes a list of frequently asked questions, tips on filling out forms, general copyright information, and links to other sites related to copyright issues.

The rights publishers buy

The copyright law specifies that a writer, illustrator or photographer generally sells one-time rights to her work unless she and the buyer agree otherwise in writing. Many publications will want more exclusive rights to your work than just one-time usage; some will even require you to sell all rights. Be sure you are monetarily compensated for the additional rights you relinquish. If you must give up all rights to a work, carefully consider the price you're being offered to determine whether you'll be compensated for the loss of other potential sales.

Writers who only give up limited rights to their work can then sell reprint rights to other publications, foreign rights to international publications, or even movie rights, should the opportunity arise. Artists and photographers can sell their work to other markets such as paper product companies who may use an image on a calendar, greeting card or mug. Illustrators and photographers may even sell original work after it has been published. There are a number of galleries throughout the U.S. that display and sell the original work of children's illustrators.

Rights acquired through the sale of a book manuscript are explained in each publisher's contract. Take time to read relevant clauses to be sure you understand what rights each contract is specifying before signing. Be sure your contract contains a clause allowing all rights to revert back to you in the event the publisher goes out of business. (You may even want to have the contract reviewed by an agent or an attorney specializing in publishing law.)

The following are the rights you'll most often sell to publishers, periodicals and producers in the marketplace:

FIRST RIGHTS. The buyer purchases the rights to use the work for the first time in any medium. All other rights remain with the creator. When material is excerpted in this way (from a soon-to-be-published book in this manner) for use in a newspaper or periodical, first serial rights are also purchased.

ONE-TIME RIGHTS. The buyer has no guarantee that she is the first to use a piece. One-time permission to run written work, illustrations or photos is acquired, and then the rights revert back to the creator.

FIRST NORTH AMERICAN SERIAL RIGHTS. This is similar to first rights, except that companies who distribute both in the U.S. and Canada will stipulate these rights to ensure that another North American company won't come out with simultaneous usage of the same work.

SECOND SERIAL (REPRINT) RIGHTS. In this case, newspapers and magazines are granted the right to reproduce a work that has already appeared in another publication. These rights are also purchased by a newspaper or magazine editor who wants to publish part of a book after the book has been published. The proceeds from reprint rights for a book are often split evenly between the author and his publishing company.

SIMULTANEOUS RIGHTS. More than one publication buys one-time rights to the same work at the same time. Use of such rights occurs among magazines with circulations that don't overlap, such as many religious publications.

ALL RIGHTS. Just as it sounds, the writer, illustrator or photographer relinquishes all rights to a piece—she no longer has any say in who acquires rights to use it. All rights are purchased by publishers who pay premium usage fees, have an exclusive format, or have other book or magazine interests from which the purchased work can generate more mileage. If a company insists on acquiring all rights to your work, see if you can negotiate for the rights to revert back to you after a reasonable period of time. If they agree to such a proposal, get it in writing. Note: Writers, illustrators and photographers should be wary of "work-for-hire" arrangements. If you sign an agreement stipulating that your work will be done as work-for-hire, you will not control the copyrights of the completed work—the company that hired you will be the copyright owner.

FOREIGN SERIAL RIGHTS. Be sure before you market to foreign publications that you have sold only North American—not worldwide—serial rights to previous markets. If so, you are free to market to publications that may be interested in material that's appeared in a North American-based periodical.

SYNDICATION RIGHTS. This is a division of serial rights. For example, if a syndicate prints portions of a book in installments in its newspapers, it would be syndicating second serial rights. The syndicate would receive a commission and leave the remainder to be split between the author and publisher.

SUBSIDIARY RIGHTS. These include serial rights, dramatic rights, book club rights or translation rights. The contract should specify what percentage of profits from sales of these rights go to the author and publisher.

DRAMATIC, TELEVISION AND MOTION PICTURE RIGHTS. During a specified time, the interested party tries to sell a story to a producer or director. Many times options are renewed because the selling process can be lengthy.

DISPLAY RIGHTS OR ELECTRONIC PUBLISHING RIGHTS. They're also known as "Data, Storage and Retrieval." Usually listed under subsidiary rights, the marketing of electronic rights in this era of rapidly expanding capabilities and markets for electronic material can be tricky. Display rights can cover text or images to be used in a CD or online, or they may cover use of material in formats not even fully developed yet. If a display rights clause is listed in your contract, try to negotiate its elimination. Otherwise, be sure to pin down which electronic rights are being purchased. Demand the clause be restricted to things designed to be read only. By doing this, you maintain your rights to use your work for things such as games and interactive software.

SOURCES FOR CONTRACT HELP ///////////////////////////////

Writers' organizations offer a wealth of information to members, including contract advice:

SOCIETY OF CHILDREN'S BOOK WRITERS AND ILLUSTRATORS members can find information in the SCBWI publication "Answers to Some Questions About Contracts." Contact SCBWI at 8271 Beverly Blvd., Los Angeles CA 90048, (323)782-1010, or visit their website: scbwi.org.

THE AUTHORS GUILD also offers contract tips. Visit their website: authorsguild.org. (Members of the guild can receive a 75-point contract review from the guild's legal staff.) See the website for membership information and application form, or contact The Authors Guild at 31 E. 28th St., 10th Floor, New York NY 10016, (212)563-5904. Fax: (212)564-5363. E-mail: staff@authorsguild.org.

STRICTLY BUSINESS

An essential part of being a freelance writer, illustrator or photographer is running your freelance business. It's imperative to maintain accurate business records to determine if you're making a profit as a freelancer. Keeping correct, organized records will also make your life easier as you approach tax time.

When setting up your system, begin by keeping a bank account and ledger for your business finances apart from your personal finances. Also, if writing, illustration or photography is secondary to another freelance career, keep separate business records for each.

You will likely accumulate some business expenses before showing any profit when you start out as a freelancer. To substantiate your income and expenses to the IRS, keep all invoices, cash receipts, sales slips, bank statements, canceled checks and receipts related to travel expenses and entertaining clients. For entertainment expenditures, record the date, place and purpose of the business meeting, as well as gas mileage. Keep records for all purchases, big and small. Don't take the small purchases for granted; they can add up to a substantial amount. File all receipts in chronological order. Maintaining a separate file for each month simplifies retrieving records at the end of the year.

Record keeping

When setting up a single-entry bookkeeping system, record income and expenses separately. Use some of the subheads that appear on Schedule C (the form used for recording income from a business) of the 1040 tax form so you can easily transfer information onto the tax form when filing your return. In your ledger, include a description of each transaction—the date, source of income (or debts from business purchases), description of what was purchased or sold, the amount of the transaction, and whether payment was by cash, check or credit card.

Don't wait until January 1 to start keeping records. The moment you first make a business-related purchase or sell an article, book manuscript, illustration or photo, begin tracking your profits and losses. If you keep records from January 1 to December 31, you're using a calendar-year accounting period. Any other accounting period is called a fiscal year.

There are two types of accounting methods you can choose from—the cash method and the accrual method. The cash method is used more often: You record income when it is received and expenses when they're disbursed.

Using the accrual method, you report income at the time you earn it rather than when it's actually received. Similarly, expenses are recorded at the time they're incurred rather than when you actually pay them. If you choose this method, keep separate records for "accounts receivable" and "accounts payable."

Satisfying the IRS

To successfully—and legally—work as a freelancer, you must know what income you should report and what deductions you can claim. But before you can do that, you must prove to the IRS you're in business to make a profit, that your writing, illustration or photography is not merely a hobby. The Tax Reform Act of 1986 says you should show a profit for three years out of a five-year period to attain professional status. The IRS considers these factors as proof of your professionalism:

- accurate financial records
- a business bank account separate from your personal account
- proven time devoted to your profession
- whether it's your main or secondary source of income
- your history of profits and losses
- the amount of training you have invested in your field
- your expertise

If your business is unincorporated, you'll fill out tax information on Schedule C of Form 1040. If you're unsure of what deductions you can take, request the IRS publication containing this information. Under the Tax Reform Act, only 30 percent of business meals, entertainment and related tips, and parking charges are deductible. Other deductible expenses allowed on Schedule C include: car expenses for business-related trips; professional courses and seminars; depreciation of office equipment, such as a computer; dues and publication subscriptions; and miscellaneous expenses, such as postage used for business needs.

If you're working out of a home office, a portion of your mortgage interest (or rent), related utilities, property taxes, repair costs and depreciation may be deducted as business expenses—under special circumstances. To learn more about the possibility of home office deductions, consult IRS Publication 587, Business Use of Your Home.

The method of paying taxes on income not subject to withholding is called "estimated tax" for individuals. If you expect to owe more than $500 at year's end and if the total amount of income tax that will be withheld during the year will be less than 90 percent of the tax shown on the current year's return, you'll generally make estimated tax payments. Estimated tax payments are made in four equal installments due on April 15, June 15, September 15, and January 15 (assuming you're a calendar-year taxpayer). For more information, request Publication 533, Self-Employment Tax.

The Internal Revenue Service's website (irs.gov) offers tips and instant access to IRS forms and publications.

Social Security tax

Depending on your net income as a freelancer, you may be liable for a Social Security tax. This is a tax designed for those who don't have Social Security withheld from their paychecks. You're liable if your net income is $400 or more per year. Net income is the difference between your income and allowable business deductions. Request Schedule SE, Computation of Social Security Self-Employment Tax, if you qualify.

If completing your income tax return proves to be too complex, consider hiring an accountant (the fee is a deductible business expense) or contact the IRS for assistance. (Check their website, irs.gov.) In addition to offering numerous publications to instruct you in various facets of preparing a tax return, the IRS also has walk-in centers in some cities.

Insurance

As a self-employed professional, be aware of what health and business insurance coverage is available to you. Unless you're a Canadian who is covered by national health insurance or a full-time freelancer covered by your spouse's policy, health insurance will no doubt be one of your biggest expenses. Under the terms of a 1985 government act (COBRA), if you leave a job with health benefits, you're entitled to continue that coverage for up to 18 months; you pay 100 percent of the premium and sometimes a small administration fee. Eventually, you must search for your own health plan. You may also choose to purchase disability and life insurance. Disability insurance is offered through many private insurance companies and state governments. This insurance pays a monthly fee that covers living and business expenses during periods of long-term recuperation from a health problem. The amount of money paid is based on the recipient's annual earnings.

Before contacting any insurance representative, talk to other writers, illustrators or photographers to learn which insurance companies they recommend. If you belong to a writers' or artists' organization, ask the organization if it offers insurance coverage for professionals. (SCBWI has a plan available to members in certain states.) Group coverage may be more affordable and provide more comprehensive coverage than an individual policy.

MIDDLE GRADE VS. YOUNG ADULT

Different audiences, different styles.

....

by Marie Lamba

OK, class. What sets a middle-grade novel apart from a young adult novel? If you said MG is for readers ages 8–12, and YA is for readers ages 13–18, then give yourself a check plus. But if you're writing for the juvenile market and that's *all* you know about these two categories, then I'm afraid you still need to stick around for the rest of this class. A book that doesn't fit within the parameters of either age category is a book you won't be able to sell.

In my work with The Jennifer De Chiara Literary Agency, I see my inbox flooded every day with queries for manuscripts that suffer from an MG/YA identity crisis. Like when a query says, "I've written a 100,000-word MG novel about a seventh-grader who falls in love and has sex for the first time." Or when one states, "In my 20,000-word YA novel, a 14-year-old holds her first sleepover and learns the meaning of true friendship." Both queries would earn a swift rejection, based on both inappropriate manuscript lengths and on content that's either too mature or too young for the audience they're targeting. Sadly, by not understanding what makes a book a true MG or a solid YA, these writers have hamstrung their chances for success, regardless of how well written their stories may be. It's like they showed up to a final exam without ever cracking a book.

On the bright side, writers who study up on the many key differences between MG and YA will be able to craft the kind of well-targeted manuscript that will make both agents and editors take notice. Pay attention, because someday your manuscript *will* be tested.

MG at a Glance

AGE OF READERS: 8–12. **LENGTH:** Generally 30,000–50,000 words (although fantasy can run longer to allow for more complex world-building). **CONTENT RESTRICTIONS:** No profanity, graphic violence or sexuality (romance, if any, is limited to a crush or a first kiss). **AGE OF**

PROTAGONIST: Typically age 10 for a younger MG novel, and up to age 13 for older, more complex books. **MIND-SET:** Focus on friends, family and the character's immediate world and relationship to it; characters react to what happens to them, with minimal self-reflection. **VOICE:** Often third person.

YA at a Glance

AGE OF READERS: 13–18. **LENGTH:** Generally 50,000–75,000 words (although there's also a length allowance for fantasy). **CONTENT RESTRICTIONS:** Profanity, graphic violence, romance and sexuality (except for eroticism) are all allowable (though not required). **AGE OF PROTAGONIST:** Ages 14–15 for a younger YA with cleaner content aimed at the middle-school crowd; for older and more edgy YA, characters can be up to 18 (but not in college). **MIND-SET:** YA heroes discover how they fit in the world beyond their friends and family; they spend more time reflecting on what happens and analyzing the meaning of things. **VOICE:** Often first person.

MG vs. YA Characters

When picking your hero's age, remember that kids "read up," which means they want to read about characters who are older than they are. So an 8-year-old protagonist won't fly for the MG category, though it'd be OK for a younger chapter book or easy reader. For the widest audience, you'll generally want your protagonist to be on the oldest side of your readership that your plot will allow. That means a 12- or even 13-year-old hero for MG, and a 17- or 18-year-old for YA (just remember your hero can't be in college yet—that would push it into the "new adult" category).

MG vs. YA Readers

Middle-grade is *not* synonymous with middle school. Books for the middle-school audience tend to be divided between the MG and YA shelves. So which shelf do those readers go to? While there is no such thing as a 'tween category in bookstores, there are degrees of maturity in both MG and YA novels that'll appeal to the younger and older sides of the middle-school crowd. A longer, more complex MG novel with characters who are 13 could take place in middle school and be considered an "upper-MG novel." But the material can't be too mature. It's still an MG novel, after all, and most readers will be younger. Writing a sweeter, more innocent YA? Then it's pretty likely that your readers will be 'tweens, that your characters should be around 15 years old, and that your book will be marketed as a "young YA."

While it's useful for you to understand these nuances as you craft your story and relate to your true audience, when it comes time to submit, don't go so far as to define your novel as upper MG or younger YA in your query. That's already pointing to a more limited readership. Instead, just stick to calling it either MG or YA when you submit, and let an interested agent draw conclusions about nuances from there.

MG vs. YA Content and Voice

What's cool to a fourth-grader differs from what a 10th-grader will idolize. Same goes for the way they speak and the way they view the world. Which is why if romance appears in an MG novel, it's limited to a crush and maybe an innocent kiss, as it is in *Shug* by Jenny Han. A YA could involve deep, true love as well as sexuality, as in *The Fault in Our Stars* by John Green. Another key difference? Overall, MG novels end on a hopeful note, while YA novels could have less optimistic endings, as in Green's tearful story. You could say that that's youth vs. experience coming into play.

When it comes to content, here's another important thing to keep in mind: There are gatekeepers between your book and your targeted audience. MG readers typically don't have direct access to their novels. To get a book, kids first go through a parent, a teacher or a librarian. While you might want to have that gritty character in your upper-MG novel drop a few four-letter words, doing so *will* hurt book sales, so choose your language wisely.

Also, think *carefully* about your content. MG is not the place for graphic or persistent violence, but can it be scary and dark? Sure—look at *Holes* by Louis Sachar, where boys are threatened by a crazy warden and nearly killed by poisonous lizards. (Note, however, that book *does* have a happy ending.)

If you're writing a YA, you don't have to worry about those gatekeepers as much. But while YA authors cover just about anything in their novels, keep in mind that *gratuitous* sex, foul language or violence won't fly in *any* great literature. And do remember that school and library support can really catapult a YA title to success. While dropping a ton of F-bombs is OK if it fits with your characters and setting, be prepared for your book to be perhaps on fewer school shelves as a result, and make sure it's worth that risk.

Exceptions to Every Rule

Like any rebellious teen can tell you, rules are made to be broken. Word counts often vary from the suggested norms. Just don't deviate too low or too high, especially for a debut. I know what you're thinking: J.K. Rowling. True, *Harry Potter and the Deathly Hallows* came close to a whopping 200,000 words, but her debut novel, *Harry Potter and the Sorcerer's Stone*, was roughly 77,000 words—which is still long for the genre, but not outrageously so for an MG fantasy. Hey, once you get as popular as Rowling, you can write doorstopper-sized tomes, too.

Content can also stray from the stated guidelines, *with good reason*. You might, say, choose to have an MG with a swear word, or with a more edgy storyline. Whatever norm you do stray from, just make sure you do so for a specific and valid purpose, that your book still fits your audience's point of view, and that you understand what deviating from the norm might mean for your book's marketability.

Whether you aim to write a YA or an MG novel, there is one thing you absolutely *must* do: Tell a story that is meaningful to your intended reader. And to do that, you must first know *who* that reader is.

So which shelf does your book belong on? Know *that* and your book will surely graduate with full honors, moving on to a long and happy future in your readers' appreciative hands.

MARIE LAMBA (marielamba.com) is author of the YA novels *What I Meant…, Over My Head* and *Drawn.* She's also associate literary agent at The Jennifer De Chiara Literary Agency (jdlit.com).

SELL YOUR PICTURE BOOK

....

by Lara Perkins

Pitching a picture book? Things are looking up. Although the Association of American Publishers reports that book sales in the children's/young adult segment declined from January to October 2013, many agents observed an uptick in picture book acquisitions throughout 2013 and into 2014. By no means a perfect measure, it's nonetheless telling that approximately 400 picture book deals were announced in Publishers Marketplace in 2013 compared to approximately 300 in 2012. Still, the market is very competitive, and going head-to-head with the classics as well as new work by high-profile authors can be daunting. It needn't be. As a literary agent specializing in children's fiction and nonfiction, I'd like to share some observations about the current picture book market and tips for crafting picture books that sell.

KNOW THE MARKET.

Picture books typically hit the shelves two to five years after acquisition, so predicting current acquisition trends from new releases is difficult—as is trying to capitalize on a perceived hot trend. Yet successful new releases can suggest the larger strengths and reader appeal that publishers are seeking. For example, the success of *Goodnight, Goodnight, Construction Site* by Sherri Duskey Rinker and Tom Lichtenheld suggests stories that infuse a lulling, dreamy bedtime sweetness into active (building, traveling) daytime play are finding an audience.

The current market also reveals strong interest in character-driven stories that have series potential (*Clark the Shark* by Bruce Hale and Guy Francis, new classics like Ian Falconer's *Olivia*) and capture a universally relatable "kid experience" in a funny, larger-than-life way (*Crankenstein* by Samantha Berger and Dan Santat, *The Dark* by Lemony Snicket and Jon Klassen, *No Fits, Nilson!* by Zachariah OHora). We're also seeing interest in off-the-wall, kid-friendly humor (*Dragons Love Tacos* by Adam Rubin and Daniel Salmieri, *The Day the*

Crayons Quit by Drew Daywalt and Oliver Jeffers); stories that cleverly turn familiar relationships upside down (*Nugget and Fang* by Tammi Sauer and Michael Slack, *Children Make Terrible Pets* by Peter Brown, *How to Babysit a Grandpa* by Jean Reagan and Lee Wildish); and books that are seasonal but work year-round (*Creepy Carrots!* by Aaron Reynolds and Peter Brown, *Bear Has a Story to Tell* by Philip C. Stead and Erin Stead).

There's significant interest in beautiful nonfiction picture books, biographies and others (*On a Beam of Light: A Story of Albert Einstein* by Jennifer Berne and Vladimir Radunsky and *Nelson Mandela* by Kadir Nelson).

Lovely, lyrical picture books with a hook for parents as well as kids are sought after (*Once Upon a Memory* by Nina Laden and Renata Liwska)—particularly for the younger set—as are innovative storytelling formats that take witty, fun narrative risks (*Battle Bunny* by Jon Scieszka, Mac Barnett and Matthew Myers). Many of these titles could fit more than one description as well.

Ideally, a new manuscript should share some proven strengths with recent successful picture books, while giving readers something new and fresh.

BEGIN WITH A STRONG IDEA.

Every picture book needs a plot and story structure. Even young picture books like Hervé Tullet's *Press Here*, concept books, and picture books with cumulative structures like Oliver Jeffers' *Stuck* or unusual formats like *Battle Bunny* must have tension, rising and falling action, and a satisfying final resolution.

Any story for young readers must tap into a universal childhood experience, no matter how wacky the premise. With *Dragons Love Tacos*, for example, hosting taco parties for dragons may not be a universal experience of childhood, but avoiding certain foods and attending parties where shenanigans ensue are. Similarly, John Rocco's *Blackout* transforms a commonplace neighborhood blackout into something magical and resonant. This universality is key to winning the hearts of parents, librarians and teachers—the gatekeepers who will share your book with kids.

Childhood experiences like bedtime rituals or the first day of school are evergreen, but a fresh angle with strong kid appeal is a must. For example, many picture books deal with fear of the dark, but *The Dark* takes an inventive approach, personifying the dark and following the relationship arc between housemates Laszlo and the dark.

To give your story that all-important kid appeal, tell it from a child's-eye point of view, even if your main character is a shark or President Obama. This is true even for the youngest picture books and nonfiction picture books. For example, Susan B. Katz's and Alicia Padrón's board book *ABC Baby Me!* brings readers directly into the perspective of a baby, and *On a Beam of Light* focuses on imagination, wonder and curiosity to bring Albert Einstein and his work to life for kids. Your main character or characters must be relatable and approach the world in a way that is recognizable to your audience.

If you're tackling a more serious subject such as loss or grief, be honest in your treatment of the subject but keep the mood positive and reassuring for this age group. For example, the final phrase in *Once Upon a Memory*, "Will you remember you once were a child?" is a beautiful nod to the passage of time and inevitable end of childhood, but framed in a gentle and child-friendly way.

Keep in mind that beloved picture books are read again and again by parents and kids. For that reason, successful picture books are filled with pitch-perfect character details that readers can continue to enjoy on the 10th or 20th or 100th reading. For example, every time I read Oliver Jeffers' *This Moose Belongs to Me*, I'm newly charmed by another hilarious character detail.

CRAFT STORIES THAT SELL.

How you choose to tell your story is as important as the story you tell. Picture book texts must be lean and mean, with exceptionally tight pacing. Although word counts can soar up to 1,200–1,300 words, most picture book texts for ages 3–8 are around 250–600 words. Infant/toddler board books will be even shorter, often with just a few words per page. With no words to spare, picture books must begin in media res, with the central tension and stakes of the story or the central concept clearly evident from the opening page. For example, the first line of This Moose Belongs to Me is "Wilfred owned a moose," which immediately establishes the central conflict and misunderstanding that drives the story.

Rhyme is understandably a hot-button issue in the picture book world, as it's no secret that rhyming texts can be a more difficult sell in today's market. However, skilled, creative rhyme can still sell very well (see Rinker and Lichtenheld's *Goodnight, Goodnight, Construction Site* or *Steam Train, Dream Train*), and even editors and agents who are hesitant about rhyme may often be swayed by terrific, well-executed stanzas coupled with a strong story and characters.

Unfortunately, rhyme all too often masks larger issues with story, character or voice. If you write in rhyme, I re-commend also composing in prose to make sure the story and characters are compelling and fully drawn independent of the rhyming structure.

Whether you write in prose or rhyme, be thoughtful about rhythm and cadence, the musicality of language and the resulting effect on mood and tone. Picture books are meant to be read aloud, and *Once Upon a Memory* is just one example of how rhythm and cadence can enhance the mood of a story.

Similarly, because kids have an experimental, whole-hearted way of interacting with the world, having a child's-eye-view approach to storytelling means employing a creative and playful use of language. For example, in *Mostly Monsterly* by Tammi Sauer and Scott Magoon, Sauer has fun using the most "monsterly" words possible: *lurched*, *growled* and especially the neologism *monsterly*!

Nothing is more fun for kids than getting the joke and being part of the story, so repeating jokes and phrases makes young readers feel like "insiders" in the best way. The key however is repetition with a difference, so the story remains surprising and forward moving. For example, in *The Day the Crayons Quit*, each crayon's letter of complaint follows a similar format but has a different voice and delightfully surprising variations that keep readers hooked and the joke fresh.

Finally, picture books are like jazz collaborations. If the author does her best work and invites the illustrator to do the same, then the whole will be stronger, more surprising and more satisfying than the sum of its parts. For example, in *The Dark*, the dark gives Laszlo a gift that is never specified in the text, but the glowing illustration says it all. Making a dummy of your work can help you judge the illustration potential and visual rhythm of your story as a whole.

KNOW THE COMPETITION—THEN SUBMIT.

If you've followed the advice above and done your best to craft a story that sells, look once again at successful new releases. Make sure you (and your beta readers) can articulate both why your picture book is likely to find an audience based on successful recent picture books and how you're doing something new and different that still has major kid appeal. If you can, then chances are you've written a picture book that can sell in today's upward-moving market.

LARA PERKINS is an associate agent and digital manager at Andrea Brown Literary Agency. She represents all categories of children's literature, from picture books through young adult.

SERIES CHARACTERS FOR YOUNG READERS

Create a character that will last.

....

by Jacqueline Mitchard

Everybody wants to write a trilogy.

"I'm picturing a trilogy," says the author of the not-quite-completed first novel submission I'm reviewing for Merit Press, the realistic young adult imprint of which I'm editor-in-chief.

"I see it as a trilogy," says the student writer whose pages I'm analyzing at a workshop.

"It has to be a trilogy," says a fellow author who writes fiction for both adults and teens, as I do. "I've done so much research, all this great stuff will never fit in one book."

Oh dear. The very words make me want to run to the nearest convenience store and knock back two whole bags of kettle chips.

Serial madness stalks the land.

For all that, a *great* trilogy, or even a great septilogy, can be a beautiful thing. There was a reason people queued up at midnight for the newest adventures of Harry Potter: They couldn't get enough.

But not every character—not even every wonderfully made character—should be the creative engine for more than one book. Picture (I promise you, you'll be rushing to overeat within moments) the *To Kill a Mockingbird* trilogy. Somebody did picture the sequel to *Gone With the Wind*; it was much anticipated and a rousing failure. Scarlett O'Hara didn't need to declare that she'd never be hungry again … again.

Sometimes the motivation behind the desire to write a series based on one character is love of that character. Sometimes it's fear, perhaps of never coming up with a character you care about so much as this one. Sometimes it's hope, driven by the entirely understandable belief that if one published book is good, how great would three published books be? Authors, though we are priests and priestesses of the age (and pure in heart), are only human and dream of midnight publication parties, the lunch box and action figure franchise, the movie, the box office sequel. Who wouldn't?

But making the choice to create a series of books needs to be based on more than all that. People used to ask me all the time what happened to the bad boy hero in my first novel, *The Deep End of the Ocean,* who's only 17 on the last page of the book. In fact, in two subsequent books a dozen years later, *No Time to Wave Goodbye* and *Second Nature: A Love Story,* I did write about exactly what happened to Vincent, but in both, he's the secondary character. These books aren't a trilogy; they don't "continue" the first story where it left off, nor should they have.

When it *is* possible to take up that story where it left off, however, teens or older children can be an ideal audience. Robin Wasserman, author of the Cold Awakening trilogy as well as the immensely popular Seven Deadly Sins series, now a popular TV miniseries, points out that teen readers love their books, especially series, "with wild abandon, the way I loved books back then, so it makes absolute sense that they'd want as much out of their favorite characters as an author was willing to give them."

Of course, adults do love series characters (such as Kinsey Millhone in Sue Grafton's stunningly popular series of the same name). But as endearingly quirky as Kinsey and others are, the success of such grown-up tales is based more on the high jinks the character gets up to rather than on the development of the character in relation to whatever life throws her way. In other words, a successful adult series character needs, more than anything, a good job description: a former police detective turned private investigator, an insurance investigator with a taste for mayhem, etc. Adult series characters are *consistent.*

Teens and kids, however, change. A strong series character for this audience, then, is often one who's on a quest for a missing piece, beyond coming of age. A great series character for middle-grade readers and teens has to be engaged in something wild or fun or sinister or diverting. These characters have to be likable (though not—and this is important—necessarily the most winning character in the book), both reliable and in the process of change. And they must come with a little something extra, too.

My own YA trilogy, The Midnight Twins, begins on New Year's Eve when identical twins Mallory and Meredith Brynn turn 13. One was born one minute before midnight, the other one minute after; one possesses the gift to see into the future, the other to see into the past. In the first book, they are terrified little girls, dreading their visions. By the time they turn 16, in the final book, they have fully experienced the glory of their power, as well as become intimately acquainted with love and death.

In my new series, a two-parter, hero Alexis Kim is on a quest to avenge the murder of her best friend—a quest complicated by the fact that Allie suffers from a rare genetic condition called xeroderma pigmentosum (XP), which means that the very light of day can kill her, and further by the fact that the monster is a respected young coach beloved by everyone *else* in the community. In the first book Allie is a protected child of illness, her life lived within the bounds set by her watchful mother and her best friends, Rob and Juliet (who also have XP). By the second, she is a warrior and a young woman in love, and she has grown powerful in her determination to beat her disease and vanquish a killer. But most important, Allie is everygirl.

With those examples in mind, let's take a closer look at what makes for a series-worthy character for MG or YA readers.

1. LIKABILITY & RELATABILITY

A great series character is usually not the most beautiful or most charismatic character because the reader needs to identify with him or her. Thus, one of the most important characteristics of a character who'll become part of a teen or a kid's life for several years is simple, relatable *likability*. Before she was on fire, it was being a loving big sister that led Katniss Everdeen to The Hunger Games. That's where we all met her, on a level to which millions of teens (and adults) could relate. She would harden into a warrior and soften into a woman, but, though brave, she's no hero. The fate thrust on her is something she accepts, not seeks.

So make sure that your primary character's biography includes flaws as well as quirks. According to Sara Pennypacker, author of seven MG *New York Times* bestsellers based on the character of Clementine, what makes a good series character is what makes a good friend, "the kind of friend you'd cry, 'Yes! Of *course*!' to if she called you up and asked, 'Want to come over and do nothing today?'"

Stand-alone characters have a wider range of appeal—they might make great friends, too, but often they're better to spend a short bit of time with. For a series character, it's more about what they're facing, how the world is treating them, what kind of trouble or heroism or brilliant adventure they're about to get into that makes readers want to go along. They should have plenty of human faults and, Pennypacker says, "not be afraid to reveal them—maybe not immediately, but pretty soon. And they should be accepting of these faults, so readers feel their own faults would be accepted. Curiosity is great in a friend and a series character: It leads to exploration and trouble!"

Pennypacker's Clementine is often in trouble; the inside of the principal's office is as familiar to her as her own bedroom, and she often winds up there for infractions that result from an excess of high spirits. Pennypacker says it's also important to remember that a series character for kids has to have a sense of humor. "After all, if we're going to hang out with each other book after book, misadventure after misadventure, both the reader and the writer want to laugh with this person."

Book after book? That character needs …

2. DURABILITY & ADAPTABILITY

A character who lasts is not the same as a character who stays the same. As a YA editor, I look for a sea of changes in characters because teens and kids are the only human beings who really *do* experience change, down to the molecular level, as a commonplace of everyday life. So how do you make your character deeply satisfying and familiar while making it possible for readers to return to people and a world they know intimately? "She has an unshakable spirit [and] genuinely feels she can save the day with her brain, wit and scrappy street smarts," says Cindy Pearlman, of the eponymous character Jex Malone, whose story will be published in May by Merit Press. Conceived as a series character by Pearlman and her partner, fellow journalist Vickie Chachere (who write under the names C.L. Gaber and V.C. Stanley), Jex is a post-millennial "girl detective" who pays both comic and genuine homage to Nancy Drew. But unlike Nancy, she's a modern girl, a child of divorce. So, Pearlman points out, she has huge trust issues that mean she's "not an easy friend" to her four besties. Plot and interiority work together so that "while solving dangerous mysteries … Jex's confidence is bolstered. In a real way, each adventure helps her deal with personal issues … and slowly, with a lot of misfires [she] learns to become a trusting and fearless young woman."

Even in a fantasy series, the secret is to root great characters squarely in the world of identifiable human emotion. My own mentor, the great fantasy author Ray Bradbury, told me that growing up in Waukegan, Ill., was the best possible preparation for writing *The Martian Chronicles*, because, even over generations and whole galaxies, human emotion is consistent. But once you create your world, how do you bring readers into it, again and again?

3. PLAUSIBILITY

All fiction requires the suspension of disbelief, so you need to work hard to establish plausibility *within* that universe. One of the most difficult things in the word world is to write the second book in a series. The challenge for a good writer is finding the balance—appealing to the reader who's meeting these characters for the first time and making sure the reader who knows the character already isn't utterly bored.

Wasserman says that a great first chapter is key. "If the first chapter can stand on its own, that's a good sign the book will as well, and once you hook the reader, you can help ease them into understanding how this story fits into a larger context." What helps is feathering in past details in the way great mystery writers do, like three-time Edgar Award winner Ruth Rendell, whose irascible Inspector Wexford has been solving crimes and dealing with his fractious daughters for decades. Don't confuse the reader by referring to Olivia's death without ever saying who Olivia was: Nothing is more frustrating. Once you've plunged into the action, introduce backstory as seamlessly and with as much literary consciousness as you can. For example, use scenes and interactions between the main character(s) and others to shade in the background, without being too obvious. It's easier with MG series characters and readers, because in realistic fiction young kids experience bigger changes while remaining recognizably themselves.

Pennypacker says, "With Clementine, I kept everything I loved about her—her creativity, her positive responses to her own flaws ("OK, fine!"), her sense of who she is, her humorous worldview—but I let her grow through some things that weren't working for her, which made me feel proud in a weirdly parental way. This might be because Clementine is based on my son, whose biggest challenges in childhood were attention issues. Clementine struggles with impulsivity, distractibility and some extra activity. If you read the books in order, you'd see that while she never outgrows these challenges, she makes believable improvements in all these areas."

4. MARKETABILITY

To make a series a stunner, it needs to comprise more than a continuation of a story. A great series needs marketability, which means that readers won't just be finding out what happened to a character, but seeing familiar-but-primary characters engaged in entirely new pursuits and adventures.

One of the reasons the characters in *What We Saw at Night*, the first book of my new series, were so deeply into extreme sports was that it was almost certain that they would live short lives—XP sufferers rarely live to see their 40th birthday. How could I continue the serial killer mystery but also inject some kind of thrill, charm and, above all, hope?

Well, I won't reveal any spoilers, but sometimes the boy next door grows up and can look pretty good to a girl. And why be a fiction writer if you can't research and invent what would be the logical way to make a fatal illness into a chronic condition (gene therapy)? As for extreme sports, quite coincidentally, the series was set on the shores of the cold and vastly beautiful Lake Superior. In the first book I sent the kids up—through parkour—to an unimaginable terror. In the second book I sent them down in the most dangerous of all extreme sports, deep diving with only the air in your lungs. And it was to an *even more* unimaginable terror.

Am I through with Allie now? Undeniably, I miss her, and there are other things she could do. But, age-wise, she's topped out as a teen protagonist, and the worst possible error to make with a series character is to spread that character too thin over yet another book. Something less than a quarter of the way to being "finished" with a character is probably a great time to move on, after, as Wasserman says, the essential fire of the stories that made the characters "scream across the page" is over.

Will readers still ask you, "Whatever happened to …?"

I hope so. You've left them feeling fulfilled, but wanting more. That's what great series do.

JACQUELYN MITCHARD is the author of the bestselling novel *The Deep End of the Ocean* and editor-in-chief of Merit Press (operated by F+W Media, parent company of WD Books).

WRITING ABOUT SENSITIVE TOPICS

YA authors talk.

....

by Kerrie Flanagan

For YA authors Ellen Hopkins, Cheryl Rainfield and Jay Asher, no topic is off limits. Between the three of them, they have addressed subjects like suicide, drug abuse, cutting, prostitution and sexual abuse. Each of their books has received high acclaim and awards alongside criticism for writing about such controversial topics for young people. Despite the critics, they plan to continue to give teens a voice by writing books about sensitive topics and showing their readers that they are not alone.

Ellen Hopkins is a poet, freelance writer, and the award-winning author of twenty nonfiction titles and five *NY Times* bestselling novels-in-verse. She has published hundreds of articles on subjects ranging from aviation to child abuse to wine growing. Hopkins mentors other writers through her position as a regional adviser for the Nevada chapter of the Society of Children's Book Writers and Illustrators (SCBWI). She is a regular speaker at schools, book festivals and writers' conferences across the US, and now throughout the world.

Cheryl Rainfield is the author of the award-winning novel *Scars*, along with three other novels for teens. She's also the author of two short story collections and two hi-lo books for reluctant teen readers. Rainfield is an incest and ritual abuse survivor, and all of her books have fragments of the abuse she experienced. Although she writes about some of the harsh things teens go through, she also writes about healing, hope and love, and finding courage and strength. She is an avid reader and lives in Toronto with her little dog Petal.

Jay Asher is the author of the young adult novels *Thirteen Reasons Why* and *The Future Of Us* and. Asher's debut novel, *Thirteen Reasons Why* spent over two years on the *New York Times* children's hardcover bestseller list, with foreign rights sold in over 30 countries and more than one million copies in print in the U.S. alone. It won multiple awards and is being developed as a movie by Universal Pictures. His second novel, *The Future of Us* (co-written with Carolyn Mackler), has sold in 15 foreign markets, and is being developed as a movie by Warner Bros.

You all write about sensitive topics. What drew you to these topics? How do you write about these issues in an authentic and genuine way that resonates with your YA audience?

Hopkins: My first book, *Crank*, about a teen's fall into meth addiction was inspired by a very real story—my daughter's. I needed the catharsis of writing it, but also was determined to turn other teens away from that path if I could. Then, when I began really looking at the teen landscape, I became aware of issues touching the lives of so many of them—abuse, neglect, the need for love at whatever cost, depression and suicide, etc. You have to talk to teens to understand the depth of their emotions. Too many adults dismiss them. You must respect them.

Rainfield: I'm drawn to write about trauma, abuse, pain, and ways of coping with that and healing because it's what I've lived through, it's what I need to talk about. I'm an incest and torture survivor; my parents were part of cults. I felt so alone growing up, and in such deep pain and fear all the time, and no one was talking about those things. I write the books that I couldn't find as a teen and that I needed. I write to let other teens (and adults) know that they're not alone; that no matter what pain or trauma they're going through someone else has been there, and that they can get through it. It will get better. They can heal. That is a huge part of what drives me.

I get so many letters from teens telling me that they stopped cutting; got help; talked to someone for the first time; or didn't kill themselves because of one of my books. Those letters mean so much to me. I wanted to die a lot as a child and teen, so knowing that my books are making such a positive difference is huge for me—and that's another thing that drives me to write what I write. My books are my way to make a positive difference in the world.

I write about trauma and abuse and its effects from my own experience; I weave them into the fiction. I vividly remember what it felt like, and that's the place I write from— honest, emotional and real. I re-experience the trauma and pain when I write my novels—in a way it gets it out—and I re-experience it, too, each time I edit my manuscripts.

It's important to me to write about both the pain and also the hope and healing. I think it's important that readers have hope. I think that's what many of us are looking for in a story—to know we're not alone, and to know that things can get better.

Asher: Nine years before I came up with the idea for *Thirteen Reasons Why*, a relative of mine attempted suicide. She was a junior in high school, the same age as the girl in my book. That's obviously where my understanding of the subject came from, but I never imagined I'd write about it, mostly because I was only interested in writing humorous books. One day, an unusual storytelling structure I'd been thinking about clicked with this subject matter, and I knew I had a book. The ability to talk about an issue important to me in a unique and powerful way intrigued me, even though I planned to work on my humorous stuff at the same time. Three years later, I was done. And, of course, it sold before any of my funny books!

I did write *Thirteen Reasons Why* with a teen audience in mind. I wanted to write about the situations from that emotional perspective, not as an adult looking back. Yes, I shaped the story to reveal the things I wanted to say, but it had to be revealed through the words of my characters, not me. I also knew, out of respect for the seriousness of what needed to be written, that I couldn't hold back any detail that would make the scenes feel however raw they needed to feel. That's caused my book to be frequently challenged, but I know it's also what made it connect to so many readers.

All three of you have had a book banned by one group or another and Ellen, you have been included in the the annual list of "Most Challenged Authors" a few times. How do you feel about this? How does this impact your decisions about topics and issues to write about in future books?

Hopkins: My motto has always been, and remains, "Arm your kids with knowledge." Every teen is faced with choices, and without understanding possible outcomes, they often rush headlong in the wrong direction. As authors, we can't tiptoe around hard truths, because those truths are part of the human condition, and fearing a challenge is a sure way to make your writing fall flat. I choose topics because my readers are dealing with the issues I write about, and I want to fairly represent not just the problem, but how it affects those facing that problem. I don't think about possible challenges at all when I write a book.

Rainfield: I find it painful when people ban or try to ban my books. They're preventing readers from reading a book that they may need, that might save their life or help them heal, that might be the only way they have of finding out that they're not alone or not crazy. That's sad and just so wrong to me. If you don't like a book, that's fine—don't read it. If you really don't want your child to read it, that's your right. But preventing other people from reading it? I don't understand how people can think that's OK.

Having my books challenged and having people try to ban them will never stop me from writing about issues that I need to write about. Issues that I know teens today are living through and needing to talk about, desperately needing to know that someone understands—issues that teachers and parents and anyone who works with teens needs to know about. I know from reader letters that many teens need the books I write. And I need to write them. So I keep writing.

Asher: When I found out *Thirteen Reasons Why* was #3 on ALA's list of the most challenged books, I was nothing but upset. When I mention my book is on that list, many people congratulate me for having my name in the company of such great authors. But I don't think there's anything cool about being on that list. I might feel different, though, if my subject matter was different. One of the main reasons I was determined to write that book is that our society has a hard time talking about suicide. When we don't talk about it, or we ban books about it, it sends a dangerous message to people who may be having those dark thoughts and who don't think anyone will understand. The day I made that list, I received an e-mail from a teen saying my book saved her life. And that's only because she had access to it! I can't be anything but upset that there are people actively trying to restrict that access.

Thirteen Reasons Why was an anomaly for the types of stories I normally consider writing. Maybe one day I'll have an idea about a similarly serious topic, and if the storyline intrigues me enough, I'll write it with the same honesty because I've been witness to the power of doing it that way. And then I'll deal with the potential controversies that may come about, because it's worth it.

When you begin writing, do you have a message you want to convey in your story? If so, what are some ways you do that without sounding condescending or preachy to your audience?

Hopkins: I don't always have a message as such, but when I do (with the Crank books, for instance), I integrate it into the story so deeply that it doesn't come across as preachy. No one ever says, "Drugs are bad" in those books, but readers have no problem at all witnessing the protagonist's downfall, or how she can't walk away in the end, even though part of her wants to. Character depth is how you accomplish it.

Rainfield: I think it's important that we tell an entertaining story that grabs readers—I try to do that especially through suspense tension, and emotion—but I also want to show readers that they are not alone, and that they can survive and heal, and that they are strong and good and lovable and deserve to be treated well. I try to have my characters gradually gain insights and healing throughout the book, more fully recognizing their strengths near the end, so that the reader comes away feeling those things, too. It helps to show the character doing and experiencing what you want readers to understand, rather than only telling what they're doing, and to really get inside

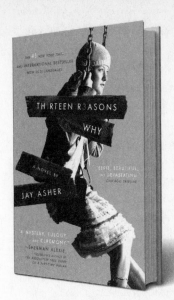 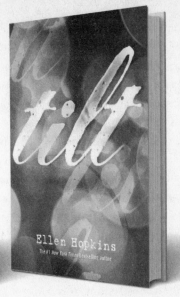 

the emotion of the character. I also try to make sure that my characters are likable; they have flaws and faults, but they also have good qualities. I try to make sure readers can relate to my characters—I do this especially through emotion. If they can't relate to a character, then I don't think the story is appealing. I get inside my characters, and put a lot of myself and my emotions and body language in them, as well as things I've observed and understood in others. I think the more distance you have from your characters, the easier it is for the reader to distance from them or judge them, or feel talked down to. But that's just my opinion; it doesn't mean I'm right. I write with my own emotion and bits of my trauma experience, and I think that helps me have a closeness to and understanding of my characters that I think my readers feel and appreciate.

Asher: I think if you're going to write about a serious issue, you're naturally going to have something you want to say because you're going to have an opinion about your topic. When the concept of *Thirteen Reasons Why* came to me, I knew my message would organically come out in the story. I didn't have to push it (or preach it). My job was simply to tell the story in an engaging way. My focus was on writing it as a suspense novel so someone who doesn't normally read sad books (like me!) would have a hard time putting it down. And if I kept your attention, you'd understand what I wanted to say.

How much research is involved when you write your books? How do you approach the research and then integrate it into your story so the story flows and doesn't sound too didactic?

Hopkins: Primary research is always best. You can research facts and statistics online, but when it comes to really understanding an issue, you have to talk to someone who's been through it. And not just one person, but many, as every experience is different and you're trying to find common denominators. Again, you're looking for truths, and you write the characters steeped in those truths. Truth is never didactic.

Rainfield: I draw on my own trauma experience for my books; I think it gives it great emotion and depth and an insider perspective. But for details I might not know, such as research about specific details about guns or how hospitals treat rape victims now, I contact experts and ask them questions. I also did a lot of research on port wine stains for *Stained*, and read how some people were treated, then drew on my own experience of being bullied and stared at for my scars to write those scenes. I try to only put in details that are necessary or that help make the story more powerful or add to the emotion of the scene, and I sprinkle them into the action and dialogue. I stay away from long passages of description or research, since I find that completely stops the forward movement of the story.

Asher: I can't begin a book until the characters feel real. With *Thirteen Reasons Why*, the girl's character felt real the moment the premise came to me. Her words and personality were strong. She had something to say! My job was to let her say it. So I chose to do very little research, other than talking to some friends about their high school years, because I didn't want statistics or anything to influence this character that already felt so real. After I finished a solid draft, I did some research to see if I was way off. It turned out that by letting the character speak, she naturally flowed through the arc of a rather typical person in a similar situation. I was actually a little surprised (and scared) that I knew to have her react in certain ways. I believe there were only two or three lines I tweaked to clarify certain points. But whether you do a lot of research or a little, if you always stay true to the character, in words and action, it's a lot easier to keep it from sounding like you're cramming information.

What should new writers keep in mind when writing about sensitive topics for a YA audience?

Hopkins: Every teen feels alone with their problems. It's fascinating, really. My readers always tell me, "I thought I was the only one going through this. Now I know I'm not, so thank you." They feel shame or fear or distress, mostly because they believe no one can understand them. When an author understands them, they become less marginalized. Write for the teen who feels alone. Show them there's a way beyond their current experience. YA authors are helping build a more positive future by arming our readers with knowledge.

Rainfield: I think using some of your own emotion and honesty in writing is so important; readers will sense if you're not being honest or you're holding back or you're afraid of the topic. You don't have to have gone through the experiences you write about; as long as you can relate to them and feel something about them, and write about that feeling honestly, your writing will speak to others. I think it helps to write about issues that you care about. It can also help to read about or talk to people who've been through those experiences if you haven't yourself. And I think it's really important to come to an issue with compassion and a lack of judgment. Otherwise, you'll alienate the readers you're trying to reach. If you can understand why someone does something, like use self-harm or drink to cope, then you help to shine light on something that others may not understand, and you'll help readers feel less alone.

Asher: Don't hold back. If something is true to the story (which sounds weird because the actual stories aren't true, but you know what I mean!), it should be in there. If you're writing about things that do happen to real people, then it's appropriate to write about only if you write it as honestly as possible. To not hold back is to be respectful of the people who actually deal with these things. It's the only way to let them know that someone understands, and to let others know what's going on.

KERRIE FLANAGAN (KerrieFlanagan.com) is a freelance writer, writing consultant, and director of Northern Colorado Writers, a group supporting and encouraging writers of all levels and genres since 2007: northerncoloradowriters.com.

CRAFTING A QUERY

How to write a great letter.

by Kara Gebhart Uhl

So you've written a book. And now you want an agent. If you're new to publishing, you probably assume that the next step is to send your finished, fabulous book out to agents, right? Wrong. Agents don't want your finished, fabulous book. In fact, they probably don't even want *part* of your finished, fabulous book—at least, not yet. First, they want your query.

A query is a short, professional way of introducing yourself to an agent. If you're frustrated by the idea of this step, imagine yourself at a cocktail party. Upon meeting someone new, you don't greet them with a boisterous hug and kiss and, in three minutes, reveal your entire life story including the fact that you were late to the party because of some gastrointestinal problems. Rather, you extend your hand. You state your name. You comment on the hors d'oeuvres, the weather, the lovely shade of someone's dress. Perhaps, after this introduction, the person you're talking to politely excuses himself. Or, perhaps, you begin to forge a friendship. It's basic etiquette, formality, professionalism—it's simply how it's done.

Agents receive hundreds of submissions every month. Often they read these submissions on their own time—evenings, weekends, on their lunch break. Given the number of writers submitting, and the number of agents reading, it would simply be impossible for agents to ask for and read entire book manuscripts off the bat. Instead, a query is a quick way for you to, first and foremost, pitch your book. But it's also a way to pitch yourself. If an agent is intrigued by your query, she may ask for a partial (say, the first three chapters of your book). Or she may ask for your entire manuscript. And only then may you be signed.

As troublesome as it may first seem, try not to be frustrated by this process. Because, honestly, a query is a really great way to help speed up what is already a monumentally slow-paced industry. Have you ever seen pictures of slush piles—those piles of unread queries on many well-known agents' desk? Imagine the size of those slush piles if they held full manuscripts instead of one-page query letters. Thinking of it this way, query letters begin to make more sense.

Here we share with you the basics of a query, including its three parts and a detailed list of dos and don'ts.

PART I: THE INTRODUCTION

Whether you're submitting a 100-word picture book or a 90,000-word novel, you must be able to sum up the most basic aspects of it in one sentence. Agents are busy. And they constantly receive submissions for types of work they don't represent. So upfront they need to know that, after reading your first paragraph, the rest of your query is going to be worth their time.

An opening sentence designed to "hook" an agent is fine—if it's good and if it works. But this is the time to tune your right brain down and your left brain up—agents desire professionalism and queries that are short and to the point. Remember the cocktail party. Always err on the side of formality. Tell the agent, in as few words as possible, what you've written, including the title, genre and length.

Within the intro you also must try to connect with the agent. Simply sending 100 identical query letters out to "Dear Agent" won't get you published. Instead, your letter should be addressed not only to a specific agency but a specific agent within that agency. (And double, triple, quadruple check that the agent's name is spelled correctly.) In addition, you need to let the agent know why you chose her specifically. A good author-agent relationship is like a good marriage. It's important that both sides invest the time to find a good fit that meets their needs. So how do you connect with an agent you don't know personally? Research.

1. Make a connection based on an author or book the agent already represents.

Most agencies have websites that list who and what they represent. Research those sites. Find a book similar to yours and explain that, because such-and-such book has a similar theme or tone or whatever, you think your book would be a great fit. In addition, many agents will list specific topics they're looking for, either on their websites or in interviews. If your book is a match, state that.

2. Make a connection based on an interview you read.

Search by agents' names online and read any and all interviews they've participated in. Perhaps they mentioned a love for X and your book is all about X. Or, perhaps they mentioned that they're looking for Y and your book is all about Y. Mention the specific interview. Prove that you've invested as much time researching them as they're about to spend researching you.

3. Make a connection based on a conference you both attended.

Was the agent you're querying the keynote speaker at a writing conference you were recently at? Mention it, specifically commenting on an aspect of his speech you liked. Even better, did you meet the agent in person? Mention it, and if there's something you can say to jog her memory about the meeting, say it. And better yet, did the agent specifically ask you to send your manuscript? Mention it.

Finally, if you're being referred to a particular agent by an author who that agent already represents—that's your opening sentence. That referral is guaranteed to get your query placed on the top of the stack.

PART II: THE PITCH

Here's where you really get to sell your book—but in only three to 10 sentences. Consider the jacket flap and its role in convincing readers to plunk down $24.95 to buy what's in between those flaps. Like a jacket flap, you need to hook an agent in the confines of very limited space. What makes your story interesting and unique? Is your story about a woman going through a midlife crisis? Fine, but there are hundreds of stories about women going through midlife crises. Is your story about a woman who, because of a midlife crisis, leaves her life and family behind to spend three months in India? Again, fine, but this story, too, already exists—in many forms. Is your story about a woman who, because of a midlife crisis, leaves her life and family behind to spend three months in India, falls in love with someone new while there and starts a new life—and family?—and then has to deal with everything she left behind upon her return? *Now* you have a hook.

Practice your pitch. Read it out loud, not only to family and friends, but to people willing to give you honest, intelligent criticism. If you belong to a writing group, workshop your pitch. Share it with members of an online writing forum. Know anyone in the publishing industry? Share it with them. Many writers spend years writing their books. We're not talking about querying magazines here, we're talking about querying an agent who could become a lifelong partner. Spend time on your pitch. Perfect it. Turn it into jacket-flap material so detailed, exciting and clear that it would be near impossible to read your pitch and not want to read more. Use active verbs. Write your pitch, put it aside for a week, then look at it again. Don't send a query simply because you finished a book. Send a query because you finished your pitch and are ready to take the next steps.

DOS AND DON'TS FOR QUERYING AGENTS

DO:

- Keep the tone professional.
- Query a specific agent at a specific agency.
- Proofread. Double-check the spelling of the agency and the agent's name.
- Keep the query concise, limiting the overall length to one page (single space, 12-point type in a commonly used font).
- Focus on the plot, not your bio, when pitching fiction.
- Pitch agents who represent the type of material you write.
- Check an agency's submission guidelines to see how it would like to be queried—for example, via e-mail or mail—and whether or not to include a SASE.
- Keep pitching, despite rejections.

DON'T:

- Include personal info not directly related to the book. For example, stating that you're a parent to three children doesn't make you more qualified than someone else to write a children's book.
- Say how long it took you to write your manuscript. Some bestselling books took 10 years to write—others, six weeks. An agent doesn't care how long it took—an agent only cares if it's good. Same thing goes with drafts—an agent doesn't care how many drafts it took you to reach the final product.
- Mention that this is your first novel or, worse, the first thing you've ever written aside from grocery lists. If you have no other publishing credits, don't advertise that fact. Don't mention it at all.
- State that your book has been edited by peers or professionals. Agents expect manuscripts to be edited, no matter how the editing was done.
- Bring up screenplays or film adaptations; you're querying an agent about publishing a book, not making a movie.
- Mention any previous rejections.
- State that the story is copyrighted with the U.S. Copyright Office or that you own all rights. Of course you own all rights. You wrote it.
- Rave about how much your family and friends loved it. What matters is that the agent loves it.
- Send flowers, baked goods or anything else except a self-addressed stamped envelope (and only if the SASE is required).
- Follow up with a phone call. After the appropriate time has passed (many agencies say how long it will take to receive a response) follow up in the manner you queried—via e-mail or mail.

PART III: THE BIO

If you write fiction, unless you're a household name, an agent is much more interested in your pitch than in who you are. If you write nonfiction, who you are—more specifically, your platform and publicity—is much more important. Regardless, these are key elements that must be present in every bio:

1. Publishing credits

If you're submitting fiction, focus on your fiction credits—previously published works and short stories. That said, if you're submitting fiction and all your previously published work is nonfiction—magazine articles, essays, etc.—that's still fine and good to mention. Just don't be overly long about it. Mention your publications in bigger magazines or well-known literary journals. If you've never had anything published, don't say you lack official credits. Simply skip this altogether and thank the agent for his time.

2. Contests and awards

If you've won many, focus on the most impressive ones and the ones that most directly relate to your work. Don't mention contests you entered and weren't named in. Also, feel free to leave titles and years out of it. If you took first place at the Delaware Writers Conference for your fiction manuscript, that's good enough. Mentioning details isn't necessary.

3. MFAs

If you've earned or are working toward a Master of Fine Arts in writing, say so and state the program. Don't mention English degrees or online writing courses.

4. Large, recognized writing organizations

Agents don't want to hear about your book club and the fact that there's always great food, or the small critique group you meet with once a week. And they really don't want to hear about the online writing forum you belong to. But if you're a member of something like the Romance Writers of America (RWA), the Mystery Writers of America (MWA), the Society of Children's Book Writers and Illustrators (SCBWI), the Society of Professional Journalists (SPJ), etc., say so. This shows you're serious about what you do and you're involved in groups that can aid with publicity and networking.

5. Platform and publicity

If you write nonfiction, who you are and how you're going to help sell the book once it's published becomes very important. Why are you the best person to write it and what do you have now—public speaking engagements, an active website or blog, substantial cred in your industry—that will help you sell this book?

Finally, be cordial. Thank the agent for taking the time to read your query and consider your manuscript. Ask if you may send more, in the format she desires (partial, full, etc.).

Think of the time you spent writing your book. Unfortunately, you can't send your book to an agent for a first impression. Your query *is* that first impression. Give it the time it deserves. Keep it professional. Keep it formal. Let it be a firm handshake—not a sloppy kiss. Let it be a first meeting that evolves into a lifetime relationship—not a rejection slip. But expect those slips. Just like you don't become lifelong friends with everyone you meet at a cocktail party, you can't expect every agent you pitch to sign you. Be patient. Keep pitching. And in the meantime, start writing that next book.

KARA GEBHART UHL, formerly a managing editor at *Writer's Digest* magazine, now freelance writers and edits in Fort Thomas, KY. She also blogs about parenting at pleiadesbee.com. Her essays have appeared on The Huffington Post, *The New York Times*' Motherlode and *TIME: Healthland*. Her parenting essay, "Apologies to the Parents I Judged Four Years Ago" was named one of *TIME*'s "Top 10 Opinions of 2012."

SAMPLE QUERY NO. 1: YOUNG ADULT
AGENT'S COMMENTS: LAUREN MACLEOD (STROTHMAN AGENCY)

Dear Ms. MacLeod,

I am seeking literary representation and hope you will consider my tween novel, REAL MERMAIDS DON'T WEAR TOE RINGS.

First zit. First crush. First … mermaid's tail?

1 Jade feels like enough of a freak-of-nature when she gets her first period at almost fifteen. She doesn't need to have it happen at the mall while trying on that XL tankini she never wanted to buy in the first place. And she really doesn't need to run into Luke Martin in the Feminine Hygiene Products **2** aisle while her dad Googles "menstruation" on his Blackberry **4** .

3 But "freak-of-nature" takes on a whole new meaning when raging hormones and bath salts bring on another metamorphosis—complete with scales and a tail. And when Jade learns she's inherited her mermaid tendencies from her late mother's side of the family, it raises the question: if Mom was once a mermaid, did she really drown that day last summer?

Jade is determined to find out. Though, how does a plus-sized, aqua-phobic mer-girl go about doing that, exactly … especially when Luke from aisle six seems to be the only person who might be able to help?

5 REAL MERMAIDS DON'T WEAR TOE RINGS is a light-hearted fantasy novel for tweens (10-14). It is complete at 44,500 words and available at your request. The first ten pages and a synopsis are included below my signature. I also have a completed chapter book for boys (MASON AND THE MEGANAUTS), should that be of interest to you.

My middle grade novel, ACADIAN STAR, was released last fall by Nimbus Publishing and has been nominated for the 2009/2010 Hackmatack Children's Choice Book Award. I have three nonfiction children's books with Crabtree Publishing to my credit (one forthcoming) as well as an upcoming early chapter book series. Thank you for taking the time to consider this project.

Kind regards,
Hélène Boudreau
www.heleneboudreau.com

1 One of the things that can really m[ake] a query letter stand out is a strong v[oice] and it seems that is one of the things [writ]ers struggle with the most. Hélène, [how]ever, knocked it out of the park with [her] query letter. I find young readers are [very] sensitive to inauthentic voices, but [I] can tell by just the first few paragra[phs] that she is going to absolutely nai[l the] tween voice in the manuscript—you [can] see this even by the way she capita[lizes] Feminine Hygiene Products **2** .

3 The first time I read this query, I [re]ally did laugh out loud. Instead of m[erely] promising me RMDWTR was funny (w[hich] it absolutely is), Hélène showed me [how] funny she can be, which made me w[ant] to request the manuscript even bef[ore I] got to her sample pages.

I also loved how clearly and with just a [few] words she could invoke an entire scene[. Hé]lène doesn't tell us Jade gets embarra[ssed] in front of a local hunk, she plops us [right] down in the middle of the pink aisle wit[h her] well-intentioned but hopelessly nerdy [dad] **4** . I felt this really spoke to her tale[nt;] if she could bring bits of a query to l[ife, I] couldn't wait to see what she could do [with] a whole manuscript. **5** And on top of [all] this, she had a phenomenal title, a bio [that] made it very clear she was ready to b[reak] out, and a hook so strong it even ma[de it] onto the cover!

Dear Ms. Humphrey,

I'm contacting you because I've read on various writing websites that you are expanding your young adult client list.

In LOSING FAITH, fifteen-year-old Brie Jenkins discovers her sister's death may not have been an accident **1**. At the funeral, an uncorroborated story surfaces about Faith's whereabouts the night of her tragic fall from a cliff. When Brie encounters a strange, evasive boy **3** at Faith's gravesite, she tries to confront him, but he disappears into a nearby forest.

Brie searches out and questions the mysterious boy, finding more information than she bargained for: Faith belonged to a secret ritualistic group, which regularly held meetings at the cliff where she died. Brie suspects foul play, but the only way to find out for sure is to risk her own life and join the secret cult. **2**

LOSING FAITH (76k/YA) will appeal to readers of **4** John Green's LOOKING FOR ALASKA and Laurie Halse Anderson's CATALYST. My published stories have won an editor's choice award in *The Greensilk Journal* and appeared in *Mississippi Crow* magazine. I'm a member of Romance Writers of America, where my manuscript is a finalist in the Florida chapter's Launching a Star Contest. For your convenience, I've pasted the first chapter at the bottom of this e-mail. Thank you for your time and consideration.

Sincerely,
Denise Jaden
www.denisejaden.com **5**

Everything about Denise's query appealed to me. She gave me a quick sentence about why she chose to query me, and then went right into the gist of her novel. **1** Her "gist" is very much a teaser, or like the back blurb of a book. She gives plot clues without revealing too much of the plot. She keeps the plot points brief and keeps the teaser moving; most important is where she ends—on a note that makes the agent curious to know more. **2** Denise also gives us vivid characters **3** in this teaser: the smart, investigative protagonist, Brie; the mysterious boy at the gravesite; the sister, Faith, who's not what she seems. By creating hints of vivid characters and quick engaging plot points in a paragraph, Denise demonstrates her storytelling ability in the query—and I suspected it would carry through to her novel. **4** Denise includes some other elements that I like to see in queries: comparisons to other well-known books (two or three is enough) and credentials that show her ability to write fiction. **5** I like, too, that she included her website—I often visit websites when considering queries.

SAMPLE QUERY NO. 3: MIDDLE GRADE
AGENT'S COMMENTS: ELANA ROTH (RED TREE LITERARY)

Dear Ms. Roth,

A boy with a hidden power and the girl who was sent to stop him have 24 hours to win a pickle contest.

1 12-year-old Pierre La Bouche is a *cornichon*. That's French for "pickle," but it also means "good-for-nothing." A middle child who gets straight C's, he's never been No. 1 at anything. When the family farm goes broke, grandfather Henri gives Pierre a mission: to save the farm by winning an international pickle contest.

2 En route to the contest, Pierre meets Aurore, the charming but less-than-truthful granddaughter of a rival farmer. She's been sent to en-snare Pierre, but after a wake up call from her conscience, she rescues him. Together, they navigate the ghostly Paris catacombs, figure out how to crash-land a plane, and duel with a black-hearted villain who will stop at nothing to capture their pickles. In their most desperate hour, it is Pierre's incredible simplicity that saves the day. Always bickering but becoming friends, Pierre and Aurore discover that anything is possible, no matter how hard it may seem.

3 *Pickle Impossible* is complete at 32,500 words. I'm a technical writer by day, optimistic novelist by night. Recently, I've interviewed a host of pickle makers and French natives. My own pickles are fermenting in the kitchen. I grew up in Toronto and live with my wife and children in Israel.

Thank you for your consideration. I hope to hear from you.

Kind Regards,

Eli Stutz

1 The first paragraph introduces the main character and the set-up. He uses concrete things to describe Pierre. He throws in the French flair of the book right away. And he doesn't beat around the bush to tell me what Pierre has to accomplish. **2** The second delves a little deeper into the plot. It gives me the complication that will drive the story forward—someone is out to stop Pierre. And then Eli accomplishes the most important trick here: He gives me some fun examples of what will happen in the book without summarizing the entire plot. That is key because I don't want to read the whole book in the query letter. But he gives me flavor. **3** The bio paragraph is straight to the point, not overcrowded with his whole life history, and also ties light-heartedly right back to the subject of the book. I loved that he tried fermenting his own pickles. (He later told me they weren't very good.) Here's the kicker. The total word count on this letter is 242 words. 242! Look how much he fits into 242 words. There's plot, character, personality and quirk. From this tightly written letter I know I'm going to get a fun, zany story. Those of you who wanted 250 words just to pitch your book, take heed! Shorter is better.

WRITING FOR BOYS (AND OTHER "RELUCTANT READERS")

by Carmela A. Martino

When it comes to boys and reading, the statistics are discouraging. In studies of students in the United States and around the world, girls, on average, score significantly higher in reading than boys. And recent research conducted by England's National Literacy Trust says that this gender gap is widening. In 2001, Jon Scieszka, the First National Ambassador of Young People's Literature, founded Guys Read to help address this problem. The GuysRead.com website is based on the principal that boys will read "if they are given reading that interests them." But not all "reluctant readers" are boys. We've invited four award-winning authors known for writing books that appeal to boys and other "reluctant readers" to share their thoughts on how to reach this audience.

MATT DE LA PEÑA is the author of five critically acclaimed young adult novels, four of which were named ALA Quick Picks for Reluctant Young Adult Readers. His most recent, *The Living* (Delacorte), won the 2014 ALA Pura Belpré Honor Award for excellence in portraying the Latino cultural experience. He also wrote the award-winning picture book *A Nation's Hope: The Story of Boxing Legend Joe Louis*, illustrated by Kadir Nelson (Dial), and the middle-grade novel, *Curse of the Ancients,* the fourth in the Infinity Ring Series (Scholastic). One of his short stories is included in *Guys Reads: Thriller*, edited by Jon Scieszka (Walden Pond), the second volume in the Guys Read anthology series. Matt received his MFA in creative writing from San Diego State University. He teaches creative writing and visits high schools and colleges throughout the country. For more about him, see his website, mattdelapena.com.

LENORE LOOK recently released the sixth book in her award-winning (and boy-friendly) Alvin Ho chapter book series: *Alvin Ho: Allergic to the Great Wall, the Forbidden Palace, and Other Tourist Attractions* (Schwartz & Wade). She is also the author of the Ruby Lu series (Atheneum) and several acclaimed picture books, including *Henry's First-Moon Birthday* (Simon & Schuster), *Uncle Peter's Amazing Chinese Wedding* (Atheneum), and, her newest, *Brush of the Gods* (Random House), a historical fiction account of the life of Wu Daozi, China's most famous painter. Lenore taught creative writing at Drew University and St. Elizabeth College in New Jersey, and frequently speaks in schools in the United States and Asia. She has also co-presented the Highlights Foundation workshop "Writing for Boys" with Bruce Coville and Rich Wallace. She lives in Hoboken, N.J., and blogs frequently at lenorelook.wordpress.com.

DAVID LUBAR has written thirty books for teens and young readers. His first novel, *Hidden Talents* (TOR Books) and his recent young-adult story collection, *Extremities: Stories of Death, Murder, and Revenge* (TOR Teen), were both ALA Quick Picks for Reluctant Young Adult Readers. His novels are on reading lists across the country, saving countless students from a close encounter with *Madame Bovary*. His Weenies short story collections have sold more than two million copies. His stories have appeared in a variety of magazines, including *Boy's Life, READ* and *Nickelodeon*. He also designed and programmed video games in a former eight-bit life. He lives in Nazareth, Pa. with his wife and various felines, and spends far too much time online, tweeting things that apparently have no effect on book sales. His website, davidlubar.com, includes a page dedicated to humor, with a section especially for children's writers.

STEVE SHEINKIN is a former textbook writer who is now making amends by writing history books kids and teens actually *want* to read. Recent titles include *Bomb: The Race to Build—and Steal—the World's Most Dangerous Weapon* (Scholastic), *The Notorious Benedict Arnold: A True Story of Adventure, Heroism, & Treachery* (Roaring Brook), *Lincoln's Grave Robbers* (Scholastic), and the newest, *The Port Chicago 50: Disaster, Mutiny, and the Fight for Civil Rights* (Roaring Brook). His books have won numerous awards, including a Newbery Honor, the Siebert Medal, and the YALSA Award for Excellence in Nonfiction for Young Adults. He also contributed a truly disturbing and disgusting story to the new *Guys*

Reads: True Stories, edited by Jon Scieszka (Walden Pond), the fifth volume in the anthology series. You can read more about him at stevesheinkin.com.

What kind of reader were you as a child? How has that influenced your writing for children and teens, and, in particular, for boys and reluctant readers?

DE LA PEÑA: Takes one to know one. Not really, but sort of. I was a big-time reluctant reader when I was in high school. I spent all my time playing ball and chasing girls. I read a lot of basketball magazines, but I couldn't penetrate novels. It wasn't until college, when I was introduced to books like Allison Walker's *The Color Purple* and Junot Díaz's *Drown* that I found a heartbeat in literature. I think a lot of artists try to make things that appeal to themselves. I do that with my books. Give me a story that feels authentic and honest, with a narrator who sounds familiar, like someone I might meet on the street, and I'm all in. Hopefully that's what my readers find when they enter my work. I also try to dig deep enough that readers will "feel" something. Reluctant readers aren't less intelligent readers. They respond to depth, too.

SHEINKIN: I loved exciting, real stories—I was never too into goblins or vampires. Probably my all-time favorite books were historical novels like *Mutiny on the Bounty* and *The Great Train Robbery*. Also anything to do with buried treasure or sharks eating people. Now, as a writer of nonfiction, I try to recapture that sense of adventure, that page-turning momentum I always loved as a young reader.

LUBAR: I devoured books of all flavors. I read fiction, biography, humor, cartoon collections, comic books, monster magazines, and a lot of science books (especially Martin Gardner's books and Isaac Asimov's collections of essays). This left me with a vast horde of semi-useful information around which to build stories, as well as an enthusiasm for knowledge for its own sake. I guess my stockpile of interesting information allows me to offer my readers all sorts of entertaining plots and plot twists.

LOOK: I cringe whenever I hear the term "reluctant reader." And to hear boys and reluctant readers always mentioned together like hydrogen and bomb, well, it's tantamount to detonating a hydrogen bomb. I'm not denying that there's a problem, but I do wonder if we're over-diagnosing a symptom (like a cough) and over-treating it, while the real illness rages elsewhere (like end-stage lung cancer). If I were a child, bored to death by books and maybe addicted to my electronic toys, and grown-ups began calling me a reluctant reader and giving me reluctant books and putting me in a reluctant group and telling my parents all about my reluctance, well, I would indeed feel pretty reluctant! Children, by nature, are not reluctant. They are open, enthusiastic, welcoming. They are explorers and adventurers. They embrace and dance. The problem is not that they are reluctant readers, the problem is that they no longer do these other things. Instead, they are scheduled to the gills and taken from one activity to the next, day after day, weekend after weekend, like a haul of fish to the canneries. They have no time, or the skill now, to fill their afternoons on their own. They have no time to idle, to let their minds wander. They have no time to wonder, to be curious. When we have robbed them of their curiosity, what use have they for books?

I was a random and voracious reader. My parents had no money for lessons or sports equipment that would improve me beyond recognition and turn me into a peach for colleges they didn't know existed. So I was at the library or at home every afternoon, reading everything that had an enticing cover, and some things that didn't. I read after school, before and after dinner, at bedtime, and then under the covers. I probably read in my dreams, too! I read so much that I was in glasses by the second grade, and in custom-fitted telescopic instruments by the time I got to high school. My random reading led me to infinite interests, so now I try to include as many of my random interests in my books as I can without being totally random.

What is it about your books that appeals to boys/reluctant readers? Were you targeting that particular audience?

SHEINKIN: I never target any particular audience; I just find stories that are compelling to me. What I try to do is take some bit of history and present it as a thriller, borrowing techniques from novels and movies. Some of the subjects I've chosen—spies, battles, grave robbing—may have particular appeal to boys, but it's not really intentional.

DE LA PEÑA: I definitely didn't start out targeting reluctant readers. I still don't (though I'm more aware of that demographic). I think it's a mistake to spend too much time worrying about target audience. It's better to write the story that moves you, revise it over and over until it hums, and let your publisher decide who to put it in front of. To be honest, I didn't even know what YA was until my first book was acquired.

LOOK: In my Alvin Ho series, as well as in my Ruby Lu books, it's all about making my young readers laugh. This is the way my dad would tell us stories when my brothers and I were growing up. They were tall tales about his childhood that kept getting more fantastical and unbelievable until we were irretrievably lost in laughter. Laughter is something that appeals to both genders and all ages. Who doesn't want to laugh? Who doesn't want to open a book and just holler? My target audience? Me! I write to make myself (or my seven-year-old self) laugh, and I just hope that my young readers will get it and jump over the edge with me.

LUBAR: I have a short attention span, so I like to keep things moving. I never let anything run on for too long. Descriptions, transitions, expositions–they all pop up, do their job, then scurry off stage. I mix dialogue and action. I keep my chapters short. I don't do this by design or to capture a certain group of readers. That's just how I write.

Many of my short stories are only two or three pages long. Even the longest ones rarely break 1,500 words. Kids can read one, and have a satisfying experience pretty quickly. They're short, but they are complete stories. I shudder when I hear them called

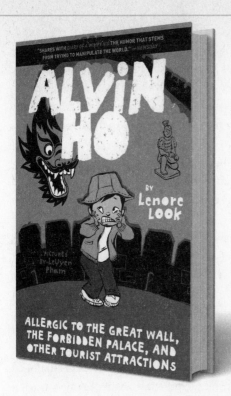

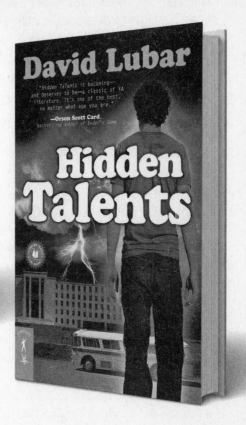

"flash fiction." They're fully fleshed out and heavily revised. I just don't spend three pages describing a hat when the story is about a vampire, or allow anyone to get long-winded when all he has to say is, "That looks like a bomb." I think the bottom line is that I have fun writing, and that fun seems to carry through to the reader. I don't write to instruct or enlighten, I write to entertain. Though the entertainment might take the form of a kid trapped in Zeno's paradox while he is walking home from school or a girl science genius creating an exothermic reaction to help her zombie friend have the right temperature in his mouth to pass his physical.

In her report, "Helping Underachieving Boys Read Well and Often," Wendy Schwartz says "boys, like all children, want to see characters like themselves." Is appealing to boys as simple as having a male main character, or is there more to it than that? Is a male protagonist a requirement, or can stories about girls appeal to boys, too?

SHEINKIN: No, I don't think having a male main character is the key factor. I, for one, loved the Little House books as a kid. I was fascinated by the details about how the family survived in such a challenging environment. I think the big thing is that readers, especially reluctant ones, have to find a story that sounds fun to them, and not like health food. I absolutely believe books and reading can appeal to these readers—it's just a matter of getting them the right book.

LUBAR: I would take it a step beyond, to the idea that the reader wants to see a character like himself. I believe we all see the main character in our own image as we read, until the various components of the main character, such as sex, age, race, body-type, etc., are revealed.

I believe a boy will read a story about an awesome girl. But I suspect, given a choice between her and an equally awesome male character, most boys would opt for the guy. There are very few rigid requirements, and writers should feel free to swim against the current when the art demands this. On the one hand, this could make a book a tougher sell. On the other, it could help the story stand out.

DE LA PEÑA: Female protagonists can definitely appeal to reluctant male readers. But if a guy reader can't identify with the sex of the protagonist he might need to identify with the "world" of the novel. Does the neighborhood feel familiar? Does the dialogue sound right? Can he identify racially or culturally? Sometimes it takes a savvy teacher or librarian to introduce that kid to a book that feels like home.

LOOK: I agree that children want to see characters like themselves, and gender is a huge part of our identity, so naturally boys will be drawn to books about boys. But a simple gender assignment isn't the trick to appealing to either boys or girls. In fact, there is no trick. There's just a lot of hard work. The greatest appeal to children is the same as for adults: honesty. Your character has to reveal what it's like to be an authentic human being. And this honesty, this authenticity is what drives us to art and why art is so important—to see ourselves as we really are, the good and the bad—it wakes us up. And when we're awake, we see the world differently, we see how to conduct our lives and how to treat our neighbors. "A book must be an axe for the frozen sea within us," Franz Kafka wrote. Children don't need axes and they're not frozen seas, but they know when a book doesn't reach them where they really live.

Are there specific craft techniques/story elements writers should focus on to hook boys and reluctant readers? For example, do books for boys need to be heavy on plot and action?

DE LA PEÑA: I think reluctant readers respond to books that, as Elmore Leonard puts it, "get to the good stuff." I do consider reader psychology. Readers like dialogue. White space on a page makes the page less daunting. Short chapters are appealing. Person-

ally, I try not to give too much internal. And I really try to keep the reader visually engaged. Also, my goal is to stay out of the way. The characters are the stars, not the writer.

SHEINKIN: I'm not a big believer in rules, or that there's ever just one right way to do things. When outlining, though, I do think a lot about how to draw readers into a story, and how to keep the action moving quickly. I map out my stories like screenwriters do, making an index card for each scene. That way I can tape them all to the wall and see whole story at once, and anticipate where any slow spots might sneak in.

LOOK: I don't know how to plot. I let my books grow organically from my characters. This means that I follow my characters from scene to scene. And each scene reveals something new about my characters. When a scene doesn't work, I throw it out. I guess this means I rely on action–something is always happening. But action is meaningless unless it reveals something new and moves your book forward.

The best hook, I think, is language. Simple, strong language that pulls you in and clutches you by the collar until the last word is mirrored in your glassy eyes. Choose your words carefully. Make metaphors. Use similes. Create images that linger in the reader's mind long after the book is closed. Make us see things differently. Write from the heart to the heart. What reader doesn't want to be entirely captivated like that?

But language alone isn't going to do it. There needs to be a sense of urgency, and a voice. I write because I feel a desperate need to say something, and in turn, my readers will feel a desperate need to read it. Then I listen for the right voice to tell it. Urgency and voice. If you don't feel the fire beneath you, and you haven't found the voice of your book, then plot and action and strong words aren't going to get you very far.

LUBAR: I think books for *kids* need plot and action, at least until the kids have acquired a solid reading habit. If we force young kids to read too much beautiful, lyrical, wandering literary prose where nothing happens, we teach them that reading isn't fun. There's plenty of time for them to discover the joys of deciphering a difficult passage or of absorbing and appreciating a three-paragraph extended metaphor after they've developed a love of reading. (Bear in mind that I am not a reading teacher, and my opinion could be close to worthless on issues such as this.)

As for craft, there I can speak with a bit of expertise, and mention some things that are intentional. Every one of my novels opens with a hook. If you pick up *Hidden Talents* or *Dunk* and look at the last sentence of any chapter, you will probably see a cliff hanger. I want the reader to turn the page. I also try to always have at least one unanswered question enticing the reader. Preferably, there will always be several, until the end. The questions can be small. (Who's knocking at the door?) Or they can be large. (Who shot the sheriff?) The larger the question, the longer you can keep from answering it without frustrating the reader. On the other hand, I don't worry about sentence length or vocabulary. I use the word I need. But I rarely need a word that would cause a reader to stop cold.

What kind of feedback have you received from boys/reluctant readers (or their teachers) about your books? Do they ask for specific subjects or types of stories?

LUBAR: Most of the requests I get are for sequels. Kids want me to follow up *Hidden Talents* and *True Talents* with a third book. Or they ask if I'm writing another story collection. (Happily, that is almost always the case.) I get lots of emails with ideas for weird and twisted short stories from kids who've read my Weenies collections and want to share their own creepy creations. I'm pretty sure every writer can make the following statement, but that doesn't make it any less awesome. I often hear from teachers or parents who tell me one of my books was the first book a child read willingly. That's my gold medallion, embossed not on the cover of my book, but on my heart.

DE LA PEÑA: A lot of girls who like my books write to say, "When are you gonna write about a girl?" A lot of readers want a sequel to a book, which I view as a huge compliment (though I never deliver). Here's something people don't realize about reluctant readers: They are incredibly loyal. If they like one of your books they will read them all. They trust you, which is an incredible honor.

LOOK: Readers tell me they love my books because they laugh through them. They say they're surprised that I use a really flawed character as a hero/heroine, but they really love that the characters are not perfect and get themselves in so much trouble. They also say that I'm describing them! Ha ha. If they only knew–I'm mostly describing myself!

SHEINKIN: The best responses I've gotten have been from kids—usually boys—who say things like, "I used to hate reading and thought history was really boring. Now I want to find out more." So yes, books do have that power! And yes, it does seem like many boys are more drawn to fact-based stories than fiction.

What advice do you have for writers who want to appeal to boys and other reluctant readers?

DE LA PEÑA: Don't "write down" to them. That's the fastest way to turn off a reluctant reader—or any kind of reader. Be as honest as humanly possible. And hone your craft. At the end of the day it all comes down to craft.

LUBAR: Don't target reluctant readers. Write an amazing book. Write about something that excites or interests you. Write about characters having awesome adventures or solving unsolvable problems. Toss your characters into a rock tumbler (metaphorically). Don't target just reluctant readers. Very few books will appeal to the entire range of reluctant readers, but yours might be the first to strike a spark for a kid. And that's priceless. That's your gold medallion.

SHEINKIN: I'd say, don't think of it that way. Find a story that *you* think is really exciting and that you would have liked as a kid. And then craft a straightforward and no-nonsense narrative. I love cooking shows, and the judges say stuff like, "I can really taste the love, the passion you put into this dish." Writing is exactly the same. If you really love your story, it will show through in the words, and that's the only way to grab and keep readers. And hey, if you can throw in some creepy or disgusting details, a few explosions, so much the better.

LOOK: Forget about appealing to anybody. Write what you're interested in. Use the simplest, strongest words. Write with a sense of urgency. Listen for the voice of your book. Don't show your work to anyone too soon. Don't ask for feedback every 30 minutes. Don't ask for reassurances every 30 seconds. Trust yourself. And just write!

FURTHER RESOURCES FOR WRITERS

Here are some additional resources on the topic:

Guys Read website founded by Jon Scieszka: GuysRead.com

June 2005 interview with Jon Scieszka by Gordon McAlpin on the inspiration behind GuysRead.com: bookslut.com/features/2005_06_005714.php

Summary of National Literacy Trust research revealing widening gender gap in boys' and girls' attitudes towards reading and writing. booktrade.info/index.php/showarticle/28849 Original report, dated 8/2010, also available at National Literacy Trust website: www.literacytrust.org.uk/search/3?q=gender&tags=

Listing, by year, of American Library Association (ALA) Young Adult Library Services Association (YALSA) Quick Picks for Reluctant Young Adult Readers: ala.org/yalsa/booklists/quickpicks

Full text of the article by Wendy Schwartz "Helping Underachieving Boys Read Well and Often"—nagc.org/index.aspx?id=341

Matt de la Peña's essay on NPR's CodeSwitch blog "Sometimes the 'Tough Teen' is Quietly Writing Stories," about his own experience of being a reluctant reader and how he connects with similar teen readers through his books and speaking engagements: npr.org/blogs/codeswitch/2013/11/11/243960103/a-reluctant-reader-turns-ya-author-for-tough-teens

A video of Matt de la Peña talking about his unlikely path to becoming an author and how he tries to appeal to reluctant readers: youtube.com/watch?v=M6uUsUnlEmk#t=15

Highlights Foundation Writing Workshops—they periodically offer a workshop on "Writing for Boys," with Lenore Look as one of the instructors: highlightsfoundation.org/upcoming-workshops/

Article: "Boys and Books: Encouraging Middle School Males to Read," by Johna Faulconer, Jessica Grant and Melissa Matsevich, East Carolina University, which includes references to additional resources: ncmle.org/journal/PDF/Feb08/Boys-and-books.pdf

CARMELA MARTINO has an M.F.A. in Writing for Children and Young Adults from Vermont College. Her most recent boy-friendly credits include a humorous short story about a baseball-loving boy and his cat in the middle-grade anthology *I Fooled You: Ten Stories of Tricks, Jokes, and Switcheroos* edited by Johanna Hurwitz (Candlewick Press), and a poem about a paralympic marathoner in *And the Crowd Goes Wild! A Global Gathering of Sports Poems*, edited by Carol-Ann Hoyte and Heidi Bee Roemer (Friesen Press). In addition to writing stories and poems for children and teens, Carmela works as a freelance writer and writing teacher. She founded TeachingAuthors.com, a blog by six children's authors who are also writing teachers. For more information, see carmelamartino.com.

TALKING CRAFT IN YOUNG ADULT

Cat Winters, Tessa Gratton & Renee Ahdieh.

....

by Ricki Schultz

So much of writing is subjective—everyone has a process and his own set of "rules." As an aspiring author, one must detangle and demystify many so-often unquantifiable concepts in order to figure out what will work best for his or her writing. As you likely know, it can be a confusing and emotional animal to conquer.

That said, three young adult writers who've Figured It Out are here to help. The award-winning **Cat Winters**, the multi-pubbed **Tessa Gratton** and new-kid-on-the-block **Renee Ahdieh** took the time to discuss their paths to publication as well as their unique takes on some of those elusive aspects of craft, in hopes that they might aid those of us trying to get where they are—on the shelves. Their practical advice on the sometimes-abstract subjects of voice, worldbuilding, plotting and more will both entertain and inspire you to pick up your pen and get out there!

Meet the Authors:

Cat Winters is the author of *In the Shadow of Blackbirds*, which was named a 2014 Morris Award Finalist, a 2014 Best Fiction for Young Adults pick, a 2013 Bram Stoker Award Nominee and a *School Library Journal* Best Book of 2013. Her upcoming titles include *The Cure for Dreaming* (Amulet Books/ Fall 2014) and *The Uninvited* (William Morrow/2015). She's also a contributor to the 2015 YA horror anthology *Slasher Girls & Monster Boys*.

Tessa Gratton's Blood Journals series (Random House 2011) has garnered her much attention, and her latest title in the United States of Asgard series, *The Strange Maid*, hit shelves in June of 2014.

Renee Ahdieh's upcoming *The Wrath and the Dawn*, the first book in her One Thousand One series (Penguin/Putnam 2015) is a YA reimagining of *The Arabian Nights* focusing on the tale of Scheherazade.

On tense and point of view: Is this a conscious decision for you? What goes into that decision?

CW: I really wanted to tell [*In the Shadow of Blackbirds*] through the voice of my protagonist, sixteen-year-old Mary Shelley Black (who was named after the author of *Frankenstein* but isn't related to her). Some of my favorite stories involving history's worst moments are told by younger narrators. Children and teens can be so much more honest about both the absurdities and the terrors of life's darkest hours. They see the humor and the pain and the gray areas between right and wrong, and they aren't afraid to reveal their true emotions.

If I had chosen a third-person point of view, I think the setting would have come across as too bleak to be enjoyable. My 1918 historical world is incredibly dark and unsettling, but I felt that seeing the time period through the eyes of a logical, resilient, candid teen would give the reader a strong sense of hope. Plus, I enjoy the intimacy of first person. This is Mary's story, so she should be the one telling it.

I briefly considered using present tense, but only because it was trendy at the time, which didn't seem a good enough reason to ignore my gut instinct to write in first-person past tense.

TG: My point of view choice is always conscious, and it depends on what level of intimacy and immediacy I want from a project. Regarding tense, for me past tense allows for more room to experiment within first person, because you can move non-linearly along the timeline of the story. Present tense is by its very nature immediate. The narrator and the reader share space and experience the story at the same time. Present tense presents more challenges to me because it's more restrictive that way. I chose it for the United States of Asgard series because the world of that series is epic in every sense of the word. I wanted my narration to be the opposite of epic: narrow, prejudiced, intimate.

RA: For me, choosing a tense comes about organically. It really amounts to how I hear the narrative in my head. I also feel most comfortable writing in third when dealing with historical elements. Since the One Thousand One series is partly inspired by the Abbasid Caliphate and the Sasanian Empire, the voice just lent itself to past tense. I also knew when I began writing the series that I wanted to write from multiple perspectives. Third person helped me achieve that flexibility without falling down a well of head-hopping confusion. Also, I just think it sounds pretty. I'm a sucker for pretty prose, and I think third person comes most naturally to me. First person has a wonderful sense of immediacy to it, and I know authors who paint gorgeous pictures in first person, but I think it's important for a writer to know his/her strengths so they can best be used to greatest effect.

CWIM: What was your path to publication?

CW: I took the long and difficult path to publication—although not by choice. I started writing the first book I would ever submit to agents in the fall of 1994. I began querying agents around 1996, but I didn't actually sign with an agent until 1998. She sent out my manuscript (a historical novel written for adults) in 1999, and the book failed to find a publisher because historical fiction was considered a "dead genre." That agent and I parted ways around 2000, and I spent the next several years writing more manuscripts and raising my two young children. In 2007, I signed with my current agent and, for about two years, she tried selling an adult suburban satire of mine that involved a vampire. No one bit (no pun intended).

In the fall of 2009, I embarked upon my first YA novel, *In the Shadow of Blackbirds*, which proved to be my success story. We sold the novel to Amulet Books in October 2011, and the book was published April 2013…eighteen and a half years after I started seriously writing for publication.

TG: I've written stories and novels in some form since I was in fifth grade, and although I went through a phase in high school where I thought I wanted to be an actor and a phase in college where I thought I wanted to go into politics and policy, I came to my senses and focused on writing as a career. After graduate school, I gave myself five years to work part-time, low-income jobs to direct all my energy at becoming a full-time author before I had to get serious about another career that could provide me with health insurance. I wrote a book, edited it, queried it to 10 agents and was rejected by all. I wrote another book, edited it, queried it to 10 agents (some the same, some different) and was rejected by all. I wrote another book, revised it, and sent it to one agent. She signed me, and eight months later (after revisions with her and several hard rejections from publishers), *Blood Magic* went to auction and I've been with Random House Books for Young Readers ever since. I signed the deal almost exactly five years after setting that goal for myself.

RA: A nerve-wracking, pride-swallowing siege! I wish I could tell this amazing tale of writing a book, getting in touch with the right people and making all the right decisions from the get-go, but that's definitely not the case. I queried one book a few years ago and made every mistake imaginable. Eventually, I wrote something else and began the painstaking process of querying it near the beginning of 2013. In April of that year, I attended the Writer's Digest Conference in New York, and I wound up meeting my agent at a seminar she was teaching. Two weeks later, she offered me representation.

Unfortunately, that book didn't sell, but I followed her very wise advice and began writing something else. When the first book in the One Thousand One series was done,

my agent sent it out to several editors. Within a week, we had multiple houses passing it along to acquisitions, and we eventually took a pre-empt from an incredibly passionate editor at Penguin/Putnam. The whole thing was insane. I don't think I slept for three days. But it's so easy for the struggles of the past to get lost in the excitement of the now. Even though this particular book sold quickly, I worked for many years to get to this place, and I have a virtual trove of this-is-why-you-suck letters to prove it. Sure, this industry is about talent and timing, but most of all, it's about tenacity.

Do you consider yourself to be a plotter or a pantser? What methods do you use to plot when an idea strikes you?

CW: I use a plotter/pantser combination of methods. Typically, I plot the book in my head and watch the events unfold as if the novel were a mental movie. I don't necessarily fill in all the details of the plot, but I figure out the basic path of the story, and I always feel better if I know the ending before I sit down to write. When I'm ready to work, I usually head straight into the first several chapters and get my momentum going.

The next step is printing out calendars for the book's setting. For *In the Shadow of Blackbirds*, I printed out four calendar pages: April, October, June and November 1918, the key months in the novel. I then penciled in all the essential plot points on those pages, sort of like using a day planner for my characters' activities. By doing so, I'm mapping out my plot, keeping track of the passage of time and visually learning how much more I need to do to build everything up before I reach the book's climax. The method is a little untraditional, but it works for me.

TG: I'm a character-arc-er. My ideas strike in the form of world and character conflict almost always. So, for me, the beginning of a project is all about figuring out the world and how the characters I'm interested in fit into that world. When I know the answers to those questions, I start mapping out my main character(s) and how I want them to change. What do they want? What do they fear most? What choice will they have to make in the emotional climax? That's the "plotting" I do, and then I tend to dive into the drafting process. To me, actual plot is the last thing to worry about. I can change plot to suit my needs and my characters.

RA: I am a crazy, crazy plotter. Whenever I meet a pantser, I bow a floor-touching obeisance to such intrepid genius. I have neither the stomach nor the ability to write without putting together a fully fleshed narrative first. When an idea strikes me, I usually spend at least a month researching and creating character arcs. Usually, I start in web form. I'll sit down and construct a character, giving him/her a name and deciding his/her features. Then, I'll determine what personality traits I want this character to embody. After that, I decide the best way to show those traits in action. Typically, these are the seeds of various scenes. Weaving them together into a story is the best part.

When writing a series, there has to be a fair amount of planning involved. How do you know what to reveal about the overarching plot and when?

RA: Again, I am a huge control freak when it comes to plotting. Usually, I function off a structure I find almost reminiscent of an action movie. I want the inciting incident to be clear from the beginning, so that readers understand the stakes early on. The idea is to maintain as much conflict and tension as you can for the full duration of the narrative. This is what prompts readers to keep turning pages. Decide what your characters think they want, and find ways to turn these desires on their heads. Give them things. Then take them away. Question their motives. Find heroes in unlikely places. But always be true to your characters. A plot is nothing without compelling characters.

And, if all else fails, kill someone. That usually does the trick.

What is the best way for writers to develop their voices—particularly when writing for children or young adults? How do you develop authentic voice?

CW: Voice is such a difficult skill to teach. I think it helps to read other books with well-developed voices so a writer can learn what strong voices sound like and observe what makes them work so brilliantly. For examples of unforgettable voices from the past decade, I highly recommend Markus Zusak's *The Book Thief*, Carrie Mesrobian's *Sex and Violence*, and Suzanne Collins's *The Hunger Games*.

Think about your characters and how they would talk; hear their voices in your head. My Mary Shelley Black character is brutally honest, so I chose to have her narrate *In the Shadow of Blackbirds* in straightforward language. When she encounters moments of distress, which happens frequently as the book progresses, her sentences turn choppy and erratic to reflect how her mind is working at the moment. For my Fall 2014 YA novel, *The Cure for Dreaming*, I opted to write from the point of view of a character who's a little awkward and shy on the outside but itching to be bolder on the inside. I consciously chose to show her growth through her voice. In the beginning, she's prone to using adverbs and hyperboles to describe her awe of events around her. Toward the end, her voice strengthens, and her language grows less flowery.

TG: I don't think this answer is any different when writing for kids than writing for adults: practice. And read. Read a lot, both in and out of your genre. Voice is one of those nearly impossible-to-define aspects of writing. You can't force it, but once you have it you can't really lose it accidentally. Voice is only identifiable across multiple projects and stories, so you have to write many things to find your own.

RA: Everyone says this, but I feel compelled to say it again: read. Read in your genre. Read outside your genre. When you come across something that rings especially true, take a step back and study the whys and the hows. In young adult fiction, I think the most authentic voices are the ones able to convey the world of a youth—the struggle for identity and the innocence of pure emotion—in an uncontrived manner. They sound natural. You can remember thinking, feeling, saying some of those things as a teen. But, most of all, this kind of voice can't be forced. The books that really make me cringe are the ones that try too hard to accomplish something that needs to be effortless by definition.

Going one further, how do you go about making sure the voice matches the time period and world in which you're writing?

CW: It helps to read primary sources from a time period: letters, diaries, newspaper articles, etc., that were written by people who actually lived in your era of choice. You'll learn common slang, general attitudes, quirks in speech, etc. For *In the Shadow of Blackbirds*, I read several firsthand accounts of the Spanish influenza, and I pored over WWI letters from soldiers writing to loved ones back home. The language of 1918, although a little corny at times, was surprisingly modern, which allowed me the opportunity to create characters who wouldn't sound completely out-of-date to twenty-first-century readers.

TG: Now this is a different subject: narrative voice and authorial voice are different things. Authorial voice is personal to a writer, and links their work across projects and genre. It overlaps with the narrative voice, but cannot be contained by it.

Narrative voice—the voice that is specific to individual projects—is all about worldbuilding for me. My characters word choices, slang, rhythm of speech, all of that has to do with the world in which they live. In the Blood books, those voices are situated within the Midwest; in the US Asgard books, the rhythm is much more poetic and grandiose, because the world is based on thousand-year-old epic poetry. This requires research, reading, sometimes talking out loud to oneself and even travel if you can manage it.

RA: If you're writing from a different world or time period, try to find books written from that time period or about that world. Study the cadence and usage. Really understand how the syntax differs from ours. Another thing I find especially helpful is poetry from that era. Oftentimes, it can be stylized and romanticized in nature, but it also definitely offers distinct voice.

Talk to us about worldbuilding. How do you approach this, and what suggestions might you have for aspiring authors with regard to doing it well? Any tips on how to go about sprinkling in details without becoming description heavy?

CW: Here are my top four worldbuilding tips:

1. Sensory details: It's so important to utilize *all five* of the senses: sight, smell, sound, touch and taste. Even if you're writing about a fantastical, made-up planet, your readers won't be able to travel along with you unless you make the world as evocative as possible.

2. Build the world through the characters' actions: Readers will lose interest if you're explaining the setting to them without your characters actually doing anything within that setting. If you want to show an ornate table inside a manor house, have your protagonist sit at that table and accidentally bump her knee on the hand-carved leg as she's scooting in her chair. Make the descriptions a part of your characters' experiences and movements.

3. Build the world through your characters' reactions: When I was writing *In the Shadow of Blackbirds*, I studied my own reactions to fear-inspiring situations. After reading a terrifying book before bedtime, I paid attention to the way my pounding heart echoed against my mattress . . . and sounded like a second heart beating inside the bed. I studied the change in my rate of breathing and the way my furniture seemed to turn into ominous creatures in the dark. Even if my readers have never found themselves in a ghostly situation or a plague like the 1918 Spanish influenza, I could help them relate to my protagonist's experiences by incorporating real human emotions and physical reactions.

4. Add little, specific details: When you reach the revising and polishing stages, look for the spots in your manuscript that seem a little bland—the places where generic details are threatening to keep your world from evolving into a full-color work of art. For example, when your character puts on his coat, tell us about the style of buttons he's fastening up to warm his chest. You're giving readers info about your character as well as his social status and needs, all by letting us know basic details about his jacket.

TG: *World* is connected to everything else. World dictates plot, character and theme, because you can't have any of those things without a world to put them in. Even if your book is a contemporary, the kind of cars, the neighborhood, the school, the names, the parental jobs—any and all of those things come from the world.

The way to sprinkle in world details is to keep in mind what your narrator knows and what your reader needs to know. Don't add more than that, ever. If you're writing first person, you cannot tell the reader anything that your narrator doesn't know and isn't willing to share. In third, you have more leeway, and that's when to keep in mind that less is more. You the author can (and should) know as much as possible about the whats, hows, and whys, but when putting in a detail ask yourself: Does this help my reader understand setting/theme/character/plot better? If not, delete! No matter how cool a detail it might be, stay strong.

RA: Build your world before you begin writing. Even if you're a pantser, have a very clear picture in your head. Then, pick and choose the things you want to stand out. I tend to have a fifty-fifty rule when it comes to creating a scene. I try to determine which half of the picture in my mind is most important, so I can leave the other half to a reader's imagination. You should never be writing about every detail in a scene. Be sensory in your descriptions. Once you share aspects of sight and sound and smell, convey other facets through action and dialogue. Pages and pages on how the bishop likes his tea offer very little insight into the bishop as a person. If it's so important, try to give it meaning and action outside of description. Description should enhance a narrative, not make it.

What's your best piece of crafting advice?

CW: I absolutely love writing dialogue and feel that conversational scenes between characters are an excellent way to both increase tension and develop complex relationships. Here's my crafting advice for verbal interactions: Write the dialogue without any actions. Get the spoken words down on paper without worrying about clarifying who's speaking and who's doing what as they talk. Let the conversation build and intensify. Allow characters to cut each other off. Use their silences and subject-changing tactics to show what they're feeling. Afterward, you can go back and fill in all the details about who's furrowing their eyebrows and who's pacing the floor or doing whatever characters are apt to do. You'll find your dialogue flowing in a much more natural rhythm when you focus first on the spoken words and second on the extra info.

TG: There's a famous quote attributed to Ernest Hemmingway that goes "write drunk, edit sober," and while it's obviously problematic for a lot of reasons, I think my best piece of crafting advice is to keep the spirit of that quote in mind when writing. Drafting, the initial writing, is a time to be wild and free, to experiment and let yourself be afraid of what you're doing. Don't hold yourself back, don't worry about craft. Revision is the time to get some distance, listen to critique and be as cold as possible to your own words and ideas. This is when you focus on the craft as much as possible.

RA: Fall in love with something. Your character. Your story. Your world. The best pieces of fiction I've ever read were obvious labors of love. Passion is the most important aspect in any creative endeavor. If you don't love it, you're not going to put in the hours and hours necessary to make it perfect. You're not going to agonize over that sentence. And you won't understand the joy of getting it just right. Destroying adverbs and learning the all-important difference between showing and telling are always important, but if you don't let yourself fall in love with your work, you're lost before you even begin.

Your character names are all very unique and feel very much like they belong within the world you've constructed. How do you come up with them? It feels like there was more involved than simply going to babynames.com!

TG: Thank you! You've hit it exactly: I use worldbuilding to come up with my names.

In the United States of Asgard books, I had very specific naming conventions that I created via researching Viking naming patterns and modern US ones. Not only do the names sound Nordic or specific to a culture in US-Asgard, but they give readers clues about the characters' backgrounds. All followers of Odin, for example, are "sons of" while followers of Freyr usually have a last name ending in "ing." Lokiskin use a matronymic naming system which reflects their god's status as a mother.

Even when my books take place in the "real world," I name my characters based on worldbuilding. I start with their parents: who are the folks who named my characters in-world? What sort of names would they choose and why? Are they Irish-American? Black? Hispanic? Daughters of the American Revolution? And I look at the Social Security Administration to find the top 100 names in the year my characters were born to pick names for secondary characters. You can look up popular names by state and region, too, which is helpful.

What kinds of research did you have to conduct for Blackbirds?

CW: I used numerous reference books that covered everything from food rationing in WWI to Harry Houdini's encounters with Spiritualism. I also studied archival letters, personal accounts of 1918, silent films, newspaper articles, advertisements, clothing catalogs, newsreels and literature from the time period, as well as historical photographs, ten of which appear in the novel. I've lived in the novel's two primary locations,

Portland, Ore., and San Diego, and I used to be a member of the San Diego Historical Society. I've included links to some of my favorite research websites and reference books at blackbirdsnovel.com.

How do you attack writing in multiple POVs, and what advice would you have for someone who's never done it before?

RA: I think it's extremely important to be aware of the perspectives you intend to write from prior to penning a single word. That way you can fully develop each voice so it's distinct. When writing multiple POVs, it's easy to fall prey to a lack of distinction between characters. Everything sounds the same, and a discerning reader will notice. Once you've determined which perspectives you intend to write from, sit back and choose keywords, phrases, gestures, thoughts that character might have. Does your heroine tend to use flowery language? Does she curse a lot? Is your hero introspective or effusive? Does he tend to languish in exposition? Once you've determined their personalities and quirks of thought and behavior, it's a lot easier to step into their shoes and write from their vantage point.

If you've never written multiple POVs, I suggest writing short stories about some of your characters. Tell a vignette from each of their pasts. Create an arc and run with it. You might even wind up with some great backstory.

RICKI SCHULTZ (rickischultz.com) is a young adult writer represented by Barbara Poelle of Irene Goodman Literary Agency.

YOUR WEB PRESENCE

3 keys to connecting with young readers online.

....

by Lee Wind

Social media is a vast space that, like the universe, keeps expanding. It's a realm where a writer can quickly become overwhelmed: websites, blogs, Listservs, apps, Facebook, Twitter, Instagram, Pinterest, Tumblr, Goodreads, YouTube, Google+, Ning, Shelfari, Red Room, Stumble-Upon and so on. Social media outlets trend: They come on the scene (Vine), they go (Myspace), and some of them are even designed to self-destruct (Snapchat). And when you're trying to build an author platform based on outreach to kid and teen readers—who tend to be even more trend-aware than adults—steering through this starry space can be especially tricky.

Here are three guiding stars to navigate the ever-changing Web.

1. KNOW WHO YOUR AUDIENCE IS—AND WHERE TO FIND THEM.

First, if this isn't immediately obvious: You need an online home. It's not enough to find out what social media networks teens are frequenting and set up profiles there. You'll also need a landing page (a website, a blog, etc.) where readers can, at minimum, find out basic information about you and your work, and link to your various social media profiles, all in one place. Consider two goals: How can you make it easy for someone who's heard about you (or one of your books) to find you? And, how can you make it easy for someone who is interested in the kind of things you write to find you?

If you're writing for middle-grade or young adult audiences, you can focus your online efforts primarily on those readers. To reach audiences younger than that, your efforts are better spent appealing to the gatekeepers who influence or oversee their reading: parents, librarians, educators and booksellers.

Many of the best author websites, though, cater to both audiences, sending young readers to one area of the site, gatekeepers to another, and even (for those active in the writing community) fellow writers to a third. Cynthia Leitich Smith, online powerhouse and best-selling author of the Tantalize series, is one example. She divides her website into the following subpages: About Cyn, Cyn's Events, Books for Kids, Books for YAs, FAQs for All, Goodies for Writers, and Children's and YA Lit Resources.

A huge part of reaching your audience is knowing where they're spending their time online and how they prefer to use those different social media spaces. Kiera Cass, bestselling YA author of the Selection trilogy, says she's found that Q&As seem to be best received on Twitter, and fan art contests draw the biggest followings on Tumblr. She cautions, however, that what's true of one author's specific audience might not be true of another's. "I'd bet it works in different places for different fandoms," she says. She recommends doing some careful trial and error to better focus your efforts where the fans respond. After all, she says, "If they're not excited, what's the point?"

2. DELIVER WHAT THAT AUDIENCE WANTS.

Once we know who we're reaching out to and where to find them, we next need to figure out what we can offer to meet our specific audience's desires. Readers of bestselling author Jeff Kinney's Diary of a Wimpy Kid series want the *fun stuff*—like the gadgety "Fortune Reader" on his website that ties into the eighth book in the series, *Hard Luck*. That's quite different from the searingly powerful poems that readers get at the website of bestselling YA novels-in-verse author Ellen Hopkins.

"We are past the days of a come-and-see website," says author Mitali Perkins, a 2012 Boston Public Library Literary Light for Children honoree. Now, she says, "It's come and chat." With that in mind, let's consider some of the most effective features successful authors are offering their young readers online.

Giveaways & Contests

Signed copies are perhaps the most common kind of giveaway. There are many ways to go about this. With authors who have the resources, an everyone-wins scenario can be a rewarding approach. Smith signs and mails bookplates to readers who request them. Catherine Ryan Hyde personally inscribes e-books via a service called Authorgraph. For his debut book launch, Greg Pincus arranged to sign at a bookstore that then mailed his books to readers who couldn't attend.

Contests are another way to build reader excitement—and keep them coming back for more. For a more limited giveaway, a contest can be as simple as having readers leave a comment to enter a drawing to win a copy of the book; these sorts of contests work especially well when you're trying to broaden your audience. Once you have an existing fan base, you might conceive of something more elaborate, such as Leviathan series author Scott Wester-feld's "Show Us Your Steampunk" photo contest on Facebook—where for a chance to win *and* be seen, fans dressed up in their best steampunk costumes and took photos of themselves holding Westerfeld's books. Prizes included signed copies and physical props from the books' cover shoots. Having fans dress up as characters from his popular fictional world was a powerful way to engage them not just with the author, but with one another, too.

FAQs, Q&As, and Resources

Creating your own Q&A or FAQ page is a simple way to serve multiple purposes. It can help with student book reports (Smith explains which of her characters would identify as *Native American* and which as *American Indian*, for example), satisfy readers' curiosity about everything from your characters to your own favorite foods, and free you up from answering the same questions over and over. Resist the urge to be overly formal. Write in *your* voice, which will almost certainly appeal to your young audience much more than any sort of "professional author" persona. For instance, check out YA award-winner Libba Bray's answer to the perennial *Where do your ideas come from?* on her FAQ page:

> From Ideaworld! It's the big mega-idea mart on the edge of town. I take my cart and roll down the aisles picking up plot, metaphor, simile, character, theme, whatever I need. Sadly, they are almost always out of stock on everything except the Enormo-Box of 100% Suck, which I already have plenty of. So then I am forced to pull ideas from everywhere—my iPod, books/newspapers/magazines/cereal boxes, urban and/or nature walks, people watching, the cats, art museums, everyday human interaction, everyday alien interaction, etc. Then I dust off the old imagination and work my bum off to try to make it into palatable story bits."

For authors whose books deal with fact or issue-driven subject matter, offering readers resources beyond the Q&A format can be a way to show that you care about your young readers, help them learn more, and ensure that they're still thinking and talking about your book long after they finish reading it. Cheryl Rainfield, whose books delve into some of the harder challenges teens face (such as *Scars*, which explores self-harm), offers website visitors "Healing and Inspiring Links" with more than 300 resources on topics like self-esteem, abuse, addiction and more.

APPS, GAMES & EXTRAS: Kiera Cass offers deleted scenes from her books on her website. She also links to Pinterest pages of images "that inspire me/remind me of my book." Readers there can then comment on those images, like or "repin" them, exponentially expanding Kiera's reach.

The lure of extras like these can also drive readers to any apps you might offer for tablet- and smartphone-happy teens. Readers of Richelle Mead's Vampire Academy series and

Bloodlines series can access the "Interactive Character Map" on her app, where they can uncover little-known facts and secrets about her main characters and see how all the members of her cast are interconnected.

Games appeal to MG and YA readers, too. In one popular model, readers can play "Crack the Code With Sammy Keyes" at Wendelin Van Draanen's website to unlock a new Sammy Keyes mystery story piece by piece.

INTERACTIVE CHALLENGES: Fan fiction can be especially popular among young reader-writers. On Scholastic's multiauthored "The 39 Clues" website, every other Friday visitors are prompted with "an explosive story starter," challenging them to reply with their best fan fiction. From there, readers engage with one another via their stories, building a community.

A close relative of fan fiction is fan art: On his blog, Westerfeld shares reader art inspired by his books and characters, from decorated objects to computer animation to hand-rendered drawings. Not getting a lot of comments on your blog? Scott's fan art posts get hundreds of comments—some more than 800!

Challenges like these can be hosted either just for fun or for prizes. Perkins, whose books and online offerings explore life between cultures, encourages her readers to be writers as well by hosting annual prose and poetry awards for "Teens Between Cultures."

VIDEOS: Bestselling YA author John Green and his brother Hank post regular videos (as the vlogbrothers) via their YouTube channel, which has developed a cult following of fans who call themselves Nerdfighters (as in nerds who are fighters in spirit, not people who go out and fight nerds). Video topics are far-reaching, as in Green's "Project for Awesome" (in which he discovers *after* doodling all over his face with permanent marker that he doesn't have a "Sharpie-face-removal-plan"). Other fan favorites include "Cooking with a 3-Year-Old: The Mac & Cheese and Communist Celery Edition," which is clocking more than a million views. While those may seem random, they're all an extension of what makes Green's books so popular in the first place; the author shows himself as funny, smart, likable and real.

AUTHENTIC CONNECTION: Sometimes, as Perkins puts it, we need to "reward responders with attention."

Young audiences are often drawn to books because they make them feel as if someone is sharing the experiences they're maturing through, and with some careful thought authors can make their websites a real-time extension of that. To that end, Hopkins offers a safe space and a sense of caring and connection that resonates with her audience. Expanding on the theme of her novel *Perfect*, her website features a "What Makes You Perfect" wall, telling visitors: "Only you can decide for you what is perfect. Share something about you that you think makes you perfect." Her readers respond in spades, opening up and sharing deep and sometimes searing truths.

YA bestseller Sarah Dessen has a separate community website (powered by Ning) called Sarah-land, the "Official Community for Sarah Dessen fans looking to talk about books, writing and all things Sarah!" Members can access forums, groups, videos, a chat space and more.

Giving our readers a place to connect with one another can be invaluable, but we should remember that readers are reaching out online because they want to know more about us, too. Don't be afraid to step out of your professional author persona and just be yourself. Hyde maintains separate author and personal pages on Facebook and Google+ but recently learned that her content needn't be so segregated. "I accidentally posted one of my #DailyGratitude photos [from my personal profile] onto my Facebook author page, and everybody liked it so much that I now share my gratitude posts with readers," she says.

Look again at the earlier examples and notice how much Bray's funny description of "Ideaworld" entices us to see if her books are just as entertaining, and how Hopkins' heartfelt offerings promise to be a natural extension of both herself as an artist and the fictional work she writes. Watch Green make that dinner with his young son, and then read the opening chapter of *The Fault in Our Stars*, and the consistency will be clear. We shouldn't pander to young readers online. Authenticity wins, every time.

3. DECIDE HOW TO BEST FOCUS YOUR TIME—AND REMEMBER WHY YOU'RE DOING THIS.

So how much of this do we have to do? Outside of having an online home, how many social media outlets do we have to be on?

There's no "have to." It's better to be actively engaged in one place, and create a following and a strong connection with readers and potential readers there, than to be sort-of-doing-the-occasional-thing everywhere. It's a bit like mixing juice from concentrate—if we dilute it too much, there's no flavor left. Aiming for one or two social media outlets is a great place to start.

Choose something, and do just that—start. Experiment. See what comes naturally, where and what your fans respond to, and what you like doing. (If you're not having fun on social media, your lack of enthusiasm will come through and negate your efforts; read Authentic Connection above.) See also what time-savers you can find. Most platforms allow you to schedule posts and updates in advance, as well as automatically move information between outlets. For example, my seven weekly blog posts at I'm Here. I'm Queer. What the Hell Do I Read? and SCBWI: The Blog are sent automatically to my Facebook page.

The coolest thing—and also sometimes the biggest pitfall—about online social media is that there are no gatekeepers. We can put stuff out there and reach our readers and potential readers directly. No agents to pitch, no editors to hear back from. The danger is we're putting stuff out there with no team vetting or filtering, so we need to be thoughtful about what we say and do and learn from our mistakes when we make them. But this is also an amazing freedom, and a chance to start our dream, right now.

Remember this, too: Unlike a print published book, there's no "done" with an online presence or platform. We don't have to get it perfect from the start. We can make it better as we go along. So figure out *your* Who, Where, What, How and Why, and steer for the stars.

LEE WIND (leewind.org) is a writer, blogger and speaker out to empower gay (GLBTQ) teens and their allies. He is based in Los Angeles.

NOTHING BUT THE TRUTH

Writing and selling nonfiction.

by Suzanne Morgan Williams and Jenny MacKay

Schools and libraries are so eager to add up-to-date, engaging nonfiction children's books to their classrooms and collections that the excitement is palpable. Why? By 2014, 45 states, District of Columbia and four U.S. Territories adopted the Common Core curriculum. Common Core State Standards list skills that U.S. students should master by the end of high school in order to prepare for college or careers. The guidelines require that students learn critical thinking and problem solving through reading, writing and speaking. They also require that half of assigned reading material for fourth-graders—rising to 70 percent or more for 12th-graders—is age-appropriate nonfiction texts focused on a variety of subjects from art to science to history. These readings should help students examine multiple voices and perspectives, make comparisons and draw conclusions. As a result, today's young library and bookstore patrons will not be satisfied with one book about snakes—they want *every* book about snakes.

Any market with an appetite for new content is good news for writers, but veteran authors of this genre know that writing nonfiction requires every bit as much craft and creativity as writing fiction. Add the requirement that every detail must be both true and provable, and nonfiction presents some unique challenges. Tackling nonfiction requires a careful assessment of one's own expertise and interests as a writer, knowledge of what publishers are seeking and can sell, and the ability to weave these elements into a compelling package for the savvy young readers a Common Core curriculum is designed to produce.

ENDLESS TOPICS

There is no formula for writing "Common Core" nonfiction books. On the contrary, New York Public Library Youth Materials Collections Specialist and Fuse #8 blogger Betsy Bird reminds us that a Common Core sticker on a book doesn't mean much: "Every work of nonfiction can be Common Core–aligned." So of all the possibilities, what subjects will resonate with readers? Fortunately, kids respond to a basic tenet of storytelling: Any interesting tale, whether freaky, heroic, sad or funny, is even better when it's true. Successful nonfiction authors find fascinating ideas everywhere. "After writing 38 books and more than 1,000 nonfiction articles for kids and about children's books and writers," says children's author Kelly Milner Halls, "I've discovered there are no boring topics, only boring ways to approach them."

Well-written true stories about everything from pirates to venomous serpents to the International Space Station will appeal to young readers. Titles with high-interest topics that connect to multiple subject areas are especially versatile since many nonfiction texts now do double duty, teaching history, science or math within language arts classes. A pirate book that explores the geometry of ocean navigation or a book about the politics of the Space Station stands a good chance of grabbing an editor's attention.

Writers who explore a small, unique angle of a broader topic may spark young readers' interests. "The biggest problem when writing nonfiction for children is keeping your focus narrow, usually much more narrow than you think," says Chris Eboch, a fiction and nonfiction writer. "Choose the one thing that most fascinates you or that you most want to share with readers. Explore it in a depth appropriate for the audience."

"Sometimes," says novelist and nonfiction author Terri Farley, "the best way to define the most interesting aspect of a broader topic is to think of a catchy subtitle. *That* is the story within the nonfiction topic." She cites the title of her nonfiction book, *Wild at Heart: Mustangs and the Young People Fighting to Save Them*, as an example.

Use the News

In the search for appropriate and interesting topics, current events are a tried and true standby in many authors' toolkits. "Topics that I propose are generally topics that are in the news and that interest me," says children's science, health and history author Connie Goldsmith. "When both those conditions are present, it's not difficult to capture an editor's attention. Editors are generally interested in books about timely topics written with genuine enthusiasm."

The world changes so rapidly that the publishing market supports a constant supply of new and current nonfiction books, especially about things like scientific inventions and medical discoveries that can progress dramatically from one year to the next. Goldsmith joins media distribution lists and subscribes to medical journals, perusing them for facts and concepts she can use in future books. When considering a new idea, she says, "Check out what books on the topic have been published elsewhere. Did you discover that other publishers have done similar books? That may or may not be a bad thing, especially if the other books are several years old." Authors sometimes feel dismayed if books already exist about their subject but if they put a fresh twist on a topic, or show editors that older books are outdated, their ideas can still work.

However, the publishing process takes longer than some writers expect. "A time-driven proposal, such as an upcoming anniversary, should be submitted many years in advance," says Ginger Wadsworth, a children's nonfiction author specializing in biography and history. "It can take a long time to find the right publisher, do the research, et cetera, before the drop-dead publishing year." Spying catchy, current topics at just the right time can take a bit of practice, but persistent writers face favorable odds.

Write What You Love, or Love What You Write

Once they have identified a few topics, nonfiction writers make choices based on their personalities, talents, knowledge and interests. Ideas with the best odds of impressing editors are ones the writer either knows about, is passionate about or both. Excitement about a subject is contagious to readers, and it transforms the labor-intensive journey of writing a nonfiction book to a rewarding experience—not a chore. "The person I think most about when selecting a topic is me," says Kirby Larson, a Newbery Honor–winning fiction and nonfiction author. "I have to be passionate about an idea before I can dive into the one, two, or even five years of research my work requires." Wadsworth agrees. "I have to admire the people I write about. It takes years to do the research and writing, and I am inviting that individual into my office, my mind and my heart forever."

Still, some authors develop a knack for tackling even tedious topics with gusto. Publishers sometimes request books on certain subjects to fill unmet needs in the marketplace, and these assignments can be lucrative for writers who are able to make almost any topic captivating. "When I agree to do the assigned book, the topic may not always wow me," says Goldsmith, "but as I research and learn more, inevitably, the topic intrigues me and I become very enthusiastic about the project."

Many authors build successful careers out of answering calls for submissions on topics other writers may overlook or feel intimidated by. "There are times paying the bills forces me to find the spark," Halls says. "When your kid needs new sneakers, you write what you have to write to land that check."

Connect with Classrooms

When selecting a subject and matching it to an age group of readers, it helps to know what kids are learning at school. Ask teachers what topics are covered in which grades, and visit websites of state departments of education to help target ideas to potential audiences. In the U.S., for example, students in fourth grade often focus on their state's history, while chemistry is traditionally a high school subject. This doesn't mean younger students aren't interested in chemistry or that high schoolers are no longer interested in the states. A creative writer can make nearly any topic appealing to readers of various ages. However, the complexity of technical concepts and emotional depth of books, as well as their lengths and design, vary greatly from the early elementary years to high school.

Aligning projects with curriculum not only helps sell them, it provides authors with opportunities for classroom visits after their books are published. Halls says, "Nonfiction often pays less than you might think, but thanks to my speaking engagements, I can spend four years researching Big Foot and still pay my bills."

CRITICAL CHOICES

Nonfiction writers must make smart choices about both the age level that matches their topic and if it is suited to a single book or a series. Book length, word choice, point of view, and other elements of a project will depend on those decisions, and requirements vary from publisher to publisher. "Nonfiction voice can be controlled by the market," says Eboch. "In some cases, this is strict. If you are one author working on a series for an educational publisher, you'll probably have to match the series voice." Authors who pitch their own projects or series may have more leeway in their storytelling voice, but the acquisition process may be more difficult. Pitching a series may be tempting, but a series needs a strong theme and material to fill multiple titles. A stand-alone book may be easier to sell.

According to Bird, simply choosing the right audience may be enough to set a book apart from the competition. "It seems like folks are writing a lot of young nonfiction," she says, "but for kids above the age of eight there's shockingly little. If you want to find the best nonfiction market right now, you should be writing for teens. YA nonfiction is near non-existent, so there's a huge gap there waiting to be filled." For nonfiction writers, it pays to be both creative and flexible, not just about the choice of concepts, facts, and themes, but about how these are presented in the finished book.

Unearthing Facts

Although there is infinite variety in topics and presentation, what remains constant among children's nonfiction writers is a commitment to solid and thorough research. Young readers are prone to believing whatever they read, so nonfiction writers are serious about their responsibility to present nothing but the facts. "Teens may be vulnerable to Internet claims, anecdotal stories and rumors, so I ensure my research is always from top-notch reputable sources such as government organizations, nonprofit organizations, and well-known medical sources," Goldsmith says. "I want my readers to trust my information."

Writing for children as opposed to adults does not mean authors can get away with less research. Halls only uses facts she can verify with three reputable sources, "because the kids deserve real evidence." Even for shorter books, nonfiction authors invest themselves fully in their research. "My first objective is to learn everything I can, even though I won't necessarily use every detail in a book," Wadsworth says. In the end, a nonfiction project is condensed from a wealth of knowledge into its most colorful, meaningful components. Diligent research can set a project apart from the competition.

Firsthand Accounts, Firsthand Research

Educational standards require students to differentiate between primary and secondary sources. Primary sources may include diaries, journals, historic documents, interviews, scientific research and personal experience. Secondary sources are derived from the originals. Authors who strive to obtain primary sources may distance themselves from less tenacious researchers.

Library and sound Internet research is the backbone of nonfiction, but most writers also interview experts and visit sites that are significant to their projects. "For my two books on Laura Ingalls Wilder, I visited almost all of her 'little houses,'" Wadsworth says. "For my book on John Muir, I walked the trails he used, observed the plants, animals, and geological features he wrote about, and more." Interviews have been a significant part of Farley's research and she suggests, "Before doing an interview read all you can find written by or about that person, give yourself a good grounding in the topic, write out a dozen questions that can't be answered 'yes' or 'no.' Then *listen* to the answers." Different topics lead writers down different research paths, but the end goal is to find and share unique details that engage and excite young readers.

Supplying Supplemental Materials

The difference between a salable nonfiction proposal and one that's not may come down to including supporting materials and backmatter. These extra features make a book visually appealing and its content more interactive. "Backmatter is your friend," says Bird. "Don't be afraid to include web resources, similar books that kids can read for more information, and Author's Notes [that give] a little context to the story."

Indispensable backmatter includes a complete list of the author's sources and a section of age-appropriate content readers can use to learn more about the topic, such as reputable Internet sites and links to audio or video files. Other options are glossaries and annotated indexes of important people or events. Sidebars and fact boxes with high-interest details can jazz up a concept, as can charts, diagrams and timelines.

Providing such elements will establish the author as a professional who understands the needs of the marketplace. However, backmatter should supplement, not outshine, the main story. "Don't leave the best stuff in the back," Bird says. "You need to balance the facts in the story with the facts at the end."

Homework

Spend time in libraries and bookstores exploring how subjects are presented to kids of different ages. Take advantage of online booksellers, too. They provide searchable databases that allow users to filter results by genre, age group, and keywords, and unlike libraries, these websites show sales rankings that can indicate books' popularity. These websites also display forthcoming book titles, making them ideal for finding the most current books on a given topic, giving authors valuable, current information about the market.

Photo Finish

When making proposals, authors can provide links to or copies of photos that illustrate their work. This gives editors a visual feel for the material and may save the publisher time. Some publishers do all photo research and pay the costs of acquiring photo permissions. Others require that authors research and pay for permissions—so writers should ask who will be responsible for these costs.

MAKING THE NONFICTION PITCH

Once a writer has chosen a topic with a unique focus and has researched it extensively, it is time to put together a submission package to send to editors or agents. Each may have distinct preferences on what to include, so authors should always check websites for current submission guidelines. Emma Dryden, a former children's book editor and publisher who now owns the editorial consulting company Drydenbks, suggests that writers prepare these things before pitching their idea:

- A mission statement that tells what the book is to be about and how the subject matter (person, event, etc.) will resonate with readers of a specific age
- A writing sample from the book, perhaps the first chapter or 1,000 words
- An annotated list of chapters or sections
- Information as to how the subject matter suits, supplements, or ties in with school curriculum and Common Core
- Information about what else exists in the market that would compete or compare with the book
- Information about the author's interest in and, if applicable, expertise in the subject matter of their book
- An indication as to what, if any, illustrations, primary sources or supplemental materials (such as maps, links, or audio) the author has and/or will be providing.

"In addition to getting a sense of the author's writing style and approach to the subject matter," Dryden says, "I expect to see enough in the proposal that proves to me the author understands the make-up of the market they want to serve with their project and that the author's done thorough research on their subject matter not just for the sake of the book they want to write, but for the sake of suiting the needs of the marketplace."

Educational or Trade?

Two types of children's nonfiction book publishers are educational and trade. Educational publishers typically produce book series with concepts developed by the publisher's staff. They hire independent contractors (work-for-hire authors) to write books for these series, usually for a fixed fee. Authors follow precise guidelines as to length, reading level and structure. Trade publishers generally accept queries from authors or author's agents and pursue projects that fit their current interests. Trade nonfiction authors may receive advances and royalties instead of flat fees.

There are pros and cons to both paths of publication. Some authors who write for pre-planned nonfiction series may feel their artistic freedom is limited. Work-for-hire income is also capped at the agreed-upon rate, and authors usually sell all rights to the publisher. Trade publishing provides more creative flexibility and potentially more income per book, but submissions face the slush pile and breaking in can be difficult. Work-for-hire arrangements, on the other hand, can provide steady paying work, multiple book contracts, and a rapid accumulation of writing credits. Many nonfiction authors write for both kinds of publishers.

BRACING FOR A CAREER IN CHILDREN'S NONFICTION

Even the most carefully prepared submission package may gather rejections, but for persistent authors who understand their market, most well-framed nonfiction books can eventually find a home. "After 30-plus years in this business, I still need to do my 'homework,' so I study the market, go to conferences and talk with other nonfiction authors," Wadsworth says. "When I get a rejection I try to be thick-skinned. Within a week, I go to my pre-prepared list of potential publishers and send the proposal out again."

Halls agrees that studying publishers' needs is part of the job. "All of my proposals have been published sooner or later because I've done my homework first. I know what each editor likes and submit to his or her published interests."

Writing nonfiction for children can be demanding, but successful nonfiction writers get to share compelling true stories that can shape young readers' lives. Halls says, "These kids, if we spark their imaginations, will change the world."

JENNY MACKAY (jennymackay.com) has an MFA in creative writing and is the author of 25 nonfiction books for teens on topics ranging from technology and sports to social issues and crime scene investigation. Her recent books include *People in the News: James Cameron* and *Gun Control* (Lucent Books). **SUZANNE MORGAN WILLIAMS** (suzannemorganwilliams.com) is the author of 11 multicultural nonfiction books for children as well as the middle grade novel *Bull Rider*. A former teacher, she has an M.Ed. and frequently leads teachers' and writers' workshops.

MAKE THEM CARE ABOUT CHARACTER

Character objective, motivation & conflict.

....

by Mary Kole

A kid reader, whether they know it or not, is picking up a book with the following request in mind: *Make me care*. That's my mantra every time I approach the slush and shelves, too. The best way to accomplish this is to introduce not only a great character but a character with Objectives and Motivations. Then the writer must imbue the character's life with enough conflict, both internal and external, to really get the story engine humming.

We root for people in life when we know their desires and goals. Will they persevere (like we want to with our own goals)? Will they fail (like we're afraid to)? We start to care once we see a person in trouble. This empathy is an important bond to create between reader and character, and you should do it as early as possible.

OBJECTIVE, MOTIVATION, AND ACTION

Objective, motivation, and action are all sides of the same pyramid. One is the desire, the other is the foundation below it, and the third serves the other two.

Objective: A character's main goal in life, whether that is a thing (the One Ring), a person (Juliet), or a value that springs from their personality or code of right and wrong (justice for all). A character can have many Objectives, but you should always know the overarching goal they're striving toward. As you'll see in the next chapter, characters can have Objectives from moment to moment, scene to scene, and then on a larger scale.

Motivation: I won't care much if you simply tell me what a person wants. Deep-seated personal drivers don't spring out of nowhere. As a reader (and an agent), I'm always asking: Why? Why does she want this? Why did he get this way? Motivation is usually explored in backstory, but whether it ends up explicitly on the page or not, the reader must get below-the-surface insight into a character's Objectives.

Action: Once your character is motivated by a goal, they act toward it. I was a theatre major, so I hope you'll allow me a digression. In acting theory, your motivation is expressed by the actions you take. For example, Blanche and Stanley are fighting in A Streetcar Named Desire. It's one scene, but Stanley first begs, then demands, then grovels to try and get through to her. His Objective is the same (get her to stay), but like a rat in a maze, he tries different avenues to achieve his goal. Keep this in mind for later.

Because life is never simple, Objectives and motivations must be complex. It's not enough to galvanize a character to action with one simple goal, nor is it sufficient to explain a strong Objective with one easy Motivation. (For example, "He was hit by a falling tree as a kid so he became a lumberjack in a twisted revenge ploy.")

We must *always* know what your characters want (each and every one of them) when we see them in a scene. Outline a character's Objectives and Motivations, and then reinforce them constantly for the reader with actions. I should be able to open the book to any page in your manuscript and intuit exactly what the characters' objectives are on that page, in that scene, in that chapter.

Once a character stops striving, we stop caring, and action loses meaning. Every choice a character makes and everything she does should have bearing on her goal. But it doesn't always have to be linear. Sometimes a character has to make a sacrifice that gets him further away from his Objective. Sometimes she's frustrated and does something completely counterproductive. Those instances are always interesting from a character standpoint, but they always have one thing in common: The goal is never out of sight, even if it's taunting your protagonist from the rearview mirror.

A good image to keep in mind is that of a bull's eye. One should be blazing brightly at the end of your manuscript. Every scene and chapter should fire an arrow toward it, even if the arrow doesn't fly straight or hit its target. Either way, the bull's eye exists is a constant reminder that there's an endgame. Don't let your plot wander too far away from the main objective.

Character needs to tie into the bull's eye, too, not just plot. Think also about your protagonist's self-doubt after a big decision, their surprise when they don't get or, better yet, achieve their Objective. What is their Interiority in the moment as something happens to bring them closer or further from their goal? Let them stumble on their path toward Objectives and make mistakes. How do they think about these in the moment? What do they learn? How do they deal with the ramifications of the mistake? We get to know a character via their actions and reactions.

Objective Tip: Don't make a protagonist's Objective entirely dependent on someone else. Make it something they can move toward. If their Objective is to borrow their brother's car and the brother says, "No," or if they need information but a character withholds it for no reason, that's a nonstarter. Where do you go from there? Make it something they have at least some power over or chance of achieving.

It's also important to remember the shadowy, hidden side of Objectives. The truth is, we don't always want what's good for us. For me, it usually boils down to sleep versus socializing. I *know* I have an early flight tomorrow but… Kids have counterproductive urges, too, and we shouldn't shield them from this quirk of human nature. What dark dreams does your character have?

Finally, most humans are not open books. If we were, therapists and self-help gurus would be out of a job. We don't always know exactly what we want, why we want it, or how to express it. Here we come to the Unconscious Objective. For some people, it's to love and be loved by others. For still others, it's to be accepted by their peers at any cost.

Characters struggling with Unconscious Objectives shouldn't be able to articulate them. But those deep desires are something that you, the writer, must absolutely think about. Readers should know what a character's driving conscious goal is, and also have a sense of the unconscious machinery or more basic human need operating underneath it all. And remember, make this but one complex part of your character and never state it outright. It is a rare person who walks around saying, "I just need love," and so your characters shouldn't either.

A CHARACTER IN CONFLICT

Another piece of the characterization puzzle is Conflict. There are two kinds of Conflict: Internal and External. Internal is what's going on in the character's mental life (self-confidence issues, fitting in, depression, etc.), External is the character's friction with relationships and the larger world (me vs. people, me vs. the world).

Internal Conflict: The issues that a character has swirling in their heads about their identity and their life in general at any one moment. This is often in reaction to events happening in the outside world. Other times, Internal Conflict exists in the character's head alone. Good sources of Internal Conflict can be: loneliness, self-consciousness, lingering heartbreak, fear of failure, etc.

External Conflict: There are two levels of External Conflict, the Interpersonal, and the Societal. Interpersonal Conflict can be a fight with a girlfriend, problems with the parents, a forced summer job, a bully at school, etc. Societal Conflict happens on a grand scale. In a dystopian society, for example, the protagonist is in conflict with the government or ruling class. Flu epidemics, famine, an authoritative regime, prevalent racism, an economic downturn, etc., are all examples of Societal Conflict.

Both Internal and External Conflict need to be present, fresh, relatable, and compelling enough to keep a reader's attention. And our access to conflict, especially in terms of how much it affects a character, is through Interiority.

You can spend weeks thinking up many layers of delicious conflict to put your character through. Just know that a balance between internal issues and external issues should be apparent from the first page. We don't want to read about a character who has achieved perfect zen piece of mind. Fiction runs on friction and trouble, especially for middle grade and young adult readers!

BALANCING INTERNAL AND EXTERNAL CONFLICT

In fiction, I'm always harping on writers to add more conflict, more stakes, more tension. But there must always be a reason behind the angst.

Conflict without the proper Motivation is melodrama. And nobody wants to read about a whiner. In this chapter's examples, the conflict never seemed over-the-top because the angst always came from a deeply frustrated desire. So make sure that every bit of conflict you write stems from somewhere—that it isn't just conflict for conflict's sake.

And keep in mind that Internal Conflict isn't enough. As we already know, if you had an entire manuscript of a teen sitting in his room, thinking about all the things that suck in his life, it would be dead in the water. (Lots of writers have tried this, I hope I can save you the trouble.)

You need to imbue your work with External Conflict, too. That means friction with other people and with the world at large. You should include this latter layer even if you're not writing a dystopian novel or an otherwise fractured world. None of us, I don't think, is truly happy with every facet of society. You don't have to dwell here, but Societal Conflict is a good layer to add to your story.

Both Objective and Motivation are essential to every novel, so are Internal and External Conflict. Really spend your time on the following exercises and make sure you're thinking through as many layers of these essential story elements as you can.

EXERCISES
Revealing Objective: What does your character want and why? What would they give up for what they want? What would they die for? What impossible thing do they crave? What is their most secret longing? What is their version of a perfect world? On the flip side, what is something they want that they probably shouldn't? Articulate these. Next to each one, write one example of how this Objective manifests itself in action. For example, "She wants a sense of home more than anything else...so she crawls into bed with her foster parents every night."

Revealing Motivation: Think of as many reasons or details as you can for each Objective and why your character wants what she wants.

Confronting Changes: How does your character come to terms with self after an emotional transition, difficult decision, or mistake? How might their reactions be surprising or unexpected? What are some of the events you're planning in your manuscript that will throw them for a loop of Internal Conflict?

Confronting Failure: What is holding your character back? What is the scene where they try to confront it? How can they fail? How do they eventually either blow past this obstacle or make peace with it? These are emotions you can harness when building conflict.

Me vs. the World: What is broken or otherwise wrong with society (in your character's estimation)? Why is this a problem for them? How can you bring your character into contact with the source of their tension? Write out how they react to society's ills in this moment; try to imagine what you can reveal about the character's true self here.

MARY KOLE (marykole.com) worked as an editorial intern at Chronicle Books and then a children's book literary agent for Andrea Brown Literary Agency and Movable Type Management. She championed a list of picture book, middle grade, and young adult writers, and a small portfolio of illustrators. Her main passion, however, is teaching the craft of writing and working directly with writers. She earned her M.F.A at the University of San Francisco, published the guidebook *Writing Irresistible Kidlit* with Writer's Digest Books in 2012 (from which this article is excerpted), and blogs at kidlit.com. Mary lives with her chef husband, Todd, and two pugs, Gertie and Olive, in Minneapolis. She currently offers rigorous and constructive freelance editorial services to writers and illustrators.

KATHY APPELT

On her greatest writing strengths and weaknesses.

by Michele Corriel

Kathi Appelt is no stranger to the publishing world, with more than 30 books for children and young adults, some of which regularly appear on the *New York Times* bestseller list.

Her poetic style, embellished with tones of magic and deep-rooted myths, resonates with both young readers as well as those on award panels.

The Underneath, her first middle grade novel, was named a National Book Award Finalist, a Newbery Honor Book, and the PEN USA Literature for Children Award. That was followed by *Keeper*, named an NCTE Notable Children's Book and a School Library Journal Best Book of the Year. Her memoir, *My Father's Summers* (Henry Holt, 2004) won the Paterson Prize for Young Adult Poetry. And Appelt was presented with the A.C. Greene Award by the Friends of Abilene Public Library, which named her a "Texas Distinguished Author."

Her newest novel, *The True Blue Scouts of Sugar Man Swamp*, named as a finalist for the National Book Awards, received starred reviews in *Kirkus, School Library Journal, Booklist, Publisher's Weekly,* and *Shelf Awareness.*

In 2014, she saw a new picture book come out, *Mogie: The Heart of the House,* illustrated by Marc Rosenthal (Atheneum). For more information, check her website, kathiappelt.com.

1. Reading your books makes me want to be a better writer. Where do you go to replenish your well?

Thank you! I find sustenance in an array of places—books, music, art. I love to take long walks. I love to go to plays. I think there is plenty for us to breathe in and to use in our own work. Whenever my well feels dry, I allow myself to have fallow ground, to just be quiet. That usually fills me up.

2. Your work always feels so organic. What's your writing process? Do you plan or do you let the story unfold?

Thanks again! I can't say that I have a tried and true process. As soon as I think I've got it all figured out, then something comes up that throws me for a loop and I have to start over from a different approach. In huge ways, my stories tend to unfold, but I'm also not saying that they unfold in unplanned ways. I do quite a bit of journaling when I'm working on a story, but then I also create plot plans and outlines. That's not to say that I have hard and firm plot points because sometimes in the writing, a surprise happens and I'll have to switch things up. It only means that I rely upon a road map.

3. Your characters are truly memorable. Do they come to you fully formed?

Oh how I wish! No. For the most part, I have to really draw them out. I have to listen to them. I have to prod. And almost always, my main character is the one I have the most trouble understanding.

4. Do you ever cry as you're writing?

Yes. And I laugh, too.

5. You've done picture books, middle grade and young adult novels. Which one is your favorite genre to write?

Whichever one is on my desk at the moment.

6. There's always a bit of myth in your novels, or magic. What is it about those tales that keep you coming back?

I do believe in magic, and I also believe that myths allow us to find the landscapes of our stories.

7. You've been a National Book Award finalist and a Newbery Honor recipient. What does that feel like and what kind of expectations does that put on your writing, if any?

I wish that every one of my writer friends, my students, etc., could have the opportunity to win one of those shiny medals. It feels very much like confirmation for the work we do, and it's a joy to be in the spotlight. As far as expectations, I think I've always wanted to write the best story I could. I don't write specifically for awards.

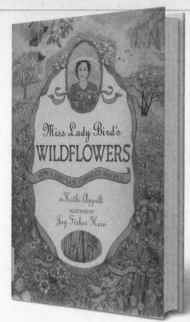

8. You've written from the perspective of raccoons, snakes, alligators, seagulls, mer men, crows, hummingbirds, and of course dogs and cats. What's next?

Actually, a girl. And also a fox. And maybe a camel.

9. Do you have a favorite character that you'd like to go back to?

I love Bubba and Beau. I miss them. I always saw Bubba as a combination of my two sons, who are now all grown up. I'd love to revisit him.

10. What is your greatest strength as a writer and what is your greatest weakness?

I think my strength is that I'm dogged. I'm not afraid to revise and revise and revise. I prefer not to discuss weaknesses. They ride on my shoulder enough as it is.

11. Did you always want to be a writer?

Yes. My first grade teacher, Mrs. Beall, told me that she thought I'd grow up to be a writer.

13. How has your process changed over the course of two dozen books?

Well, when I started out as a writer, I wrote on paper with a pencil. Now I only rarely do that.

14. With *The True Blue Scouts of Sugar Man Swamp* the plot has quite a few twists and turns. Did you know where you were going when you started?

Sort of. Whenever I start out with a story, I always try to figure out where I'm going and how the story is supposed to end. If I have at least a vague ending, then I can start typing. If I don't know the ending, I find myself spinning in circles. It's not pretty. So, I spend a lot of time trying to see that finish line.

MICHELE CORRIEL is a children's book author and freelance writer living and working in Belgrade, Mont. Her work is as varied as the life she's led, from the rock/art venues of New York City to the rural backroads of the West. Michele has received a number of awards for her nonfiction magazine work as well as her poetry. Her latest picture book, *Weird Rocks* (Mountain Press), explores geology for young rock hounds and her middle novel, *Fairview Felines: A Newspaper Mystery* (Ambush Books), is also available as an audio book.

LOREN LONG

On breaking in, agents, and the art of both writing and illustrating.

....

by Kara Gebhart Uhl

Author/illustrator Loren Long was drawing long before he was writing. After getting a B.A. in graphic design/art studio at University of Kentucky and completing graduate studies at the American Academy of Art in Chicago, Long worked as an illustrator at Gibson Greeting Card Company in Cincinnati.

A freelancer in the 1990s, his editorial illustrations appeared in major magazines and newspapers, including *Forbes*, *TIME*, *Atlantic Monthly* and *Sports Illustrated*. Long then began illustrating book covers for Harper Collins, Penguin, Houghton Mifflin and the National Geographic Society. Eventually an editor asked him to illustrate his first picture book, *I Dream of Trains* by Angela Johnson. This earned him a Golden Kite Award for best picture book illustration from the Society of Children's Book Writers and Illustrators.

Today Long is the No. 1 *New York Times* bestselling illustrator of President Barack Obama's picture book *Of Thee I Sing*, the re-illustrated edition of *The Little Engine That Could* by Watty Piper, and *Mr. Peabody's Apples* by Madonna. He's also the author/illustrator of *The New York Times* bestselling picture books *Otis, Otis and the Tornado, Otis and the Puppy* and *An Otis Christmas*.

Long's newest book, *Otis and the Scarecrow*, will publish this fall. For more information about Long visit lorenlong.com and otisthetractor.com. You also can find him on Facebook and Twitter.

You've written that "all those years of illustrating for magazines developed my visual storytelling abilities." Can you please expand on that, detailing why that's particularly important as a picture book writer/illustrator?

In my days of illustrating for the editorial markets (magazines) there were times I would have a one or two-day turnaround. The deadlines were crazy as opposed to months for children's picture books. It was hard to do your best work under those limitations. But with little time, it trained me to simplify the concept. Just like a picture book, a magazine would give you an article (like a manuscript) and ask you to make a picture or two to accompany the text. I would start my brainstorming by trying to boil down the article into one sentence, asking myself, What is this article saying? That would help me conceptualize ideas for telling the story of the article in the simplest terms possible. Often, that is the strongest way to visually communicate. This helps me now, in the same way, get to the heart of a story (or even a moment in a story) that I'm illustrating.

What inspired your career shifts and transitions, and what drew you to the book publishing industry?

From the start, I dreamed large. I wanted to do the biggest national work possible. I didn't know what that work was exactly but I have always felt that if someone else is doing it, why can't I? Incidentally, I wasn't thinking of children's book work at that time in my career.

I also knew that dreams like these would not happen overnight and I was content to walk slowly toward those dreams—no matter how long it would take. Greeting card companies were one of the few places employing illustrators full time so it was a great start.

But after a few years, I wanted to work at home, be my own boss and work for clients all over the country. So I left and ended up spending nearly 10 years doing mostly magazines. This helped me shape the style and direction in my work making it identifiable. The shift into publishing came from sending samples to art directors at publishing houses asking for book covers or picture book projects (it can still be that easy by the way). I started getting book cover assignments, which led to my first picture book project. I then found what I loved most.

Tell me about your agent, Steven Malk at Writers House. When did he enter the picture? Did he seek you out or did you seek him? And why do you think it's important for author/illustrators to team up with an agent?

In the beginning of my children's publishing career, I didn't have an agent and didn't want one. I already had work and didn't need help getting new projects. I worked very hard to earn a place in the industry and didn't see the point in giving an agent 15 percent of my income. So I worked on my own with the help of a good contract attorney to help me sort through the details of a contract. I kept my head down but sometimes wondered if an agent could help me make decisions, as my career got more complicated.

I knew of Steve Malk at Writers House because he represents many of the best in the field (in my humble opinion). I worked with Jon Scieszka on *Trucktown*. Steve is Jon's agent. Steve reached out to me back then and we hit it off on a personal level, which was important to me. We kept in touch and later he invited me to an event he was hosting during the Summer SCBWI convention in Los Angeles.

I've been working with Steve for three years now and the relationship has greatly enhanced my work and my life, really. He helps me make decisions from a broader, more knowledgeable vantage point than I ever could make going solo. I worked most of my career without an agent but now feel that it is a good idea to have one, especially if you're starting out. They can help you find work in the beginning. My advice to new people trying to get into the publishing world: Try to get an agent. Try to land an agent while you're trying to get the attention of art directors and editors. An agent knows the field, has contacts, and can take away the long and frustrating learning curve. But again, I'd simultaneously reach out to editors and art directors while looking for that agent.

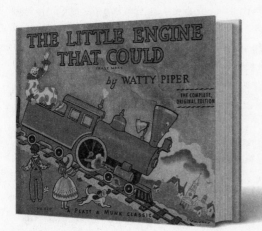

Your early work in the picture book field was as illustrator only. Many writers simply know that they shouldn't team up with an illustrator on their own—rather, that partnership is up to the publisher. So how does it work? Did Malk pitch your portfolio to publishers or did publishers seek you out for projects?

I was fortunate to have cultivated a "style" or a "look" in the years before I began working in publishing. As mentioned, I sent postcards and was lucky that publishers began calling me to do mostly YA book covers. All it can take is one and soon, every publisher sees your work. An editor from a different house saw a jacket I did and sent me a manuscript for my first picture book. It's worth stating that I was 39 when I got that first break. It didn't come easy or quick for me. But I never needed an agent in the beginning—I had work.

How do you know if a project is a good fit? Do you have to feel a connection to the story? Have you turned down projects and if so, why?

I have to connect with a text if I'm going to make it into my book. When you illustrate a book that someone else writes, it becomes just as much your as it is theirs. I have to love the story, the subject, and even what and whom the book is for. Even if you're brand new in the field and in need of work, it is important to love and embrace a story if you're going to spend months working on it and your name will be on the cover. I know many starting out are waiting for the phone to ring and it may seem crazy to turn something down. But if you don't love the story, it likely won't result in the kind of book you can further your career with.

In your Note to the Reader in your re-illustrated version of Watty Piper's *The Little Engine That Could*, you wrote, "Even today, as an adult, a father myself, I can still hear my mother's voice and that familiar cadence as she would read those powerful words to me. I can see the rocking chair we would sit in together in my bedroom, and I still feel the warmth of those moments." Tell me more about the powerful timelessness of picture books and what you hope to achieve with your own works in regards to that.

I love the coveted place in our society that is the picture book. I love everything about it—the education, creative development, quality time and love that two people experience when reading together. Otis represents my search for the experience I had in those tender moments in my life when I was on my mother's lap and she was reading books to me like *The Little Engine That Could*. It's a safe harbor for a child and those moments will be with that child forever.

It's humbling to me to know that one of my books will be that warm, safe place that a child will take with them for life.

Tell me about your experience illustrating President Barack Obama's picture book *Of Thee I Sing*.

I love what President Obama's *Of Thee I Sing* says to his daughters, my sons and the children of America. It's such a positive, inspiring, patriotic book. I hope that every child gets to hear its message. I love the book and am honored that my art will live in the book forever.

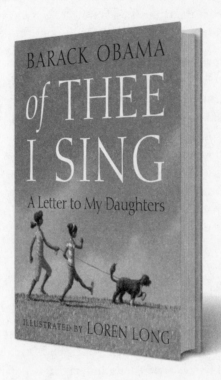

Your 2008 holiday picture book *Drummer Boy* was your first solo effort as both writer and illustrator. How did your previous work as illustrator only help you with the craft of writing?

I never dreamed I would write and become a published author. I was content illustrating someone else's story. But after doing so for a number of books I began to have ideas of my own and I realized that if I can tell a story with pictures, I am already writing in a sense. I don't claim to be an accomplished writer, but I can tell a story. The ideas are the hard part. In the case of *Drummer Boy*, that story is a story of a toy lost and found, so the plot line was dictated by what I thought would be dramatic to illustrate. So the visual thoughts came first. I just had to try not to mess it up with my words.

In works that you both write and illustrate, please describe your process. What comes first—the words or the illustrations? What do you find easiest and what's most difficult?

I pretty much write the story first with little thought about visuals. I may think to myself, *This will make a great scene* or *That will be fun to draw* here or there but for the most part I'm trying to find the story first, knowing that the art is a different challenge. The art is rarely easy. I struggle with certain phases in the art of every book I do. This said I still used to say the art is easiest but lately I'm trying to challenge myself visually and stylistically so the art is scary.

What is a typical working day like in the life of Loren Long? What does your studio look like? Do you keep a strict schedule? What tips do you have for other writers and/or illustrators who work from home?

My family life dictates my work life. When the boys are in school, I am up with them and get to work some time after they leave. When they're home for summer break, I keep summer hours.

I wish I could tell you that I keep a strict disciplined work schedule, but I don't. It's a creative endeavor and I have deadlines that stretch a year or two away. I'm not a morning person but I don't work nights or weekends anymore until I'm on the last month of a book.

You have received much success in your career, including earning SCBWI's Golden Kite Award in 2003 and repeatedly appearing on the *New York Times* bestseller list. What advice do you have to writers and/or illustrators in terms of success and fame?

The best advice I can give on this matter is do the very best you can to reach your own potential. And don't compare yourself to everybody else and what they are doing and who's getting this starred review and winning that award. It's wasted time and energy because you have no control over what happens and what people think about others or what they think about you. Be the best you can be and let the rest go. Once the art leaves your studio, it's out of your control.

Otis, the tractor and title character in now five books and a sticker/activity book, is well loved. What inspired the first book and what was it about Otis, the character, that made him worthy of a series? What advice do you have for author/illustrators who are considering a series character for the picture book market?

Otis has been an unexpected treat in my career. The first book was inspired by a loosely told story my wife and sons made up when they were in preschool and a tractor I drove on a horse farm in my college days in Lexington, Ky. I never set out to write a character that would become a series. I wrote the first story as if it would be a stand-alone book. I suppose there is something in Otis's character and personality that hits a soft spot in children and their parents, and teachers and librarians. My publisher and I were happy to revisit the character with more stories. He's a noble little tractor that I truly love to write and paint. I don't see anything wrong with setting out to write a character for a series but be careful not to manufacture grand fame and success of a particular character in your head before it has even become book one.

What are your thoughts on the current picture book market?

I think it's an exciting time in the picture book market. For me, it's the most fulfilling work I've ever done as a working artist. It's a field that I believe is viable and will last in varying forms well into the future. No matter what the device, grown-up people will always read and look at stories with children. It is an increasingly competitive field to break into but well worth the effort.

KARA GEBHART UHL is a Fort Thomas, Ky.-based freelance writer and editor who blogs about parenting at pleiadesbee.com.

JAMES DASHNER

On revision, world-building and why being a movie buff helps your writing.

....

by Donna Gambale Kuzma

James Dashner's first young adult novel, *The Maze Runner* (Delacorte), was released in October 2009 amid much buzz, and it certainly lived up to readers' expectations. *Kirkus* selected *The Maze Runner* as one of the best young adult books of 2009, and both it and its sequel, *The Scorch Trials*, made the *New York Times* bestseller list. Summer 2014 saw the major motion picture release of *The Maze Runner*'s film adaptation.

Dashner's success didn't come overnight, though. When *The Maze Runner* hit bookstores, he'd been writing for 10 years and had already published four middle grade books regionally with a small press. He broke onto the national scene in 2008 with his second middle grade fantasy series, The 13th Reality, which began with *The Journal of Curious Letters* (Shadow Mountain). The first three books have been published thus far, with two more to come.

Before becoming a full-time writer, Dashner worked as an accountant, a job he was ecstatic to quit. Here, he talks about the perils of revision, his advice for aspiring writers, how being a movie buff improves his writing, and what he's learned about thriving in the business. For more on Dashner, visit jamesdashner.com.

Why do you choose to write for children and teens?

That was the age when I personally fell in love with reading, and there's a magic about it that I love to experience over and over again. I also like how you can get away with almost anything in books for younger readers—mixing genres, throwing in humor and crazy creatures and horror and romance, all in the same book. It's just fun. There's the easy answer.

What challenges did you come across when plotting the three-book arc of the Maze Runner trilogy? How much did you know from the beginning, and what was a surprise?

It's a complex story, and it's been a challenge to make sure every little thing ties together. My editor (Krista Marino) has been brilliant in helping with that. I did know the overall story arc from the beginning, though many, many things were changed along the way. Now that we're almost done with revisions on the third book, I feel very relieved. I think readers will be very satisfied with how it all ends.

How has being a movie buff helped your writing?

More than I can possibly express. Movies are an important part of my life, and I see almost every single one that comes out. They really help the idea factory in my brain churn and stay fresh. Often I'll go see a movie in the middle of the day, and some of my best writing comes right after doing so. There's just something about seeing an entire story arc in two hours, with all the scenes and dialogue and characters and visuals. I love it.

You've done national book tours for _The Maze Runner_ and _The Scorch Trials_. Any advice for an author embarking on his or her first tour?

Enjoy every minute of it. It's a high honor for a publisher to choose to spend money on you, and they treat you really well while you're out and about. Enjoy the hotels, the food, the people, the bookstores, everything. Expect to be tired—lots of early mornings and airports. I think my biggest advice is to never complain or act like a prima donna. For one, you'll anger aspiring writers who would do anything to be in your shoes, and two, it makes you look like a sourpuss and turns people off. Smile even if you don't feel like it!

How do you balance your writing schedule when you're writing two series and promoting your newest release?

It's not easy, that's for sure. Ideally I like to separate them as much as possible—two or three months on one at a time. But that doesn't always work out, so then I try to split it between morning and afternoon, things like that. The hardest is when I have to write or edit while on tour.

You mentioned on your blog that you worked hard in your revisions for _The Maze Runner_ to differentiate your large cast of characters—and it worked! How did you make them so distinct?

Developing the characters for that story was difficult because they've had their memories erased, and it really hit me how much you pull from a character's prior experiences to flush out their personality and traits. But I worked on doing it through their dialogue and interactions with each other, as well as their reactions to situations. I always start with a defining trait for each person, then let my mind expand and fill in the blanks.

There's heavy world-building in both your 13th Reality series and in the Maze Runner books. How do you develop the world of your story?

It's somewhat similar to my characters. Very much so, actually. When I envision a certain aspect of my world, I begin with one or two obvious descriptions or features then let my mind naturally expand upon it. A lot of it comes as I'm actually writing.

You're a huge fan of writers' conferences. What helpful tips can you pass along to conference-goers?

You can't overstate the importance of conferences. Almost every published author I know can trace some bit of their success back to a conference or someone they met at a conference. Be prepared; attend every class you possibly can; and most importantly, network like crazy. Meet the agents and editors and other writers. It will all come back to help you at some point.

Who are your favorite YA authors?

That's a hard one because I know so many and I'd hate to hurt anyone's feelings by leaving them out. Better to say who I loved to read when I was that age: Judy Blume, Madeleine L'Engle, Tolkien, Stephen King. How's that for variety?

What's your favorite part of promoting your books? What do you find most effective?

I love interacting with my readers, hearing from them, meeting them, etc. I'm so glad we live in this age of blogs and e-mail and Twitter and all that. That makes it a lot of fun. I would say the most effective method of marketing is to get people talking about them— word of mouth. And the Internet is probably the most valuable way to make that happen. Other than the obvious, of course, which is make sure your book doesn't stink!

Tell us about when you found out you hit the *New York Times* bestseller list for *The Maze Runner*. Where were you, what were you doing, who were you with, and what was your exact reaction?

Great question! Fittingly, I was in the middle of a movie at the theater. Embarrassingly, I was all by myself, which is very typical on a weekday afternoon. But I knew we had a chance to hit the list, so when I saw my agent was calling, I ran out of the theater and ended up having to call him back because I wasn't fast enough. He told me the great news, and it really overwhelmed me. The *NY Times* isn't really the greatest indicator of sales, per se, but there's just something so symbolic about it, and I felt like I'd reached a major milestone. It was something I'd dreamed about my whole life. After sharing the

joy with my agent, I then called my wife, and then my mom. And, I'll admit it, a few tears were shed. It's a day I'll never forget. I'm proud to say we've spent several months on the list now!

What have you learned about maintaining positive relationships with agents, editors and others in the business?

It's extremely important. Never burn a bridge. Never. It's a small world in this industry, and you never know what might come back to help you or haunt you. Most of the successful authors I know are genuinely good people and aren't jerks. That had to have helped their publishing journey in some regard. Who wants to work with a jerk? So, don't be a jerk.

What does your workspace look like? Do you have any rituals or superstitions you follow when you write?

We moved about a year ago and I finally have my own office. It's my favorite place in the world besides a bookstore or library (where I often go to work for a change of scenery). I have a comfy couch, a comfy chair and ottoman, a desk, lots of bookshelves. It's heaven. I don't really have any rituals or anything. I just sit down and go at it. But one thing that helps me: movie soundtrack music. Things like *Lord of the Rings, Aliens, The Matrix, Braveheart.* Those really bring out my creative juices and help me visualize what I'm writing.

What's your favorite murdered darling from your books—the one character, scene, plot or even line that you really wanted to keep but ultimately had to cut?

One of my 13th Reality books had a really dark, horrifying scene that I loved. I'd channeled my evil Stephen King side to write it. But, in the end, my editor thought it was *too* dark and I reluctantly agreed to change it significantly. What's so wrong with scarring someone for life?

What do you do when you get stuck on a scene or chapter, or have general writer's block?

It's certainly a sinking feeling when that happens, but honestly, I don't suffer from writer's block very often. I think the problem that hits me is before I even sit down with my laptop, I just feel a general lack of desire to write. What snaps me out of that is to read for a bit or watch a movie. Or exercise. That time is better spent than staring at a computer screen or writing dreck.

You've admitted to not being a fan of revision, but of course there's no avoiding it. How do you tackle the evil beast?

Guilty! It's certainly not my favorite part. I'm all about the original creative process—the first draft. But I'm also smart enough to know that revisions are equally important. I don't want a bad product landing in the hands of my readers, so it's actually not that hard to get motivated to do what needs to be done. But I do find myself having to be a little more disciplined in terms of setting daily goals to get the task completed. I always give myself a day or two off after reading the initial editorial letter, however. It needs to sink in and I have to get over my depression, psyche myself up. For some reason our brain convinces us that *this* time, your editor thought it was *perfect*.

What's the best advice you have for aspiring writers?

Attend conferences, write every day and be persistent. Please don't listen to all the negative stuff. Yes, be realistic. But shoot for the stars. If I'd listened to every naysayer who tried to tell me that I could never make a living doing this, I would've given up. But those things always went in one ear and out the other with me. You can do it.

DONNA GAMBALE KUZMA works an office job by day, writes young adult novels by night, and travels when possible. She is a contributing editor for the Guide to Literary Agents Blog and was a contributor for the 2012 and 2013 *Children's Writer's & Illustrator's Market*. She freelances as a copyeditor and proofreader of both fiction and nonfiction. You can find her on Twitter (@donnagambale) and online at firstnovelsclub.com, where she blogs about writing, reading, networking, and the rest of life.

RED FOX ROUNDUP

5 writers from one agency discuss breaking in, agent/client relationships and more.

....

by Kara Gebhart Uhl

//

About a decade ago literary agent Karen Grencik sold Sarah Wilson's *George Hogglesberry, Grade School Alien* to editor Abigail Samoun. The book won the Society of Children's Book Writers & Illustrators (SCBWI) Golden Kite Award. Fast forward to 2011, when Grencik and Samoun teamed up again, this time to form Red Fox Literary, a boutique agency specializing in picture books, middle grade and young adult titles.

Today Grencik and Samoun represent a successful and varied group of writers and illustrators. We reached out to five of Red Fox's clients, asking them about everything from breaking in, how to have a successful agent/client relationship, the market today and perseverance. For more on Red Fox, visit redfoxliterary.com. For more on each writer/illustrator, see below.

MARSHA DIANE ARNOLD is an award-winning picture book author with 11 traditional books, two digital apps and an e-book to her credit. Her work includes *Heart of a Tiger, Roar of a Snore* and the popular digital app, Prancing Dancing Lily. Arnold also is the creator of the e-course "Writing Wonderful Character-Driven Picture Books" at The Children's Book Academy (childrensbookacademy. com/writing-character-driven-stories.html), where she also writes a monthly blog. Three of her upcoming books are *A Welcome Song for Baby* from Tamarind Books in the U.K., *Lost.Found.* from Neal Porter Books, and *Waiting for Snow* with Kate O'Sullivan of Houghton Mifflin. When not creating imaginative worlds and wacky characters at her home in northern California, Arnold enjoys traveling the world, scuba diving, gardening and, like her characters, always trying new things. Learn more at marshadianearnold.com.

ANN INGALLS has been writing for all of her adult life, both as an early childhood and special education teacher, and as a freelance writer. She is the author of 25 books in print or forthcoming. Her first picture book, *Little Piano Girl*, was published in 2010 and was a finalist for the first-ever SCBWI Crystal Kite Award. *Ice Cream Soup*, an early reader, was published in spring of 2013 by Penguin, and her early-reader series for Scholastic, Biggety Bat, will launch in 2014. Ann's first picture-book app, Do-Si-Do-Bots, will be published in 2014 by Two Little Birds and Little Bahalia. Learn more at anningalls.com.

CHRIS PALLACE is a dad, husband, writer, game designer, professional artist, amateur cook and intermediate juggler. He also co-owns Bent Castle Workshops (bentcastle.com), which produces top-notch games and playing cards. He is currently teamed up with Kevin Serwacki in writing and illustrating *Joey and Johnny the Ninjas*, the first in a series for HarperCollins, available 2015. Serwacki and Pallace also have a distinctive love of power tools and currently use them to produce Fairy Doors, but that's another story.

MIRANDA PAUL is a freelance writer, children's book author and creator of RateYourStory.org. One of her bravest literary achievements involved reciting a poem while nestled in a crocodile pit. Paul is the author of *One Plastic Bag* (Lerner/Millbrook, 2015); *Water is Water* (Neal Porter Books/Roaring Brook/Macmillan, 2015); and *Helping Hands* (Lerner/Millbrook, 2016). Besides writing and teaching for The Children's Book Academy (childrensbookacademy.com), she loves traveling, spending time with family, fighting injustice and hosting backyard brick-oven pizza parties. Learn more at MirandaPaul.com.

KEVIN SERWACKI was born in Nairobi Kenya and graduated from RIT with a degree in Illustration. He settled in Rochester, NY and for 20 years he made a full-time career out of art. His Illustrations have been used in various publications throughout Rochester including the *Democrat and Chronicle*, *Rochester Magazine* and *Geneseo*. He has taught children's cartooning classes in the Monroe County Public Library system and worked as a teaching artist for ArtPeace. His first children's picture book, *Doorknob the Rabbit and the Carnival of Bugs*, was published by Tricycle Press in 2005. Currently Serwacki has teamed with fellow artist Christopher Pallace to design, write and illustrate a series of illustrated novels titled *Joey and Johnny the Ninjas* (2015, Balzer and Bray). The two have a studio in the Hungerford Building in Rochester, where they make tiny little doors for fairies and larger creations for humans. Learn more at serwacki.com.

How did you break into the children's book market? And what tips do you have for fellow writers/illustrators who hope to be published someday?

ARNOLD: When my children were small, I began writing about their daily adventures, which led to my award-winning syndicated column, *homegrown treasures*. I had to come up with new ideas and write about them every week, for 10 years. It was great writing practice. The column was followed by children's magazine stories; then in 1995, my dream of writing a picture book came to fruition with the publication of *Heart of a Tiger* by Dial Books for Young Readers.

Ten more picture books followed, but then came my seven-year drought. The publishing industry had changed, my editors left the industry, and I felt no connection to some of the picture books being published. When rain finally broke my drought in 2013, it felt as if I was "breaking into" the children's book market all over again. And it felt heavenly—four manuscripts to three top publishing houses.

This time, when I "broke in," I had an agent to assist me and the stories I wrote were very different from the ones I'd written earlier—shorter and more visual. Personally, I've never used the phrase "break in." Finding a publisher for our work seems more like a steady climb, a passionate striving, a happy synchronicity.

If you want to be published, it's important to study the craft and art of children's book writing. There are many sources on the Internet to assist you in your quest. Find the ones that call to you. One of the many is The Children's Book Academy (childrensbookacademy.com) where there are classes and blogs, including mine, to learn from. Also, join SCBWI (scbwi.org), an international organization specifically for writers and illustrators who create for children and young adults. There you will find knowledge, advice and support.

Enjoy your path, have patience and be tenacious. Remember that writing for children is not only fun, it's a serious business. What we write in our stories strongly affects children's lives.

INGALLS: *Babytalk Magazine* published the first piece I ever sent out. It was the story about our daughter's birth and diagnosis of a multiple heart defect. (She's fine by the way.) Following that, I wrote a short story for *Reminisce Magazine* about my childhood. Having these few writing credits gave me a bit of credibility as a writer and the confidence to try my hand at what I really loved to do—write picture books. *Little Piano Girl*, the childhood story of jazz legend, Mary Lou Williams, was the first picture book

I sold. I co-authored that with my sister, Maryann Macdonald. We passed our manuscript back and forth online or in conversation about 100 times until we were satisfied with the product. Both her critique group and mine provided suggestions for clarification or interest. I cannot recommend a single thing that is more important than the help of a serious critique group.

PALLACE: I have a creative partner that I work really well with. But the part I want to stress for this question is I was prepared to *not* break into the children's book market. I mean that literally. When we [Pallace and Serwacki] started working on *Joey and Johnny the Ninjas* I knew that it was good, but I knew there was a lot of good stuff out there not getting published. I tried to not worry about it.

So, with *Joey and Johnny the Ninjas*, Kevin and I were prepared to not get picked up by a publishing house. We had two different plans to self-publish and were prepared to give it a year to see where it took us. The most dangerous thing you can do is wait for someone else to give you a hand up. Be proactive. Take your ideas, make them real and see where they lead you.

PAUL: I freelanced for years before I sold my first traditional picture book. I'd accumulated more than a hundred magazine, newspaper and digital storybook credits, mostly through work-for-hire assignments for children's and adult markets. I'd obtained a B.A. in English and took additional writing courses, and won a picture book mentorship from the SCBWI in my state.

At a 2012 writing event, an editor described what he was looking to acquire. I felt one of the manuscripts I'd been working on was a perfect fit. I submitted it to him, and he referred my work to the editor at Lerner who eventually bought it. In a surprising twist of fate, I was working on a query to Karen Grencik of Red Fox Literary the same week that editor contacted me. When I let Karen know of the publisher's strong interest, she read my manuscript that day. It's hard to believe that was nearly two years ago!

[Regarding tips for writers,] Focus less on getting published and more on craft and building a body of work. I feel like I wasted a lot of time dwelling on the "published" part and, like many aspiring writers, sent out a few queries too early.

SERWACKI: I began trying to get published around 1995. I started with books about getting published—this seemed obvious. I found the books both helpful and exhausting. They required lots of work, preparation, perseverance, positive energy and other qualities that I didn't think I had. The advice I listened to was enrolling myself in a local network of aspiring writers and illustrators—RACWI (Rochester Area Children's Book Writers and Illustrators). They acted as my cheerleaders and guidance counselors, which both bolstered my self esteem and forced me to confront my flaws. ... From there I joined SCBWI. This gave me access to large conferences that exposed me to professional editors, agents, and an even larger network of potential friends and supporters.

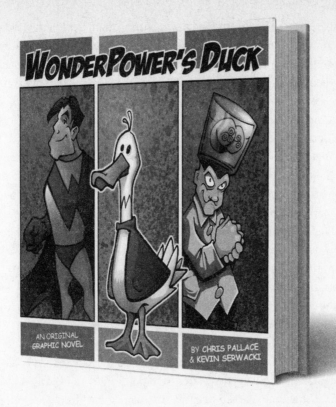

It was not easy to go to those things. They were good, useful and necessary, but I also dreaded them because they made me feel *so* small and unimportant. I was just another person desperately waving my arms in the hope that an editor would notice me.

But I *did* get noticed at the 1999 New York mid-year conference. They had a room set up for illustrators and I paid for a space to display one of my illustrations. My odd style earned me a few business cards from a couple of editors [including] Candlewick Press. I was deeply encouraged by the look of jealousy I received from the artist next to me.

This business card earned me the attention of a woman from SCBWI who was organizing a small portfolio review show in NYC. She invited me to attend. One of the perks of this show was all the artwork would be reviewed by a real-life children's book agent. This is how I met Ronnie Ann Herman of the Herman Agency. She liked my unusual style and offered to represent me right away. I knew how big this was, and I was terrified.

Ronnie worked very hard for me and managed to sell my first children's picture book, *Doorknob the Rabbit and the Carnival of Bugs* (2005 Tricycle Press). … The second book I wrote didn't catch the interest of any publishers and I was finding the process of making books to be very isolating. This led me to assume that I was done with books and I started to pursue sculpture instead. Ronnie and I parted ways on good terms.

But I wasn't done with books. The best thing that I got from my experience with *Doorknob*, was Abigail, my editor. I decided we were friends within five seconds of our first phone conversation. Until I spoke to her, I was afraid of the editing process. … Her edits did nothing but improve my book. … After the book was done *she* decided that we were going to work together again. And she meant it.

She kept in touch with me and every so often would gently and sweetly encourage me to try books again, and I would gently and sweetly ignore her. I was doing sculptural work with my good friend Chris Pallace. I liked this work better because it involved constant collaboration.

Eventually Abi made me an offer that I couldn't ignore. She was going to become an agent and despite my apparent reluctance to do books she wanted to represent me. This is when it finally occurred to me to apply the same formula that was working so well in sculpture to writing books. Chris was the perfect collaborator—he's creative, funny, and he enjoys working out plots, which is something I don't enjoy. Together we compiled a list of 30 book ideas and picked one to team up on.

The first book we chose to work on was a children's graphic novel called *Captain WonderPower's Duck*. It was a cute book, and it proved that Chris and I could write and draw as a team, but it didn't get any bites from publishers. In hindsight I understand why: The main character worked well in a single story, but there was nothing to lend itself to future books. … We were being artists and we weren't thinking in business or revenue terms. Thankfully, Abi was. She looked at our list of ideas and she told us to work on the one called *Joey and Johnny the Ninjas* … We heard nothing for almost a year and then we got four offers in the same week. … We went with HarperCollins because we liked the immediate connection we felt with our editor, Donna Bray. She laughed in all the right places, and that means a lot to us.

What's necessary in a positive agent/client relationship? And what value is there in having an agent in today's market?

ARNOLD: I sold my first 11 manuscripts without an agent, but the publishing industry has changed. It's very important to have an agent in today's marketplace. Because of the deluge of manuscripts, many unready and unsuitable, coming into publishing houses, most houses are closed to unsolicited submissions, even from published authors.

I'm lucky to have the marvelous Karen Grencik of Red Fox Literary as my agent. What I love about Karen is that she loves my work! Well, most of it. Personally, I need a cheerleader in my corner; Karen is my cheerleader. She's supportive and kind, but not afraid to say "no" if she feels a manuscript isn't ready. And we have what is perhaps the most important element in a positive relationship: trust.

INGALLS: I have been extraordinarily lucky to have snagged Karen Grencik at Red Fox Literary. She is relentless in her support of her clients. She offered me representation after reading a picture book manuscript I sent called "Mtoto and His Pig." She sent that around a number of times to no avail. Karen and I have a cooperative arrangement whereby I send out work and so does she. More importantly, she reads and considers my work, offers a suggestion or two, and handles all contract negotiations. For that, I'm extremely grateful. I consider her to be a very good friend. She is above all, a very kind and respectful person.

PALLACE: I'm very lucky to have Abigail Samoun as my agent. Why? Three big reasons: To sell a book to a publisher you need to find the right person, at the right time, and make the right connection with them. A good agent is going to know the publishers, when to set up a meeting, and maybe even what they're looking for. Your agent will be actively working to make the best fit [and] give the best possible first impression of you and your work to the publisher.

Additionally, producing your book is a job, but so is selling it. When you take both tasks onto yourself, you're going to be working two jobs requiring very different skill sets. And if this is your first book, then chances are you're currently employed doing something else, too. A good agent is going make selling your book their job. This is going to save you time and, for me, time is one of the most valuable commodities there is.

Third: Writing, drawing and creating is hard. If you're doing it right, it means a lot to you. Unless you're brilliantly lucky you're going to get a lot of 'no' when you submit your work. You can take a 'no.' I believe its good for you, but it's still hard to hear. Rejection or (even worse) no response at all can take a toll on your creative output. Your agent is an extra level of separation between you and the word 'no' allowing you to focus on producing your work with minimal distraction.

PAUL: I think necessities for a successful agent/client relationship include: patience, honesty and realistic expectations. Before I had representation, I wrote a blog post inviting the "Agent Fairy" to visit and take away all the stress of submitting my work. I laugh now, at the thought that an agent would poof away all of a writer's responsibilities (other than writing, of course). My agent has definitely eased the load—and seems to have a magical work-around-the-clock ability—but I think of her as a partner and colleague and not as a fairy godmother.

I remember getting one rejection letter nearly two years after I submitted! A benefit of having an agent in today's market is getting your work read in a timely fashion, by the actual editor to whom you're submitting. (Warning: Getting your work read quickly also means rejections may pour in quickly!) Having an agent proved invaluable when my second book received multiple offers—who wants to deal with the stress of turning down an offer!?

SERWACKI: Abi is the reason that I got back into books after giving up on them. She used her knowledge of the book market to guide us when deciding which project to work on. She kept us on task by giving us deadlines. She knew which editors would have an interest in our work. She kept us out of the slush pile. She knew what to fight for in our contract—we would have been utterly lost without her. She forced us to read *every* agonizing, boring word of that contract line by line. I might count this as the one black mark I have against her. She acted as a sounding board for both story ideas and marketing ideas.

What are your three top craft tips you can offer?

ARNOLD: It seems elementary, dear Watson, but you must read your work aloud. Not only that, read it aloud as you write and after you write, again and again. You want your words to be lyrical and rhythmical, with no stumbles and no trips of the tongue.

Some may not consider it a craft tip, but I think it's vital for children's writers and illustrators to be playful. Make odd observations, things others might not notice. Quirkiness is fun! Trust where your playfulness and creativity take you.

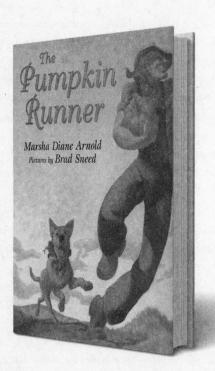

Thirdly, think about your picture book story as much as you write it. Visualize it in your mind. Make a dummy, just for your own purposes, to get a feel for how the words and images will work on the pages. Do this even if you aren't an illustrator, especially if you aren't an illustrator. Simply imagine the image or make a line sketch.

INGALLS: First and foremost, study the marketplace. Since I've worked as a writer, there have been a number of changes, most notably, the length of picture book manuscripts. Editors have always sought stories that will stand the test of time. They want pieces that have if not a universal appeal, at least some that ring true to multiple audiences, perhaps the young child and his/her caregiver who incidentally has the purchasing power.

Write regularly. I work about 40 hours a week either critiquing other writers' work, doing research, studying the market and trends, promoting my work, doing school or library visits and writing. The bulk of my time is spent writing and rewriting. If you only have two hours a week to work at your craft, organize your time accordingly or develop a plan that works for you.

PALLACE: A reliable sounding board is invaluable. Don't go to the person who always thinks you're brilliant. Be sure to ask the guy who will tell you if, indeed, 'these jeans make your ass look big.'

Joey and Johnny the Ninja is a collaboration on all levels—the concept, the writing, the drawing, even the editing and plotting. Because Kevin Serwacki and I work well together this makes for a better book. We kick the ideas around quite a bit before they ever hit the page and are not shy about declaring something as 'not funny' or 'too sappy.' When I pitch an idea I can see his thoughts on it before the words reach his lips. I don't always agree with him, but it forces me to rethink. Decide if an idea is worth fighting for, or if it's best to let it go.

Keep notes. Thanks to computers it is much easier to keep organized notes on characters, subjects, gags and minutia. Pretty much anytime I see, or think, of something that sparks an idea I tuck it away for potential later use.

I keep files on all my characters in a book—everything from motivations and personality, to height and eye color. Nothing fancy, just some quickly jotted down words so I can look it up if I ever need to. Note-taking is one of the things that has really allowed me to come to terms with "killing your babies." Those ideas cut from the piece go into a file. They might not work here, or now. They might never see the light of day, but they're not gone.

The character is king. I've got nothing against a driving plot, or an unexpected twist, but without characters, it's just a history textbook. Most of what happens in my writing is there because someone set it in motion. Even if I dropped a meteor on the book, it would be the characters' choices that make the event interesting rather than the event itself. Whenever I am stuck, or in doubt about what will happen next, I think about my characters' goals and/or how they would react to their current situation. This occasionally steers the plot in a new and unexpected way, but it always feels more true in the end.

PAUL: Don't rush. Growing up, my mom said "haste makes waste" so much I loathed the phrase. It pains me to admit it, but Mom was right. Take time to write and revise. Put stories away. Consider alternate endings. Let feedback stew or process for weeks or months, not days. Know that some of what you write will never be published, and be OK with that.

Read. Read the classics, read what's new, read the loud bestsellers and quiet award winners. If your local booksellers and librarians don't know you by name, you're not reading enough. Read things similar to what you're working on. Read stuff that has nothing to do with what you're writing. Don't rely on your memory to remember what you've read. Take notes and document what strikes you. Dissect strategies that authors use and keep a log. This will help you fill your writing toolbox.

SERWACKI: I was hugely experimental with my illustration and this led to a success, but it also led to a failure. The success part was that my work didn't look like anybody else's, which allowed me to stand out in the crowd when I exhibited. I was surrounded by hundreds of artists who worked in watercolor and ink. Their work was professional and probably more skilled than my stuff but they all blended together. I got an editor's business card because of that.

But the failure of my experimental work was that I became so obsessed with creating techniques that looked different that I produced very little actual finished work. Set aside some time to experiment, but make certain you are also leaving time to create finished work in a style that you can successfully duplicate. Art directors need to know what they are getting when they buy your artwork.

The one part of writing that makes the experience sometimes unenjoyable for me are the moments of complete inactivity—those moments when you just don't have the flow and every time you look at the clock it seems another three hours have gone by and you have nothing but one bad paragraph to show for it. I combat that by making sure I have another activity close by that involves the use of my hands. I make small doors that I sell as fairy doors. They take a long time to make because I have to glue small planks of painted wood down one at a time. It's completely brainless but time-consuming work. It occupies the part of my brain that gets stressed when it notices that time is ticking by. When that stress goes away, the words usually start flowing. And even if they don't, I still end up with some work getting done.

[Also] I have an iPad and just like anybody else I use it to watch movies. The iPad has a handy function that allows you to take a photo of anything on the screen when you push both buttons at the same time. I *love* this function! When I was in college our illustration professor quite rightfully insisted that we get photo reference of everything before we drew it. If I wanted to paint an apple, I'd have to take a photo. I have files with hundred of photos from all the movies I've watched. I separate them into categories such as, facial expressions, locations, inspiration, Kung Fu poses, crowd scenes, body types … it's a reference file for every possible thing I can think of. I use these files to draw from but I'll also flip through them to see if any of the images spark an idea for a character or situation. It's easy visual brainstorming.

What are your thoughts on today's publishing market? Is it on the upswing? Are there any particular trends writers/illustrators need to consider?

ARNOLD: Last year was a positive one for me, so right now I find the publishing world a positive place. But there's no doubting, it's tough out there.

Picture books were thought to be on the slide several years ago, but I think they're on the upswing. There are many opportunities, in many different formats. Besides my traditional picture books, I have an e-book and am delighted with the digital apps Fat Red Couch is developing for me. If you love traditional publishing, as I do, I think it's standing strong. Digital works will never replace holding a physical book in our hands, near a friend or family member who reads it to or with you.

Regarding trends, I think it's something for authors to be aware of, but not to think about too much. Our work as writers and illustrators is to write, to draw, to create—not to worry about the industry.

INGALLS: It seems to me that author/illustrators are having a bit more success of late. I'm seeing some very charming books imagined by these talented individuals. As a picture book writer first and foremost, I know that more than half of a story is told by the illustrations, sometimes the entire story. Think wordless books or a book that sold recently that had just 14 words—one for each spread. I read recently that of the approximately 1 million manuscripts circulating at this time, about 1 percent will receive some consideration. That is not to say that they will make it to publication. The competition is very stiff. Don't be dismayed and don't give up. And remember this: It's never too late to do what you really want to do.

PALLACE: Never do it for the money. Experience says there are easier ways to make it. If you've got a story to tell, tell it. Make it the best story you can. I'm sure there is a certain type of author who has the skill to identify a trend and mine it for gold. I count myself lucky not to be one of them. Tell *your* story.

Creation should come from the heart. There is something inside you that you are going to share with the reader. If you filter that idea through what you think will be popular you're only going to dilute it. Better to write down what you want to say, instead of what you think they wish to hear.

PAUL: Those are the million-dollar questions. I don't know if the market is on the up-swing. I just stay positive and keep writing. I guess it's important to be aware of trends, but I think many debut authors will stand out with a manuscript that's fresh, original or different. To me, one exciting trend is that creative nonfiction and picture book biographies are being released by a broader range of publishers.

SERWACKI: I don't know very much about the publishing market and trends aren't something that I think about consciously. I'm certainly affected by trends every time I watch a movie, read a book or see advertising, but I don't set myself to directly follow them. I draw and write about things that I really want to draw and write about. This keeps it fun and interesting for me, and hopefully my readers.

So much of success in this industry revolves around perseverance. Please talk about your personal perseverance and provide any insight you have for a fellow writer/illustrator who is struggling with rejection.

ARNOLD: My first book, *Heart of a Tiger*, was rejected thirteen times before I found the editor who loved it as much as I did. The story was close to my heart and I didn't want to give up on it. I'm so glad I didn't. It's my top award winner and was in print for 17 years. One of the awards it garnered was the Ridgway award for Best First Book by a New Author. The perseverance paid off.

I don't think there's much I can share to ease the pain of rejection. Even bestselling authors feel it, whether from editors, reviewers or readers. I still feel it. The best we can do is to live in balance, remember what is most important (for me that's family, friends and our natural world), and to keep striving for our dream. When our creation is ready, we must be brave and let it go. We must send out our best work and keep sending it out.

INGALLS: Perseverance is absolutely the name of the game. I have worked and re-worked some manuscripts for over six years. Some will sell and others won't. Editors may have feelings one way or another—many are not in agreement about what needs to change for a particular piece to sell. They have to consider their own lists, and the trends that they see coming down the pike before I do.

Receiving a rejection is just an acknowledgement that work is out on submission and being reviewed. It's always so much better to get a comment or two, but at least the work is out. If it never sees the light of day on an editor's computer monitor or on his or her desk, it can never sell. Having the courage to rework a piece, place it before the eyes and ears of a critique group or two, and then an editor or several is what has to happen before a manuscript will make it to print or in digital format. At this point in my career, I've had maybe 200 sales and I have about a thousand (I'm guessing) rejections. But so what? It's the process that is important before the product becomes a reality. Enjoy the process!

PALLACE: The trick is, don't make it hard to keep going. Always have something that you can push forward on. Never hinge everything on getting to 'yes.'

When I was a kid I wanted to either make comics, or work for the Muppets. After college I had an opportunity in the fantasy gaming industry and immediately had some really rewarding work at some very unfortunate pay. Shortly after, the real world kicked into high gear. Loans needed to be paid, rent, car, art supplies, girlfriend (now wife). I took a job as a graphic designer. It was't glamorous, but it was good. I did this for quite a while, never losing sight of my inspirations. I drew and I plotted and I wrote, but it was all private. None of it was reaching the world, and I could feel something was wrong.

Things changed in 2004 when I quit my job. I partnered up with a friend to start a gaming company called Bent Castle Workshops. This was the single most frightening thing I have ever done. It wasn't even the financial pressure, though there was plenty of that, it was the *freedom*. Freedom can be scary.

I was talented, I was determined and I wasn't ready. Bent Castle was my gauntlet. Making a game was a lot harder than I thought, and our first game was released due to stubbornness alone. Ben and I just pushed forward no matter what, and learned how to do better the next time. Then we did it again, and again.

While the gaming world was opening up to me, the world of books was not. I had been working on an ABC superhero book. It was perfect match for my background and research told me there wasn't any other book like it on the market. Right before I was ready to submit to publishers a member of my children's book writers' group somberly told me that they just read the listing for an another ABC superhero book. It was written by a known comic book artist. I checked it out. It was good. I was crushed.

In 2010 Kevin Serwacki, a friend I had worked with on many freelance projects, and I decided to write a children's graphic novel. … Spent the better part of a year on it, but never quite got it off the ground—but we did get a round of pleasant rejections. Still, it had value. Just like I had cut my teeth on the gaming world, [it] gave me real insight into graphic novels. …

Kevin and my writing styles lean toward world building, so we were very interested in doing a series. … We spent 4 months fine-tuning, [and] put together a 75-page graphic novel (pencils only), and a layout for the next the books. We developed the characters and the world until we felt we had an ample playground to explore. Then we gave it to Abi, and about a year later we were lucky to get multiple offers.

PAUL: An editor once said my book—which took me eight years from idea to final draft—was probably not commercial enough to sell as a debut. I could have argued with him during our critique session, but I did not. I could have given up on it. (I almost did.) I could have blogged a "told you so!" post after the book sold to another publisher. I did not. I took the feedback and incorporated it into that book, making it better. I kept my notes from the conference and studied what that editor was looking to publish. I considered carefully which of my other manuscripts fit that imprint's needs. I worked tirelessly on revising my next book and ended up selling it to that very editor. A few months later, when I told him in person how "lucky" I felt, he said this: "I think people make their own luck."

Don't let rejection cripple you. I grew my thick skin at a young age through participating in drama. From countless, frightening auditions to directors' orders (yelled through a megaphone), rejection and critique go hand in hand with performing arts. Experience in theatre helped me develop a professional expectation that feedback, revision and collaboration are always part of the creative process. These on-stage skills translate well to writing and publishing.

SERWACKI: The best piece of information that I was ever given regarding the subject of perseverance was "the one thing that all successful people have in common is that they have more failures under their belts." I think it takes years of experience to hear this and fully believe it. I was a teaching artist for many years and I would repeat this over and over and over in the hopes that my students would embrace it and understand it. More often than not I would witness them fail and then refuse to attempt that thing again. It was very frustrating.

I get why it's tough. Failure hurts and we spend our lives being taught to avoid and fear it. But after years of struggling as an artist I can now look back and see where all my failures brought me. I can track every single success I've ever had back to what was originally a failure. Once you embrace the fact that failure *must* occur in order to prepare you for success, it doesn't hurt quite so much.

KARA GEBHART UHL is a Fort Thomas, Ky.-based freelance writer and editor who blogs about parenting at pleiadesbee.com.

LAUREN DESTEFANO

On why you should focus on the writing and the rest will come.

....

by Ricki Schultz

A lot of information exists out there about writing and publishing—how to craft, what conferences to attend, how to build platform, and much more. For young adult author Lauren DeStefano, much of that can be overwhelming. Likewise, it can keep aspiring authors from what she says should be their focus: the writing.

While the Connecticut native recognizes these things are significant to a writing career, what she deems most important—and what's worked for her—is finding one's own writing process (or lack thereof, when need be), allowing characters to dictate the stories (instead of the other way around) and embracing rejection. The rest will come.

So, why are we bogged down in distraction? Why are we so concerned with being the perfect client, the perfect author to acquire, that we focus on the wrong things? Such ideas about perfection creep their way into DeStefano's works as well. Her interest in man's unnatural quest for perfection is explored in both her debut dystopian series, the acclaimed Chemical Garden Trilogy, as well as in the *utopian* series she's currently penning, The Internment Chronicles (both Simon & Schuster).

Lucky for us, the Albertus Magnus College alum was nice enough to spare a few moments to share her story, wax poetic about surviving in this industry and offer some insight on how to thrive as an aspiring author.

Are you a plotter or a pantser? According to your website, you wrote the initial draft of Wither in about a month—followed by months of editing. What does a typical writing day/week look like for you? What is your schedule?

I think the most popular question any author receives is about his or her writing process. I'd love to give you a profound or even remotely helpful answer, but the truth is that I just make it up as I go. I have fun. I write until it begins to feel like I want to claw my face off and then I stop, and I start again when it feels like there's magic brewing. Sometimes I don't write for weeks, or months. Sometimes I write a few sentences and call it a day. Sometimes I write for six hours and then have cake for dinner. There's no planning involved.

Looking at your FAQs on your website, it appears you landed your agent after doing research and going through the query trenches—and that you didn't live out some non-querying fairy tale. That will give many writers a lot of hope! Please tell us a little bit about your query journey.

I sent out so many queries that I stopped counting after 140, and eventually hooked the interest of a small handful. Ultimately the most promising responses I got from agents was: "Try me again with your next project."

Of those agents, Barbara [Poelle, of the Irene Goodman Agency] was the only one to follow up three months later to ask if I was writing anything new and if there was anything she could do to help/encourage the process. I found that to go way above and beyond what I would have expected or what I'd heard from my fellow query colleagues. Long story short, Wither happened.

How do/did you deal with rejections?

Rejections have never bothered me. They've never been a source of contention. The way I see it, there isn't just one person out there whose "no" can define a writer's career or life. In the early stages when we were submitting to editors, I took comfort in rejection, as weird as that might sound. It wasn't until we landed my first book deal that I was thrown into unfamiliar waters and scared out of my mind.

I also used to think that being published meant that the rest of my writing career would be a series of yes's and open doors. I had that wrong. There are more opportunities for a published writer to hear "no" than there are for an aspiring author.

You pitched 20 potential manuscript ideas to your agent, and the idea for Wither was #15, according to your site. How many manuscripts did you write before you started/sold Wither?

The 20 potential manuscript thing was actually a writing exercise my agent asked me to do. At the time, I was overwhelmed and didn't think anything viable would come of it. Shows how little I know.

Aside from the 20 manuscript ideas in that exercise, I wrote three manuscripts before *Wither*.

I read in an interview that you started out writing adult fiction. How did you come to start writing YA? Any interest in going back ever?

Wither was sort of a weird accident. I meant to write a short story, possibly for teens. It turned into a full-on YA novel, and I enjoyed the ride so much that I got in line again. But yes, I would love to go back to adult one day. I keep searching for that right adult story, but it hasn't come to me yet.

Your books thus far have been written in first person, present tense. What draws you to this point of view? What do you find are the advantages (or disadvantages) of writing in this and other tenses, and how do you know which is best for a given story or series?

I was attracted to first person present tense because I liked the urgency, but it isn't a style I used in my older manuscripts and I've got a few things in the works that are written in a different style. I like to play around and see what speaks to me. I end up throwing away a lot of unfinished stories this way, but it's worth it when I find one that catches.

As a series writer, you know a thing or two about weaving in backstory. What methods do you use to approach this? Any rules you follow or tips to impart?

I make it up as I go. But I don't do any dictating; I let my characters tell me what they're thinking and where they want to go, and if what I'm planning for them is wrong. They always know what they're doing, even if I don't.

Can you speak about setting? One of the many things that makes the Chemical Garden Trilogy unique is that it's set in a post-apocalyptic Florida. What went into that decision—why Florida? How do you think it might have affected the series if you'd set it somewhere more overused like New York or Los Angeles? In general, how do you feel your settings enhance your characters and plots? (Is this a calculated thing?)

I wouldn't say that the settings enhance the characters. To me, it seems more like the characters are the ones who affect the settings. Yes, *Wither* is set in Florida, but it doesn't look like the Florida we know today. Things are broken. There are small, contained areas of wealth and beauty, and the rest is a dilapidated failure caused by an attempt to make things perfect. The characters did that.

I hear a lot of people say that humans are at the top of the food chain, but the way I see it, humans are able to master technology, and it's that technology that gives us the upper hand. It's a bit unnatural if you think about it. So I like to plop my characters in

a certain setting and see what roads they build, what towers they climb, if they make a metropolis or destroy one instead.

How do you push through roadblocks?

I don't. If I hit a roadblock, I back up and figure out where I went wrong. A roadblock means I'm writing something that doesn't belong, like a body rejecting an organ transplant. You can't force the organ to comply; you have to take it out and hope the next one is a match.

You're very active on Twitter, and you've got quite a following. How did you build your platform (how much of it happened post publication, post *New York Times* bestseller list, etc.), and what should all new writers be doing?

All new writers should be writing.

I had no social media accounts until after my books were sold, and even then, nobody really knew or cared who I was until my first book had been out for a while. I see so many aspiring authors asking what they should be blogging about and agonizing over how to get more followers when they should be writing their books. What's important is that a writer is focused on his or her story, being true to those characters, being respectful of his or her language, and telling a story that is worthy of the reader's time. Do that, and I guarantee people will follow you.

The Chemical Garden trilogy as well the Internment Chronicles both have, in part, to do with the idea of perfection—in the latter, it's more to be about a perfect society while, in the former, it's concerning man's quest for perfection. Where did this interest spark for you? And, for fun, what would you consider to be a perfect day?

> I've always been interested in the human condition. I watch a lot of documentaries, but my favorites are the ones about food—the packaging, the farming, the marketing. If you go to the grocery store, even the raw vegetables have stickers on them, and the numbers on those stickers are meant to identify which products use which pesticides and which products are genetically modified. There isn't a lot of nature in our diets or in our overall society, and this is something that fascinates me. I suppose a story about trying to make things perfect, rather than natural, stemmed from there.
>
> A perfect day for me would involve lots of napping.

What is one thing you wish you'd known when you started writing?

> It's probably best that I didn't know anything. I've experienced things in this industry that would have scared me off. And my advice to any aspiring writer seeking publishing knowledge would be to not over-research publishing. Just focus on writing that story and take it one day at a time.

RICKI SCHULTZ (rickischultz.com) is a young adult writer represented by Barbara Poelle of Irene Goodman Literary Agency.

JANE YOLEN

On telling the story that needs to be told.

....

by Nancy Parish

The daughter of two writers, Jane Yolen published her first poem while still a student at Smith College. Since then, she's written picture books, folk tales, middle grade fiction, young adult novels, story collections and science fiction. In all, she's seen more than 300 of her works in print. Her picture book *Owl Moon,* won the Caldecott for illustrator, John Shoenherr.

Jane's also received a National Book Award nomination, two Nebulas, a World Fantasy Award, SCBWI's Golden Kite Award, three Mythopoeic awards, two Christopher Medals and the Jewish Book Award. She's the recipient of the Kerlan Award for her body of work and the Catholic Library's Regina Medal. She's also received six honorary doctorates in literature. It's no wonder she's been called the American Hans Christian Andersen and the Aesop for the twentieth century.

Somehow, she also finds time to be on the Board of Advisors for SCBWI, the organization she helped nurture in its infancy. There, she kindly shares the wisdom that comes with such a diverse and storied career. Learn more at janeyolen.com.

What advice would you give the 21-year-old Jane Yolen just starting out in this business?

Three things: BIC: Butt in chair; there is no time fairy; reinvention is as important as invention.

Your novel, *The Devil's Arithmetic,* is an emotional piece about the Holocaust. How can writers tap into emotion like that so that their work resonates with readers?

I read everything out loud as I write which somehow gets me more into the moment. Perhaps it is because I hear the characters' voices that way. Or the rhythms of the sentences. Or because as a skim reader, I tend to miss too much, even in my own books unless I slow down the process by reading out loud.

How do you know when a manuscript is ready to be sent out into the world?

That is a question I am still asking myself! Maybe when I can no longer stand it. Maybe when I have gone over it five more times and changed nothing. But whenever it comes back, I find things that need fixing, so you see—I don't *really* know the answer!

In the *How Do Dinosaurs…* books, how do you decide what to put in the text and what can be shown in Mark Teague's awesome illustrations?

I have been doing picture books so long (and the How Do Dino books since 1998—the first one was published in 2000) that it's second nature to me. And still, once I see the illustrations, I make word adjustments.

In *B.U.G. (Big Ugly Guy)*, you mesh the main character's Jewish heritage with some folklore elements. Where do these ideas come from?

> Well, I'm Jewish and a folklorist manqué, and the golem is a Jewish folklore character. Not a big stretch there!

B.U.G. (Big Ugly Guy) has a boy for the main character. Do you write differently when writing for boys versus girls?

> I have to work harder to get the boy's voice right.

You write in so many different genres—science fiction, poetry, picture books, young adult and middle grade. How do you balance your time?

> I don't balance the time so much as balance the ongoing projects. I often work on three to five things in the same day, some for as little as a few minutes, some for hours. The book (poem, story, essay, speech) lets me know when I've reached that day's limit or my attention wavers—whichever comes first.

Are there any scenes or chapters from your novels that you regret cutting? If so, which ones?

> There's always a chance before the book is in print to make more chances, restoring cuts or making more. But I don't take time rethinking the book once it's out there. If I have the book in hand, I move on. Regret spoils the release. I am already way into the next thing.

You've said that it's dangerous to fall in love with your own words. Care to elaborate?

> The advice "murder your darlings" isn't talking about characters but about those overly precious and usually overwritten bits of writing we get on the first, second, even third go-round of a book. He meant we must be ruthless with our prose. I had an editor at the very beginning of my career who warned me, "You are incredibly facile. Don't be beguiled by your facility." I take that caution very seriously.

Where do you see the publishing industry headed? Should we be excited or scared?

> I had a vision right after Steve Jobs died, an actual visual-auditory vision (I thought only saints got those!) of Jobs up in a heavenly pub having a drink and passionate discussion with an old man dressed in a long black robe with a stiff white collar and a long grey beard. I realized by his guttural accent that the old man was Johannes Gutenberg and the two of them were discussing the Delivery of Story. They were both in agreement that Story was a fundamental component of human life, but acknowledged that they were at two ends of the delivery system.

I'm both excited and scared, possibly because at 75, I'm not sure I will live long enough to see where this wheel turn is heading.

What three authors, living or dead, would you most want to have lunch with? Why?

Emily Dickinson because, well, wouldn't you want to? Isak Dinesen, so she could tell me stories as she used to tell them to Finch-Hatton. James Thurber (who was a drinking buddy of my dad's) because he gave me permission when in high school to make his *White Deer* into a musical and I want to explain to him why I never did.

Editors and agents frequently mention that they are most interested in manuscripts with a strong voice. What do you think constitutes a strong voice and what tips do you have for writers struggling with voice?

I recently read a short story by my granddaughter Alison Stemple (remember that name, though she's only 15 right now) and she already has a strong authorial voice. As I explained to her, some (few) people are born with a storyteller's voice while most writers—even well-known writers—struggle to achieve one. It's basically unteachable, but when you come upon the good ones, you know it zero to the bone!

You were one of the first members of SCBWI, and the organization has grown to be a great resource for writers. Are there any areas where you feel the organization can improve?

I am worried that writers publishing in traditional markets are being swamped by impatient writers publishing their own work. I worry about holding the line on excellence. I worry that we don't do enough in the organization to keep our well-known published writers. And I still think it's the best damned writing organization on the planet.

Do you feel writers need to embrace social media to be successful? Why?

I think writers need to write. What media you write for, how you write, who you perceive as your audience is *your* business, not mine. Some people (I'm thinking particularly about Neil Gaiman, Cory Doctorow, John Scalzi) have used social media to tremendous effect and have built themselves enormous audiences. (It doesn't hurt they are all dynamite writers!) But many of the people flogging their own books and stories and poems on social media are either fairly transparent and inept at it, or they are not particularly good writers to begin with. The rest of us fall into the can't-be-bothered or takes-too-much-of-my-writing-time categories.

And actually, I should be off writing right now!

NANCY PARISH writes the blog thesoundandfurry.blogspot.com. Her articles and a recurring column entitled "Footnotes" have appeared in the Guide to Literary Agents Blog. 12 years ago, she founded the Cincinnati SCBWI group. When she's not working or writing, she's attempting to teach her two cats how to fetch their own toys.

SHERRI DUSKEY RINKER

On breaking the rules and overnight success.

....

by Kara Gebhart Uhl

Author Sherri Duskey Rinker's story of success is an author's dream. A working mom, she sent her first picture book, *Goodnight, Goodnight, Construction Site*, to Chronicle. The publishing house pulled it out of the slush pile and tapped bestselling illustrator Tom Lichtenheld to handle the art. It hit No. 1 on *The New York Times* bestseller list.

Rinker's love of picture books began at an early age, "thanks to an indulgent grandmother who bought me books and read to me constantly," she says in her online bio. In college she pursued a journalism major and an art history minor from Southern Illinois University. After receiving a B.A. in Visual Communications, she worked in the graphic design field for 25 years, designing logos, sales materials and corporate identity items.

Now a full-time author whose second picture book, *Steam Train, Dream Train* (also illustrated by Tom Lichtenheld), also hit No. 1 on *The New York Times* bestseller list, Rinker has several projects in the works. First is a book coming out in 2016 with Balzer + Bray, illustrated by Patrick McDonnell, titled *Since There Was You*. "I'm really excited about it because it feels like a next step in terms of my writing style and subject matter," Rinker says. "And, it's been fun and interesting exploring with another editor. (Alessandra Balzer is *amazing*.) Of course, it's scary, too: 'Can I be successful outside of Chronicle and Tom Lichtenheld?'"

In addition, Rinker is working on a character book with Chronicle, as well as a possible sequel to *Goodnight, Goodnight, Construction Site*. "And, I have three other manuscripts sitting in various forms with my agent," she says. "I'm really smitten with them and I'm praying that Amy can find them wonderful homes. I'm enjoying the exploration right now. My goal for this year is to start work on a nonfiction book and also to write a picture book prequel to a book that I've loved for a long time. We'll see."

Read on to learn more about her thoughts on rhyming picture books, writing while parenting and the necessity of an agent. For more on Rinker, visit sherriduskeyrinker.com.

For fellow writers who have outside full-time jobs, how do you know when it's time to quit the day job and devote all your working hours to the craft? And how do you work through the worry that accompanies such a decision?

I have been extremely blessed by the success of *Goodnight, Goodnight, Construction Site* and, thanks to BookScan, I had a rough idea of what that was earning. In addition, my second book was about to debut—along with a big promotional tour—and I had just sold a third manuscript. Leaving the graphic design/marketing world had been a goal for me for some time: I just wasn't feeling happy or fulfilled with the work any longer. I consulted with my agent about my decision, and the timing just seemed right. So far, it's proved to be the right decision.

You wrote your first picture book, *Goodnight, Goodnight, Construction Site*, while working full-time and caring for your two children. What was the writing process like?

The process of writing the initial manuscript was much like you'd suspect: stealing time during the night while the family was in bed! The manuscript probably took me about a month, but mostly because I submitted a concept layout with the manuscript, and I labored over that.

The editing process was very much a family affair: consulting with my boys over rhyme and meter, and getting technical help from my husband and youngest son—my field experts.

So many agents and editors insist they don't want rhyming picture books yet you chose to rhyme. Did you consider it a risk pre-submission? Why did you feel rhyme was best for your book?

This is where I think that ignorance paid off: I didn't set out to "get published," so I didn't do any research prior. *Goodnight, Goodnight, Construction Site* came to me, really, as a gift: the concept, the title—all of it. I remember getting the idea one evening and feeling like I was hit by a bullet. So, I wrote it the way it came to me: in verse. Once I had the manuscript, I needed to figure out how to get it someplace, and I did some very cursory research into how that whole process worked—agents versus unagented, etc.

Since *Goodnight, Goodnight, Construction Site* was sold, I've read countless accounts from agents, editors, writers, etc., about how rhyming manuscripts are frowned upon. My response: Thank goodness I didn't know any better. (And, as a side note, as a mom who has read hundreds and hundreds of books out loud, I love rhyming books—and so did my boys.) I guess that rules are made to be broken, right?

You submitted your book, unagented, to Chronicle. How long did it take to be discovered in the slush pile? And because that is so many writers' dream, please describe what that first phone call was like.

I sent one manuscript to one publisher: Chronicle. I had a list of publishers, and my plan was to submit exclusively, one-by-one, politely thanking them after each rejection. Chronicle's submission policy at the time stated that rejection could be assumed if no communication was received in three months. After three months and one week, Mary Colgan, my first editor at Chronicle, left a voicemail message on my home phone number, letting me know that Chronicle was interested. I listened to that message at least 20 times—and even woke up in the middle of the night to hear it again, just to make sure I hadn't dreamt it. Needless to say, it was the phone call that changed my life.

I read that, given your graphic design background, you submitted Goodnight, Goodnight, Construction Site with a concept layout. What did that entail and do you believe it helped your submission?

This makes me laugh every time I talk about it, because it reminds me of how little I knew! … The concept sketch cracks me up because it is so completely opposite of how the book ultimately looked.

I often get questions about that board, though, and I'll tell you this: Envision a table of editors sitting together on a Tuesday evening opening slush pile envelopes. Is it *possible* that an oversized envelope and a colorful visual helped to give my submission a second look? It probably didn't hurt.

Once under contract with Chronicle, what was the editing process like?

Gut-wrenching and painful! In hindsight, the edits weren't even particularly large or complex, but I was new, and I took every suggestion *so* personally. I've edited other books since then, and I'm learning to loosen my grip and view the process as more dynamic and collaborative. But it was initially a very emotional time, for sure.

As I understand your agent, Amy Rennert of The Amy Rennert Agency, found you. When did that happen? Were you looking for an agent? Why did you ultimately decide to sign with an agent and is it something you would recommend to children's writers?

I had poked around at the idea of getting an agent when I thought that *Steam Train* might get an offer. I casually queried three houses: one declined and two never communicated at all. After that, I just felt like I'd leave the process up to fate, since that seemed to be the way my author career evolved anyway. After all, I'd done well with *Goodnight, Goodnight, Construction Site* and wasn't even 100 percent sure that I wanted, or needed, an agent.

In April of 2011, just after *Goodnight, Goodnight, Construction Site* had debuted, I was in New York for my first set of school visits and to meet my publishing team at BookExpo America. *Goodnight, Goodnight, Construction Site* hit *The New York Times* for the first time that week. I was sitting on a plane on a runway at LaGuardia when I checked my email and saw a communication from Amy with the words, "Possible Representation?" in the subject line. My heart skipped a beat, for sure!

Amy represents some huge names in children's books: Tom Lichtenheld, Amy Krouse Rosenthal, Eric Litwin. I called Tom and talked about his experience with Amy and, needless to say, everything fell into place. She negotiated *Steam Train* for me the following week.

At this point in my career, I cannot imagine trying to do this without an agent. Was it necessary to getting my first book published? No. Is it necessary for moving forward from this point, making solid decisions, getting manuscript critiques and direction: Yes. Absolutely.

How did *Steam Train, Dream Train* come about? How did the writing process differ from *Goodnight, Goodnight, Construction Site*?

The initial process was similar: I had an idea, wrote it and sent it in. But, once Chronicle bought *Steam Train*, the evolution was far bigger and more dynamic. Tom Lichtenheld was part of the process from the beginning, and we worked collaboratively. Tom envisioned the animal crew and asked me to write to bring in that element. I viewed some of his sketches and made requests. The book became, I think, the best part of both of us, creatively speaking, and took on a life of its own.

After the overwhelming success of *Goodnight, Goodnight, Construction Site*, did you worry about the so-called sophomore slump?

I'll relay a conversation that I had with Tom Lichtenheld about this just before *Steam Train, Dream Train* debuted, that I think will sum this up:

Me: "I just worry that *Steam Train* won't do as well as our first book."

Tom: "Don't worry. It won't.

Bottom line: *Goodnight, Goodnight, Construction Site* is a once-in-a-lifetime success. I realize that. I had hoped that my second book would be respected and well-received, and I'm grateful that it has been. Ultimately, I just want to produce the best work that I can, write from a place of love and gratitude, hope that I'm being divinely guided, keep myself, my intentions and my actions positive, and team with the best possible people. I try very hard to let the rest go and leave it up to God. That's the goal, anyway. (I admit I'm a bit of a worrier, and I like control—so it's a constant struggle. But, getting older helps.)

Many publishers are interested in various novelty formats to accompany books for younger readers. Fans of your work can now buy all sorts of merchandise, including a matching game, lacing cards and a personalized lunch box. What sort of involvement do you have as an author with these products and how has it impacted your success?

Honestly, it's been really fun to see the different interpretations of the book. Chronicle is very gracious in allowing me some input and the opportunity to make suggestions. Along with Tom Lichtenheld's watchful eye, I think they do an amazing job.

The ancillary and merchandising items have given the book greater visibility. Is that a good thing for me as an author? Definitely. I'm incredibly grateful.

As I understand you do many school visits/presentations. How many do you do each year and what do these entail? What tips do you have for authors new to public speaking?

I aim to do at least a few presentations a month. The last year has brought so many changes (writing as a full-time job, the book tour, a move to a new town for my family and getting my sons settled into new schools) that I've pulled back a little from promoting my visits, but it's an enjoyable part of my new career.

In terms of advice, I feel completely inadequate to offer any, but from my own experience I can tell you that presenting has been an evolution. It's taken time for me to make presentations my own and to feel like they're relevant to my experience, voice and perspective. And, I'm sure that the process will be ever-evolving. I think that just trying to be genuine to your own strengths is probably the best starting point.

Goodnight, Goodnight, Construction Site debuted at No. 10 on The New York Times bestseller list. How did that—practically overnight—success impact your life?

After some initial on-and-off, *Goodnight, Goodnight, Construction Site* took to *The New York Times* and has remained on the list for 124 weeks. Even as I write this I find it unbelievably surreal. I'm so blessed

Of course, the *New York Times* presence has been a huge help to my career: Obviously, my manuscripts get seen, and the publicity and success help in terms of booking presentations and author visits. But, the publishing industry has incredibly high standards. I still write manuscripts that are declined; my editors are still tough on me. The road is definitely easier for me—but not easy. And that's as it should be.

Please tell me about the lulling language in both *Goodnight, Goodnight, Construction Site* and *Steam Train, Dream Train*. Did you envision these books as bedtime stories from the beginning, and how did language play a role in that decision?

From the beginning, both of my books were bedtime books. Bedtime was always when I read to my boys, so it was an obvious fit for me. And, from its inception, *Goodnight, Goodnight, Construction Site* was a marrying of a truck book with a bedtime book—which was something I felt was missing from picture book offerings.

Several reviewers have talked about the ingenuity of marrying a truck book with a bedtime story in order to reach a typically boy audience. Did you have a specific audience in mind when writing *Goodnight, Goodnight, Construction Site*?

My own son, a truck obsessed little guy with a tireless (literally!) passion for the vehicles, inspired the book. So, I guess he was the target audience. Fortunately, he represents a large group.

What does your typical work day look like? Do you set daily goals? Do you work from home and if so, what does your office look like? How do you manage your time while also raising two children?

We've converted the formal dining room of the house into my office, so I'm right in the thick of the household—for better or worse. I love that I see the kids get off the bus, and that I'm right there when they get home. But, when I'm really on a roll and want to focus on getting something on paper, it can be hard.

If the boys are off school, I need to sneak in writing in the morning before the day gets going. During the summer, it's nearly impossible for me to get much done, and so I just try to make peace with that and enjoy spending time with the kids. During the school year, I try to capitalize on the boys' time at school—and sometimes that works, and sometimes that doesn't. Of course, a sick child, a snow day—that throws everything off. I have dozens of themes, subjects and ideas, and I just try to get them on paper when I can. I'm always jotting down bits and pieces onto my iPhone so that I don't forget them.

I don't set daily goals, but I set yearly goals. That way, my hope is that everything balances out over time. If I over-schedule or put uber-specific demands on myself, I stress myself out and ultimately feel disappointed in myself. I'm learning to lighten up.

KARA GEBHART UHL is a Fort Thomas, Ky.-based freelance writer and editor who blogs about parenting at pleiadesbee.com.

ANNIE BARROWS

*On transitioning from editor to author,
and knowing the market.*

by Kara Gebhart Uhl

Annie Barrows has the distinction of being a bestselling writer (for both children and adults) and an editor of bestselling books. Her love of the written word blossomed early. Born in California in 1962, Barrows says she spent most of her childhood at the library—so much time, in fact, that the library hired her to shelve books at the age of 12.

After attending University of California at Berkeley and receiving a B.A. in medieval history, she opted for a career in publishing, hoping she'd get to continue her favorite pastime professionally—read. Her first job was proofreader at an art magazine and later, editor at a textbook publishing company. In 1988, Chronicle Books hired her as an editorial assistant and she moved up the ranks eventually earning a senior editor title. During her time at Chronicle, Barrows acquired *Griffin & Sabine,* the publishing firm's first *New York Times* bestseller.

In 1996, after receiving a Masters of Fine Arts in Creative Writing from Mills College and having a baby, Barrows chose to trade in her title of editor for that of author. She wrote several nonfiction books (topics included fortune-telling and opera) before diving into children's books. *Ivy and Bean,* the first book in her children's series of the same name, was published in 2006, and was named an ALA Notable Book for 2007. She's since written nine additional books for the series, which appears regularly on *The New York Times* bestseller list. In 2008, Bloomsbury USA published her novel for older children, *The Magic Half.* Its sequel, *Magic in the Mix,* will be published fall 2014.

Barrows also is the co-author, with her aunt, Mary Ann Shaffer, of *The New York Times* bestseller *The Guernsey Literary and Potato Peel Pie Society,* published by The Dial Press in 2008.

Today Barrows lives in northern California with her husband and two daughters. She is currently working on a new novel for adults and says she has a number of children's projects up her sleeve.

Here she talks about her transition from editor to author, MFAs, her writing and editing processes, and the importance of knowing the market.

What was your role at Chronicle Books and looking back, how has it impacted your career as author today?

I started at Chronicle as an editorial assistant, which meant that I did everything from Xeroxing to reading manuscripts to climbing around the dumpster to find lost galleys to line editing. I liked all of it (it was a pretty clean dumpster) and I learned a lot really fast. I was promoted up the editorial chain in two directions, both as an acquiring editor and as a managing editor. At Chronicle, managing editors were in charge of the editorial process, including copyediting and proofing, and the production schedules. As an acquiring editor, I was most interested in buying books that combined art and text in innovative ways. Because I was on both the production and acquisition sides of publishing, my education was unusually broad, and I think it's been instrumental in my career for the following reasons: First, I'm not afraid of (most) editors; I'm not afraid to reject their edits; and I can usually validate my arguments. Some of the most impassioned writing of my life has been about single quotation marks. Second, I'm sympathetic to editors. They lead a harassed life, constantly being shaken down by art directors, marketers, salespeople, publishers, and their own Profit and Loss statements. They barely have time to read, much less to think about what a manuscript could become. I'm familiar [with] the pressures they're under and the marks they're obliged to hit, and I operate under the assumption that the more I can do, the easier their jobs are (and the happier I am). Third, I think anyone who's spent time working at Chronicle Books ends up with the ability to articulate her opinions about visual matters, which turns out to be quite a rare skill. I thought everyone could do it until I started working with other publishers and realized that most editors—and authors—can't say why a cover is or isn't working. They know why, intuitively, but they can't talk about it, and therefore, they can't manipulate it. It's been amazingly useful, being able to talk about art, not only because it gives me more input on the visuals in my books, but also because it impresses people.

Tell me about the transition from editor to writer, including your time earning an MFA in Creative Writing at Mills College. Do you recommend aspiring writers look into MFA programs?

My transmogrification from editor to writer was very slow and as pragmatic as such a ridiculous career move could be. As I noted above, I had two jobs at Chronicle. When I decided to get an MFA, I quit one of them (the managing one) and kept the other (the acquiring one), so I worked at Chronicle part-time during my MFA. It was only after I finished the program and had a kid that I finally left for good, and even then, I was still freelancing as an editor.

As for recommending an MFA, yeah, sure—I would never say it's *necessary*; but being in a program does force you to produce work, and it allows you to spend time with smart people who care about writing and reading. In MFAs, as in so many things, the key to happiness is low expectations. As long as you don't expect that you'll come out of the program with a contract or even a publishable manuscript (and as long as you're not permanently impoverishing yourself to attend), an MFA program can be great.

I do worry that the proliferation of MFA programs is going to result in a great sanding of the American voice. The concerns of the academy—and no matter what they think, MFA instructors are members of the academy—reflect a verbose yet narrow slice of the world, and as MFA graduates come to dominate both publishing and writing, I fear that we will end up with nothing to read but books on subjects that interest the academy, like for instance murder, apocalypse and addiction. Boring!

As a writer, you first published adult nonfiction. What inspired your first children's book, Ivy and Bean?

By about 2002, I didn't have anything left to say to grownups. I was spending all my time with kids, I was reading only kids' books, and I was finding grownups increasingly tedious. And then, in 2003, my older daughter began to read early chapter books. I was appalled at their limited quantity and even more appalled at their limited quality. They're seven, not mentally defective, I remember saying to myself. In fact, kids seemed so much funnier, more interesting and more creative than adults that I was jealous, and I wanted to see if I could think like they did. So I gave it a try, and that was the beginning of *Ivy and Bean*.

Children's books range from board books to young adult—what drew you to the early chapter book category? And what tips do you have for writers looking to break into this category?

I have the same advice for anyone who's interested in writing for children, regardless of category or age group, and here it is: Children don't need to be fixed. They're fine the way they are.

I've been saying this for years, and mostly, adults nod and smile and pay not the slightest bit of attention. Generally, adults think that children's books should instruct their readers, that the job of the children's author is to make children better, more understanding, more like—ahem—the author himself. It's pathetic, really.

While writing the Ivy and Bean series you also helped your late aunt, Mary Ann Shaffer, finish the bestselling adult historical novel, *The Guernsey Literary and Potato Peel Pie Society*, published in 2008. Was it difficult to be writing for two completely different audiences at the same time?

For me, it's impossible to write for adults and kids at the same time. During my deepest deadline desperation about *Guernsey Literary*, I did try to write an Ivy and Bean at the same time, and I found I couldn't do it. I can alternate by weeks, but not within a day. I find writing for kids to be much trickier mentally than writing for adults. Because I am writing for someone I am not (a kid), I'm obliged to leave myself behind in a way that's extremely difficult. The brain orientation is harder for kids' books, but the actual writing is harder for adult books.

What does your typical workday look like? Do you set daily goals? How do you manage your time while also raising two children?

I love my typical workday! I love it when all the real people go away and I am left with my imaginary friends to carry on our complicated relationships. I generally start my day by taking care of anything that's currently in the process of being published—galleys, cover sketches, publicity matters. Then I read a couple of publishing newsletters, so I'm on top of the buzz. Then I get down to business. I begin by reading what I did the day before and then taking it from where I left off. I tend to have large goals—finish manuscript by April—rather than small goals—get to page 38—because I'm not a very good predictor of what's going to be difficult. Some scenes I dread turn out to be easy, and vice versa. I work until the late afternoon, when (a) I get tired of myself and (b) my family comes home from school. It works out nicely.

Describe your writing process. Do you work from home and if so, what does your office look like? Do you outline? Do you work on multiple projects at once?

I can't work anywhere *but* home. My office is at the top of my house, as far from the madding crowd as I can get, with a big window that looks out on a circle of trees (and on my neighbors' back yard, which isn't as interesting as one could wish). I clean my office when I'm between books; as I'm hardly ever between books, my office is a mess most of the time. It's ringed with books I've used for various projects, including encyclopedias of ghost sightings, medieval saints, regional American slang, costume history, the trees of the eastern United States and the history of music, as well as a collection of 1938 *LIFE* magazines, the WPA Guide to West Virginia, and my favorite reference book of all time, *English Through the Ages*. That's a sample. My floor houses more books, including a lot of my own, and various piles of paper. My desk, on the other hand, has pretensions; papers and files have taken over the front, but in the back there are artifacts of my career (a key to the city of Evanston, Ill.) and relics of my youth, including one actual reliquary, currently unoccupied.

An honest description of my writing process would fill a medium-sized and deeply uninteresting book because it changes with each work I write. For Ivy and Bean books, I collect ideas in a manila file folder. These ideas can be as simple as three words jotted on a sticky note, or they can be a full description of a weird thing I saw a kid doing. Some of them are plots and some are just jokes, but I read through the whole file when I'm sitting down to write a book because it puts me in the Ivy and Bean mood. Then I write a one-sentence story line. Then I write a one-page synopsis. Then I stare out my window for about four hours, and then I sit down and write the first page, which always surprises the heck out of me. Discovering where I'll begin is my favorite part of the whole process.

What's your editing process like? I read that you rewrote the first *Ivy and Bean* six times. Was that while under contract with a publisher or on your own, before submission? Why is the art of rewriting so important?

I despise rewriting. I love the euphoria of the first draft, which is to me like lighting matches must be to a pyromaniac; I love making myself laugh, finding a fabulous word, playing with my adorable characters. By the time I finish my first draft of a manuscript, I'm convinced it's the most gorgeous book in the world. Grim experience has taught me that this isn't true, so I stuff my nice manuscript in a drawer and I don't look at it for a couple of weeks. When I take it out and read it, it has inexplicably transformed into a mediocre if not downright crappy book. I have to rewrite it. In fact, I usually have to restructure the plot and then rewrite every sentence. Bah. I rewrite it at least twice—though I usually don't have to replot more than once—and then I read the manuscript out loud, preferably to a kid. That's when I find out that my language is too complicated or my description is too boring or my audience has no idea what a bungee cord is. So I rewrite it again to fix those problems. Then, finally, I give it to my editor, who usually finds a very good reason why I should write it yet again. It's a good thing that the illustration, design and printing process takes a year, during which period my bitterness dissipates, allowing my heart to swell with love for my book once again, just in time for publication.

Character likeability is so important in children's work, especially series, and this is something you've clearly accomplished with Ivy and Bean, opposites who are best friends. What tips do you have for writers who wish to create series characters for younger readers?

I'm not sure I thought about likeability per se when I invented Ivy and Bean. I just knew that I liked them. Anyone who's creating a main character must face the complexity of humans honestly. Sure, it's easier to drop a blanket characteristic over an entire character—for example: girlyness—and assign attributes accordingly, but it's boring and dishonest, too, because that's not how people are. You can have an emblematic tertiary character, but primaries and secondaries need to be satisfyingly real, i.e., complicated. In the long run, you make it easier for yourself if your major characters are multi-layered, because there are more things they're likely to do. A girly dresser who's profoundly interested in entomology is going to give you a lot more scope for story than a girly dresser who hates dirt.

You've written that "*The Magic Half* is a catalog of my favorite daydreams: a tiny door in an enchanted house, time travel, and twins." Tell me more about the inspiration for this book and how plot and character came about.

To some extent, I write in order to have something to read, and this was particularly true of *The Magic Half*. It was the kind of book I read a lot as a child, what I call "domestic magic," which takes place in the world we know, with a magic element added.

Unfortunately, this genre has almost gone extinct, due to an epidemic of fantasy books, which generally take place in a different world or our world with quite different inhabitants. I wanted to read a tale of domestic magic, and I wanted the magic element to be time-travel, because I will never get over my disappointment at not having had that experience. I went looking for such a book and came up empty-handed. So I wrote my own. Actually, I wrote 40 pages of it, and then got busy with something else. Later, my daughter found the 40 pages and was infuriated when I told her that there wasn't any more. I finished it so she would stop griping. I don't know why people say that kids have a deleterious effect on one's career.

In late 2012, I was completely fed up with a manuscript I was working on, and for relief, I began to think again about Miri and Molly, the heroines of *The Magic Half*. This turned into the sequel to that book, which will be coming out this fall and is titled *Magic in the Mix*. I guess this proves that working on multiple projects is fruitful, if only in [the] great Robert Benchley tradition of accomplishing a dozen small tasks in order to avoid a single big one.

As someone who has had success as both editor and writer, what advice do you have for fellow children's writers trying to break into the market?

The first caveat: There are a million ways to be a successful writer, and not all of them include being published. The second caveat: Any single piece of advice about publishing has so many exceptions and special dispensations and is so immediately outmoded that it's almost useless.

Nonetheless, here goes: If you want to be published, it is necessary to become familiar with the marketplace. What's being published, what's being talked about, what's popular with children, with teachers and with parents? These are things you need to know, and once you know them, you need to scrutinize your manuscript's viability in terms of what you've learned. Are there a million books like it? (That's bad.) Are there no books at all like it? (That's bad, too.) Who's the audience? (No fair saying everybody.) Where will it be shelved in a bookstore? What category does it fit into? Is it longer than other books in that category? (Cut it.) And finally, does your projected audience like it? (Your projected audience can't be related to you.)

If familiarizing yourself with the marketplace fills you with gloom and boredom, that's fine! Don't do it! Enjoy writing and enjoy reading your works to your friends and family. That's a wonderful outcome. But if you want your work to be published and read by people you don't know, you have an obligation to try to understand publishing. Good luck.

You've written 10 Ivy and Bean books. Do you have more in the works? And if you have an end date for the series in mind, how does that come about? How do you know when it's time to leave beloved characters alone and move on?

I don't think I'll ever be willing to say that I'm finished with Ivy and Bean. I love them. But I am—and they are—on hiatus at the moment. I began writing the Ivy and Bean books in 2003 (though the first one wasn't published until 2006), which means I've spent more than a decade with them. I still find them charming, and I still think seven-year-olds are wonderful, but I need a break. While I was writing books nine and 10, I kept having the feeling that I was writing a sentence I'd written before—and that, more than anything, persuaded me that I should stop for a while. The thought of producing a repetitive or flimsy Ivy and Bean book makes me miserable. But just the other day, I got this great new idea . . .

Your website is a fan favorite, not only with the humor and tone you take in your online writing but also with your extras, such as the Ivy and Bean Babysitter Test and tips on how to bug your older sister. Why do you think it's important for today's children's writers to have an online presence?

I hate to say websites are necessary because I like to maintain the illusion (delusion?) that good writing is the only true necessity. But honestly? Websites are necessary. Everyone over the age of two has been trained to believe that there's *more* to every piece of art than what has been given to them by its creator, that there's some hunk of secret material just behind the thing itself that will add to their satisfaction. Maybe they're right. In any case, that's what a website is: more—more fun, more information, more marketing. It's a place to put all the stuff your editor wouldn't allow you to put in the book, where kids on book-report duty can get the required biographical data on the author, where events can be advertised, where you can proudly display your meticulous research, and where despairing fans can get a little tide-over as they await the next publication day.

14. What are you working on now? And what do you hope to be working on in the future?

I'm busy with three different books right now. In Fall 2014, *Magic in the Mix,* the sequel to *Magic Half,* will be published, and we're currently at the cover-sketch and galleys-on-the-way stage, which is very exciting. Also in Fall 14, there will be a fill-in journal called *Ivy + Bean + Me,* which contains a lot of writing prompts (e.g., "Something I Did That Was Probably Not a Good Idea") as well as commentary from Ivy and Bean, some Ivy and Bean story openers for the kids to finish at will, and, as usual, suggestions for making life more interesting. And then, of course, there's my novel for adults, which I've been working on for about five years. I think—I hope—I'm in the home stretch now. It's utterly brilliant, in my opinion.

As for the future, there are several books I want to write, both for kids and for grownup people. On the other hand, there are days when I think I'll give up on writing and go back to editing. And there are still other days when I think I'll go back to school and become an etymologist.

KARA GEBHART UHL is a Fort Thomas, Ky.-based freelance writer and editor who blogs about parenting at pleiadesbee.com.

CINDA WILLIAMS CHIMA

On how she found her voice.

by *Victoria A. Selvaggio*

Like many writers, Cinda Williams Chima was fascinated with the world of reading and writing at an early age. It was a fascination that remained with her even as she pursued other endeavors such as working in advertising typing ad copy, becoming a dietitian, teaching nutrition and dietetics at the University of Akron in Ohio and writing a nutrition column for the *Cleveland Plain Dealer*.

It wasn't until her children were born that she came back to her true passion: storytelling. And fans of her young adult contemporary fantasy series Heir Chronicles (*The Warrior Heir* (2006), *The Wizard Heir* (2007), *The Dragon Heir* (2008), *The Enchanter Heir* (2013), all from Hyperion) and Chima's bestselling young adult high fantasy Seven Realms series (*The Demon King* (2009), *The Exiled Queen* (2010), *The Gray Wolf Throne* (2011), and *The Crimson Crown* (2012), all from Hyperion) couldn't be happier.

The starred reviews in *Kirkus* and VOYA (among others), to numerous state awards lists, and the bestseller lists: the *New York Times*, *USA Today* and *Publishers Weekly*, accredit Chima's determination to hone her craft while continuing to thrive in this ever-changing market.

Here, Chima shows that "becoming published" has brought forth greater things than succeeding in that first contract. Being able to prosper in the fascinating world of reading and writing while having the opportunity to find her "own" voice has been life changing. Join her, as she highlights her own writer tips from immersing herself in the publishing industry to collaborating her strengths and weaknesses as a writer. Want more? Check out Chima's website: cindachima.com

First, your website is amazing! The documentation provides viewers with a vast amount of information, set up almost like layers of a story. Explain why having a website and/or other social media is important for writers, even if one is unpublished. On the other side of that, I hear from writers that blogging/tweeting is too time consuming; how do you find a good balance in being active in social media while remembering the importance of writing time?

One mistake many new writers make is focusing too much on promotion and social media at the expense of their writing time. Most of us don't have the luxury of writing full time, especially in the beginning. It's especially critical to protect writing time if you're juggling multiple commitments. The work comes first, before blogging and tweeting and website development. Trying to sell substandard work is like trying to roll a boulder uphill—lots of sweat and effort, little progress.

I don't think it's necessary to have a website before publication, but it is important to have a "home" on the web. Even a blog can serve as a point of contact, and many hosting sites provide templates that enable anyone to produce a professional site. It's better to have a professional-looking, up-to-date blog than an amateurish, clunky, out-of-date website. Readers respond better to a blog that provides information and value. They won't return to a site that is purely promotion.

Use the resources that are available to you. My website is thorough and frequently updated because I am married to the web designer. He puts a high priority on my requests. Some writers design their own websites; others hire a professional. If you have to pay for every little update, you'll need other avenues to deliver timely news to readers that you can manage yourself. Some writers incorporate a blog into their websites, which is an easy way to add updates to the site.

Facebook can be a useful point of contact on the web. Many authors have a "fan page" separate from their personal Facebook pages. It's easy to post news, images and updates on Facebook. Twitter is another social media outlet that can make it easy to make frequent, brief contact with readers and colleagues, and provide just-in-time updates about events and publishing news.

Above all, pick and choose where you want to spend your time. If you enjoy social media, if you're good at it, have at it. But don't try to be everywhere at once.

Once you are shopping a project, be aware that agents and editors may visit your social media sites to see if you're the kind of person that they might want to work with. Make sure that you are presenting a professional, creative, rational (e.g. not sociopathic) face to the world.

Knowing you personally, and having the opportunity to hear your presentations, I understand the concept of finding your own voice. Share with readers the connection you feel with writing and the writing community. Moreover, how has this process brought you to a place where you feel you finally belong?

A writing community can be nourishing to a writer, personally and professionally. Because writing is a solitary endeavor, other writers can provide important validation and context, answering the "Is it just me?" and "Am I crazy?" questions. From a professional standpoint, peer writers are usually the best source of critique, especially early on. Peer critique can help you get your work to the point where you can benefit from a critique from an editor or agent. It can be challenging to find the right "fit" in a critique group, but it's worthwhile to keep looking. Networking with other writers can open the door to new resources and new opportunities and great friendships.

I am constantly noting to other writers and illustrators how you continue to immerse yourself in the publishing industry. In addition to belonging to many writers' organizations, you present at numerous conferences and events. You also register and attend many as a participant. Why do you feel this is important?

Attending conferences and events is part of the process of creating a writing community. In "real life," many of us live and work with people who are free of the writing disease. Even if they are supportive, it can be draining to constantly explain, defend and justify the time we claim for writing.

Other writers "get it." They speak the language, and they don't ask annoying questions about when you're going to finally get a publisher or make the *New York Times* list. Like nobody else, they understand the pain of rejection and the visceral wound of a bad review, because they have been there.

Conferences and workshops can also be a good place to meet writers who might be good critique partners. My first critique group grew out of a fiction-writing workshop I took at a local library.

Not all writers enjoy teaching. I do. I've always been a teacher of one sort or another. I often present at conferences and teach writing workshops. I find that prepping for a workshop sharpens my own skills, and clarifies my thinking about the process. I love devising ways to deliver concepts and content that writers can apply right away. It's especially rewarding to teach writing workshops to teens, because I see my teen self in them. I wrote my first novels in junior high, but I had no formal training or exposure to other writers until I was an adult.

Conferences can be a great place to make contact with agents and editors, and figure out who might be a good "fit" for you. You may feel that all the power is in the agent's hands, but, in truth, you are interviewing each other. Agents need great books to sell. If you have written a great book, then they need you.

You'll get the most out of editor and agent contacts at conferences if you spend the time up front to make sure the work is ready for prime time before you pitch it. Don't spend time polishing your query letter when the work itself isn't there yet.

Again, prioritize. Some would-be writers become conference junkies who get very little actual writing done. Don't fall into that trap. Writing is like tennis—you will not improve without practice, no matter how many workshops you take. If you have limited time, spend it writing, and pick and choose the conferences that are most likely to meet your needs.

What other ways besides writers' organizations, conferences and events, allow you to be current with today's market and trends? What reference books or materials are on your must-have list? Do you have a reading regimen and if so, how does that improve your productivity?

Stephen King once said, "If you don't have time to read, you don't have the time (or the tools) to write." I agree. Much of my education in writing comes from a lifetime of reading.

Reading in the genre you intend to write is an education on craft as well as in the market. Nobody should be writing for teens who hasn't read several dozen recent teen books. The ones you read twenty years ago don't count. Reading a range of books has an additional benefit. It's only human to mimic the strong writer voices you've encountered. Reading widely helps a writer develop her own voice.

I have an entire shelf of writing references, some of which I've read, and some of which I just like looking at. Some I consult when I'm putting together a workshop or program. I have a list of writing references that I've found useful on my website.

These days, I spend more time reading in my genre. My to-read shelf is always groaning—it's hard to keep up. If a book is causing a stir, especially in my target audience, I want to know why. I want to know what it is about that book that connects with readers.

I have an author page on Goodreads, and when readers ask me what I've read lately, I often point them to my "bookshelves" there.

As for trends, I think it's important to be aware of trends, but not to be a slave to them. Really and truly, nobody knows what the next big thing is going to be until it happens. Write the book that only you can write. Write the book that's in your heart—that's the one that is most likely to be successful.

Moving on to your publication journey, share a little about the bumps in the road—submissions, rejections, writing while working a day job and raising a family. What advice can you give to other writers as they experience their own bumps in the road?

Bumps in my road to publication? More like barricades and detours. I've been writing since third grade, so I'm not exactly an example of an overnight success. My first published pieces were freelance work—personal essays about parenting, feature articles for newspapers, and so on. I eventually made a conscious decision to turn away from nonfiction and focus on novels. My sons were teens at the time, and we all enjoyed reading fantasy, so I decided to write something we could all enjoy reading. The result was *The Warrior Heir*. After much self-education, much revision, and lots more practice, it became my first published novel.

It took me four years to find the right agent, partly because the work was not really ready when I first sent it out. I did not find my agent through a referral or contact at a conference—I researched agents and sent out queries. Finding an agent was the key to publication for me.

Nobody should go into writing in hopes of making a fortune. It does happen, but that attitude can be the path to disillusionment and heartbreak. Successful writers love the process of writing (well, most of the time). Real writers must write. If that's the case, it's like this wonderful bonus to be able to make a living at it.

I kept my day job until I had three books published. My third book made the *New York Times* list, so I was able to sign a contract for three more. I had access to health insurance and money saved up, so I took the plunge.

Ahhh, the sweet success of publication. But again, knowing you personally—you remain so grounded! Describe what it feels like to receive a great contract and even more so, validation. What tips can you share with writers on things you know now and wished you knew then?

In publishing, as in love, there is really nothing like the first time—that first agent phone call, that first yes from an editor, holding your book in your hands for the very first time. That look on your spouse's face when that hobby you had suddenly becomes a business.

What do I wish I'd known?

Focus on craft first. The very best thing you can do for your writing career is to write a fantastic book—the kind of book that every agent and editor wants to see in their inbox.

Finding an agent will not solve all your problems, even if it's a great agent. Finding a publisher will not solve all your problems, even if it's one of the Big Five. No author ever believes that her publisher is doing enough promotion for her book. Not everyone will like your book, no matter how good it is.

When you began The Heir Chronicles, did you see this as a series? Do you still have plans to write *The Sorcerer Heir*?

When I'd finished *The Warrior Heir*, I was so enthralled with my magical world and my characters that I immediately wrote the *The Wizard Heir*. I stopped then, because it can be off-putting to publishers to be pitched a nine-book series from a debut author. I think the best position to be in as a debut author is to write a stand-alone book with series potential.

As it worked out, my publisher bought The Heir Chronicles one book at a time. It was only after *The Dragon Heir* made the *Times* list that they offered me a three-book contract (for The Seven Realms.)

It was challenging to return to the Heir series after a four-year hiatus. But it was also fun to revisit characters I loved and create new ones.

The Sorcerer Heir is scheduled for fall 2014.

How was writing The Seven Realms series different from The Heir Chronicles?

I had such fun writing this series, which was set in a world I created for an adult high fantasy series that I never published. I knew the characters and the world very well going in, and so there was a lot less wandering in the wilderness. I've always loved high fantasy (think Lord of the Rings, Eragon, Tamora Pierce's novels) but I was wary about writing it for teens. Reading high fantasy is sometimes akin to hacking through a thicket of words. I was determined to make my work accessible to readers who are not committed fantasy fans.

With so many years dedicated to both series, how did you stay on track? What tips can you share with writers on staying focused when writing a series and/or a stand-alone novel?

What's important is finding the process that works for you. Some writers develop an outline for their series so they know what needs to happen in each installment. Some writers also do a lot of prework—character profiles and world-building, language, etc., before they even begin.

I am a plunger—I sold The Seven Realms series based on a 60-page sample and a one-paragraph summary for each book. It ended up being four books, and the 60 pages appeared in book three. I do keep a table of characters, magical terminology, places, and so on so I (hopefully) don't mess up. For The Seven Realms, I began drawing a map, adding places and landscape features as I needed them—sort of as-you-go world-building.

In addition to both series, how did you handle the revision process? Writers can either find this task daunting or exciting. Share your feelings.

I'm just nerdy enough to enjoy revision after the death plunge of the first draft. In revision, I can take that ugly thing I wrote and make it pretty.

All writers have strengths and weaknesses. What are your strengths? What are your weaknesses? Explain how you learned to collaborate them.

One of my strengths is that I do love the process of writing. I think that's the key to persistence when everyone is saying no to you. I'm told that I'm skilled at building characters who live and breathe and leap off the page, and places that suck the reader in.

A weakness that I share with many writers is that editor in my head—that relentless voice that tells me that I'm faking it, that I don't know what I'm doing, and so on. I often use daily word count goals when writing a first draft to force myself to soldier on in the face of that. I also have learned that my editor sleeps late, so I am most productive in the morning.

What are your future writing plans and goals? Have you considered writing in any other genres?

I have been so very happy in teen fantasy—I have no immediate plans to make a change. But I will never live long enough to write all of the ideas I have, in all of the genres I would like to try.

Writers often only hear about the success stories of authors (huge advances, three-book deals, numerous publishing houses interested in the manuscript) while the "bad stuff" seems to dissipate. Obviously, all the success stories come

hand-in-hand with a tremendous amount of work and pressure. Share some of the "bad stuff" you've had to work through while noting how you've managed to stay so grounded.

Some books are more difficult to birth than others. It doesn't necessarily get easier. Gene Wolfe once said, "You never learn how to write a novel. You just learn how to write the novel that you're writing." With the next one, you start all over again. Depressing, isn't it? The difference between a first novel and successive novels is that maybe you have the memory of succeeding in the past. And that's reassuring.

....

VICTORIA A. SELVAGGIO (vickiscorner.com) is the regional advisor for SCBWI: Northern Ohio (ohionorth.scbwi.org). Writing all genres, she immerses herself in the publishing industry daily. When she is not reading and/or writting or planning her next event, she's busy working her part-time day job and operating her part-time business.

....

DEBBIE DADEY

On how to keep the writing fire alive over many years.

·····································

by Kerrie Flanagan

Award-winning children's author Debbie Dadey is living the dream. Since 1990, she has published 158 books, selling over 47 million copies. She is best known for her chapter book series with co-author Marcia Thornton Jones, The Adventures of the Bailey School Kids, published by Scholastic. Her latest series, The Mermaid Tales, currently has nine books, and is a solo venture by Dadey. These chapter books for young readers, published by Simon & Schuster, combine the fantasy world of mermaids with ocean facts and ecology.

Before becoming a full-time writer, Dadey was a first grade teacher and a librarian in Kentucky. She and Jones worked in the same elementary school. They discussed how great it would be to write for children and decided that together, they would try it. They wrote every day during their 20-minute lunch break or before and after school, took writing courses, attended conferences and did extensive research. Eventually they started sending out their work. For over a year they tried to sell a book with no luck. A small success, the sale of a greeting card, gave them the incentive to keep going.

After a frustrating day when the students would not listen or do their work, Dadey and Jones joked that they would have to sprout horns and grow 10 feet tall for the kids to pay attention. This idea about a teacher who might be a monster became the premise for their first book, *Vampires Don't Wear Polka Dots* that eventually became part of the bestselling Bailey School Kids series.

What is your writing process?

I definitely outline. For the ones I have under contract I will write a synopsis and then my editor will choose which idea she likes best. For books that are already sold, I'll send an outline to my editor. She will look at it and tweak it a little. Then I can write the book quicker, instead of writing it all wrong and having to rewrite it. I will then take her outline and her suggestions and write the story.

My outlines are brief, a couple of sentences for each chapter. It's enough to give me a focus, but not enough to say the book is already written in outline form. Some people write such a specific outline that it doesn't give any room for fun surprises to happen in the story.

I write or rewrite a chapter or two a day, print it out, and put it by my bed. I read it before I go to bed at night and make changes. The next day I will take those changes and put them into the computer. That helps me get going on the story and back into where I was the day before.

With all these books you have already written, how do you continue to come up with new ideas?

I have an idea file that I have in my desk. Anytime I come up with a snippet or see something in a magazine or in a newspaper and I think it will be fun to write about, I tear it out and I stick it in there because I know I won't remember. Or if I have an interesting dream, I'll try to jot it down quickly before I forget and put it in the file.

Right now I have lots of ideas I want to write about, but if there is ever an opportunity to write something new, I can go to that idea file. Sometimes I use the ideas for entire books, and sometimes I use the ideas for things to happen in a book.

What are your thoughts on social media and the role it plays in your writing life?

One thing I wish I had done earlier is social media. I think it is important in today's day and age. I use my social media sites to hopefully appeal to the teachers and the parents. It helps to get the word out there about my stories.

Sometimes I feel like I am beating my head against the wall and I am not sure what is the best answer. I try to find a balance between writing as much as I can and doing as much social media as I can comfortably. I think you have to do what you are comfortable with.

I have a little bit of a set Facebook schedule that helps me. On Tuesday I do trivia, Wednesday I try to do something for writers, Thursday I try to post something for reluctant readers and the other days I do whatever floats my boat.

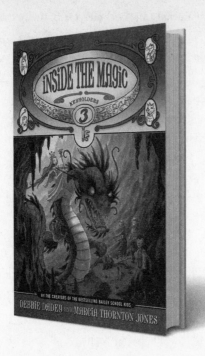

You write for a younger audience. Are there any cautions when using social media with your readers?

Yes, and that is why I hesitated a long time before doing it. I figured anyone reading my books should not be on Facebook. I do have some kids who write to me there, but then I always direct them to my website where I have a place they can write to me called Kids Talk. I preview every question and make sure they don't put their full names, addresses and phone numbers (and some of them do) and if they do, I take all that out before I make it live.

You do a great job weaving humor into your books. What do you think is important for writers to keep in mind when writing humor for children?

If it's not funny to me, it won't be funny to a kid. I think unusual or unexpected situations can be funny. And underwear is always funny.

Yesterday I was trying to think of something funny and I had to walk away from the computer and do some housekeeping things. Then I kept thinking, what would be funny. I started jotting down ideas. Then I did more housework and then it came to me. Sometimes doing something totally unrelated can free up my mind a bit.

I love funny stories. I don't think you can ever have too much funny in a story. The times that I have written safe haven't been as successful as the times I've pushed the envelope. It makes writing more fun and hopefully makes the reading more fun.

You and Marcia wrote more than 60 books together. What is the process of co-authoring a book like and how were you able to sustain a successful working relationship for so long?

We complement each other. I write short and snappy, Marcia writes more long and literary. Putting the two together is like a whole new style. When we first started writing, neither one of us knew what we were doing and we were unsure. We kept each other going. It is so easy to get depressed when you get those rejections. You want to quit. Having a partner can ease that rejection.

We pretty much work the same way I do by myself. We will come up with a synopsis. We'll do an outline and then toss that back and forth over the Internet. When we first started doing this, we would underline everything we changed or highlight it. Now we just change it. Then we take the outline and one of us starts the story. Usually I start them because I like to do that. I will write one or two chapters, then send it to Marcia, then she will makes some changes and suggestions, then write a couple more chapters, then send it back to me and we go back and forth that way.

Your newest series got you out of the Bailey School and into the ocean. Do you have to do a lot of research about the ocean for this series?

I started out with tons of books on my desk. Now I have one really good reference book I use. I've had a lot of fun infusing this into the story and throwing in tidbits about the ocean. In the back of the book is a glossary that tells the real truth about all the ocean creatures.

In each story, the mermaids go to a school. You might not be aware of this, but when you are a mermaid you don't go to school until third grade. They of course have lessons in school. Whatever they are learning about in school is the focus of the book. For instance, *The Secret Seahorse* has information about seahorses. In another one, *Dream of the Blue Turtle*, a leatherback turtle comes to visit their classroom. The mermaids learn about leatherback turtles and a little ecology because one of the main reasons for the deaths of the turtles is that they eat plastic bags put into the ocean.

What advice would you give your early writer self?

Have fun writing and don't be afraid to take chances. Don't write what everybody else is writing. Write what you want to write. Every time I have done something unusual, it has been successful. The times I have done what everybody else is doing, not so much luck.

How do you stay motivated and inspired after 20 years?

I remember what my dad told me when I first started writing: "Debbie, if other people can write books, so can you." I took that to heart and try to remember that when it is darkest before the dawn.

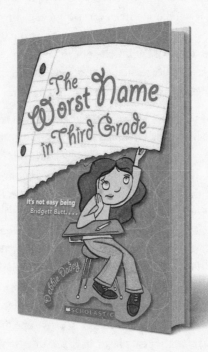

KERRIE FLANAGAN (KerrieFlanagan.com) is a freelance writer, writing consultant, and director of Northern Colorado Writers, a group supporting and encouraging writers of all levels and genres since 2007: northerncoloradowriters.com.

LAURA RESAU

On the 3 things all writers should be doing to better their careers.

by Kerrie Flanagan

With seven YA and middle grade books under her belt, award-winning author Laura Resau is making her mark in the literary world. Since her first novel, *What the Moon Saw*, debuted in 2006, her books have received rave reviews from *Kirkus* and *Publishers Weekly* and have won many awards. Her books *Red Glass* and *The Queen of Water* were on Oprah's kids reading lists in 2008 and 2012.

Her use of vivid imagery and her amazing ability to capture the cultural essence of the places she incorporates into her novels stems from her time living and traveling in Latin America and Europe as well as her love for written language.

Resau holds a master's degree in cultural anthropology and believes her schooling effects not only what she writes, but also how she approaches her writing. It taught her to look at the big picture and pay attention to the social, economic and political circumstances that inform a situation.

Her books have dealt with serious topics like immigration, undocumented families, refugee experiences, human rights, social justice, child slavery and anxiety disorders, but Resau doesn't approach her novels as a vehicle to discuss the issues. By writing fiction from a deep place with an anthropological perspective, Resau feels she can reach tens of thousands more readers than she could writing academic articles.

How did you become interested in writing and explain your path to getting your first book published.

My first attempts were very short little stories. I loved when teachers gave creative writing assignments. But I hadn't met any writers before in my life so I didn't think it was a realistic profession. As a kid and teen I thought I could be a primatologist or an archaeologist and that got me interested in the field of anthropology. It seemed more realistic than being a writer.

After I graduated from college I wanted to immerse myself in another culture and have adventures. I ended up living in Oaxaca, Mexico for two years as an English teacher and later as an anthropologist. While in Mexico, I recorded my experiences and other people's stories and it started coming together into a novel in my head. That ended up becoming my first book, *What the Moon Saw*. At the time it still seemed like a pipe dream to be a writer and get a book published. So I still thought I was going to be an anthropologist.

After Mexico I went to grad school for anthropology. That year in grad school I would spend the first two hours of the day working on my book and then I would do my anthropology work. I realized I felt most alive, most passionate about life those first two hours of the morning when I was writing my children's book. After I got my master's degree, I had originally planned to get my Ph.D. and be a professor, but as I reflected on my life and what made me feel alive and happy to be on Earth, I realized it was writing.

Once I made that commitment to be a writer, I pieced together jobs while I worked on writing my book. I started attending SCBWI conferences and writing workshops, and I started getting to know writers in the community and forming friendships. I haphazardly started submitting my work to agents and editors. In retrospect I can see I didn't do it in a very strategic way. Over the course of a couple of years I randomly sent stuff out and got rejected.

My luck changed a little when I got a story published in *Cricket* magazine. I got to know the main editor and I mentioned to her I had a manuscript. She read it and gave me a wonderful, thoughtful critique. I followed her advice and the manuscript became so much stronger as a result. Because of some changes in the company she wasn't able to make me an offer on the book but she helped me get my manuscript into good shape.

The next place I submitted it, Delacorte, accepted it. After I got the offer, one of my writing friends gave me the number of her agent. He didn't feel the book was a good fit for him but knew Erin Murphy of the Erin Murphy Literary Agency. He thought the book would be a great fit with her. It was.

I finished *What the Moon Saw* around 2000 and then I just started revising. In 2001 I had a solid draft of it. It wasn't until 2005 that I got the contract. Since I had been revising this book so much, I had time to write most of my second book, *Red Glass*. I gave it to Erin and she said it was a perfect next book. The editor at Delacorte really like it and published it. I have published all seven of my books with Delacorte.

Now that you are on the other side of the series, what did you enjoy most about the process and what was the biggest challenge?

The whole reason I decided to do a series because after my first I kept getting a lot of reader mail saying they'd like to see sequels to *What the Moon Saw* and *Red Glass*. When teens love the characters, they really want to see more. With those two book I felt like they were complete and I didn't need to continue developing those worlds.

But with my third book, *Indigo Notebook*, I went in to it knowing I would stick with these characters. When readers really get involved in the world and characters you create it's wonderful to be able to give them another book. That was the most rewarding thing.

The challenging part for me was the deadlines. With a trilogy, the readers (and publishers) really want your next book to come out not much longer than a year apart. I felt an obligation to the readers to stick to that schedule. That was hard because with my other books I had the luxury of years. I could spend two hours thinking of the right word. The kind of time pressure involved in writing a trilogy was a new feeling and honestly, kind of stressful. I am the kind of person who gets lots of ideas and I write my ideas down in my notebook and I start developing them and it was hard because there were a couple of books I really wanted to write while I was involved in the Notebook trilogy.

Star in the Forest was one of those books. I felt really guilty writing it because I wasn't supposed to be working on it. But I had to write it. I wrote that book incredibly fast because I felt like I was playing hooky from what I was supposed to be doing. I was worried I would get in trouble with my editor when the agent sent it to her. It all worked out fine because Delacorte wanted to publish it. During this time, I also finally got my book *Queen of Water* that took almost seven years to write from start to finish, in good enough shape that my editor wanted to publish that too.

So, I had the trilogy, but I also had these other two books. I was working on rough drafts, writing, revising, copyediting, page proofing and promoting the books coming out. All this stuff was happening at one time, plus being a new mother was stressful. That was the downside.

Did you take a break from writing after that?

I took a break but not from writing. If I go more than a couple days without writing I get really grumpy and cranky. After I finished the trilogy I told my agent I wanted to have a break from deadlines. I kept writing every day, but I wanted to be able to have fun and explore. I wanted to have a year of just being playful and write whatever I wanted to do.

  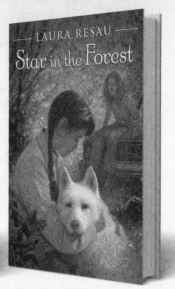

For me it worked well. I know some writers need deadlines and work best under pressure. My particular personality responds better to having free time to play.

How did all this deadline writing impact your writing.

I think it made me realize that I can do it. That I am capable of writing a book in a short period time under pressure. Now when I don't have that pressure it feels really wonderful and delightful and luxurious. It was stressful at the time but I do think that ultimately it gave me more confidence in myself as a writer.

You have had amazing experiences living abroad and traveling. How have those experiences influenced your writing?

When I am immersing myself in a culture that is unfamiliar to me I do tend to approach it as an anthropologist; constantly making observations and writing them down, asking lots of questions and asking if I can participate in anything from cooking to healing rituals. Getting that kind of immersive experience that an anthropologist gets is good for writers. Most the materials for my books came from my notes I took while having these kinds of experiences.

Many of the dramas that happen in my books happened to me in real life. Like being stung by a scorpion, which is something in *What the Moon Saw.* I got myself into many sticky situations on buses. In *What the Moon Saw* the girls are on bus going over remote mountains in southern Mexico. There is a storm during rainy season and the bus starts sliding off the edge of a cliff. That exact same thing happened to me. We had to save ourselves by climbing out the window because the door was stuck and wouldn't open. A lot of these kinds of adventures I had find their way into my books.

You weave different languages throughout your books. Do you have any advice for writers wanting to do this in their books?

When I read books with words from other languages, I do get frustrated if I can't figure it out through context. I do feel it is my obligation as the author to give the reader enough clues so they can fairly easily figure it out without too much brain power. Usually the words I keep in the original language are words that might not have a great translation in English or they have a certain connotation in the native language that doesn't translate well to English.

Like *comal*. It is a clay plate that you make tortillas on in rural Mexico, but clay plate sounds kind of clunky. I use the word comal and I think it evokes smoky kitchens, homemade tortillas and women with callused fingertips.

In most of my books, I have a glossary and pronunciation guide in the back and I found that a lot of people are OK without that, but there are some readers who will get caught up. It will stop them and keep them from enjoying the book if they can't get a definitive sense of what the word means and how to say it.

Do you have to do a lot research for your books?

I do believe my primary mode of research is participant observation, which is what an anthropologist would call it. I do as many daily activities with people as I can, take notes and ask questions. For me that is important because I get a more multi-sensory experience; smelling the smells, tasting the food, feeling the air.

I am good at listening very carefully to what people tell me and remembering it in great detail. This is something I became good at when I was doing my anthropology field research. I could make information last for six or seven hours in my head, but then I would have to race to my notebook and write it all down. I think you develop the skill to hold those things in your memory for a few hours until you can get near a notebook.

I also supplement that research with Internet research, book research and I like watching documentaries. But I do feel that is more of a limited value than actually being there.

How valuable is a writer's group to the success of a writer?

I think it is incredibly valuable. My writer's group has been an important part of my life for over a decade. We meet every two weeks and critique a portion of peoples' work and give feedback. We devote half of the meeting to updating each other on our writing lives. It has always been a supporting and encouraging atmosphere. Obviously, you get good tangible feedback for revising so you can make your work stronger, but I think for me my writer's group has functioned as an amazing psychological and emotional support for me. They helped me get through the rejections of my first manuscript and helped me hang in there and keep submitting.

After I got the contract for *What the Moon Saw*, I was floundering a bit. I thought I would do a short story collection. My writing group had read a huge chunk of what was to become *Red Glass*. I had abandoned it because I felt like it was way too complicated and the characters were too zany. I didn't know how it would all fit together. They asked me about it and wondered why I hadn't finished it. They loved the characters and wanted to see what happened to them. I got it out, started working on it more and after revising I felt confident enough to show it to my agent and she loved it.

I wonder if it weren't for my writing group if I would have ever finished that manuscript or even seen any value in it. Now, it is one of my most popular books and has won the most awards.

As a writer you don't always see the value in your own work. You can't always determine what's working and what's not working. I think you need other eyes to see that and to tell you. There were probably a number of projects I would have abandoned if it weren't for my writing group's encouragement.

What are three things you believe all writers should be doing?

The first one is I think writers should be writing in a journal or diary reflecting on their writing process. Reflecting on their work in progress. Reflecting on their feelings about writing at that particular time. Reflecting on their goals, their progress toward their goals and their frustrations along the way. Reflecting on why they write and what they love about their current project.

The second is making sure their priority is writing and not social media and promotion. There are different ways to do this. One thing I do is use program Freedom that disconnects me from wireless for a set period of time. Most mornings before I start messing around with email or Facebook I will set Freedom for a couple hours, so all I have to do is creative writing. Make creative writing a priority before getting involved with all the other distractions of technology, social media and modern life.

The last one is to set goals and hold yourself accountable. At the beginning of each year, I write a few goals, then I break those goals down into smaller steps. I think as writers we need to structure our time and hold ourselves accountable.

What has been your biggest key to success?

A lot of it has to do with actually finishing stuff. I know many extremely talented writers who for whatever reason don't take that step of fully realizing their creative vision. Sometimes perfectionism is holding them back and sometimes self doubt is holding them back and sometimes external criticism is holding them back. As writers we have to be aware of all the obstacles that are going to present themselves to us.

In my case I've had to deal with anxiety issues my whole life and different fears, rational and irrational. Through constantly reflecting on my emotional state, in regards to writing, I feel like I've been able to find ways to deal with those fears and anxieties that come with writing. For me the most important thing is finishing the project despite the difficulties and despite my doubts and despite the perfectionist urges I have. For those writers who actually commit to finishing something, they are much closer to having their book published and making their career a reality.

KERRIE FLANAGAN (KerrieFlanagan.com) is a freelance writer, writing consultant, and director of Northern Colorado Writers, a group supporting and encouraging writers of all levels and genres since 2007: northerncoloradowriters.com.

FIRST BOOKS

Hear from debut authors of picture books, board books, middle grade & young adult.

compiled by Chuck Sambuchino

There's something fresh and amazing about debut novels that's inspiring to other writers. It's with that in mind that we collected 13 successful debuts from the past year and sat down to ask the authors questions about how they broke in, what they did right and what advice they have for scribes who are trying to follow in their footsteps. These are writers of picture books, middle grade stories and young adult novels—same as you—who saw their work come to life through hard work and determination. Read on to learn more about their individual journeys.

PICTURE BOOKS

❶ CINDY JENSON-ELLIOTT
(CINDYJENSONELLIOTT.COM)
Weeds Find a Way **(BEACH LANE BOOKS)**

QUICK TAKE: "An exploration of the ways weeds adapt to survive and thrive in nature."

WRITES FROM: San Diego

PRE-BOOK: I teach gardening, science, reading and writing. My first year in the garden, we had an abundance of weeds. I began to pull them out, then realized what a marvelous resource they were—free plants! A free science lesson in plant adaptations! I looked for a resource to teach about weeds and found that there was none. So I wrote one.

TIME FRAME: I contemplated weeds for about 4 months, then I spent about 5 months writing and revising, taking the manuscript to my critique group, and revising again. Then I took the manuscript to a conference to get a critique from an editor. Turning it into a book has taken five years—a year to revise and find an artist. Two years for the artist to do sketches. A year to do art, and a year to produce the book.

ENTER THE AGENT: I did not have an agent when I sold *Weeds Find a Way* and my next book, *Dig In*. I sold them both to an editor at the same conference, the San Diego SCBWI Spring Conference. Four years after selling them, I am now represented by Stefanie von Borstel of Full Circle Literary.

WHAT I LEARNED: Most people don't know that most writers do not making a full living with their writing. Most writers have other jobs, too, and that's fine. We write because we have an internal need and drive and joy in writing. I have learned to define success on my own terms.

WHAT I DID RIGHT: I have given myself the gift of time and hard work to make this particular dream of mine come true. I began to take classes, go to conferences, ask questions. Steven Malk, agent at Writers House, told me about SCBWI, and I became a member and began going to meetings. I also began trying to sell articles, and talking to people I knew who wrote. I got into a critique group and got some helpful feedback and began submitting articles and querying magazines and newspapers. I am an overnight success after 15 years of hard work.

ADVICE FOR WRITERS: Give yourself time to learn to write well. Be nice to yourself and others. No one gets rich doing this, but we can all help make the world a kinder, more beautiful and appreciative place by what we do.

NEXT UP: I just sold a picture book biography of Ansel Adams to Christy Ottaviano at Henry Holt, and that will be out in 2016. Meanwhile, I keep writing, teaching, gardening, and giving people more ways to connect with nature.

❷ PAT ZIETLOW MILLER (PATZIETLOWMILLER.COM)
Sophie's Squash (**SCHWARTZ & WADE**)

QUICK TAKE: "Sophie falls in love with a butternut squash, names it Bernice, and is convinced their friendship will endure forever."

WRITES FROM: Madison, Wis.

PRE-BOOK: I was writing as a newspaper reporter, magazine editor and corporate communicator. When I was 39, I suddenly realized the obvious: If I wanted to publish books for children, I had to actually sit down and write them.

TIME FRAME: I wrote the first draft of *Sophie's Squash* in a week or so. But getting through the many revisions it took for the book to reach its final form took about four years. (I was also working on other manuscripts during this time.)

ENTER THE AGENT: My agent is Ammi-Joan Paquette of the Erin Murphy Literary Agency. I did not have an agent when I sold *Sophie's Squash* to Schwartz & Wade. I submitted through the slush pile. But I started working with Joan soon after S&W offered to buy the book. I had seen her speak at an SCBWI conference in Iowa, and I followed up with a query. I sent her several stories I had in progress, we talked on the phone and it all worked out.

WHAT I DID RIGHT: I really studied picture books when I started trying to write them. I read hundreds. I analyzed how they were structured, how the page turns worked and how the stories were paced. I'd always read picture books for fun, but I hadn't ever tried to figure out exactly why I loved them.

WHAT I WOULD HAVE DONE DIFFERENT: I would have been a little more confident. I attended several conferences where I lurked in corners because I was too shy to talk to the authors and editors. There was no reason for me to be scared.

ADVICE FOR WRITERS: I have two pieces of advice that are going to sound like they contradict each other, but I'm sharing them anyway because they're both true. 1) Don't assume your book is done before it really is. The biggest thing I learned is that a book can *always* be better. Make sure you've put in the time to revise. Get a professional edit. 2) But don't be so scared that your book is not perfect that you never submit. I also meet writers who have been diligently working on their manuscripts for years but haven't submitted them because they're terrified of getting a "no." Be responsible, do your homework and submit properly, but do submit.

NEXT UP: There will be a sequel called *Sophie's Seeds*, and I have three other books that are in the process of being published.

③ KIT CHASE (TRAFALGARSSQUARE.COM)
Oliver's Tree **(PUTNAM JUVENILE)**

QUICK TAKE: "Being an elephant has its drawbacks when it comes to playing with friends, but with a little love and imagination, Oliver's friends come up with the perfect play-thing."

WRITES FROM: I write from my home in Southern California, or the beach, or the car.

PRE-BOOK: I had an online children's art shop where I sold my artwork. I was lucky because my editor found me via my Etsy shop and took a liking to a piece I had done. She asked me if I had a story based on the characters in the piece, and from that *Oliver's Tree* was born.

TIME FRAME: From start to finish, this book took about two years to write and illustrate.

WHAT I LEARNED: I was surprised and shocked to see exactly how much design work an artist has to do for a picture book. Integrating text into the pictures and finding the best way for each page to tell a story is harder than you would think. I was quite surprised.

WHAT I DID RIGHT: I kept working the sketches and rewording the story until it was just right.

WHAT I WOULD HAVE DONE DIFFERENT: I would have paid more attention to the design and layout of other picture books before even considering creating one myself.

PLATFORM: I have an Etsy shop and a website, which has developed a lot of followers and fans. I also have a blog where I post from time to time and where we did some giveaways. I am constantly adding to my Pinterest boards and sending out tweets, and we've been sending out promotional items for the book through these venues.

NEXT UP: Finishing up books two and three in the Oliver, Charlie and Lulu series.

BOARD BOOKS

④ SARAH JONES (SARAHLUCIAJONES.COM)
Orange Triangle Fox (**BLUE MANATEE PRESS**)

QUICK TAKE: "A concept book teaching colors, animals and shapes to children through simple and fun-shaped forest creatures, such as the red square owl and yellow star frog."

WRITES FROM: Cincinnati

PRE-BOOK: This board book is truly my start in this industry. I have always been interested in art, which lead me to study painting, new media, and art education in college and grad school. It wasn't until I started working at Blue Manatee Children's Bookstore in 2011 that I became so very passionate about children's books.

TIME FRAME: Once I had the idea for *Orange Triangle Fox*, I completed the art and layout within a few weeks. The idea came to me nearly fully formed, and creating the illustrations to go along with it was the fun part for me. That first version that I pitched to Blue Manatee Press is what is in print today.

WHAT I DID RIGHT: The best thing I did to aid me in this process is getting to know my audience. I run three weekly story times and make daily book recommendations to children and adults of all kinds. Knowing what makes both kids and adults smile, and what keeps them engaged, is key. I have also made a huge effort to pick the brain of every author and illustrator who did a signing at the bookstore; they have been a wealth of knowledge and support.

PLATFORM: Hosting a popular musical story time at Blue Manatee, I have had a built-in platform of wonderful readers and fans from the start. Upon the release of *Orange Triangle Fox*, they were the first to buy copies and sing praises (apart from my fantastic family). Being a part of this local, independent and much-loved bookstore has shown me the most loyal and supportive community of readers.

ADVICE FOR WRITERS: Visit libraries, bookstores and schools, and talk to the people inside!

NEXT UP: More Books! I have another concept board book out right now called *Bunnies Near and Far*, which teaches counting and opposites with funny bunnies and a catchy rhyme.

MIDDLE GRADE

⑤ DANA LEVY (DANAALISONLEVY.COM)
The Misadventures of the Family Fletcher
(PENGUIN RANDOM HOUSE)

QUICK TAKE: "A family with four boys, two dads, and a cantankerous new neighbor tackles the mayhem and madness of the new school year."

WRITES FROM: New England

PRE-NOVEL: I write freelance nonfiction for a variety of corporate and academic clients, but fiction is my first love. When the idea for *The Misadventures of the Family Fletcher* came along, I was excited to write something my own kids could read. And every night when I finished writing, I'd read them what I had. It was great motivation! They'd come home from school and the first words I'd hear were, "Did you write the next chapter? Are you going to read it tonight?!" They offered some pretty great suggestions, too.

ENTER THE AGENT: My agent is Marietta Zacker from the Nancy Gallt Literary Agency. I had done lots of research on agents, and during the online writing conference WriteOnCon, I heard Marietta give a webcast. She said, "Your story is your gold—be true to it." It really resonated. So I queried her, and got pulled out of the slush! Lucky me.

WHAT I LEARNED: The piece I've had to learn for myself is how to let go. Let go of total control of the book, let go of the timeline, let go of a lot of things. A *story* can be very personal. A *book*, well, that's a collaborative group effort.

WHAT I DID RIGHT: I think the cost of doing business, especially in the age of the Internet, is to know the industry. There is so much good information out there, on how to write a good query letter, on how to research agents, on how to work on the craft of writing. There is no excuse for not being savvy. I also learned not to take rejection too personally.

PLATFORM: I have an adorable website, a Facebook author page, a Tumblr, and a Twitter account.

ADVICE FOR WRITERS: Find other authors to be your tribe. Find critique partners, commiserators, brainstormers, celebrators.

NEXT UP: I'm working on a few things at once, including another middle grade contemporary story!

⑥ RACHEL SEARLES
(RACHELSEARLES.COM)
The Lost Planet **(FEIWEL & FRIENDS)**

QUICK TAKE: "A boy with no memory races across the galaxy seeking to outrun his enemies and find his identity with the help of a few unlikely allies."

WRITES FROM: Venice Beach, Calif.

PRE-NOVEL: I had wanted to write a book for a long time (since I was six?), but this was the first book I ever finished.

TIME FRAME: It took me about two years to write the first 30,000 words, but a New Year's resolution motivated me to try to start writing 1,000 words a day, and I finished the first draft four months later. I spent another year and a half on revisions with critique partners before I started sending it out.

ENTER THE AGENT: My agent is Joanna Volpe of New Leaf Literary, and I never actually queried her. She was holding a random drawing for a full manuscript critique, and I won the the drawing! I was beyond thrilled when her critique came with an offer of representation.

WHAT YOU LEARNED: Not everyone is going to love your work. Some people will, but others might be lukewarm on it, and you have to learn that that's not an objective review of your talent. People just have wildly different tastes, and no book will work for everyone. You have to learn to be confident in your own work, and buck up and move on.

WHAT I DID RIGHT: I did my research on the industry and proper business etiquette (it matters!), and more importantly, I spent a *lot* of time revising my book. My critique partners were invaluable for this.

ADVICE FOR WRITERS: Be professional, and stay persistent even when it gets tough. If getting published were a snap, everyone would be doing it. It takes a lot of grit to keep working on a manuscript until you barely want to look at it anymore, and then wade through the query and submission trenches, possibly multiple times. But the payoff when you finally reach your goal is well worth it.

NEXT UP: I'm currently revising the sequel to *The Lost Planet*, and working on an outline for the third book.

⑦ HEIDI SCHULZ
(HEIDISCHULZBOOKS.COM)
Hook's Revenge (DISNEY-HYPERION)

QUICK TAKE: "Jocelyn Hook, 13-year-old daughter of the late Captain Hook, seeks to avenge his death at the jaws of the Neverland crocodile."

WRITES FROM: Salem, Ore.

PRE-NOVEL: Before *Hook's Revenge*, the majority of my writing was in the form of blog posts, and the bulk of my storytelling took place in my daughter's bedroom before she fell asleep. Though I always wanted to write fiction, I was slow coming around to it.

TIME FRAME: I finished the draft in 2011 and spent the first half of 2012 rewriting, revising and shaping the story into something I could begin querying agents with.

ENTER THE AGENT: I happened to see agent Janet Reid (The Query Shark) invite writers to query her at a particular date and time, and she would give personal feedback. I expected nothing more than a note telling me why she was rejecting my manuscript, but she surprised me with a kind referral to her then-colleague, Brooks Sherman. A month later, he contacted me to set up a phone call. We spent an hour discussing what could be done to strengthen and improve the manuscript. I hung up the phone and got right to work. When it was ready, I sent him my revision. He offered the next week.

WHAT I DID RIGHT: I can't discount the power of Twitter. Besides being a wonderful community of other writers, it offers a wealth of information and the opportunity to make personal connections. Following Janet Reid led to a referral to my agent. Conversations about my book after signing with him led to early editor interest.

PLATFORM: I have both personal and author Facebook pages. I have accounts on Goodreads, Pinterest, Instagram and Google Plus that I use (and/or ignore) to varying degrees, but as I mentioned before, I find Twitter to be the most valuable, and most enjoyable, part of my author platform. I think that's the key. An online presence is important, but I don't think you have to be everywhere.

ADVICE FOR WRITERS: Be brave and be bold (but stay within the boundaries of professionalism).

NEXT UP: My picture book debut, *Giraffes Ruin Everything*, comes out with Bloomsbury Kids in 2016.

YOUNG ADULT

⑧ JULIE MURPHY
(JULIEMURPHYWRITES.COM)
Side Effects May Vary **(BALZAR + BRAY/HARPERCOLLINS)**

QUICK TAKE: "When 16-year-old Alice is diagnosed with leukemia, she makes a list of things to do and people to ruin; all her scores are settled until she goes into remission."

WRITES FROM: Dallas/Fort Worth, Texas

PRE-NOVEL: My degree is in political science, and I actually found myself writing young adult during a gap year between my bachelor's and my master's. During that year, I wrote two manuscripts, one of which was *Side Effects May Vary*. (I have yet to go back to school. Definitely one of these days.)

TIME FRAME: *Side Effects May Vary* was a bit of a whirlwind experience. I wrote it, signed with an agent, and sold the manuscript in seven months. I penned the first draft during NaNoWriMo, and after revising for two months, I queried.

ENTER THE AGENT: My agent is Molly Jaffa of Folio Literary Management. I queried her with my first manuscript, which she rejected. When I queried for my second novel, she said yes.

WHAT I DID RIGHT: I think what made a world of difference was taking the time to find trust-worthy critique partners.

PLATFORM: After selling my book, I dropped my blog and have concentrated my efforts on Twitter, Facebook and Tumblr. I think it's important for every writer to be on Twitter, but other than that, let yourself gravitate to the social media where you are most comfortable. Obviously, your platform will vary based on the type of book you write.

ADVICE FOR WRITERS: Be open to critical feedback. No matter how incredible your story is, an editor and/or agent can't really work with someone who's not willing to be flexible and consider different options. Whether it's a critique partner, editor or agent, surround yourself with people whose taste you trust. They won't always be right, but neither will you.

NEXT UP: My sophomore novel is currently titled *Dumplin'* and will be out in 2015!

⑨ LYDIA KANG (LYDIAKANG.COM)
Control (DIAL)

QUICK TAKE: "A 17-year-old girl aligns herself with a foster home full of genetic freaks to save a sister with a secret trait."

WRITES FROM: Omaha, Neb.

PRE-NOVEL: I had published poetry and creative nonfiction. I'd written two other YA novels that taught me a lot but never got published.

TIME FRAME: It took me 2–3 weeks to write an outline, then three months to write the first draft. After I got some really amazing beta reader feedback, I revised heavily for another three months, and then queried.

ENTER THE AGENT: I had to pick between two offers of representation, and chose Eric Myers of The Spieler Agency. He submitted *Control* to editors about a month after he became my agent and we had a pre-empt within two weeks. It was a dream come true!

WHAT I LEARNED: Becoming friends with many other debut authors and sharing our contract-to-publication experience has been priceless and unexpected. I don't know what I would do without the Lucky 13s (a group of debut young adult and middle grade authors).

WHAT I DID RIGHT: Once I realized how competitive it was to get an agent and be published, I knew it would take a lot of hard work to create something of substance that would stand out. I never assumed my agent or editor would "fix" it later.

PLATFORM: I'm on Twitter, I blog, Tumblr, Facebook, and am on Pinterest and Goodreads. I have a Medical Mondays series on my blog where I offer free advice to other writers about their fictional medical questions. That helped build my platform within the writing and publishing community.

ADVICE FOR WRITERS: Read a lot and analyze how your favorite authors write prose and plot their stories. They'll teach you everything!

NEXT UP: *Control*'s sequel came out in 2014. I'm also looking into doing more sci-fi, fantasy and even historical in the future.

⑩ LIVIA BLACKBURNE
(LIVIABLACKBURNE.COM)
Midnight Thief **(DISNEY-HYPERION)**

QUICK TAKE: "An acrobatic thief takes a mysterious job with the Assassins Guild, and a young knight stumbles upon her trail."

WRITES FROM: Los Angeles

PRE-NOVEL: I published a nonfiction essay, "From Words to Brain," with a small digital press on the neuroscience of reading.

TIME FRAME: I started writing a novel in high school. Eventually I got to about 60 pages. Then I went to college and stopped writing. When I turned 25, I took out the old manuscript. The most interesting character was the heroine's best friend, Kyra. So I took Kyra and rewrote the manuscript to be about her. It took me about two years to finish.

ENTER THE AGENT: I initially wanted to self-publish my novel, but my writer friends suggested I query a few agents. As irony would have it, I got an offer fairly quickly, and decided to give the traditional pathway a try. My agent is Jim McCarthy of Dystel & Goderich Literary Management.

WHAT I LEARNED: Just how important your first book is to your career. The sales numbers color your record from then on, and it also determines the books you write after that.

WHAT I DID RIGHT: I didn't start querying until the manuscript was absolutely ready. I got a few full requests at conferences, but I waited a year before I sent it to those agents. It was hard to wait, but I knew I only had one chance. My manuscript went through my critique group and beta readers (about 20 total) before I started querying.

WHAT I WOULD HAVE DONE DIFFERENT: I would've revised even more before the manuscript went on submission to editors. Because the more offers you have for your manuscript, the higher your advance, and the more support and publicity your book will ultimately get.

PLATFORM: To gain readers for my fiction, I recently self-published a novella called *Poison Dance* that's related to *Midnight Thief*. I've been doing a lot of promotion for the novella, as well as giving it away for reviews in hopes of building buzz and gaining readers.

ADVICE FOR WRITERS: Get critique partners that you can trust.

NEXT UP: I'm exploring the possibility of a sequel to *Midnight Thief*, as well as some ideas for unrelated works.

⑪ REBECCA PETRUCK
(REBECCAPETRUCK.COM)
Steering Toward Normal (**AMULET BOOKS**)

QUICK TAKE: "When eighth-grade classmates discover they are half brothers, the poop flies (for real—there are cows)."

WRITES FROM: Wilmington, N.C.

PRE-NOVEL: I wrote a lot of different things—picture books, nonfiction articles, fantasy, adult literary, humor, etc. None were published, and that wasn't really the point. I was writing to find what fit best. I entered an M.F.A. program that did not have a children's writing component, but everything I wrote—even the pages for my application—featured teens.

TIME FRAME: *Steering Toward Normal* was my M.F.A. thesis. Prior to my defense in December 2006, I rewrote the entire manuscript in six weeks. After graduating, I shoved it into a drawer feeling I never wanted to see those pages again! Years later, a chance conversation with an author at a conference inspired me to read my old story again.

ENTER THE AGENT: I met my agent, Kate Testerman of kt literary, the old-fashioned way: a query slush pile. I sent 46 queries, received requests from nine, revise and resubmits from three, and an offer from Kate. In a way, querying really is a numbers game.

WHAT I DID RIGHT: I attended as many writing conferences and retreats with agents and editors present as possible, and I always submitted work to be critiqued by them. That kind of access to publishing professionals is worth every dollar.

WHAT I WOULD HAVE DONE DIFFERENT: I would have done more yoga! I wasn't prepared for all the *waiting*, and it took its toll. Every step on the path to publication involves waiting. I signed with Kate during Christmas 2010 and *Steering Toward Normal* was published May 2014. That's three and a half years of sudden bursts of joy interspersed with bouts of anxiety—and just a lot of simple waiting. Yoga. Seriously. Do it.

ADVICE FOR WRITERS: Listen to rejection. I see inexperienced writers dismiss rejection as the reader "not getting it" or "not liking them," then go on to submit the same work to another 50 agents/editors. Rejection can be a gift. If feedback is fairly consistent, then it highlights an issue with your story.

NEXT UP: My latest work-in-progress is inspired by a *National Geographic* article about the nutritional value of eating insects.

⑫ ROMILY BERNARD (ROMILYBERNARD.COM)
Find Me (HARPERTEEN)

QUICK TAKE: "A teenage hacker trying to get out of the game gets black-mailed into finding a classmate's rapist."

WRITES FROM: Atlanta, Ga.

PRE-BOOK: I'd written women's fiction, chick-lit and historical romance. Almost every agent I submitted to said, "Wow, like your voice, but, um, the heroine is kind of … grouchy." Then, in 2010, I decided to try writing YA. Suddenly, my heroines weren't grouchy. They were spunky.

TIME FRAME: I wrote *Find Me* in about nine months. After I was agented, we spent another four months rewriting it twice.

ENTER THE AGENT: I'm repped by the amazing Sarah Davies of Greenhouse Literary. I found her online then cross-referenced her information with *Publishers Weekly* deals and supplemented that by researching her current authors.

BIGGEST LEARNING EXPERIENCES: For an industry that trades in dreams, publishing is still about *product*. That sounds heartless, but it's not. It means we have to make hard decisions about what's right for the book, but also what's right for the market. Scary? Yes. But you have to trust the people you surround yourself with. I researched publishers the same way I researched agents, so, when I accepted HarperCollins' offer, I knew what caliber of professional I was getting. The trick? I have to get out of the way and let them do their job.

DO DIFFERENT NEXT TIME: I would have found YA sooner. But I think, for me, going through all those failed novels was part of the process. At BEA this year, someone told me I was an overnight success. I told her 246 agent rejections over four years begged to differ.

PLATFORM: I blog with the Doomsdaises.

ADVICE FOR WRITERS: Learn to separate constructive criticism from negative criticism. There are going to be people who are *never* going to like your writing. Ignore those people.

NEXT UP: The sequel, *Remember Me,* is due out fall 2014

⑬ Shane Burcaw
(laughingatmynightmare.tumblr.com)
Laughing at My Nightmare (**ROARING BROOK PRESS**)

QUICK TAKE: "A young adult memoir about the humorous (and sometimes serious) aspects of living with a severely debilitating physical disability."

WRITES FROM: Bethlehem, Pa.

PRE-BOOK: I was writing my blog, which shares the name of my book. As my number of followers climbed into the hundreds of thousands, I realized a book might be in order. I got an agent, we found a publisher, and it has been a big adventure ever since!

TIME FRAME: I wrote most of this book the summer between my junior and senior years of college. A majority of the later stage writing and editing happened once I resumed school for my senior year. Balancing the two was quite the challenge.

ENTER THE AGENT: My agent is Tina Wexler of ICM Partners. I queried 25 agents and got offers from four of them. During the process of choosing one of the four, a friend introduced me to Tina (who I had not originally queried) and she took a look at my proposal and also offered to represent me!

WHAT I LEARNED: Editing takes longer than I expected. I didn't anticipate how much back and forth there would be between my editor and I. The other thing I learned is that having an established platform (which I had from my blog) goes a long way in helping to get offers from agents and publishers.

WHAT I DID RIGHT: I didn't give up after the first few denials from agents, and I also didn't jump at the first agent who offered to represent me.

I WISH I WOULD HAVE DONE DIFFERENT: I'd have taken a year off of school to focus on writing. Juggling the two was not easy.

PLATFORM: I continue to blog to keep my platform strong and committed. I also do speaking engagements for my nonprofit and always plug the book at the end.

ADVICE FOR WRITERS: Query agents until your fingers hurt. You might get a lot of denials, but if your story is truly worthwhile, eventually you'll get that *yes*.

NEXT UP: Fiction!

DEBUT ILLUSTRATORS

First-time illustrators tell their stories and share advice.

....

by Jodell Sadler

There are few moments as pristine as getting that call to do your first book as an illustrator, whether it's a cover, a picture book, or older genre project. With this moment in mind, we collected nine successful debut illustrators and asked them about their first experiences and what helped them cross over to the world of professional children's illustrations. How did they explore craft and make their works stand out? How did they establish their own style? How did they find representation? And what advice do they have for illustrators looking to break in? Learn and explore more about their individual journeys here.

PICTURE BOOKS

① THEODORE TAYLOR III (THEODORE3.COM)
When the Beat Was Born: DJ Kool Herc and the Creation of Hip Hop **(ROARING BROOK PRESS)**

THE BOOK: A biography about the life of DJ Kool Herc and how he became partly responsible for giving birth to hip-hop in the late 1970s.

AWARDS: 2014 Coretta Scott King/Steptoe winner.

HOW I GOT STARTED: I've been carrying a sketchbook with me since elementary school. When it came to deciding what major to pursue after high school, I decided art would be best. Soon I became a student in the Communication Arts (previously Illustration) department at Virginia Commonwealth University. After graduation I began freelancing small jobs outside of my day job as a web designer, creating posters for a local children's theater and doing many album covers.

SOURCE OF INSPIRATION: My style is inspired by many sources, including street art, comic books, animation, printmaking and children's books from my childhood.

WORKING WITH AN ART DIRECTOR: It was great! First, we started with sketches of what the characters in the book might look like. We then went into planning the pages with rough sketches and ideas. Once we decided what each page would look like, I created more detailed sketches and added colors. Once that was finalized I began work on the final drawings.

WHAT HELPED ME STAND OUT: I believe I stood out because of the many music-inspired illustrations I had in my portfolio. I enjoy drawing musicians as a way to connect my two favorite hobbies, music and drawing.

PORTFOLIO/ONLINE: I've had a a personal portfolio website in some form since middle school. Other than that, I've been an active member of DeviantART for 11 years, have much of my artwork on Flickr (which is how my publisher discovered my work), and I post frequently on Tumblr.

ADVICE FOR OTHERS: Don't be afraid to share your artwork online. When I was in school there was a lot of suspicion about the safety of sharing work online, but the benefits far outweigh the consequences in my experience. You never know who may be looking at your work!

② Greg Pizzoli (gregpizzoli.com)
The Watermelon Seed (DISNEY/HYPERION)

THE BOOK: A crocodile faces his fear of swallowing a watermelon seed.

AWARDS: 2014 Geisel Medal.

HOW THE BOOK HAPPENED: My editor at Disney-Hyperion saw my work at a portfolio showcase hosted by SCBWI. I was lucky enough to win an honor award at both the NY and LA SCBWI conferences, and when I wrote *The Watermelon Seed*, my editor, who had seen my work at that first conference, was able to acquire it for publication soon after.

HOW I GOT STARTED: I got my MFA in Book Arts/Printmaking and made hand-printed and sewn children's books as part of my graduate thesis. After graduating, I slowly got jobs here and there, and focused on improving my portfolio and drawing skills. Eventually I had enough work to leave my day job and focus on writing and illustrating full time. Been doing that for about three years. I absolutely love it.

DEVELOPMENT: The first draft was something like 2,500 words, and the final book is 140. A lot of the process was just cutting things away and working to make the humor sit front and center, without being self-conscious.

QUICK PIC: The art for the book was drawn with a brush pen on board, and then scanned in and color separated in Photoshop. The big fills of color were screenprinted, which is what gives it that texture and hand-made quality. All of the seeds in the book were made using a rubber stamp that I had made custom.

WHAT I LEARNED: I learned a lot about pacing a book and what makes for a good storytime. I also learned exactly how much collaboration goes into the book process.

PORTFOLIO AND PLATFORM: I have a website and I share stuff on Twitter, Facebook, and Tumblr. When I was first starting out, I sent out a lot of postcards and zines, and I often think I should start that up again (I actually think it's fun), but for now I mostly do online stuff.

ADVICE FOR ILLUSTRATORS: Draw! Draw more! And draw kids. It's the one thing I say over and over when people ask me to review their portfolios for the children's market: DRAW KIDS.

③ JACOB GRANT (JACOBGRANT.ME)
Scaredy Kate (BARRON'S EDUCATIONAL SERIES)

THE BOOK: Kate has a problem. She's terrified of her aunt's big bulldog. Kate's aunt calls the dog Cookie … Kate calls it a *monster*.

THE BOOK DEAL: Once I had finally taken the plunge and decided to put everything I have towards writing and illustrating picture books, I made a newbie mistake. Instead of finishing the art for a quarter of the book, I completed the whole thing. I was naive but wanted to prove to myself that I could finish a picture book. Being tenacious, I pushed on with another book, and by some miracle, it found its way into the hands of an editor at Barron's.

HOW I GOT STARTED: In 2006, I graduated from the Art Academy of Cincinnati with a BFA in graphic design. I had always loved illustration, but graphic design seemed stable, so I spent the next 5 years working as a designer. Soon after, I found myself unemployed due to downsizing, so I immediately got to work on finishing my first picture book.

SOURCE OF INSPIRATION: Much of my inspiration comes from animation. Hayao Miyazaki's films like *Spirited Away* are packed with brilliant ideas and beautiful art. I'm also greatly inspired by the multitude of artists and writers that come together to create cartoons like "Adventure Time" and "Steven Universe."

WHAT I LEARNED: If you can stand up and explain why you made the decisions you made about story or artwork, editors will often respond to that. In the end, you must be flexible and willing to compromise.

ART REPRESENTATIVE: I initially got in touch with my literary agent, Steven Chudney, when I sent out *Scaredy Kate* for representation. He had shown some interest, but because the book had already sold to Barron's, I came back to Steven with my next picture book. I signed on, we made some edits and he sent the book out. Within four days I had a two-book deal with Feiwel and Friends at Macmillan.

WHAT I DID RIGHT: I kept working at it despite the failure of my first book.

PORTFOLIO AND PLATFORM: Having a personal website is essential. I don't think anyone will take you seriously unless you have some level of online presence. It's also important to have an active sketch blog where you can share work and keep up with other artists.

ADVICE FOR ILLUSTRATORS: I'd feel silly giving advice to old pros as I still have much to learn myself. My advice for illustrators who are starting out would be the following:

1. Fake It Till You Make It. I truly believe the difference between people who are pursuing their passion and those that wish they could, is simply being willing to work for it and act like you know what you're doing.

2. Work Hard. This goes without saying. I don't feel I deserve this career unless I'm pushing myself to work it like any job, but harder. Monday thru Friday I work on picture books from 7-5. Evenings and weekends I sketch and play around with media and colors. If you really want it, you have to put in the work.

3. Join SCBWI. The Society of Children's Book Writers and Illustrators is the greatest tool at your disposal. Membership is affordable, and the resources and expertise they provide are invaluable. Attending the New York winter conference was an eye-opener and made me realize the bar is much higher than I ever would've guessed. The conferences aren't cheap, but they're worth every penny.

4. Find or Start a Critique Group. SCBWI is a big help in finding a group of people to share honest critique with. You can try to find a group through your local chapter or a group that just communicates through email. Thinking about other peoples work in a critical and constructive manner will help give you a fresh perspective on your own.

5. Some other Helpful Bits: (1) Basics, a standard picture book is 16 spreads. First page is the title page, and page 2-3 are the dedication and copyright. After that you have 14 spreads and one end page to tell your story. (2) Start your illustrations for a book in the middle. By the middle of the book, the reader will be more involved in the story than analyzing the artwork. The work you create later in production will always be stronger. (Thanks to Mo Willems for this one.) (3) A book with a horizontal format is about a place. A vertical format is about a character.

6. Finally, two helpful resources that have better advice than I can offer. You'll have to look these up online, but they should be relatively easy to find: "Pixar's 22 Rules of Storytelling," and Mo Willems's "How to Write in 4 Easy Steps, 4 Kinda Harder Steps, and 1 Pretty Much Impossible Step."

④ TEAGAN WHITE (TEAGANWHITE.COM)
Adventures with Barefoot Critters (TUNDRA BOOKS)

THE BOOK: An ABC book that follows a cast of animals (a brother and sister fox, a deer, a squirrel, and triceratops) through seasons and months of creative activities.

THE BOOK DEAL: *Adventures with Barefoot Critters* was conceived while at The Minneapolis College of Art & Design (MCAD). I had little experience with children's illustration, character design, or writing but had an assignment to create an ABC book, so I decided to develop it into a full dummy for my final project. I posted a few samples on my website, and shortly after graduation, Nicole Tugeau contacted me about representation, and soon after that, an editor from Tundra Books asked me about developing the project into a picture book.

HOW I GOT STARTED: I've been working as a freelance illustrator since high school. After developing a web presence, I started getting better freelance illustration opportunities with bigger clients like Nike. Children's illustration was something I fell into it. I had doodles of animal characters for a project during school and fell in love with the watercolor style, so I just kept doing those drawings until I found myself with a children's agent.

SOURCE OF INSPIRATION: The characters and scenes in my children's work are directly inspired by nature. An extremely important part of my non-children's illustration process is weekly adventures I go on—wandering along animal paths through the woods, walking on frozen swamps, squelching along muddy riverbanks.

WHAT I LEARNED: To let go of the little things and know your editor is probably right.

ART REPRESENTATIVE: My agent, Nicole Tugeau, found me on Behance.net in summer 2012.

WHAT I DID RIGHT: I've been told that my children's illustrations, despite being contemporary in terms of style, have a nostalgic that really appeals to people. I also try to pack my illustrations with a lot of specific details.

PORTFOLIO AND PLATFORM: Behance.net (art directors, editors, and agencies browse for specific projects), Instagram, Twitter, Facebook, Society6, Tumblr, and Pinterest.

ADVICE FOR ILLUSTRATORS: Make work about what you're interested in and what excites you! The strongest work comes from something you're passionate about, not from imitation.

⑤ KATE NELMS (KATENELMS.BLOGSPOT. COM)

See What a Seal Can Do, written by Chris Butterworth
(CANDLEWICK)

THE BOOK: An informative guide all about seals.

HOW I GOT STARTED: Apart from spending most of my childhood and teenage years drawing anything and everything, I went to an art college and studied graphic design for two years, before going on to study illustration at Bristol U.W.E, graduating with a BA.

WHAT LEAD ME TO MY FIRST ILLUSTRATION JOB: One day I decided to paint a ringed seal swimming underwater. When I'd finished painting it, I sent it out and promptly received an email back, explaining that an author had recently submitted text for a book about a grey seal, and they wanted me to show illustrative examples. I got straight to it and after some very positive feedback, I was given the rough text for the book and asked to produce some quick thumbnails in response to it. After what felt like forever waiting to find out whether I'd got the job, I received an email asking if I wanted to do it.

SOURCE OF INSPIRATION: My inspiration is being outside and experiencing nature. I grow a lot of flowers, fruit, and veggies so I am outside in all weathers, listening to the bird songs, noticing paw prints in the mud, and finding a sleepy old toad behind a flower pot. I love the honesty and the beauty of all of it: natural textures, animal markings, intricate patterns on the bark of a giant Oak tree, or the perfect structure of a bird feather. I strive to achieve this raw texture, so that readers really feel as though they might reach out and touch it.

WHAT I LEARNED: I learned how there is so much thought and effort that goes into a book. Taking the time to understand another creature's life and how they see the world, it is a very humbling experience and will never be forgotten.

ADVICE FOR ILLUSTRATORS: Keep developing your own style and try not to impair your expressions to a way that you feel might appeal to others the most. Illustrate the world around you how you feel it best, and if you have days where nothing seems to be working, don't panic! It happens, and you haven't finally 'lost the knack,' although it can feel like it. Try something new from time to time, new mediums or a totally new angle, try with your opposite hand, try with your toes!

PICTURE BOOKS, MIDDLE GRADE, GRAPHIC NOVELS

6 MARIS WICKS (MARISWICKS.TUMBLR.COM)
Primates: The Fearless Science of Jane Goodall, Dian Fossey, and Birute Galdikas, written by Jim Ottaviani (**TANGLEWOOD PRESS**)

THE BOOK: A detailed account of the three greatest primatologists of the last century.

HOW I GOT STARTED: I graduated with a BFA in Illustration from the Rhode Island School of Design. I took a few children's book classes in college and a comics class, but it was [only later] that I knew I wanted to make science comics. Soon, I was contacted by First Second Books for *Primates*, written by Jim Ottaviani.

AUDITIONING: First Second asked me to audition for *Primates*. Immediately upon receiving the script, I read it twice through and drew up character designs of the three main characters (and their respective primates of study), and three fully colored sample pages from the story.

SOURCE OF INSPIRATION: My early influences were books by Edward Gorey, Maurice Sendak, Eric Carle, James Marshall, Arnold Lobel, and also Sesame Street. In college, I read everything from Hergé's "TinTin" to Mazzucchelli/Miller's *Batman: Year One* to Craig Thompson's *Good-bye, Chunky Rice*.

WHAT I LEARNED: All those weird jobs I worked before I put on my illustrator hat were not superfluous! Every thing I've learned from every place I've worked has helped to make me a better writer/illustrator.

ART REPRESENTATIVE: I am represented by Bernadette Baker-Baughman of Victoria Sanders & Associates. Once I was presented with a contract for *Primates*, I asked around for agent suggestions and was recommended to Bernadette because she had represented a number of other comics illustrators and writers.

WHAT I DID RIGHT: I embrace my simple, cartoony style of drawing. For me, it was this similar style of illustration that engaged me the most as a kid: abstract enough from reality to be interesting, but still energetic enough to tell a great story. I like to think of my drawing style as "deceptively simple."

ADVICE FOR ILLUSTRATORS: Experiment. Now, more than ever, illustrators have their hands in many different pots. I know folks who created self-published mini comics for years and now they work in animation, or superhero comic artists who have editorial illustrations in *The New Yorker*. There are connections—both creative and professional—all over the place.

PICTURE BOOKS AND APPS

⑦ PAMELA BARON (PAMELABARON.COM)
A Shiver of Sharks (**LITTLE BAHALIA BOOKS**)

THE BOOK: A guide to groupings of animals in the ocean.

HOW I GOT STARTED: I got into drawing through my love of comics during my early teenage years. Although I soon became curious about other forms of art, I still always craved painting. So during college, I switched majors to illustration.

MY FIRST BOOK: Once upon a time, Stacey Williams of Little Bahalia Publishing searched the Internet for an illustrator that could combine the elements of animation and traditional illustration. After searching far and wide through the never-ending catacombs of online portfolios, she came across a (my) series of whimsical bird paintings that caught her eye. She approached the illustrator who happened to have a special place in her heart for animation. The match was perfect and there was much rejoicing.

QUICK PIC: The cover for *A Shiver of Sharks* received the 2013 Digital Book Award for cover design. When most people look at this cover, they see a flat image. But a lot of my inspiration for approaching this project came from the beauty and grace of Indonesian shadow puppetry I saw at a school assembly as a kid. In order for Stacey and her team to be able to animate the creatures, I needed to create "digital puppets." From the different layers of coral to each individual shark tooth, everything was hand painted separately. After I finished painting, I digitally cut them out and reassembled them in the form you see, each page having up to a 100+ different layers of moveable parts.

WHAT I LEARNED: There is great benefit in good communication.

WHAT I DID RIGHT: Stacey really values my interests outside of my identity as an illustrator. I would have never been able to explore that side of myself without the freedom I was given and the encouragement of family and friends.

ADVICE FOR ILLUSTRATORS: "The willingness to allow the beast to roam freely is the source of the power of the image. I always look for my beast. I love my beast and I fear him." ~ Al DeCredico

PICTURE BOOKS AND EARLY READERS

⑧ CALE ATKINSON (CALE.CA)
Muddy, Mud, Bud **(PENGUIN YOUNG READERS)**

THE BOOK: "Bud the car loves to be muddy. But when he thinks a car wash will help him get muddier, he's in for a big surprise."

THE DEAL: I decided I wanted to develop one of my book ideas into a near-final state (in writing and illustration). Upon sending it to my rep to get some feedback, she was excited and confident that the book could be sent out to publishers. I got great feedback from Disney Hyperion, and after working with the editor, I got an offer!

HOW I GOT STARTED: When the time came, I decided against post-secondary school and instead self taught myself, using the Internet as a great learning tool, plus countless late night hours busily practicing away. I got my first jobs mostly by getting my art out there and not being afraid to email people/companies.

WHAT I LEARNED: It has been an amazing learning experience in seeing the different steps a book goes through from the initial "pitch" to receiving a publisher's offer. I think like so many other mediums in the arts industry, you have to be open to receiving feedback and working with others to develop and hone your idea to make it the best it can be.

ART REPRESENTATIVE: I first met Nicole through an email I sent when dipping my feet in the rep waters to see if any out there would be interested in representing a young hooligan with more of an animation background. She was so positive right from her first reply and has been a huge help in my illustration career ever since!

WHAT I DID RIGHT: I think passion really shows through a project in the end. You just have to be yourself and make what excites you. As far as getting it out into the world, don't be afraid to show your work and don't be afraid to keep sending it until you get a reply!

PORTFOLIO AND PLATFORM: I currently have a Behance gallery set up through my rep Nicole's Tugeau2 website. I also have a personal blog, tumblr, and vimeo site showcasing current work. Twitter has also been a wonderful tool in getting my artwork out a well as connecting with many wonderful inspiring people!

ADVICE FOR ILLUSTRATORS: Make time for those little things you want to do just because you are excited or inspired to do them. It's amazing what can come out of having fun and sketching for no end reason. I came up with a bookwhile randomly doodling, not sitting thinking of book ideas.

MIDDLE GRADE COVERS

⑨ KIRBI FAGAN (KIRBIILLUSTRATIONS.COM)
Deadly Delicious (CREATESPACE)

MY FIRST BOOK ILLUSTRATION PROJECT: I was a finalist in the Ron L. Hubbard Future Illustrator's contest. Months later they asked me to create an illustration for their Vol. 30. That next week, I was hired for two middle grade novel covers.

HOW I GOT STARTED: After graduating art school, I set up shop in my parent's basement and started doing artwork for anything that paid while keeping my eyes on the publishing industry. I emailed art directors, sent postcards, and attended conventions. As I improved over those months, the work I wanted finally came.

FIRST ILLUSTRATION/BOOK PROJECT: I was so thrilled to receive a story that resonated with me. *Deadly Delicious* by Karen Kincy is a story of a young witch name Josephine, who runs into a bit of trouble with some cake-eating zombies. There is some young love and lots of magical action! My favorite part of the story is when a dog, named Flash, ate a love spell meant for Josephine's crush. He was my favorite character, so I made sure there was room for him on the cover.

WHAT I LEARNED: The best thing for the work can sometimes be to rest. Taped to my desk is a note that says, "stop rushing." Whenever I come back to work after taking some time off, somehow I always have a new solution to whatever was bothering me.

ART REPRESENTATIVE: I represent myself… for now! Waiting for "the one."

PORTFOLIO AND PLATFORM: My website and blog are my homefront online, but I also frequent Facebook, Pinterest, Instragram, and (my favorite) Twitter.

ADVICE FOR ILLUSTRATORS: Don't work for free; it devalues the entire industry. Stay positive. Do all things with eagerness and passion. Try to embrace where you are in your artistic development and not where you think you should be.

JODELL SADLER earned her MFA in Writing for Children & Young Adults from Hamline University in 2009, and jumped into Agenting in 2012. She hosts Writer's Digest tutorials on Picture Book Pacing, Editing, Ten Tips To Write Heart Into Picture Books, 25 Tips to Get an Agent's Attention, and more. She serves as the Book Look columnist for SCBWI-Illinois.org, and presents at SCBWI and other events. For more, visit sadlercreativeliterary.com.

NEW AGENT SPOTLIGHTS

Learn about new reps seeking clients.

....

by Chuck Sambuchino

///

One of the most common recurring work blog items I get complimented on (besides my headshot, which my wife has called "semi-dashing … almost") is my "New Agent Alerts," a series where I spotlight new/newer literary reps who are open to queries and looking for clients right now.

This is due to the fact that newer agents are golden opportunities for aspiring authors because they are actively building their client list. They're hungry to sign new clients and start the ball rolling with submissions to editors and books sold. Whereas an established agent with 40 clients may have little to no time to consider new writers' work let alone help them shape it, a newer agent may be willing to sign a promising writer whose work is not a guaranteed huge payday.

THE CONS AND PROS OF NEWER AGENTS

At writing conferences, a frequent question I get is "Is it OK to sign with a new agent?" The question comes about because people value experience, and wonder about the skill of someone who's new to the scene. The concern is an interesting one, so let me try to list out the downsides and upsides to choosing a rep who's in her first few years agenting.

The cons
- They are likely less experienced in contract negotiations.
- They likely know fewer editors at this point than a rep who's been in business a while, meaning there is a less likely chance they can help you get published. This is a big, justified point—and writers' foremost concern.
- They are likely in a weaker position to demand a high advance for you.

- New agents come and some go. This means if your agent is in business for a year or two and doesn't find the success for which they hoped, they could bail on the biz altogether. That leaves you without a home. If you sign with an agent who's been in business for 14 years, however, chances are they won't quit tomorrow.

The pros

- They are actively building their client list—and that means they are anxious to sign new writers and lock in those first several sales.
- They are usually willing to give your work a longer look. They may be willing to work with you on a project to get it ready for submission, whereas a more established agent has lots of clients and no time—meaning they have no spare moments to help you with shaping your novel or proposal.
- With fewer clients under their wing, you should get more attention than you would with an established rep.
- If they've found their calling and don't seem like they're giving up any time soon (and keep in mind, most do continue on as agents), you could have a decades-long relationship that pays off with lots of books.
- Just as they may have little going for them, they also have little going against them. An established agent once told me that a new agent is in a unique position because they have no duds under their belt. Their slate is clean.

HOW CAN YOU DECIDE FOR YOURSELF?

1. FACTOR IN IF THEY'RE PART OF A LARGER AGENCY. Agents share contacts and resources. If your agent is the new girl at an agency with five people, those other four agents will help her (and you) with submissions. In other words, she's new, but not alone.

2. LEARN WHERE THE AGENT CAME FROM. Has she been an apprentice at the agency for two years? Was she an editor for seven years and just switched to agenting? If they already have a few years in publishing under their belt, they're not as green as you may think. Agents don't become agents overnight.

3. ASK WHERE SHE WILL SUBMIT THE WORK. This is a big one. If you fear the agent lacks proper contacts to move your work, ask straight out: "What editors do you see us submitting this book to, and have you sold to them before?" The question tests their plan for where to send the manuscript and get it in print.

4. ASK THEM "WHY SHOULD I SIGN WITH YOU?" This is another straight-up question that gets right to the point. If she's new and has little/no sales at that point, she can't respond with "I sell tons of books and I make it rain cash money!! Dolla dolla bills, y'all!!!" She can't rely on her track record to entice you. So what's her sales pitch? Weigh her enthusiasm, her plan for the book, her promises of hard work and anything else she tells you. In the publishing business, you want communication and enthusiasm from agents (and editors). Both are invaluable. What's the point of signing with a huge agent when they don't return your e-mails and consider your book last on their list of priorities for the day?

5. IF YOU'RE NOT SOLD, YOU CAN ALWAYS SAY NO. It's as simple as that. Always query new/newer agents because, at the end of the day, just because they offer representation doesn't mean you have to accept.

NEW AGENT SPOTLIGHTS ("AGENTS & ART REPS" SECTION)

Peppered throughout this book's large number of agency listings (in the "Agents & Art Reps" listings section) are sporadic "New Agent Alert" sidebars. Look them over to see if these newer reps would be a good fit for your work. Always read personal information and submission guidelines carefully. Don't let an agent reject you because you submitted work incorrectly. Wherever possible, we have included a website address for their agency, as well as their Twitter handle for those reps that tweet.

Also please note that as of when this book went to press in 2014, all these agents were still active and looking for writers. That said, I cannot guarantee every one is still in their respective position when you read this, nor that they have kept their query inboxes open. I urge you to visit agency websites and double check before you query. (This is always a good idea in any case.) Good luck!

CHUCK SAMBUCHINO (chucksambuchino.com, @chucksambuchino on Twitter) edits the *Guide to Literary Agents* (guidetoliteraryagents.com/blog) as well as the *Children's Writer's & Illustrator's Market*. His pop-humor books include *How to Survive a Garden Gnome Attack* (film rights optioned by Sony) and *Red Dog / Blue Dog: When Pooches Get Political* (reddog-bluedog.com). Chuck's other writing books include *Formatting & Submitting Your Manuscript, 3rd. Ed.,* as well as *Create Your Writer Platform*. Besides that, he is a sleep-depreived new father, husband, guitarist, dog owner, and cookie addict.

GLOSSARY OF INDUSTRY TERMS

AAR. Association of Authors' Representatives.

ABA. American Booksellers Association.

ABC. Association of Booksellers for Children.

ADVANCE. A sum of money a publisher pays a writer or illustrator prior to the publication of a book. It is usually paid in installments, such as one half on signing the contract, one half on delivery of a complete and satisfactory manuscript. The advance is paid against the royalty money that will be earned by the book.

ALA. American Library Association.

ALL RIGHTS. The rights contracted to a publisher permitting the use of material anywhere and in any form, including movie and book club sales, without additional payment to the creator.

ANTHOLOGY. A collection of selected writings by various authors or gatherings of works by one author.

ANTHROPOMORPHIZATION. The act of attributing human form and personality to things not human (such as animals).

ASAP. As soon as possible.

ASSIGNMENT. An editor or art director asks a writer, illustrator or photographer to produce a specific piece for an agreed-upon fee.

B&W. Black and white.

BACKLIST. A publisher's list of books not published during the current season but still in print.

BEA. BookExpo America.

BIENNIALLY. Occurring once every 2 years.

BIMONTHLY. Occurring once every 2 months.

BIWEEKLY. Occurring once every 2 weeks.

BOOK PACKAGER. A company that draws all elements of a book together, from the initial concept to writing and marketing strategies, then sells the book package to a book publisher and/or movie producer. Also known as book producer or book developer.

BOOK PROPOSAL. Package submitted to a publisher for consideration usually consisting of a synopsis and outline as well as sample chapters.

BUSINESS-SIZE ENVELOPE. Also known as a #10 envelope. The standard size used in sending business correspondence.

CAMERA-READY. Refers to art that is completely prepared for copy camera platemaking.

CAPTION. A description of the subject matter of an illustration or photograph; photo captions include persons' names where appropriate. Also called cutline.

CBC. Children's Book Council.

CLEAN-COPY. A manuscript free of errors and needing no editing; it is ready for typesetting.

CLIPS. Samples, usually from newspapers or magazines, of a writer's published work.

CONCEPT BOOKS. Books that deal with ideas, concepts and large-scale problems, promoting an understanding of what's happening in a child's world. Most prevalent are alphabet and counting books, but also includes books dealing with specific concerns facing young people (such as divorce, birth of a sibling, friendship or moving).

CONTRACT. A written agreement stating the rights to be purchased by an editor, art director or producer and the amount of payment the writer, illustrator or photographer will receive for that sale. (See the article "Running Your Business.")

CONTRIBUTOR'S COPIES. The magazine issues sent to an author, illustrator or photographer in which her work appears.

CO-OP PUBLISHER. A publisher that shares production costs with an author but, unlike subsidy publishers, handles all marketing and distribution. An author receives a high percentage of royalties until her initial investment is recouped, then standard royalties. (*Children's Writer's & Illustrator's Market* does not include co-op publishers.)

COPY. The actual written material of a manuscript.

COPYEDITING. Editing a manuscript for grammar usage, spelling, punctuation and general style.

COPYRIGHT. A means to legally protect an author's/illustrator's/photographer's work. This can be shown by writing the creator's name and the year of the work's creation.

COVER LETTER. A brief letter, accompanying a complete manuscript, especially useful if responding to an editor's request for a manuscript. May also accompany a book proposal.

CUTLINE. See caption.

DIVISION. An unincorporated branch of a company.

DUMMY. A loose mock-up of a book showing placement of text and artwork.

ELECTRONIC SUBMISSION. A submission of material by e-mail or Web form.

FINAL DRAFT. The last version of a polished manuscript ready for submission to an editor.

FIRST NORTH AMERICAN SERIAL RIGHTS. The right to publish material in a periodical for the first time, in the U.S. or Canada. (See the article "Running Your Business.")

F&GS. Folded and gathered sheets. An early, not-yet-bound copy of a picture book.

FLAT FEE. A one-time payment.

GALLEYS. The first typeset version of a manuscript that has not yet been divided into pages.

GENRE. A formulaic type of fiction, such as horror, mystery, romance, fantasy, suspense, thriller, science fiction or Western.

GLOSSY. A photograph with a shiny surface as opposed to one with a non-shiny matte finish.

GOUACHE. Opaque watercolor with an appreciable film thickness and an actual paint layer.

HALFTONE. Reproduction of a continuous tone illustration with the image formed by dots produced by a camera lens screen.

HARD COPY. The printed copy of a computer's output.

HARDWARE. Refers to all the mechanically-integrated components of a computer that are not software—circuit boards, transistors and the machines that are the actual computer.

HI-LO. High interest, low reading level.

HOME PAGE. The first page of a website.

IBBY. International Board on Books for Young People.

IMPRINT. Name applied to a publisher's specific line of books.

INTERNET. A worldwide network of computers that offers access to a wide variety of electronic resources.

IRA. International Reading Association.

IRC. International Reply Coupon. Sold at the post office to enclose with text or artwork sent to a recipient outside your own country to cover postage costs when replying or returning work.

KEYLINE. Identification of the positions of illustrations and copy for the printer.

LAYOUT. Arrangement of illustrations, photographs, text and headlines for printed material.

LINE DRAWING. Illustration done with pencil or ink using no wash or other shading.

MASS MARKET BOOKS. Paperback books directed toward an extremely large audience sold in supermarkets, drugstores, airports, newsstands, online retailers and bookstores.

MECHANICALS. Paste-up or preparation of work for printing.

MIDDLE GRADE OR MID-GRADE. See middle reader.

MIDDLE READER. The general classification of books written for readers approximately ages 9–12. Often called middle grade or mid-grade.

MS (MSS). Manuscript(s).

MULTIPLE SUBMISSIONS. See simultaneous submissions.

NCTE. National Council of Teachers of English.

ONE-TIME RIGHTS. Permission to publish a story in periodical or book form one time only. (See the article "Running Your Business.")

OUTLINE. A summary of a book's contents; often in the form of chapter headings with a descriptive sentence or two under each heading to show the scope of the book.

PACKAGE SALE. The sale of a manuscript and illustrations/photos as a "package" paid for with one check.

PAYMENT ON ACCEPTANCE. The writer, artist or photographer is paid for her work at the time the editor or art director decides to buy it.

PAYMENT ON PUBLICATION. The writer, artist or photographer is paid for her work when it is published.

PICTURE BOOK. A type of book aimed at preschoolers to 8-year-olds that tells a story using a combination of text and artwork, or artwork only.

PRINT. An impression pulled from an original plate, stone, block, screen or negative; also a positive made from a photographic negative.

PROOFREADING. Reading text to correct typographical errors.

QUERY. A letter to an editor or agent designed to capture interest in an article or book you have written or propose to write. (See the article "Before Your First Sale.")

READING FEE. Money charged by some agents and publishers to read a submitted manuscript. (*Children's Writer's & Illustrator's Market* does not include agencies that charge reading fees.)

REPRINT RIGHTS. Permission to print an already published work whose first rights have been sold to another magazine or book publisher. (See the article "Running Your Business.")

RESPONSE TIME. The average length of time it takes an editor or art director to accept or reject a query or submission, and inform the creator of the decision.

RIGHTS. The bundle of permissions offered to an editor or art director in exchange for printing a manuscript, artwork or photographs. (See the article "Running Your Business.")

ROUGH DRAFT. A manuscript that has not been checked for errors in grammar, punctuation, spelling or content.

ROUGHS. Preliminary sketches or drawings.

ROYALTY. An agreed percentage paid by a publisher to a writer, illustrator or photographer for each copy of her work sold.

SAE. Self-addressed envelope.

SASE. Self-addressed, stamped envelope.

SCBWI. The Society of Children's Book Writers and Illustrators.

SECOND SERIAL RIGHTS. Permission for the reprinting of a work in another periodical after its first publication in book or magazine form. (See the article "Running Your Business.")

SEMIANNUAL. Occurring every 6 months or twice a year.

SEMIMONTHLY. Occurring twice a month.

SEMIWEEKLY. Occurring twice a week.

SERIAL RIGHTS. The rights given by an author to a publisher to print a piece in one or more periodicals. (See the article "Running Your Business.")

SIMULTANEOUS SUBMISSIONS. Queries or proposals sent to several publishers at the same time. Also called multiple submissions. (See the article "Before Your First Sale.")

SLANT. The approach to a story or piece of artwork that will appeal to readers of a particular publication.

SLUSH PILE. Editors' term for their collections of unsolicited manuscripts.

SOFTWARE. Programs and related documentation for use with a computer.

SOLICITED MANUSCRIPT. Material that an editor has asked for or agreed to consider before being sent by a writer.

SPAR. Society of Photographers and Artists Representatives.

SPECULATION (SPEC). Creating a piece with no assurance from an editor or art director that it will be purchased or any reimbursements for material or labor paid.

SUBSIDIARY RIGHTS. All rights other than book publishing rights included in a book contract, such as paperback, book club and movie rights. (See the article "Running Your Business.")

SUBSIDY PUBLISHER. A book publisher that charges the author for the cost of typesetting, printing and promoting a book. Also called a vanity publisher. (Note: *Children's Writer's & Illustrator's Market* does not include subsidy publishers.)

SYNOPSIS. A brief summary of a story or novel. Usually a page to a page and a half, single-spaced, if part of a book proposal.

TABLOID. Publication printed on an ordinary newspaper page turned sideways and folded in half.

TEARSHEET. Page from a magazine or newspaper containing your printed art, story, article, poem or photo.

THUMBNAIL. A rough layout in miniature.

TRADE BOOKS. Books sold in bookstores and through online retailers, aimed at a smaller audience than mass market books, and printed in smaller quantities by publishers.

TRANSPARENCIES. Positive color slides; not color prints.

UNSOLICITED MANUSCRIPT. Material sent without an editor's, art director's or agent's request.

VANITY PUBLISHER. See subsidy publisher.

WORK-FOR-HIRE. An arrangement between a writer, illustrator or photographer and a company under which the company retains complete control of the work's copyright. (See the article "Running Your Business.")

YA. See young adult.

YOUNG ADULT. The general classification of books written for readers approximately ages 12–16. Often referred to as YA.

YOUNG READER. The general classification of books written for readers approximately ages 5–8.

BOOK PUBLISHERS

///

There's no magic formula for getting published. It's a matter of getting the right manuscript on the right editor's desk at the right time. Before you submit it's important to learn publishers' needs, see what kind of books they're producing and decide which publishers your work is best suited for. *Children's Writer's & Illustrator's Market* is but one tool in this process. (Those just starting out, turn to Quick Tips for Writers & Illustrators on page 6.)

To help you narrow down the list of possible publishers for your work, we've included several indexes at the back of this book. The **Subject Index** lists book and magazine publishers according to their fiction and nonfiction needs or interests. The **Age-Level Index** indicates which age groups publishers cater to. The **Photography Index** indicates which markets buy photography for children's publications.

If you write contemporary fiction for young adults, for example, and you're trying to place a book manuscript, go first to the Subject Index. Locate the fiction categories under Book Publishers and copy the list under Contemporary. Then go to the Age-Level Index and highlight the publishers on the Contemporary list that are included under the Young Adults heading. Read the listings for the highlighted publishers to see if your work matches their needs.

Remember, *Children's Writer's & Illustrator's Market* should not be your only source for researching publishers. Here are a few other sources of information:

• The Society of Children's Book Writers and Illustrators (SCBWI) offers members an annual market survey of children's book publishers for the cost of postage or free online at scbwi. org (SCBWI membership information can also be found at scbwi.org).

• The Children's Book Council website (cbcbooks.org) gives information on member publishers.

• If a publisher interests you, send a SASE for submission guidelines or check publishers' websites for guidelines *before* submitting. To quickly find guidelines online, visit The Colossal Directory of Children's Publishers at signaleader.com.

• Check publishers' websites. Many include their complete catalogs that you can browse. Web addresses are included in many publishers' listings.

• Spend time at your local bookstore to see who's publishing what. While you're there, browse through *Publishers Weekly* and *The Horn Book*.

SUBSIDY & SELF-PUBLISHING

Some determined writers who receive rejections from royalty publishers may look to subsidy and co-op publishers as an option for getting their work into print. These publishers ask writers to pay all or part of the costs of producing a book. We strongly advise writers and illustrators to work only with publishers who pay them. For this reason, we've adopted a policy not to include any subsidy or co-op publishers in *Children's Writer's & Illustrator's Market* (or any other Writer's Digest Books market books).

If you're interested in publishing your book just to share it with friends and relatives, self-publishing is a viable option, but it involves time, energy, and money. You oversee all book production details. Check with a local printer for advice and information on cost or check online for print-on-demand publishing options (which are often more affordable).

Whatever path you choose, keep in mind that the market is flooded with submissions, so it's important for you to hone your craft and submit the best work possible. Competition from thousands of other writers and illustrators makes it more important than ever to research publishers before submitting—read their guidelines, look at their catalogs, check out a few of their titles and visit their websites.

ABBEVILLE FAMILY

Abbeville Press, 137 Varick St., New York NY 10013. (212)366-5585. **Fax:** (212)366-6966. **E-mail:** abbeville@abbeville.com. **Website:** www.abbeville.com. "Our list is full for the next several seasons." Publishes 8 titles/year. 10% of books from first-time authors.

○ Not accepting unsolicited book proposals at this time.

FICTION Picture books: animal, anthology, concept, contemporary, fantasy, folktales, health, hi-lo, history, humor, multicultural, nature/environment, poetry, science fiction, special needs, sports, suspense. Average word length 300-1,000 words.

HOW TO CONTACT Please refer to website for submission policy.

ILLUSTRATION Works with approx 2-4 illustrators/year. Uses color artwork only.

PHOTOGRAPHY Buys stock and assigns work.

⊘ ABRAMS BOOKS FOR YOUNG READERS

115 W. 18th St., New York NY 10011. **Website:** www.abramsyoungreaders.com.

○ Abrams no longer accepts unsolicited mss or queries.

ILLUSTRATION Illustrations only: Do not submit original material; copies only. Contact: Chad Beckerman, art director.

ALADDIN

Simon & Schuster, 1230 Avenue of the Americas, 4th Floor, New York NY 10020. (212)698-7000. **Website:** www.simonandschuster.com. Aladdin also publishes Aladdin M!X, for those readers too old for kids' books, but not quite ready for adult or young adult novels. **Contact:** Bethany Buck, VP and publisher; Fiona Simpson, editorial director, Karen Nagel, executive editor; Russell Gordon, exec. art director; Karin Paprocki, art director. Aladdin publishes picture books, beginning readers, chapter books, middle grade and tween fiction and nonfiction, and graphic novels and nonfiction in hardcover and paperback, with an emphasis on commercial, kid-friendly titles. Publishes hardcover/paperback originals and imprints of Simon & Schuster Children's Publishing Children's Division.

HOW TO CONTACT Simon & Schuster does not review, retain or return unsolicited materials or artwork. "We suggest prospective authors and illustrators submit their mss through a professional literary agent."

⊘ AMULET BOOKS

Imprint of Abrams 115 W. 18th St., New York NY 10001. **Website:** www.amuletbooks.com. **Contact:** Susan Van Metre, vice president/publisher; Tamar Brazis, editorial director; Cecily Kaiser, publishing director. 10% of books from first-time authors.

○ Does not accept unsolicited mss or queries.

FICTION Middle readers: adventure, contemporary, fantasy, history, science fiction, sports. Young adults/teens: adventure, contemporary, fantasy, history, science fiction, sports, suspense.

ILLUSTRATION Works with 10-12 illustrators/year. Uses both color and b&w. Query with samples. Contact: Chad Beckerman, art director. Samples filed.

PHOTOGRAPHY Buys stock images and assigns work.

ANAPHORA LITERARY PRESS

5755 E. River Road, #2201, Tucson AZ 85750. (520)425-4266. **E-mail:** director@anaphoraliterary.com. **Website:** anaphoraliterary.com. **Contact:** Anna Faktorovich, editor-in-chief. "In the Winter of 2010, Anaphora began accepting book-length single-author submissions. We are actively seeking single- and multiple-author books in fiction (poetry, novels, and short story collections) and nonfiction (academic, legal, business, journals, edited and un-edited dissertations, biographies, and memoirs). E-mail submissions. Profits are split 50/50 with writers. We do not offer any free contributor copies." Publishes in trade paperback originals and reprints; mass market paperback originals and reprints. Publishes 3 titles/year. 50% of books from first-time authors. 100% from unagented writers.

FICTION "We are actively seeking submissions at this time. The genre is not as important as the quality of work. You should have a completed full-length ms ready to be emailed or mailed upon request."

NONFICTION "We are actively seeking quality writing that is original, innovative, enlightening, intellectual and otherwise a pleasure to read. Our primary focus in nonfiction is literary criticism; but, there are many other areas of interest."

HOW TO CONTACT Looking for single and multiple-author books in fiction (poetry, novels, and short story collections). Query. Submit ms, bio, summary, and marketing plan via e-mail. Reviews artwork. 200 queries/year; 100 mss/year Responds in 1 week on queries, proposals, and mss. Publishes 2 months after acceptance.

TERMS Pays 20-30% royalty on retail price. "Book profits are shared with authors." Catalog and guidelines available online at website.

TIPS "Our audience is academics, college students and graduates, as well as anybody who loves literature. Proofreading your work is very important. See the website for specific submission requirements."

ARBORDALE PUBLISHING

612 Johnnie Dodds, Suite A2, Mt. Pleasant SC 29464. (843)971-6722. **Fax:** (843)216-3804. **E-mail:** katie hall@arbordalepublishing.com. **E-mail:** donnager man@arbordalepublishing.com. **Website:** www.ar bordalepublishing.com. **Contact:** Donna German and Katie Hall, editors. "The picture books we publish are usually, but not always, fictional stories that relate to animals, nature, the environment, math, and science. All books should subtly convey an educational theme through a warm story that is fun to read and that will grab a child's attention. Each book has a 3-5 page 'For Creative Minds' section to reinforce the educational component. This section will have a craft and/or game as well as 'fun facts' to be shared by the parent, teacher, or other adult. Authors do not need to supply this information. Mss. should be fewer than 1,500 words and meet all of the following 4 criteria: Fun to read—mostly fiction with nonfiction facts woven into the story; National or regional in scope; Must tie into early elementary school curriculum; must be marketable through a niche market such as a zoo, aquarium, or museum gift shop." Publishes hardcover, trade paperback, and electronic originals. Publishes 20 titles/year. 50% of books from first-time authors. 100% from unagented writers.

FICTION Picture books: animal, folktales, nature/environment, math-related. Word length—picture books: no more than 1,500.

NONFICTION "We are not looking for mss. about: pets (dogs or cats in particular); new babies; local or state-specific; magic; biographies; history-related; ABC books; poetry; series; young adult books or novels; holiday-related books. We do not consider mss. that have been previously published in any way, including e-books or self-published."

HOW TO CONTACT Accepts electronic submissions only. Snail mail submissions are discarded without being opened. Accepts electronic submissions only. Snail mail submissions are discarded without being opened. 2,000 mss received/year. Acknowledges re-ceipt of ms submission within 1 week. Publishes book 18 months after acceptance. May hold onto mss of interest for 1 year until acceptance.

ILLUSTRATION Works with 20 illustrators/year. Prefers to work with illustrators from the US and Canada. Uses color artwork only. Submit Web link or 2-3 electronic images. Contact: Donna German. "I generally keep submissions on file until I match the manuscripts to illustration needs."

TERMS Pays 6-8% royalty on wholesale price. Pays small advance. Book catalog and guidelines available online.

TIPS "Please make sure that you have looked at our website to read our complete submission guidelines and to see if we are looking for a particular subject. Manuscripts must meet all four of our stated criteria. We look for fairly realistic, bright and colorful art-no cartoons. We want the children excited about the books. We envision the books being used at home and in the classroom."

ATHENEUM BOOKS FOR YOUNG READERS

Simon & Schuster, 1230 Avenue of the Americas, New York NY 10020. **Website:** kids.simonandschuster.com. **Contact:** Caitlyn Dlouhy, editorial director; Justin Chanda, vice president/publisher; Reka Simonsen, executive editor; Anne Zafian, vice president. Publishes hardcover originals.

FICTION All in juvenile versions. "We have few specific needs except for books that are fresh, interesting and well written. Fad topics are dangerous, as are works you haven't polished to the best of your ability. We also don't need safety pamphlets, ABC books, coloring books and board books. In writing picture book texts, avoid the coy and 'cutesy,' such as stories about characters with alliterative names." Agented submissions only. No paperback romance-type fiction.

NONFICTION Publishes hardcover originals, picture books for young kids, nonfiction for ages 8-12 and novels for middle-grade and young adults. Types of books include biography, historical fiction, history, nonfiction. Publishes 60 titles/year. 100% require freelance illustration. Agented submissions only.

TERMS Guidelines for #10 SASE.

TIPS "Study our titles."

AZRO PRESS

PMB 342, 1704 Llano St. B, Santa Fe NM 87505. (505)989-3272. **Fax:** (505)989-3832. **E-mail:** books@

azropress.com; azropress@gmail.com. **Website:** www.
azropress.com. **Contact:** Gae Eisenhardt.

"We like to publish illustrated children's books
by Southwestern authors and illustrators. We
are always looking for books with a Southwestern look or theme." Note that this market will
open and close itself to submissions at different times during the year. The best thing to do
is check the website and see if the publisher is
currently open to submissions.

FICTION Picture books: animal, history, humor, na-
ture/environment. Young readers: adventure, animal,
hi-lo, history, humor. Average word length: picture
books—1,200; young readers—2,000-2,500.

NONFICTION Picture books: animal, geography,
history. Young readers: geography, history.

HOW TO CONTACT Responds to queries/mss in 3-4
months. Publishes book 1-2 years after acceptance.

ILLUSTRATION Accepts material from international
illustrators. Works with 3 illustrators/year. Uses color
and b&w artwork. Reviews ms/illustration packages.
Reviews work for future assignments. Query with
samples. Submit samples to illustrations editor. Responds in 3-4 months. Samples not returned. Samples
are filed.

TERMS Pays authors royalty of 5-10% based on
wholesale price. Pays illustrators by the project
($2,000) or royalty of 5%. Catalog available for #10
SASE and 3 first-class stamps or online.

BAILIWICK PRESS

309 East Mulberry St., Fort Collins CO 80524.
(970)672-4878. **Fax:** (970)672-4731. **E-mail:** info@
bailiwickpress.com. **Website:** www.bailiwickpress.
com. "We're a micro-press that produces books and
other products that inspire and tell great stories. Our
motto is 'books with something to say.' We are now
considering submissions, agented and unagented, for
children's and young adult fiction. We're looking for
smart, funny, and layered writing that kids will clam-
or for. Authors who already have a following have a
leg up. We are only looking for humorous children's
fiction. Please do not submit work for adults. Illustrated fiction is desired but not required. (Illustrators
are also invited to send samples.) Make us laugh out
loud, ooh and aah, and cry, 'Eureka!'"

HOW TO CONTACT "Please read the Aldo Zelnick
series to determine if we might be on the same page,
then fill out our submission form. Please do not send

submissions via snail mail or phone calls. **You must
complete the online submission form to be considered.** If, after completing and submitting the form,
you also need to send us an e-mail attachment (such as
sample illustrations or excerpts of graphics), you may
e-mail them to aldozelnick@gmail.com." Responds
in 6 months.

ILLUSTRATION Illustrated fiction desired but not
required. Send samples.

BALZER & BRAY

HarperCollins Children's Books, 195 Broadway, New
York NY 10007. **Website:** www.harpercollinschild
rens.com. "We publish bold, creative, groundbreak-
ing picture books and novels that appeal directly to
kids in a fresh way." Publishes 10 titles/year. **Co-pub-
lishers:** Donna Bray and Alessandra Balzer, who are
also both VPs.

FICTION picture books, young readers: adventure,
animal, anthology, concept, contemporary, fantasy,
history, humor, multicultural, nature/environment,
poetry, science fiction, special needs, sports, suspense.
Middle readers, young adults/teens: adventure, animal, anthology, contemporary, fantasy, history, humor, multicultural, nature/environment, poetry, science fiction, special needs, sports, suspense.

NONFICTION "We will publish very few nonfiction
titles, maybe 1-2 per year."

HOW TO CONTACT Contact editor. Agented submissions only. Agented submissions only. Publishes
book 18 months after acceptance.

ILLUSTRATION Works with 10 illustrators/year.
Uses both color and b&w. Illustrations only: send
tearsheets to be kept on file. Responds only if interested. Samples are not returned.

PHOTOGRAPHY Works on assignment only.

TERMS Offers advances. Pays illustrators by the project.

BANTAM BOOKS

Imprint of Random House, Inc., 1745 Broadway, New
York NY 10019. (212)782-9000. **Website:** www.ban-
tam-dell.atrandom.com.

Not seeking mss at this time.

BEHRMAN HOUSE INC.

11 Edison Place, Springfield NJ 07081. (973)379-7200.
Fax: (973)379-7280. **E-mail:** customersupport@beh
rmanhouse.com. **Website:** www.behrmanhouse.com.
Publishes books on all aspects of Judaism: history,
cultural, textbooks, holidays. "Behrman House pub-

lishes quality books of Jewish content—history, Bible, philosophy, holidays, ethics—for children and adults." 12% of books from first-time authors.

NONFICTION All levels: Judaism, Jewish educational textbooks. Average word length: young reader—1,200; middle reader—2,000; young adult—4,000.

HOW TO CONTACT Submit outline/synopsis and sample chapters. Submit outline/synopsis and sample chapters. Responds in 1 month to queries; 2 months to mss. Publishes book 18 months after acceptance.

ILLUSTRATION Works with 6 children's illustrators/year. Reviews ms/illustration packages from artists. "Query first." Illustrations only: Query with samples; send unsolicited art samples by mail. Responds to queries in 1 month; mss in 2 months.

PHOTOGRAPHY Purchases photos from freelancers. Buys stock and assigns work. Uses photos of families involved in Jewish activities. Uses color and b&w prints. Photographers should query with samples. Send unsolicited photos by mail. Submit portfolio for review.

TERMS Pays authors royalty of 3-10% based on retail price or buys ms outright for $1,000-5,000. Offers advance. Pays illustrators by the project (range: $500-5,000). Book catalog free on request.

TIPS Looking for "religious school texts" with Judaic themes or general trade Judaica.

○ BERKLEY BOOKS

Penguin Group (USA) Inc., 375 Hudson St., New York NY 10014. **Website:** us.penguingroup.com/. **Contact:** Leslie Gelbman, president and publisher. The Berkley Publishing Group publishes a variety of general nonfiction and fiction including the traditional categories of romance, mystery and science fiction. Publishes paperback and mass market originals and reprints. Publishes 500 titles/year.

○ "Due to the high volume of manuscripts received, most Penguin Group (USA) Inc. imprints do not normally accept unsolicited mss. The preferred and standard method for having mss considered for publication by a major publisher is to submit them through an established literary agent."

FICTION No occult fiction.

NONFICTION No memoirs or personal stories.

HOW TO CONTACT Prefers agented submissions. Prefers agented submissions.

BETHANY HOUSE PUBLISHERS

Division of Baker Publishing Group, 6030 E. Fulton Rd., Ada MI 49301. (616)676-9185. **Fax:** (616)676-9573. **Website:** bakerpublishinggroup.com/bethanyhouse. Bethany House Publishers specializes in books that communicate Biblical truth and assist people in both spiritual and practical areas of life. While we do not accept unsolicited queries or proposals via telephone or e-mail, we will consider 1-page queries sent by fax and directed to adult nonfiction, adult fiction, or young adult/children. Publishes hardcover and trade paperback originals, mass market paperback reprints. Publishes 90-100 titles/year. 2% of books from first-time authors. 50% from unagented writers.

○ All unsolicited mss returned unopened.

HOW TO CONTACT Responds in 3 months to queries. Publishes a book 1 year after acceptance.

TERMS Pays royalty on net price. Pays advance. Book catalog for 9x12 envelope and 5 first-class stamps. Guidelines available online.

TIPS "Bethany House Publishers' publishing program relates Biblical truth to all areas of life—whether in the framework of a well-told story, of a challenging book for spiritual growth, or of a Bible reference work. We are seeking high-quality fiction and nonfiction that will inspire and challenge our audience."

⊕ BLOOMSBURY SPARK

Imprint of Bloomsbury USA, 1385 Broadway, 5th Floor, New York NY 10008. **Website:** www.bloomsbury.com/us/bloomsbury-spark.

○ Bloomsbury Spark is a one-of-a-kind, global, digital imprint from Bloomsbury Publishing dedicated to publishing a wide array of exciting fiction eBooks to teen, YA and new adult readers. Launched in Autumn 2013, our outstanding list features multiple genres: romance, contemporary, dystopian, paranormal, sci-fi, mystery, thriller, and more.

HOW TO CONTACT If you have a manuscript between 25 and 60K words long, then please send it to us at the editors of the following -emails, along with a query, a brief biography, and links to your online presence: For submissions in the United States and Canada: BloomsburySparkUS@bloomsbury.com. For submissions in the United Kingdom, Europe and ROW: BloomsburySparkUK@bloomsbury.com. For submissions in Australia: BloomsburySparkAUS@

bloomsbury.com. For submissions in India: Blooms
burySparkINDIA@bloomsbury.com

TERMS "We offer standard eBook royalty rates. Specific terms of compensation will be discussed if we're
interested in acquiring your book."

BOYDS MILLS PRESS

Highlights for Children, Inc., 815 Church St., Honesdale PA 18431. (570)253-1164. **E-mail:** contact@boyd
smillspress.com. **Website:** www.boydsmillspress.com.
Boyds Mills Press publishes picture books, nonfiction,
activity books, and paperback reprints. Their titles
have been named notable books by the International
Reading Association, the American Library Association, and the National Council of Teachers of English.
They've earned numerous awards, including the National Jewish Book Award, the Christopher Medal, the
NCTE Orbis Pictus Honor, and the Golden Kite Hon-
or. **Contact:** Elizabeth Van Doren, editorial director;
Robbin Gourley, senior art director; Tim Gillner and
Barbara Grzeslo, art directors.

🖝 Boyds Mills Press welcomes unsolicited submissions from published and unpublished
writers and artists. Submit a ms with a cover
letter of relevant information, including experience with writing and publishing. Label the
package "Manuscript Submission" and include
an SASE. For art samples, label the package
"Art Sample Submission."

FICTION Interested in picture books and middle
grade fiction. Do not send a query first. Send the entire ms of picture book or the first 3 chapters and a
plot summary for middle grade fiction (will request
the balance of ms if interested).

NONFICTION Include a detailed bibliography with
submission. Highly recommends including an expert's review of your ms and a detailed explanation
of the books in the marketplace that are similar to the
one you propose. References to the need for this book
(by the National Academy of Sciences or by similar
subject-specific organizations) will strengthen your
proposal. If you intend for the book to be illustrated
with photos or other graphic elements (charts, graphs,
etc.), it is your responsibility to find or create those elements and to include with the submission a permissions budget, if applicable. Finally, keep in mind that
good children's nonfiction has a narrative quality—a
story line—that encyclopedias do not; please consider
whether both the subject and the language will appeal to children.

HOW TO CONTACT Responds to mss within 3
months.

ILLUSTRATION Illustrators submitting a picture
book should include the ms, a dummy, and a sample reproduction of the final artwork that reflects the
style and technique you intend to use. Do not send
original artwork.

TERMS Catalog available online. Guidelines available online.

BRIGHT RING PUBLISHING, INC.

P.O. Box 31338, Bellingham WA 98228. (360)592-9201.
Fax: (360)592-4503. **E-mail:** maryann@brightring.
com. **Website:** www.brightring.com. **Contact:** Mary-
Ann Kohl, editor.

🖝 Bright Ring is not accepting manuscript submissions as of when this book went to press in
2014, but check the website for when it reopens
to submissions.

CALKINS CREEK

Boyds Mills Press, 815 Church St., Honesdale PA
18431. **Website:** www.calkinscreekbooks.com. "We
aim to publish books that are a well-written blend of
creative writing and extensive research, which emphasize important events, people, and places in U.S.
history." **Senior editor:** Carolyn Yoder.

HOW TO CONTACT Submit outline/synopsis and
3 sample chapters. Submit outline/synopsis and 3
sample chapters.

ILLUSTRATION Accepts material from international
illustrators. Works with 25 (for all Boyds Mills Press
imprints) illustrators/year. Uses both color and b&w.
Reviews ms/illustration packages. For ms/illustration
packages: Submit ms with 2 pieces of final art. Submit ms/illustration packages to address above, label
package "Manuscript Submission." Reviews work for
future assignments. If interested in illustrating future
titles, query with samples. Submit samples to address
above. Label package "Art Sample Submission."

PHOTOGRAPHY Buys stock images and assigns
work. Submit photos to: address above, label package "Art Sample Submission." Uses color or b&w 8×10
prints. For first contact, send promo piece (color or
b&w).

TERMS Pays authors royalty or work purchased outright. Guidelines online.

TIPS "Read through our recently published titles and review our catalog. When selecting titles to publish, our emphasis will be on important events, people, and places in U.S. history. Writers are encouraged to submit a detailed bibliography, including secondary and primary sources, and expert reviews with their submissions."

Ⓐ CANDLEWICK PRESS

99 Dover St., Somerville MA 02144. (617)661-3330. **Fax:** (617)661-0565. **E-mail:** bigbear@candlewick. com. **Website:** www.candlewick.com. "Candlewick Press publishes high-quality, illustrated children's books for ages infant through young adult. We are a truly child-centered publisher." Publishes hardcover and trade paperback originals, and reprints. Publishes 200 titles/year. 5% of books from first-time authors.

Ⓞ Candlewick Press is not accepting unagented queries or unsolicited mss at this time.

FICTION Picture books: animal, concept, contemporary, fantasy, history, humor, multicultural, nature/ environment, poetry. Middle readers, young adults: contemporary, fantasy, history, humor, multicultural, poetry, science fiction, sports, suspense/mystery.

NONFICTION Picture books: concept, biography, geography, nature/environment. Young readers: biography, geography, nature/environment.

HOW TO CONTACT "We do not accept editorial queries or submissions online. If you are an author or illustrator and would like us to consider your work, please read our submissions policy (online) to learn more."

ILLUSTRATION Works with approx. 40 illustrators/ year. "We prefer to see a range of styles from artists along with samples showing strong characters (human or animals) in various settings with various emotions." **Art director:** Kristen Nobles.

TERMS Pays authors royalty of 2½-10% based on retail price. Offers advance.

TIPS "We no longer accept unsolicited mss. See our website for further information about us."

CAPSTONE PRESS

Capstone Young Readers, 1710 Roe Crest Dr., North Mankato MN 56003. **Website:** www.capstonepub. com. The Capstone Press imprint publishes nonfiction with accessible text on topics kids love to capture interest and build confidence and skill in beginning, struggling, and reluctant readers, grades pre-K-9.

FICTION Send fiction submissions via e-mail (author. sub@capstonepub.com). Include the following, in the body of the e-mail: sample chapters, rèsumè, and a list of previous publishing credits.

NONFICTION Send nonfiction submissions via postal mail. Include the following: rèsumè, cover letter, and up to 3 writing samples.

HOW TO CONTACT Responds only if submissions fit needs. Mss and writing samples will not be returned. If you receive no reply within 6 months, you should assume the editors are not interested.

ILLUSTRATION Send fiction illustration submissions via e-mail (il.sub@capstonepub.com). Include the following, in the body of the e-mail: sample artwork, rèsumè, and a list of previous publishing credits. For nonfiction illustrations, send via e-mail (nf. il.sub@capstonepub.com) sample artwork (2-4 pieces) and a list of previous publishing credits.

TERMS Catalog available upon request. Guidelines available online.

CAROLRHODA LAB

Part of Lerner Publishing Group. 1251 Washington Ave. N., Minneapolis MN 55401. **Website:** www.lernerbooks.com/carolrhodalab/. **Contact:** Andrew Karre, editorial director. Carolrhoda Lab is dedicated to distinctive, provocative, boundary-pushing fiction for teens and their sympathizers. Carolrhoda Lab probes and examines the young-adult condition one novel at a time, affording YA authors and readers an opportunity to explore and experiment with thoughts, ideas, and paradigms in the human condition. Adolescence is an experience we share and a condition from which some of us never quite recover. All of us at Carolrhoda Lab are proud to proclaim our lifelong adolescence and our commitment to publishing exceptional fiction about the teenage experience.

HOW TO CONTACT Carolrhoda accepts limited solicited submissions from unagented authors. Announcements of these solicitations appear on their blog at irregular intervals. Carolrhoda does not regularly accept unsolicited submissions or queries from unagented or unreferred authors, so please do not submit anything unless the imprint puts out a specific call for it. Note that if you attended a conference where an editor spoke, you may submit for the time the editor specified at the conference. Please refer to the conference in the subject line of your email.

See if the imprint is soliciting here: http://carolrhoda.blogspot.com/2007/11/solicted-submissions.html.

ⒶCARTWHEEL BOOKS

Imprint of Scholastic Trade Division, 557 Broadway, New York NY 10012. (212)343-6100. **Website:** www.scholastic.com. Cartwheel Books publishes innovative books for children, up to age 8. "We are looking for 'novelties' that are books first, play objects second. Even without its gimmick, a Cartwheel Book should stand alone as a valid piece of children's literature." Publishes novelty books, easy readers, board books, hardcover and trade paperback originals.

FICTION Again, the subject should have mass market appeal for very young children. Humor can be helpful, but not necessary. Mistakes writers make are a reading level that is too difficult, a topic of no interest or too narrow, or mss that are too long.

NONFICTION Cartwheel Books publishes for the very young, therefore nonfiction should be written in a manner that is accessible to preschoolers through 2nd grade. Often writers choose topics that are too narrow or "special" and do not appeal to the mass market. Also, the text and vocabulary are frequently too difficult for our young audience.

HOW TO CONTACT Accepts mss from agents only. Accepts mss from agents only.

TERMS Guidelines available free.

TIPS Audience is young children, ages 0-8. Know what types of books the publisher does. Some mss that don't work for one house may be perfect for another. Check out bookstores or catalogs to see where your writing would "fit" best.

CEDAR FORT, INC.

2373 W. 700 S, Springville UT 84663. (801)489-4084. **Fax:** (801)489-1097. **Website:** www.cedarfort.com. **Contact:** Shersta Gatica, acquisitions editor. "Each year we publish well over 100 books, and many of those are by first-time authors. At the same time, we love to see books from established authors. As one of the largest book publishers in Utah, we have the capability and enthusiasm to make your book a success, whether you are a new author or a returning one. We want to publish uplifting and edifying books that help people think about what is important in life, books people enjoy reading to relax and feel better about themselves, and books to help improve lives. Although we do put out several children's books each year, we are extremely selective. Our children's books

must have strong religious or moral values, and must contain outstanding writing and an excellent storyline." Publishes hardcover, trade paperback originals and reprints, mass market paperback and electronic reprints. Publishes 120 titles/year. 60% of books from first-time authors. 95% from unagented writers.

HOW TO CONTACT Submit completed ms. Query with SASE; submit proposal package, including outline, 2 sample chapters; or submit completed ms. Receives 200 queries/year; 600 mss/year. Responds in 1 month on queries; 2 months on proposals; 4 months on mss. Publishes book 10-14 months after acceptance.

TERMS Pays 10-12% royalty on wholesale price. Pays $2,000-50,000 advance. Catalog and guidelines available online at website.

TIPS "Our audience is rural, conservative, mainstream. The first page of your ms is very important because we start reading every submission, but good writing and plot keep us reading."

ⒸCHARLESBRIDGE PUBLISHING

85 Main St., Watertown MA 02472. (617)926-0329. **Fax:** (617)926-5720. **E-mail:** tradeart@charlesbridge.com. **Website:** www.charlesbridge.com. "Charlesbridge publishes high-quality books for children, with a goal of creating lifelong readers and lifelong learners. Our books encourage reading and discovery in the classroom, library, and home. We believe that books for children should offer accurate information, promote a positive worldview, and embrace a child's innate sense of wonder and fun. To this end, we continually strive to seek new voices, new visions, and new directions in children's literature." Publishes hardcover and trade paperback nonfiction and fiction, children's books for the trade and library markets. Publishes 30 titles/year. 10-20% of books from first-time authors. 80% from unagented writers. **Contact:** Yolanda Scott, editorial director; Alyssa Pusey, senior editor; Julie Ham, editor; Susan Sherman, art director.

Ⓠ "We're always interested in innovative approaches to a difficult genre, the nonfiction picture book."

FICTION Strong stories with enduring themes. Charlesbridge publishes both picture books and transitional bridge books (books ranging from early readers to middle-grade chapter books). Our fiction titles include lively, plot-driven stories with strong, engaging characters. No alphabet books, board books, coloring books, activity books, or books with audio-tapes or CD-ROMs.

NONFICTION Strong interest in nature, environment, social studies, and other topics for trade and library markets.

HOW TO CONTACT Exclusive submissions only. "Charlesbridge accepts unsolicited manuscripts submitted exclusively to us for a period of 3 months. 'Exclusive Submission' should be written on all envelopes and cover letters." Please submit only 1 or 2 mss at a time. For picture books and shorter bridge books, please send a complete ms. For fiction books longer than 30 ms pages, please send a detailed plot synopsis, a chapter outline, and 3 chapters of text. Mss should be typed and double-spaced. Please do not submit material by email, by fax, or on a computer disk. Illustrations are not necessary. Please make a copy of your ms, as we cannot be responsible for submissions lost in the mail. Include your name and address on the first page of your ms and in your cover letter. Be sure to list any previously published work or relevant writing experience. Responds in 3 months. Publishes ms 2-4 years after acceptance.

TERMS Pays royalty. Pays advance. Guidelines available online.

TIPS "To become acquainted with our publishing program, we encourage you to review our books and visit our website where you will find our catalog."

CHICAGO REVIEW PRESS

814 N. Franklin St., Chicago IL 60610. (312)337-0747. **Fax:** (312)337-5110. **E-mail:** frontdesk@chicagoreviewpress.com. **Website:** www.chicagoreviewpress.com. **Contact:** Cynthia Sherry, publisher; Yuval Taylor, senior editor; Jerome Pohlen, senior editor; Lisa Reardon, senior editor. "Chicago Review Press publishes high-quality, nonfiction, educational activity books that extend the learning process through hands-on projects and accurate and interesting text. We look for activity books that are as much fun as they are constructive and informative."

Chicago Review Press does not publish fiction.

NONFICTION Young readers, middle readers and young adults: activity books, arts/crafts, multicultural, history, nature/environment, science. "We're interested in hands-on, educational books; anything else probably will be rejected." Average length: young readers and young adults—144-160 pages.

HOW TO CONTACT Enclose cover letter and no more than a table of contents and 1-2 sample chapters; prefers not to receive e-mail queries. Responds in 2 months. Publishes a book 1-2 years after acceptance.

ILLUSTRATION Works with 6 illustrators/year. Uses primarily b&w artwork. Reviews ms/illustration packages from artists. Submit 1-2 chapters of ms with corresponding pieces of final art. Illustrations only: Query with samples, résumé. Responds only if interested. Samples returned with SASE.

PHOTOGRAPHY Buys photos from freelancers ("but not often"). Buys stock and assigns work. Wants "instructive photos. We consult our files when we know what we're looking for on a book-by-book basis." Uses b&w prints.

TERMS Pays authors royalty of 7.5-12.5% based on retail price. Offers advances of $3,000-6,000. Pays illustrators by the project (range varies considerably). Pays photographers by the project (range varies considerably). Book catalog available for $3. Ms guidelines available for $3.

TIPS "We're looking for original activity books for small children and the adults caring for them—new themes and enticing projects to occupy kids' imaginations and promote their sense of personal creativity. We like activity books that are as much fun as they are constructive. Please write for guidelines so you'll know what we're looking for."

CHILDREN'S BRAINS ARE YUMMY (CBAY) BOOKS

PO Box 670296, Dallas, TX 75367. (512) 789-1004. **E-mail:** submissions@cbaybooks.com. **Website:** www.cbaybooks.com. **Contact:** Madeline Smoot, publisher. "CBAY Books currently focuses on quality fantasy and science fiction books for the middle grade and teen markets." Publishes 8 titles/year. 30% of books from first-time authors.

As of this book going to print in 2014, this market was not accepting unsolicited submissions. Check the website for updates and changes.

ILLUSTRATION Accepts international material. Works with 0-1 illustrators/year. Uses color artwork only. Reviews artwork. Send manuscripts with dummy. Send resume and tearsheets. Send samples to Madeline Smoot. Responds to queries only if interested.

PHOTOGRAPHY Buy stock images.

TERMS Pays authors royalty 10-15% based on wholesale price. Offers advances against royalties. Average amount $500. Brochure and guidelines online.

CHILDREN'S PRESS/FRANKLIN WATTS

Imprint of Scholastic, Inc., 90 Old Sherman Turnpike, Danbury CT 06816. Part of Scholastic Library Publishing. **Website:** www.scholastic.com/internationalschools/childrenspress.htm. Publishes nonfiction hardcover originals.

○ "Children's Press publishes 90% nonfiction for the school and library market, and 10% early reader fiction and nonfiction. Our books support textbooks and closely relate to the elementary and middle-school curriculum. Franklin Watts publishes nonfiction for middle and high school curriculum."

NONFICTION "We publish nonfiction books that supplement the school curriculum." No fiction, poetry, folktales, cookbooks or novelty books.

HOW TO CONTACT Does not accept unsolicited mss.

TERMS Book catalog for #10 SASE.

TIPS Most of this publisher's books are developed inhouse; less than 5% come from unsolicited submissions. However, they publish several series for which they always need new books. Study catalogs to discover possible needs.

CHILD WELFARE LEAGUE OF AMERICA

1726 M St. NW, Suite 500, Washington DC 20036. **E-mail:** books@cwla.org. **Website:** www.cwla.org/pubs. CWLA is a privately supported, nonprofit, membership-based organization committed to preserving, protecting, and promoting the well-being of all children and their families. Publishes hardcover and trade paperback originals.

HOW TO CONTACT Submit complete ms and proposal with outline, TOC, sample chapter, intended audience, and SASE.

TERMS Book catalog and ms guidelines online.

TIPS "We are looking for positive, kid-friendly books for ages 3-9. We are looking for books that have a positive message—a feel-good book."

CHRONICLE BOOKS FOR CHILDREN

680 Second St., San Francisco CA 94107. (415)537-4200. **Fax:** (415)537-4460. **E-mail:** submissions@chroniclebooks.com. **Website:** www.chroniclekids.com. "Chronicle Books for Children publishes an eclectic mixture of traditional and innovative children's books. Our aim is to publish books that inspire young readers to learn and grow creatively while helping them discover the joy of reading. We're looking for quirky, bold artwork and subject matter. Currently emphasizing picture books. De-emphasizing young adult." Publishes hardcover and trade paperback originals. Publishes 50-60 titles/year. 6% of books from first-time authors. 25% from unagented writers.

FICTION Does not accept proposals by fax, via e-mail, or on disk. When submitting artwork, either as a part of a project or as samples for review, do not send original art.

NONFICTION "We're always looking for the new and unusual. We do accept unsolicited manuscripts and we review all proposals. However, given the volume of proposals we receive, we are not able to personally respond to unsolicited proposals unless we are interested in pursuing the project."

HOW TO CONTACT Submit complete ms (picture books); submit outline/synopsis and 3 sample chapters (for older readers). Will not respond to submissions unless interested. Will not consider submissions by fax, e-mail or disk. Do not include SASE; do not send original materials. No submissions will be returned. Submit via mail or e-mail (prefers e-mail for adult submissions; only by mail for children's submissions). Submit proposal (guidelines online) and allow 3 months for editors to review. If submitting by mail, do not include SASE since our staff will not return materials. Responds to queries in 1 month. Publishes a book 1-3 years after acceptance.

ILLUSTRATION Works with 40-50 illustrators/year. Wants "unusual art, graphically strong, something that will stand out on the shelves. Fine art, not mass market." Reviews ms/illustration packages from artists. "Indicate if project **must** be considered jointly, or if editor may consider text and art separately." Illustrations only: Submit samples of artist's work (not necessarily from book, but in the envisioned style). Slides, tearsheets and color photocopies OK. (No original art.) Dummies helpful. Résumé helpful. Samples suited to our needs are filed for future reference. Samples not suited to our needs will be recycled. Queries and project proposals responded to in same time frame as author query/proposals."

TERMS Pays 8% royalty. Pays variable advance. Book catalog for 9x12 envelope and 3 first-class stamps. Guidelines available online.

TIPS "We are interested in projects that have a unique bent to them—be it in subject matter, writing style, or illustrative technique. As a small list, we are looking for books that will lend our list a distinctive flavor. Primarily we are interested in fiction and nonfiction picture books for children ages up to 8 years, and nonfiction books for children ages up to 12 years. We publish board, pop-up, and other novelty formats as well as picture books. We are also interested in early chapter books, middle grade fiction, and young adult projects."

CLARION BOOKS

Houghton Mifflin Co., 215 Park Ave. S., New York NY 10003. **Website:** www.houghtonmifflinbooks.com; www.hmco.com. **Contact:** Dinah Stevenson, vice president and publisher; Anne Hoppe, senior executive editor; Jennifer B. Greene, senior editor (contemporary fiction, picture books for all ages, nonfiction); Jennifer Wingertzahn, editor (fiction, picture books); Lynne Polvino, editor (fiction, nonfiction, picture books); Christine Kettner, art director. "Clarion Books publishes picture books, nonfiction, and fiction for infants through grade 12. Avoid telling your stories in verse unless you are a professional poet." Publishes hardcover originals for children. Publishes 50 titles/year.

○   "We are no longer responding to your unsolicited submission unless we are interested in publishing it. Please do not include a SASE. Submissions will be recycled, and you will not hear from us regarding the status of your submission unless we are interested. We regret that we cannot respond personally to each submission, but we do consider each and every submission we receive."

FICTION "Clarion is highly selective in the areas of historical fiction, fantasy, and science fiction. A novel must be superlatively written in order to find a place on the list. Mss that arrive without an SASE of adequate size will not be responded to or returned. Accepts fiction translations."

NONFICTION No unsolicited mss.

HOW TO CONTACT Submit complete ms. No queries, please. Send to only one Clarion editor. Query with SASE. Submit proposal package, sample chapters, SASE. Responds in 2 months to queries. Publishes a book 2 years after acceptance.

ILLUSTRATION Pays illustrators royalty; flat fee for jacket illustration.

TERMS Pays 5-10% royalty on retail price. Pays minimum of $4,000 advance. Guidelines for #10 SASE or online.

TIPS "Looks for freshness, enthusiasm—in short, life."

CONCORDIA PUBLISHING HOUSE

3558 S. Jefferson Ave., St. Louis MO 63118. (314)268-1187. **Fax:** (314)268-1329. **E-mail:** publicity@cph.org; sarah.steiner@cph.org. **Website:** www.cph.org. **Contact:** Sarah Steiner, production editor for professional and academic books. "Concordia Publishing House produces quality resources that communicate and nurture the Christian faith and ministry of people of all ages, lay and professional. These resources include curriculum, worship aids, books, and religious supplies. We publish approximately 30 quality children's books each year. We boldly provide Gospel resources that are Christ-centered, Bible-based and faithful to our Lutheran heritage." Publishes hardcover and trade paperback originals.

NONFICTION Picture books, young readers, young adults: Bible stories, activity books, arts/crafts, concept, contemporary, religion. "All books must contain explicit Christian content."

HOW TO CONTACT Submit complete ms (picture books); submit outline/synopsis and samples for longer mss. May also query. Responds in 1 month to queries; 3 months to mss.

ILLUSTRATION Works with 20 illustrators/year. Illustrations only: Query with samples. Contact: Norm Simon, art director. Responds only if interested. Samples filed.

TERMS Pays authors royalties based on retail price or work purchased outright ($750-2,000). Ms guidelines for 1 first-class stamp and a #10 envelope.

TIPS "Do not send finished artwork with the manuscript. If sketches will help in the presentation of the manuscript, they may be sent. If stories are taken from the Bible, they should follow the Biblical account closely. Liberties should not be taken in fantasizing Biblical stories."

CRAIGMORE CREATIONS

2900 SE Stark St., Suite 1A, Portland OR 97124. (503)477-9562. **E-mail:** info@craigmorecreations.com. **Website:** www.craigmorecreations.com.

NONFICTION "We publish books that make time travel seem possible: nonfiction that explores pre-history and Earth sciences for children.

HOW TO CONTACT Submit proposal package. See website for detailed submission guidelines. Submit proposal package.

CREATIVE COMPANY

P.O. Box 227, Mankato, MN 56002, (800)445-6209. **Fax:** (507)388-2746. **E-mail:** info@thecreativecompany.us. **Website:** www.thecreativecompany.us. **Contact:** Aaron Frisch. The Creative Company has two imprints: Creative Editions (picture books), and Creative Education (nonfiction series). Publishes 140 titles/year.

○ "We are currently not accepting fiction submissions."

NONFICTION Picture books, young readers, young adults: animal, arts/crafts, biography, careers, geography, health, history, hobbies, multicultural, music/dance, nature/environment, religion, science, social issues, special needs, sports. Average word length: young readers—500; young adults—6,000.

HOW TO CONTACT Submit outline/synopsis and 2 sample chapters, along with division of titles within the series. Responds in 3 months to queries/mss. Publishes a book 2 years after acceptance.

PHOTOGRAPHY Buys stock. Contact: Tricia Kleist, photo editor. Model/property releases not required; captions required. Uses b&w prints. Submit cover letter, promo piece. Ms and photographer guidelines available for SAE.

TERMS Guidelines available for SAE.

TIPS "We are accepting nonfiction, series submissions only. Fiction submissions will not be reviewed or returned. Nonfiction submissions should be presented in series (4, 6, or 8) rather than single."

CRICKET BOOKS

Imprint of Carus Publishing, 70 E. Lake St., Suite 300, Chicago IL 60601. (603)924-7209. **Fax:** (603)924-7380. **Website:** www.cricketmag.com. **Contact:** Submissions Editor. Cricket Books publishes picture books, chapter books, and middle-grade novels. Publishes hardcover originals. Publishes 5 titles/year.

○ Currently not accepting queries or mss. Check website for submissions details and updates.

HOW TO CONTACT Publishes ms 18 months after acceptance.

ILLUSTRATION Works with 4 illustrators/year. Uses color and b&w. Illustration only: Please send artwork submissions via e-mail to: mail@cicadamag.com. Make sure "portfolio samples—cricket books" is the subject line of the e-mail. The file should be 72 dpi RGB jpg format. **Contact:** John Sandford. Responds only if interested.

TERMS Pays up to 10% royalty on retail price. Average advance: $1,500 and up.

TIPS "Take a look at the recent titles to see what sort of materials we're interested in, especially for nonfiction. Please note that we aren't doing the sort of strictly educational nonfiction that other publishers specialize in."

⊕ KATHY DAWSON BOOKS

Penguin Group, 375 Hudson St., New York NY 10014. (212)366-2000. **Website:** www.us.penguingroup.com/static/pages/publishers/yr/kathydawson.html;http://kathydawsonbooks.tumblr.com. **Contact:** Kathy Dawson, vice-president and publisher. Kathy Dawson Books will launch its first list in Winter 2014. The imprint's mission statement: Publish stellar novels with unforgettable characters for children and teens that expand their vision of the world, sneakily explore the meaning of life, celebrate the written word, and last for generations. The imprint strives to publish tomorrow's award contenders: quality books with strong hooks in a variety of genres with universal themes and compelling voices—books that break the modl and the heart.

HOW TO CONTACT Accepts fiction queries via snail mail only. Include cover sheet with one-sentence elevator pitch, main themes, author version of catalog copy for book, first 10 pages of ms (double-spaced, Times Roman, 12 point type), and publishing history. No SASE needed. Responds only if interested. Responds only if interested.

TERMS Guidelines available online.

⊘ DELACORTE PRESS

Imprint of Random House Publishing Group, 1745 Broadway, New York NY 10019. (212)782-9000. **Website:** www.randomhouse.com. Publishes middle grade and young adult fiction in hard cover, trade paperback, mass market and digest formats. Publishes middle grade and young adult fiction in hardcover, trade paperback, mass market and digest formats.

All other query letters or ms submissions must be submitted through an agent or at the request of an editor. No e-mail queries.

DIAL BOOKS FOR YOUNG READERS

Imprint of Penguin Group USA, 375 Hudson St., New York NY 10014. (212)366-2000. **Website:** www. penguin.com/youngreaders. **Contact:** Lauri Hornik, president/publisher; Kathy Dawson, associate publisher; Namrata Tripathi, editorial director; Kate Harrison, senior editor; Liz Waniewski, editor; Alisha Niehaus, editor; Jessica Garrison, editor; Lily Malcom, art director. "Dial Books for Young Readers publishes quality picture books for ages 18 months-6 years; lively, believable novels for middle readers and young adults; and occasional nonfiction for middle readers and young adults." Publishes hardcover originals. Publishes 50 titles/year. 20% of books from first-time authors.

FICTION Especially looking for lively and well-written novels for middle grade and young adult children involving a convincing plot and believable characters. The subject matter or theme should not already be overworked in previously published books. The approach must not be demeaning to any minority group, nor should the roles of female characters (or others) be stereotyped, though we don't think books should be didactic, or in any way message-y. No topics inappropriate for the juvenile, young adult, and middle grade audiences. No plays.

HOW TO CONTACT Accepts unsolicited queries and up to 10 pages for longer works and unsolicited mss for picture books. "Due to the overwhelming number of unsolicited manuscripts we receive, we at Dial Books for Young Readers have had to change our submissions policy: As of August 1, 2005, Dial will no longer respond to your unsolicited submission unless interested in publishing it. Please do not include SASE with your submission. You will not hear from Dial regarding the status of your submission unless we are interested, in which case you can expect a reply from us within four months. We accept entire picture book manuscripts and a maximum of 10 pages for longer works (novels, easy-to-reads). When submitting a portion of a longer work, please provide an accompanying cover letter that briefly describes your manuscript's plot, genre (i.e. easy-to-read, middle grade or YA novel), the intended age group, and your publishing credits, if any." 5,000 queries received/year. Responds in 4-6 months to queries.

ILLUSTRATION Send nonreturnable samples, no originals, to Lily Malcolm. Show children and animals.

TERMS Pays royalty. Pays varies advance. Book catalog for 9x12 envelope and 4 first-class stamps.

TIPS "Our readers are anywhere from preschool age to teenage. Picture books must have strong plots, lots of action, unusual premises, or universal themes treated with freshness and originality. Humor works well in these books. A very well-thought-out and intelligently presented book has the best chance of being taken on. Genre isn't as much of a factor as presentation."

DISNEY HYPERION BOOKS FOR CHILDREN

Website: www.hyperionbooksforchildren.com. **Contact:** Rotem Moscovich, senior editor; Stephanie Owens Lurie, associate publisher; Emily Meehan, editorial director; Kevin Lewis, executive editor.

FICTION Picture books, early readers, middle readers, young adults: adventure, animal, anthology (short stories), contemporary, fantasy, history, humor, multicultural, poetry, science fiction, sports, suspense/mystery. Middle readers, young adults: commercial fiction.

NONFICTION Narrative nonfiction for elementary schoolers.

HOW TO CONTACT All submissions must come via an agent.

ILLUSTRATION Works with 100 illustrators/year. "Picture books are fully illustrated throughout. All others depend on individual project." Illustrations only: Submit résumé, business card, promotional literature or tearsheets to be kept on file. Responds only if interested. Original artwork returned at job's completion.

PHOTOGRAPHY Works on assignment only. Provide résumé, business card, promotional literature or tearsheets to be kept on file.

DIVERSION PRESS

E-mail: diversionpress@yahoo.com. **Website:** www. diversionpress.com. Publishes hardcover, trade and mass market paperback originals. Publishes 5-10 titles/year. 75% of books from first-time authors. 100% from unagented writers.

FICTION "We will happily consider any children's or young adult books if they are illustrated. If your story has potential to become a series, please address that in your proposal. Fiction short stories and poetry will be considered for our anthology series. See website for details on how to submit your ms."

NONFICTION "The editors have doctoral degrees and are interested in a broad range of academic works. We are also interested in how-to, slice of life, and other nonfiction areas." Does not review works that are sexually explicit, religious, or put children in a bad light.

HOW TO CONTACT Send query/proposal first. Mss accepted by request only. Responds in 2 weeks to queries. Responds in 1 month to proposals. Publishes ms 1-2 years after acceptance.

TERMS Pays 10% royalty on wholesale price. Guidelines available online.

TIPS "Read our website and blog prior to submitting. We like short, concise queries. Tell us why your book is different, not like other books. Give us a realistic idea of what you will do to market your book—that you will actually do. We will ask for more information if we are interested."

▲ DK PUBLISHING

Penguin Random House, 375 Hudson St., New York NY 10014. **Website:** www.dk.com. **Contact:** John Searcy; Nancy Ellwood, editorial director. "DK publishes photographically illustrated nonfiction for children of all ages."

○ DK Publishing does not accept unagented mss or proposals.

DNA PRESS & NARTEA PUBLISHING

DNA Press, P.O. Box 9311, Glendale CA 91226. **E-mail:** editors@dnapress.com. **Website:** www.dna press.com. Book publisher for young adults, children, and adults. Publishes hardcover and trade paperback originals. Publishes 10 titles/year. 90% of books from first-time authors. 100% from unagented writers.

FICTION All books should be oriented to explaining science even if they do not fall 100% under the category of science fiction.

NONFICTION "We publish business, real estate and investment books."

HOW TO CONTACT Submit complete ms. 500 queries received/year. 400 mss received/year. Responds in 6 weeks to mss. Publishes book 8 months after acceptance.

TERMS Pays 10-15% royalty. Book catalog and ms guidelines free.

TIPS Quick response, great relationships, high commission/royalty.

DUTTON CHILDREN'S BOOKS

Penguin Group (USA), Inc., 375 Hudson St., New York NY 10014. **E-mail:** duttonpublicity@ us.penguingroup.com. **Website:** www.penguin.com. **Contact:** Julie Strauss-Gabel, VP and Publisher; Sara Reynolds, art director. Dutton Children's Books publishes high-quality fiction and nonfiction for readers ranging from preschoolers to young adults on a variety of subjects. Currently emphasizing middle grade and young adult novels that offer a fresh perspective. De-emphasizing photographic nonfiction and picture books that teach a lesson. Approximately 80 new hardcover titles are published every year, fiction and nonfiction for babies through young adults. Publishes hardcover originals as well as novelty formats. Publishes 100 titles/year. 15% of books from first-time authors.

○ "Cultivating the creative talents of authors and illustrators and publishing books with purpose and heart continue to be the mission and joy at Dutton."

FICTION Dutton Children's Books has a diverse, general interest list that includes picture books; easy-to-read books; and fiction for all ages, from first chapter books to young adult readers.

HOW TO CONTACT Query. Responds only in interested.

TERMS Pays royalty on retail price. Offers advance.

EAKIN PRESS

P.O. Box 331779, Fort Worth TX 76163. **Phone/Fax:** (817)344-7036. **Website:** www.eakinpress.com. **Contact:** Kris Gholson, associate publisher. "Our top priority is to cover the history and culture of the Southwest, especially Texas and Oklahoma. We also have successfully published titles related to ethnic studies. We publish very little fiction, other than for children." Publishes hardcover and paperback originals and reprints.

○ No electronic submissions.

FICTION Juvenile fiction for grades K-12, preferably relating to Texas and the Southwest or contemporary. No adult fiction.

NONFICTION Juvenile nonfiction: includes biographies of historic personalities, prefer with Texas or regional interest, or nature studies; and easy-read illustrated books for grades 1-3.

HOW TO CONTACT Query or submit outline/synopsis Submit sample chapters, bio, synopsis, publishing credits, SASE. Responds in up to 1 year to queries.

TERMS Book catalog for $1.25. Guidelines available online.

⊘ EDUPRESS, INC.

P.O. Box 8610, Madison WI 53708. (920)563-9571 ext. 332. **Fax:** (920)563-7395. **E-mail:** edupress@high smith.com; LBowie@highsmith.com. **Website:** www. edupressinc.com. **Contact:** Liz Bowie. Edupress, Inc., publishes supplemental curriculum resources for PK-6th grade. Currently emphasizing reading and math materials, as well as science and social studies.

⊘   "Our mission is to create products that make kids want to go to school!"

HOW TO CONTACT Submit complete ms via mail or e-mail with "Manuscript Submission" as the subject line. Responds in 2-4 months. Publishes ms 1-2 years after acceptance.

ILLUSTRATION Query with samples. Contact: Cathy Baker, product development manager. Responds only if interested. Samples returned with SASE.

PHOTOGRAPHY Buys stock.

TERMS Work purchased outright from authors. Catalog available on website.

TIPS "We are looking for unique, research-based, quality supplemental materials for Pre-K through eighth grade. We publish all subject areas in many different formats, including games. Our materials are intended for classroom and home schooling use."

EERDMANS BOOKS FOR YOUNG READERS

2140 Oak Industrial Dr. NE, Grand Rapids MI 49505. **E-mail:** youngreaders@eerdmans.com. **Website:** www.eerdmans.com/youngreaders. **Contact:** Acquisitions Editor. "We are seeking books that encourage independent thinking, problem-solving, creativity, acceptance, kindness. Books that encourage moral values without being didactic or preachy. Board books, picture books, middle reader fiction, young adult fiction, nonfiction, illustrated storybooks. A submission stands out when it's obvious that someone put time into it—the publisher's name and address are spelled correctly, the package is neat, and all of our submission requirements have been followed precisely. We look for short, concise cover letters that explain why the ms fits with our list, and/or how the ms fills an important need in the world of children's literature. Send exclusive ms submissions to acquisitions editor. We regret that due to the volume of material we receive, we cannot comment on ms we are unable to accept."

⊘   "We seek to engage young minds with words and pictures that inform and delight, inspire and entertain. From board books for babies to picture books, nonfiction, and novels for children and young adults, our goal is to produce quality literature for a new generation of readers. We believe in books!"

FICTION Picture books: animal, contemporary, folktales, history, humor, multicultural, nature/environment, poetry, religion, special needs, social issues, sports, suspense. Young readers: animal, contemporary, fantasy, folktales, history, humor, multicultural, poetry, religion, special needs, social issues, sports, suspense. Middle readers: adventure, contemporary, fantasy, history, humor, multicultural, nature/environment, problem novels, religion, social issues, sports, suspense. Young adults/teens: adventure, contemporary, fantasy, folktales, history, humor, multicultural, nature/environment, problem novels, religion, sports, suspense. Average word length: picture books—1,000; middle readers—15,000; young adult—45,000. "Right now we are not acquiring books that revolve around a holiday. (No Christmas, Thanksgiving, Easter, Halloween, Fourth of July, Hanukkah books.) We do not publish retold or original fairy tales, nor do we publish books about witches or ghosts or vampires."

NONFICTION Middle readers: biography, history, multicultural, nature/environment, religion, social issues. Young adults/teens: biography, history, multicultural, nature/environment, religion, social issues. Average word length: 35,000.

HOW TO CONTACT Send exclusive ms submissions (marked so on outside of envelope) to acquisitions editor. 6,000 mss received/year. Responds to mss in 3-4 months. Publishes middle reader and YA books 1 year after acceptance; publishes picture books in 2-3 years.

ILLUSTRATION Accepts material from international illustrators. Works with 10-12 illustrators/year. Uses color artwork primarily. Reviews work for future assignments. If interested in illustrating future titles, send promo sheet. Submit samples to Gayle Brown, Art Director. Samples not returned. Samples filed.

TERMS Pays 5-7% royalty on retail.

TIPS "Find out who Eerdmans is before submitting a manuscript. Look at our website, request a catalog, and check out our books."

🅐 EGMONT USA

443 Park Ave. S, New York NY 10016. (212)685-0102. **Website:** www.egmontusa.com. **Contact:** Andrea Cascardi, managing director and publisher; Regina Griffin, executive editor; Greg Ferguson, senior editor; Ruth Katcher, editor-at-large; Alison Weiss, assistant editor. Specializes in trade books. Publishes 1 picture book/year; 2 young readers/year; 20 middle readers/year; 20 young adult/year. "Egmont USA publishes quality commercial fiction. We are committed to editorial excellence and to providing first-rate care for our authors. Our motto is that we turn writers into authors and children into passionate readers." 25% of books from first-time authors.

○ "Unfortunately, Egmont USA is not currently able to accept unsolicited submissions; we only accept submissions from literary agents."

FICTION Young readers: adventure, animal, contemporary, humor, multicultural. Middle readers: adventure, animal, contemporary, fantasy, humor, multicultural, problem novels, science fiction, special needs. Young adults/teens: adventure, animal, contemporary, fantasy, humor, multicultural, paranormal, problem novels, religion, science fiction, special needs.

HOW TO CONTACT Query or submit completed ms. Responds to queries in 4 weeks; mss in 6 weeks. Publishes book 18 months after acceptance.

ILLUSTRATION Only interested in agented in material. Works with 5 illustrators/year. Uses both color and b&w. Illustrations only: Query with samples. Responds only if interested. Samples are not returned. Send art samples to Greg Ferguson (gregferguson@egmont.com).

TERMS Pays authors royalties based on retail price.

ENETE ENTERPRISES

3600 Mission #10, San Diego CA 92109. **E-mail:** EneteEnterprises@gmail.com. **Website:** www.EneteEnterprises.com. **Contact:** Shannon Enete, editor. Publishes trade paperback originals, mass market paperback originals, electronic originals. Publishes 6 titles/year. 95% of books from first-time authors. 100% from unagented writers.

NONFICTION "Actively seeking books about healthcare / medicine. More specifically: back care, emergency medicine, international medicine, healthcare, insurance, EMT or Paramedic, or alternative medicine."

HOW TO CONTACT Submit query, proposal, or ms by e-mail according to guidelines (do not forget a marketing plan). Submit query, proposal, or ms by e-mail. 270 queries received/year. Responds to queries/proposals in 1 month; mss in 1-3 months. Publishes book 3-6 months after acceptance.

TERMS Pays royalties of 1-15%. Guidelines available on website.

TIPS "Send me your best work. Do not rush a draft."

FACTS ON FILE, INC.

Infobase Learning, 132 W. 31st St., 17th Floor, New York NY 10001. (800)322-8755. **Fax:** (800)678-3633. **E-mail:** llikoff@factsonfile.com; custserv@factsonfile.com. **Website:** www.factsonfile.com. **Contact:** Laurie Likoff, editorial director (science, fashion, natural history); Justine Ciovacco (science, nature, juvenile); Owen Lancer, senior editor (American history, women's studies); James Chambers, trade editor (health, pop culture, true crime, sports); Jeff Soloway, acquisitions editor (language/literature); Erika Arroyo, art director. Facts on File produces high-quality reference materials on a broad range of subjects for the school library market and the general nonfiction trade. Publishes hardcover originals and reprints. Publishes 135-150 titles/year. 25% from unagented writers.

NONFICTION "We publish serious, informational books for a targeted audience. All our books must have strong library interest, but we also distribute books effectively to the trade. Our library books fit the junior and senior high school curriculum." No computer books, technical books, cookbooks, biographies (except YA), pop psychology, humor, fiction or poetry.

HOW TO CONTACT Query or submit outline and sample chapter with SASE. No submissions returned without SASE. Responds in 2 months to queries.

ILLUSTRATION Commissions line art only.

TERMS Pays 10% royalty on retail price. Pays $5,000-10,000 advance. Book catalog available free. Guidelines available online.

TIPS "Our audience is school and public libraries for our more reference-oriented books and libraries, schools and bookstores for our less reference-oriented informational titles."

FARRAR, STRAUS & GIROUX FOR YOUNG READERS

Macmillan Children's Publishing Group, 18 W. 18th St., New York NY 10011. (212)741-6900. **Fax:** (212)633-2427. **E-mail:** childrens-editorial@fsgbooks. com. **Website:** www.fsgkidsbooks.com. **Contact:** Joy Peskin, vice-president; Margaret Ferguson, editorial director; Wesley Adams, executive editor; Janine O'Malley, senior editor; Frances Foster, Frances Foster Books; Robbin Gourley, art director.

FICTION All levels: all categories. "Original and well-written material for all ages."

NONFICTION All levels: all categories. "We publish only literary nonfiction."

HOW TO CONTACT Submit cover letter, first 50 pages by mail only.

ILLUSTRATION Works with 30-60 illustrators/year. Reviews ms/illustration packages from artists. Submit ms with 1 example of final art, remainder roughs. Do not send originals. Illustrations only: Query with tearsheets. Responds if interested in 3 months. Samples returned with SASE; samples sometimes filed.

TERMS Book catalog available by request. Ms guidelines online.

TIPS "Study our catalog before submitting. We will see illustrators' portfolios by appointment. Don't ask for criticism and/or advice—due to the volume of submissions we receive, it's just not possible. Never send originals. Always enclose SASE."

Ⓐ FEIWEL AND FRIENDS

Macmillan Children's Publishing Group, 175 Fifth Ave., New York NY 10010. (646)307-5151. E-mail: info@feiwelandfriends.com. **Website:** http:// us.macmillan.com/feiwelandfriends.aspx. Feiwel and Friends is a publisher of innovative children's fiction and nonfiction literature, including hardcover, paperback series, and individual titles. The list is eclectic and combines quality and commercial appeal for readers ages 0-16. The imprint is dedicated to "book by book" publishing, bringing the work of distinctive and oustanding authors, illustrators, and ideas to the marketplace. **Contact:** Jean Feiwel, publisher; Liz Szabla, editorial director.

Ⓞ This market does not accept unsolicited mss due to the volume of submissions; they also do not accept unsolicited queries for interior art. The best way to submit a ms is through an agent.

TERMS Catalog available online.

FIRST EDITION DESIGN PUBLISHING

P.O. Box 20217, Sarasota FL 34276. (941)921-2607. **Fax:** (617)866-7510. **E-mail:** support@firstedition design.com. **E-mail:** submission@firsteditiondesign. com. **Website:** www.firsteditiondesignpublishing. com. **Contact:** Deborah E. Gordon, executive editor; Tom Gahan, marketing director. Publishes 750+ titles/year. 45%% of books from first-time authors. 95%% from unagented writers.

HOW TO CONTACT Submit complete ms electronically. Send complete ms electronically. Accept to publish time is 1 week to 2 months.

TERMS Pays royalty 30-70% on retail price. Guidelines available free on request or online at website.

TIPS "Follow our FAQs listed on our website."

Ⓐ FIRST SECOND

Macmillan Children's Publishing Group, 175 5th Ave., New York NY 10010. **E-mail:** mail@firstsecondbooks. com. **Website:** http://us.macmillan.com/firstsecond. aspx; www.firstsecondbooks.com. **Contact:** Mark Siegel, editorial director; Calista Brill, editor; Colleen Venable, designer. First Second is a publisher of graphic novels and an imprint of Macmillan Children's Publishing Group.

Ⓞ First Second does not accept unsolicited submissions.

FICTION Considers any graphic novel project in almost any genre, for any age. Interested in fiction of all kinds. Not all titles may be suitable for young readers, but First Second does not publish pornography or books with gratuitous violence. Interested in authors with a unique and sincere voice. Consider signing an agent or receiving a referral from a cartoonist that First Second knows. This is the best way to receive a response.

HOW TO CONTACT Responds in about 6 weeks.

TERMS Catalog available online.

Ⓞ FIVE STAR PUBLICATIONS, INC.

P.O. Box 6698, Chandler AZ 85246. (480)940-8182. **Fax:** (480)940-8787. **E-mail:** info@fivestarpublica tions.com. **Website:** www.fivestarpublications.com. Publishes 7 middle readers/year. **Contact:** Linda F. Radke, president. "Helps produce and market award-winning books."

Ⓞ "Five Star Publications publishes and promotes award-winning fiction, nonfiction, cookbooks, children's literature and professional guides.

More information about Five Star Publications, Inc., a 25-year leader in the book publishing/book marketing industry, is available online at our website."

ILLUSTRATION Works with 3 illustrators/year. Reviews ms/illustration packages from artists. Query. Illustrations only: Query with samples. Responds only if interested. Samples filed.

PHOTOGRAPHY Buys stock and assigns work. Works on assignment only. Submit letter.

TIPS "Not only do we want to recognize and honor accomplished authors in the field of children's literature, but we also want to highlight and reward up-and-coming newly published authors, as well as younger published writers."

FLUX

Llewellyn Worldwide, Ltd., Llewellyn Worldwide, Ltd., 2143 Wooddale Dr., Woodbury, MN 55125. (651)312-8613. **Fax:** (651)291-1908. **Website:** www.fluxnow.com; fluxnow.blogspot.com. **Contact:** Brian Farrey, acquisitions editor. "Flux seeks to publish authors who see YA as a point of view, not a reading level. We look for books that try to capture a slice of teenage experience, whether in real or imagined worlds." Publishes 21 titles/year. 50% of books from first-time authors.

○ Does not accept unsolicited mss.

FICTION Young Adults: adventure, contemporary, fantasy, history, humor, problem novels, religion, science fiction, sports, suspense. Average word length: 50,000.

HOW TO CONTACT Accepts agented submissions only.

TERMS Pays royalties of 10-15% based on wholesale price. Book catalog and guidelines available on website.

TIPS "Read contemporary teen books. Be aware of what else is out there. If you don't read teen books, you probably shouldn't write them. Know your audience. Write incredibly well. Do not condescend."

FREE SPIRIT PUBLISHING, INC.

(612)338-2068. **Fax:** (612)337-5050. **E-mail:** acquisitions@freespirit.com. **Website:** www.freespirit.com. "We believe passionately in empowering kids to learn to think for themselves and make their own good choices." Publishes trade paperback originals and reprints. Publishes 12-18 titles/year. 5% of books from first-time authors. 75% from unagented writers.

○ Free Spirit does not accept general fiction, poetry or storybook submissions.

FICTION "We will consider fiction that relates directly to select areas of focus. Please review catalog and author guidelines (both available online) for details before submitting proposal. If you'd like material returned, enclose a SASE with sufficient postage."

NONFICTION "Many of our authors are educators, mental health professionals, and youth workers involved in helping kids and teens." No general fiction or picture storybooks, poetry, single biographies or autobiographies, books with mythical or animal characters, or books with religious or New Age content. "We are not looking for academic or religious materials, or books that analyze problems with the nation's school systems."

HOW TO CONTACT Accepts queries only—not submissions—by e-mail. Query with cover letter stating qualifications, intent, and intended audience and market analysis (how your book stands out from the field), along with your promotional plan, outline, 2 sample chapters, resume, SASE. Do not send original copies of work. Responds to proposals in 4-6 months.

ILLUSTRATION Works with 5 illustrators/year. Submit samples to creative director for consideration. If appropriate, samples will be kept on file and artist will be contacted if a suitable project comes up. Enclose SASE if you'd like materials returned.

PHOTOGRAPHY Uses stock photos. Does not accept photography submissions.

TERMS Pays advance. Book catalog and ms guidelines online.

TIPS "Our books are issue-oriented, jargon-free, and solution-focused. Our audience is children, teens, teachers, parents and youth counselors. We are especially concerned with kids' social and emotional well-being and look for books with ready-to-use strategies for coping with today's issues at home or in school-written in everyday language. We are not looking for academic or religious materials, or books that analyze problems with the nation's school systems. Instead, we want books that offer practical, positive advice so kids can help themselves, and parents and teachers can help kids succeed."

FREESTONE/PEACHTREE, JR.

1700 Chattahoochee Ave., Atlanta GA 30318. (404)876-8761. **Fax:** (404)875-2578. **E-mail:** hello@peachtree-online.com. **Website:** www.peachtree

-online.com. **Contact:** Helen Harriss, acquisitions; Loraine Joyner, art director; Melanie McMahon Ives, production manager. Publishes 4-8 titles/year.

○ Freestone and Peachtree, Jr. are imprints of Peachtree Publishers. See the listing for Peachtree for submission information. No e-mail or fax queries or submissions, please.

FICTION Middle Readers: adventure, animal, history, nature/environment, sports. Young Adults: fiction, history, biography, mystery, adventure. Does not want to see science fiction, religion, or romance.

NONFICTION Picture books, young readers, middle readers, young adults: history, sports. Picture books: animal, health, multicultural, nature/environment, science, social issues, special needs.

HOW TO CONTACT Submit 3 sample chapters by postal mail only. No query necessary. Responds in 6 months-1 year. Publishes book 1-2 years after acceptance.

ILLUSTRATION Works with 10-20 illustrators/year. Responds only if interested. Samples not returned; samples filed. Originals returned at job's completion.

TERMS Pays authors royalty. Pays illustrators by the project or royalty. Pays photographers by the project or per photo.

○ FULCRUM PUBLISHING

4690 Table Mountain Dr., Suite 100, Golden CO 80403. **E-mail:** info@fulcrum-books.com. **Website:** www.fulcrum-books.com. **Contact:** T. Baker, acquisitions editor.

NONFICTION Middle and early readers: Western history, nature/ environment, Native American.

HOW TO CONTACT Submit complete ms or submit outline/synopsis and 2 sample chapters. "Publisher does not send response letters unless we are interested in publishing." Do not send SASE.

PHOTOGRAPHY Works on assignment only.

TERMS Pays authors royalty based on wholesale price. Offers advances. Catalog for SASE. Guidelines online.

TIPS "Research our line first. We look for books that appeal to the school market and trade. "

GIBBS SMITH

P.O. Box 667, Layton UT 84041. (801)544-9800. **Fax:** (801)544-8853. **E-mail:** duribe@gibbs-smith.com. **Website:** www.gibbs-smith.com. **Contact:** Suzanne Taylor, associate publisher and creative director (children's activity books); Jennifer Grillone, art acquisi-

tions. Publishes 3 titles/year. 50% of books from first-time authors. 50% from unagented writers.

NONFICTION Middle readers: activity, arts/crafts, cooking, how-to, nature/environment, science. Average word length: picture books—under 1,000 words; activity books—under 15,000 words.

HOW TO CONTACT Submit an outline and writing samples for activity books; query for other types of books. Responds to queries and mss in 2 months. Publishes ms 1-2 years after acceptance.

ILLUSTRATION Works with 2 illustrators/year. Reviews ms/illustration packages from artists. Query. Submit ms with 3-5 pieces of final art. Illustrations only: Query with samples; provide résumé, promo sheet, slides (duplicate slides, not originals). Responds only if interested. Samples returned with SASE; samples filed.

TERMS Pays illustrators by the project or royalty of 2% based on retail price. Sends galleys to authors; color proofs to illustrators. Original artwork returned at job's completion. Pays authors royalty of 2% based on retail price or work purchased outright ($500 minimum). Offers advances (average amount: $2,000). Book catalog available for 9×12 SAE and $2.30 postage. Ms guidelines available by e-mail.

TIPS "We target ages 5-11. We do not publish young adult novels or chapter books."

○ DAVID R. GODINE, PUBLISHER

15 Court Square, Suite 320, Boston MA 02108. (617)451-9600. **Fax:** (617)350-0250. **E-mail:** info@godine.com. **Website:** www.godine.com. "We publish books that matter for people who care."

○ This publisher is no longer considering unsolicited mss of any type. Only interested in agented material.

HOW TO CONTACT Only interested in agented material.

ILLUSTRATION Only interested in agented material. Works with 1-3 illustrators/year. "Please do not send original artwork unless solicited. Almost all of the children's books we accept for publication come to us with the author and illustrator already paired up. Therefore, we rarely use freelance illustrators."

○ GOLDEN BOOKS FOR YOUNG READERS GROUP

1745 Broadway, New York NY 10019. **Website:** www.randomhouse.com. **Contact:** Kristen Depken; Michelle Nagler, associate publisher director; Caroline

Abbey, senior editor. "Random House Books aims to create books that nurture the hearts and minds of children, providing and promoting quality books and a rich variety of media that entertain and educate readers from 6 months to 12 years." 2% of books from first-time authors.

○ Random House-Golden Books does not accept unsolicited mss, only agented material. They reserve the right not to return unsolicited material.

TERMS Pays authors in royalties; sometimes buys mss outright. Book catalog free on request.

GREENHAVEN PRESS

27500 Drake Rd., Farmington Hills MI 48331. **E-mail:** betz.deschenes@cengage.com. **Website:** www.gale.com/greenhaven. **Contact:** Betz Des Chenes. Publishes 220 young adult academic reference titles/year. 50% of books by first-time authors. Greenhaven continues to print quality nonfiction anthologies for libraries and classrooms. "Our well-known Opposing Viewpoints series is highly respected by students and librarians in need of material on controversial social issues." Greenhaven accepts no unsolicited mss. Send query, resume, and list of published works by e-mail. Work purchased outright from authors; write-for-hire, flat fee.

NONFICTION Young adults (high school): controversial issues, social issues, history, literature, science, environment, health.

Ⓐ GREENWILLOW BOOKS

HarperCollins Children's Books, 195 Broadway., New York NY 10007. (212)207-7000. **Website:** www.greenwillowblog.com. **Contact:** Virginia Duncan, vice president/publisher; Paul Zakris, art director. Publishes hardcover originals, paperbacks, e-books, and reprints. Publishes 40-50 titles/year.

○ Does not accept unsolicited mss. "Unsolicited mail will not be opened and will not be returned."

HOW TO CONTACT Publishes ms 2 years after acceptance.

TERMS Pays 10% royalty on wholesale price for first-time authors. Offers variable advance.

GROSSET & DUNLAP PUBLISHERS

Penguin Putnam Inc., 375 Hudson St., New York NY 10014. **Website:** www.penguingroup.com. **Contact:** Francesco Sedita, vice president/publisher. Grosset & Dunlap publishes children's books that show children that reading is fun, with books that speak to their interests, and that are affordable so that children can build a home library of their own. Focus on licensed properties, series and readers. "Grosset & Dunlap publishes high-interest, affordable books for children ages 0-10 years. We focus on original series, licensed properties, readers and novelty books." Publishes hardcover (few) and mass market paperback originals. Publishes 140 titles/year.

HOW TO CONTACT All book formats except for picture books. Submit a summary and the first chapter or 2 for longer works. All book formats except for picture books. Submit a summary and the first chapter or 2 for longer works.

TERMS Pays royalty. Pays advance.

TIPS "Nonfiction that is particularly topical or of wide interest in the mass market; new concepts for novelty format for preschoolers; and very well-written easy readers on topics that appeal to primary graders have the best chance of selling to our firm."

GRYPHON HOUSE, INC.

P.O. Box 10, 6848 Leon's Way, Lewisville NC 27023. **Website:** www.gryphonhouse.com. **Contact:** Kathy Charner, editor-in-chief. "Gryphon House publishes books that teachers and parents of young children (birth-age 8) consider essential to their daily lives." Publishes parent and teacher resource books, textbooks. Recently published *Reading Games*, by Jackie Silberg; *Primary Art*, by MaryAnn F. Kohl; *Teaching Young Children with Autism Spectrum Disorder*, by Clarissa Willis; *The Complete Resource Book for Infants*, by Pam Schiller. "At Gryphon House, our goal is to publish books that help teachers and parents enrich the lives of children from birth through age 8. We strive to make our books useful for teachers at all levels of experience, as well as for parents, caregivers, and anyone interested in working with children." Query. Submit outline/synopsis and 2 sample chapters. Responds to queries/mss in 6 months. Publishes a book 18 months after acceptance. Will consider simultaneous submissions, e-mail submissions. Book catalog and ms guidelines available via website or with SASE. "We are looking for books of creative, participatory learning experiences that have a common conceptual theme to tie them together. The books should be on subjects that parents or teachers want to do on a daily basis." Publishes trade paperback originals. Publishes 12-15 titles/year.

NONFICTION Currently emphasizing social-emotional intelligence and classroom management; de-emphasizing literacy after-school activities.

HOW TO CONTACT "We prefer to receive a letter of inquiry and/or a proposal, rather than the entire manuscript. Please include: the proposed title, the purpose of the book, table of contents, introductory material, 20-40 sample pages of the actual book. In addition, please describe the book, including the intended audience, why teachers will want to buy it, how it is different from other similar books already published, and what qualifications you possess that make you the appropriate person to write the book. If you have a writing sample that demonstrates that you write clear, compelling prose, please include it with your letter." Responds in 3-6 months to queries.

ILLUSTRATION Works with 4-5 illustrators/year. Uses b&w realistic artwork only. Query with samples, promo sheet. Responds in 2 months. Samples returned with SASE; samples filed. Pays illustrators by the project.

PHOTOGRAPHY Pays photographers by the project or per photo. Sends edited ms copy to authors. Original artwork returned at job's completion.

TERMS Pays royalty on wholesale price. Guidelines available online.

HARLEQUIN TEEN

Harlequin, 233 Broadway, Ste. 1001, New York NY 10279. **Website:** www.harlequin.com; www.harlequinteen.com. **Contact:** Natashya Wilson, executive editor; Annie Stone, editor; T.S. Ferguson, associate editor.. Harlequin Teen is a single-title program dedicated to building authors and publishing unique, memorable young-adult fiction. Stories with the unforgettable romance, characters and atmosphere of Stephenie Meyer's Twilight saga, the witty humor of Meg Cabot's Princess Diaries novels, the edgy emotion of Jay Asher's *Th1rteen R3asons Why*, the thrilling danger of Suzanne Collins's *Hunger Games*, the futuristic world-building of Scott Westerfeld's *Uglies*, and the power of Marcus Zusak's *The Book Thief* are examples of the range and depth of projects that Harlequin Teen seeks.

This market is currently accepting agented submissions only.

FICTION Harlequin Teen looks for fresh, authentic fiction featuring extraordinary characters and extraordinary stories set in contemporary, paranormal, fantasy, science-fiction, and historical worlds. Wants commercial, high-concept stories that capture the teen experience and will speak to readers with power and authenticity. All subgenres are welcome, so long as the book delivers a relevant reading experience that will resonate long after the book's covers are closed. Expects that most stories will include a compelling romantic element.

HOW TO CONTACT Have agent include a query letter and a synopsis of 500-1,000 words, along with a full or partial ms (50,000-100,000 words). Submit via a hard copy or as an e-mail attachment.

HARPERCOLLINS CHILDREN'S BOOKS/HARPERCOLLINS PUBLISHERS

This publisher has a number of imprints underneath it. HarperCollins Children's Books, 195 Broadway, New York NY 10007. (212)207-7000. **E-mail:** Dana.fritts@Harpercollins.com; Kate.engbring@Harpercollins.com. **Website:** www.harpercollins.com. HarperCollins, one of the largest English language publishers in the world, is a broad-based publisher with strengths in academic, business and professional, children's, educational, general interest, and religious and spiritual books, as well as multimedia titles. Publishes hardcover and paperback originals and paperback reprints. Publishes 500 titles/year.

FICTION "We look for a strong story line and exceptional literary talent."

NONFICTION No unsolicited mss or queries.

HOW TO CONTACT Agented submissions only. All unsolicited mss returned. Agented submissions only. Unsolicited mss returned unopened. Responds in 1 month, will contact only if interested. Does not accept any unsolicted texts.

TERMS Negotiates payment upon acceptance. Catalog available online.

TIPS "We do not accept any unsolicited material."

HARPERTEEN

HarperCollins Children's Books, 195 Broadway, New York NY 10007. (212)207-7000. **Fax:** (212)702-2583. **E-mail:** Jennifer.Deason@harpercollins.com. **Website:** www.harpercollins.com. HarperTeen is a teen imprint that publishes hardcovers, paperback reprints and paperback originals. Publishes 100 titles/year.

HarperCollins Children's Books is not accepting unsolicited and/or unagented mss or queries. Unfortunately the volume of these submissions is so large that they cannot receive the attention they deserve. Such submissions will not be reviewed or returned.

HOLIDAY HOUSE, INC.

425 Madison Ave., New York NY 10017. (212)688-0085. **Fax:** (212)421-6134. **E-mail:** info@holiday-house.com. **Website:** holidayhouse.com. **Contact:** Mary Cash, vice president and editor-in-chief; Grace Maccarone, executive editor; Claire Counihan, director of art and design. "Holiday House publishes children's and young adult books for the school and library markets. We have a commitment to publishing first-time authors and illustrators. We specialize in quality hardcovers from picture books to young adult, both fiction and nonfiction, primarily for the school and library market." Publishes hardcover originals and paperback reprints. Publishes 50 titles/year. 5% of books from first-time authors. 50% from unagented writers.

FICTION Children's books only.

HOW TO CONTACT Query with SASE. No phone calls, please. Please send the entire ms, whether submitting a picture book or novel. Send ms via U.S. Mail. "We do not accept certified or registered mail. There is no need to include a SASE. We do not consider submissions by e-mail or fax. Please note that you do not have to supply illustrations. However, if you have illustrations you would like to include with your submission, you may send detailed sketches or photocopies of the original art. Do not send original art." Responds in 4 months. Publishes 1-2 years after acceptance.

ILLUSTRATION Accepting art samples, not returned.

TERMS Pays royalty on list price, range varies. Agent's royalty. Guidelines for #10 SASE.

TIPS "We need manuscripts with strong stories and writing."

HOUGHTON MIFFLIN HARCOURT BOOKS FOR CHILDREN

Imprint of Houghton Mifflin Trade & Reference Division, 222 Berkeley St., Boston MA 02116. (617)351-5000. **Fax:** (617)351-1111. **E-mail:** children's_books@hmco.com. **Website:** www.houghtonmifflinbooks.com. **Contact:** Erica Zappy, associate editor; Kate O'Sullivan, senior editor; Anne Rider, executive editor; Margaret Raymo, editorial director. Houghton Mifflin Harcourt gives shape to ideas that educate, inform, and above all, delight. Query with SASE. Submit sample chapters, synopsis. Faxed or e-mailed manu-scripts and proposals are not considered. Complete submission guidelines available on website. Publishes hardcover originals and trade paperback originals and reprints. Publishes 100 titles/year. 10% of books from first-time authors. 60% from unagented writers.

○ Does not respond to or return mss unless interested.

NONFICTION Interested in innovative books and subjects about which the author is passionate.

HOW TO CONTACT Submit complete ms. Query with SASE. Submit sample chapters, synopsis. 5,000 queries received/year. 14,000 mss received/year. Responds in 4-6 months to queries. Publishes ms 2 years after acceptance.

TERMS Pays 5-10% royalty on retail price. Pays variable advance. Guidelines available online.

TIPS Faxed or e-mailed mss and proposals are not considered.

IDEALS CHILDREN'S BOOKS AND CANDYCANE PRESS

2630 Elm Hill Pike, Suite 100, Nashville TN 37214. **Website:** www.idealsbooks.com.

FICTION Picture books: animal, concept, history, religion. Board books: animal, history, nature/environment, religion. Ideals publishes for ages 4-8, no longer than 800 words; CandyCane publishes for ages 2-5, no longer than 500 words.

NONFICTION Ideals publishes for ages 4-8, no longer than 800 words; CandyCane publishes for ages 2-5, no longer than 500 words.

HOW TO CONTACT Submit complete ms. Submit complete ms.

IDEALS PUBLICATIONS INC.

2630 Elm Hill Pike, Suite 100, Nashville TN 37214. (615)781-1451. **E-mail:** idealsinfo@guideposts.org. **Website:** www.idealsbooks.com. "Ideals Publications publishes 20-25 new children's titles a year, primarily for 2-8 year-olds. Our backlist includes more than 400 titles, and we publish picture books, activity books, board books, and novelty and sound books covering a wide array of topics, such as Bible stories, holidays, early learning, history, family relationships, and values. Our bestselling titles include *The Story of Christmas, The Story of Easter, Seaman's Journal, How Do I Love You?, God Made You Special* and *A View at the Zoo*. Through our dedication to publishing high-quality and engaging books, we never forget our obligation to our littlest readers to help create those special moments with books."

FICTION Ideals Children's Books publishes fiction and nonfiction picture books for children ages 4 to 8. Subjects include holiday, inspirational, and patriotic themes; relationships and values; and general fiction. Mss should be no longer than 800 words. CandyCane Press publishes board books and novelty books for children ages 2 to 5. Subject matter is similar to Ideals Children's Books, with a focus on younger children. Mss should be no longer than 250 words.

ILLUMINATION ARTS

P.O. Box 1865, Bellevue WA 98009. **Website:** www. illumin.com. **Contact:** Ruth Thompson, editorial director.

O   "Note that our submission review process is on hold until notice on website so submissions are not currently being reviewed." Normal requirements include no electronic or CD submissions for text or art. Considers simultaneous submissions.

FICTION Word length: Prefers under 1,000, but will consider up to 1,500 words.

TERMS Pays authors and illustrators royalty based on wholesale price. Book fliers available for SASE.

TIPS "Read our books or visit website to see what our books are like. Follow submission guidelines found on website. Be patient. We are unable to track unsolicited submissions."

IMPACT PUBLISHERS, INC.

P.O. Box 6016, Atascadero CA 93423. **E-mail:** submissions@impactpublishers.com. **Website:** www.impact publishers.com. **Contact:** Freeman Porter, submissions editor. "Our purpose is to make the best human services expertise available to the widest possible audience. We publish only popular psychology and self-help materials written in everyday language by professionals with advanced degrees and significant experience in the human services." Publishes 3-5 titles/year. 20% of books from first-time authors.

NONFICTION Young readers, middle readers, young adults: self-help.

HOW TO CONTACT Query or submit complete ms, cover letter, résumé. Responds in 3 months.

ILLUSTRATION Works with 1 illustrator/year. Not accepting freelance illustrator queries.

TERMS Pays authors royalty of 10-12%. Offers advances. Book catalog for #10 SASE with 2 first-class stamps. Guidelines for SASE.

TIPS "Please do not submit fiction, poetry or narratives."

JEWISH LIGHTS PUBLISHING

LongHill Partners, Inc., Sunset Farm Offices, Rt. 4, P.O. Box 237, Woodstock VT 05091. (802)457-4000. **Fax:** (802)457-4004. **E-mail:** editorial@jewishlights. com; sales@jewishlights.com. **Website:** www.jew ishlights.com. **Contact:** Tim Holtz, art acquisitions. "Jewish Lights publishes books for people of all faiths and all backgrounds who yearn for books that attract, engage, educate and spiritually inspire. Our authors are at the forefront of spiritual thought and deal with the quest for the self and for meaning in life by drawing on the Jewish wisdom tradition. Our books cover topics including history, spirituality, life cycle, children, self-help, recovery, theology and philosophy. We do not publish autobiography, biography, fiction, haggadot, poetry or cookbooks. At this point we plan to do only two books for children annually, and one will be for younger children (ages 4-10)." Publishes hardcover and trade paperback originals, trade paperback reprints. Publishes 30 titles/year. 50% of books from first-time authors. 75% from unagented writers.

FICTION Picture books, young readers, middle readers: spirituality. "We are not interested in anything other than spirituality."

NONFICTION Picture book, young readers, middle readers: activity books, spirituality. "We do *not* publish haggadot, biography, poetry, or cookbooks."

HOW TO CONTACT Query with outline/synopsis and 2 sample chapters; submit complete ms for picture books. Query. Responds in 3 months to queries. Publishes ms 1 year after acceptance.

TERMS Pays authors royalty of 10% of revenue received; 15% royalty for subsequent printings. Book catalog and ms guidelines online.

TIPS "We publish books for all faiths and backgrounds that also reflect the Jewish wisdom tradition. Explain in your cover letter why you're submitting your project to us in particular. Make sure you know what we publish."

JOURNEYFORTH

Imprint of BJU Press, 1700 Wade Hampton Blvd., Greenville SC 29614. (864)242-5100, ext. 4350. **Fax:** (864)298-0268. **E-mail:** jb@bju.edu. **Website:** www.

journeyforth.com. **Contact:** Nancy Lohr. "Small independent publisher of trustworthy novels and biographies for readers pre-school through high school from a conservative Christian perspective, Christian living books, and Bible studies for adults." Publishes paperback originals. Publishes 25 titles/year. 10% of books from first-time authors. 8% from unagented writers.

FICTION Young readers, middle readers, young adults: adventure, animal, contemporary, fantasy, folktales, history, humor, multicultural, nature/environment, problem novels, suspense/mystery. Average word length: young readers—10,000-12,000; middle readers—10,000-40,000; young adult/teens—40,000-60,000. "Our fiction is all based on a moral and Christian worldview." Does not want short stories.

NONFICTION Young readers, middle readers, young adult: biography. Average word length: young readers—10,000-12,000; middle readers—10,000-40,000; young adult/teens—40,000-60,000. Christian living, Bible studies, church and ministry, church history. "We produce books for the adult Christian market that are from a conservative Christian worldview."

HOW TO CONTACT Fiction: Query or submit outline/synopsis and 5 sample chapters. "Do not send stories with magical elements. We are not currently accepting picture books. We do not publish: romance, science fiction, poetry and drama." Nonfiction: Query or submit outline/synopsis and 5 sample chapters. Responds to queries in 4 weeks; mss in 3 months. Publishes book 12-15 months after acceptance. Will consider previously published work. Submit 5 sample chapters, synopsis, SASE. Responds in 1 month to queries. Responds in 3 months to manuscripts. Publishes book 12-18 months after acceptance.

ILLUSTRATION Works with 2- 4 illustrators/year. Query with samples. Send promo sheet; will review website portfolio if applicable. Responds only if interested. Samples returned with SASE; samples filed.

TERMS Pays authors royalty based on wholesale price. Pays illustrators by the project. Originals returned to artist at job's completion. Pays royalty. Book catalog available free. Guidelines online.

TIPS "Study the publisher's guidelines. No picture books and no submissions by e-mail."

◯ KAMEHAMEHA PUBLISHING

Website: www.kamehamehapublishing.org. "Kamehameha Schools Press publishes in the areas of Hawaiian history, Hawaiian culture, Hawaiian language and Hawaiian studies."

FICTION Young reader, middle readers, young adults: biography, history, multicultural, Hawaiian folklore.

NONFICTION Young reader, middle readers, young adults: biography, history, multicultural, Hawaiian folklore.

HOW TO CONTACT Responds in 3 months. Publishes ms 2 years after acceptance.

ILLUSTRATION Uses color and b&w artwork. Illustrations only: Query with samples. Responds only if interested. Samples not returned.

TERMS Work purchased outright from authors or by royalty agreement. Call or write for book catalog.

TIPS "Writers and illustrators must be knowledgeable in Hawaiian history/culture and be able to show credentials to validate their proficiency. Greatly prefer to work with writers/illustrators available in the Honolulu area."

KANE/MILLER BOOK PUBLISHERS

Kane/Miller: A Division of EDC Publishing, 4901 Morena Blvd., Suite 213, San Diego CA 92117. (858)456-0540. **Fax:** (858)456-9641. **E-mail:** submissions@kanemiller.com. **Website:** www.kanemiller.com. **Contact:** Editorial Department. "Kane/Miller Book Publishers is a division of EDC Publishing, specializing in award-winning children's books from around the world. Our books bring the children of the world closer to each other, sharing stories and ideas, while exploring cultural differences and similarities. Although we continue to look for books from other countries, we are now actively seeking works that convey cultures and communities within the US. We are looking for picture book fiction and nonfiction on those subjects that may be defined as particularly American: sports such as baseball, historical events, American biographies, American folk tales, etc. We are committed to expanding our early and middlegrade fiction list. We're interested in great stories with engaging characters in all genres (mystery, fantasy, adventure, historical, etc.) and, as with picture books, especially those with particularly American subjects. All submissions sent via USPS should be sent to: Editorial Department. Please do not send anything requiring a signature. Work submitted for consideration may also be sent via e-mail. Please send either the complete picture book ms, the published book (with a summary and outline in English, if that is not the language of origin) or a synopsis of the work and two sample chapters. Do not send originals. Illustrators may send color copies, tear sheets, or other non-returnable illustration samples. If you have a website with additional samples of your work, please include the web address. Please do not send original artwork, or samples on CD. A SASE must be included if you send your submission via USPS; otherwise you will not receive a reply. If we wish to follow up, we will notify you."

○ "We like to think that a child reading a Kane/Miller book will see parallels between his own life and what might be the unfamiliar setting and characters of the story. And that by seeing how a character who is somehow or in some way dissimilar—an outsider—finds a way to fit comfortably into a culture or community or situation while maintaining a healthy sense of self and self-dignity, she might be empowered to do the same."

FICTION Picture Books: concept, contemporary, health, humor, multicultural. Young Readers: contemporary, multicultural, suspense. Middle Readers: contemporary, humor, multicultural, suspense.

HOW TO CONTACT Responds in 90 days to queries.

KAR-BEN PUBLISHING

Lerner Publishing Group, 241 First Ave., N, Minneapolis MN 55401. (612)215-6229. **Fax:** 612-332-7615. **E-mail:** Editorial@Karben.com. **Website:** www.karben.com. Publishes hardcover, trade paperback and electronic originals. Publishes 10-15 titles/year. 20% of books from first-time authors. 70% from unagented writers.

FICTION "We seek picture book mss of about 1,000 words on Jewish-themed topics for children." Picture books: Adventure, concept, folktales, history, humor, multicultural, religion, special needs; must be on a Jewish theme. Average word length: picture books–1,000. Recently published titles: *The Count's Hanukkah Countdown, Sammy Spider's First Book of Jewish Holidays, The Cats of Ben Yehuda Street.*

NONFICTION "In addition to traditional Jewish-themed stories about Jewish holidays, history, folktales and other subjects, we especially seek stories that reflect the rich diversity of the contemporary Jewish community." Picture books, young readers: activity books, arts/crafts, biography, careers, concept, cooking, history, how-to, multicultural, religion, social is-

sues, special needs; must be of Jewish interest. No textbooks, games, or educational materials.

HOW TO CONTACT Submit full ms. Picture books only. Submit completed ms. 800 mss received/year. Responds in 6 weeks. Most manuscripts published within 2 years.

TERMS Pays 5% royalty on NET sale. Pays $500-2,500 advance. Book catalog available online; free upon request. Guidelines available online.

TIPS "Authors: Do a literature search to make sure similar title doesn't already exist. Illustrators: Look at our online catalog for a sense of what we like—bright colors and lively composition."

KREGEL PUBLICATIONS

Kregel, Inc., P.O. Box 2607, Grand Rapids MI 49501. (616)451-4775. **Fax:** (616)451-9330. **E-mail:** kregelbooks@kregel.com. **Website:** www.kregelpublications.com. **Contact:** Dennis R. Hillman, publisher. "Our mission as an evangelical Christian publisher is to provide—with integrity and excellence—trusted, Biblically based resources that challenge and encourage individuals in their Christian lives. Works in theology and Biblical studies should reflect the historic, orthodox Protestant tradition." Publishes hardcover and trade paperback originals and reprints. Publishes 90 titles/year. 20% of books from first-time authors. 35% from unagented writers.

○ Finds works through The Writer's Edge and Christian Manuscript Submissions manuscript screening services.

FICTION Fiction should be geared toward the evangelical Christian market. Wants books with fast-paced, contemporary storylines presenting a strong Christian message in an engaging, entertaining style.

NONFICTION "We serve evangelical Christian readers and those in career Christian service."

HOW TO CONTACT Publishes ms 16 months after acceptance.

TERMS Pays royalty on wholesale price. Pays negotiable advance. Guidelines online.

TIPS "Our audience consists of conservative, evangelical Christians, including pastors and ministry students."

⊕ LEDGE HILL PUBLISHING

P.O. Box 337, Alton NH 03809. **E-mail:** info@ledgehillpublishing.com. **Website:** www.ledgehillpublishing.com. **Contact:** Amanda Eason. Publishes hardcover, trade paperback, and mass market paperback originals. Publishes 10-15 titles/year. 100% of books from first-time authors. 100% from unagented writers.

HOW TO CONTACT Submit proposal package, including syopsis and 4 sample chapters or submit complete ms. Submit proposal package including an outline, 3 sample chapters or submit complete ms. 20-40 queries received/year. 15-30 mss received/year. Responds in 1 month to queries and proposals; 2 months to mss. Publishes ms 3 months after acceptance.

TERMS Pays 2-15% royalty. Book catalog available online at website. Guidelines free on request by e-mail or online at website.

LEE & LOW BOOKS

95 Madison Ave., #1205, New York NY 10016. (212)779-4400. **E-mail:** general@leeandlow.com. **Website:** www.leeandlow.com. **Contact:** Louise May, editor-in-chief (multicultural children's fiction/non-fiction). "Our goals are to meet a growing need for books that address children of color, and to present literature that all children can identify with. We only consider multicultural children's books. Currently emphasizing material for 5-12 year olds. Sponsors a yearly New Voices Award for first-time picture book authors of color. Contest rules online at website or for SASE." Publishes hardcover originals and trade paperback reprints. Publishes 12-14 titles/year. 20% of books from first-time authors. 50% from unagented writers.

FICTION Picture books, young readers: anthology, contemporary, history, multicultural, poetry. Picture book, middle reader: contemporary, history, multicultural, nature/environment, poetry, sports. Average word length: picture books—1,000-1,500 words. "We do not publish folklore or animal stories."

NONFICTION Picture books: concept. Picture books, middle readers: biography, history, multicultural, science and sports. Average word length: picture books—1,500-3,000.

HOW TO CONTACT Submit complete ms. Submit complete ms. Receives 100 queries/year; 1,200 mss/year. Responds in 6 months to mss if interested. Publishes book 2 years after acceptance.

ILLUSTRATION Works with 12-14 illustrators/year. Uses color artwork only. Reviews ms/illustration packages from artists. Contact: Louise May. Illustrations only: Query with samples, résumé, promo sheet and tearsheets. Responds only if interested. Samples

returned with SASE; samples filed. Original artwork returned at job's completion.

PHOTOGRAPHY Buys photos from freelancers. Works on assignment only. Model/property releases required. Submit cover letter, résumé, promo piece and book dummy.

TERMS Pays net royalty. Pays authors advances against royalty. Pays illustrators advance against royalty. Photographers paid advance against royalty. Book catalog available online. Guidelines available online or by written request with SASE.

TIPS "Check our website to see the kinds of books we publish. Do not send mss that don't fit our mission."

LEGACY PRESS

P.O. Box 261129, San Diego CA 92196. (858)277-1167. **E-mail:** john.gregory@rainbowpublishers.com. **Website:** www.rainbowpublishers.com. Publishes 4 young readers/year; 4 middle readers/year; 4 young adult titles/year. 50% of books by first-time authors. "Our mission is to publish Bible-based, teacher resource materials that contribute to and inspire spiritual growth and development in kids ages 2-12."

NONFICTION Young readers, middle readers, young adult/teens: activity books, arts/crafts, how-to, reference, religion.

HOW TO CONTACT Responds to queries in 6 weeks, mss in 3 months.

TERMS For authors work purchased outright (range: $500 and up). Pays illustrators by the project (range: $300 and up). Sends galleys to authors.

TIPS "Our Rainbow imprint publishes reproducible books for teachers of children in Christian ministries, including crafts, activities, games and puzzles. Our Legacy imprint publishes titles for children such as devotionals, fiction and Christian living. Please see website and study the market before submitting material."

ARTHUR A. LEVINE BOOKS

Scholastic, Inc., 557 Broadway, New York NY 10012. (212)343-4436. **Fax:** (212)343-6143. **E-mail:** arthura levinebooks@scholastic.com. **Website:** www. arthuralevinebooks.com. **Contact:** Arthur A. Levine, VP/publisher; Cheryl Klein, executive editor; Emily Clement, assistant editor. Imprint of Scholastic, Inc. Publishes hardcover, paperback, and e-book editions.

FICTION "Arthur A. Levine is looking for distinctive literature, for children and young adults, for whatever's extraordinary." Averages 18-20 total titles/year.

HOW TO CONTACT Query. Please follow submission guidelines. Responds in 1 month to queries; 5 months to mss. Publishes a book 18 months after acceptance.

TERMS Guidelines online.

Ⓐ LITTLE, BROWN AND CO. BOOKS FOR YOUNG READERS

Hachette Book Group USA, 237 Park Ave., New York NY 10017. (212)364-1100. **Fax:** (212)364-0925. **E-mail:** pamela.gruber@hbgusa.com. **Website:** www.lb-kids.com; www.lb-teens.com. **Contact:** Pamela Gruber. "Little, Brown and Co. Children's Publishing publishes all formats including board books, picture books, middle grade fiction, and nonfiction YA titles. We are looking for strong writing and presentation, but no predetermined topics." Only interested in solicited agented material. Publishes 100-150 titles/year. **Contact:** Megan Tingley, executive VP and publisher; Alvina Ling, executive editorial director; Andrea Spooner, editorial director; Jennifer Bailey Hunt, executive editor; Elizabeth Bewley and Connie Hsu, senior editors, Mary-Kate Gaudet, editor, Dave Caplan, creative director, Patti Ann Harris, executive art director.

FICTION Picture books: humor, adventure, animal, contemporary, history, multicultural, folktales. Young adults: contemporary, humor, multicultural, suspense/mystery, chick lit. Multicultural needs include "any material by, for and about minorities." Average word length: picture books—1,000; young readers—6,000; middle readers—15,000- 50,000; young adults—50,000 and up.

NONFICTION Writers should avoid looking for the 'issue' they think publishers want to see, choosing instead topics they know best and are most enthusiastic about/inspired by. Middle readers, young adults: arts/crafts, history, multicultural, nature, self help, social issues, sports, science. Average word length: middle readers—15,000-25,000; young adults—20,000-40,000.

HOW TO CONTACT Agented submissions only. Agented submissions only. Responds in 1 month to queries; 2 months to proposals and mss. Publishes ms 2 years after acceptance.

ILLUSTRATION Works with 40 illustrators/year. Illustrations only: Query art director with b&w and color samples; provide résumé, promo sheet or tearsheets to be kept on file. Does not respond to art samples. Do not send originals; copies only. Accepts illustration samples by postal mail or e-mail.

PHOTOGRAPHY Works on assignment only. Model/property releases required; captions required. Publishes photo essays and photo concept books. Uses 35mm transparencies. Photographers should provide résumé, promo sheets or tearsheets to be kept on file.

TERMS Pays authors royalties based on retail price. Pays illustrators and photographers by the project or royalty based on retail price. Sends galleys to authors; dummies to illustrators. Pays negotiable advance.

TIPS "In order to break into the field, authors and illustrators should research their competition and try to come up with something outstandingly different."

LUCKY MARBLE BOOKS

PageSpring Publishing, P.O. Box 21133, Columbus OH 43221. **E-mail:** yaeditor@pagespringpublishing.com. **Website:** www.luckymarblebooks.com. "Lucky Marble Books publishes novel-length young adult and middle grade fiction. We are looking for engaging characters and well-crafted plots that keep our readers turning the page. We accept e-mail queries only; see our website for details." Publishes trade paperback and electronic originals.

HOW TO CONTACT Submit proposal package via e-mail. Include synopsis and 3 sample chapters. Responds in 3 months to queries and mss. Publishes ms 6-9 months after acceptance.

TERMS Pays royalty. Guidelines online.

TIPS "We love books that jump right into the story and sweep us along!"

MAGINATION PRESS

750 First St. NE, Washington DC 20002. (202)336-5618. **Fax:** (202)336-5624. **E-mail:** rteeter@apa.org. **Website:** www.apa.org. **Contact:** Kristine Enderle, managing editor. Magination Press is an imprint of the American Psychological Association. "We publish books dealing with the psycho/therapeutic resolution of children's problems and psychological issues with a strong self-help component." Submit complete ms. Materials returned only with SASE. Publishes 12 titles/year. 75% of books from first-time authors.

FICTION All levels: psychological and social issues, self-help, health, parenting concerns and, special needs. Picture books, middle school readers.

NONFICTION All levels: psychological and social issues, self-help, health, multicultural, special needs.

HOW TO CONTACT Responds to queries in 1-2 months; mss in 2-6 months. Publishes a book 18-24 months after acceptance.

ILLUSTRATION Works with 10-15 illustrators/year. Reviews ms/illustration packages. Will review artwork for future assignments. Responds only if interested, or immediately if SASE or response card is included. "We keep samples on file."

MARTIN SISTERS PUBLISHING, LLC

E-mail: submissions@martinsisterspublishing.com. **Website:** www.martinsisterspublishing.com. **Contact:** Denise Melton, Publisher/Editor (Fiction/nonfiction); Melissa Newman, Publisher/Editor (Fiction/nonfiction). Firm/imprint publishes trade and mass market paperback originals; electronic originals. Publishes 12 titles/year. 75% of books from first-time authors. 100% from unagented writers.

HOW TO CONTACT Send query letter only. Send query letter only. Responds in 1 month on queries, 2 months on proposals, 3-6 months on mss. Time between acceptance of ms and publication is 6 months.

TERMS Pays 7.5% royalty/max on retail price. No advance offered. Catalog and guidelines available online.

⭕ MASTER BOOKS

P.O. Box 726, Green Forest AR 72638. (870)438-5288. **Fax:** (870)438-5120. **E-mail:** submissions@newleaf press.net; craig@newleafpress.net. **Website:** www. masterbooks.net. **Contact:** Craig Froman, acquisitions editor. Publishes 3 middle readers/year; 2 young adult nonfiction titles/year; 20 adult trade books/year. 10% of books from first-time authors.

NONFICTION Picture books: activity books, animal, nature/environment, creation. Young readers, middle readers, young adults: activity books, animal, biography Christian, nature/environment, science, creation.

HOW TO CONTACT Submission guidelines on website. Responds in 4 months. Publishes book 1 year after acceptance.

TERMS Pays authors royalty of 3-15% based on wholesale price. Book catalog available upon request. Guidelines online.

TIPS "All of our children's books are creation-based, including topics from the Book of Genesis. We look also for home school educational material that would be supplementary to a home school curriculum."

MARGARET K. MCELDERRY BOOKS

Imprint of Simon & Schuster Children's Publishing Division, 1230 Sixth Ave., New York NY 10020.

(212)698-7200. **Website:** www.simonsayskids.com. **Contact:** Justin Chanda, vice president; Karen Wojtyla, editorial director; Gretchen Hirsch, associate editor; Emily Fabre, assistant editor; Ann Bobco, executive art director.. "Margaret K. McElderry Books publishes hardcover and paperback trade books for children from pre-school age through young adult. This list includes picture books, middle grade and teen fiction, poetry, and fantasy. The style and subject matter of the books we publish is almost unlimited. We do not publish textbooks, coloring and activity books, greeting cards, magazines, pamphlets, or religious publications." Publishes 30 titles/year. 15% of books from first-time authors. 50% from unagented writers.

FICTION We will consider any category. Results depend on the quality of the imagination, the artwork, and the writing. Average word length: picture books—500; young readers—2,000; middle readers—10,000-20,000; young adults—45,000-50,000. No unsolicited mss.

NONFICTION Looks for originality of ideas, clarity and felicity of expression, well-organized plot and strong characterization (fiction) or clear exposition (nonfiction); quality. Accept query letters with SASE only for picture books; query letter with first 3 chapters, SASE for middle grades and young adult novels. No unsolicited mss.

HOW TO CONTACT Send query letter with SASE.

TERMS Pays authors royalty based on retail price. Pays illustrator royalty of by the project. Pays photographers by the project. Original artwork returned at job's completion. Offers $5,000-8,000 advance for new authors. Guidelines for #10 SASE.

TIPS "Read! The children's book field is competitive. See what's been done and what's out there before submitting. We look for high quality: an originality of ideas, clarity and felicity of expression, a well organized plot, and strong character-driven stories. We're looking for strong, original fiction, especially mysteries and middle grade humor. We are always interested in picture books for the youngest age reader. Study our titles."

MEDALLION MEDIA GROUP

100 S. River St., Aurora IL 60506. (630)513-8316. **E-mail:** emily@medallionmediagroup.com. **E-mail:** submissions@medallionmediagroup.com. **Website:** medallionmediagroup.com. **Contact:** Emily Steele,

editorial director. "We are an independent, innovative publisher looking for compelling, memorable stories told in distinctive voices." Publishes trade paperback, hardcover, e-book originals, book apps, and TREEbook™.

FICTION Word count: 40,000-90,000 for YA; 60,000-120,000 for all others. No short stories, anthologies, erotica.

NONFICTION Agented only.

HOW TO CONTACT Submit first 3 consecutive chapters and a synopsis through our online submission form. Please query. Responds in 2-3 months to mss. Publishes ms 1-2 years after acceptance.

TERMS Offers advance. Guidelines online.

TIPS "We are not affected by trends. We are simply looking for well-crafted, original, compelling works of fiction and nonfiction. Please visit our website for the most current guidelines prior to submitting anything to us."

MERIT PRESS

A division of Adams Media (part of F+W Media), 57 Littlefield St, Avon, MA 02322. (508)427-7100. **E-mail:** meritpress@fwmedia.com. **Website:** www.adamsmedia.com/merit-press-books. **Contact:** Jacquelyn Mitchard, editor-in-chief.

○ Focuses on contemporary YA, usually based in reality.

FICTION "Natural is good; a little bit of supernatural (as in, perhaps foreseeing the future) is okay, too. Normal is great (at least until something happens) but not paranormal. What we are not seeking right now is tryphids, blood drinkers, flesh eaters and even yetis (much though we love them)."

HOW TO CONTACT "We do accept direct submissions as well as submissions from literary agents. We don't accept submissions in hard copy. Send full or partial manuscripts and queries to meritpress@fwmedia.com."

TIPS "I want to publish the next *Carrie, The Book Thief, National Velvet, Tuck Everlasting, Mr. and Mrs. Bo Jo Jones,* and *The Outsiders.* These will be the classics for a new generation, and they're being written right now. Since suspense (noir or pastel, comic or macabre) is my love, I hope I have a sense for finding those stories. As it turns out, a big part of my vocation, at this point in my career, is the desire to discover and nurture great new writers, and to put great books in the hands of great readers."

MERIWETHER PUBLISHING LTD.

885 Elkton Dr., Colorado Springs CO 80907. (719)594-9916. **Fax:** (719)594-4422. **E-mail:** editor@meriwether.com. **Website:** www.meriwether.com. **Contact:** Ted Zapel; Rhonda Wray. "Our niche is drama. Our books cover a wide variety of theatre subjects from play anthologies to theatrecraft. We publish books of monologs, duologs, short one-act plays, scenes for students, acting textbooks, how-to speech and theatre textbooks, improvisation and theatre games. We also publish anthologies of Christian sketches. We do not publish works of fiction or devotionals." 75% of books from first-time authors.

FICTION Middle readers, young adults: anthology, contemporary, humor, religion. "We publish plays, not prose-fiction. Our emphasis is comedy plays instead of educational themes."

NONFICTION Middle readers: activity books, how-to, religion, textbooks. Young adults: activity books, drama/theater arts, how-to church activities, religion. Average length: 250 pages.

HOW TO CONTACT Responds to queries in 3 weeks, mss in 2 months or less. Publishes book 6-12 months after acceptance.

ILLUSTRATION "We do our illustration in house."

TERMS Pays authors royalty of 10% based on retail or wholesale price.

TIPS "We are currently interested in finding unique treatments for theater arts subjects: scene books, how-to books, musical comedy scripts, monologs and short comedy plays for teens."

MILKWEED EDITIONS

1011 Washington Ave. S., Suite 300, Minneapolis MN 55415. (612)332-3192. **Fax:** (612)215-2550. **E-mail:** submissions@milkweed.org. **Website:** www.milkweed.org. Publishes 3-4 middle readers/year. 25% of books by first-time authors. **Contact:** Patrick Thomas, editor and program director. "Milkweed Editions publishes with the intention of making a humane impact on society, in the belief that literature is a transformative art uniquely able to convey the essential experiences of the human heart and spirit. To that end, Milkweed Editions publishes distinctive voices of literary merit in handsomely designed, visually dynamic books, exploring the ethical, cultural, and esthetic issues that free societies need continually to address." Publishes hardcover, trade paperback, and electronic originals; trade paperback and electronic reprints. Publishes 15-20 titles/year. 25% of books from first-time authors. 75% from unagented writers.

FICTION Novels for adults and for readers 8-13. High literary quality. For adult readers: literary fiction, nonfiction, poetry, essays. Middle readers: adventure, contemporary, fantasy, multicultural, nature/environment, suspense/mystery. Average length: middle readers—90-200 pages. No romance, mysteries, science fiction.

HOW TO CONTACT Query with SASE, submit completed ms. Responds in 6 months. Publishes book in 18 months.

TERMS Pays authors variable royalty based on retail price. Offers advance against royalties. Pays varied advance from $500-10,000. Book catalog online. Guidelines online.

TIPS "We are looking for excellent writing with the intent of making a humane impact on society. Please read submission guidelines before submitting and acquaint yourself with our books in terms of style and quality before submitting. Many factors influence our selection process, so don't get discouraged. Nonfiction is focused on literary writing about the natural world, including living well in urban environments."

THE MILLBROOK PRESS

Lerner Publishing Group, 1251 Washington Ave N, Minneapolis MN 55401. **Website:** www.lernerbooks.com. **Contact:** Carol Hinz, editorial director. "Millbrook Press publishes informative picture books, illustrated nonfiction titles, and inspiring photo-driven titles for grades K–5. Our authors approach curricular topics with a fresh point of view. Our fact-filled books engage readers with fun yet accessible writing, high-quality photographs, and a wide variety of illustration styles. We cover subjects ranging from the parts of speech and other language arts skills; to history, science, and math; to art, sports, crafts, and other interests. Millbrook Press is the home of the best-selling Words Are CATegorical® series and Bob Raczka's Art Adventures."

"We do not accept unsolicited manuscripts from authors. Occasionally, we may put out a call for submissions, which will be announced on our website."

MITCHELL LANE PUBLISHERS, INC.

P.O. Box 196, Hockessin DE 19707. (302)234-9426. **Fax:** (866)834-4164. **E-mail:** barbaramitchell@mitchelllane.com. **Website:** www.mitchelllane.com. **Contact:** Barbara Mitchell, publisher. Publishes hardcover and library bound originals. Publishes 80 titles/year. 0% of books from first-time authors. 90% from unagented writers.

NONFICTION Young readers, middle readers, young adults: biography, nonfiction, and curriculum-related subjects. Average word length: 4,000-50,000 words. Recently published: *My Guide to US Citizenship, Rivers of the World* and *Vote America*.

HOW TO CONTACT Query with SASE. All unsolicited mss discarded. 100 queries received/year. 5 mss received/year. Responds only if interested to queries. Publishes ms 1 year after acceptance.

ILLUSTRATION Works with 2-3 illustrators/year. Reviews ms/illustration packages from artists. Query. Illustration only: Query with samples; send résumé, portfolio, slides, tearsheets. Responds only if interested. Samples not returned; samples filed.

PHOTOGRAPHY Buys stock images. Needs photos of famous and prominent minority figures. Captions required. Uses color prints or digital images. Submit cover letter, résumé, published samples, stock photo list.

TERMS Work purchased outright from authors (range: $350-2,000). Pays illustrators by the project (range: $40-400). Book catalog available free.

TIPS "We hire writers on a 'work-for-hire' basis to complete book projects we assign. Send résumé and writing samples that do not need to be returned."

MOODY PUBLISHERS

Moody Bible Institute, 820 N. LaSalle Blvd., Chicago IL 60610. (800)678-8812. **Fax:** (312)329-4157. **E-mail:** authors@moody.edu. **Website:** www.moodypublishers.org. "The mission of Moody Publishers is to educate and edify the Christian and to evangelize the non-Christian by ethically publishing conservative, evangelical Christian literature and other media for all ages around the world, and to help provide resources for Moody Bible Institute in its training of future Christian leaders." Publishes hardcover, trade, and mass market paperback originals. Publishes 60 titles/year. 1% of books from first-time authors. 80% from unagented writers.

NONFICTION "We are no longer reviewing queries or unsolicited manuscripts unless they come to us through an agent. Unsolicited proposals will be returned only if proper postage is included. We are not able to acknowledge the receipt of your unsolicited proposal."

HOW TO CONTACT Agented submissions only. Does not accept unsolicited nonfiction submissions. 1,500 queries received/year. 2,000 mss received/year. Responds in 2-3 months to queries. Publishes book 1 year after acceptance.

TERMS Royalty varies. Book catalog for 9×12 envelope and 4 first-class stamps. Guidelines for SASE and on website.

TIPS "In our fiction list, we're looking for Christian storytellers rather than teachers trying to present a message. Your motivation should be to delight the reader. Using your skills to create beautiful works is glorifying to God."

❹ NATIONAL GEOGRAPHIC CHILDREN'S BOOKS

1145 17th St. NW, Washington DC 20090-8199. (800)647-5463. **Website:** www.ngchildrensbooks. org. **Contact:** Nancy Feresten, senior vice-president of kids publishing and media; Jennifer Emmett, vice-president and editorial director; Eva Absher, design director. National Geographic Children's Books provides quality nonfiction for children and young adults by award-winning authors.

○ This market does not currently accept unsolicited mss.

NOMAD PRESS

2456 Christain St., White River Junction VT 05001. (802)649-1995. **Fax:** (802)649-2667. **E-mail:** rachel@ nomadpress.net; info@nomadpress.net. **Website:** www.nomadpress.net. **Contact:** Alex Kahan, publisher. "We produce nonfiction children's activity books that bring a particular science or cultural topic into sharp focus. Nomad Press does not accept unsolicited manuscripts. If authors are interested in contributing to our children's series, please send a writing resume that includes relevant experience/expertise and publishing credits."

○ Nomad Press does not accept picture books or fiction.

NONFICTION Middle readers: activity books, history, science. Average word length: middle readers—30,000.

HOW TO CONTACT Responds to queries in 3-4 weeks. Publishes book 1 year after acceptance.

TERMS Pays authors royalty based on retail price or work purchased outright. Offers advance against royalties. Catalog available on website.

TIPS "We publish a very specific kind of nonfiction children's activity book. Please keep this in mind when querying or submitting."

NORTH ATLANTIC BOOKS

2526 MLK Jr. Way, Berkeley CA 94704. **Website:** www. northatlanticbooks.com. **Contact:** Douglas Reil, associate publisher; Erin Wiegand, senior acquisitions editor. Publishes hardcover, trade paperback, and electronic originals; trade paperback and electronic reprints. Publishes 60 titles/year. 50% of books from first-time authors. 75% from unagented writers.

FICTION "We only publish fiction on rare occasions."

NONFICTION "See our submission guidelines on our website."

HOW TO CONTACT Submit proposal package including an outline, 3-4 sample chapters, and "a 75-word statement about the book, your qualifications as an author, marketing plan/audience, for the book, and comparable titles." Submit proposal package including an outline, 3-4 sample chapters, and "a 75-word statement about the book, your qualifications as an author, marketing plan/audience, for the book, and comparable titles." Receives 200 mss/year. Responds in 3-6 months. Publishes ms 14 months after acceptance.

TERMS Pays royalty percentage on wholesale price. Book catalog free on request (if available). Guidelines online.

◔ ONSTAGE PUBLISHING

190 Lime Quarry Rd., Suite 106-J, Madison AL 35758-8962. (256)461-0661. **E-mail:** onstage123@knology. net. **Website:** www.onstagepublishing.com. **Contact:** Dianne Hamilton, senior editor. At this time, we only produce fiction books for ages 8-18. We are adding an eBook only side of the house for mysteries for grades 6-12. See our website for more information. We will not do anthologies of any kind. Query first for nonfiction projects as nonfiction projects must spark our interest. Now accepting e-mail queries and submissions. For submissions: Put the first 3 chapters in the body of the e-mail. Do not use attachments! We will no longer return any mss. Only an SASE envelope is needed. Send complete ms if under 20,000 words, otherwise send synopsis and first 3 chapters. 80% of books from first-time authors.

○ To everyone who has submitted a ms, we are currently about 6 months behind. We should get back on track eventually. Please feel free to submit your ms to other houses. OnStage Publishing understands that authors work very hard to produce the finished ms and we do not have to have exclusive submission rights. Please let us know if you sell your ms. Meanwhile, keep writing and we'll keep reading for our next acquisitions.

FICTION Middle readers: adventure, contemporary, fantasy, history, nature/environment, science fiction, suspense/mystery. Young adults: adventure, contemporary, fantasy, history, humor, science fiction, suspense/mystery. Average word length: chapter books—4,000-6,000 words; middle readers—5,000 words and up; young adults—25,000 and up. Recently published *China Clipper* by Jamie Dodson (an adventure for boys ages 12+); *Huntsville, 1892: Clara* (a chapter book for grades 3-5). "We do not produce picture books."

ILLUSTRATION Reviews ms/illustration packages from artists. Submit with 3 pieces of final art. **Contact:** Dianne Hamilton, senior editor. Illustrations only. Samples not returned.

TERMS Pays authors/illustrators/photographers advance plus royalties.

TIPS "Study our titles and get a sense of the kind of books we publish, so that you know whether your project is likely to be right for us."

ORCHARD BOOKS

557 Broadway, New York NY 10012. **E-mail:** mcroland@scholastic.com. **Website:** www.scholastic.com. **Contact:** Ken Geist, vice president/editorial director; David Saylor, vice president/creative director. Publishes 20 titles/year. 10% of books from first-time authors.

○ Orchard is not accepting unsolicited mss.

FICTION Picture books, early readers, and novelty: animal, contemporary, history, humor, multicultural, poetry.

TERMS Most commonly offers an advance against list royalties.

TIPS "Read some of our books to determine first whether your manuscript is suited to our list."

ⒶⒸ CHRISTY OTTAVIANO BOOKS

Macmillan Children's Publishing Group, 175 Fifth Ave., New York NY 10010. Part of Henry Holt Books for Young Readers. **Website:** http://us.macmillan.com/all/editorslist/general/christyottavianobooks.

○ The line's broad scope features author-illustrators and encompasses literary and commercial picture books and fiction for all ages with a focus on the middle-grade market. Books that encourage imagination and free-thinking, foster a sense of family and community, target the feelings of children, and speak directly to young people's interests as they explore various milestones—contemporary classics that both challenge and entertain inquisitive readers.

BOOKS The imprint's first books include *The Scrambled States of America Talent Show* by Laurie Keller; *Masterpiece* by Elise Broach; *Larry and the Meaning of Life* by Janet Tashjian; *Piper Reed, The Great Gypsy* by Kimberly Willis Holt; *Ralph's World Rocks* by Ralph Covert, illustrated by Charise Mericle Harper; and *Wild Boars Cook* by Meg Rosoff, illustrated by Sophie Blackall.

Ⓒ OUR SUNDAY VISITOR, INC.

200 Noll Plaza, Huntington IN 46750. **E-mail:** jlindsey@osv.com. **Website:** www.osv.com. **Contact:** Jacquelyn Lindsey; David Dziena; Bert Ghezzi; Cindy Cavnar; Tyler Ottinger, art director. "We are a Catholic publishing company seeking to educate and deepen our readers in their faith. Currently emphasizing devotional, inspirational, Catholic identity, apologetics, and catechetics." Publishes paperback and hardbound originals. Publishes 40-50 titles/year.

○ Our Sunday Visitor, Inc. is publishing only those children's books that are specifically Catholic. See website for specific submission guidelines.

NONFICTION Prefers to see well-developed proposals as first submission with annotated outline and definition of intended market; Catholic viewpoints on family, prayer, and devotional books, and Catholic heritage books. Picture books, middle readers, young readers, young adults.

HOW TO CONTACT Query, submit complete ms, or submit outline/synopsis and 2-3 sample chapters. Responds in 2 months. Publishes ms 1-2 years after acceptance.

TERMS Pays authors royalty of 10-12% net. Pays illustrators by the project (range: $25-1,500). Book catalog for 9×12 envelope and first-class stamps; ms guidelines available online.

TIPS "Stay in accordance with our guidelines."

RICHARD C. OWEN PUBLISHERS, INC.

P.O. Box 585, Katonah NY 10536. (914)232-3903; (800)262-0787. **E-mail:** richardowen@rcowen.com. **Website:** www.rcowen.com. **Contact:** Richard Owen, publisher. "We publish child-focused books, with inherent instructional value, about characters and situations with which five-, six-, and seven-year-old children can identify—books that can be read for meaning, entertainment, enjoyment and information. We include multicultural stories that present minorities in a positive and natural way. Our stories show the diversity in America." Not interested in lesson plans, or books of activities for literature studies or other content areas. Submit complete ms and cover letter.

○ "Due to high volume and long production time, we are currently limiting to nonfiction submissions only."

NONFICTION "Our books are for kindergarten, first- and second-grade children to read on their own. The stories are very brief—under 1,000 words—yet well structured and crafted with memorable characters, language, and plots. Picture books, young readers: animals, careers, history, how-to, music/dance, geography, multicultural, nature/environment, science, sports. Multicultural needs include: Good stories respectful of all heritages, races, cultural—African-American, Hispanic, American Indian." Wants lively stories. No "encyclopedic" type of information stories. Average word length: under 500 words.

HOW TO CONTACT Responds to mss in 1 year. Publishes book 2-3 years after acceptance.

ILLUSTRATION Works with 20 illustrators/year. Uses color artwork only. Illustration only: Send color copies/reproductions or photos of art or provide tearsheets; do not send slides or originals. Include SASE and cover letter. Responds only if interested; samples filed.

TERMS Pays authors royalty of 5% based on net price or outright purchase (range: $25-500). Offers no advances. Pays illustrators by the project (range: $100-2,000) or per photo (range: $100-150). Book catalog available with SASE. Ms guidelines with SASE or online.

TIPS "We don't respond to queries or e-mails. Please do not fax or e-mail us. Because our books are so brief, it is better to send an entire manuscript. We publish story books with inherent educational value for young readers—books they can read with enjoyment and success. We believe students become enthusiastic, independent, life-long learners when supported and guided by skillful teachers using good books. The professional development work we do and the books we publish support these beliefs."

PAGESPRING PUBLISHING

P.O. Box 2113, Columbus OH 43221. **E-mail:** ps@pagespringpublishing.com. **E-mail:** yaeditor@pagespringpublishing.com; weditor@pagespringpublishing.com. **Website:** www.pagespringpublishing.com. "PageSpring Publishing publishes young adult and middle grade titles under the Lucky Marble Books imprint and women's fiction under the Cup of Tea imprint. See imprint websites for submission details." Publishes trade paperback and electronic originals. Publishes 10-20 titles/year.

HOW TO CONTACT Submit proposal package including synopsis and 3 sample chapters. Responds to queries in 1 month. Publishes ms 6 months after acceptance.

TERMS Pays royalty on wholesale price. Guidelines online.

PAULINE BOOKS & MEDIA

50 St. Paul's Ave., Boston MA 02130. (617)522-8911. **Fax:** (617)541-9805. **E-mail:** design@paulinemedia.com; editorial@paulinemedia.com. **Website:** www.pauline.org. "Submissions are evaluated on adherence to Gospel values, harmony with the Catholic tradition, relevance of topic, and quality of writing." For board books and picture books, the entire manuscript should be submitted. For easy-to-read, young readers, and middle reader books and teen books, please send a cover letter accompanied by a synopsis and two sample chapters. "Electronic submissions are encouraged. We make every effort to respond to unsolicited submissions within 2 months." Publishes trade paperback originals and reprints. Publishes 40 titles/year. 15% of books from first-time authors. 5% from unagented writers.

FICTION Children's and teen fiction only. We are now accepting submissions for easy-to-read and middle reader chapter, and teen fiction. Please see our Writer's Guidelines.

NONFICTION Picture books, young readers, middle readers, teen: religion and fiction. Average word length: picture books—500-1,000; young readers—8,000-10,000; middle readers—15,000-25,000;

teen--30,000-50,000. Recently published *Shine: Choices to Make God Smile*, the Christopher Award-winning picture book by Genny Monchamp; *Forever You: A Book About Your Soul and Body* by Nicole Lataif; *My First Book of Saints; The Mass Explained for Kids* and *Teens Share the Word*. No memoir/autobiography, poetry, or strictly nonreligious works considered.

HOW TO CONTACT "Submit proposal package, including synopsis, 2 sample chapters, and cover letter; complete ms." Submit proposal package, including outline, 1-2 sample chapters, cover letter, synopsis, intended audience and proposed length. Responds in 2 months to queries, proposals, & mss. Publishes a book approximately 11-18 months after acceptance.

ILLUSTRATION Works with 10-15 illustrators/year. Uses color and black-and-white- artwork. Illustrations only: Send résumé and 4-5 color samples. Samples and résumés will be kept on file unless return is requested and SASE provided.

TERMS Varies by project, but generally are royalties with advance. Flat fees sometimes considered for smaller works. Book catalog available online. Guidelines available online & by e-mail.

TIPS "Manuscripts may or may not be explicitly catechetical, but we seek those that reflect a positive worldview, good moral values, awareness and appreciation of diversity, and respect for all people. All material must be relevant to the lives of readers and must conform to Catholic teaching and practice."

PAULIST PRESS

997 MacArthur Blvd., Mahwah NJ 07430. (201)825-7300. **Fax:** (201)825-8345. **Website:** www.paulist press.com. **Contact:** Mark-David Janus, CSP, publisher. "Paulist Press publishes ecumenical theology, Roman Catholic studies, and books on scripture, liturgy, spirituality, church history, and philosophy, as well as works on faith and culture. Our publishing is oriented toward adult-level nonfiction. We do not publish poetry or works of fiction, and we have scaled back our involvement in children's publishing."

HOW TO CONTACT Receives 250 submissions/year. Responds in 3 months to queries and proposals; 3-4 months on mss. Publishes a book 18-24 months after acceptance.

TERMS Royalties and advances are negotible. Illustrators sometimes receive a flat fee when all we need

are spot illustrations. Book catalog available online. Guidelines available online and by e-mail.

ⓐ PEACE HILL PRESS

Affiliate of W.W. Norton, 18021 The Glebe Ln., Charles City VA 23030. (804)829-5043. **Fax:** (804)829-5704. **E-mail:** info@peacehillpress.com. **Website:** www.peace hillpress.com. **Contact:** Peter Buffington, acquisitions editor. Publishes hardcover and trade paperback originals. Publishes 4-8 titles/year.

TERMS Pays 6-10% royalty on retail price. Pays $500-1,000 advance.

PEACHTREE CHILDREN'S BOOKS

Peachtree Publishers, Ltd., 1700 Chattahoochee Ave., Atlanta GA 30318-2112. (404)876-8761. **Fax:** (404)875-2578. **E-mail:** hello@peachtree-online.com. **Website:** www.peachtree-online.com. **Contact:** Helen Harriss, submissions editor. "We publish a broad range of subjects and perspectives, with emphasis on innovative plots and strong writing." Publishes hardcover and trade paperback originals. Publishes 30 titles/year. 25% of books from first-time authors. 25% from unagented writers.

FICTION Looking for very well-written middle grade and young adult novels. No adult fiction. No collections of poetry or short stories; no romance or science fiction.

NONFICTION No e-mail or fax queries of mss.

HOW TO CONTACT Submit complete ms with SASE. Submit complete ms with SASE, or summary and 3 sample chapters with SASE. Responds in 6 months and mss. Publishes ms 1 year after acceptance.

TERMS Pays royalty on retail price. Book catalog for 6 first-class stamps. Guidelines available online.

PELICAN PUBLISHING COMPANY

1000 Burmaster St., Gretna LA 70053. (504)368-1175. **Fax:** (504)368-1195. **E-mail:** editorial@pelicanpub.com. **Website:** www.pelicanpub.com. **Contact:** Nina Kooij, editor-in-chief. "We believe ideas have consequences. One of the consequences is that they lead to a best-selling book. We publish books to improve and uplift the reader. Currently emphasizing business and history titles." Publishes 20 young readers/year; 1 middle reader/year. "Our children's books (illustrated and otherwise) include history, biography, holiday, and regional. Pelican's mission is to publish books of quality and permanence that enrich the lives of those who read them." Publishes hardcover, trade paperback and mass market paperback originals and reprints.

FICTION We publish no adult fiction. Young readers: history, holiday, science, multicultural and regional. Middle readers: Louisiana History. Multicultural needs include stories about African-Americans, Irish-Americans, Jews, Asian-Americans, and Hispanics. Does not want animal stories, general Christmas stories, "day at school" or "accept yourself" stories. Maximum word length: young readers—1,100; middle readers—40,000. No young adult, romance, science fiction, fantasy, gothic, mystery, erotica, confession, horror, sex, or violence. Also no psychological novels.

NONFICTION "We look for authors who can promote successfully. We require that a query be made first. This greatly expedites the review process and can save the writer additional postage expenses." Young readers: biography, history, holiday, multicultural. Middle readers: Louisiana history, holiday, regional. No multiple queries or submissions.

HOW TO CONTACT Query with SASE. Submit outline, clips, 2 sample chapters, SASE. Query with SASE. Responds in 1 month to queries; 3 months to mss. Publishes a book 9-18 months after acceptance.

ILLUSTRATION Works with 20 illustrators/year. Reviews ms/illustration packages from artists. Query first. Illustrations only: Query with samples (no originals). Responds only if interested. Samples returned with SASE; samples kept on file.

TERMS Pays authors in royalties; buys ms outright "rarely." Illustrators paid by "various arrangements." Advance considered. Book catalog and ms guidelines online.

TIPS "We do extremely well with cookbooks, popular histories, and business. We will continue to build in these areas. The writer must have a clear sense of the market and knowledge of the competition. A query letter should describe the project briefly, give the author's writing and professional credentials, and promotional ideas."

Ⓐ PHILOMEL BOOKS

Imprint of Penguin Group (USA), Inc., 375 Hudson St., New York NY 10014. (212)414-3610. **Website:** www.us.penguingroup.com. **Contact:** Michael Green, president/publisher; Semadar Megged, art director. "We look for beautifully written, engaging manuscripts for children and young adults." Publishes hardcover originals. Publishes 8-10 titles/year. 5% of books from first-time authors. 20% from unagented writers.

FICTION All levels: adventure, animal, boys, contemporary, fantasy, folktales, historical fiction, humor, sports, multicultural. Middle readers, young adults: problem novels, science fiction, suspense/mystery. No concept picture books, mass-market "character" books, or series. Average word length: picture books—1,000; young readers—1,500; middle readers—14,000; young adult—20,000. No series or activity books. No generic, mass-market oriented fiction.

NONFICTION Picture books.

HOW TO CONTACT No unsolicited mss.

ILLUSTRATION Works with 8-10 illustrators/year. Reviews ms/illustration packages from artists. Query with art sample first. Illustrations only: Query with samples. Send résumé and tearsheets. Responds to art samples in 1 month. Original artwork returned at job's completion. Samples returned with SASE or kept on file.

TERMS Pays authors in royalties. Average advance payment "varies." Illustrators paid by advance and in royalties. Pays negotiable advance. Book catalog for 9×12 envelope and 4 first-class stamps. Guidelines for #10 SASE.

TIPS Wants "unique fiction or nonfiction with a strong voice and lasting quality. Discover your own voice and own story and persevere." Looks for "something unusual, original, well written. Fine art or illustrative art that feels unique. The genre (fantasy, contemporary, or historical fiction) is not so important as the story itself and the spirited life the story allows its main character."

Ⓞ PIANO PRESS

P.O. Box 85, Del Mar CA 92014. (619)884-1401. **Fax:** (858)755-1104. **E-mail:** pianopress@pianopress.com. **Website:** www.pianopress.com. **Contact:** Elizabeth C. Axford, editor. "We publish music-related books, either fiction or nonfiction, coloring books, songbooks, and poetry."

FICTION Picture books, young readers, middle readers, young adults: folktales, multicultural, poetry, music. Average word length: picture books—1,500-2,000.

NONFICTION Picture books, young readers, middle readers, young adults: multicultural, music/dance. Average word length: picture books—1,500-2,000.

HOW TO CONTACT Responds to queries in 3 months; mss in 6 months. Publishes book 1 year after acceptance.

ILLUSTRATION Works with 1 or 2 illustrators/year. Reviews ms/illustration packages from artists. Illustrations only: Query with samples. Responds in 3 months. Samples returned with SASE; samples filed.

PHOTOGRAPHY Buys stock and assigns work. Looking for music-related, multicultural. Model/property releases required. Uses glossy or flat, color or b&w prints. Submit cover letter, résumé, client list, published samples, stock photo list.

TERMS Pays authors, illustrators, and photographers royalty of 5-10% based on retail price. Book catalog available for #10 SASE and 2 first-class stamps.

TIPS "We are looking for music-related material only for any juvenile market. Please do not send non-music-related materials. Query first before submitting anything."

PIÑATA BOOKS

Imprint of Arte Publico Press, University of Houston, 4902 Gulf Fwy, Bldg 19, Rm 100, Houston TX 77204-2004. (713)743-2845. **Fax:** (713)743-3080. **E-mail:** submapp@mail.uh.edu. **Website:** www.latinoteca.com/arte-publico-press. **Contact:** Nicolas Kanellos, director. "Piñata Books is dedicated to the publication of children's and young adult literature focusing on U.S. Hispanic culture by U.S. Hispanic authors. Arte Publico's mission is the publication, promotion and dissemination of Latino literature for a variety of national and regional audiences, from early childhood to adult, through the complete gamut of delivery systems, including personal performance as well as print and electronic media." Publishes hardcover and trade paperback originals. Publishes 10-15 titles/year. 80% of books from first-time authors.

○ Accepts material from U.S./Hispanic authors only (living abroad OK). Mss, queries, synopses, etc., are accepted in either English or Spanish.

NONFICTION Piñata Books specializes in publication of children's and young adult literature that authentically portrays themes, characters and customs unique to U.S. Hispanic culture.

HOW TO CONTACT Submissions made through online submission form. Responds in 2-3 months to queries; 4-6 months to mss. Publishes book 2 years after acceptance.

ILLUSTRATION Works with 6 illustrators/year. Uses color artwork only. Reviews ms/illustration packages from artists. Query or send portfolio (slides, color copies). Illustrations only: Query with samples or send résumé, promo sheet, portfolio, slides, client list

and tearsheets. Responds only if interested. Samples not returned; samples filed.

TERMS Pays 10% royalty on wholesale price. Pays $1,000-3,000 advance. Book catalog and ms guidelines available via website or with #10 SASE.

TIPS "Include cover letter with submission explaining why your manuscript is unique and important, why we should publish it, who will buy it, etc."

PINEAPPLE PRESS, INC.

P.O. Box 3889, Sarasota FL 34230. (941)739-2219. **Fax:** (941)739-2296. **E-mail:** info@pineapplepress.com. **Website:** www.pineapplepress.com. **Contact:** June Cussen, executive editor. "We are seeking quality nonfiction on diverse topics for the library and book trade markets. Our mission is to publish good books about Florida." Publishes hardcover and trade paperback originals. Publishes 25 titles/year. 50% of books from first-time authors. 95% from unagented writers.

FICTION Picture books, young readers, middle readers, young adults: animal, folktales, history, nature/environment.

NONFICTION Picture books: animal, history, nature/environmental, science. Young readers, middle readers, young adults: animal, biography, geography, history, nature/environment, science. Recently published *Those Magical Manatees*, by Jan Lee Wicker and *Those Beautiful Butterflies*, by Sarah Cussen. We will consider most nonfiction topics when related to Florida.

HOW TO CONTACT Query or submit outline/synopsis and 3 sample chapters. Query or submit outline/synopsis and intro and 3 sample chapters. 1,000 queries received/year. 500 mss received/year. Responds to queries/samples/mss in 2 months. Publishes a book 1 year after acceptance.

ILLUSTRATION Works with 2 illustrators/year. Reviews ms/illustration packages from artists. Query with nonreturnable samples. Contact: June Cussen, executive editor. Illustrations only: Query with brochure, nonreturnable samples, photocopies, résumé. Responds only if interested. Samples returned with SASE, but prefers nonreturnable; samples filed.

TERMS Pays authors royalty of 10-15%. Book catalog for 9×12 SAE with $1.25 postage. Guidelines available online.

TIPS "Quality first novels will be published, though we usually only do one or two novels per year and they must be set in Florida. We regard the author/editor relationship as a trusting relationship with communication open both ways. Learn all you can about the publishing process and about how to promote your book once it is published. A query on a novel without a brief sample seems useless."

THE POISONED PENCIL

Poisoned Pen Press, 6962 E. 1st Ave., Suite 103, Scottsdale AZ 85251. (480)945-3375. **Fax:** (480)949-1707. **E-mail:** info@thepoisonedpencil.com. **E-mail:** www. thepoisonedpencil.submittable.com/submit. **Website:** www.thepoisonedpencil.com. **Contact:** Ellen Larson, editor. Publishes trade paperback and electronic originals.

🔾 Accepts young adult mysteries only.

FICTION "We publish only young adult mystery novels, 45,000 to 90,000 words in length. For our purposes, a young adult book is a book with a protagonist between the ages of 13 and 18. We are looking for both traditional and cross-genre young adult mysteries. We encourage off-beat approaches and narrative choices that reflect the complexity and ambiguity of today's world. Submissions from teens are very welcome. Avoid serial killers, excessive gore, and vampires (and other heavy supernatural themes). We only consider authors who live in the US or Canada, due to practicalities of marketing promotion. Avoid coincidence in plotting. Avoid having your sleuth leap to conclusions rather than discover and deduce. Pay attention to the resonance between character and plot; between plot and theme; between theme and character. We are looking for clean style, fluid storytelling, and solid structure. Unrealistic dialogue is a real turn-off."

HOW TO CONTACT Submit proposal package including synopsis, complete ms, and cover letter. 250 submissions received/year. Responds in 6 weeks to mss. Publishes ms 15 months after acceptance.

TERMS Pays 9-15% for trade paperback; 25-35% for eBooks. Pays advance of $1,000. Guidelines online.

TIPS "Our audience is young adults and adults who love YA mysteries."

Ⓐ PRICE STERN SLOAN, INC.

Penguin Group, 375 Hudson St., New York NY 10014. (212)366-2000. **Website:** us.penguingroup.com/static/pages/publishers/index.html. **Contact:** Francesco Sedita, vice-president/publisher. "Price Stern Sloan publishes quirky mass market novelty series for childrens as well as licensed movie tie-in books." Price

Stern Sloan only responds to submissions it's interested in publishing.

🔾 Price Stern Sloan does not accept e-mail submissions.

FICTION Publishes picture books and novelty/board books including Mad Libs Movie and Television Tie-ins, and unauthorized biographies. All book formats except for picture books. "We publish unique novelty formats and fun, colorful paperbacks and activity books. We also publish the Book with Audio Series *Wee Sing* and *Baby Loves Jazz*."

HOW TO CONTACT Agented submissions only.

TERMS Book catalog online.

TIPS "Price Stern Sloan publishes unique, fun titles."

Ⓐ PUFFIN BOOKS

Imprint of Penguin Group (USA), Inc., 375 Hudson St., New York NY 10014. (212)366-2000. **Website:** www.penguinputnam.com. **Contact:** Kristin Gilson, editorial director. "Puffin Books publishes high-end trade paperbacks and paperback reprints for preschool children, beginning and middle readers, and young adults." Publishes trade paperback originals and reprints. Publishes 175-200 titles/year. 1% of books from first-time authors. 5% from unagented writers.

NONFICTION "Women in history books interest us."

HOW TO CONTACT No unsolicited mss. Agented submissions only. Receives 600 queries and mss/year. Responds in 5 months. Publishes book 1 year after acceptance.

ILLUSTRATION Reviews artwork. Send color copies.

PHOTOGRAPHY Reviews photos. Send color copies.

TERMS Royalty varies. Pays varies advance. Book catalog for 9×12 SAE with 7 first-class stamps.

TIPS "Our audience ranges from little children 'first books' to young adult (ages 14-16). An original idea has the best luck."

Ⓐ PUSH

Scholastic, 557 Broadway, New York NY 10012. **E-mail:** dlevithan@scholastic.com. **Website:** www.thisispush.com. PUSH publishes new voices in teen literature. Publishes 6-9 titles/year. 50% of books from first-time authors.

🔾 PUSH does not accept unsolicited mss or queries, only agented or referred fiction/memoir.

TIPS "We only publish first-time writers (and then their subsequent books), so authors who have published previously should not consider PUSH. Also, for young writers in grades 7-12, we run the PUSH Novel Contest with the Scholastic Art & Writing Awards. Every year it begins in October and ends in March. Rules can be found on our website."

Ⓐ G.P. PUTNAM'S SONS HARDCOVER

Imprint of Penguin Group (USA), Inc., 375 Hudson, New York NY 10014. (212)366-2000. **Fax:** (212)366-2664. **Website:** www.penguinputnam.com. **Contact:** Jennifer Besser, vice-president and publisher; Nancy Paulsen, president and publisher (also publishes Nancy Paulsen Books); Cecilia Yung, vice-president and art director; Arianne Lewin, executive editor; Stacey Barney, editor. Publishes hardcover originals.

FICTION Agented submissions only.

HOW TO CONTACT Agented submissions only.

TERMS Pays variable royalties on retail price. Pays varies advance. Request book catalog through mail order department.

RAINBOW PUBLISHERS

P.O. Box 261129, San Diego CA 92196. (858)277-1167. **E-mail:** editor@rainbowpublishers.com. **Website:** www.rainbowpublishers.com; www.legacypresskids.com. "Our mission is to publish Bible-based, teacher resource materials that contribute to and inspire spiritual growth and development in kids ages 2-12."

NONFICTION Young readers, middle readers, young adult/teens: activity books, arts/crafts, how-to, reference, religion.

HOW TO CONTACT Responds to queries in 6 weeks; mss in 3 months.

ILLUSTRATION Works with 25 illustrators/year. Reviews ms/illustration packages from artists. Submit ms with 2-5 pieces of final art. Illustrations only: Query with samples. Responds in 6 weeks. Samples returned with SASE; samples filed.

TERMS Pays illustrators by the project (range: $300 and up). For authors work purchased outright (range: $500 and up).

TIPS "Our Rainbow imprint publishes reproducible books for teachers of children in Christian ministries, including crafts, activities, games and puzzles. Our Legacy imprint publishes titles for children such as devotionals, fiction and Christian living. Please write for guidelines and study the market before submitting material."

RAIN TOWN PRESS

1111 E. Burnside St. #309, Portland OR 97214. (503)962-9612. **E-mail:** submissions@raintownpress.com. **Website:** www.raintownpress.com. **Contact:** Misty V'Marie, acquisitions editor; Ellery Harvey, art director. Publishes 1-4 middle readers; 1-4 young adult titles/year. 100% of books from first-time authors.

Ⓠ "We are Portland, Oregon's first independent press dedicated to publishing literature for middle grade and young adult readers. We hope to give rise to their voice, speaking directly to the spirit they embody through our books and other endeavors. The gray days we endure in the Pacific Northwest are custom-made for reading a good book—or in our case, making one. The rain inspires, challenges, and motivates us. To that end, we say: Let it drizzle. We will soon publish picture books."

FICTION Middle Readers/YA/Teens: Wants adventure, animal, contemporary, fantasy, folktales, graphic novels, health, hi-lo, history, humor, multicultural, nature/environment, problem novels, sci-fi, special needs, sports. Catalog available on website.

NONFICTION Middle Readers/YA/Teens: biography, concept, graphic novels, hi-lo, how-to.

HOW TO CONTACT Query. Submit complete ms. Query. Submit outline/synopsis and 2 sample chapters. Responds in 1-6 months. Publishes ms 1 year after acceptance.

ILLUSTRATION Reviews ms/illustration packages from artists (will review packages for future titles); uses both color and b&w. Submit query, link to online portfolio. Originals not returned. Does not show dummies to illustrators.

PHOTOGRAPHY Buys stock images and assigned work. Model/property releases required with submissions. Photo captions required. Use high-res digital materials. Send cover letter, client list, portolio (online preferred).

TERMS Pays 8-15% royalty on net sales. Does not pay advance. Catalog online. Guidelines online.

TIPS "The middle grade and YA markets have sometimes very stringent conventions for subject matter, theme, etc. It's most helpful if an author knows his/her genre inside and out. Read, read, read books that have successfully been published for your genre. This will ultimately make your writing more marketable. Also, follow a publisher's submission guidelines to a tee. We try to set writers up for success. Send us what we're looking for."

RAZORBILL

Penguin Group, 375 Hudson St., New York NY 10014. (212)414-3448. **Fax:** (212)414-3343. **E-mail:** laura. schechter@us.penguingroup.com; ben.schrank@ us.penguingroup.com. **Website:** www.razorbillbooks. com. **Contact:** Gillian Levinson, assistant edtor; Jessica Rothenberg, editor; Brianne Mulligan, editor; Casey McIntyre, associate publisher; Deborah Kaplan, vice president and executive art director. "This division of Penguin Young Readers is looking for the best and the most original of commercial contemporary fiction titles for middle grade and YA readers. A select quantity of nonfiction titles will also be considered." Publishes 30 titles/year.

FICTION Middle Readers: adventure, contemporary, graphic novels, fantasy, humor, problem novels. Young adults/teens: adventure, contemporary, fantasy, graphic novels, humor, multicultural, suspense, paranormal, science fiction, dystopian, literary, romance. Average word length: middle readers—40,000; young adult—60,000.

NONFICTION Middle readers and young adults/ teens: concept.

HOW TO CONTACT Submit cover letter with up to 30 sample pages. Submit cover letter with up to 30 sample pages. Responds in 1-3 months. Publishes book 1-2 after acceptance.

TERMS Offers advance against royalties.

TIPS "New writers will have the best chance of acceptance and publication with original, contemporary material that boasts a distinctive voice and well-articulated world. Check out www.razorbillbooks.com to get a better idea of what we're looking for."

RENAISSANCE HOUSE

465 Westview Ave., Englewood NJ 07631. (201)408-4048. **E-mail:** info@renaissancehouse.net. **Website:** www.renaissancehouse.net. Publishes biographies, folktales, coffee table books, instructional, textbooks, adventure, picture books, juvenile and young adult. Specializes in multicultural and bilingual titles, Spanish-English. Submit manuscript; e-mail submissions. Children's, educational, multicultural, and textbooks. Represents 80 illustrators. 95% of artwork handled is children's book illustration. Currently open to illustrators seeking representation. Open to both new and established illustrators.

FICTION Picture books: animal, folktales, multicultural. Young readers: animal, anthology, folktales, multicultural. Middle readers, young adult/teens: anthology, folktales, multicultural, nature/environment.

HOW TO CONTACT Responds to queries/mss in 2 weeks. Publishes ms 1 year after acceptance.

ILLUSTRATION Works with 25 illustrators/year. Uses color and b&w artwork. Reviews ms/illustration packages from artists. Send ms with dummy. Contact: Sam Laredo. Contact: Raquel Benatar. Responds in 3 weeks. Samples not returned; samples filed.

⊕ RIPPLE GROVE PRESS

P.O. Box 491, Hubbardston MA 01452. **E-mail:** submit@ripplegrovepress.com. **Website:** www.ripplegrovepress.com. Ripple Grove Press is a family-owned children's picture book publishing company started in 2013. "Our mission is to create picture books that come from life experiences, elegant imagination, and the deep passion in our hearts. We want each book to enlighten a child's mind with fun and wonder. Ripple Grove Press searches for a powerful 'timeless' feel in each book we publish. Our stories will make you laugh, think, or keep you guessing and dreaming." Publishes hardcover originals. Publishes 3-10 titles/year.

FICTION "Our focus is picture books for children aged 2-6. We want something unique, sweet, funny, touching, offbeat, colorful, surprising, charming, different, and creative."

HOW TO CONTACT Submit completed ms. Accepts submissions by mail and e-mail. Please submit a cover letter including a summary of your story, the age range of the story, a brief biography of yourself, and contact information. Submit completed mss only. Accepts submissions by mail and e-mail. Please submit a cover letter including a summary of your story, the age range of the story, a brief biography of yourself, and contact information. Responds to queries within 3 months. Average length of time between acceptance of a book-length ms and publication is 12-18 months.

TERMS Authors receive between 10-12% royalty on net receipt. Guidelines available online.

TIPS Also targeting the adults reading to the children. "We create books that children and adults want to read over and over again. Our books showcase art as well as stories and tie them together to create a unique and creative product."

Ⓐ ROARING BROOK PRESS

Macmillan Children's Publishing Group, 175 Fifth Ave., New York NY 10010. (646)307-5151. **E-mail:**

david.langva@roaringbrookpress.com. **E-mail:** press.inquiries@macmillanusa.com. **Website:** us.macmillan.com/RoaringBrook.aspx. **Contact:** David Langva; Simon Boughton, VP and publisher; Nancy Mercadeo, executive editor. Roaring Brook Press is an imprint of Macmillan, a group of companies that includes Henry Holt and Farrar, Straus & Giroux. Roaring Brook is not accepting unsolicited mss.

FICTION Picture books, young readers, middle readers, young adults: adventure, animal, contemporary, fantasy, history, humor, multicultural, nature/environment, poetry, religion, science fiction, sports, suspense/mystery.

NONFICTION Picture books, young readers, middle readers, young adults: adventure, animal, contemporary, fantasy, history, humor, multicultural, nature/environment, poetry, religion, science fiction, sports, suspense/mystery.

HOW TO CONTACT Not accepting unsolicited mss or queries

ILLUSTRATION Works with 25 illustrators/year. Illustrations only: Query with samples. Do not send original art; copies only through the mail. Samples returned with SASE.

TERMS Pays authors royalty based on retail price.

TIPS "You should find a reputable agent and have him/her submit your work."

ROSEN PUBLISHING

29 E. 21st St., New York NY 10010. (800)237-9932. **Fax:** (888)436-4643. **Website:** www.rosenpublishing.com. Artists and writers should contact customer service team through online form for information about contributing to Rosen Publishing. Rosen Publishing is an independent educational publishing house, established to serve the needs of students in grades Pre-K-12 with high interest, curriculum-correlated materials. Rosen publishes more than 700 new books each year and has a backlist of more than 7,000.

○ Note: Rosen Publishing is a difficult market to break into.

SASQUATCH BOOKS

1904 Third Ave., Suite 710, Seattle WA 98101. (206)467-4300. **Fax:** (206)467-4301. **E-mail:** ttabor@sasquatchbooks.com. **Website:** www.sasquatchbooks.com. **Contact:** Gary Luke, editorial director; Terence Maikels, acquisitions editor; Heidi Lenze, acquisitions editor. "Sasquatch Books publishes books for and from the Pacific Northwest, Alaska, and Califor-nia is the nation's premier regional press. Sasquatch Books' publishing program is a veritable celebration of regionally written words. Undeterred by political or geographical borders, Sasquatch defines its region as the magnificent area that stretches from the Brooks Range to the Gulf of California and from the Rocky Mountains to the Pacific Ocean. Our top-selling Best Places® travel guides serve the most popular destinations and locations of the West. We also publish widely in the areas of food and wine, gardening, nature, photography, children's books, and regional history, all facets of the literature of place. With more than 200 books brimming with insider information on the West, we offer an energetic eye on the lifestyle, landscape, and worldview of our region. Considers queries and proposals from authors and agents for new projects that fit into our West Coast regional publishing program. We can evaluate query letters, proposals, and complete mss." Publishes regional hardcover and trade paperback originals. Publishes 30 titles/year. 20% of books from first-time authors. 75% from unagented writers.

○ "When you submit to Sasquatch Books, please remember that the editors want to know about you and your project, along with a sense of who will want to read your book."

FICTION Young readers: adventure, animal, concept, contemporary, humor, nature/environment.

NONFICTION "We are seeking quality nonfiction works about the Pacific Northwest and West Coast regions (including Alaska to California). The literature of place includes how-to and where-to as well as history and narrative nonfiction." Picture books: activity books, animal, concept, nature/environment.

HOW TO CONTACT Query first, then submit outline and sample chapters with SASE. Send submissions to The Editors. E-mailed submissions and queries are not recommended. Please include return postage if you want your materials back. Responds to queries in 3 months. Publishes book 6-9 months after acceptance.

ILLUSTRATION Accepts material from international illustrators. Works with 5 illustrators/year. Uses both color and b&w. Reviews ms/illustration packages. For ms/illustration packages: Query. Submit ms/illustration packages to The Editors. Reviews work for future assignments. If interested in illustrating future titles, query with samples. Samples returned with SASE. Samples filed.

TERMS Pays royalty on cover price. Pays wide range advance. Book catalog for 9×12 envelope and 2 first-class stamps. Guidelines available online.

TIPS "We sell books through a range of channels in addition to the book trade. Our primary audience consists of active, literate residents of the West Coast."

SCARLETTA PRESS

10 S. 5th St., Suite 1105, Minneapolis MN 55402. (612)455-0252. **Website:** www.scarlettapress.com. Publishes 8-12 titles/year. 50% of books from first-time authors. 85% from unagented writers.

- "We accept submissions only during our reading period September 1-June 1."

FICTION Does not publish plays, screenplays, short story collections, or poetry.

HOW TO CONTACT Submit cover letter with synopsis, 1-2 sample chapters.

TERMS Pays 10-20% royalty. Guidelines online.

TIPS "Read our submission guidelines carefully before submitting."

Ⓐ SCHOLASTIC LIBRARY PUBLISHING

90 Old Sherman Turnpike, Danbury CT 06816. (203)797-3500. **Fax:** (203)797-3197. **E-mail:** slpservice@scholastic.com. **Website:** www.scholastic.com/librarypublishing. **Contact:** Phil Friedman, vice president/publisher; Kate Nunn, editor-in-chief; Marie O'Neil, art director. "Scholastic Library is a leading publisher of reference, educational, and children's books. We provide parents, teachers, and librarians with the tools they need to enlighten children to the pleasure of learning and prepare them for the road ahead. Publishes informational (nonfiction) for K-12; picture books for young readers, grades 1-3." Publishes hardcover and trade paperback originals.

- Accepts agented submissions only.

FICTION Publishes 1 picture book series, Rookie Readers, for grades 1-2. Does not accept unsolicited mss.

NONFICTION Photo-illustrated books for all levels: animal, arts/crafts, biography, careers, concept, geography, health, history, hobbies, how-to, multicultural, nature/environment, science, social issues, special needs, sports. Average word length: young readers—2,000; middle readers—8,000; young adult—15,000.

HOW TO CONTACT Does not accept fiction proposals. Query; submit outline/synopsis, resume, and/or list of publications, and writing sample. SASE required for response.

ILLUSTRATION Works with 15-20 illustrators/year. Uses color artwork and line drawings. Illustrations only: Query with samples or arrange personal portfolio review. Responds only if interested. Samples returned with SASE. Samples filed. Do not send originals. No phone or e-mail inquiries; contact only by mail.

TERMS Pays authors royalty based on net or work purchased outright. Pays illustrators at competitive rates.

Ⓐ SCHOLASTIC PRESS

Imprint of Scholastic, Inc., 557 Broadway, New York NY 10012. (212)343-6100. **Fax:** (212)343-4713. **Website:** www.scholastic.com. **Contact:** David Saylor, editorial director, Scholastic Press, creative director and associate publisher for all Scholastic hardcover imprints. Scholastic Press publishes fresh, literary picture book fiction and nonfiction; fresh, literary non-series or nongenre-oriented middle grade and young adult fiction. Currently emphasizing subtly handled treatments of key relationships in children's lives; unusual approaches to commonly dry subjects, such as biography, math, history, or science. De-emphasizing fairy tales (or retellings), board books, genre, or series fiction (mystery, fantasy, etc.). Publishes hardcover originals. Publishes 60 titles/year. 1% of books from first-time authors.

FICTION Looking for strong picture books, young chapter books, appealing middle grade novels (ages 8-11) and interesting and well-written young adult novels. Wants fresh, exciting picture books and novels--inspiring, new talent.

HOW TO CONTACT Agented submissions and previously published authors only. 2,500 queries received/year. Responds in 3 months to queries; 6-8 months to mss. Publishes book 2 years after acceptance.

ILLUSTRATION Works with 30 illustrators/year. Uses both b&w and color artwork. Illustrations only: Query with samples; send tearsheets. Responds only if interested. Samples returned with SASE. Original artwork returned at job's completion.

TERMS Pays royalty on retail price. Pays variable advance.

TIPS "Read *currently* published children's books. Revise, rewrite, rework and find your own voice, style and subject. We are looking for authors with a strong and unique voice who can tell a great story and have the ability to evoke genuine emotion. Children's publishers are becoming more selective, looking for irresistible talent and fairly broad appeal, yet still very willing to take risks, just to keep the game interesting."

Ⓐ SCHWARTZ & WADE BOOKS

Random House Children's Books, 1745 Broadway, New York NY 10019. **Website:** www.randomhousekids.com. Schwartz & Wade Books is an imprint of Random House Children's Books, co-directed by Anne Schwartz and Lee Wade, who take a unique approach to the creative process and believe that the best books for children grow from a seamless collaboration between editorial and design.

Ⓞ This market does not accept unsolicited submissions, proposals, mss, or submission queries. Recommends that authors work with an established literary agent.

SEEDLING CONTINENTAL PRESS

520 E. Bainbridge St., Elizabethtown PA 17022. **E-mail:** bspencer@continentalpress.com. **Website:** www.continentalpress.com. **Contact:** Megan Bergonzi. Publishes books for classroom use only for the beginning reader in English. "Natural language and predictable text are requisite. Patterned text is acceptable, but must have a unique story line. Poetry, books in rhyme and full-length picture books are not being accepted. Illustrations are not necessary."

FICTION Young readers: adventure, animal, folktales, humor, multicultural, nature/environment. Does not accept texts longer than 12 pages or over 300 words. Average word length: young readers—100.

NONFICTION Young readers: animal, arts/crafts, biography, careers, concept, multicultural, nature/environment, science. Does not accept texts longer than 12 pages or over 300 words. Average word length: young readers—100.

HOW TO CONTACT Submit complete ms. Submit complete ms. Responds to mss in 6 months. Publishes book 1-2 years after acceptance.

ILLUSTRATION Works with 8-10 illustrators/year. Uses color artwork only. Reviews ms/illustration packages from artists. Submit ms with dummy. Illustrations only: Color copies or line art. Responds only if interested. Samples returned with SASE only; samples filed if interested.

PHOTOGRAPHY Buys photos from freelancers. Works on assignment only. Model/property releases required. Uses color prints and 35mm transparencies. Submit cover letter and color promo piece.

TERMS Work purchased outright from authors.

TIPS "See our website. Follow writers' guidelines carefully and test your story with children and educators."

Ⓐ SIMON & SCHUSTER BOOKS FOR YOUNG READERS

Imprint of Simon & Schuster Children's Publishing, 1230 Avenue of the Americas, New York NY 10020. (212)698-7000. **Fax:** (212)698-2796. **Website:** www.simonsayskids.com. "Simon and Schuster Books For Young Readers is the Flagship imprint of the S&S Children's Division. We are committed to publishing a wide range of contemporary, commercial, award-winning fiction and nonfiction that spans every age of children's publishing. BFYR is constantly looking to the future, supporting our foundation authors and franchises, but always with an eye for breaking new ground with every publication. We publish high-quality fiction and nonfiction for a variety of age groups and a variety of markets. Above all, we strive to publish books that we are passionate about." Publishes hardcover originals. Publishes 75 titles/year.

Ⓞ No unsolicited mss. All unsolicited mss returned unopened.

NONFICTION Picture books: concept. All levels: narrative, current events, biography, history. "We're looking for picture books or middle grade nonfiction that have a retail potential. No photo essays."

HOW TO CONTACT Agented submissions only. Agented submissions only. Publishes ms 2-4 years after acceptance.

ILLUSTRATION Works with 70 illustrators/year. Do not submit original artwork. Does not accept unsolicited or unagented illustration submissions.

TERMS Pays variable royalty on retail price. Guidelines online.

TIPS "We're looking for picture books centered on a strong, fully-developed protagonist who grows or changes during the course of the story; YA novels that are challenging and psychologically complex; also imaginative and humorous middle-grade fiction. And we want nonfiction that is as engaging as fiction. Our imprint's slogan is 'Reading You'll Remember.' We aim to publish books that are fresh, accessible and family-oriented; we want them to have an impact on the reader."

SKINNER HOUSE BOOKS

The Unitarian Universalist Association, 25 Beacon St., Boston MA 02108. (617)742-2100 ext. 603. **Fax:** (617)742-7025. **E-mail:** bookproposals@uua.org. **Website:** www.uua.org/publications/skinnerhouse. **Contact:** Betsy Martin. "We publish titles in Unitarian Universalist faith, liberal religion, history, biography, worship, and issues of social justice. Most of our children's titles are intended for religious education or worship use. They reflect Unitarian Universalist values. We also publish inspirational titles of poetic prose and meditations. Writers should know that Unitarian Universalism is a liberal religious denomination committed to progressive ideals. Currently emphasizing social justice concerns." Publishes trade paperback originals and reprints. Publishes 10-20 titles/year. 50% of books from first-time authors. 100% from unagented writers.

FICTION All levels: anthology, multicultural, nature/environment, religion.

NONFICTION All levels: activity books, multicultural, music/dance, nature/environment, religion.

HOW TO CONTACT Query or submit proposal with cover letter, TOC, 2 sample chapters. Query or submit proposal with cover letter, TOC, 2 sample chapters. Responds to queries in 3 weeks. Publishes book 1 year after acceptance.

ILLUSTRATION Works with 2 illustrators/year. Uses both color and b&w. Reviews ms/illustration packages from artists. Query. Contact: Suzanne Morgan, design director. Responds only if interested. Samples returned with SASE.

PHOTOGRAPHY Buys stock images and assigns work. Contact: Suzanne Morgan, design director. Uses inspirational types of photo's. Model/property releases required; captions required. Uses color, b&w. Submit cover letter, resume.

TERMS Book catalog for 6×9 SAE with 3 first-class stamps. Guidelines online.

TIPS "From outside our denomination, we are interested in manuscripts that will be of help or interest to liberal churches, Sunday School classes, parents, ministers, and volunteers. Inspirational/spiritual and children's titles must reflect liberal Unitarian Universalist values."

Ⓐ LIZZIE SKURNICK BOOKS

Ig Publishing, 392 Clinton Ave., Brooklyn NY 11238. (718)797-0676. **E-mail:** lizzie@lizzieskurnickbooks.com; robert@igpub.com. **Website:** http://lizzieskurnickbooks.com; http://igpub.com. **Contact:** Lizzie Skurnick, editor-in-chief; Robert Lasner, editor-in-chief (editorial and media inquiries); Elizabeth Clementson, publisher. Lizzie Skurnick Books, an imprint of Ig Publishing, is devoted to reissuing the very best in young adult literature, from the classics of the 1930s and 1940s to the social novels of the 1970s and 1980s. Among the authors already published, and to be published, are Lois Duncan, Ellen Crawford, Ernest J. Gaines, Lila Perl, Berthe Amoss, Sandra Scoppettone, M.E. Kerr, Sydney Taylor, Norma Klein, Brenda Wilkinson, Norma Fox Mazer, and Joan Lowery Nixon. The imprint also publishes some new children's book titles, but wishes to receive submissions from agented writers only.

Ⓞ Ig does not accept unsolicited mss, either by e-mail or regular mail. If you have a ms that you would like Ig to take a look at, send a query to the attention of Robert Lasner, editor-in-chief. If interested, they will contact. All unsolicited mss will be discarded. Prefers queries by e-mail only.

SLEEPING BEAR PRESS

315 East Eisenhower Pkwy, Suite 200, Ann Arbor MI 48108. (800)487-2323. **Fax:** (734)794-0004. **E-mail:** customerservice@sleepingbearpress.com. **Website:** www.sleepingbearpress.com. **Contact:** Heather Hughes.

Ⓞ Currently not accepting ms submissions or queries at this time. "Please check back for further updates."

FICTION Picture books: adventure, animal, concept, folktales, history, multicultural, nature/environment, religion, sports. Young readers: adventure, animal, concept, folktales, history, humor, multicultural, nature/environment, religion, sports. Average word length: picture books—1,800.

TERMS Book catalog available via e-mail.

SPINNER BOOKS

University Games, 2030 Harrison St., San Francisco CA 94107. (415)503-1600. **Fax:** (415)503-0085. **E-mail:** info@ugames.com. **Website:** www.ugames.com. "Spinners Books publishes books of puzzles, games and trivia."

NONFICTION Picture books: games & puzzles.

HOW TO CONTACT Query. Responds to queries in 3 months; mss in 2 months only if interested. Publishes book 6 months after acceptance.

ILLUSTRATION Only interested in agented material. Uses both color and b&w. Illustrations only: Query with samples. Responds in 3 months only if interested. Samples not returned.

STANDARD PUBLISHING

Standex International Corp., 8805 Governor's Hill Dr., Suite 400, Cincinnati OH 45249. (800)543-1353. **E-mail:** customerservice@standardpub.com. **E-mail:** adultministry@standardpub.com; ministrytochildren@standardpub.com; ministrytoyouth@standardpub.com. **Website:** www.standardpub.com. Publishes resources that meet church and family needs in the area of children's ministry.

TERMS Guidelines and current publishing objectives available online.

STERLING PUBLISHING CO., INC.

Owned by Barnes & Noble Booksellers, 387 Park Ave. S., 11th Floor, New York NY 10016. (212)532-7160. **Fax:** (212)981-0508. **E-mail:** ragis@sterlingpublishing.com. **E-mail:** info@sterlingpublishing.com. **Website:** www.sterlingpublishing.com. "Sterling publishes highly illustrated, accessible, hands-on, practical books for adults and children." Publishes hardcover and paperback originals and reprints. 15% of books from first-time authors.

"Our mission is to publish high-quality books that educate, entertain, and enrich the lives of our readers."

FICTION Picture books. "At present we do not accept fiction."

NONFICTION Proposals on subjects such as crafting, decorating, outdoor living, and photography should be sent directly to Lark Books at their Asheville, North Carolina offices. Complete guidelines can be found on the Lark site: www.larkbooks.com/submissions. Publishes nonfiction only.

HOW TO CONTACT Submit outline, publishing history, 1 sample chapter (typed and double-spaced), SASE. "Explain your idea. Send sample illustrations where applicable. For children's books, please submit full mss. We do not accept electronic (e-mail) submissions. Be sure to include information about yourself with particular regard to your skills and qualifications in the subject area of your submission. It is help-

ful for us to know your publishing history—whether or not you've written other books and, if so, the name of the publisher and whether those books are currently in print."

ILLUSTRATION Works with 50 illustrators/year. Reviews ms/illustration packages from artists. Illustrations only: Send promo sheet. Contact: Karen Nelson, creative director. Responds in 6 weeks. Samples returned with SASE; samples filed.

PHOTOGRAPHY Buys stock and assigns work. Contact: Karen Nelson.

TERMS Pays royalty or work purchased outright. Offers advances (average amount: $2,000). Catalog online. Guidelines online.

TIPS "We are primarily a nonfiction activities-based publisher. We have a picture book list, but we do not publish chapter books or novels. Our list is not trend-driven. We focus on titles that will backlist well. "

STOREY PUBLISHING

210 MASS MoCA Way, North Adams MA 01247. (800)793-9396. **Fax:** (413)346-2196. **E-mail:** webmaster@storey.com. **Website:** www.storey.com. **Contact:** Deborah Balmuth, editorial director (building, sewing, gift). "The mission of Storey Publishing is to serve our customers by publishing practical information that encourages personal independence in harmony with the environment. We seek to do this in a positive atmosphere that promotes editorial quality, team spirit, and profitability. The books we select to carry out this mission include titles on gardening, small-scale farming, building, cooking, homebrewing, crafts, part-time business, home improvement, woodworking, animals, nature, natural living, personal care, and country living. We are always pleased to review new proposals, which we try to process expeditiously. We offer both work-for-hire and standard royalty contracts." Publishes hardcover and trade paperback originals and reprints. Publishes 40 titles/year. 25% of books from first-time authors. 60% from unagented writers.

HOW TO CONTACT 600 queries received/year. 150 mss received/year. Responds in 1 month to queries; 3 months to proposals/mss. Publishes book 2 years after acceptance.

TERMS We offer both work-for-hire and standard royalty contracts. Pays advance. Book catalog available free. Guidelines online.

SYNERGEBOOKS

948 New Highway 7, Columbia TN 38401. (863)956-3015. **Fax:** (863)588-2198. **E-mail:** synergebooks@aol.com. **Website:** www.synergebooks.com. **Contact:** Debra Staples, publisher/acquisitions editor. "SynergEbooks is first and foremost a digital publisher, so most of our marketing budget goes to those formats. Authors are required to direct-sell a minimum of 100 digital copies of a title before it's accepted for print." Publishes trade paperback and electronic originals. Publishes 40-60 titles/year. 95% of books from first-time authors. 99.9% from unagented writers.

FICTION SynergEbooks publishes at least 40 new titles a year, and only 1-5 of those are put into print in any given year.

HOW TO CONTACT Submit proposal package, including synopsis, 1-3 sample chapters, and marketing plans. 250 queries received/year.

TERMS Pays 15-40% royalty; makes outright purchase. Book catalog and guidelines online.

TIPS "At SynergEbooks, we work with the author to promote their work."

TANGLEWOOD BOOKS

P.O. Box 3009, Terre Haute IN 47803. **E-mail:** ptierney@tanglewoodbooks.com. **Website:** www.tanglewoodbooks.com. **Contact:** Kairi Hamlin, acquisitions editor; Peggy Tierney, publisher. "Tanglewood Press strives to publish entertaining, kid-centric books." Publishes 10 titles/year. 20% of books from first-time authors.

FICTION Picture books: adventure, animal, concept, contemporary, fantasy, humor. Average word length: picture books—800.

HOW TO CONTACT Not currently accepting submissions. Responds to mss in up to 18 months. Publishes book 2 years after acceptance.

ILLUSTRATION Accepts material from international illustrators. Works with 3-4 illustrators/year. Uses both color and b&w. Reviews ms/illustration packages. For ms/illustration packages: Send ms with sample illustrations. Submit ms/illustration packages to Peggy Tierney, publisher. If interested in illustrating future titles, query with samples. Submit samples to Peggy Tierney, publisher. Samples not returned. Samples filed.

TERMS Illustrators paid by the project for covers and small illustrations; royalty of 3-5% for picture books. Author sees galleys for review. Illustrators see dummies for review. Originals returned to artist at job's completion. Guidelines online.

TIPS "Please see lengthy 'Submissions' page on our website."

ⓐ KATHERINE TEGEN BOOKS

HarperCollins Children's Books, 195 Broadway, New York NY 10007. **Website:** www.harpercollins.com/. **Contact:** Katherine Tegen, vice-president and publisher; Anica Mrose Rissi, executive editor; Claudia Gabel, executive editor. Katherine Tegen Books publishes high-quality, commercial literature for children of all ages, including teens. Talented authors and illustrators who offer powerful narratives that are thought-provoking, well-written, and entertaining are the core of the Katherine Tegen Books imprint.

Ⓞ Katherine Tegen Books accepts agented work only.

TILBURY HOUSE

Wordsplice Studio, Inc., Tilbury House Publishers, 12 Starr Street, Thomaston ME 04861. (800)582-1899. **Fax:** (207)582-8772. **E-mail:** tilbury@tilburyhouse.com. **Website:** www.tilburyhouse.com. **Contact:** Karen Fisk, associate children's book editor; Jonathan Eaton, publisher; Fran Hodgkins, director of editorial, design, and promotion. Publishes 10 titles/year.

FICTION Picture books: multicultural, nature/environment. Special needs include books that teach children about tolerance and honoring diversity. Recently published *The Eye of the Whale*, by Jennifer O'Connell, illustrated by Jennifer O'Connell; *The Secret Pool*, by Kimberly Ridley, illustrated by Rebekah Raye

NONFICTION Regional adult biography/history/maritime/nature, and children's picture books that deal with issues, such as bullying, multiculturalism, etc.

HOW TO CONTACT Submit complete ms or outline/synopsis. Submit complete ms or outline/synopsis. Responds to mss in 2 months. Publishes ms 1 year after acceptance.

ILLUSTRATION Works with 2-3 illustrators/year. Illustrations only: Query with samples. Responds in 1 month. Samples returned with SASE. Original artwork returned at job's completion.

PHOTOGRAPHY Buys photos from freelancers. Works on assignment only.

TERMS Pays royalty based on wholesale price. Book catalog available free. Guidelines available online.

TIPS "We are always interested in stories that will encourage children to understand the natural world and the environment, as well as stories with social justice themes. We really like stories that engage children to become problem solvers as well as those that promote respect, tolerance and compassion." We do not publish books with personified animal characters; historical fiction; chapter books; fantasy."

Ⓐ TOR BOOKS

175 Fifth Ave., New York NY 10010. **Website:** www.tor-forge.com. **Contact:** Juliet Pederson, publishing coordinator. Publishes Publishes 5-10 middle readers/year; 5-10 young adult titles/year. titles/year.

○ Tor Books is the "world's largest publisher of science fiction and fantasy, with strong category publishing in historical fiction, mystery, western/Americana, thriller, YA."

FICTION Average word length: middle readers—30,000; young adults—60,000-100,000.

NONFICTION Middle readers and young adult: geography, history, how-to, multicultural, nature/environment, science, social issues. Does not want to see religion, cooking. Average word length: middle readers—25,000-35,000; young adults—70,000.

HOW TO CONTACT "We do not accept queries."

TERMS Pays author royalty. Pays illustrators by the project. Book catalog available for 9x12 SAE and 3 first-class stamps. See website for latest submission guidelines.

TIPS "Know the house you are submitting to, familiarize yourself with the types of books they are publishing. Get an agent. Allow him/her to direct you to publishers who are most appropriate. It saves time and effort."

TU BOOKS

Lee & Low Books, 95 Madison Ave., Ste. #1205, New York NY 10016. (212)779-4400. **Fax:** (212)683-1894. **E-mail:** tu@leeandlow.com. **Website:** www.leeandlow.com/p/tu.mhtml. **Contact:** Stacy Whitman, editorial director. Fantasy, science fiction, and myster: these genres draw in young readers like no other. Tu Books focuses on multicultural versions of these genres, publishing books for children and young adults that focus on diverse settings and characters in fantastic stories that are open to readers from many cultures around the world.

FICTION Focuses on well-told, exciting, adventurous fantasy, science fiction, and mystery novels featuring people of color set in worlds inspired by non-Western folklore or culture. Looking specifically for stories for both middle grade (ages 8-12) and young adult (ages 12-18) readers.

HOW TO CONTACT Tu Books is temporarily closed for submissions. Check website for when submissions will re-open. Mss should be sent through postal mail only. Mss shoudl be accompanied by a cover letter that includes a brief biography of the author, including publishing history. The letter should also state if the manuscript is a simultaneous or an exclusive submission. Include a synopsis and the first 3 chapters of the novel. Include full contact information on the cover letter and the first page of hte ms. Responds only if interested.

ILLUSTRATION Tu Books will consider fantasy, science fiction, and mystery artwork for book covers and spot illustrations, for novels aimed at older readers (ages 8-18). Artists should send a postcard sample with the address of their website porfolio, along with a rèsumè and/or cover letter as well as color copies, tear sheets, or other non-returnable illustration samples.

TERMS Guidelines available online.

TURN THE PAGE PUBLISHING LLC

P.O. Box 3179, Upper Montclair NJ 07043. **E-mail:** rlentin@turnthepagepublishing.com. **E-mail:** inquiry@turnthepagepublishing.com. **Website:** www.turnthepagepublishing.com. **Contact:** Roseann Lentin, editor-in-chief; Ann Kolakowski, editor. Publishes hardcover, trade paperback, electronic originals and trade paperback, electronic reprints. Publishes 12-15 titles/year. 95% of books from first-time authors. 100% from unagented writers.

FICTION "We like new, fresh voices who are not afraid to 'step outside the box,' with unique ideas and storylines. We prefer 'edgy' rather than 'typical.'"

HOW TO CONTACT Submit proposal package including synopsis and 3 sample chapters. Submit proposal package including outline, 3 sample chapters, author bio. Receives 100 queries/year; 50 mss/year. Responds in 2-3 months. Publishes ms 8 months after acceptance.

TERMS Pays 8-15% royalty on retail price. Book catalog online. Guidelines by e-mail.

TIPS "Our audience is made up of intelligent, sophisticated, forward-thinking, progressive readers, who are not afraid to consider reading something different to Turn the Page of their lives. We're an independent publisher, we're avant-garde, so if you're looking for run of the mill, don't submit here."

❹ TYNDALE HOUSE PUBLISHERS, INC.

351 Executive Dr., Carol Stream IL 60188. (800)323-9400. **Fax:** (800)684-0247. **Website:** www.tyndale.com. **Contact:** Katara Washington Patton, acquisitions; Talinda Iverson, art acquisitions. "Tyndale House publishes practical, user-friendly Christian books for the home and family." Publishes hardcover and trade paperback originals and mass paperback reprints. Publishes 15 titles/year.

FICTION "Christian truths must be woven into the story organically. No short story collections. Youth books: character building stories with Christian perspective. Especially interested in ages 10-14. We primarily publish Christian historical romances, with occasional contemporary, suspense, or standalones."

HOW TO CONTACT Agented submissions only. No unsolicited mss.

ILLUSTRATION Uses full-color for book covers, b&w or color spot illustrations for some nonfiction. Illustrations only: Query with photocopies (color or b&w) of samples, résumé.

PHOTOGRAPHY Buys photos from freelancers. Works on assignment only.

TERMS Pays negotiable royalty. Pays negotiable advance. Guidelines online.

TIPS "All accepted manuscripts will appeal to Evangelical Christian children and parents."

URJ PRESS

633 Third Ave., 7th Floor, New York NY 10017. (212)650-4120. **Fax:** (212)650-4119. **E-mail:** press@urj.org. **Website:** www.urjbooksandmusic.com. **Contact:** Michael H. Goldberg, editor-in-chief. "URJ publishes textbooks for the religious classroom, children's tradebooks and scholarly work of Jewish education import--no adult fiction and no YA fiction." Publishes hardcover and trade paperback originals. Publishes 22 titles/year. 70% of books from first-time authors. 90% from unagented writers.

◐ URJ Press publishes books related to Judaism.

NONFICTION Picture books, young readers, middle readers: religion. Average word length: picture books—1,500.

HOW TO CONTACT Submit proposal package, outline, bio, 1-2 sample chapters. 500 queries received/year. 400 mss received/year. Responds in 4 months. Publishes book 18-24 months after acceptance.

ILLUSTRATION Works with 5 illustrators/year. Reviews ms/illustration packages from artists. Send ms with dummy. Illustrations only: Send portfolio to be kept on file. Responds in 2 months. Samples returned with SASE. Looking specifically for Jewish themes.

PHOTOGRAPHY Buys stock and assigns work. Uses photos with Jewish content. Prefers modern settings. Submit cover letter and promo piece.

TERMS Pays 3-5% royalty on retail price. Makes outright purchase of $500-2,000. Pays $500-2,000 advance. Book catalog and ms guidelines online.

TIPS "Look at some of our books. Have an understanding of the Reform Judaism community. In addition to bookstores, we sell to Jewish congregations and Hebrew day schools."

❹ VIKING CHILDREN'S BOOKS

375 Hudson St., New York NY 10014. **E-mail:** avery studiopublicity@us.penguingroup.com. **Website:** www.penguingroup.com. **Contact:** Catherine Frank, executive editor. "Viking Children's Books is known for humorous, quirky picture books, in addition to more traditional fiction. We publish the highest quality fiction, nonfiction, and picture books for preschoolers through young adults." Publishes hardcover originals. Publishes 70 titles/year.

◐ Does not accept unsolicited submissions.

FICTION All levels: adventure, animal, contemporary, fantasy, history, humor, multicultural, nature/environment, poetry, problem novels, romance, science fiction, sports, suspense/mystery.

NONFICTION All levels: biography, concept, history, multicultural, music/dance, nature/environment, science, and sports.

HOW TO CONTACT Accepts agented mss only. Agented submissions only. Responds in 6 months. Publishes book 1-2 years after acceptance.

ILLUSTRATION Works with 30 illustrators/year. Responds to artist's queries/submissions only if interested. Samples returned with SASE only or samples filed. Originals returned at job's completion.

TERMS Pays 2-10% royalty on retail price or flat fee. Pays negotiable advance.

TIPS "No 'cartoony' or mass-market submissions for picture books."

◑ WEIGL PUBLISHERS INC.

350 Fifth Ave. 59th Floor, New York NY 10118. (866)649-3445. **Fax:** (866)449-3445. **E-mail:** linda@weigl.com. **Website:** www.weigl.com. **Contact:**

Heather Kissock, acquisitions. Publishes 25 young readers/year; 40 middle readers/year; 20 young adult titles/year. "Our mission is to provide innovative high-quality learning resources for schools and libraries worldwide at a competitive price." Publishes 85 titles/year. 15% of books from first-time authors.

NONFICTION Young readers: animal, biography, geography, history, multicultural, nature/environment, science. Middle readers: animal, biography, geography, history, multicultural, nature/environment, science, social issues, sports. Young adults: biography, careers, geography, history, multicultural, nature/environment, social issues. Average word length: young readers—100 words/page; middle readers—200 words/page; young adults—300 words/page.

HOW TO CONTACT Query by e-mail only. Publishes book 6-9 months after acceptance.

ILLUSTRATION Pays illustrators by the project. Catalog available on website.

PHOTOGRAPHY Pays per photo.

TERMS Catalog online.

WHITE MANE KIDS

73 W. Burd St., P.O. Box 708, Shippensburg PA 17257. (717)532-2237. **Fax:** (717)532-6110. **E-mail:** marketing@whitemane.com. **Website:** www.whitemane.com. **Contact:** Harold Collier, acquisitions editor.

FICTION Middle readers, young adults: history (primarily American Civil War). Average word length: middle readers—30,000. Does not publish picture books.

NONFICTION Middle readers, young adults: history. Average word length: middle readers—30,000. Does not publish picture books.

HOW TO CONTACT Query. Submit outline/synopsis and 2-3 sample chapters. Responds to queries in 1 month, mss in 3 months. Publishes book 18 months after acceptance.

ILLUSTRATION Works with 4 illustrators/year. Illustrations used for cover art only. Responds only if interested. Samples returned with SASE.

PHOTOGRAPHY Buys stock and assigns work. Submit cover letter and portfolio.

TERMS Pays authors royalty of 7-10%. Pays illustrators and photographers by the project. Book catalog and writer's guidelines available for SASE.

TIPS "Make your work historically accurate. We are interested in historically accurate fiction for middle and young adult readers. We do *not* publish picture

books. Our primary focus is the American Civil War and some America Revolution topics."

ALBERT WHITMAN & COMPANY

250 S. Northwest Hwy., Suite 320, Park Ridge IL 60068. (800)255-7675. **Fax:** (847)581-0039. **E-mail:** submissions@awhitmanco.com. **Website:** www.albertwhitman.com. Albert Whitman & Company publishes books for the trade, library, and school library market. Interested in reviewing the following types of projects: Picture book manuscripts for ages 2-8; novels and chapter books for ages 8-12; young adult novels; nonfiction for ages 3-12 and YA; art samples showing pictures of children. Best known for the classic series The Boxcar Children® Mysteries. Publishes in original hardcover, paperback, boardbooks. Publishes 60 titles/year. 10% of books from first-time authors. 50% from unagented writers.

🔘 "We are no longer reading unsolicited queries and manuscripts sent through the US mail. We now require these submissions to be sent by e-mail. You must visit our website for our guidelines, which include instructions for formatting your e-mail. E-mails that do not follow this format may not be read. We read every submission within 4 months of receipt, but we can no longer respond to every one. If you do not receive a response from us after four months, we have declined to publish your submission."

TERMS Guidelines online.

WILLIAMSON BOOKS

2630 Elm Hill Pike, Suite 100, Nashville TN 37214. **E-mail:** pjay@guideposts.org. **Website:** www.idealsbooks.com. Publishes "very successful nonfiction series (Kids Can! Series) on subjects such as history, science, arts/crafts, geography, diversity, multiculturalism. Little Hands series for ages 2-6, Kaleidoscope Kids series (age 7 and up) and Quick Starts for Kids! series (ages 8 and up). Our goal is to help every child fulfill his/her potential and experience personal growth."

NONFICTION Hands-on active learning books, animals, African-American, arts/crafts, Asian, biography, diversity, careers, geography, health, history, hobbies, how-to, math, multicultural, music/dance, nature/environment, Native American, science, writing and journaling. Does not want to see textbooks, picture books, fiction. "Looking for all things African American, Asian American, Hispanic, Latino, and Native American including crafts and traditions, as well as their history, biographies, and personal retrospectives of growing up in U.S. for grades pre K-8th. We are looking for books in which learning and doing are inseparable."

HOW TO CONTACT Query with annotated TOC/synopsis and 1 sample chapter. Responds in 4 months. Publishes book 1 year after acceptance.

ILLUSTRATION Works with at least 2 illustrators and 2 designers/year. "We're interested in expanding our illustrator and design freelancers." Uses primarily 2-color and 4-color artwork. Responds only if interested. Samples returned with SASE; samples filed.

PHOTOGRAPHY Buys photos from freelancers; uses archival art and photos.

TERMS Pays authors advance against future royalties based on wholesale price or purchases outright. Pays illustrators by the project. Pays photographers per photo. Guidelines available for SASE.

TIPS "Please do not send any fiction or picture books of any kind—those should go to Ideals Children's Books. Look at our books to see what we do. We're interested in interactive learning books with a creative approach packed with interesting information, written for young readers ages 3-7 and 8-14. In nonfiction children's publishing, we are looking for authors with a depth of knowledge shared with children through a warm, embracing style. Our publishing philosophy is based on the idea that all children can succeed and have positive learning experiences. Children's lasting learning experiences involve their participation."

WINDRIVER PUBLISHING, INC.

3280 Madison Ave., Ogden UT 84403. (801)689-7440. **E-mail:** info@windriverpublishing.com. **Website:** www.windriverpublishing.com. **Contact:** E. Keith Howick, Jr., president; Gail Howick, vice president/editor-in-chief. "Authors who wish to submit book proposals for review must do so according to our Submissions Guidelines, which can be found on our website, along with an on-line submission form, which is our preferred submission method. We do not accept submissions of any kind by e-mail." Publishes hardcover originals and reprints, trade paperback originals, and mass market originals. Publishes 8 titles/year. 95% of books from first-time authors. 90% from unagented writers.

HOW TO CONTACT Not accepting submissions at this time. Does not accept unsolicited mss. 1,000 queries received/year. 300 mss received/year. Responds in 1-2 months to queries; 4-6 months to proposals/mss. Publishes book 1 year after acceptance.

TERMS Book catalog online. Guidelines online.

TIPS "We do not accept manuscripts containing graphic or gratuitous profanity, sex, or violence. See online instructions for details."

🅐 PAULA WISEMAN BOOKS

1230 Sixth Ave., New York NY 10020. (212)698-7272. **Fax:** (212)698-2796. **E-mail:** paula.wiseman@simonandschuster.com; sylvie.frank@simonandschuster.com. **Website:** kids.simonandschuster.com. Publishes 20 titles/year. 10% of books from first-time authors.

FICTION Considers all categories. Average word length: picture books—500; others standard length.

NONFICTION Picture books: animal, biography, concept, history, nature/environment. Young readers: animal, biography, history, multicultural, nature/environment, sports. Average word length: picture books—500; others standard length.

HOW TO CONTACT Does not accept unsolicited or unagented mss.

ILLUSTRATION Works with 15 illustrators/year. Does not accept unsolicited or unagented illustrations or submissions.

WORDSONG

815 Church St., Honesdale PA 18431. **Fax:** (570)253-0179. **E-mail:** submissions@boydsmillspress.com; eagarrow@boydsmillspress.com. **Website:** www.wordsongpoetry.com. "We publish fresh voices in contemporary poetry."

FICTION Submit complete ms or submit through agent. Label package "Manuscript Submission" and include SASE. "Please send a book-length collection of your own poems. Do not send an initial query."

NONFICTION Submit complete ms or submit through agent. Label package "Manuscript Submission" and include SASE. "Please send a book-length collection of your own poems. Do not send an initial query."

HOW TO CONTACT Responds to mss in 3 months.

ILLUSTRATION Works with 7 illustrators/year. Reviews ms/illustration packages from artists. Submit complete ms with 1 or 2 pieces of art. Illustrations only: Query with samples best suited to the art (postcard, 8½ × 11, etc.). Label package "Art Sample

Submission." Responds only if interested. Samples returned with SASE.

PHOTOGRAPHY Assigns work.

TERMS Pays authors royalty or work purchased outright.

TIPS "Collections of original poetry, not anthologies, are our biggest need at this time. Keep in mind that the strongest collections demonstrate a facility with multiple poetic forms and offer fresh images and insights. Check to see what's already on the market and on our website before submitting."

○ WORLD BOOK, INC.

233 N. Michigan Ave., Suite 2000, Chicago IL 60601. (312)729-5800. **Fax:** (312)729-5600. **Website:** www.worldbook.com. **Contact:** Paul A. Kobasa, editor-in-chief. World Book, Inc. (publisher of The World Book Encyclopedia), publishes reference sources and nonfiction series for children and young adults in the areas of science, mathematics, English-language skills, basic academic and social skills, social studies, history, and health and fitness. "We publish print and non-print material appropriate for children ages 3-14. WB does not publish fiction, poetry, or wordless picture books."

NONFICTION Young readers: animal, arts/crafts, careers, concept, geography, health, reference. Middle readers: animal, arts/crafts, careers, geography, health, history, hobbies, how-to, nature/environment, reference, science. Young adult: arts/crafts, careers, geography, health, history, hobbies, how-to, nature/environment, reference, science.

HOW TO CONTACT Submit outline/synopsis only; no mss. Responds to queries in 2 months. Publishes book 18 months after acceptance.

ILLUSTRATION Works with 10-30 illustrators/year. Illustrations only: Query with samples. Responds only if interested. Samples returned with SASE; samples filed "if extra copies and if interested."

PHOTOGRAPHY Buys stock and assigns work. Needs broad spectrum; editorial concept, specific natural, physical and social science spectrum. Model/property releases required; captions required. Submit cover letter, résumé, promo piece (color and b&w).

TERMS Payment negotiated on project-by-project basis.

ZUMAYA PUBLICATIONS, LLC

3209 S. Interstate 35, Austin TX 78741. **E-mail:** business@zumayapublications.com. **E-mail:** acquisitions@zumayapublications.com. **Website:** www.zumayapublications.com. **Contact:** Adrienne Rose, acquisitions editor. Publishes trade paperback and electronic originals and reprints. Publishes 20-25 titles/year. 5% of books from first-time authors. 98% from unagented writers.

○ "We accept only electronic queries; all others will be discarded unread. A working knowledge of computers and relevant software is a necessity, as our production process is completely digital."

FICTION "We are currently oversupplied with speculative fiction and are reviewing submissions in SF, fantasy and paranormal suspense by invitation only. We are much in need of GLBT and YA/middle grade, historical and western, New Age/inspirational (no overtly Christian materials, please), non-category romance, thrillers. As with nonfiction, we encourage people to review what we've already published so as to avoid sending us more of the same, at least, insofar as the plot is concerned. While we're always looking for good specific mysteries, we want original concepts rather than slightly altered versions of what we've already published."

NONFICTION "The easiest way to figure out what we're looking for is to look at what we've already done. Our main nonfiction interests are in collections of true ghost stories, ones that have been investigated or thoroughly documented, memoirs that address specific regions and eras from a 'normal person' viewpoint and books on the craft of writing. That doesn't mean we won't consider something else."

HOW TO CONTACT Electronic query only. 1,000 queries received/year. 100 mss received/year. Responds in 6 months to queries and proposals; 9 months to mss. Publishes book 2 years after acceptance.

TERMS Guidelines online.

TIPS "We're catering to readers who may have loved last year's best seller but not enough to want to read 10 more just like it. Have something different. If it does not fit standard pigeonholes, that's a plus. On the other hand, it has to have an audience. And if you're not prepared to work with us on promotion and marketing, particularly via social media, it would be better to look elsewhere."

CANADIAN & INTERNATIONAL BOOK PUBLISHERS

///

While the United States is considered the largest market in children's publishing, the children's publishing world is by no means strictly dominated by the U.S. After all, the most prestigious children's book extravaganza in the world occurs each year in Bologna, Italy, at the Bologna Children's Book Fair and some of the world's most beloved characters were born in the United Kingdom (i.e., Winnie-the-Pooh and Mr. Potter).

In this section you'll find book publishers from English-speaking countries around the world from Canada, Australia, New Zealand and the United Kingdom. The listings in this section look just like the U.S. Book Publishers section; and the publishers listed are dedicated to the same goal—publishing great books for children.

Like always, be sure to study each listing and research each publisher carefully before submitting material. Determine whether a publisher is open to U.S. or international submissions, as many publishers accept submissions only from residents of their own country. Some publishers accept illustration samples from foreign artists, but do not accept manuscripts from foreign writers. Illustrators do have a slight edge in this category as many illustrators generate commissions from all around the globe. Visit publishers' websites to be certain they publish the sort of work you do. Visit online bookstores to see if publishers' books are available there. Write or e-mail to request catalogs and submission guidelines.

When mailing requests or submissions out of the United States, remember that U.S. postal stamps are useless on your SASE. Always include International Reply Coupons (IRCs) with your SAE. Each IRC is good for postage for one letter. So if you want the publisher to return your manuscript or send a catalog, be sure to enclose enough IRCs to pay the postage. For more help visit the United State Postal Service website at www.usps.com/global. Visit www.timeanddate.com/worldclock and American Computer Resources, Inc.'s International

Calling Code Directory at www.the-acr.com/codes/cntrycd.htm before calling or faxing internationally to make sure you're calling at a reasonable time and using the correct numbers.

As in the rest of *Children's Writer's & Illustrator's Market*, the maple leaf symbol identifies Canadian markets. Look for the international symbol throughout *Children's Writer's & Illustrator's Market* as well. Several of the Society of Children's Book Writers and Illustrator's (SCBWI) international conferences are listed in the Conferences & Workshops section along with other events in locations around the globe. Look for more information about SCBWI's international chapters on the organization's website, scbwi.org.

⊙ ☺ ANNICK PRESS, LTD.

15 Patricia Ave., Toronto ON M2M 1H9, Canada. (416)221-4802. **Fax:** (416)221-8400. **E-mail:** annick press@annickpress.com. **Website:** www.annickpress. com. **Contact:** Rick Wilks, director; Colleen MacMillan, associate publisher; Sheryl Shapiro, creative director. "Annick Press maintains a commitment to high quality books that entertain and challenge. Our publications share fantasy and stimulate imagination, while encouraging children to trust their judgment and abilities." Publishes 5 picture books/year; 6 young readers/year; 8 middle readers/year; 9 young adult titles/year. Publishes picture books, juvenile and YA fiction and nonfiction; specializes in trade books. Publishes 25 titles/year. 20% of books from first-time authors. 80-85% from unagented writers.

⊙ Does not accept unsolicited mss.

FICTION Publisher of children's books. Publishes hardcover and trade paperback originals. Average print order: 9,000. First novel print order: 7,000. Plans 18 first novels this year. Averages 25 total titles/year. Distributes titles through Firefly Books Ltd. Juvenile, young adult. Not accepting picture books at this time.

HOW TO CONTACT 5,000 queries received/year. 3,000 mss received/year. Publishes a book 2 years after acceptance.

TERMS Pays authors royalty of 5-12% based on retail price. Offers advances (average amount: $3,000). Pays illustrators royalty of 5% minimum. Book catalog and guidelines available online.

☺ BOREALIS PRESS, LTD.

8 Mohawk Crescent, Napean ON K2H 7G6, Canada. (613)829-0150. **Fax:** (613)829-7783. **E-mail:** drt@bo realispress.com. **Website:** www.borealispress.com. "Our mission is to publish work that will be of lasting interest in the Canadian book market." Currently emphasizing Canadian fiction, nonfiction, drama, poetry. De-emphasizing children's books. Publishes hardcover and paperback originals and reprints. Publishes 20 titles/year. 80% of books from first-time authors. 95% from unagented writers.

FICTION Only material Canadian in content and dealing with significant aspects of the human situation.

NONFICTION Only material Canadian in content. Looks for style in tone and language, reader interest, and maturity of outlook.

HOW TO CONTACT Query with SASE. Submit clips, 1-2 sample chapters. *No unsolicited mss.* Submit outline, 2 sample chapters. Responds in 2 months to queries; 4 months to mss. Publishes book 18 months after acceptance.

TERMS Pays 10% royalty on net receipts; plus 3 free author's copies. Book catalog online. Guidelines online.

☺ THE BRUCEDALE PRESS

P.O. Box 2259, Port Elgin ON N0H 2C0, Canada. (519)832-6025. **E-mail:** info@brucedalepress.ca. **Website:** brucedalepress.ca. The Brucedale Press publishes books and other materials of regional interest and merit, as well as literary, historical, and/or pictorial works. Publishes hardcover and trade paperback originals. Publishes 3 titles/year. 75% of books from first-time authors. 100% from unagented writers.

⊙ Accepts works by Canadian authors only. Submissions accepted in September and March ONLY.

HOW TO CONTACT 50 queries received/year. 30 mss received/year. Publishes book 1 year after acceptance.

TERMS Pays royalty. Book catalog for #10 SASE (Canadian postage or IRC) or online. Guidelines available online.

TIPS Our focus is very regional. In reading submissions, I look for quality writing with a strong connection to the Queen's Bush area of Ontario. All authors should visit our website, get a catalog, and read our books before submitting.

☻ BUSTER BOOKS

9 Lion Yard, Tremadoc Rd., London WA SW4 7NQ, United Kingdom. 020 7720 8643. **Fax:** 022 7720 8953. **E-mail:** enquiries@michaelomarabooks.com. **Website:** www.busterbooks.co.uk. "We are dedicated to providing irresistible and fun books for children of all ages. We typically publish black-and-white nonfiction for children aged 8-12 novelty titles-including doodle books."

HOW TO CONTACT Submit synopsis and sample text. Prefers synopsis and sample text over complete ms.

TIPS "We do not accept fiction submissions. Please do not send original artwork as we cannot guarantee its safety." Visit website before submitting.

CHILD'S PLAY (INTERNATIONAL) LTD.

Children's Play International, Ashworth Rd. Bridgemead, Swindon, Wiltshire SN5 7YD, United Kingdom. **E-mail:** allday@childs-play.com; neil@childs-play.com; office@childs-play.com. **Website:** www.childs-play.com. **Contact:** Sue Baker, Neil Burden, manuscript acquisitions. Specializes in nonfiction, fiction, educational material, multicultural material. Produces 30 picture books/year; 10 young readers/year; 2 middle readers/year. "A child's early years are more important than any other. This is when children learn most about the world around them and the language they need to survive and grow. Child's Play aims to create exactly the right material for this all-important time." Publishes 45 titles/year. 20% of books from first-time authors.

"Due to a backlog of submissions, Child's Play is currently no longer able to accept anymore manuscripts."

FICTION Picture books: adventure, animal, concept, contemporary, folktales, multicultural, nature/environment. Young readers: adventure, animal, anthology, concept, contemporary, folktales, humor, multicultural, nature/environment, poetry. Average word length: picture books—1,500; young readers—2,000.

NONFICTION Picture books: activity books, animal, concept, multicultural, music/dance, nature/environment, science. Young readers: activity books, animal, concept, multicultural, music/dance, nature/environment, science. Average word length: picture books—2,000; young readers—3,000.

HOW TO CONTACT Publishes book 2 years after acceptance.

ILLUSTRATION Accepts material from international illustrators. Works with 10 illustrators/year. Uses color artwork only. Reviews ms/illustration packages. For ms/illustration packages: Query or submit ms/illustration packages to Sue Baker, editor. Reviews work for future assignments. If interested in illustrating future titles, query with samples, CD, website address. Submit samples to Annie Kubler, art director. Responds in 10 weeks. Samples not returned. Samples filed.

TIPS "Look at our website to see the kind of work we do before sending. Do not send cartoons. We do not publish novels. We do publish lots of books with pictures of babies/toddlers."

CHRISTIAN FOCUS PUBLICATIONS

Geanies House, Fearn, Tain Ross-shire Scotland IV20 1TW, United Kingdom. 44 (0) 1862 871 011. **Fax:** 44 (0) 1862 871 699. **E-mail:** info@christianfocus.com. **Website:** www.christianfocus.com. **Contact:** Catherine Mackenzie, publisher. Specializes in Christian material, nonfiction, fiction, educational material. Publishes 22-32 titles/year. 2% of books from first-time authors.

FICTION Picture books, young readers, adventure, history, religion. Middle readers: adventure, problem novels, religion. Young adult/teens: adventure, history, problem novels, religion. Average word length: young readers—5,000; middle readers—max 10,000; young adult/teen—max 20,000.

NONFICTION All levels: activity books, biography, history, religion, science. Average word length: picture books—5,000; young readers—5,000; middle readers—5,000-10,000; young adult/teens—10,000-20,000.

HOW TO CONTACT Query or submit outline/synopsis and 3 sample chapters. Will consider electronic submissions and previously published work. Query or submit outline/synopsis and 3 sample chapters. Will consider electronic submissions and previously published work. Responds to queries in 2 weeks; mss in 3 months. Publishes book 1 year after acceptance.

ILLUSTRATION Works on 15-20 potential projects. "Some artists are chosen to do more than one. Some projects just require a cover illustration, some require full color spreads, others black and white line art." **Contact:** Catherine Mackenzie, children's editor. Responds in 2 weeks only if interested. Samples are not returned.

PHOTOGRAPHY "We only purchase royalty free photos from particular photographic associations. However portfolios can be presented to our designer." **Contact:** Daniel van Straaten. Photographers should send cover letter, résumé, published samples, client list, portfolio.

TIPS "Be aware of the international market as regards writing style/topics as well as illustration styles. Our company sells rights to European as well as Asian countries. Fiction sales are not as good as they were. Christian fiction for youngsters is not a product that is performing well in comparison to nonfiction such as Christian biography/Bible stories/church history, etc."

COTEAU BOOKS

Thunder Creek Publishing Co-operative Ltd., 2517 Victoria Ave., Regina SK S4P 0T2, Canada. (306)777-

0170. **Fax:** (306)522-5152. **E-mail:** coteau@coteau books.com. **Website:** www.coteaubooks.com. **Contact:** Geoffrey Ursell, publisher. "Our mission is to publish the finest in Canadian fiction, nonfiction, poetry, drama, and children's literature, with an emphasis on Saskatchewan and prairie writers. De-emphasizing science fiction, picture books." Publishes trade paperback originals and reprints. Publishes 12 titles/year. 25% of books from first-time authors. 90% from unagented writers.

FICTION *Canadian authors only.* No science fiction. No children's picture books.

NONFICTION *Canadian authors only.*

HOW TO CONTACT Submit hard copy query, bio, complete ms, SASE. Submit hard copy query, bio, 3-4 sample chapters, SASE. 200 queries received/year. 40 mss received/year. Responds in 3 months. Publishes book 1 year after acceptance.

TERMS Pays 10% royalty on retail price. Book catalog available free. Guidelines online.

TIPS "Look at past publications to get an idea of our editorial program. We do not publish romance, horror, or picture books but are interested in juvenile and teen fiction from Canadian authors. Submissions, even queries, must be made in hard copy only. We do not accept simultaneous/multiple submissions. Check our website for new submission timing guidelines."

DUNDURN PRESS, LTD.

3 Church St., Suite 500, Toronto ON M5E 1M2, Canada. (416)214-5544. **E-mail:** info@dundurn.com. **Website:** www.dundurn.com. **Contact:** Acquisitions Editor. Dundurn publishes books by Canadian authors. Publishes hardcover, trade paperback, and ebook originals and reprints. 25% of books from first-time authors. 50% from unagented writers.

○ "We do not publish poetry, short stories, children's books for readers under seven years of age, or picture books."

FICTION No romance, science fiction, or experimental.

HOW TO CONTACT "Until further notice, we will not be accepting any unsolicited fiction manuscripts." Submit cover letter, synopsis, CV, table of contents, writing sample, e-mail contact. Accepts submissions via postal mail only. Do not submit original materials. Submissions will not be returned. 600 queries received/year. Responds in 3 months to queries. Publishes ms 1-2 year after acceptance.

TERMS Guidelines online.

FABER & FABER LTD

Bloomsbury House, 74-77 Great Russell St., London WC1B 3DA, United Kingdom. (020)7465-0045. **Fax:** (020)7465-0034. **Website:** www.faber.co.uk. **Contact:** Lee Brackstone, Hannah Griffiths, Angus Cargill, (fiction); Walter Donohue, (film); Dinah Wood, (plays); Julian Loose, Neil Belton, (nonfiction); Paul Keegan, (poetry); Belinda Matthews, (music); Suzy Jenvy, Julia Wells, (children's). Faber & Faber have rejuvenated their nonfiction, music and children's titles in recent years and the film and drama lists remain market leaders. Publishes hardcover and paperback originals and reprints. Publishes 200 titles/year.

○ Faber & Faber will consider unsolicited proposals for poetry only.

HOW TO CONTACT *No unsolicited fiction submissions. No unsolicited nonfiction submissions.* Responds in 3 months to mss.

TERMS Pays royalty. Pays varying advances with each project. Book catalog available online.

TIPS "Explore the website and downloadable book catalogues thoroughly to get a feel for the lists in all categories and genres."

DAVID FICKLING BOOKS

31 Beamont St., Oxford En OX1 2NP, United Kingdom. (018)65-339000. **Fax:** (018)65-339009. **E-mail:** submissions@davidficklingbooks.com. **Website:** www.davidficklingbooks.co.uk. **Contact:** Hannah Featherstone, editor. David Fickling Books is a story house. Publishes 12-20 titles/year.

FICTION Considers all categories.

HOW TO CONTACT Submit cover letter and 3 sample chapters as PDF attachment saved in format "Author Name_Full Title." Responds to mss in 3 months, if interested.

ILLUSTRATION Reviews ms/illustration packages from artists. Illustrations only: query with samples.

PHOTOGRAPHY Submit cover letter, résumé, promo pieces.

TERMS Guidelines online.

TIPS "We adore stories for all ages, in both text and pictures. Quality is our watch word."

FITZHENRY & WHITESIDE LTD.

195 Allstate Pkwy., Markham ON L3R 4T8, Canada. (905)477-9700. **Fax:** (905)477-9179. **E-mail:** fitzkids@ fitzhenry.ca; godwit@fitzhenry.ca; charkin@fitzhen

ry.ca. **Website:** www.fitzhenry.ca/. **Contact:** Sharon Fitzhenry, president; Cathy Sandusky, children's publisher; Christie Harkin, submissions editor. Emphasis on Canadian authors and illustrators, subject or perspective. Publishes 15 titles/year. 10% of books from first-time authors.

HOW TO CONTACT Publishes book 1-2 years after acceptance.

ILLUSTRATION Works with approximately 10 illustrators/year. Reviews ms/illustration packages from artists. Submit outline and sample illustration (copy). Illustrations only: Query with samples and promo sheet. Samples not returned unless requested.

PHOTOGRAPHY Buys photos from freelancers. Buys stock and assigns work. Captions required. Uses b&w 8×10 prints; 35mm and 4×5 transparencies, 300+ dpi digital images. Submit stock photo list and promo piece.

TERMS Pays authors 8-10% royalty with escalations. Offers "respectable" advances for picture books, split 50/50 between author and illustrator. Pays illustrators by project and royalty. Pays photographers per photo.

TIPS "We respond to quality."

FRANCES LINCOLN CHILDREN'S BOOKS

Frances Lincoln, 74-77 White Lion St., Islington, London N1 9PF, United Kingdom. 00442072844009. **E-mail:** fl@franceslincoln.com. **Website:** www.franceslincoln.com. "Our company was founded by Frances Lincoln in 1977. We published our first books two years later, and we have been creating illustrated books of the highest quality ever since, with special emphasis on gardening, walking and the outdoors, art, architecture, design and landscape. In 1983, we started to publish illustrated books for children. Since then we have won many awards and prizes with both fiction and nonfiction children's books." Publishes 100 titles/year. 6% of books from first-time authors.

FICTION Average word length: picture books—1,000; young readers—9,788; middle readers—20,653; young adults—35,407.

NONFICTION Average word length: picture books—1,000; middle readers—29,768.

HOW TO CONTACT Query by e-mail. Query by e-mail. Responds in 6 weeks to mss. Publishes book 18 months after acceptance.

ILLUSTRATION Works with approx 56 illustrators/year. Uses both color and b&w. Reviews ms/illustra-tion packages from artist. Sample illustrations. Illustrations only: Query with samples. Responds only if interested. Samples are returned with SASE. Samples are kept on file only if interested.

PHOTOGRAPHY Buys stock images and assign work. Uses children, multicultural photos. Submit cover letter, published samples, or portfolio.

FRANKLIN WATTS

338 Euston Rd., London NW1 3BH, United Kingdom. +44 (0)20 7873 6000. **Fax:** +44 (0)20 7873 6024. **E-mail:** ad@hachettechildrens.co.uk. **Website:** www.franklinwatts.co.uk. Franklin Watts is well known for its high quality and attractive information books, which support the National Curriculum and stimulate children's enquiring minds. Reader Development is one of Franklin Watts' specialisations; the list offers titles on a wide array of subjects for beginner readers. It is also the proud publisher of many award-winning authors/illustrators, including Mick Manning and Brita Granstrom.

Generally does not accept unsolicited mss.

GROUNDWOOD BOOKS

110 Spadina Ave. Suite 801, Toronto ON M5V 2K4, Canada. (416)363-4343. **Fax:** (416)363-1017. **E-mail:** ssutherland@groundwoodbooks.com. **Website:** www.houseofanansi.com. Publishes 13 picture books/year; 3 young readers/year; 5 middle readers/year; 5 young adult titles/year, approximately 2 nonfiction titles/year.

FICTION Recently published: *Lily and Taylor,* by Elise Moser; *The Servant,* by Fatima Sherafeddine; *Black Flame,* by Gerelchimeg Blackcrane; *The Spotted Dog Last Seen,* by Jessica Scott Kerrin.

NONFICTION Recently published: *Looks Like Daylight- Voices of Indigenous Kids,* by Deborah Ellis. Picture books recently published: *Oy, Feh, So?,* by Cary Fagan, illustrated by Gary Clement; *once Upon a Northern Night,* by Jean E. Pendziwol, illustrated by Isabelle Arsenault; *Northwest Passage,* by Stan Rogers, illustrated by Matt James; *The Voyage,* by Veronica Salinas, illustrated by Camilla Engman; *Out the Window,* by Cybèle Young.

HOW TO CONTACT Submit synopsis and sample chapters. Responds to mss in 6-8 months.

TERMS Offers advances. Visit website for guidelines: www.houseofanansi.com/Groundwoodsubmissions.aspx.

☉ KIDS CAN PRESS

25 Dockside Dr., Toronto ON M5A 0B5, Canada. (416)479-7000. **Fax:** (416)960-5437. **E-mail:** info@kidscan.com; kkalmar@kidscan.com. **Website:** www.kidscanpress.com. U.S. address: 2250 Military Rd., Tonawanda, NY 14150.. **Contact:** Corus Quay, acquisitions.

Kids Can Press is currently accepting unsolicited mss from Canadian adult authors only.

FICTION Picture books, young readers: concepts. "We do not accept young adult fiction or fantasy novels for any age." Adventure, animal, contemporary, folktales, history, humor, multicultural, nature/environment, special needs, sports, suspense/mystery. Average word length: picture books 1,000-2,000; young readers 750-1,500; middle readers 10,000-15,000; young adults over 15,000.

NONFICTION Picture books: activity books, animal, arts/crafts, biography, careers, concept, health, history, hobbies, how-to, multicultural, nature/environment, science, social issues, special needs, sports. Young readers: activity books, animal, arts/crafts, biography, careers, concept, history, hobbies, how-to, multicultural. Middle readers: cooking, music/dance. Average word length: picture books 500-1,250; young readers 750-2,000; middle readers 5,000-15,000.

HOW TO CONTACT Submit outline/synopsis and 2-3 sample chapters. For picture books submit complete ms. Submit outline/synopsis and 2-3 sample chapters. For picture books submit complete ms. Responds in 6 months only if interesed. Publishes book 18-24 months after acceptance.

ILLUSTRATION Works with 40 illustrators/year. Reviews ms/illustration packages from artists. Send color copies of illustration portfolio, cover letter outlining other experience. Contact: Art Director. Illustrations only: Send tearsheets, color photocopies. Responds only if interested.

☉ LITTLE TIGER PRESS

1 The Coda Centre, 189 Munster Rd., London En SW6 6AW, United Kingdom. (44)20-7385 6333. **E-mail:** info@littletiger.co.uk; malperin@littletiger.co.uk. **Website:** www.littletigerpress.com.

FICTION Picture books: animal, concept, contemporary, humor. Average word length: picture books—750 words or fewer.

ILLUSTRATION Digital submissions preferred please send in digital samples as pdf or jpeg attachments to artsubmissions@littletiger.co.uk. Files should be flattened and no bigger than 1 mb per attachment. Include name and contact details on any attachments. Printed submissions please send in printed color samples as A4 printouts. Do not send in original artwork as we cannot be held responsible for unsolicited original artwork being lost or damaged in the post. We aim to acknowledge unsolicited material and to return material if so requested within 3 months. Please include SAE if return of material is requested.

TIPS "Every reasonable care is taken of the manuscripts and samples we receive, but we cannot accept responsibility for any loss or damage. Try to read or look at as many books on the Little Tiger Press list before sending in your material. Refer to our website for further details."

☉ MANOR HOUSE PUBLISHING, INC.

452 Cottingham Crescent, Ancaster ON L9G 3V6, Canada. **E-mail:** mbdavie@manor-house.biz. **Website:** www.manor-house.biz. **Contact:** Mike Davie, president (novels, poetry, and nonfiction). Publishes hardcover, trade paperback, and mass market paperback originals reprints. Publishes 5-6 titles/year. 90% of books from first-time authors. 90% from unagented writers.

FICTION Stories should have Canadian settings and characters should be Canadian, but content should have universal appeal to wide audience.

NONFICTION "We are a Canadian publisher, so mss should be Canadian in content and aimed as much as possible at a wide, general audience. At this point in time, we are only publishing books by Canadian citizens residing in Canada."

HOW TO CONTACT Query via e-mail. Submit proposal package, clips, bio, 3 sample chapters. Submit complete ms. Query via e-mail. Submit proposal package, outline, bio, 3 sample chapters. Submit complete ms. 30 queries received/year; 20 mss received/year. Queries and mss to be sent by e-mail only. "We will respond in 30 days if interested-if not, there is no response. Do not follow up unless asked to do so." Publishes book 1 year after acceptance.

TERMS Pays 10% royalty on retail price. Book catalog available online. Guidelines available via e-mail.

TIPS "Our audience includes everyone—the general public/mass audience. Self-edit your work first, make sure it is well written with strong Canadian content."

☺ ORCA BOOK PUBLISHERS

P.O. Box 5626, Stn. B, Victoria BC V8R 6S4, Canada. **Fax:** (877)408-1551. **E-mail:** orca@orcabook.com. **Website:** www.orcabook.com. **Contact:** Amy Collins, editor (picture books); Sarah Harvey, editor (young readers); Andrew Wooldridge, editor (juvenile and teen fiction); Bob Tyrrell, publisher (YA, teen).. Publishes hardcover and trade paperback originals, and mass market paperback originals and reprints. Publishes 30 titles/year. 20% of books from first-time authors. 75% from unagented writers.

○ Only publishes Canadian authors.

FICTION Picture books: animals, contemporary, history, nature/environment. Middle readers: contemporary, history, fantasy, nature/environment, problem novels, graphic novels. Young adults: adventure, contemporary, hi-lo (Orca Soundings), history, multicultural, nature/environment, problem novels, suspense/mystery, graphic novels. Average word length: picture books—500-1,500; middle readers—20,000-35,000; young adult—25,000-45,000; Orca Soundings—13,000-15,000; Orca Currents—13,000-15,000. No romance, science fiction.

NONFICTION Only publishes Canadian authors.

HOW TO CONTACT Query with SASE. Submit proposal package, outline, clips, 2-5 sample chapters, SASE. Query with SASE. 2,500 queries received/year. 1,000 mss received/year. Responds in 1 month to queries; 2 months to proposals and mss. Publishes book 12-18 months after acceptance.

ILLUSTRATION Works with 8-10 illustrators/year. Reviews ms/illustration packages from artists. Submit ms with 3-4 pieces of final art. "Reproductions only, no original art please." Illustrations only: Query with samples; provide résumé, slides. Responds in 2 months. Samples returned with SASE; samples filed.

TERMS Pays 10% royalty. Book catalog for 8½x11 SASE. Guidelines available online.

TIPS "Our audience is students in grades K-12. Know our books, and know the market."

☺ PICCADILLY PRESS

5 Castle Rd., London NW1 8PR, United Kingdom. (44)(207)267-4492. **Fax:** (44)(207)267-4493. **E-mail:** books@piccadillypress.co.uk. **Website:** www.piccadillypress.co.uk. "Piccadilly Press is the perfect choice for variety of reading for everyone aged 2-16! We're an independent publisher, celebrating 26 years of specialising in teen fiction and nonfiction, childrens fiction, picture books and parenting books by highly acclaimed authors and illustrators and fresh new talents too. We hope you enjoy reading the books as much as we enjoy publishing them."

FICTION Picture books: animal, contemporary, fantasy, nature/environment. Young adults: contemporary, humor, problem novels. Average word length: picture books—500-1,000; young adults—25,000-35,000.

NONFICTION Young adults: self help (humorous). Average word length: young adults—25,000-35,000.

HOW TO CONTACT Submit complete ms for picture books or submit outline/synopsis and 2 sample chapters for YA. Enclose a brief cover letter and SASE for reply. Submit outline/synopsis and 2 sample chapters. Responds to mss in 6 weeks.

ILLUSTRATION Illustrations only: Query with samples (do not send originals).

TIPS "Take a look in bookshops to see if there are many other books of a similar nature to yours--this is what your book will be competing against, so make sure there is something truly unique about your story. Looking at what else is available will give you ideas as to what topics are popular, but reading a little of them will also give you a sense of the right styles, language and length appropriate for the age-group."

☺ RAINCOAST BOOK DISTRIBUTION, LTD.

2440 Viking Way, Richmond BC V6V 1N2, Canada. (604)448-7100. **Fax:** (604)270-7161. **E-mail:** info@raincoast.com. **Website:** www.raincoast.com. Publishes hardcover and trade paperback originals and reprints. Publishes 60 titles/year. 10% of books from first-time authors. 40% from unagented writers.

FICTION *No unsolicited mss.*

NONFICTION *No unsolicited mss.*

HOW TO CONTACT Query with SASE. 3,000 queries received/year. Publishes book within 2 years of acceptance.

TERMS Pays 8-12% royalty on retail price. Pays $1,000-6,000 advance. Book catalog for #10 SASE.

☺☺ RANDOM HOUSE CHILDREN'S BOOKS

61-63 Uxbridge Rd., London En W5 5SA, United Kingdom. (44)(208)231-6000. **Fax:** (44)(208)231-6737. **E-mail:** enquiries@randomhouse.co.uk; lduffy@randomhouse.co.uk. **Website:** www.kidsatrandomhouse.

co.uk. **Contact:** Philippa Dickinson, managing director. Publishes 250 titles/year.

Ⓞ Only interested in agented material.

FICTION Picture books: adventure, animal, anthology, contemporary, fantasy, folktales, humor, multicultural, nature/environment, poetry, suspense/mystery. Young readers: adventure, animal, anthology, contemporary, fantasy, folktales, humor, multicultural, nature/environment, poetry, sports, suspense/mystery. Middle readers: adventure, animal, anthology, contemporary, fantasy, folktales, humor, multicultural, nature/environment, problem novels, romance, sports, suspense/mystery. Young adults: adventure, contemporary, fantasy, humor, multicultural, nature/environment, problem novels, romance, science fiction, suspense/mystery. Average word length: picture books—800; young readers—1,500-6,000; middle readers—10,000-15,000; young adults—20,000-45,000.

ILLUSTRATION Works with 50 illustrators/year. Reviews ms/illustration packages from artists. Query with samples. Contact: Margaret Hope. Samples are returned with SASE (IRC).

PHOTOGRAPHY Buys photos from freelancers. Contact: Margaret Hope. Photo captions required. Uses color or b&w prints. Submit cover letter, published samples.

TERMS Pays authors royalty. Offers advances.

TIPS "Although Random House is a big publisher, each imprint only publishes a small number of books each year. Our lists for the next few years are already full. Any book we take on from a previously unpublished author has to be truly exceptional. Manuscripts should be sent to us via literary agents."

🌑 RANSOM PUBLISHING

Radley House, 8 St. Cross Road, Winchester Hampshire SO23 9HX, United Kingdom. +44 (0) 01962 862307. **Fax:** +44 (0) 05601 148881. **E-mail:** ransom@ransom.co.uk. **Website:** www.ransom.co.uk. **Contact:** Jenny Ertle, editor. Independent UK publisher with distribution in English speaking markets throughout the world. Specializes in books for reluctant and struggling readers. "Our high-quality, visually stimulating, age appropriate material has achieved wide acclaim for its ability to engage and motivate those who either can't or won't read." One of the few English language publishers to publish books with very high interest age and very low reading age.

Has a developing list of children's books for home and school use. Specializes in phonics and general reading programs. Publishes paperback originals.

FICTION Easy reading for young adults. Books for reluctant and struggling readers.

HOW TO CONTACT Accepts unsolicited mss. Query with SASE or submit outline/proposal. Prefers queries by e-mail. Include estimated word count, brief bio, list of publishing credits. Responds to mss in 3-4 weeks.

TERMS Pays 10% royalty on net receipts. Ms guidelines by e-mail.

☼ RONSDALE PRESS

3350 W. 21st Ave., Vancouver BC V6S 1G7, Canada. (604)738-4688. **Fax:** (604)731-4548. **E-mail:** ronsdale@shaw.ca. **Website:** ronsdalepress.com. **Contact:** Ronald B. Hatch (fiction, poetry, nonfiction, social commentary); Veronica Hatch (YA novels and short stories). "Ronsdale Press is a Canadian literary publishing house that publishes 12 books each year, four of which are young adult titles. Of particular interest are books involving children exploring and discovering new aspects of Canadian history." Publishes trade paperback originals. Publishes 12 titles/year. 40% of books from first-time authors. 95% from unagented writers.

FICTION Young adults: Canadian novels. Average word length: middle readers and young adults—50,000. Recently published *Torn from Troy*, by Patrick Bowman (ages 10-14); *Hannah & The Salish Sea*, by Carol Anne Shaw (ages 10-14); *Dark Times*, edited by Ann Walsh (anthology of short stories, ages 10 and up); *Outlaw in India*, by Philip Roy; *Freedom Bound*, by Jean Rae Baxter (ages 10-14).

NONFICTION Middle readers, young adults: animal, biography, history, multicultural, social issues. Average word length: young readers—90; middle readers—90. "We publish a number of books for children and young adults in the age 10 to 15 range. We are especially interested in YA historical novels. We regret that we can no longer publish picture books."

HOW TO CONTACT Submit complete ms. Submit complete ms. 40 queries received/year. 800 mss received/year. Responds to queries in 2 weeks; mss in 2 months. Publishes book 1 year after acceptance.

ILLUSTRATION Works with 2 illustrators/year. Reviews ms/illustration packages from artists. Requires only cover art. Responds in 2 weeks. Samples returned with SASE. Originals returned to artist at job's completion.

TERMS Pays 10% royalty on retail price. Book catalog for #10 SASE. Guidelines available online.

TIPS "Ronsdale Press is a literary publishing house, based in Vancouver, and dedicated to publishing books from across Canada, books that give Canadians new insights into themselves and their country. We aim to publish the best Canadian writers."

SECOND STORY PRESS

20 Maud St., Suite 401, Toronto ON M5V 2M5, Canada. (416)537-7850. **Fax:** (416)537-0588. **E-mail:** info@secondstorypress.ca; marketing@secondstorypress.com. **Website:** www.secondstorypress.ca.

FICTION Considers non-sexist, non-racist, and non-violent stories, as well as historical fiction, chapter books, picture books.

NONFICTION Picture books: biography.

HOW TO CONTACT Accepts appropriate material from residents of Canada only. Submit complete ms or submit outline and sample chapters by postal mail only. No electronic submissions or queries.

TAFELBERG PUBLISHERS

Imprint of NB Publishers, P.O. Box 879, Cape Town 8000, South Africa. (27)(21)406-3033. **Fax:** (27)(21)406-3812. **E-mail:** kristin@nb.co.za. **Website:** www.tafelberg.com. **Contact:** Danita van Romburgh, editorial secretary; Louise Steyn, publisher. General publisher best known for Afrikaans fiction, authoritative political works, children's/youth literature, and a variety of illustrated and nonillustrated nonfiction. Publishes 10 titles/year.

FICTION Picture books, young readers: animal, anthology, contemporary, fantasy, folktales, hi-lo, humor, multicultural, nature/environment, scient fiction, special needs. Middle readers, young adults: animal (middle reader only), contemporary, fantasy, hi-lo, humor, multicultural, nature/environment, problem novels, science fiction, special needs, sports, suspense/mystery. Average word length: picture books—1,500-7,500; young readers—25,000; middle readers—15,000; young adults—40,000.

HOW TO CONTACT Submit complete ms. Submit outline, information on intended market, bio, and 1-2 sample chapters. Responds to queries in 2 weeks; mss in 6 months. Publishes book 1 year after acceptance.

ILLUSTRATION Works with 2-3 illustrators/year. Reviews ms/illustration packages from artists. Send ms with dummy or e-mail and jpegs. Contact: Louise Steyn, publisher. Illustrations only: Query with brochure, photocopies, résumé, URL, JPEGs. Responds only if interested. Samples not returned.

TERMS Pays authors royalty of 15-18% based on wholesale price.

TIPS "Writers: Story needs to have a South African or African style. Illustrators: I'd like to look, but the chances of getting commissioned are slim. The market is small and difficult. Do not expect huge advances. Editorial staff attended or plans to attend the following conferences: IBBY, Frankfurt, SCBWI Bologna."

THISTLEDOWN PRESS LTD.

401 2nd Ave., Saskatoon SK S7K 2C3, Canada. (306)244-1722. **Fax:** (306)244-1762. **E-mail:** editorial@thistledownpress.com. **Website:** www.thistledownpress.com. **Contact:** Allan Forrie, publisher.

"Thistledown originates books by Canadian authors only, although we have co-published titles by authors outside Canada. We do not publish children's picture books."

FICTION Middle readers, young adults: adventure, anthology, contemporary, fantasy, humor, poetry, romance, science fiction, suspense/mystery, short stories. Average word length: young adults—40,000.

HOW TO CONTACT Submit outline/synopsis and sample chapters. *Does not accept mss.* Do not query by e-mail. Responds to queries in 4 months. Publishes book 1 year after acceptance.

ILLUSTRATION Prefers agented illustrators but "not mandatory." Works with few illustrators. Illustrations only: Query with samples, promo sheet, slides, tearsheets. Responds only if interested. Samples returned with SASE; samples filed.

TERMS Pays authors royalty of 10-12% based on net dollar sales. Pays illustrators and photographers by the project (range: $250-750). Book catalog free on request. Guidelines available for #10 envelope and IRC.

TIPS "Send cover letter including publishing history and SASE."

TRADEWIND BOOKS

(604)662-4405. **E-mail:** tradewindbooks@mail.lycos.com. **Website:** www.tradewindbooks.com. **Contact:** Michael Katz, publisher; Carol Frank, art director; R. David Stephens, senior editor. "Tradewind Books publishes juvenile picture books and young adult novels. Requires that submissions include evidence that author has read at least 3 titles published by Tradewind Books." Publishes hardcover and trade paperback originals. Publishes 5 titles/year. 15% of books from first-time authors. 50% from unagented writers.

FICTION Picture books: adventure, multicultural, folktales. Average word length: 900 words.

HOW TO CONTACT Send complete ms for picture books. *YA novels by Canadian authors only. Chapter books by US authors considered.* Responds to mss in 2 months. Publishes book 3 years after acceptance.

ILLUSTRATION Works with 3-4 illustrators/year. Reviews ms/illustration packages from artists. Send illustrated ms as dummy. Illustrations only: Query with samples. Responds only if interested. Samples returned with SASE; samples filed.

TERMS Pays 7% royalty on retail price. Pays variable advance. Book catalog and ms guidelines online.

USBORNE PUBLISHING

83-85 Saffron Hill, London En EC1N 8RT, United Kingdom. (44)207430-2800. **Fax:** (44)207430-1562. **E-mail:** mail@usborne.co.uk. **Website:** www.usborne.com. "Usborne Publishing is a multiple-award winning, world-wide children's publishing company publishing almost every type of children's book for every age from baby to young adult."

FICTION Young readers, middle readers: adventure, contemporary, fantasy, history, humor, multicultural, nature/environment, science fiction, suspense/mystery, strong concept-based or character-led series. Average word length: young readers—5,000-10,000; middle readers—25,000-50,000; young adult—50,000-100,000.

ILLUSTRATION Works with 100 illustrators per year. Illustrations only: Query with samples. Samples not returned; samples filed.

PHOTOGRAPHY Contact: Usborne Art Department. Submit samples.

TERMS Pays authors royalty.

TIPS "Do not send any original work and, sorry, but we cannot guarantee a reply."

WEIGL EDUCATIONAL PUBLISHERS, LTD.

350 5th Ave., 59th Floor, New York NY 10118. (403)233-7747. **Fax:** (403)233-7769. **E-mail:** linda@

weigl.com; av2books@weigl.com. **Website:** www.weigl.ca. "Textbook publisher catering to juvenile and young adult audience (K-12)." Makes outright purchase. Responds ASAP to queries. Query with SASE. Publishes hardcover originals and reprints, school library softcover. Publishes 40 titles/year. 100% from unagented writers.

TERMS Book catalog available for free.

WHITECAP BOOKS, LTD.

210 - 314 W. Cordova St., Vancouver BC V6B 1 E8, Canada. (604)681-6181. **Fax:** (905)477-9179. **E-mail:** jeffreyb@whitecap.ca. **Website:** www.whitecap.ca. "Whitecap Books is a general trade publisher with a focus on food and wine titles. Although we are interested in reviewing unsolicited ms submissions, please note that we only accept submissions that meet the needs of our current publishing program. Please see some of most recent releases to get an idea of the kinds of titles we are interested in." Publishes hardcover and trade paperback originals. Publishes 40 titles/year. 20% of books from first-time authors. 90% from unagented writers.

FICTION No children's picture books or adult fiction.

NONFICTION Young children's and middle reader's nonfiction focusing mainly on nature, wildlife and animals. "Writers should take the time to research our list and read the submission guidelines on our website. This is especially important for children's writers and cookbook authors. We will only consider submissions that fall into these categories: cookbooks, wine and spirits, regional travel, home and garden, Canadian history, North American natural history, juvenile series-based fiction." "At this time, we are not accepting the following categories: self-help or inspirational books, political, social commentary, or issue books, general how-to books, biographies or memoirs, business and finance, art and architecture, religion and spirituality."

HOW TO CONTACT See guidelines. Submit cover letter, synopsis, SASE via ground mail. See guidelines online at website. 500 queries received/year; 1,000 mss received/year. Responds in 2-3 months to proposals. Publishes book 1 year after acceptance.

ILLUSTRATION Works with 1-2 illustrators/year. Uses color artwork only. Reviews ms/illustration packages from artists. Query. Contact: Rights and Acquisitions. Illustrations only: Send postcard sample with tearsheets. Contact: Michelle Furbacher, art director. Responds only if interested.

PHOTOGRAPHY Only accepts digital photography. Submit stock photo list. Buys stock and assigns work. Model/property releases required.

TERMS Pays royalty. Pays negotiated advance. Catalog and guidelines available online at website.

TIPS "We want well-written, well-researched material that presents a fresh approach to a particular topic."

MAGAZINES

Children's magazines are a great place for unpublished writers and illustrators to break into the market. Writers, illustrators and photographers alike may find it easier to get book assignments if they have tearsheets from magazines. Having magazine work under your belt shows you're professional and have experience working with editors and art directors and meeting deadlines.

But magazines aren't merely a breaking-in point. Writing, illustration and photo assignments for magazines let you see your work in print quickly, and the magazine market can offer steady work and regular paychecks (a number of them pay on acceptance). Book authors and illustrators may have to wait a year or two before receiving royalties from a project. The magazine market is also a good place to use research material that didn't make it into a book project you're working on. You may even work on a magazine idea that blossoms into a book project.

TARGETING YOUR SUBMISSIONS

It's important to know the topics typically covered by different children's magazines. To help you match your work with the right publications, we've included several indexes in the back of this book. The **Subject Index** lists both book and magazine publishers by the fiction and nonfiction subjects they're seeking.

If you're a writer, use the Subject Index in conjunction with the **Age-Level Index** to narrow your list of markets. Targeting the correct age group with your submission is an important consideration. Many rejection slips are sent because a writer has not targeted a manuscript to the correct age. Few magazines are aimed at children of all ages, so you must be certain your manuscript is written for the audience level of the particular magazine you're submitting to. Magazines for children (just as magazines for adults) may also target a specific gender.

Each magazine has a different editorial philosophy. Language usage also varies between periodicals, as does the length of feature articles and the use of artwork and photographs. Reading magazines *before* submitting is the best way to determine if your material is appropriate. Also, because magazines targeted to specific age groups have a natural turnover in readership every few years, old topics (with a new slant) can be recycled.

If you're a photographer, the **Photography Index** lists children's magazines that use photos from freelancers. Using it in combination with the subject index can narrow your search. For instance, if you photograph sports, compare the Magazine list in the Photography Index with the list under Sports in the Subject Index. Highlight the markets that appear on both lists, then read those listings to decide which magazines might be best for your work.

Since many kids' magazines sell subscriptions through direct mail or schools, you may not be able to find a particular publication at bookstores or newsstands. Check your local library, or send for copies of the magazines you're interested in. Most magazines in this section have sample copies available and will send them for a SASE or small fee.

Also, many magazines have submission guidelines and theme lists available for a SASE. Check magazines' websites, too. Many offer excerpts of articles, submission guidelines, and theme lists and will give you a feel for the editorial focus of the publication.

Watch for the Canadian icon and International icon symbols. These publications' needs and requirements may differ from their U.S. counterparts.

ADVOCATE, PKA'S PUBLICATION

1881 Little Westkill Rd., Prattsville NY 12468. (518)299-3103. **Website:** Advocatepka.weebly.com; www.facebook.com/Advocate/PKAPublications; www.facebook.com/GaitedHorseAssociation. advoad@localnet.com. **Contact:** Patricia Keller, publisher. *Advocate, PKA's Publication*, published bimonthly, is an advertiser-supported tabloid using "original, previously unpublished works, such as feature stories, essays, 'think' pieces, letters to the editor, profiles, humor, fiction, poetry, puzzles, cartoons, or line drawings. Advocates for good writers and quality writings. We publish art, fiction, photos and poetry. *Advocate's* submitters are talented people of all ages who do not earn their livings as writers. We wish to promote the arts and to give those we publish the opportunity to be published." Estab. 1987. Circ. 7,000.

○ "This publication has a strong horse orientation." Includes Gaited Horse Association newsletter. Horse-oriented stories, poetry, art and photos are currently needed.

FICTION Middle readers, young adults/teens, adults: adventure, animal, contemporary, fantasy, folktales, health, humorous, nature/environment, problem-solving, romance, science fiction, sports, suspense/mystery. Looks for "well written, entertaining work, whether fiction or nonfiction." Buys approximately 42 mss/year. Prose pieces should not exceed 1,500 words. Wants to see more humorous material, nature/environment and romantic comedy. "Nothing religious, pornographic, violent, erotic, pro-drug or anti-enviroment." Send complete ms.

NONFICTION Middle readers, young adults/teens: animal, arts/crafts, biography, careers, concept, cooking, fashion, games/puzzles, geography, history, hobbies, how-to, humorous, interview/profile, nature/environment, problem-solving, science, social issues, sports, travel. Buys 10 mss/year. Prose pieces should not exceed 1,500 words. Send complete ms.

POETRY Wants "nearly any kind of poetry, any length." Occasionally comments on rejected poems. No religious or pornographic poetry. Pays 2 contributor copies.

HOW TO CONTACT Responds to queries in 6 weeks; mss in 2 months. Publishes ms 2-18 months after acceptance.

ILLUSTRATION Uses b&w artwork only. Uses cartoons. Reviews ms/illustration packages from artists. Submit a photo print (b&w or color), an excellent copy of work (no larger than 8×10) or original. Prints in black and white but accepts color work that converts well to gray scale. Illustrations only: "Send previous unpublished art with SASE, please." Responds in 2 months. Samples returned with SASE; samples not filed. Credit line given.

PHOTOS Buys photos from freelancers. Model/property releases required. Uses color and b&w prints (no slides). Send unsolicited photos by mail with SASE. Responds in 2 months. Wants nature, artistic and humorous photos.

TERMS Acquires first rights for mss, artwork, and photographs. Pays on publication with contributor's copies. Sample copy: $5 (includes guidelines). Subscription: $18.50 (6 issues). Previous three issues are on our website.

TIPS "Please, no simultaneous submissions, work that has appeared on the Internet, pornography, overt religiosity, anti-environmentalism or gratuitous violence. Artists and photographers should keep in mind that we are a b&w paper. Please do not send postcards. Use envelope with SASE."

AMERICAN CAREERS

Career Communications, Inc., 6701 W. 64th St., Suite 210, Overland Park KS 66202. (800)669-7795. **E-mail:** ccinfo@carcom.com. **Website:** www.carcom.com; www.americancareersonline.com. **Contact:** Mary Pitchford, editor-in-chief; Jerry Kanabel, art director. "*American Careers* provides career, salary, and education information to middle school and high school students. Self-tests help them relate their interests and abilities to future careers." Estab. 1989. Circ. 500,000.

NONFICTION Query by mail only with published clips. Length: 300-1,000 words. Pays $100-450.

HOW TO CONTACT Accepts queries by mail.

PHOTOS State availability. Captions, identification of subjects, model releases required. Negotiates payment individually.

TERMS Buys all rights. Makes work-for-hire assignments. Byline given. Pays 1 month after acceptance. No kill fee. 10% freelance written. Sample copy for $4. Guidelines for #10 SASE.

TIPS "Letters of introduction or query letters with samples and résumés are ways we get to know writers. Samples should include how-to articles and career-related articles. Articles written for teenagers also would make good samples. Short feature articles on careers, career-related how-to articles, and self-assessment tools (10-20 point quizzes with scoring information) are primarily what we publish."

AMERICAN CHEERLEADER

Macfadden Performing Arts Media LLC, 110 William St., 23rd Floor, New York NY 10038. (646)459-4800. **Fax:** (646)459-4900. **E-mail:** editors@americancheerleader.com. **Website:** www.americancheerleader.com. **Contact:** Marisa Walker, editor-in-chief. Bimonthly magazine covering high school, college, and competitive cheerleading. "We try to keep a young, informative voice for all articles—'for cheerleaders, by cheerleaders.'" Estab. 1995. Circ. 200,000.

NONFICTION Needs young adults: biography, interview/profile (sports personalities), careers, fashion, beauty, health, how-to (cheering techniques, routines, pep songs, etc.), problem-solving, sports, cheerleading-specific material. Query by e-mail; provide résumé, business card, and tearsheets to be kept on file. "We're looking for authors who know cheerleading." Length: 750-2,000 words. Pays $100-250 for assigned articles; $100 maximum for unsolicited articles.

HOW TO CONTACT Editorial lead time 3 months. Responds in 4 weeks to queries. Responds in 2 months to mss. Publishes ms an average of 4 months after acceptance. Accepts queries by mail, e-mail, online submission form.

ILLUSTRATION Reviews ms/illustration packages from artists. Illustrations only: Query with samples; arrange portfolio review. Responds only if interested. Samples filed. Originals not returned at job's completion. Credit line given.

PHOTOS State availability. Model releases required. Reviews transparencies, 5x7 prints. Offers $50/photo.

TERMS Buys all rights. Byline given. Pays on publication. Offers 25% kill fee. 30% freelance written. Sample copy for $2.95. Guidelines free.

TIPS "We invite proposals from freelance writers who are involved in or have been involved in cheerleading—i.e., coaches, sponsors, or cheerleaders. Our writing style is upbeat and 'sporty' to catch and hold the attention of our teenaged readers. Articles should be broken down into lots of sidebars, bulleted lists, Q&As, etc."

APPLESEEDS

30 Grove St., Suite C, Peterborough NH 03458. (800)821-0115. **Fax:** (603)924-7380. **E-mail:** susanbuckleynyc@gmail.com. **Website:** www.cobblestonepub.com. **Contact:** Susan Buckley, editor. *AppleSeeds* is a 36-page, multidisciplinary, nonfiction social studies magazine from Cobblestone Publishing for ages 6-9 (primarily grades 3 and 4). Each issue focuses on 1 theme.

○ *Does not accept unsolicited mss.*

NONFICTION Query only (via e-mail). See website for submission guidelines and theme list.

HOW TO CONTACT Accepts queries by e-mail only.

ILLUSTRATION Contact Ann Dillon at Cobblestone. See website for illustration guidelines.

TERMS Buys all rights. Sample copy for $6.95 + $2 s&h. Guidelines available on website.

TIPS "Submit queries specifically focused on the theme of an upcoming issue. We generally work 6 months ahead on themes. We look for unusual perspectives, original ideas, and excellent scholarship. Writers should check our website for current guidelines, topics, and query deadlines. We use very little fiction. Illustrators should not submit unsolicited art."

AQUILA

Studio 2, 67A Willowfield Rd., Eastbourne BN22 8AP, United Kingdom. (44)(132)343-1313. **Fax:** (44)(132)373-1136. **E-mail:** info@aquila.co.uk. **Website:** www.aquila.co.uk. **Contact:** Jackie Berry, editor. *"Aquila* is an educational magazine for readers ages 8-13 including factual articles (no pop/celebrity material), arts/crafts, and puzzles." Entire publication aimed at juvenile market. Estab. 1993. Circ. 40,000.

FICTION Young Readers: animal, contemporary, fantasy, folktales, health, history, humorous, multicultural, nature/environment, problem solving, religious, science fiction, sports, suspense/mystery. Middle Readers: animal, contemporary, fantasy, folktales, health, history, humorous, multicultural, nature/environment, problem solving, religious, romance, science fiction, sports, suspense/mystery. Buys 6-8 mss/year. Query with published clips. Length: 1,000-1,500 words. Pays £90 for short story and £80/episode for serial.

NONFICTION Considers Young Readers: animal, arts/crafts, concept, cooking, games/puzzles, health, history, how-to, interview/profile, math, nature/environment, science, sports. Middle Readers: animal, arts/crafts, concept, cooking, games/puzzles, health, history, interview/profile, math, nature/environment, science, sports. Buys 48 mss/year. Query. Length: 600-800 words. Pays £50-75/feature.

HOW TO CONTACT Editorial lead time is 1 year. Responds to queries in 6-8 weeks. Publishes ms 1 year after acceptance.

ILLUSTRATION Color artwork only.Works on assignment only. For first contact, query with samples. Submit samples to Jackie Berry, Editor. Responds only if interested. Samples not returned. Samples filed.

TERMS Buys exclusive magazine rights. Pays on publication. Sample copy for £5. Writer's guidelines online at website.

TIPS "We only accept a high level of educational material for children ages 8-13 with a good standard of literacy and ability."

○ ASK

ePals Media, 70 E. Lake St., Suite 800, Chicago IL 60601. **E-mail:** ask@askmagkids.com. **Website:** www.cricketmag.com. **Contact:** Liz Huyck, editor. Magazine published 9 times/year covering science for children ages 6-9. "*ASK* is a magazine of arts and sciences for curious kids who like to find out how the world works." Estab. 2002.

NONFICTION Needs young readers, middle readers: science, engineering, invention, machines, archaeology, animals, nature/environment, history, history of science. "*ASK* commissions most articles but welcomes queries from authors on all nonfiction subjects. Particularly looking for odd, unusual, and interesting stories likely to interest science-oriented kids. Writers interested in working for *ASK* should send a résumé and writing sample (including at least 1 page unedited) for consideration." Average word length: 150-1,600.

ILLUSTRATION Buys 10 illustrations/issue; 60 illustrations/year. Works on assignment only. For illustrations, send query with samples.

PHOTOS Buys 10 illustrations/issue; 60 illustrations/year. Works on assignment only. For illustrations, send query with samples.

TERMS Byline given. Visit www.cricketmag.com/19-Submission-Guidelines-for-ASK-magazine-for-children-ages-6-9 for current issue theme list and calendar.

◉ AUSTRALASIAN JOURNAL OF EARLY CHILDHOOD

Early Childhood Australia, P.O. Box 86, Deakin West ACT 2600, Australia. (61)(2)6242-1800. **Fax:** (61)(2)6242-1818. **E-mail:** publishing@earlychildhood.org.au. **Website:** www.earlychildhoodaustralia.org.

au. **Contact:** Chris Jones, publishing manager. Nonprofit early childhood advocacy organization, acting in the interests of young children aged from birth to 8 years of age, their families and those in the early childhood field. Specialist publisher of early childhood magazines, journals, and booklets.

NONFICTION Needs essays. Send complete ms. Length: Magazine articles, 600-1,000 words; research-based papers, 3,000-6,500 words; submissions for booklets, approximately 5,000 words.

TERMS Guidelines available online.

BABYBUG

70 East Lake St., Suite 800, Chicago IL 60601. **E-mail:** babybug@babybugmagkids.com. **Website:** www.cricketmag.com/babybug; www.babybugmagkids.com. **Contact:** Submissions editor. *Babybug* is a look-and-listen magazine for babies and toddlers ages 6 months-3 years. Publishes 9 issues per year. Estab. 1994. Circ. 45,000.

FICTION Very short, clear fiction. rhythmic, rhyming Length: 6 sentences maximum. Up to 25¢/word. Payment after publication. Rights vary.

NONFICTION very short clear fiction submittable. cricketmag.com; www.cricketmag.com/submissions Six sentence maximum Pays up to 25¢ per word. Payment after publication. Rights vary.

POETRY "We are especially interested in rhythmic and rhyming poetry. Poems may explore a baby's day or they may be more whimsical." Pays up to $3/line; $25 minimum. Payment after publication. Rights vary.

HOW TO CONTACT Responds in 6 months to mss.

ILLUSTRATION Uses color artwork only. Works on assignment only. Reviews ms/illustration packages from artists. "The manuscripts will be evaluated for quality of concept and text before the art is considered." Contact: Suzanne Beck. Illustrations only: Send tearsheets or photo prints/photocopies with SASE. "Submissions without SASE will be discarded." Responds in 3 months. Samples filed.

PHOTOS Pays $500/spread; $250/page.

TERMS Byline given. 50% freelance written. Guidelines available online.

TIPS "Imagine having to read your story or poem—out loud—50 times or more! That's what parents will have to do. Babies and toddlers demand, 'Read it again!' Your material must hold up under repetition. And humor is much appreciated by all."

BOYS' LIFE

Boy Scouts of America, P.O. Box 152079, 1325 West Walnut Hill Lane, Irving TX 75015. (972)580-2366. **Fax:** (972)580-2079. **Website:** www.boyslife.org. **Contact:** J.D. Owen, editor-in-chief; Michael Goldman, managing editor; Paula Murphey, senior editor. *Boys' Life* is a monthly 4-color general interest magazine for boys 7-18, most of whom are Cub Scouts, Boy Scouts or Venturers. Estab. 1911. Circ. 1.1 million.

FICTION Needs All fiction is assigned.

NONFICTION Scouting activities and general interests (nature, Earth, health, cars, sports, science, computers, space and aviation, entertainment, history, music, animals, how-to's, etc.) Query with SASE. No phone queries. Averge word length for articles: 500-1,500 words, including sidebars and boxes. Average word length for columns: 300-750. Pay ranges from $400-1,500.

HOW TO CONTACT Responds to queries/mss in 2 months. Publishes approximately one year after acceptance. Accepts queries by mail.

ILLUSTRATION Buys 10-12 illustrations/issue; 100-125 illustrations/year. Works on assignment only. Reviews ms/illustration packages from artists. "Query first." Illustrations only: Send tearsheets. Responds to art samples only if interested. Samples returned with SASE. Original artwork returned at job's completion. Works on assignment only.

PHOTOS Photo guidelines free with SASE. Boy Scouts of America Magazine Division also publishes *Scouting* magazine. "Most photographs are from specific assignments that freelance photojournalists shoot for *Boys' Life*. Interested in all photographers, but do not send unsolicited images." Pays $500 base editorial day rate against placement fees, plus expenses. **Pays on acceptance.** Buys one-time rights.

TERMS Buys one-time rights. Byline given. Pays on acceptance. 75% freelance written. Prefers to work with published/established writers; works with small number of new/unpublished writers each year. Sample copies for $3.95 plus 9x12 SASE. Guidelines available online.

TIPS "We strongly recommend reading at least 12 issues of the magazine before submitting queries. We are a good market for any writer willing to do the necessary homework. Write for a boy you know who is 12. Our readers demand punchy writing in relatively short, straightforward sentences. The editors demand well-reported articles that demonstrate high standards of journalism. We follow the *Associated Press* manual of style and usage. Learn and read our publications before submitting anything."

BOYS' QUEST

P.O. Box 227, Bluffton OH 45817-0227. (419)358-4610, ext. 101. **Fax:** (419)358-8020. **Website:** www.funforkidzmagazines.com. **Contact:** Marilyn Edwards, editor. Bimonthly magazine. "*Boys' Quest* is a magazine created for boys from 5 to 14 years, with youngsters 8, 9 and 10 the specific target age. Our point of view is that every young boy deserves the right to be a young boy for a number of years before he becomes a young adult." Estab. 1995. Circ. 10,000.

FICTION Picture-oriented material, young readers, middle readers: adventure, animal, history, humorous, multicultural, nature/environment, problem-solving, sports. Does not want to see violence, teenage themes. Buys 30 mss/year. Query or send complete ms (preferred). Send SASE with correct postage. No faxed or e-mailed material. Length: 200-500 words.

NONFICTION Needs nonfiction pieces that are accompanied by clear photos. Articles accompanied by photos with high resolution are far more likely to be accepted than those that need illustrations. Query or send complete ms (preferred). Send SASE with correct postage. No faxed or e-mailed material. Length: 500 words.

POETRY Reviews poetry. Limit submissions to 6 poems. Length: 21 lines maximum.

HOW TO CONTACT Responds to queries in 2 weeks; mss in 2 weeks (if rejected); 6 weeks (if scheduled). Accepts queries by mail.

ILLUSTRATION Buys 10 illustrations/issue; 60-70 illustrations/year. Uses b&w artwork only. Works on assignment only. Reviews ms/illustration packages from artists. Illustrations only: Query with samples, tearsheets. Responds in 1 month only if interested and a SASE. Samples returned with SASE; samples filed. Credit line given.

PHOTOS Photos used for support of nonfiction. "Excellent photographs included with a nonfiction story is considered very seriously." Model/property releases required. Uses b&w, 5x7 or 3x5 prints. Query with samples; send unsolicited photos by mail. Responds in 3 weeks. "We use a number of photos, printed in b&w, inside the magazine. These photos support the articles." $5/photo.

TERMS Buys first North American serial rights for mss. Byline given. Pays on publication. Guidelines and open themes available for SASE, or visit www.funforkidz.com and click on 'Writers' at the bottom of the homepage.

TIPS "First be familiar with our magazines. We are looking for lively writing, most of it from a young boy's point of view—with the boy or boys directly involved in an activity that is both wholesome and unusual. We need nonfiction with photos and fiction stories—around 500 words—puzzles, poems, cooking, carpentry projects, jokes and riddles. Nonfiction pieces that are accompanied by b&w photos are far more likely to be accepted than those that need illustrations. We will entertain simultaneous submissions as long as that fact is noted on the ms."

BREAD FOR GOD'S CHILDREN

P.O. Box 1017, Arcadia FL 34265. (863)494-6214. **Fax:** (863)993-0154. **E-mail:** bread@breadministries.org. **Website:** www.breadministries.org. **Contact:** Judith M. Gibbs, editor. An interdenominational Christian teaching publication published 6-8 times/year written to aid children and youth in leading a Christian life. Estab. 1972. Circ. 10,000 (U.S. & Canada).

FICTION "We are looking for writers who have a solid knowledge of Biblical principles and are concerned for the youth of today living by those principles. Our stories must be well written, with the story itself getting the message across—no preaching, moralizing, or tag endings." Young readers, middle readers, young adult/teen: adventure, religious, problem-solving, sports. Looks for "teaching stories that portray Christian lifestyles without preaching." Buys approximately 10-15 mss/year. Send complete ms. Length: young children—600-800 words; older children—900-1,500 words. Pays $40-50.

NONFICTION All levels: how-to. "We do not want anything detrimental to solid family values. Most topics will fit if they are slanted to our basic needs." Buys 3-4 mss/year. Length: 500-800 words.

HOW TO CONTACT Responds to mss in 6 months. Publishes ms an average of 6 months after acceptance. Accepts queries by mail.

ILLUSTRATION "The only illustrations we purchase are those occasional good ones accompanying an accepted story."

TERMS Pays on publication. Pays $30-50 for stories; $30 for articles. Sample copies free for 9×12 SAE and 5 first-class stamps (for 2 copies). Buys first rights. Byline given. No kill fee. 10% freelance written. Three sample copies for 9x12 SAE and 5 first-class stamps. Guidelines for #10 SASE.

TIPS "We want stories or articles that illustrate overcoming obstacles by faith and living solid, Christian lives. Know our publication and what we have used in the past. Know the readership and publisher's guidelines. Stories should teach the value of morality and honesty without preaching. Edit carefully for content and grammar."

BRILLIANT STAR

1233 Central St., Evanston IL 60201. (847)853-2354. **E-mail:** brilliant@usbnc.org; sengle@usbnc.org. **Website:** www.brilliantstarmagazine.org. **Contact:** Susan Engle, associate editor; Amethel Parel-Sewell, art director. "*Brilliant Star* presents Bahá'í history and principles through fiction, nonfiction, activities, interviews, puzzles, cartoons, games, music, and art. Universal values of good character, such as kindness, courage, creativity, and helpfulness are incorporated into the magazine." Estab. 1969.

FICTION Needs middle readers: contemporary, fantasy, folktale, multicultural, nature/environment, problem-solving, religious. Submit complete ms. Length: 700-1,400 words.

NONFICTION Middle readers: arts/crafts, games/puzzles, geography, how-to, humorous, multicultural, nature/environment, religion, social issues. Query. Length: 300-700 words.

POETRY "We only publish poetry written by children at the moment."

ILLUSTRATION Reviews ms/illustration packages from artists. Illustrations only; query with samples. Contact: Aaron Kreader, graphic designer. Responds only if interested. Samples kept on file. Credit line given.

PHOTOS Buys photos with accompanying ms only. Model/property release required; captions required. Responds only if interested.

TERMS Buys first rights and reprint rights for mss, artwork, and photos. Byline given. Pays 2 contributor's copies. Guidelines available for SASE or via e-mail.

TIPS "*Brilliant Star*'s content is developed with a focus on children in their 'tween' years, ages 8-12. This is a period of intense emotional, physical, and psychological development. Familiarize yourself with the interests and challenges of children in this age range. Protagonists in our fiction are usually in the upper part of our age range: 10-12 years old. They solve their problems without adult intervention. We appreciate seeing a sense of humor but not related to bodily functions or put-downs. Keep your language and concepts age-appropriate. Use short words, sentences, and paragraphs. Activities and games may be submitted in rough or final form. Send us a description of your activity along with short, simple instructions. We avoid long, complicated activities that require adult supervision. If you think they will be helpful, please try to provide step-by-step rough sketches of the instructions. You may also submit photographs to illustrate the activity."

CADET QUEST MAGAZINE

1333 Alger St. SE, Grand Rapids MI 49507. (616)241-5616. **Fax:** (616)241-5558. **E-mail:** submissions@calvinistcadets.org. **Website:** www.calvinistcadets.org. **Contact:** G. Richard Broene, editor. Magazine published 7 times/year. *Cadet Quest Magazine* shows boys 9-14 how God is at work in their lives and in the world around them. Estab. 1958. Circ. 6,000.

◯ Accepts submissions by mail or by e-mail (must include ms in text of e-mail). Will not open attachments.

FICTION Middle readers, boys/early teens: adventure, arts/craft, games/puzzles, hobbies, humorous, multicultural, religious, science, sports. Fast-moving stories that appeal to a boy's sense of adventure or sense of humor are welcome. Needs adventure, religious. spiritual, sports Avoid preachiness. Avoid simplistic answers to complicated problems. Avoid long dialogue and little action. No fantasy, science fiction, fashion, horror, or erotica. Send complete ms. Length: 900-1,500 words. Pays 4-6¢/word, and 1 contributor's copy.

NONFICTION Needs how-to, humor, inspirational, interview, personal experience. informational Send complete ms. Length: 500-1,500 words. Pays 4-6¢/word.

HOW TO CONTACT Responds in 2 months to mss. Publishes ms an average of 4-11 months after acceptance.

ILLUSTRATION Buys 2 illustrations/issue; buys 12 illustrations/year. Works on assignment only. Reviews ms/illustration packages from artists.

PHOTOS Pays $20-30 for photos purchased with ms.

TERMS Buys first North American serial rights, buys one-time rights, buys second serial (reprint) rights, buys simultaneous rights. Rights purchased vary with author and material. Byline given. Pays on acceptance. No kill fee. 40% freelance written. Works with a small number of new/unpublished writers each year. Sample copy for 9x12 SASE. Guidelines for #10 SASE.

TIPS "Best time to submit stories/articles is early in the year (January-April). Also remember readers are boys ages 9-14. Stories must reflect or add to the theme of the issue and be from a Christian perspective."

CALLIOPE

30 Grove St., Suite C, Peterborough NH 03458-1454. (603)924-7209. **Fax:** (603)924-7380. **E-mail:** customerservice@caruspub.com. **Website:** www.cobblestonepub.com. **Contact:** Rosalie Baker and Charles Baker, co-editors; Lou Waryncia, editorial director; Ann Dillon, art director. Magazine published 9 times/year covering world history (East and West) through 1800 AD for 8 to 14-year-old kids. Articles must relate to the issue's theme. Lively, original approaches to the subject are the primary concerns of the editors in choosing material. Estab. 1990. Circ. 13,000.

FICTION Middle readers and young adults: adventure, folktales, plays, history, biographical fiction. Material must relate to forthcoming themes. Needs adventure, historical. biographical, retold legends Length: no more than 1,000 words. Pays 20-25¢/word.

NONFICTION Needs essays, general interest, historical, how-to, crafts/woodworking, humor, interview, personal experience, photo feature, technical, travel. recipes Query with writing sample, 1-page outline, bibliography, SASE. Length: 400-1000 words/feature articles; 300-600 words/supplemental nonfiction. Pays 20-25¢/word.

HOW TO CONTACT If interested, responds 5 months before publication date. Accepts queries by mail.

PHOTOS "Illustrations only: Send tearsheets, photocopies. Original work returned upon job's completion (upon written request). Buys photos from freelancers. Wants photos pertaining to any upcoming themes. Uses b&w/color prints, 35mm transparencies and 300 DPI digital images. Send unsolicited photos by mail (on speculation). Buys all rights for mss and artwork." If you have photographs pertaining to any upcoming theme, please contact the editor by mail or fax, or send them with your query. You may also send images on speculation. Model/property release preferred. Reviews b&w prints, color slides. Reviews photos with or without accompanying manuscript. We buy one-time use. Our suggested fee range for professional quality photographs follows: ¼ page to full page b/w $15-100; color $25-100. Please note that fees for non-professional quality photographs are negotiated. Cover fees are set on an individual basis for one-time use, plus promotional use. All cover images are color. Prices set by museums, societies, stock photography houses, etc., are paid or negotiated. Photographs that are promotional in nature (e.g., from tourist agencies, organizations, special events, etc.) are usually submitted at no charge. Pays on publication. Credit line given. Buys one-time rights; negotiable.

TERMS Buys all rights. Byline given. Pays on publication. Kill fee. 50% freelance written. Sample copy for $5.95, $2 shipping and handling, and 10x13 SASE. Guidelines available online.

TIPS "A query must consist of the following to be considered: a brief cover letter stating subject and word length of the proposed article; a detailed one-page outline explaining the information to be presented in the article; a bibliography of materials the author intends to use in preparing the article; a SASE. Writers new to *Calliope* should send a writing sample with query. In all correspondence, please include your complete address as well as a telephone number where you can be reached. A writer may send as many queries for one issue as he or she wishes, but each query must have a separate cover letter, outline and bibliography as well as a SASE. Telephone and e-mail queries are not accepted. Handwritten queries will not be considered. Queries may be submitted at any time, but queries sent well in advance of deadline may not be answered for several months."

CARUS PUBLISHING COMPANY

30 Grove St., Suite C, Peterborough NH 03458. **Website:** www.cricketmag.com. "We do not accept e-mailed submissions. Mss must be typed and accompanied by an SASE so that we may respond to your submission. Mss without an accompanying SASE will not be considered. Unfortunately, we are unable to return mss. Please do not send us your only copy. When submitting poetry, please send us no more than 6 poems at a time. Be sure to include phone and e-mail contact information. Please allow us up to 8

months for careful consideration of your submission. No phone calls, please."

See listings for *Babybug, Cicada, Click, Cricket, Ladybug, Muse, Spider* and *ASK*. Carus Publishing owns Cobblestone Publishing, publisher of *AppleSeeds, Calliope, Cobblestone, Dig, Faces* and *Odyssey*.

CATHOLIC FORESTER

Catholic Order of Foresters, 355 Shuman Blvd., P.O. Box 3012, Naperville IL 60566-7012. **Fax:** (630)983-3384. **E-mail:** magazine@catholicforester.org. **Website:** www.catholicforester.org. **Contact:** Editor; art director. Quarterly magazine for members of the Catholic Order of Foresters, a fraternal insurance benefit society. "*Catholic Forester* is a quarterly magazine filled with product features, member stories, and articles affirming fraternalism, unity, friendship, and true Christian charity among members. Although a portion of each issue is devoted to the organization and its members, a few freelance pieces are published in most issues. These articles cover varied topics to create a balanced issue for the purpose of informing, educating, and entertaining our readers." Estab. 1883. Circ. 77,000.

FICTION Needs humorous, religious. inspirational 1-5 Length: 500-1,500 words. Pays 50¢/word.

NONFICTION Needs health and wellness, money management and budgeting, parenting and family life, insurance, nostalgia, humor, inspirational, religious. Will consider previously published work. Send complete ms by mail, fax, or e-mail. Rejected material will not be returned without accompanying SASE. Length: 500-1,000 words. Pays 50¢/word.

POETRY Length: 15 lines maximum. Pays 30¢/word.

HOW TO CONTACT Editorial lead time 6 months. Responds in 3 months to mss.

ILLUSTRATION Buys 2-4 illustrations/issue. Uses color artwork only.

PHOTOS State availability. Negotiates payment individually.

TERMS Buys first North American serial rights. Pays on acceptance. 5% freelance written. Sample copy for 9x12 SAE and 4 first-class stamps. Guidelines available on website.

TIPS "Our audience includes a broad age spectrum, ranging from youth to seniors. A good children's story with a positive lesson or message would rate high on our list."

☺ CHEMMATTERS

1155 16th St., NW, Washington DC 20036. (202)872-6164. **Fax:** (202)833-7732. **E-mail:** chemmatters@acs.org. **Website:** www.acs.org/chemmatters. **Contact:** Patrice Pages, editor; Cornithia Harris, art director. Covers content covered in a standard high school chemistry textbook. Estab. 1983.

NONFICTION Query with published clips. Pays $500-1,000 for article. Additional payment for mss/illustration packages and for photos accompanying articles.

HOW TO CONTACT Responds to queries/mss in 4 weeks. Publishes ms 6 months after acceptance. Accepts queries by mail, e-mail.

ILLUSTRATION Buys 3 illustrations/issue; 12 illustrations/year. Uses color artwork only. Works on assignment only. Reviews ms/illustration packages from artists. Query. Illustrations only: Query with promo sheet, résumé. Samples returned with self-addressed stamped envelope; samples not filed. Credit line given.

PHOTOS Looking for photos of high school students engaged in science-related activities. Model/property release required; captions required. Uses color prints, but prefers high-resolution PDFs. Query with samples. Responds in 2 weeks.

TERMS Minimally buys first North American serial rights, but prefers to buy all rights, reprint rights, electronic rights for mss. Buys all rights for artwork; non-exclusive first rights for photos. Pays on acceptance. Sample copies free for 10x13 SASE and 3 first-class stamps. Writer's guidelines free for SASE (available as e-mail attachment upon request).

TIPS "Be aware of the content covered in a standard high school chemistry textbook. Choose themes and topics that are timely, interesting, fun, *and* that relate to the content and concepts of the first-year chemistry course. Articles should describe real people involved with real science. Best articles feature young people making a difference or solving a problem."

CICADA MAGAZINE

Cricket Magazine Group, 70 E. Lake St., Suite 800, Chicago IL 60601. **E-mail:** cicada@cicadamag.com. **Website:** www.cricketmag.com/cicada. **Contact:** Submissions editor. Bimonthly literary magazine for ages 14 and up. Publishes 6 issues per year. Estab. 1998. Circ. 10,000.

FICTION Realistic, contemporary and historical fiction as well as humor, mysteries, fantasy and science fiction. Length: 9,000 words maximum Pays up to 25¢/word.

NONFICTION Needs essays, personal experience. First-person experiences of interest to teens and young adult readers. submittable.cricketmag.com; www.cricketmag.com/submissions Length: 5,000 words maximum; Pays up to 25¢/word.

POETRY Reviews serious, humorous, free verse, rhyming. Length: 25 lines maximum. Pays up to $3/line ($25 minimum).

HOW TO CONTACT Responds in 3-6 months to mss.

ILLUSTRATION Buys 10 illustrations/issue; 60 illustrations/year. Uses color artwork for cover; b&w for interior. Works on assignment only. Reviews ms/illustration packages from artists. "To submit samples, e-mail a link to your online portfolio to: cicada@cicadamag.com. You may also e-mail a sample up to a maximum attachment size of 50 KB. We will keep your samples on file and contact you if we find an assignment that suits your style."

PHOTOS Wants documentary photos (clear shots that illustrate specific artifacts, persons, locations, phenomena, etc., cited in the text) and "art" shots of teens in photo montage/lighting effects etc.

TERMS Pays after publication. Guidelines available online at submittable.cricketmag.com or www.cricketmag.com/submissions

TIPS "Quality writing, good literary style, genuine teen sensibility, depth, humor, good character development, avoidance of stereotypes. Read several issues to familiarize yourself with our style."

CLICK

Carus Publishing, 30 Grove St., Suite C, Peterborough NH 03458. **E-mail:** click@caruspub.com. **Website:** www.cricketmag.com. **Contact:** Amy Tao, editor; Deb Porter, art director. Magazine covering areas of interest for children ages 3-7. "*Click* is a science and exploration magazine for children ages 3-7. Designed and written with the idea that it's never too early to encourage a child's natural curiosity about the world, *Click*'s 40 full-color pages are filled with amazing photographs, beautiful illustrations, and stories and articles that are both entertaining and thought-provoking."

○ *Does not accept unsolicited mss.*

FICTION Wants short stories suitable for children 3-7. "*Click* seeks stories that contain and explain nonfiction concepts within them. Since it is part of *Click*'s mission to encourage children to question, observe, and explore, successful stories often show children engaged in finding out about their universe—with the help of supportive, but not all-knowing, adults." Query. Length: 600-1,000 words.

NONFICTION Query with résumé and writing samples. Length: 200-400 words.

POETRY Wants poems suitable for ages 3-7. Query.

ILLUSTRATION Buys 10 illustrations/issue; 100 illustrations/year. Works on assignment only. Query with samples. Responds only if interested. Credit line given.

TERMS Guidelines online.

TIPS "The best way for writers to understand what *Click* is looking for is to read the magazine. Writers are encouraged to examine several past copies before submitting an article or story."

COBBLESTONE

Carus Publishing, 30 Grove St., Suite C, Peterborough NH 03458. (800)821-0115. **Fax:** (603)924-7380. **E-mail:** customerservice@caruspub.com. **Website:** www.cobblestonepub.com. Covers American history for ages 9-14. "We are interested in articles of historical accuracy and lively, original approaches to the subject at hand. Writers are encouraged to study recent *Cobblestone* back issues for content and style. All material must relate to the theme of a specific upcoming issue in order to be considered. To be considered, a query must accompany each individual idea (however, you can mail them all together) and must include the following: a brief cover letter stating the subject and word length of the proposed article, a detailed one-page outline explaining the information to be presented in the article, an extensive bibliography of materials the author intends to use in preparing the article, a SASE. Authors are urged to use primary resources and up-to-date scholarly resources in their bibliography. Writers new to COBBLESTONE® should send a writing sample with the query. If you would like to know if your query has been received, please also include a stamped postcard that requests acknowledgment of receipt. In all correspondence, please include your complete address as well as a telephone number where you can be reached. A writer may send as many queries for one issue as he or she wishes, but each query must have a separate cover letter, outline, bibliography, and SASE. All queries must be typed. Please do not send unsolicited manuscripts—queries only! Prefers to work with published/established writers.

Each issue presents a particular theme, making it exciting as well as informative. Half of all subscriptions are for schools. All material must relate to monthly theme." Circ. 15,000.

◯ *Cobblestone* stands apart from other children's magazines by offering a solid look at one subject and stressing strong editorial content, color photographs throughout, and original illustrations." *Cobblestone* themes and deadline are available on website or with SASE.

FICTION Needs adventure, historical. biographical, retold legends, folktales, multicultural Query. Length: 800 words maximum. Pays 20-25¢/word.

NONFICTION Needs historical, humor, interview, personal experience, photo feature, travel, crafts, recipes, activities. Query with writing sample, 1-page outline, bibliography, SASE. Length: 800 words/feature articles; 300-600 words/supplemental nonfiction; 700 words maximum/activities. Pays 20-25¢/word.

POETRY Serious and light verse considered. Must have clear, objective imagery. Length: 100 lines maximum. Pays on an individual basis. Acquires all rights.

HOW TO CONTACT Accepts queries by mail, fax.

ILLUSTRATION Reviews ms/illustration packages from artists. Query. Illustrations only: Send photocopies, tearsheets, or other nonreturnable samples. "Illustrators should consult issues of *Cobblestone* to familiarize themselves with our needs." Responds to art samples in 1 month. Samples are not returned; samples filed. Original artwork returned at job's completion (upon written request). Credit line given. Illustrators: "Submit color samples, not too juvenile. Study past issues to know what we look for. The illustration we use is generally for stories, recipes and activities."

PHOTOS Captions, identification of subjects required, model release. Reviews contact sheets, transparencies, prints. $15-100/b&w. Pays on publication. Credit line given. Buys one-time rights. Our suggested fee range for professional quality photographs follows: ¼ page to full page b/w $15 to $100; color $25 to $100. Please note that fees for non-professional quality photographs are negotiated.

TERMS Buys all rights. Byline given. Pays on publication. Offers 50% kill fee. 50% freelance written. Guidelines available on website or with SASE; sample copy for $6.95, $2 shipping/handling, 10x13 SASE.

TIPS "Review theme lists and past issues to see what we're looking for."

MAGAZINES

COLLEGEXPRESS MAGAZINE

Carnegie Communications, LLC, 2 LAN Dr., Suite 100, Westford MA 01886. **E-mail:** info@carne giecomm.com. **Website:** www.collegexpress.com. *CollegeXpress Magazine*, formerly *Careers and Colleges*, provides juniors and seniors in high school with editorial, tips, trends, and websites to assist them in the transition to college, career, young adulthood, and independence.

○ Distributed to 760,000 homes of 15- to 17-year-olds and college-bound high school graduates, and 10,000 high schools.

NONFICTION Needs Young adults/teens: careers, college, health, how-to, humorous, interview/profile, personal development, problem-solving, social issues, sports, travel. Query. Length: 1,000-1,500 words.

HOW TO CONTACT Responds to queries in 6 weeks. Accepts queries by mail, e-mail.

ILLUSTRATION Buys 2 illustrations/issue; buys 8 illustrations/year. Works on assignment only. Reviews samples online. Query first. Credit line given.

TERMS Buys all rights. Byline given. Pays on acceptance plus 45 days. Contributor's guidelines available electronically.

TIPS "Articles with great quotes, good reporting, good writing. Rich with examples and anecdotes. Must tie in with the objective to help teenaged readers plan for their futures. Current trends, policy changes and information regarding college admissions, financial aid, and career opportunities."

CRICKET

70 E. Lake St., Suite 800, Chicago IL 60601. **E-mail:** cricket@cricketmagkids.com. **Website:** www.crick etmag.com/ckt-cricket-magazine-for-kids-ages-9-14; www.cricketmagkids.com. **Contact:** Submissions editor. Monthly magazine for children ages 9-14. "*Cricket* is a monthly literary magazine for ages 9-14." Publishes 9 issues per year. Estab. 1973. Circ. 73,000.

FICTION Needs realistic, contemporary, historic, humor, mysteries, fantasy, science fiction, folk/fairy tales, legend, myth. No didactic, sex, religious, or horror stories. Submit complete ms. Length: 1,200-1,800 words. Pays up to 25¢/word.

NONFICTION Biography, history, science, technology, natural history, social science, geography, foreign culture, travel, adventure, sports. Submittable. cricketmag.com; www.cricketmag.com/submissions. Length: 1,200-1,800 words. Pays up to 25¢/word.

POETRY Reviews poems. Serious, humorous, nonsense rhymes. Length: 35 lines maximum. Pays up to $3/line.

HOW TO CONTACT Responds in 3-6 months to mss. Accepts queries by mail.

ILLUSTRATION Buys 22 illustrations (7 separate commissions)/issue; 198 illustrations/year. Preferred theme for style: "stylized realism; strong people, especially kids; good action illustration; whimsical and humorous. All media, generally full color." Reviews ms/illustration packages from artists, "but reserves option to re-illustrate." Send complete ms with sample and query. Illustrations only: Provide link to web site or tearsheets and good quality photocopies to be kept on file. SASE required for response/return of samples.

TERMS Byline given. Pays on publication. Guidelines available online at submittable.cricketmag.com or www.cricketmag.com/submissions.

TIPS Writers: "Read copies of back issues and current issues. Adhere to specified word limits. *Please* do not query." Would currently like to see more fantasy and science fiction. Illustrators: "Send only your best work and be able to reproduce that quality in assignments. Put name and address on *all* samples. Know a publication before you submit."

DAVEY AND GOLIATH'S DEVOTIONS

Evangelical Lutheran Church in America, ELCA Churchwide Ministries, 8765 W. Higgins Rd., Chicago IL 60631. **E-mail:** daveyandgoliath@elca.org. **E-mail:** cllsub@augsburgfortress.com. **Website:** www.daveyandgoliath.org. "*Davey and Goliath's Devotions* is a magazine with concrete ideas that families can use to build Biblical literacy and share faith and serve others. It includes Bible stories, family activities, crafts, games, and a section of puzzles and mazes."

○ This is a booklet of interactive conversations and activities related to weekly devotional material. Used primarily by Lutheran families with elementary school-age children.

NONFICTION Needs religious. If you are interested in writing weekly content or puzzles or games, query with samples. Follow Weekly Content or Puzzles and Games Content guidelines, available online.

TERMS Buys all rights. Pays on acceptance of final ms.

TIPS "Pay attention to details in the sample devotional. Follow the process laid out in the information for prospective writers. Ability to interpret Bible texts appropriately for children is required. Content must be doable and fun for families on the go."

DIG

Cobblestone Publishing, 30 Grove St., Suite C, Peterborough NH 03450. (603)924-7209. **Fax:** (603)924-7380. **E-mail:** cfbakeriii@meganet.net. **Website:** www.cobblestonepub.com. **Contact:** Rosalie Baker, editor; Lou Waryncia, editorial director; Ann Dillon, art director. An archaeology magazine for kids ages 9-14. Publishes entertaining and educational stories about discoveries, artifacts, and archaeologists. Estab. 1999.

FICTION Query. "Writers new to *Dig* should send a writing sample with query." Multiple queries accepted, may not be answered for many months. Length: up to 800 words. Pays 20-25¢/printed word.

NONFICTION Query. "A query must consist of all of the following to be considered: a brief cover letter stating the subject and word length of the proposed article, a detailed one-page outline explaining the information to be presented in the article, a bibliography of materials the author intends to use in preparing the article, and an SASE. Writers new to *Dig* should send a writing sample with query." Multiple queries accepted; may not be answered for many months. Length: 700-800 words for feature articles; 300-600 words for supplemental nonfiction; up to 700 words for activities. Pays 20-25¢/printed word for feature articles and supplemental nonfiction. Pays activities, puzzles, and games on an individual basis.

ILLUSTRATION Buys 10-15 illustrations/issue; 60-75 illustrations/year. Prefers color artwork. Works on assignment only. Reviews ms/illustration packages from artists. Query. Illustrations only: Query with samples. Arrange portfolio review. Send tearsheets. Responds in 2 months only if interested. Samples not returned; samples filed. Credit line given.

PHOTOS Uses anything related to archaeology, history, artifacts, and current archaeological events that relate to kids. Uses color prints and 35mm transparencies and 300 dpi digital images. Provide résumé, promotional literature, or tearsheets to be kept on file. Responds only if interested.

TERMS Buys all rights for mss. Buys first North American rights for photos. Pays on publication. Sample copy for $6.95 + $2 s&h.

TIPS "We are looking for writers who can communicate archaeological concepts in a conversational, interesting, informative, and *accurate* style for kids."

Writers should have some idea where photography can be located to support their articles."

DIG MAGAZINE

Carus Publishing Co., 30 Grove St., Suite C, Peterborough NH 03458. (603)924-7209. **Fax:** (603)924-7380. **Website:** www.digonsite.com. **Contact:** Rosalie Baker, editor. Magazine published 9 times/year covering archaeology for kids ages 9-14. *Dig* lets young people share in the thrill of archaeological discovery while learning about the cultural, scientific, and architectural traits and beliefs of different societies. Recent developments in the field of archaeology form the magazine's core subject matter. Estab. 1999. Circ. 20,000.

NONFICTION Needs personal experience, photo feature, travel, archaeological excavation reports. Query with published clips. Length: 100-1,000 words. Pays 20-25¢/word.

POETRY Query. Length: up to 100 lines.

HOW TO CONTACT Editorial lead time 1 year. Responds in several months. Publishes ms an average of 1 year after acceptance. Accepts queries by mail.

PHOTOS State availability. Identification of subjects required. Negotiates payment individually.

TERMS Buys all rights. Byline given. Pays on publication. No kill fee. 75% freelance written. Sample copy for $5.95 with 8x11 SASE or $10 without SASE. Guidelines available online.

TIPS "Please remember that this is a children's magazine for kids ages 9-14 so the tone is as kid-friendly as possible given the scholarship involved in researching and describing a site or a find."

DRAMATICS MAGAZINE

Educational Theatre Association, 2343 Auburn Ave., Cincinnati OH 45219. (513)421-3900. **E-mail:** dcorathers@schooltheatre.org. **Website:** http://schooltheatre.org. **Contact:** Don Corathers, editor. *Dramatics* is for students (mainly high school age) and teachers of theater. Mix includes how-to (tech theater, acting, directing, etc.), informational, interview, photo feature, humorous, profile, technical. *Dramatics* wants student readers to grow as theater artists and become a more discerning and appreciative audience. Material is directed to both theater students and their teachers, with strong student slant. Tries to portray the theater community in all its diversity. Estab. 1929. Circ. 35,000.

FICTION Young adults: drama (one-act and full-length plays). "We prefer unpublished scripts that have been produced at least once." Does not want to see plays that show no understanding of the conventions of the theater. No plays for children, no Christmas or didactic "message" plays. Submit complete ms. Buys 5-9 plays/year. Emerging playwrights have better chances with résumé of credits. Length: 750-3,000 words. Pays $100-500 for plays.

NONFICTION Needs young adults: arts/crafts, careers, how-to, interview/profile, multicultural (all theater-related). Submit complete ms. Length: 750-3,000 words. Pays $50-500 for articles.

HOW TO CONTACT Publishes ms 3 months after acceptance.

ILLUSTRATION Buys 0-2 illustrations/year. Works on assignment only. Arrange portfolio review; send résumé, promo sheets and tearsheets. Responds only if interested. Samples returned with SASE; sample not filed. Credit line given. Pays up to $100 for illustrations.

PHOTOS Buys photos with accompanying ms only. Looking for "good-quality production or candid photography to accompany article. We very occasionally publish photo essays." Model/property release and captions required. Prefers hi-res JPG files. Will consider prints or transparencies. Query with résumé of credits. Responds only if interested.

TERMS Byline given. Pays on acceptance. Sample copy available for 9x12 SAE with 4-ounce first-class postage. Guidelines available for SASE.

TIPS "Obtain our writer's guidelines and look at recent back issues. The best way to break in is to know our audience—drama students, teachers, and others interested in theater—and write for them. Writers who have some practical experience in theater, especially in technical areas, have an advantage, but we'll work with anybody who has a good idea. Some freelancers have become regular contributors."

FACES

Cobblestone Publishing, 30 Grove St., Suite C, Peterborough NH 03458. (603)924-7209; (800)821-0115. **Fax:** (603)924-7380. **E-mail:** customerservice@caruspub.com. **Website:** www.cobblestonepub.com. "Published 9 times/year, *Faces* covers world culture for ages 9-14. It stands apart from other children's magazines by offering a solid look at one subject and stressing strong editorial content, color photographs throughout, and original illustrations. *Faces* offers an equal balance of feature articles and activities, as well as folktales and legends." Estab. 1984. Circ. 15,000.

FICTION Needs ethnic, historical. retold legends/folktales, original plays Length: 800 words maximum. Pays 20-25¢/word.

NONFICTION Needs historical, humor, interview, personal experience, photo feature, travel. recipes, activities, crafts Query with writing sample, 1-page outline, bibliography, SASE. Length: 800 words/feature articles; 300-600/supplemental nonfiction; 700 words maximum/activities. Pays 20-25¢/word.

POETRY Serious and light verse considered. Must have clear, objective imagery. Length: 100 lines maximum. Pays on an individual basis.

HOW TO CONTACT Accepts queries by mail, e-mail.

ILLUSTRATION "Submit b&w samples, not too juvenile. Study past issues to know what we look for. The illustration we use is generally for retold legends, recipes and activities." Buys 3 illustrations/issue; buys 27 illustrations/year. Preferred theme or style: Material that is meticulously researched (most articles are written by professional anthropologists); simple, direct style preferred, but not too juvenile. Works on assignment only. Roughs required. Reviews ms/illustration packages from artists. Illustrations only: Send samples of b&w work. "Illustrators should consult issues of *Faces* to familiarize themselves with our needs." Responds to art samples only if interested. Samples returned with SASE. Original artwork returned at job's completion (upon written request). Credit line given.

PHOTOS Wants photos relating to forthcoming themes. "Contact the editor by mail or fax, or send photos with your query. You may also send images on speculation." Captions, identification of subjects, model releases required. Reviews contact sheets, transparencies, prints. Pays $15-100/b&w; $25-100/color; cover fees are negotiated.

TERMS Buys all rights. Byline given. Pays on publication. Offers 50% kill fee. 90-100% freelance written. Sample copy for $6.95, $2 shipping and handling, 10 x 13 SASE. Guidelines with SASE or online.

TIPS "Writers are encouraged to study past issues of the magazine to become familiar with our style and content. Writers with anthropological and/or travel experience are particularly encouraged; *Faces* is about world cultures. All feature articles, recipes and activities are freelance contributions."

FCA MAGAZINE

Fellowship of Christian Athletes, 8701 Leeds Rd., Kansas City MO 64129. (816)921-0909; (800)289-0909. **Fax:** (816)921-8755. **E-mail:** mag@fca.org. **Website:** www.fca.org/mag. **Contact:** Clay Meyer, editor; Matheau Casner, creative director. Published 6 times/year. "We seek to serve as a ministry tool of the Fellowship of Christian Athletes by informing, inspiring, and involving coaches, athletes, and all whom they influence, that they may make an impact for Jesus Christ." Estab. 1959. Circ. 80,000.

NONFICTION Needs inspirational, interview (with name athletes and coaches solid in their faith), personal experience, photo feature. "Articles should be accompanied by at least 3 quality photos." Query. Considers electronic sumbissions via e-mail. Length: 1,000-2,000 words. Pays $150-400 for assigned and unsolicited articles.

HOW TO CONTACT Responds to queries/mss in 3 months. Publishes ms an average of 4 months after acceptance.

PHOTOS Purchases photos separately. Looking for photos of sports action. Uses color prints and high resolution electronic files of 300 dpi or higher. State availability. Reviews contact sheets. Payment based on size of photo.

TERMS Buys first rights and second serial (reprint) rights. Byline given. Pays on publication. No kill fee. 50% freelance written. Prefers to work with published/established writers, but works with a growing number of new/unpublished writers each year. Sample copy for $2 and 9x12 SASE with 3 first-class stamps. Guidelines available at www.fca.org/mag/media-kit.

TIPS "Profiles and interviews of particular interest to coed athlete, primarily high school and college age. Our graphics and editorial content appeal to youth. The area most open to freelancers is profiles on or interviews with well-known athletes or coaches (male, female, minorities) who have been or are involved in some capacity with FCA."

THE FRIEND MAGAZINE

The Church of Jesus Christ of Latter-day Saints, 50 E. North Temple St., Salt Lake City UT 84150. (801)240-2210. **E-mail:** friend@ldschurch.org. **Website:** www.lds.org/friend. **Contact:** Paul B. Pieper, editor; Mark W. Robison, art director. Monthly magazine for 3-12 year olds. "The *Friend* is published by The Church of Jesus Christ of Latter-day Saints for boys and girls up to 12 years of age." Estab. 1971. Circ. 275,000.

FICTION Wants illustrated stories and "For Little Friends" stories. See guidelines online.

NONFICTION Needs historical, humor, inspirational, religious, adventure, ethnic, nature, family- and gospel-oriented puzzles, games, cartoons. Query by mail or e-mail first. Length: 1,000 words maximum. Pays $100-150 (400 words and up) for stories; $20 minimum for activities and games.

POETRY "We are looking for easy-to-illustrate poems with catchy cadences. Poems should convey a sense of joy and reflect gospel teachings. Also brief poems that will appeal to preschoolers." Length: 20 lines maximum. Pays $30 for poems.

HOW TO CONTACT Responds in 2 months to mss.

ILLUSTRATION Illustrations only: Query with samples; arrange personal interview to show portfolio; provide résumé and tearsheets for files.

TERMS Buys all rights for mss. "Authors may request rights to have their work reprinted after their ms is published." Pays on acceptance. Sample copy for $1.50, 9x12 envelope, and 4 first-class stamps.

FUN FOR KIDZ

P.O. Box 227, Bluffton OH 45817-0227. (419)358-4610. **Fax:** (419)358-8020. **Website:** http://funforkidz.com. **Contact:** Marilyn Edwards, articles editor. "*Fun for Kidz* is a magazine created for boys and girls ages 5-14, with youngsters 8, 9, and 10 the specific target age. The magazine is designed as an activity publication to be enjoyed by both boys and girls on the alternative months of *Hopscotch* and *Boys' Quest* magazines." Estab. 2002.

○ *Fun for Kidz* is theme-oriented. Send SASE for theme list and writer's guidelines or visit www.funforkidz.com and click on 'Writers' at the bottom of the homepage.

FICTION Needs picture-oriented material, young readers, middle readers: adventure, animal, history, humorous, problem-solving, multicultural, nature/environment, sports. Submit complete ms with SASE, contact info, and notation of which upcoming theme your content should be considered for. Length: 300-700 words. Pays minimum 5¢/word.

NONFICTION Needs picture-oriented material, young readers, middle readers: animal, arts/crafts, cooking, games/puzzles, history, hobbies, how-to, humorous, problem-solving, sports, carpentry projects.

Submit complete ms with SASE, contact info, and notation of which upcoming theme your content should be considered for. Length: 300-700 words. Pays minimum 5¢/word for articles; variable rate for games and projects, etc.

HOW TO CONTACT Responds in 2 weeks to queries; 6 weeks to mss. Accepts queries by mail.

ILLUSTRATION Works on assignment mostly. "We are anxious to find artists capable of illustrating stories and features. Our inside art is pen and ink." Query with samples. Samples kept on file.

PHOTOS "We use a number of b&w photos inside the magazine; most support the articles used."

TERMS Buys first North American serial rights. Byline given. Pays on acceptance. Sample copy for $6 in US, $8 for Canada, and $10.50 internationally.

TIPS "Our point of view is that every child deserves the right to be a child for a number of years before he or she becomes a young adult. As a result, *Fun for Kidz* looks for activities that deal with timeless topics, such as pets, nature, hobbies, science, games, sports, careers, simple cooking, and anything else likely to interest a child."

GIRLS' LIFE

Monarch Publishing, 4529 Harford Rd., Baltimore MD 21214. (410)426-9600. **Fax:** (866)793-1531. **E-mail:** writeforGL@girlslife.com. **Website:** www.girlslife.com. **Contact:** Jessica D'Argenio Waller, fashion editor; Chun Kim, art director. Bimonthly magazine covering girls ages 9-15. Estab. 1994. Circ. 363,000.

FICTION "We accept short fiction. They should be stand-alone stories and are generally 2,500-3,500 words."

NONFICTION Needs book excerpts, essays, general interest, how-to, humor, inspirational, interview, new product, travel. Query by mail with published clips. Submit complete mss on spec only. "Features and articles should speak to young women ages 10-15 looking for new ideas about relationships, family, friends, school, etc. with fresh, savvy advice. Front-of-the-book columns and quizzes are a good place to start." Length: 700-2,000 words. Pays $350/regular column; $500/feature.

HOW TO CONTACT Editorial lead time 4 months. Responds in 1 month to queries. Publishes ms an average of 3 months after acceptance. Accepts queries by mail, e-mail.

PHOTOS State availability with submission if applicable. Reviews contact sheets, negatives, transparencies. Negotiates payment individually. Captions, identification of subjects, model releases required. State availability. Captions, identification of subjects, model releases required. Reviews contact sheets, negatives, transparencies. Negotiates payment individually.

TERMS Buys all rights. Byline given. Pays on publication. Sample copy for $5 or online. Guidelines available online.

TIPS "Send thought-out queries with published writing samples and detailed résumé. Have fresh ideas and a voice that speaks to our audience-not down to them. And check out a copy of the magazine or visit girlslife.com before submitting."

◷ GREEN TEACHER

Green Teacher, 95 Robert St., Toronto ON M2S 2K5, Canada. (416)960-1244. **Fax:** (416)925-3474. **E-mail:** tim@greenteacher.com; info@greenteacher.com. **Website:** www.greenteacher.com. **Contact:** Tim Grant, co-editor; Brandon Quigley, editorial assistant. "*Green Teacher* is a magazine that helps youth educators enhance environmental and global education inside and outside of schools." Estab. 1991. Circ. 15,000.

NONFICTION multicultural, nature, environment Query. Submit one-page summary or outline. Length: 1,500-3,500 words.

HOW TO CONTACT Responds to queries in 1 week. Publishes ms 8 months after acceptance. Accepts queries by mail, e-mail.

ILLUSTRATION Buys 3 illustrations/issue from freelancers; 10 illustrations/year from freelancers. B&w artwork only. Works on assignment only. Reviews ms/illustration packages from artists. Query with samples; tearsheets. Responds only if interested. Samples not returned. Samples filed. Credit line given.

PHOTOS Purchases photos both separately and with accompanying mss. "Activity photos, environmental photos." Uses b&w prints. Query with samples. Responds only of interested.

TERMS Pays on acceptance.

GUIDE

55 W. Oak Ridge Dr., Hagerstown MD 21740. (301)393-4037. **Fax:** (301)393-4055. **E-mail:** guide@rhpa.org. **Website:** www.guidemagazine.org. **Contact:** Randy Fishell, editor; Brandon Reese, designer. "*Guide* is a Christian story magazine for young people ages 10-14. The 32-page, 4-color publication is pub-

lished weekly by the Review and Herald Publishing Association. Our mission is to show readers, through stories that illustrate Bible truth, how to walk with God now and forever." Estab. 1953.

NONFICTION Send complete ms. "Each issue includes 3-4 true stories. *Guide* does not publish fiction, poetry, or articles (devotionals, how-to, profiles, etc.). However, we sometimes accept quizzes and other unique nonstory formats. Each piece should include a clear spiritual element." Length: 1,000-1,200 words. Pays 7-10¢/word.

HOW TO CONTACT Responds in 6 weeks to mss. Accepts queries by mail, e-mail.

TERMS Buys first serial rights. Byline given. Pays on acceptance. Sample copy free with 6x9 SAE and 2 first-class stamps. Guidelines available on website.

TIPS "Children's magazines want mystery, action, discovery, suspense, and humor—no matter what the topic. For us, truth is stronger than fiction."

HIGHLIGHTS FOR CHILDREN

803 Church St., Honesdale PA 18431. (570)253-1080. **Fax:** (570)251-7847. **Website:** www.highlights.com. **Contact:** Christine French Cully, editor-in-chief. Monthly magazine for children up to ages 3-12. "This book of wholesome fun is dedicated to helping children grow in basic skills and knowledge, in creativeness, in ability to think and reason, in sensitivity to others, in high ideals, and worthy ways of living—for children are the world's most important people. We publish stories for beginning and advanced readers. Up to 500 words for beginning readers, up to 800 words for advanced readers." Estab. 1946. Circ. approximately 1.5 million.

FICTION Meaningful stories appealing to both girls and boys, up to age 12. Vivid, full of action. Engaging plot, strong characterization, lively language. Prefers stories in which a child protagonist solves a dilemma through his or her own resources. Seeks stories that the child ages 8-12 will eagerly read, and the younger child will like to hear when read aloud (500-800 words). Stories require interesting plots and a number of illustration possiblities. Also need rebuses (picture stories 100 words), stories with urban settings, stories for beginning readers (100-500 words), sports and humorous stories, adventures, holiday stories, and mysteries. We also would like to see more material of 1-page length (300 words), both fiction and factual. Needs adventure, fantasy, historical, humorous. ani-

mal, contemporary, folktales, multi-cultural, problem-solving, sports No sotries glorifying war, crime or violence. Send complete ms. Pays $100 minimum plus 2 contributor's copies.

NONFICTION "Generally we prefer to see a manuscript rather than a query. However, we will review queries regarding nonfiction." Length: 800 words maximum. Pays $25 for craft ideas and puzzles; $25 for fingerplays; $150 and up for articles.

POETRY Lines/poem: 16 maximum ("most poems are shorter"). Considers simultaneous submissions ("please indicate"); no previously published poetry. No e-mail submissions. "Submit typed manuscript with very brief cover letter." Occasionally comments on submissions "if manuscript has merit or author seems to have potential for our market." Guidelines available for SASE. Responds "generally within one month." Always sends prepublication galleys. Pays 2 contributors copies; "money varies." Acquires all rights.

HOW TO CONTACT Responds in 2 months to queries. Accepts queries by mail.

PHOTOS Reviews electronic files, color 35mm slides, photos.

TERMS Buys all rights. Pays on acceptance. 80% freelance written. Sample copy free. Guidelines on website in "Company" area.

TIPS "Know the magazine's style before submitting. Send for guidelines and sample issue if necessary." Writers: "At *Highlights* we're paying closer attention to acquiring more nonfiction for young readers than we have in the past." Illustrators: "Fresh, imaginative work encouraged. Flexibility in working relationships a plus. Illustrators presenting their work need not confine themselves to just children's illustrations as long as work can translate to our needs. We also use animal illustrations, real and imaginary. We need crafts, puzzles and any activity that will stimulate children mentally and creatively. Know our publication's standards and content by reading sample issues, not just the guidelines. Avoid tired themes, or put a fresh twist on an old theme so that its style is fun and lively. Write what inspires you, not what you think the market needs. We are pleased that many authors of children's literature report that their first published work was in the pages of *Highlights*. It is not our policy to consider fiction on the strength of the reputation of the author. We judge each submission on its own merits. Query with simple letter to establish whether the nonfiction subject is likely to be of interest. Expert reviews and complete bibliography required for non-fiction. A beginning writer should first become familiar with the type of material that *Highlights* publishes. Include special qualifications, if any, of author. Write for the child, not the editor. Write in a voice that children understand and relate to. Speak to today's kids, avoiding didactic, overt messages. Even though our general principles haven't changed over the years, we are contemporary in our approach to issues. Avoid worn themes."

HOPSCOTCH

P.O. Box 164, Bluffton OH 45817. (419)358-4610. **Fax:** (419)358-8020. **E-mail:** customerservice@funforkidz. com ("we do not accept submissions via e-mail"). **Website:** www.hopscotchmagazine.com. **Contact:** Marilyn Edwards, editor. "For girls from ages 5-14, featuring traditional subjects—pets, games, hobbies, nature, science, sports, etc.—with an emphasis on articles that show girls actively involved in unusual and/or worthwhile activities." Estab. 1989. Circ. 14,000.

FICTION Needs picture-oriented material, young readers, middle readers: adventure, animal, history, humorous, nature/environment, sports, suspense/mystery. Does not want to see stories dealing with dating, sex, fashion, hard rock music. Submit complete ms. Length: 300-700 words.

NONFICTION Picture-oriented material, young readers, middle readers: animal, arts/crafts, biography, cooking, games/puzzles, geography, hobbies, how-to, humorous, math, nature/environment, science. "Need more nonfiction with quality photos about a *Hopscotch*-age girl involved in a worthwhile activity." Query or submit complete ms. Length: 400-700 words.

HOW TO CONTACT Responds in 2 weeks to queries; 5 weeks to mss.

ILLUSTRATION Buys approximately 10 illustrations/issue. "Generally, the illustrations are assigned after we have purchased a piece (usually fiction). Occasionally, we will use a painting—in any given medium—for the cover, and these are usually seasonal." Uses b&w artwork only for inside; color for cover. Reviews ms/illustration packages from artists. Query first or send complete ms with final art. Illustrations only: Send résumé, portfolio, client list, and tearsheets. Responds to art samples only if interested and SASE in

1 month. Samples returned with SASE. Credit line given.

PHOTOS Purchases photos separately (cover only) and with accompanying ms only. Looking for photos to accompany article. Model/property releases required. Uses 5x7, b&w prints; 35mm transparencies. B&w photos should go with ms. Should show girl or girls ages 6-12.

TERMS Byline given. Pays on publication.

TIPS "Remember we publish only 6 issues a year, which means our editorial needs are extremely limited. Please look at our guidelines and our magazine. Remember, we use far more nonfiction than fiction. Guidelines and current theme list can be downloaded from our website. If decent photos accompany the piece, it stands an even better chance of being accepted. We believe it is the responsibility of the contributor to come up with photos. Please remember, our readers are 6-12 years—most are 8-10—and your text should reflect that. Many magazines try to entertain first and educate second. We try to do the reverse. Our magazine is more simplistic, like a book to be read from cover to cover. We are looking for wholesome, nondated material."

☺ HORSEPOWER

Box 670, Aurora ON L4G 4J9, Canada. (800)505-7428. **Fax:** (905)841-1530. **E-mail:** ftdesk@horse-canada. com. **Website:** www.horsepowermagazine.ca. **Contact:** Susan Stafford, managing editor. Bimonthly 16-page magazine, bound into *Horse Canada*, a bimonthly family horse magazine. "*Horsepower* offers how-to articles and stories relating to horse care for kids ages 6-16, with a focus on safety." Estab. 1988. Circ. 17,000.

☺ *Horsepower no longer accepts fiction.*

NONFICTION Needs Middle readers, young adults: arts/crafts, biography, careers, fashion, games/puzzles, health, history, hobbies, how-to, humorous, interview/profile, problem-solving, travel. Submit complete ms. Length: 500-1,200 words.

HOW TO CONTACT Responds to mss in 3 months.

ILLUSTRATION Buys 3 illustrations/year. Reviews ms/illustration packages from artists. Contact: Editor. Query with samples. Responds only if interested. Samples returned with SASE; samples kept on file. Credit line given.

PHOTOS Looks for photos of kids and horses, instructional/educational, relating to riding or horse care. Uses color matte or glossy prints. Query with samples. Responds only if interested. Accepts TIFF or JPEG 300 dpi, disk or e-mail. Children on horseback must be wearing riding helmets or photos cannot be published.

TERMS Buys one-time rights for mss. Pays on publication. Guidelines available for SASE.

TIPS "Articles must be easy to understand, yet detailed and accurate. How-to or other educational features must be written by, or in conjunction with, a riding/teaching professional. Fiction is not encouraged, unless it is outstanding and teaches a moral or practical lesson. Note: Preference will be given to Canadian writers and photographers due to Canadian content laws. Non-Canadian contributors accepted on a very limited basis."

HUNGER MOUNTAIN

Vermont College of Fine Arts, 36 College St., Montpelier VT 05602. (802)828-8517. **E-mail:** hungermtn@vcfa.edu. **Website:** www.hungermtn.org. "We accept picture book, middle grade, YA and YA crossover work (text only—for now). We're looking for polished pieces that entertain, that show the range of adolescent experience, and that are compelling, creative and will appeal to the devoted followers of the kid-lit craft, as well as the child inside us all." Monthly online publication and annual perfect-bound journal covering high quality fiction, poetry, creative nonfiction, craft essaus, writing for children, and artwork. Accepts high quality work from unknown, emerging, or successful writers. No genre fiction, drama, or academic articles, please. *Hunger Mountain* is about 200 pages, 7x10, professionally printed, perfect-bound, with full-bleed color artwork on cover. Press run is 1,000; 10,000 visits online monthly. Single copy: $10; subscription: $12/year, $22 for 2 years. Make checks payable to Vermont College of Fine Arts. Member: CLMP. Estab. 2002.

◯ Uses online submissions manager.

FICTION "We look for work that is beautifully crafted and tells a good story, with characters that are alive and kicking, storylines that stay with us long after we've finished reading, and sentences that slay us with their precision." Needs adventure, high quality short stories and short shorts. No genre fiction, meaning science fiction, fantasy, horror, erotic, etc. Submit ms using online submissions manager. Length: no more than 10,000 words. Pays $25-100.

NONFICTION "We welcome an array of traditional and experimental work, including, but not limited to, personal, lyrical, and meditative essays, memoirs, collages, rants, and humor. The only requirements are recognition of truth, a unique voice with a firm command of language, and an engaging story with multiple pressure points." Submit complete ms using online submissions manager. Length: no more than 10,000 words.

POETRY Submit 3-10 poems at a time. All poems should be in ONE file. "We look for poetry that is as much about the world as about the self, that's an invitation, an opening out, a hand beckoning. We like poems that name or identify something essential that we may have overlooked. We like poetry with acute, precise attention to both content and diction." Submit using online submissions manager. No light verse, humor/quirky/catchy verse, greeting card verse.

HOW TO CONTACT Responds in 4 months to mss. Publishes ms an average of 1 year after acceptance. Accepts queries by online submission form.

PHOTOS Send photos. Reviews contact sheets, transparencies, prints, GIF/JPEG files. Slides preferred. Negotiates payment individually.

TERMS Buys first worldwide serial rights. Byline given. Pays on publication. No kill fee. Sample copy for $10. Writer's guidelines online.

TIPS "Mss must be typed, prose double-spaced. Poets submit at least 3 poems. No multiple genre submissions. Fresh viewpoints and human interest are very important, as is originality. We are committed to publishing an outstanding journal of the arts. Do not send entire novels, mss, or short story collections. Do not send previously published work."

INSIGHT

The Review and Herald Publishing Association, 55 W. Oak Ridge Dr., Hagerstown MD 21740. (301)393-4038. **E-mail:** insight@rhpa.org. **Website:** www.insight magazine.org. Weekly magazine covering spiritual life of teenagers. *Insight* publishes true dramatic stories, interviews, and community and mission service features that relate directly to the lives of Christian teenagers, particularly those with a Seventh-day Adventist background. Estab. 1970. Circ. 8,000.

NONFICTION Needs how-to, teen relationships and experiences, humor, interview, personal experience, photo feature, religious. Send complete ms. Length:

500-1,000 words. Pays $25-150 for assigned articles. Pays $25-125 for unsolicited articles.

HOW TO CONTACT Editorial lead time 6 months. Responds in 1 month to mss. Publishes ms an average of 4 months after acceptance. Accepts queries by mail, e-mail, fax.

PHOTOS State availability. Model releases required. Reviews contact sheets, negatives, transparencies, prints. Negotiates payment individually.

TERMS Buys first rights, buys second serial (reprint) rights. Byline given. Pays on publication. No kill fee. 80% freelance written. Sample copy for $2 and #10 SASE. Guidelines available online.

TIPS "Skim 2 months of *Insight*. Write about your teen experiences. Use informed, contemporary style and vocabulary. Follow Jesus' life and example."

JACK AND JILL

U.S. Kids, 1100 Waterway Blvd., Indianapolis IN 46206-0567. (317)634-1100. **E-mail:** editor@saturdayeveningpost.com. **Website:** www.jackandjillmag.org. Bimonthly magazine published for children ages 8-12. Estab. 1938. Circ. 200,000.

○ "Please do not send artwork. We prefer to work with professional illustrators of our own choosing."

FICTION Submit complete ms via postal mail; no e-mail submissions. "The tone of the stories should be fun and engaging. Stories should hook readers right from the get-go and pull them through the story. Humor is very important! Dialogue should be witty instead of just furthering the plot. The story should convey some kind of positive message. Possible themes could include self-reliance, being kind to others, appreciating other cultures, and so on. There are a million positive messages, so get creative! Kids can see preachy coming from a mile away, though, so please focus on telling a good story over teaching a lesson. The message—if there is one—should come organically from the story and not feel tacked on." Needs Young readers and middle readers: adventure, contemporary, folktales, health, history, humorous, nature, sports. Length: 600-800 words. Pays 30¢/word.

NONFICTION Needs Young readers, middle readers: animal, arts, crafts, cooking, games, puzzles, history, hobbies, how-to, humorous, interviews, profile, nature, science, sports. Submit complete ms via postal mail; no e-mail submissions. Queries not accepted. "We are especially interested in features or Q&As with regular kids (or groups of kids) in the *Jack and Jill* age group who are engaged in unusual, challenging, or interesting activities. No celebrity pieces please." Length: 700 words. Pays 30¢/word.

POETRY Submit via postal mail; no e-mail submissions. Wants light-hearted poetry appropriate for the age group. Mss must be typewritten with poet's contact information in upper right-hand corner of each poem's page. SASE required. Pays $25-50.

HOW TO CONTACT Responds to mss in 3 months. Publishes ms an average of 8 months after acceptance.

ILLUSTRATION Buys 15 illustrations/issue; 90 illustrations/year. Credit line given.

TERMS Buys all rights. Byline given. Pays on publication. 50% freelance written. Guidelines available online.

TIPS "We are constantly looking for new writers who can tell good stories with interesting slants—stories that are not full of outdated and time-worn expressions. We like to see stories about kids who are smart and capable, but not sarcastic or smug. Problem-solving skills, personal responsibility, and integrity are good topics for us. Obtain current issues of the magazine and study them to determine our present needs and editorial style."

JUNIOR BASEBALL

(203)210-5726. **E-mail:** publisher@juniorbaseball.com. **Website:** www.juniorbaseball.com. **Contact:** Jim Beecher, publisher. Bimonthly magazine focused on youth baseball players ages 7-17 (including high school) and their parents/coaches. Edited to various reading levels, depending upon age/skill level of feature. Estab. 1996. Circ. 20,000.

NONFICTION Needs how-to, skills, tips, features, how-to play better baseball, etc., interview, with major league players; only on assignment, personal experience, from coaches' or parents' perspective. Query. Length: 500-1,000 words. Pays $50-100.

HOW TO CONTACT Editorial lead time 3 months. Responds in 2 weeks to queries; 1 month to mss. Publishes ms an average of 4 months after acceptance.

PHOTOS Photos can be e-mailed in 300 dpi JPEGs. State availability. Captions, identification of subjects required. Reviews 35mm transparencies, 3x5 prints. Offers $10-100/photo; negotiates payment individually.

TERMS Buys all rights. Byline given. Pays on publication. No kill fee. 25% freelance written. Sample copy for $5 or for free online.

TIPS "Must be well-versed in baseball! Have a child who is very involved in the sport, or have extensive hands-on experience in coaching baseball, at the youth, high school, or higher level. We can always use accurate, authoritative skills information, and good photos to accompany is a big advantage! This magazine is read by experts. No fiction, poems, games, puzzles, etc." Does not want first-person articles about your child.

THE KERF

College of the Redwoods, 883 W. Washington Blvd., Crescent City CA 95531. **E-mail:** ken-letko@redwoods.edu. **Website:** www.redwoods.edu/Departments/english/poets&writers/clm.htm. **Contact:** Ken Letko. *The Kerf*, published annually in fall, features "poetry that speaks to the environment and humanity." Wants "poetry that exhibits an environmental consciousness." Considers poetry by children and teens. Estab. 1995.

○ *The Kerf* is 54 pages, digest-sized, printed via Docutech, saddle-stapled, with CS2 coverstock. Receives about 1,000 poems/year, accepts up to 3%. Press run is 400 (150 shelf sales); 100 distributed free to contributors and writing centers. Has published poetry by Ruth Daigon, Alice D'Alessio, James Grabill, George Keithley, and Paul Willis.

POETRY Submit up to 5 poems (7 pages maximum) at a time. Reads submissions January 15-March 31 only.

TERMS Sample: $5. Make checks payable to College of the Redwoods.

KEYS FOR KIDS

Box 1001, Grand Rapids MI 49501-1001. (616)647-4950. **Fax:** (616)647-4950. **E-mail:** hazel@cbhministries.org. **Website:** www.cbhministries.org. **Contact:** Hazel Marett, fiction editor. "CBH Ministries is an international Christian ministry based on the gospel of Jesus Christ, which produces and distributes excellent media resources to evangelize and disciple kids and their families." Estab. 1982.

FICTION Buys 40 mss/year. Needs religious. "Tell a story (not a Bible story) with a spiritual application." Submit complete ms. Length: 375-400 words. Pays $25 for stories.

TERMS Buys reprint rights or first rights for mss. Pays on acceptance. Sample copy for 6x9 SAE and 3 first-class stamps. Guidelines for SASE.

TIPS "Be sure to follow guidelines after studying sample copy of the publication."

KIDS LIFE MAGAZINE

1426 22nd Ave., Tuscaloosa AL 35401. (205)345-1193. **E-mail:** kidslife@comcast.net. **Website:** www.kidslifemagazine.com. **Contact:** Mary Jane Turner, publisher. "*Kids Life Magazine*, established in 2000, prides itself in bringing you a publication that showcases all the Tuscaloosa area has to offer its families. Not only does our community offer many activities and family-oriented events, we also have wonderful shopping and dining!" Estab. 2000. Circ. 30,000.

LADYBUG

700 E. Lake St., Suite 800, Chicago IL 60601. **E-mail:** ladybug@ladybugmagkids.com. **Website:** www.cricketmag.com/ladybug; ladybugmagkids.com. **Contact:** Submissions editor. Monthly magazine for children ages 3-6. *LADYBUG Magazine* is an imaginative magazine with art and literature for young children (ages 3-6). Publishes 9 issues per year. Estab. 1990. Circ. 125,000.

FICTION imaginative contemporary stories, original retellings of fairy and folk tales, multicultural stories Submit complete ms, include SASE. Length: 800 words maximum. Pays up to 25¢/word.

NONFICTION gentle nonfiction, action rhymes, finger plays, crafts and activities Send complete ms, SASE. Length: 400-700 words. Pays 25¢/word minimum.

POETRY Wants poetry that is "rhythmic, rhyming; serious, humorous." Length: 20 lines maximum. Pays up to $3/line ($25 minimum).

HOW TO CONTACT Responds in 6 months to mss.

ILLUSTRATION Prefers "bright colors; all media, but uses watercolor and acrylics most often; same size as magazine is preferred but not required." To be considered for future assignments: Submit promo sheet, slides, tearsheets, color and b&w photocopies. Responds to art samples in 3 months. Submissions without SASE will be discarded.

TERMS Byline given. Pays on publication. Guidelines available online at submittable.cricketmag.com or www.cricketmag.com/submissions.

LEADING EDGE

4087 JKB, Provo UT 84602. **E-mail:** editor@leading edgemagazine.com; fiction@leadingedgemagazine. com; art@leadingedgemagazine.com. **Website:** www. leadingedgemagazine.com. **Contact:** Diane Cardon, senior editor. Semiannual magazine covering science fiction and fantasy. "We strive to encourage developing and established talent and provide high-quality speculative fiction to our readers." Does not accept mss with sex, excessive violence, or profanity. "*Leading Edge* is a magazine dedicated to new and upcoming talent in the fields of science fiction and fantasy." Estab. 1981. Circ. 200.

○ Accepts unsolicited submissions.

FICTION Needs fantasy, science fiction. Send complete ms with cover letter and SASE. Include estimated word count. Length: 15,000 words maximum. Pays 1¢/word; $10 minimum.

POETRY "Publishes 2-4 poems per issue. Poetry should reflect both literary value and popular appeal and should deal with science fiction- or fantasy-related themes. Submit 1 or more poems at a time. No e-mail submissions. Cover letter is preferred. Include name, address, phone number, length of poem, title, and type of poem at the top of each page. Please include SASE with every submission." Pays $10 for first 4 pages; $1.50/each subsequent page.

HOW TO CONTACT Responds in 2-4 months to mss. Publishes ms an average of 2-4 months after acceptance.

ILLUSTRATION Buys 24 illustrations/issue; 48 illustrations/year. Uses b&w artwork only. Works on assignment only. Contact: Art Director. Illustrations only: Send postcard sample with portfolio, samples, URL. Responds only if interested. Samples filed. Credit line given.

TERMS Buys first North American serial rights. Byline given. Pays on publication. No kill fee. 90% freelance written. Single copy: $5.95. "We no longer provide subscriptions, but *Leading Edge* is now available on Amazon Kindle, as well as print-on-demand." Guidelines available online at website.

TIPS "Buy a sample issue to know what is currently selling in our magazine. Also, make sure to follow the writer's guidelines when submitting."

THE LOUISVILLE REVIEW

Spalding University, 851 S. Fourth St., Louisville KY 40203. (502)585-9911, ext. 2777. **Fax:** (502)992-2409. **E-mail:** louisvillereview@spalding.edu. **Website:** www.louisvillereview.org. **Contact:** Kathleen Driskell, associate editor. *The Louisville Review*, published twice/year, prints all kinds of poetry. Has a section devoted to poetry by children and teens (grades K-12) called The Children's Corner. Has published poetry by Wendy Bishop, Gary Fincke, Michael Burkard, and Sandra Kohler. *The Louisville Review* is 150 pages, digest-sized, flat-spined. Receives about 700 submissions/year, accepts about 10%. Single copy: $8; subscription: $14/year, $27/2 years, $40/3 years (foreign subscribers add $6/year for s&h). Estab. 1976.

POETRY Considers simultaneous submissions; no previously published poems. Accepts submissions via online manager; please see website for more information. "Poetry by children must include permission of parent to publish if accepted. Address those submissions to The Children's Corner." Reads submissions year round. Pays in contributors copies.

TERMS Sample: $5.

LYRICAL PASSION POETRY E-ZINE

P.O. Box 17331, Arlington VA 22216. **Website:** http://lyricalpassionpoetry.yolasite.com. **Contact:** Raquel D. Bailey, founding editor. Founded by award-winning poet Raquel D. Bailey, *Lyrical Passion Poetry E-Zine* is an attractive monthly online literary magazine specializing in Japanese short-form poetry. Publishes quality artwork, well-crafted short fiction, and poetry in English by emerging and established writers. Literature of lasting literary value will be considered. Welcomes the traditional to the experimental. Poetry works written in German will be considered if accompanied by translations. Offers annual short-fiction and poetry contests. Estab. 2007. Circ. 500 online visitors/month.

FICTION Send complete mss, typed, double-spaced. Cover letter preferred.

POETRY Multiple submissions are permitted, but no more than 3 submissions in a 6-month period. Submissions from minors should be accompanied by a cover letter from parent with written consent for their child's submission to be published on the website with their child's first initial and last name accompanied by their age at the time of submission. Does not want: dark, cliché, limerick, erotica, extremely explicit, violent, or depressing literature. Free-verse poetry length: between 1 and 40 lines.

HOW TO CONTACT Responds in 2 months. Publishes ms 1 month after acceptance. Accepts queries by e-mail.

TERMS Acquires first-time rights, electronic rights (must be the first literary venue to publish online or in any electronic format). Rights revert to poets upon publication. Guidelines and upcoming themes available on website.

MUSE

Cricket Magazine Group, 70 E. Lake St., Suite 800, Chicago IL 60601. **E-mail:** muse@musemagkids. com. **Website:** www.cricketmag.com. "The goal of *Muse* is to give as many children as possible access to the most important ideas and concepts underlying the principal areas of human knowledge. Articles should meet the highest possible standards of clarity and transparency aided, wherever possible, by a tone of skepticism, humor, and irreverence." All articles are commissioned. To be considered for assignments, experienced science writers may send a résumé and 3 published clips. Estab. 1996. Circ. 40,000.

○ *Muse is not accepting unsolicited mss or queries.*

NONFICTION Middle readers, young adult: animal, arts, history, math, nature/environment, problem-solving, science, social issues.

ILLUSTRATION Works on assignment only. Credit line given. Send prints or tearsheets, but please, no portfolios or original art, and above all, *do not send samples that need to be returned.*

PHOTOS Needs vary. Query with samples to photo editor.

NATIONAL GEOGRAPHIC KIDS

National Geographic Society, 1145 17th St. NW, Washington DC 20036. **Website:** www.kids.nation algeographic.com. **Contact:** Catherine Hughes, science editor; Andrea Silen, associate editor; Jay Sumner, photo director. Magazine published 10 times/year. "It's our mission to find fresh ways to entertain children while educating and exciting them about their world." Estab. 1975. Circ. 1.3 million.

○ We do not want poetry, sports, fiction, or story ideas that are too young—our audience is between ages 6-14."

NONFICTION Needs general interest, humor, interview, technical, travel. animals, human interest, science, technology, entertainment, archaeology, pets, history, paleontology Query with published clips and

résumé. Length: 100-1,000 words. Pays $1/word for assigned articles.

HOW TO CONTACT Editorial lead time 6+ months. Publishes ms an average of 6 months after acceptance. Accepts queries by mail.

PHOTOS State availability. Captions, identification of subjects, model releases required. Reviews contact sheets, negatives, transparencies, prints. Negotiates payment individually.

TERMS Buys all rights. Makes work-for-hire assignments. Byline given. Pays on acceptance. Offers 10% kill fee. 70% freelance written. Sample copy for #10 SASE. Guidelines online.

TIPS "Submit relevant clips. Writers must have demonstrated experience writing for kids. Read the magazine before submitting. Send query and clips via snail mail—materials will not be returned. No SASE required unless sample copy is requested."

NATURE FRIEND MAGAZINE

4253 Woodcock Lane, Dayton VA 22821. (540)867-0764. **E-mail:** info@naturefriendmagazine.com; ed itor@naturefriendmagazine.com; photos@nature friendmagazine.com. **Website:** www.naturefriend-magazine.com. **Contact:** Kevin Shank, editor. Monthly children's magazine covering creation-based nature. "*Nature Friend* includes stories, puzzles, science experiments, nature experiments—all submissions need to honor God as creator." Estab. 1982. Circ. 13,000.

○ Picture-oriented material and conversational material needed.

NONFICTION Needs how-to, nature, photo feature, science experiments (for ages 8-12), articles about interesting/unusual animals. Send complete ms. Length: 250-900 words. Pays 5¢/word.

HOW TO CONTACT Editorial lead time 4 months. Responds in 6 months to mss.

PHOTOS Send photos. Captions, identification of subjects required. Reviews prints. Offers $20-75/photo.

TERMS Buys first rights, buys one-time rights. Byline given. Pays on publication. No kill fee. 80% freelance written. Sample copy for $5 postage paid. Guidelines available on website.

TIPS "We want to bring joy and knowledge to children by opening the world of God's creation to them. We endeavor to create a sense of awe about nature's Creator and a respect for His creation. We'd like to see more submissions on hands-on things to do with a nature theme (not collecting rocks or leaves—real stuff). Also looking for good stories that are accompanied by good photography."

NEW MOON GIRLS

New Moon Girl Media, P.O. Box 161287, Duluth MN 55816. (218)728-5507. **Fax:** (218)728-0314. **E-mail:** girl@newmoon.org. **Website:** www.newmoon.org. Bimonthly magazine covering girls ages 8-14, edited by girls ages 8-14. "*New Moon Girls* is for every girl who wants her voice heard and her dreams taken seriously. *New Moon* celebrates girls, explores the passage from girl to woman, and builds healthy resistance to gender inequities. The *New Moon* girl is true to herself, and *New Moon Girls* helps her as she pursues her unique path in life, moving confidently into the world." Estab. 1992. Circ. 30,000.

In general, all material should be pro-girl and feature girls and women as the primary focus.

FICTION Prefers girl-written material. All girl-centered. Needs adventure, fantasy, historical, humorous, slice-of-life vignettes. Send complete ms. Length: 900-1,600 words. Pays 6-12¢/word.

NONFICTION Needs essays, general interest, humor, inspirational, interview, opinion, personal experience, written by girls, photo feature, religious, travel, multicultural/girls from other countries. Send complete ms. Publishes nonfiction by adults in Herstory and Women's Work departments only. Length: 600 words. Pays 6-12¢/word.

POETRY No poetry by adults.

HOW TO CONTACT Editorial lead time 6 months. Responds in 2 months to mss. Publishes ms an average of 6 months after acceptance. Accepts queries by mail, e-mail, fax.

ILLUSTRATION Buys 6-12 illustrations/year from freelancers. *New Moon* seeks 4-color cover illustrations. Reviews ms/illustrations packages from artists. Query. Submit ms with rough sketches. Illustration only: Query; send portfolio and tearsheets. Samples not returned; samples filed. Responds in 6 months only if interested. Credit line given.

PHOTOS State availability. Captions, identification of subjects required. Negotiates payment individually.

TERMS Buys all rights. Byline given. Pays on publication. 25% freelance written. Sample copy for $7.50 or online. Guidelines available at website.

TIPS "We'd like to see more girl-written feature articles that relate to a theme. These can be about any-

thing the girl has done personally, or she can write about something she's studied. Please read *New Moon Girls* before submitting to get a sense of our style. Writers and artists who comprehend our goals have the best chance of publication. We love creative articles—both nonfiction and fiction—that are not condescending to our readers. Keep articles to suggested word lengths; avoid stereotypes. Refer to our guidelines and upcoming themes."

POCKETS

The Upper Room, P.O. Box 340004, Nashville TN 37203. (615)340-7333. **Fax:** (615)340-7267. **E-mail:** pockets@upperroom.org. **Website:** pockets.upper room.org. **Contact:** Lynn W. Gilliam, editor. Magazine published 11 times/year. "*Pockets* is a Christian devotional magazine for children ages 8-12. All submissions should address the broad theme of the magazine. Each issue is built around one theme with material which can be used by children in a variety of ways. Scripture stories, fiction, poetry, prayers, art, graphics, puzzles and activities are included. Submissions do not need to be overtly religious. They should help children experience a Christian lifestyle that is not always a neatly-wrapped moral package, but is open to the continuing revelation of God's will. Seasonal material, both secular and liturgical, is desired." Estab. 1981.

Does not accept e-mail or fax submissions.

NONFICTION Picture-oriented, young readers, middle readers: cooking, games/puzzles. "*Pockets* seeks biographical sketches of persons, famous or unknown, whose lives reflect their Christian commitment, written in a way that appeals to children." Does not accept how-to articles. "Nonfiction reads like a story." Multicultural needs include: stories that feature children of various racial/ethnic groups and do so in a way that is true to those depicted. Length: 400-1,000 words. Pays 14¢/word.

POETRY Considers poetry by children. Length: 4-20 lines. Pays $25 minimum.

HOW TO CONTACT Responds in 8 weeks to mss. Publishes ms an average of 1 year after acceptance.

PHOTOS Send 4-6 close-up photos of children actively involved in peacemakers at work activities. Send photos, contact sheets, prints, or digital images. Must be 300 dpi. Pays $25/photo.

TERMS Buys first North American serial rights. Byline given. Pays on acceptance. No kill fee. 60% freelance written. Each issue reflects a specific theme. Guidelines on website.

TIPS "Theme stories, role models, and retold scripture stories are most open to freelancers. Poetry is also open. It is very helpful if writers read our writers' guidelines and themes on our website."

RAINBOW RUMPUS

P.O. Box 6881, Minneapolis MN 55406. (612)721-6442. **E-mail:** fictionandpoetry@rainbowrumpus.org; admin@rainbowrumpus.org. **Website:** www.rainbowrumpus.org. **Contact:** Beth Wallace, fiction editor. "*Rainbow Rumpus* is the world's only online literary magazine for children and youth with lesbian, gay, bisexual, and transgender (LGBT) parents. We are creating a new genre of children's and young adult fiction. Please carefully read and observe the guidelines on our website. All fiction and poetry submissions should be sent via our contact page. Be sure to select the 'Submissions' category. A staff member will be in touch with you shortly to obtain a copy of your ms." Estab. 2005. Circ. 300 visits/day.

FICTION Needs All levels: adventure, animal, contemporary, fantasy, folktales, history, humorous, multicultural, nature/environment, problem solving, science fiction, sports, suspense/mystery. "Stories should be written from the point of view of children or teens with lesbian, gay, bisexual, or transgender parents or other family members, or who are connected to the LGBT community. Stories featuring families of color, bisexual parents, transgender parents, family members with disabilities, and mixed-race families are particularly welcome." Length: "Stories for 4- to 12-year-old children should be approximately 800 to 2,500 words in length. Stories for 13- to 18-year-olds may be as long as 5,000 words." Pays $300/story.

NONFICTION Needs interview, profile. social issues Query. Length: 800-5,000 words. Pays $75/story.

ILLUSTRATION Buys 1 illustration/issue. Uses both b&w and color artwork. Reviews ms/illustration packages from artists: Query. Illustrations only: Query with samples. Contact: Beth Wallace, fiction editor. Samples not returned; samples filed depending on the level of interest. Credit line given.

TERMS Buys first North American online rights for mss; may request print anthology and audio or recording rights. Byline given. Pays on publication. Writer's guidelines available on website.

TIPS "Emerging writers encouraged to submit. You do not need to be a member of the LGBT community to participate."

RED LIGHTS

2740 Andrea Drive, Allentown PA 18103-4602. (212)875-9342. **E-mail:** mhazelton@rcn.com; marilynhazelton@rcn.com. **Contact:** Marilyn Hazelton, editor. *red lights tanka journal*, published biannually in January and June, is devoted to English-language tanka and tanka sequences. Wants "print-only tanka, mainly 'free-form' but also strictly syllabic 5-7-5-7-7; will consider tanka sequences and tan-renga." Considers poetry by children and teens. Has published poetry by Sanford Goldstein, Michael McClintock, Laura Maffei, Linda Jeannette Ward, Jane Reichhold, and Michael Dylan Welch. *red lights* is 36-40 pages, offset-printed, saddle-stapled, with Japanese textured paper cover; copies are numbered. Single copy: $10; subscription: $20 U.S., $22 USD Canada, $26 USD foreign. Make checks payable to *red lights* in the U.S. Estab. 2004.

SCIENCE WEEKLY

P.O. Box 70638, Chevy Chase MD 20813. (301)680-8804. **Fax:** (301)680-9240. **E-mail:** scienceweekly@erols.com. **Website:** www.scienceweekly.com. **Contact:** Dr. Claude Mayberry, publisher. *Science Weekly* uses freelance writers to develop and write an entire issue on a single science topic. Send résumé only, not submissions. Authors preferred within the greater D.C./Virginia/Maryland area. *Science Weekly* works on assignment only. Estab. 1984. Circ. 200,000.

Ⓞ   Submit resume only.

NONFICTION Young readers, middle readers (K-6th grade): science/math education, education, problem-solving.

TERMS Pays on publication. Sample copy free with SAE and 3 first-class stamps.

Ⓐ   SEVENTEEN MAGAZINE

300 W. 57th St., 17th Floor, New York NY 10019. (917)934-6500. **Fax:** (917)934-6574. **E-mail:** mail@seventeen.com. **Website:** www.seventeen.com. Monthly magazine covering topics geared toward young adult American women. "We reach 14.5 million girls each month. Over the past six decades, *Seventeen* has helped shape teenage life in America. We represent an important rite of passage, helping to define, socialize and empower young women. We create notions of beauty and style, proclaim what's hot

in popular culture and identify social issues." Estab. 1944. Circ. 2,000,000.

○ *Seventeen* no longer accepts fiction submissions.

NONFICTION Needs young adults: careers, cooking, hobbies, how-to, humorous, interview/profile, multicultural, social issues. Query. Length: 200-2,000 words.

ILLUSTRATION *Only interested in agented material.* Buys 10 illustrations/issue; 120 illustrations/year. Works on assignment only. Reviews ms/illustration packages. Illustrations only: Query with samples. Responds only if interested. Samples not returned; samples filed. Credit line given.

PHOTOS Looking for photos to match current stories. Model/property releases required; captions required. Uses color, 8×10 prints; 35mm, 2¼×2¼, 4×5 or 8×10 transparencies. Query with samples or résumé of credits, or submit portfolio for review. Responds only if interested.

TERMS Buys first North American serial rights, first rights, or all rights for mss. Buys exclusive rights for 3 months. Byline sometimes given. Pays on publication. Writer's guidelines for SASE.

TIPS "Send for guidelines before submitting."

SHINE BRIGHTLY

GEMS Girls' Clubs, 1333 Alger St., SE, Grand Rapids MI 49507. (616)241-5616. **Fax:** (616)241-5558. **E-mail:** shinebrightly@gemsgc.org. **Website:** www.gemsgc. org. **Contact:** Kathryn Miller, executive director; Kelli Gilmore, managing editor. Monthly magazine (with combined June/July, August summer issue). "Our purpose is to lead girls into a living relationship with Jesus Christ and to help them see how God is at work in their lives and the world around them. Puzzles, crafts, stories, and articles for girls ages 9-14." Estab. 1970. Circ. 17,000.

FICTION Does not want "unrealistic stories and those with trite, easy endings. We are interested in manuscripts that show how girls can change the world." Needs adventure experiences girls could have in their hometowns or places they might realistically visit, ethnic, historical, humorous, mystery, religious, omance, slice-of-life vignettes, suspense,. Believable only. Nothing too preachy. Submit complete ms in body of e-mail. No attachments. Length: 700-900 words. Pays up to $35, plus 2 copies.

NONFICTION Needs humor, inspirational, seasonal and holiday, interview, personal experience, photo feature, religious, travel, adventure, mystery. Submit complete ms in body of e-mail. No attachments. Length: 100-800 words. Pays up to $35, plus 2 copies.

POETRY Limited need for poetry. Pays $5-15.

HOW TO CONTACT Responds in 2 months to mss. Publishes ms an average of 1 year after acceptance.

ILLUSTRATION Samples returned with SASE. Credit line given.

PHOTOS Purchased with or without ms. Appreciate multicultural subjects. Reviews 5x7 or 8x10 clear color glossy prints. Pays $25-50 on publication.

TERMS Buys first North American serial rights, buys second serial (reprint) rights, buys simultaneous rights. Byline given. Pays on publication. No kill fee. 80% freelance written. Works with new and published/established writers. Sample copy with 9x12 SASE with 3 first class stamps and $1. Guidelines available online.

TIPS Writers: "Please check our website before submitting. We have a specific style and theme that deals with how girls can impact the world. The stories should be current, deal with pre-adolescent problems and joys, and help girls see God at work in their lives through humor as well as problem-solving." Prefers not to see anything on the adult level, secular material, or violence. Writers frequently oversimplify the articles and often write with a Pollyanna attitude. An author should be able to see his/her writing style as exciting and appealing to girls ages 9-14. The style can be fun, but also teach a truth. Subjects should be current and important to *SHINE brightly* readers. Use our theme update as a guide. We would like to receive material with a multicultural slant."

SKIPPING STONES: A MULTICULTURAL LITERARY MAGAZINE

P.O. Box 3939, Eugene OR 97403-0939. (541)342-4956. **E-mail:** editor@skippingstones.org. **Website:** www.skippingstones.org. **Contact:** Arun Toké, editor. "*Skipping Stones* is an award-winning multicultural, nonprofit magazine designed to promote cooperation, creativity and celebration of cultural and ecological richness. We encourage submissions by children of color, minorities and under-represented populations. We want material meant for children and young adults/teenagers with multicultural or ecological awareness themes. Think, live and write as if you were a child, tween or teen. We want material that gives insight to cultural celebrations, lifestyle, customs and traditions, glimpse of daily life in other countries and cultures. Photos, songs, artwork are most welcome if they illustrate/highlight the points. Translations are invited if your submission is in a language other than English." Themes may include cultural celebrations, living abroad, challenging disability, hospitality customs of various cultures, cross-cultural understanding, African, Asian and Latin American cultures, humor, international understanding, turning points and magical moments in life, caring for the earth, spirituality, and multicultural awareness. *Skipping Stones* is magazine-sized, saddle-stapled, printed on recycled paper. Published quarterly during the school year (4 issues). Estab. 1988. Circ. 1,400 print, plus Web.

FICTION Middle readers, young adult/teens: contemporary, meaningful, humorous. All levels: folktales, multicultural, nature/environment. Multicultural needs include: bilingual or multilingual pieces; use of words from other languages; settings in other countries, cultures or multi-ethnic communities. Needs adventure, ethnic, historical, humorous, multicultural, international, social issues .No suspense or romance stories. Send complete ms. Length: 1,000 words maximum. Pays 6 contributor's copies.

NONFICTION Needs essays, general interest, humor, inspirational, interview, opinion, personal experience, photo feature, travel. All levels: animal, biography, cooking, games/puzzles, history, humorous, interview/profile, multicultural, nature/environment, creative problem-solving, religion and cultural celebrations, sports, travel, social and international awareness. Does not want to see preaching, violence or abusive language. Send complete ms. Length: 1,000 words maximum. Pays 6 contributors copies.

POETRY Submit up to 5 poems at a time. Considers simultaneous submissions; no previously published poems. Accepts e-mail submissions. Cover letter is preferred. "Include your cultural background, experiences, and the inspiration behind your creation." Time between acceptance and publication is 6-9 months. "A piece is chosen for publication when most of the editorial staff feel good about it." Seldom comments on rejected poems. Publishes multi-theme issues. Responds in up to 4 months. Length: 30 lines maximum. Pays 2 contributors copies, offers 40% discount for more copies and subscription, if desired.

HOW TO CONTACT Editorial lead time 3-4 months. Responds only if interested. Send nonreturnable sam-

ples. Publishes ms an average of 4-8 months after acceptance. Accepts queries by mail, e-mail.

ILLUSTRATION Prefers illustrations by teenagers and young adults. Will consider all illustration packages. Manuscript/illustration packages: Query; submit complete ms with final art; submit tearsheets. Responds in 4 months. Credit line given.

PHOTOS Black & white photos preferred, but color photos with good contrast are welcome. Needs: youth 7-17, international, nature, celebrations. Send photos. Captions required. Reviews 4X6 prints, low-res JPEG files. Offers no additional payment for photos.

TERMS Buys first North American serial rights, nonexclusive reprint, and electronic rights. Byline given. No kill fee. 80% freelance written. Sample: $7. Subscription: $25. Guidelines available online or for SASE.

TIPS "Be original and innovative. Use multicultural, nature, or cross-cultural themes. Multilingual submissions are welcome."

SPARKLE

GEMS Girls' Clubs, 1333 Alger St. SE, Grand Rapids MI 49507. (616)241-5616. **Fax:** (616)241-5558. **E-mail:** kelli@gemsgc.org. **Website:** www.gemsgc.org. **Contact:** Kelli Gilmore, managing editor; Lisa Hunter, art director/photo editor. Bimonthly magazine for girls ages 6-9. Mission is to prepare young girls to live out their faith and become world-changers. Strives to help girls make a difference in the world. Looks at the application of scripture to everyday life. Also strives to delight the reader and cause the reader to evalute her own life in light of the truth presented. Finally, attempts to teach practical life skills. Estab. 2002. Circ. 9,000.

FICTION Young readers: adventure, animal, contemporary, ethnic/multcultural, fantasy, folktale, health, history, humorous, music and musicians, mystery, nature/environment, problem-solving, religious, recipes, service projects, slice-of-life, sports, suspense/mystery, vignettes, interacting with family and friends. Send complete ms. Length: 100-400 words. Pays $35 maximum.

NONFICTION Young readers: animal, arts/crafts, biography, careers, cooking, concept, games/puzzles, geography, health, history, hobbies, how-to, humor, inspirational, interview/profile, math, multicultural, music/drama/art, nature/environment, personal experience, photo feature, problem-solving, quizzes, recipes, religious, science, social issues, sports, travel. Looking for inspirational biographies, stories from Zambia, and ideas on how to live a green lifestyle Send complete ms. Length: 100-400 words. Pays $35 maximum.

POETRY Prefers rhyming. "We do not wish to see anything that is too difficult for a first grader to read. We wish it to remain light. The style can be fun, but also teach a truth." No violence or secular material.

HOW TO CONTACT Editorial lead time 3 months. Responds in 3 weeks to queries; 3 months to mss. Accepts queries by mail, e-mail.

ILLUSTRATION Buys 1-2 illustrations/issue; 8-10 illustrations/year. Uses color artwork only. Works on assignment only. Reviews ms/illustration packages from artists. Send ms with dummy. Illustrations only: send promo sheet. Contact: Sara DeRidder. Responds in 3 weeks only if interested. Samples returned with SASE; samples filed. Credit line given.

PHOTOS Send photos. Identification of subjects required. Reviews at least 5X7 clear color glossy prints, GIF/JPEG files on CD. Offers $25-50/photo.

TERMS Buys first North American serial rights, buys first rights, buys one-time rights, buys second serial (reprint) rights, buys simultaneous rights. Byline given. Pays on publication. Offers $20 kill fee. 80% freelance written. Sample copy for 9x13 SAE, 3 first-class stamps, and $1 for coverage/publication cost. Writer's guidelines for #10 SASE or online.

TIPS "Keep it simple. We are writing to 1st-3rd graders. It must be simple yet interesting. Manuscripts should build girls up in Christian character but not be preachy. They are just learning about God and how He wants them to live. Manuscripts should be delightful as well as educational and inspirational. Writers should keep stories simple but not write with a 'Pollyanna' attitude. Authors should see their writing style as exciting and appealing to girls ages 6-9. Subjects should be current and important to *Sparkle* readers. Use our theme as a guide. We would like to receive material with a multicultural slant."

SPIDER

Cricket Magazine Group, 70 East Lake St., Suite 300, Chicago IL 60601. (312)701-1720. **Fax:** (312)701-1728. **Website:** www.cricketmag.com. **Contact:** Marianne Carus, editor-in-chief; Suzanne Beck, managing art director. Monthly reading and activity magazine for children ages 6-9. "*Spider* introduces children to the highest quality stories, poems, illustrations, articles, and activities. It was created to foster in beginning readers a love of reading and discovery that will last a lifetime. We're looking for writers who respect children's intelligence." Estab. 1994. Circ. 70,000.

FICTION Stories should be easy to read. Recently published work by Polly Horvath, Andrea Cheng, and Beth Wagner Brust. Needs fantasy, humorous, science fiction. folk tales, fairy tales, fables, myths No romance, horror, religious. Submit complete ms and SASE. Length: 300-1,000 words. Pays 25¢/word maximum.

NONFICTION Submit complete ms, bibliography, SASE. Length: 300-800 words. Pays 25¢/word maximum.

POETRY Length: 20 lines maximum. Pays $3/line maximum.

HOW TO CONTACT Responds in 6 months to mss.

ILLUSTRATION Buys 5-10 illustrations/issue; 45-90 illustrations/year. Uses color artwork only. "We prefer that you work on flexible or strippable stock, no larger than 20×22 (image area 19×21). This will allow us to put the art directly on the drum of our separator's laser scanner. Art on disk CMYK, 300 dpi. We use more realism than cartoon-style art." Works on assignment only. Reviews ms/illustration packages from artists. Illustrations only: Send promo sheet and tearsheets. Responds in 3 months. Samples returned with SASE; samples filed. Credit line given.

PHOTOS Buys photos from freelancers. Buys photos with accompanying ms only. Model/property releases and captions required. Uses 35mm, 2¼×2¼ transparencies or digital files. Send unsolicited photos by mail; provide résumé and tearsheets. Responds in 3 months. For art samples, it is especially helpful to see pieces showing children, animals, action scenes, and several scenes from a narrative showing a character in different situations. Send photocopies/tearsheets. Also considers photo essays (prefers color, but b&w is also accepted). Captions, identification of subjects, model releases required. Reviews contact sheets, transparencies, 8×10 prints.

TERMS Byline given. Pays on publication. 85% freelance written. Guidelines available online.

TIPS "We'd like to see more of the following: engaging nonfiction, fillers, and 'takeout page' activities; folktales, fairy tales, science fiction, and humorous stories. Most importantly, do not write down to children."

STONE SOUP

Children's Art Foundation, P.O. Box 83, Santa Cruz CA 95063-0083. (831)426-5557. **E-mail:** editor@stonesoup.com. **Website:** http://stonesoup.com. **Contact:** Ms. Gerry Mandel, editor. Bimonthly magazine of writing and art by children age 13 under, including fiction, poetry, book reviews, and art. *Stone Soup* is 48 pages, 7x10, professionally printed in color on heavy stock, saddle-stapled, with coated cover with full-color illustration. Receives 5,000 poetry submissions/year, accepts about 12. Press run is 15,000. Subscription: $37/year (U.S.). "We have a preference for writing and art based on real-life experiences; no formula stories or poems. We only publish writing by children ages 8 to 13. We do not publish writing by adults." Estab. 1973.

○ "Stories and poems from past issues are available online."

FICTION Needs adventure, ethnic, experimental, fantasy, historical, humorous, mystery, science fiction, slice-of-life vignettes, suspense. "We do not like assignments or formula stories of any kind." Send complete ms; no SASE. Length: 150-2,500 words. Pays $40 for stories, a certificate and 2 contributors copies, plus discounts.

NONFICTION Needs historical, personal experience. book reviews Submit complete ms; no SASE. Pays $40, a certificate and 2 contributor's copies, plus discounts.

POETRY Wants free verse poetry. Does not want rhyming poetry, haiku, or cinquain. Pays $40/poem, a certificate, and 2 contributor's copies, plus discounts.

HOW TO CONTACT Publishes ms an average of 4 months after acceptance.

TERMS Buys all rights. Pays on publication. 100% freelance written. Sample copy by phone only. Guidelines available online.

TIPS "All writing we publish is by young people ages 13 and under. We do not publish any writing by adults. We can't emphasize enough how important it is to read a couple of issues of the magazine. You can read stories and poems from past issues online. We have a strong preference for writing on subjects that mean a lot to the author. If you feel strongly about something that happened to you or something you observed, use that feeling as the basis for your story or poem. Stories should have good descriptions, realistic dialogue, and a point to make. In a poem, each word must be chosen carefully. Your poem should present a view of your subject, and a way of using words that are special and all your own."

TC MAGAZINE (TEENAGE CHRISTIAN)

HU Box 10750, Searcy AR 72149. (501)279-4530. **E-mail:** editor@tcmagazine.org; write@tcmagazine.org. **Website:** www.tcmagazine.org. "*TC Magazine* is published by the Mitchell Center for Leadership & Ministry. We are dedicated to the idea that it is not only possible, but entirely excellent to live in this world with a vibrant and thriving faith. That, and an awesome magazine." Estab. 1961.

FICTION Does not want fiction.

HOW TO CONTACT Accepts queries by e-mail.

ILLUSTRATION Works on assignment only. Send ms with dummy. Illustrations only. Responds only if interested.

PHOTOS Buys photos separately. Model/property release required. Uses hi-res color digital photos. E-mail. Responds only if interested.

TERMS Pays on publication. Guidelines online.

TURTLE MAGAZINE FOR PRESCHOOL KIDS

U.S. Kids, 1100 Waterway Blvd., Indianapolis IN 46202. **Website:** www.turtlemag.org. Bimonthly magazine for children ages 3-5. *Turtle Magazine for Preschool Kids* uses read-aloud stories, especially suitable for bedtime or naptime reading, for children ages 2-5. Also uses poems, simple science experiments, easy recipes and health-related articles. Wants light-hearted poetry appropriate for the age group. Estab. 1978. Circ. 300,000.

FICTION Picture-oriented material: health-related, medical, history, humorous, multicultural, nature/environment, problem-solving. Avoid stories in which the characters indulge in unhealthy activities. *Queries are not accepted.* Send complete ms. Length: 350 words maximum. Pays $70 minimum and 10 contributor's copies.

NONFICTION Picture-oriented material: cooking, health, sports, simple science. "We use very simple experiments illustrating basic science concepts. These should be pretested. We also publish simple, healthful recipes." Submit complete ms. *Queries are not accepted.* Length: 350 words maximum. Pays $70 minimum and 2 contributors copies.

POETRY Especially looking for short poems (4-12 lines) and slightly longer action rhymes to foster creative movement in preschoolers. Also uses short verse on inside front cover and back cover. Pays $35 minimum.

HOW TO CONTACT Responds in 3 months to queries.

TERMS Buys all rights. Byline given. Pays on publication. No kill fee. Sample copy for $3.99. Guidelines free with SASE and on website.

TIPS "Writers should present their material in a way that is appropriate for kids, but which does not talk down to them. Reading our editorial guidelines is not enough. Careful study of current issues will acquaint writers with each title's personality, various departments, and regular features. We are looking for more short rebus stories, easy science experiments, and simple, nonfiction health articles. We are trying to include more material for our youngest readers. Material must be entertaining and written from a healthy lifestyle perspective. Our need for health-related material, especially features that encourage fitness, is ongoing. Health subjects must be age-appropriate. When writing about them, think creatively and lighten up! Always keep in mind that in order for a story or article to educate preschoolers, it first must be entertaining--warm and engaging, exciting, or genuinely funny. Here the trend is toward leaner, lighter writing. There will be a growing need for interactive activities. Writers might want to consider developing an activity to accompany their concise manuscripts."

YOUNG RIDER

P.O. Box 8237, Lexington KY 40533. (859)260-9800. **Fax:** (859)260-9814. **E-mail:** yreditor@bowtieinc. com. **Website:** www.youngrider.com. **Contact:** Lesley Ward, editor. The Magazine for Horse and Pony Lovers. "*Young Rider* magazine teaches young people, in an easy-to-read and entertaining way, how to look after their horses properly, and how to improve their riding skills safely." Estab. 1994.

FICTION Young adults: adventure, animal, horses. "We would prefer funny stories, with a bit of conflict, which will appeal to the 13-year-old age group. They should be written in the third person, and about kids." Buys 4-5 short stories/year. Length: 800-1,000 words. Pays $150.

NONFICTION Young adults: animal, careers, famous equestrians, health (horse), horse celebrities, riding. Query with published clips. Length: 800-1,000 words. Pays $200/story.

HOW TO CONTACT Rsponds to queries in 2 weeks. Publishes ms 6-12 months after acceptance.

ILLUSTRATION Buys 2 illustrations/issue; 10 illustrations/year. Works on assignment only. Reviews ms/ illustration packages from artists. Query. Contact: Lesley Ward, editor. Illustrations only: Query with samples. Contact: Lesley Ward, editor. Responds in 2 weeks. Samples returned with SASE. Credit line given.

PHOTOS Buys photos with accompanying ms only. Uses high-res digital images only—in focus, good light. Model/property release required; captions required. Query with samples. Responds in 2 weeks.

TERMS Buys first North American serial rights for mss, artwork, photos. Byline given. Pays on publication. Sample copy for $3.50. Guidelines for SASE.

TIPS "Fiction must be in third person. Read magazine before sending in a query. No 'true story from when I was a youngster.' No moralistic stories. Fiction must be up-to-date and humorous, teen-oriented. No practical or how-to articles—all done in-house."

AGENTS & ART REPS

///

This section features listings of literary agents and art reps who either specialize in, or represent a good percentage of, children's writers and/or illustrators. While there are a number of children's publishers who are open to non-agented material, using the services of an agent or rep can be beneficial to a writer or artist. Agents and reps can get your work seen by editors and art directors more quickly. They are familiar with the market and have insights into which editors and art directors would be most interested in your work. Also, they negotiate contracts and will likely be able to get you a better deal than you could get on your own.

Agents and reps make their income by taking a percentage of what writers and illustrators receive from publishers. The standard percentage for agents is 10 to 15 percent; art reps generally take 25 to 30 percent. We have not included any agencies in this section that charge reading fees.

WHAT TO SEND

When putting together a package for an agent or rep, follow the guidelines given in their listings. Most agents open to submissions prefer initially to receive a query letter describing your work. For novels and longer works, some agents ask for an outline and a number of sample chapters, but you should send these only if you're asked to do so. Never fax or e-mail query letters or sample chapters to agents without their permission. Just as with publishers, agents receive a large volume of submissions. It may take them a long time to reply, so you may want to query several agents at one time. It's best, however, to have a complete manuscript considered by only one agent at a time. Always include a self-addressed, stamped envelope (SASE).

For initial contact with art reps, send a brief query letter and self-promo pieces, following the guidelines given in the listings. If you don't have a flier or brochure, send photocopies. Always include a SASE.

For those who both write and illustrate, some agents listed will consider the work of author/illustrators. Read through the listings for details.

As you consider approaching agents and reps with your work, keep in mind that they are very choosy about who they take on to represent. Your work must be high quality and presented professionally to make an impression on them. For more information on approaching agents and additional listings, see *Guide to Literary Agents* (Writer's Digest Books). For additional listings of art reps see *Artist's & Graphic Designer's Market* (Writer's Digest Books).

AN ORGANIZATION FOR AGENTS

In some listings of agents you'll see references to AAR (The Association of Authors' Representatives). This organization requires its members to meet an established list of professional standards and code of ethics.

The objectives of AAR include keeping agents informed about conditions in publishing and related fields; encouraging cooperation among literary organizations; and assisting agents in representing their author-clients' interests. Officially, members are prohibited from directly or indirectly charging reading fees. They offer writers a list of member agents on their website. They also offer a list of recommended questions an author should ask an agent and other FAQs, all found on their website. They can be contacted at AAR, 676A 9th Ave. #312, New York NY 10036. (212)840-5777. E-mail: aarinc@mindspring.com. Website: www.aar-online.org.

AGENTS

A+B WORKS

E-mail: query@aplusbworks.com. **Website:** aplusb works.com. **Contact:** Amy Jameson, Brandon Jameson. Estab. 2004.

- Prior to her current position, Ms. Jameson worked at Janklow & Nesbit Associates.

REPRESENTS nonfiction books, novels. **Considers these nonfiction areas:** creative nonfiction. **Considers these fiction areas:** middle grade, women's, young adult.

HOW TO CONTACT Query via e-mail only. "Please review our submissions policies first. Send queries to query@aplusbworks.com."

ADAMS LITERARY

7845 Colony Rd., C4 #215, Charlotte NC 28226. (704)542-1440. **Fax:** (704)542-1450. **E-mail:** info@adamsliterary.com. **E-mail:** submissions@adamslit erary.com. **Website:** www.adamsliterary.com. **Contact:** Tracey Adams, Josh Adams, Quinlan Lee. Member of AAR. Other memberships include SCBWI and WNBA. Currently handles: juvenile books.

MEMBER AGENTS Tracey Adams, Josh Adams, Quinlan Lee.

REPRESENTS Considers these fiction areas: middle grade, picture books, young adult.

- Represents "the finest children's book authors and artists."

HOW TO CONTACT Contact through online form on website only. Send e-mail if that is not operating correctly. All submissions and queries should first be made through the online form on website. Will not review—and will promptly recycle—any unsolicited submissions or queries received by mail. Before submitting work for consideration, review complete guidelines. Responds in 6 weeks. "While we have an established client list, we do seek new talent—and we accept submissions from both published and aspiring authors and artists."

TERMS Agent receives 15% commission on domestic sales; 20% on foreign sales. Offers written contract.

RECENT SALES *Exposed*, by Kimberly Marcus (Random House); *The Lemonade Crime*, by Jacqueline Davies (Houghton Mifflin); *Jane Jones: Worst Vampire Ever*, by Caissie St. Onge (Random House).

TIPS "Guidelines are posted (and frequently updated) on our website."

FAYE BENDER LITERARY AGENCY

19 Cheever Place, Brooklyn NY 11231. **E-mail:** info@fbliterary.com. **Website:** www.fbliterary.com. **Contact:** Faye Bender. Estab. 2004. Member of AAR.

MEMBER AGENTS Faye Bender.

REPRESENTS nonfiction books, novels, juvenile. **Considers these nonfiction areas:** biography, memoirs, popular culture, women's issues, women's studies, young adult, narrative, health, popular science. **Considers these fiction areas:** commercial, literary, middle grade, women's, young adult.

- "I choose books based on the narrative voice and strength of writing. I work with previously published and first-time authors." Faye does not represent picture books, genre fiction for adults (western, romance, horror, science fiction, fantasy), business books, spirituality, or screenplays.

HOW TO CONTACT Please submit a query letter and ten sample pages to info@fbliterary.com (no attachments). "Due to the volume of e-mails, we can't respond to everything. If we are interested, we will be in touch as soon as we possibly can. Otherwise, please consider it a pass."

RECENT SALES Liane Moriarty's *The Husband's Secret* (Amy Einhorn Books); Rebecca Stead's *Liar & Spy* (Wendy Lamb Books); Kristin Cashore's *Bitterblue* (Dial); Dayna Lorentz's No Safety in Numbers series (Dial).

TIPS "Please keep your letters to the point, include all relevant information, and have a bit of patience."

BOOKSTOP LITERARY AGENCY

67 Meadow View Rd., Orinda CA 94563. (925)254-2664. **Fax:** (925)254-2668. **E-mail:** kendra@booksto pliterary.com; info@bookstopliterary.com. **Website:** www.bookstopliterary.com. Estab. 1983.

- "Special interest in Hispanic, Asian American, and African American writers; quirky picture books; clever adventure/mystery novels; and authentic and emotional young adult voices."

HOW TO CONTACT Send: cover letter, entire ms for picture books; first 30 pages of novels; proposal and sample chapters OK for nonfiction. E-mail submissions: Paste cover letter and first 10 pages of ms into body of e-mail, send to info@bookstopliterary.com. Send sample illustrations only if you are an illustrator.

TERMS AGENT RECEIVES 15% commission on domestic sales. Offers written contract, binding for 1 year.

BRADFORD LITERARY AGENCY

5694 Mission Center Rd., #347, San Diego CA 92108. (619)521-1201. **E-mail:** queries@bradfordlit.com. **Website:** www.bradfordlit.com. **Contact:** Laura Bradford, Natalie Lakosil, Sarah LaPolla. Estab. 2001. Member of AAR, RWA, SCBWI, ALA. Represents 50 clients. 20% of clients are new/unpublished writers. Currently handles: nonfiction books 5%, novels 95%.

REPRESENTS Considers these nonfiction areas: biography, business, creative nonfiction, humor, memoirs, parenting, self-help. **Considers these fiction areas:** erotica, middle grade, mystery, paranormal, picture books, romance, thriller, women's, young adult.

> Actively seeking many types of romance (historical, romantic suspense, paranormal, category, contemporary, erotic). Does not want to receive poetry, screenplays, short stories, westerns, horror, new age, religion, crafts, cookbooks, gift books.

HOW TO CONTACT Accepts e-mail queries only; send to queries@bradfordlit.com (or sarah@bradfordlit if contacting Sarah LaPolla). The entire submission must appear in the body of the e-mail and not as an attachment. The subject line should begin as follows: QUERY: (the title of the ms or any short message that is important should follow). For fiction: e-mail a query letter along with the first chapter of ms and a synopsis. Include the genre and word count in cover letter. Nonfiction: e-mail full nonfiction proposal including a query letter and a sample chapter. Accepts simultaneous submissions. Responds in 2-4 weeks to queries. Responds in 10 weeks to mss. Obtains most new clients through solicitations.

TERMS Agent receives 15% commission on domestic sales. Agent receives 20% commission on foreign sales. Offers written contract, non-binding for 2 years; 45-day notice must be given to terminate contract. Charges for extra copies of books for foreign submissions.

RECENT SALES Sold 68 titles in the last year. *All Fall Down*, by Megan Hart (Mira Books); *Body and Soul*, by Stacey Kade (Hyperion Children's); *All Things Wicked*, by Karina Cooper (Avon); *Circle Eight: Matthew*, by Emma Lang (Kensington Brava); *Midnight Enchantment*, by Anya Bast (Berkley Sensation); *Out-*

post, by Ann Aguirre (Feiwel and Friends); *The One That I Want*, by Jennifer Echols (Simon Pulse); *Catch Me a Cowboy*, by Katie Lane (Grand Central); *Back in a Soldier's Arms*, by Soraya Lane (Harlequin); *Enraptured*, by Elisabeth Naughton (Sourcebooks); *Wicked Road to Hell*, by Juliana Stone (Avon); *Master of Sin*, by Maggie Robinson (Kensington Brava); *Chaos Burning*, by Lauren Dane (Berkley Sensation); *If I Lie*, by Corrine Jackson (Simon Pulse); *Renegade*, by J.A. Souders (Tor).

WRITERS CONFERENCES RWA National Conference; Romantic Times Booklovers Convention.

ANDREA BROWN LITERARY AGENCY, INC.

1076 Eagle Dr., Salinas CA 93905. (831)422-5925. **E-mail:** andrea@andreabrownlit.com; caryn@andreabrownlit.com; lauraqueries@gmail.com; jennifer@andreabrownlit.com; kelly@andreabrownlit.com; jennL@andreabrownlit.com; jamie@andreabrownlit.com; jmatt@andreabrownlit.com; lara@andreabrownlit.com. **Website:** www.andreabrownlit.com. **Contact:** Andrea Brown, president. Member of AAR. 10% of clients are new/unpublished writers.

> Prior to opening her agency, Ms. Brown served as an editorial assistant at Random House and Dell Publishing and as an editor with Knopf.

MEMBER AGENTS Andrea Brown (President); Laura Rennert (Senior Agent); Caryn Wiseman (Senior Agent); Kelly Sonnack (Agent); Jennifer Rofé (Agent); Jennifer Laughran (Agent); Jamie Weiss Chilton (Agent); Jennifer Mattson (Associate Agent); Lara Perkins (Associate Agent, Digital Manager).

REPRESENTS nonfiction, fiction, juvenile books. **Considers these nonfiction areas:** juvenile nonfiction, memoirs, young adult, narrative. **Considers these fiction areas:** juvenile, literary, picture books, women's, young adult, middle grade, all juvenile genres.

> Specializes in "all kinds of children's books—illustrators and authors." 98% juvenile books. Considers: nonfiction, fiction, picture books, young adult.

HOW TO CONTACT For picture books, submit complete ms. For fiction, submit query letter, first 10 pages. For nonfiction, submit proposal, first 10 pages. Illustrators: submit a query letter and 2-3 illustration samples (in jpeg format), link to online portfolio, and text of picture book, if applicable. "We only accept queries via e-mail. No attachments, with the excep-

REBECCA PODOS
(REES LITERARY AGENCY)

reesagency.com

@RebeccaPodos

ABOUT REBECCA: Rebecca Podos (Rees Literary Agency) is a graduate of the MFA Writing, Literature and Publishing program at Emerson College, whose own fiction has appeared in *Glimmer Train, Glyph, CAJE, Bellows American Review, Paper Darts*, and *SmokeLong Quarterly.*

SHE IS SEEKING: young adult fiction of all kinds, including contemporary, emotionally driven stories, mystery, romance, urban and historical fantasy, horror, and sci-fi. Occasionally, she also considers literary and commercial adult fiction, new adult, and narrative nonfiction.

HOW TO QUERY: Send a query letter and the first few chapters (pasted in the e-mail) to Rebecca@reesagency.com.

tion of jpeg illustrations from illustrators." Visit the agents' bios on our website and choose only one agent to whom you will submit your e-query. Send a short e-mail query letter to that agent with QUERY in the subject field. Accepts simultaneous submissions. If we are interested in your work, we will certainly follow up by e-mail or by phone. However, if you haven't heard from us within 6 to 8 weeks, please assume that we are passing on your project. Obtains most new clients through referrals from editors, clients and agents. Check website for guidelines and information.

TERMS Agent receives 15% commission on domestic sales. Agent receives 25% commission on foreign sales. Offers written contract.

RECENT SALES *The Scorpio Races*, by Maggie Stiefvater (Scholastic); *The Raven Boys*, by Maggie Stiefvater (Scholastic); *Wolves of Mercy Falls* series, by Maggie Stiefvater (Scholastic); *The Future of Us*, by Jay Asher; *Triangles*, by Ellen Hopkins (Atria); *Crank*, by Ellen Hopkins (McElderry/S&S); *Burned*, by Ellen Hopkins (McElderry/S&S); *Impulse*, by Ellen Hopkins (McElderry/S&S); *Glass*, by Ellen Hopkins (McElderry/S&S); *Tricks*, by Ellen Hopkins (McElderry/S&S); *Fallout*, by Ellen Hopkins (McElderry/S&S); *Perfect*, by Ellen Hopkins (McElderry/S&S); *The Strange Case of Origami Yoda*, by Tom Angleberger (Amulet/Abrams); *Darth Paper Strikes Back*, by Tom Angleberger (Amulet/Abrams); *Becoming Chloe*, by Catherine Ryan Hyde (Knopf); Sasha Cohen autobiography (HarperCollins); *The Five Ancestors*, by Jeff Stone (Random House); *Thirteen Reasons Why*, by Jay Asher (Penguin); *Identical*, by Ellen Hopkins (S&S).

WRITERS CONFERENCES SCBWI; Asilomar; Maui Writers' Conference; Southwest Writers' Conference; San Diego State University Writers' Conference; Big Sur Children's Writing Workshop; William Saroyan Writers' Conference; Columbus Writers' Conference; Willamette Writers' Conference; La Jolla Writers' Conference; San Francisco Writers' Conference; Hilton Head Writers' Conference; Pacific Northwest Conference; Pikes Peak Conference.

TIPS "ABLA is consistently ranked #1 in juvenile sales in Publishers Marketplace. Several clients have placed in the top 10 of the NY Times Bestseller List in the last year, including Tom Angleberger, Jay Asher, Ellen Hopkins, and Maggie Stiefvater. Awards recently won by ABLA clients include the Michael L. Printz Honor, the APALA Asian/Pacific Award and Honor, Charlotte Zolotow Honor, Cybils Award, EB White Read Aloud Award and Honor, Edgar Award Nominee, Indies Choice Honor Award, Jack Ezra Keats New Writer Award, Odyssey Honor Audiobook, Orbis Pictus Honor, Pura Belpré Illustrator Honor Book; SCBWI Golden Kite Award; Stonewall Honor; Texas Bluebonnet Award; Theodore Seuss Geisel Honor; William C. Morris YA Debut Award."

❶ KIMBERLEY CAMERON & ASSOCIATES

1550 Tiburon Blvd., #704, Tiburon CA 94920. **Fax:** (415)789-9191. **E-mail:** info@kimberleycameron.com. **Website:** www.kimberleycameron.com. **Contact:** Kimberley Cameron. Member of AAR. 30% of clients are new/unpublished writers.

Kimberley Cameron & Associates (formerly The Reece Halsey Agency) has had an illustrious client list of established writers, including the estate of Aldous Huxley, and has represented Upton Sinclair, William Faulkner, and Henry Miller.

MEMBER AGENTS Kimberley Cameron; **Elizabeth Kracht**, liz@kimberleycameron.com (literary, commercial, women's, thrillers, mysteries, and YA with crossover appeal); **Pooja Menon**, pooja@kimberleycameron.com (international stories, literary, historical, commercial, fantasy and high-end women's fiction; in nonfiction, she's looking for adventure & travel memoirs, journalism & human-interest stories, and self-help books addressing relationships and the human psychology from a fresh perspective); **Amy Cloughley**, amyc@kimberleycameron.com (literary and upmarket fiction, women's, mystery, narrative nonfiction); **Mary C. Moore** (literary fiction; she also loves a good commercial book; commercially she is looking for unusual fantasy, grounded science fiction, and atypical romance; strong female characters and unique cultures especially catch her eye); **Ethan Vaughan** (no submissions).

REPRESENTS Considers these nonfiction areas: creative nonfiction, psychology, self-help, travel. Considers these fiction areas: commercial, fantasy, historical, literary, mystery, romance, science fiction, thriller, women's, young adult.

⚷ "We are looking for a unique and heartfelt voice that conveys a universal truth."

HOW TO CONTACT We accept e-mail queries only. Please address all queries to one agent only. Please send a query letter in the body of the e-mail, written in a professional manner and clearly addressed to the agent of your choice. Attach a one-page synopsis and the first fifty pages of your manuscript as separate Word or PDF documents. We have difficulties opening other file formats. Include "Author Submission" in the subject line. If submitting nonfiction, attach a nonfiction proposal. Obtains new clients through recommendations from others, solicitations.

TERMS Agent receives 15% on domestic sales; 10% on film sales. Offers written contract, binding for 1 year.

WRITERS CONFERENCES Texas Writing Retreat; Pacific Northwest Writers Association Conference; Women's Fiction Festival in Matera, Italy; Willamette Writers Conference; San Francisco Writers Conference; Book Passage Mystery and Travel Writers Conferences; Chuckanut Writers Conference; many others.

TIPS "Please consult our submission guidelines and send a polite, well-written query to our e-mail address."

⊕ COMPASS TALENT

6 East 32nd Street, 6th Floor, New York NY 10016. (646)376-7718. **E-mail:** query@compasstalent.com. **Website:** www.compasstalent.com. **Contact:** Heather Schroder.

REPRESENTS Considers these nonfiction areas: cooking, creative nonfiction, foods, history, memoirs, science. Considers these fiction areas: commercial, juvenile, literary, mainstream.

HOW TO CONTACT Please send a query describing your project, along with a sample chapter and some information about yourself to query@compasstalent.com. Allow eight weeks for a response. Please do not send your material to us through the mail.

RECENT SALES A full list of agency clients is available on the website.

◯ DON CONGDON ASSOCIATES INC.

110 William St., Suite 2202, New York NY 10038. (212)645-1229. **Fax:** (212)727-2688. **E-mail:** dca@doncongdon.com. **Website:** doncongdon.com. **Contact:** Michael Congdon, Susan Ramer, Cristina Con-

cepcion, Maura Kye Casella, Katie Kotchman, Katie Grimm. Member of AAR. Represents 100 clients.

REPRESENTS Considers these nonfiction areas: anthropology, archeology, autobiography, biography, child guidance, cooking, creative nonfiction, current affairs, dance, environment, film, foods, government, health, history, humor, language, law, literature, medicine, memoirs, military, music, parenting, popular culture, politics, psychology, satire, science, technology, theater, travel, true crime, war, women's issues, women's studies. **Considers these fiction areas:** action, adventure, contemporary issues, crime, detective, literary, mainstream, middle grade, mystery, police, short story collections, suspense, thriller, women's, young adult.

8━━ Especially interested in narrative nonfiction and literary fiction.

HOW TO CONTACT "For queries via e-mail, you must include the word 'Query' and the agent's full name in your subject heading. Please also include your query and sample chapter in the body of the e-mail, as we do not open attachments for security reasons. Please query only one agent within the agency at a time." Responds in 3 weeks to queries. Responds in 1 month to mss. Obtains most new clients through recommendations from other authors.

TERMS Agent receives 15% commission on domestic sales. Agent receives 19% commission on foreign sales. Charges client for extra shipping costs, photocopying, copyright fees, book purchases.

RECENT SALES This agency represents many best-selling clients such as David Sedaris and Kathryn Stockett.

TIPS "Writing a query letter with an SASE is a must. We cannot guarantee replies to foreign queries via standard mail. No phone calls. We never download attachments to e-mail queries for security reasons, so please copy and paste material into your e-mail."

JILL CORCORAN LITERARY AGENCY

777 Silver Spur Rd., Suite 219, Roling Hills Estates CA 90274. **Website:** http://jillcorcoranliteraryagen cy.com; http://jillcorcoran.blogspot.com. **Contact:** Jill Corcoran. Jill Corcoran represents picture books, chapter books, middle grade, and young adult, plus a select list of adult nonfiction. Previously worked with the Herman Agency for 4 years.

○ Note: Jill is currently closed to submissions and queries except from authors who she has met from conferences or referrals from editors and agents. She will be accepting new queries in the fall.

RECENT SALES Recent titles: *Guy-Write: What Every Guy Writer Needs to Know*, by Ralph Fletcher; *Kiss, Kiss Good Night*, by Kenn Nesbitt; *The Plot Whisperer: Secrets of Story Structure Any Writer Can Master*, by Martha Alderson; *Blind Spot*, by Laura Ellen; *How I Lost You*, by Janet Gurtler.

○ CORVISIERO LITERARY AGENCY

275 Madison Ave., 14th Floor, New York NY 10016. (646)942-8396. **Fax:** (646)217-3758. **E-mail:** contact@ corvisieroagency.com. **E-mail:** query@corvisieroag ency.com. **Website:** www.corvisieroagency.com. **Contact:** Marisa A. Corvisiero, senior agent and literary attorney.

MEMBER AGENTS Marisa A. Corvisiero, senior agent and literary attorney; Saritza Hernandez, senior agent; Sarah Negovetich, junior agent; Doreen McDonald, junior agent; Rebecca Simas, junior agent; Cate Hart, junior agent.

HOW TO CONTACT Accepts submissions via e-mail only. Include 5 pages of complete and polished ms pasted into the body of an e-mail, and a 1-2 page synopsis. For nonfiction, include a proposal instead of the synopsis. All sample pages must be properly formatted into 1 inch margins, double-spaced lines, Times New Roman black font size 12.

TIPS "For tips and discussions on what we look for in query letters and submissions, please take a look at Marisa A. Corvisiero's blog: Thoughts From A Literary Agent."

CURTIS BROWN, LTD.

10 Astor Place, New York NY 10003-6935. (212)473-5400. **E-mail:** gknowlton@cbltd.com. **Website:** www. curtisbrown.com. **Contact:** Ginger Knowlton. Alternate address: Peter Ginsberg, president at CBSF, 1750 Montgomery St., San Francisco CA 94111; (415)954-8566. Member of AAR. Signatory of WGA.

MEMBER AGENTS Ginger Clark (science fiction, fantasy, paranormal romance, literary horror, and young adult and middle grade fiction); Katherine Fausset (adult fiction and nonfiction, including literary and commercial fiction, journalism, memoir, lifestyle, prescriptive and narrative nonfiction); Holly Frederick; Peter Ginsberg, President; Elizabeth Harding, Vice President (represents authors and illustrators of juvenile, middle grade and young adult fiction); **Steve Kasdin** (commercial fiction, including mysteries/thrillers, romantic suspense—emphasis on the suspense, and historical fiction; narrative nonfiction, including biography, history and current affairs; and young adult fiction, particularly if it has adult crossover appeal); **Ginger Knowlton**, Executive Vice President (authors and illustrators of children's books in all genres); **Timothy Knowlton**, Chief Executive Officer; **Jonathan Lyons** (biographies, history, science, pop culture, sports, general narrative nonfiction, mysteries, thrillers, science fiction and fantasy, and young adult fiction); **Laura Blake Peterson**, Vice President (memoir and biography, natural history, literary fiction, mystery, suspense, women's fiction, health and fitness, children's and young adult, faith issues and popular culture); **Maureen Walters**, Senior Vice President (working primarily in women's fiction and nonfiction projects on subjects as eclectic as parenting & child care, popular psychology, inspirational/motivational volumes as well as a few medical/nutritional books); **Mitchell Waters** (literary and commercial fiction and nonfiction, including mystery, history, biography, memoir, young adult, cookbooks, self-help and popular culture).

REPRESENTS nonfiction books, novels, short story collections, juvenile. **Considers these nonfiction areas:** animals, anthropology, art, biography, business, computers, cooking, crafts, creative nonfiction, current affairs, education, ethnic, film, gardening, government, health, history, how-to, humor, language, memoirs, military, money, multicultural, music, New Age, philosophy, photography, popular culture, psychology, recreation, regional, science, self-help, sex, sociology, software, spirituality, sports, translation, travel, true crime. **Considers these fiction areas:** adventure, confession, detective, erotica, ethnic, experimental, fantasy, feminist, gay, historical, horror, humor, juvenile, literary, mainstream, middle grade, military, multicultural, multimedia, mystery, New Age, occult, picture books, regional, religious, romance, spiritual, sports, thriller, translation, women's, young adult.

HOW TO CONTACT "Send us a query letter, a synopsis of the work, a sample chapter and a brief resume. Illustrators should send 1-2 samples of published work, along with 6-8 color copies (no original art). Please send all book queries to our address, Attn: Query Department. Please enclose a stamped, self-addressed envelope for our response and return postage if you wish to have your materials returned to you. We typically respond to queries within 6 to 8 weeks." Note that some agents list their e-mail on the agency website and are fine with e-mail submissions. Note if the submission/query is being considered elsewhere. Responds in 3 weeks to queries; 5 weeks to mss. Obtains most new clients through recommendations from others, solicitations, conferences.

TERMS Agent receives 15% commission on domestic sales; 20% on foreign sales. Offers written contract. 75-day notice must be given to terminate contract. Charges for some postage (overseas, etc.).

RECENT SALES This agency prefers not to share information on specific sales.

D4EO LITERARY AGENCY

7 Indian Valley Rd., Weston CT 06883. (203)544-7180. **Fax:** (203)544-7160. **Website:** www.d4eoliterary agency.com. **Contact:** Bob Diforio. Represents 100+ clients. 50% of clients are new/unpublished writers. Currently handles: nonfiction books 70%, novels 25%, juvenile books 5%.

Prior to opening his agency, Mr. Diforio was a publisher.

MEMBER AGENTS Bob Diforio (referrals only); Mandy Hubbard (middle grade, young adult, and genre romance); Kristin Miller-Vincent (closed to queries); Bree Odgen (children's, young adult, juvenile nonfiction, graphic novels, pop culture, art books, genre horror, noir, genre romance, historical, hard sci-fi); Samantha Dighton (closed to queries); Joyce Holland (currently closed to submissions).

REPRESENTS nonfiction books, novels. **Considers these nonfiction areas:** juvenile, art, biography, business, child, current affairs, gay, health, history, how-to, humor, memoirs, military, money, psychology, religion, science, self-help, sports, true crime, women's. **Considers these fiction areas:** adventure, detective, erotica, historical, horror, humor, juvenile, literary, mainstream, middle grade, mystery, picture books, romance, sports, thriller.

HOW TO CONTACT Each of these agents has a different submission e-mail and different tastes regarding how they review material. See all on their individual agent pages on the agency website. Responds in 1 week to queries. Obtains most new clients through recommendations from others.

TERMS Agent receives 15% commission on domestic sales. Agent receives 25% commission on foreign sales.

MARIA VICENTE
(P.S. LITERARY AGENCY)

psliterary.com

@MsMariaVicente

ABOUT MARIA: Maria has a B.A. in English Literature from Carleton University and a B.Ed. from The University of Western Ontario.

SHE IS SEEKING: literary and commercial fiction, new adult, young adult, middle grade, high-concept picture books, and nonfiction proposals in the pop culture, pop psychology, design, and lifestyle categories. She has a particular interest in magical realism, fiction with visual components, and nonfiction inspired by online culture.

HOW TO QUERY: query@psliterary.com. Limit your query to one page and include the following: an introduction (the title and category of your work and an estimated word count), a brief overview (similar to back-cover copy), and a writer's bio (a little bit about yourself and your background). Do not send attachments or submit a full-length manuscript/proposal unless requested. In your e-mail subject line, have it read "Query for Maria: [Book Title]."

Offers written contract, binding for 2 years; 60-day notice must be given to terminate contract. Charges for photocopying and submission postage.

◑ LIZA DAWSON ASSOCIATES

350 Seventh Ave., Suite 2003, New York NY 10001. (212)465-9071. **Website:** www.lizadawsonassociates. com. **Contact:** Anna Olswanger. Member of AAR. Other memberships include MWA, Women's Media Group. Represents 50+ clients. 30% of clients are new/unpublished writers.

◖ Prior to becoming an agent, Ms. Dawson was an editor for 20 years, spending 11 years at William Morrow as vice president and 2 years at Putnam as executive editor. Ms. Blasdell was a senior editor at HarperCollins and Avon. Ms. Olswanger is an author.

MEMBER AGENTS Liza Dawson (plot-driven literary fiction, historicals, thrillers, suspense, parenting books, history, psychology [both popular and clinical], politics, narrative nonfiction and memoirs); **Caitlin Blasdell** (science fiction, fantasy (both adult and young adult), parenting, business, thrillers and women's fiction); **Anna Olswanger** (gift books for adults, young adult fiction and nonfiction, children's illustrated books, and Judaica); **Havis Dawson** (business books, how-to and practical books, spirituality, fantasy, Southern-culture fiction and military memoirs); **Hannah Bowman** (commercial fiction, especially science fiction and fantasy; women's fiction; cozy mysteries; romance; young adult; also nonfiction in the areas of mathematics, science, and spirituality); **Monica Odom** (literary fiction, women's fiction, voice-driven memoir, nonfiction in the areas of pop culture, food and cooking, history, politics, and current affairs).

REPRESENTS nonfiction books, novels and gift books (Olswanger only). **Considers these nonfiction areas:** autobiography, biography, business, cooking, current affairs, health, history, medicine, memoirs, parenting, popular culture, politics, psychology, sociology, women's issues, women's studies. **Considers these fiction areas:** commercial, fantasy, historical, literary, mystery, regional, romance, science fiction, suspense, thriller, women's, young adult, fantasy and science fiction (Blasdell only).

8—⚊ This agency specializes in readable literary fiction, thrillers, mainstream historicals, women's fiction, academics, historians, business, journalists, and psychology.

HOW TO CONTACT Query by e-mail only. No phone calls. Each of these agents has their own specific submission requirements, which you can find online at their website. querymonica@LizaDawsonAssociates.com; queryHannah@LizaDawsonAssociates.com; queryhavis@LizaDawsonAssociates.com; queryanna@LizaDawsonAssociates.com; queryCaitlin@LizaDawsonAssociates.com; queryliza@LizaDawsonAssociates.com. Responds in 4 weeks to queries; 8 weeks to mss. Obtains most new clients through recommendations from others, conferences.

TERMS Agent receives 15% commission on domestic sales. Agent receives 20% commission on foreign sales. Offers written contract.

ⓘ THE JENNIFER DECHIARA LITERARY AGENCY

31 East 32nd St., Suite 300, New York NY 10016. (212)481-8484. **Fax:** (212)481-9582. **Website:** www.jdlit.com.

MEMBER AGENTS Jennifer DeChiara, jenndec@aol.com (literary, commercial, women's fiction [no bodice-rippers, please], chick-lit, mysteries, suspense, thrillers; for nonfiction: LGBTQ, memoirs, books about the arts and performing arts, behind-the-scenes-type books, and books about popular culture); Stephen Fraser, stephenafraser@verizon.net (one-of-a-kind picture books; strong chapter book series; whimsical, dramatic, or humorous middle grade; dramatic or high-concept young adult; powerful and unusual nonfiction; nonfiction with a broad audience on topics as far-reaching as art history, theater, film, literature, and travel); Marie Lam-

ba, marie.jdlit@gmail.com (young adult and middle grade fiction, along with general and women's fiction and some memoir); Linda Epstein, linda.p.epstein@gmail.com (young adult, middle grade, literary fiction, quality upscale commercial fiction, vibrant narrative nonfiction, compelling memoirs, health and parenting books, cookbooks); Roseanne Wells, queryroseanne@gmail.com (literary fiction, YA, middle grade, narrative nonfiction, select memoir, science [popular or trade, not academic], history, religion [not inspirational], travel, humor, food/cooking, and similar subjects).

REPRESENTS nonfiction books, novels, juvenile. **Considers these nonfiction areas:** art, cooking, creative nonfiction, film, foods, gay/lesbian, health, history, humor, literature, memoirs, parenting, popular culture, religious, science, theater, travel. **Considers these fiction areas:** commercial, literary, middle grade, mystery, picture books, suspense, thriller, women's, young adult.

HOW TO CONTACT Each agent has their own e-mail submission address and submission instructions. Accepts simultaneous submissions. Obtains most new clients through recommendations from others, conferences, query letters.

TERMS Agent receives 15% commission on domestic sales. Agent receives 20% commission on foreign sales. Offers written contract.

ⓘ DEFIORE & CO.

47 E. 19th St., 3rd Floor, New York NY 10003. (212)925-7744. **Fax:** (212)925-9803. **E-mail:** info@defioreandco.com; submissions@defioreandco.com. **Website:** www.defioreandco.com. Member of AAR.

◯ Prior to becoming an agent, Mr. DeFiore was publisher of Villard Books (1997-1998), editor-in-chief of Hyperion (1992-1997), and editorial director of Delacorte Press (1988-1992).

MEMBER AGENTS Brian DeFiore (popular nonfiction, business, pop culture, parenting, commercial fiction); Laurie Abkemeier (memoir, parenting, business, how-to/self-help, popular science); Kate Garrick (literary fiction, memoir, popular nonfiction); Matthew Elblonk (young adult, popular culture, narrative nonfiction); Caryn Karmatz-Rudy (popular fiction, self-help, narrative nonfiction); Adam Schear (commercial fiction, humor, YA, smart thrillers, historical fiction, and quirky debut literary novels. For nonfiction: popular science, politics, popular culture, and current events); **Meredith Kaffel** (smart upmarket women's fiction, literary fiction [especially debut] and literary thrillers, narrative nonfiction, nonfiction about science and tech, sophisticated pop culture/humor books); **Rebecca Strauss** (literary and commercial fiction, women's fiction, urban fantasy, romance, mystery, YA, memoir, pop culture, and select nonfiction); **Debra Goldstein** (nonfiction books on how to live better).

REPRESENTS nonfiction books, novels. **Considers these nonfiction areas:** autobiography, biography, business, child guidance, cooking, economics, foods, how-to, inspirational, money, multicultural, parenting, popular culture, politics, psychology, religious, science, self-help, sports, young adult. **Considers these fiction areas:** ethnic, literary, mainstream, middle grade, mystery, paranormal, romance, short story collections, suspense, thriller, women's, young adult.

⊶ "Please be advised that we are not considering children's picture books, poetry, adult science fiction and fantasy, romance, or dramatic projects at this time."

HOW TO CONTACT Query with SASE or e-mail to submissions@defioreandco.com. "Please include the word 'Query' in the subject line. All attachments will be deleted; please insert all text in the body of the e-mail. For more information about our agents, their individual interests, and their query guidelines, please visit our 'About Us' page on our website." There is more information (details, sales) for each agent on the agency website. Accepts simultaneous submissions. Obtains most new clients through recommendations from others.

TERMS Agent receives 15% commission on domestic sales. Agent receives 20% commission on foreign sales. Offers written contract; 10-day notice must be given to terminate contract. Charges clients for photocopying and overnight delivery (deducted only after a sale is made).

WRITERS CONFERENCES Maui Writers Conference; Pacific Northwest Writers Conference; North Carolina Writers' Network Fall Conference.

⦿ SANDRA DIJKSTRA LITERARY AGENCY

1155 Camino del Mar, PMB 515, Del Mar CA 92014. (858)755-3115. **Fax:** (858)794-2822. **E-mail:** elise@dijkstraagency.com. **Website:** www.dijkstraagency.com. Member of AAR. Other memberships include Authors Guild, PEN West, PEN USA, Organization of American Historians, Poets and Editors, MWA. Represents 100+ clients. 30% of clients are new/unpublished writers.

MEMBER AGENTS Sandra Dijkstra, president (adult only). Other acquiring agents: **Elise Capron** (adult only), **Jill Marr** (adult only), **Thao Le** (adult and YA), **Roz Foster** (adult and YA), **Jessica Watterson** (adult and YA).

REPRESENTS nonfiction books, novels. **Considers these nonfiction areas:** biography, business, creative nonfiction, design, history, memoirs, psychology, science, self-help, narrative. **Considers these fiction areas:** commercial, horror, literary, middle grade, science fiction, suspense, thriller, women's, young adult.

HOW TO CONTACT "Please see guidelines on our website, and note that we only accept e-mail submissions. Due to the large number of unsolicited submissions we receive, we are only able to respond to those submissions in which we are interested." Accepts simultaneous submissions. Responds to queries of interest within 6 weeks.

TERMS Works in conjunction with foreign and film agents. Agent receives 15% commission on domestic sales and 20% commission on foreign sales. Offers written contract. No reading fee.

TIPS "Remember that publishing is a business. Do your research and present your project in as professional a way as possible. Only submit your work when you are confident that it is polished and ready for prime-time. Make yourself a part of the active writing community by getting stories and articles published, networking with other writers, and getting a good sense of where your work fits in the market."

⦿ DUNHAM LITERARY, INC.

110 William St., Suite 2202, New York NY 10038. (212)929-0994. **E-mail:** dunhamlit@yahoo.com. **E-mail:** query@dunhamlit.com. **Website:** www.dunhamlit.com. **Contact:** Jennie Dunham. Member of AAR. SCBWI Represents 50 clients. 15% of clients are new/unpublished writers. Currently handles: nonfiction books 25%, novels 25%, juvenile books 50%.

○ Prior to opening her agency, Ms. Dunham worked as a literary agent for Russell & Volkening. The Rhoda Weyr Agency is now a division of Dunham Literary, Inc.

REPRESENTS nonfiction, fiction, novels, juvenile books. **Considers these nonfiction areas:** anthropology, archeology, biography, cultural interests, environment, ethnic, health, history, language, literature, medicine, popular culture, politics, psychology, science, technology, women's issues, women's studies. **Considers these fiction areas:** ethnic, juvenile, literary, mainstream, picture books, young adult.

HOW TO CONTACT Query with SASE. Responds in 3 weeks to queries; 2 months to mss. Obtains most new clients through recommendations from others, solicitations.

TERMS Agent receives 15% commission on domestic sales. Agent receives 20% commission on foreign sales.

RECENT SALES Sales include *The Bad Kitty Series*, by Nick Bruel (Macmillan); *The Little Mermaid*, by Robert Sabuda (Simon & Schuster); *Transformers*, by Matthew Reinhart (Little, Brown); *The Gollywhopper Games* and Sequels, by Jody Feldman (HarperCollins); *Learning Not to Drown*, by Anna Shinoda (Simon & Schuster); *The Things You Kiss Goodbye*, by Leslie Connor (HarperCollins); *Gangsterland*, by Tod Goldberg (Counterpoint); *Ancestors and Others*, by Fred Chappell (Macmillan), *Forward From Here*, by Reeve Lindbergh (Simon & Schuster).

○ DUNOW, CARLSON, & LERNER AGENCY

27 W. 20th St., Suite 1107, New York NY 10011. (212)645-7606. **E-mail:** mail@dclagency.com. **Website:** www.dclagency.com. Member of AAR.

MEMBER AGENTS Jennifer Carlson (narrative nonfiction writers and journalists covering current events and ideas and cultural history, as well as literary and upmarket commercial novelists); **Henry Dunow** (quality fiction—literary, historical, strongly written commercial—and voice-driven nonfiction across a range of areas—narrative history, biography, memoir, current affairs, cultural trends and criticism, science, sports); **Erin Hosier** (nonfiction: popular culture, music, sociology and memoir); **Betsy Lerner** (nonfiction writers in the areas of psychology, history, cultural studies, biography, current events, business; fiction: literary, dark, funny, voice driven); **Yishai Seidman** (broad range of fiction: literary, postmodern, and thrillers; nonfiction: sports, music, and pop culture); **Amy Hughes** (nonfiction in the areas of history, cultural studies, memoir, current events, wellness, health, food, pop culture, and biography; also literary fiction); **Eleanor Jackson** (literary, commercial, memoir, art, food, science and history); **Julia**

Kenny (fiction—adult, middle grade and YA—and is especially interested in dark, literary thrillers and suspense).

REPRESENTS nonfiction books, novels, juvenile. **Considers these nonfiction areas:** art, biography, creative nonfiction, cultural interests, current affairs, foods, health, history, memoirs, music, popular culture, psychology, science, sociology, sports. **Considers these fiction areas:** commercial, literary, mainstream, middle grade, mystery, picture books, thriller, young adult.

HOW TO CONTACT Query via snail mail with SASE, or by e-mail. No attachments. Responds if interested.

RECENT SALES A full list of agency clients is on the website.

① DYSTEL & GODERICH LITERARY MANAGEMENT

1 Union Square W., Suite 904, New York NY 10003. (212)627-9100. **Fax:** (212)627-9313. **Website:** www.dystel.com. Estab. 1994. Member of AAR. Other membership includes SCBWI. Represents 600+ clients.

MEMBER AGENTS Jane Dystel; Miriam Goderich (literary and commercial fiction as well as some genre fiction, narrative nonfiction, pop culture, psychology, history, science, art, business books, and biography/memoir); **Stacey Kendall Glick** (narrative nonfiction including memoir, parenting, cooking and food, psychology, science, health and wellness, lifestyle, current events, pop culture, YA, middle grade, and select adult contemporary fiction); **Michael Bourret** (middle grade and young adult fiction, commercial adult fiction, and all sorts of nonfiction, from practical to narrative; he's especially interested in food- and cocktail-related books, memoir, popular history, politics, religion [though not spirituality], popular science, and current events); **Jim McCarthy** (literary women's fiction, underrepresented voices, mysteries, romance, paranormal fiction, narrative nonfiction, memoir, and paranormal nonfiction); **Jessica Papin** (literary and smart commercial fiction, narrative nonfiction, history with a thesis, medicine, science and religion, health, psychology, women's issues); **Lauren E. Abramo** (smart commercial fiction and well-paced literary fiction with a unique voice, including middle grade, YA, and adult and a wide variety of narrative nonfiction including science, interdisciplinary cultural studies, pop culture, psychology, reportage,

NEW AGENT SPOTLIGHT

BETH PHELAN
(BENT LITERARY)

thebentagency.com

@beth_phelan

ABOUT BETH: "After graduating from New York University, I found my footing as an intern with the Levine Greenberg Literary Agency. Since then, I've held positions at Waxman Leavell Literary and Howard Morhaim Literary Agency. As a literary agent, my favorite stories are told with humor and sprinkled with surprises. I live in Brooklyn with a neurotic chihuahua."

SHE IS SEEKING: fiction for young adults and middle grade readers, select commercial and literary adult fiction, and nonfiction by way of lifestyle, cooking/food writing, humor, pop culture, LGBT and pets/animals. For adult fiction, she leans toward new adult, suspense, thriller, and mystery.

HOW TO QUERY: Review any online submissions guideline updates on the agency website, then e-mail phelanqueries@thebentagency.com.

media, contemporary culture, and history); **John Rudolph** (picture book author/illustrators, middle grade, YA, commercial fiction for men, nonfiction); **Rachel Stout** (literary fiction, narrative nonfiction, and believable and thought-provoking YA as well as magical realism); **Sharon Pelletier** (witty literary fiction and smart commercial fiction featuring female characters, narrative nonfiction).
REPRESENTS nonfiction books, novels, cookbooks. **Considers these nonfiction areas:** animals, anthropology, archeology, autobiography, biography, business, child guidance, cultural interests, current affairs, economics, ethnic, gay/lesbian, health, history, humor, inspirational, investigative, medicine, metaphysics, military, New Age, parenting, popular culture, psychology, religious, science, technology, true crime, women's issues, women's studies. **Considers these fiction areas:** action, adventure, commercial, crime, detective, ethnic, family saga, gay, lesbian, literary, mainstream, middle grade, mystery, picture

books, police, suspense, thriller, women's, young adult.
☛ "We are actively seeking fiction for all ages, in all genres." No plays, screenplays, or poetry.
HOW TO CONTACT Query via e-mail. The varying e-mail addresses for each agent are on the agency website under "Who We Are and What We're Looking For." Accepts simultaneous submissions. Responds in 6 to 8 weeks to queries; within 8 weeks to mss. Obtains most new clients through recommendations from others, solicitations, conferences.
TERMS Agent receives 15% commission on domestic sales. Agent receives 19% commission on foreign sales. Offers written contract.
WRITERS CONFERENCES Backspace Writers' Conference; Pacific Northwest Writers' Association; Pike's Peak Writers' Conference; Writers League of Texas; Love Is Murder; Surrey International Writers Conference; Society of Children's Book Writers and Illustrators; International Thriller Writers; Willamette Writ-

ers Conference; The South Carolina Writers Workshop Conference; Las Vegas Writers Conference; Writer's Digest; Seton Hill Popular Fiction; Romance Writers of America; Geneva Writers Conference.

TIPS "DGLM prides itself on being a full-service agency. We're involved in every stage of the publishing process, from offering substantial editing on mss and proposals, to coming up with book ideas for authors looking for their next project, negotiating contracts and collecting monies for our clients. We follow a book from its inception through its sale to a publisher, its publication, and beyond. Our commitment to our writers does not, by any means, end when we have collected our commission. This is one of the many things that makes us unique in a very competitive business."

⭘ EAST/WEST LITERARY AGENCY, LLC

1158 26th St., Suite 462, Santa Monica CA 90403. (310)573-9303. **Fax:** (310)453-9008. **E-mail:** dwarren@eastwestliteraryagency.com. **Contact:** Deborah Warren. Estab. 2000. Currently handles: juvenile books 90%, adult books 10%.

MEMBER AGENTS Deborah Warren, founder.

REPRESENTS Considers these fiction areas: middle grade, picture books, young adult.

HOW TO CONTACT By referral only. Submit proposal and first 3 sample chapters, table of contents (2 pages or fewer), synopsis (1 page). For picture books, submit entire ms. Requested submissions should be sent by mail as a Word document in Courier, 12-pt., double-spaced with 1.20-inch margin on left, ragged right text, 25 lines per page, continuously paginated, with all your contact info on the first page. Only responds if interested, no need for SASE. Responds in 60 days. Obtains new clients through recommendations from others.

TERMS Agent receives 15% commission on domestic sales. Agent receives 25% commission on foreign sales. Offers written contract; 30-day notice must be given to terminate contract. Charges for out-of-pocket expenses, such as postage and copying.

EDEN STREET LITERARY

P.O. Box 30, Billings NY 12510. **E-mail:** info@edenstreetlit.com. **E-mail:** submissions@edenstreetlit.com. **Website:** www.edenstreetlit.com. **Contact:** Liza Voges. Eden Street represents over 40 authors and author-illustrators of books for young readers from pre-school through young adult. Their books

have won numerous awards over the past 25 years. Eden Street prides themselves on tailoring services to each client's goals, working in tandem with them to achieve literary, critical, and commercial success. Welcomes the opportunity to work with additional authors and illustrators.

⭘ This market gives priority to members of the Society of Children's Writers and Illustrators.

RECENT SALES Recent Titles: *Dream Dog*, by Lou Berger; *Biscuit Loves the Library*, by Alyssa Capucilli; *The Scraps Book*, by Lois Ehlert; *Two Bunny Buddies*, by Kathryn O. Galbraith; *Between Two Worlds*, by Katherine Kirkpatrick.

HOW TO CONTACT Send an e-mail (to submissions@edenstreetlit.com) with a picture book ms or dummy; a synopsis and 3 chapters of a middle-grade or YA novel; or a proposal and 3 sample chapters for nonfiction.

EDUCATIONAL DESIGN SERVICES LLC

5750 Bou Ave, Suite 1508, N. Bethesda MD 20852. **E-mail:** blinder@educationaldesignservices.com. **Website:** www.educationaldesignservices.com. **Contact:** B. Linder. Estab. 1981. 80% of clients are new/unpublished writers.

☞ "We specialize in educational materials to be used in classrooms (in class sets), for staff development or in teacher education classes." Actively seeking educational, text materials. Not looking for picture books, story books, fiction; no illustrators.

HOW TO CONTACT Query by e-mail or with SASE or send outline and 1 sample chapter. Considers simultaneous queries and submissions if so indicated. Returns material only with SASE. Responds in 6-8 weeks to queries/mss. Obtains clients through recommendations from others, queries/solicitations, or through conferences.

TERMS Agent receives 15% commission on domestic sales; 25% on foreign sales. Offers written contract, binding until any party opts out. Terminate contract through certified letter.

RECENT SALES *How to Solve Word Problems in Mathematics*, by Wayne (McGraw-Hill); *Preparing for the 8th Grade Test in Social Studies*, by Farran-Paci (Amsco); *Minority Report*, by Gunn-Singh (Scarecrow Education); *No Parent Left Behind*, by Petrosino & Spiegel (Rowman & Littlefield); *Teaching Test-taking Skills* (R&L Education); *10 Languages You'll Need*

Most in the Classroom, by Sundem, Krieger, Pickiewicz (Corwin Press*); Kids, Classrooms & Capital Hill,* by Flynn (R&L Education); *Bully Nation,* by Susan Eva Porter (Paragon House).

◑ ETHAN ELLENBERG LITERARY AGENCY

548 Broadway, #5-E, New York NY 10012. (212)431-4554. **Fax:** (212)941-4652. **E-mail:** agent@ethanellenberg.com. **Website:** ethanellenberg.com. **Contact:** Ethan Ellenberg. Estab. 1984. Represents 80 clients. 10% of clients are new/unpublished writers. Currently handles: nonfiction books 25%, novels 75%.

○ Prior to opening his agency, Mr. Ellenberg was contracts manager of Berkley/Jove and associate contracts manager for Bantam.

MEMBER AGENTS Denise Little: deniselitt@aol.com. (accepts romance, paranormal, YA, science fiction, fantasy, Christian fiction, and commercial nonfiction. Send a short query letter telling about your writing history, and including the first 15 pages of the work you want her to represent. If she is interested in your work, she'll reply to you within four weeks); **Evan Gregory** (accepting clients).

REPRESENTS nonfiction books, novels, children's books. **Considers these nonfiction areas:** biography, current affairs, health, history, medicine, military, science, technology, war, narrative. **Considers these fiction areas:** commercial, fantasy, literary, mystery, romance, science fiction, suspense, thriller, women's, young adult, children's (all types).

⚷ "This agency specializes in commercial fiction—especially thrillers, romance/women's, and specialized nonfiction. We also do a lot of children's books." "Actively seeking commercial fiction as noted above—romance/fiction for women, science fiction and fantasy, thrillers, suspense and mysteries. Our other two main areas of interest are children's books and narrative nonfiction. We are actively seeking clients, follow the directions on our website." Does not want to receive poetry, short stories, or screenplays.

HOW TO CONTACT Query by e-mail. Paste the query, synopsis and first 50 pages into the e-mail. For nonfiction, paste the proposal. For picture books, paste the entire text. Accepts simultaneous submissions. Responds in 2 weeks to queries (no attachments); 4-6 weeks to mss.

TERMS Agent receives 15% commission on domestic sales. Agent receives 10% commission on foreign sales. Offers written contract. Charges clients (with their consent) for direct expenses limited to photocopying and postage.

WRITERS CONFERENCES RWA National Conference; Novelists, Inc.; and other regional conferences.

TIPS We do consider new material from unsolicited authors. Write a good, clear letter with a succinct description of your book. We prefer the first 3 chapters when we consider fiction. For all submissions, you must include an SASE or the material will be discarded. It's always hard to break in, but talent will find a home. Check our website for complete submission guidelines. We continue to see natural storytellers and nonfiction writers with important books.

⊘ THE ELAINE P. ENGLISH LITERARY AGENCY

4710 41st St. NW, Suite D, Washington DC 20016. (202)362-5190. **Fax:** (202)362-5192. **E-mail:** queries@elaineenglish.com. **E-mail:** elaine@elaineenglish.com. **Website:** www.elaineenglish.com/literary.php. **Contact:** Elaine English, Lindsey Skouras. Member of AAR. Represents 20 clients. 25% of clients are new/unpublished writers. Currently handles: novels 100%.

○ Ms. English has been working in publishing for more than 20 years. She is also an attorney specializing in media and publishing law.

MEMBER AGENTS Elaine English (novels).

REPRESENTS novels. **Considers these fiction areas:** historical, multicultural, mystery, suspense, thriller, women's, romance (single title, historical, contemporary, romantic, suspense, chick lit, erotic), general women's fiction. The agency is slowly but steadily acquiring in all mentioned areas.

⚷ Actively seeking women's fiction, including single-title romances. Does not want to receive any science fiction, time travel, or picture books.

HOW TO CONTACT Not accepting queries as of 2014. Keep checking the website for further information and updates. Responds in 4-8 weeks to queries; 3 months to requested submissions. Obtains most new clients through recommendations from others, conferences, submissions.

TERMS Agent receives 15% commission on domestic sales. Agent receives 20% commission on foreign sales. Offers written contract; 30-day notice must be given to terminate contract. Charges only for shipping expenses; generally taken from proceeds.

RECENT SALES Have been to Sourcebooks, Tor, Harlequin.

WRITERS CONFERENCES RWA National Conference; Novelists, Inc.; Malice Domestic; Washington Romance Writers Retreat, among others.

🔵 FLANNERY LITERARY

1140 Wickfield Ct., Naperville IL 60563. (630)428-2682. **Fax:** (630)428-2683. **E-mail:** jennifer@flannery-literary.com. **Contact:** Jennifer Flannery. Represents 40 clients. 50% of clients are new/unpublished writers. Currently handles: juvenile books 100%.

REPRESENTS Considers these fiction areas: juvenile, middle grade, young adult.

🔑 This agency specializes in children's and young adult fiction and nonfiction. It also accepts picture books. 100% juvenile books.

HOW TO CONTACT Query by mail with SASE. "Multiple queries are fine, but please inform us. Mail that requires a signature will be returned to sender, as we are not always available to sign for mail." Responds in 2 weeks to queries; 1 month to mss. Obtains new clients through referrals and queries.

TERMS Agent receives 15% commission on domestic sales. Agent receives 20% commission on foreign sales. Offers written contract, binding for life of book in print; 1-month notice must be given to terminate contract.

TIPS "Write an engrossing, succinct query describing your work. We are always looking for a fresh new voice."

🔵 FOLIO LITERARY MANAGEMENT, LLC

The Film Center Building, 630 Ninth Ave., Suite 1101, New York NY 10036. (212)400-1494. **Fax:** (212)967-0977. **Website:** www.foliolit.com. Member of AAR. Represents 100+ clients.

◯ Prior to creating Folio Literary Management, Mr. Hoffman worked for several years at another agency; Mr. Kleinman was an agent at Graybill & English; Ms. Wheeler was an agent at Creative Media Agency.

MEMBER AGENTS Scott Hoffman; Jeff Kleinman; Paige Wheeler; Frank Weimann; Michelle Brower; Claudia Cross; Jita Fumich; Michael Harriot; Molly Jaffa; Erin Harris; Erin Niumata; Katherine Latshaw; Ruth Pomerance; Marcy Posner; Steve Troha; Emily van Beek; Melissa Sarver White; Maura Teitelbaum.

REPRESENTS nonfiction books, novels, short story collections. **Considers these nonfiction areas:** animals, art, biography, business, child guidance, cooking, creative nonfiction, economics, environment, foods, health, history, how-to, humor, inspirational, memoirs, military, parenting, popular culture, politics, psychology, religious, satire, science, self-help, technology, war, women's issues, women's studies. **Considers these fiction areas:** commercial, erotica, fantasy, horror, literary, middle grade, mystery, picture books, religious, romance, thriller, women's, young adult.

🔑 No poetry, stage plays, or screenplays.

HOW TO CONTACT Query via e-mail only (no attachments). Read agent bios online for specific submission guidelines and e-mail addresses. Responds in 1 month to queries.

TIPS "Please do not submit simultaneously to more than one agent at Folio. If you're not sure which of us is exactly right for your book, don't worry. We work closely as a team, and if one of our agents gets a query that might be more appropriate for someone else, we'll always pass it along. It's important that you check each agent's bio page for clear directions as to how to submit, as well as when to expect feedback."

🔵 FOREWORD LITERARY

E-mail: info@forewordliterary.com. **Website:** forewordliterary.com/. **Contact:** Laurie McLean.

MEMBER AGENTS Laurie McLean (referrals only); **Gordon Warnock**, querygordon@forewordliterary.com (nonfiction: memoir [adult, new adult, YA, graphic], cookbooks and food studies, political and current events, pop-science, pop-culture [also punk culture and geek culture], self-help, how-to, humor, pets, business and career; Fiction: high-concept commercial fiction, literary fiction, new adult, contemporary YA, graphic novels); **Pam van Hylckama Vlieg**, querypam@forewordliterary.com (young adult, middle grade, romance, genre fiction [urban fantasy, paranormal, and epic/high fantasy], pop culture nonfiction and adult picture books); **Connor Goldsmith**, queryconnor@forewordliterary.com (sci-fi, fantasy, horror, thrillers, upmarket commercial, literary, LGBT, many nonfiction categories); **Jen Karsbaek**, queryjen@forewordliterary.com (women's fiction, upmarket commercial fiction, historical fiction, and literary fiction); **Emily Keyes**, queryemily@forewordliterary.com (mostly YA and MG, but also com-

JESSICA NEGRON
(TALCOTT NOTCH LITERARY)

talcottnotch.net

ABOUT JESSICA: She attended University of New Haven. For five years she interned with various local publications in both an editorial and design capacity until finally she found a place with Talcott Notch.

SHE IS SEEKING: all kinds of young adult and adult fiction, but leans toward science fiction and fantasy (and all the little subgenres), romance (the steamier, the better), and thrillers.

HOW TO QUERY: jnegron@talcottnotch.net. Paste the first 10 pages of your manuscript in the e-mail after your query. Address your query to Jessica.

mercial fiction which includes fantasy & science fiction, women's fiction, new adult fiction, along with pop culture and humor titles); **Sara Sciuto** (juvenile books, picture books).

REPRESENTS Considers these nonfiction areas: animals, film, gay/lesbian, history, how-to, humor, memoirs, music, popular culture, politics, science, theater. **Considers these fiction areas:** commercial, fantasy, gay, horror, lesbian, literary, mainstream, middle grade, mystery, new adult, paranormal, picture books, romance, science fiction, suspense, thriller, women's, young adult.

HOW TO CONTACT E-query. Each agent has a different query e-mail and style. Check their individual pages on the website for the latest updated info. Accepts simultaneous submissions.

RECENT SALES *Hollow World*, by Michael J. Sullivan; *Looking For Home: Hope Springs*, by Sarah M. Eden; *Free Agent*, by J.C. Nelson.

WRITERS CONFERENCES San Diego State University Writers' Conference, San Francisco Writers Conference, WNBA Pitch-O-Rama, LDS Storymakers Conference, SFWA Nebula Awards, Book Expo America, Ellen Hopkins' Ventana Sierra, Romance Writers of America Conference, Central Coast Writ-

ers Conference, World Fantasy Con, and many more. The agency website lists all.

◐ FOUNDRY LITERARY + MEDIA

33 West 17th St., PH, New York NY 10011. (212)929-5064. **Fax:** (212)929-5471. **Website:** www.foundry media.com.

MEMBER AGENTS Peter McGuigan, pmsubmissions@foundrymedia.com; **Yfat Reiss Gendell**, yrg submissions@foundrymedia.com (practical nonfiction projects in the areas of health and wellness, diet, lifestyle, how-to, and parenting and a broad range of narrative nonfiction that includes humor, memoir, history, science, pop culture, psychology, and adventure/travel stories); **Stéphanie Abou**, sasu bmissions@foundrymedia.com; **Mollie Glick**, mg submissions@foundrymedia.com (literary fiction, young adult fiction, narrative nonfiction, and a bit of practical nonfiction in the areas of popular science, medicine, psychology, cultural history, memoir and current events); **Stephen Barbara**, sbsubmis sions@foundrymedia.com (books for young readers, and adult fiction and nonfiction); **David Patterson**, dpsubmissions@foundrymedia.com (narrative and idea-driven nonfiction, with an emphasis on journalists, public figures, and scholars); **Chris Park**, cpsub missions@foundrymedia.com (memoirs, narrative nonfiction, sports books, Christian nonfiction and character-driven fiction); **Hannah Brown Gordon**, hbgsubmissions@foundrymedia.com (stories and narratives that blend genres, including thriller, suspense, historical, literary, speculative, memoir, pop-science, psychology, humor, and pop culture); **Brandi Bowles**, bbsubmissions@foundrymedia.com (literary and commercial fiction, especially high-concept novels that feature strong female bonds and psychological or scientific themes); **Kirsten Neuhaus**, knsubmissions@foundrymedia.com (platform-driven narrative nonfiction, in the areas of lifestyle [beauty/fashion/relationships], memoir, business, current events, history and stories with strong female voices, as well as smart, upmarket, and commercial fiction); **Jessica Regel**, jrsubmissions@foundrymedia.com (young adult and middle grade books, as well as a select list of adult general fiction, women's fiction, and adult nonfiction); **Anthony Mattero**, amsubmissions@foundrymedia.com (smart, platform-driven, nonfiction particularly in the genres of pop-culture, humor, music, sports, and pop-business).

REPRESENTS Considers these nonfiction areas: creative nonfiction, current affairs, diet/nutrition, health, history, how-to, humor, medicine, memoirs, music, parenting, popular culture, psychology, science, sports, travel. **Considers these fiction areas:** commercial, historical, humor, literary, middle grade, suspense, thriller, women's, young adult.

HOW TO CONTACT Target one agent only. Send queries to the specific submission e-mail of the agent. For fiction: send query, synopsis, author bio, first three chapters—all pasted in the e-mail. For nonfiction, send query, sample chapters, table of contents, author bio (all pasted).

RECENT SALES *Tell the Wolves I'm Home*, by Carol Rifka Blunt; *The Rathbones*, by Janice Clark; *This is Your Captain Speaking*, by Jon Methven; *The War Against the Assholes* and *The November Criminals*, by Sam Munson; *Ready Player One*, by Ernest Cline.

TIPS "Consult website for each agent's submission instructions."

◐ FULL CIRCLE LITERARY, LLC

7676 Hazard Center Dr., Suite 500, San Diego CA 92108. **E-mail:** submissions@fullcircleliterary.com. **Website:** www.fullcircleliterary.com. **Contact:** Lilly Ghahremani, Stefanie Von Borstel. Represents 55 clients. 60% of clients are new/unpublished writers. Currently handles: nonfiction books 70%, novels 10%, juvenile books 20%.

○ Before forming Full Circle, Ms. Von Borstel worked in both marketing and editorial capacities at Penguin and Harcourt; Ms. Ghahremani received her law degree from UCLA, and has experience in representing authors on legal affairs.

MEMBER AGENTS Lilly Ghahremani; Stefanie Von Borstel; Adriana Dominguez; Taylor Martindale (multicultural voices).

REPRESENTS nonfiction books, juvenile. **Considers these nonfiction areas:** creative nonfiction, design, how-to, popular culture, women's issues. **Considers these fiction areas:** literary, middle grade, picture books, women's, young adult.

⚷ "Our full-service boutique agency, representing a range of nonfiction and children's books (limited fiction), provides a one-stop resource for authors. Our extensive experience in the realms of law and marketing provide Full Circle clients with a unique edge." "Actively seeking nonfiction by authors with a unique and strong platform, projects that offer new and diverse viewpoints, and literature with a global or multicultural perspective. We are particularly interested in books with a Latino or Middle Eastern angle and books related to pop culture." Does not want to receive "screenplays, poetry, commercial fiction or genre fiction (horror, thriller, mystery, Western, sci-fi, fantasy, romance, historical fiction)."

HOW TO CONTACT Agency accepts e-queries. Put "Query for [Agent]" in the subject line. Send a 1-page query letter (in the body of the e-mail) including a description of your book, writing credentials and author highlights. Following your query, please include the first 10 pages or complete picture book manuscript text within the body of the e-mail. For nonfiction, include a proposal with one sample chapter. Accepts simultaneous submissions. Obtains most new clients through recommendations from others, solicitations, conferences.

TERMS Agent receives 15% commission on domestic sales. Agent receives 20% commission on foreign sales. Offers written contract; up to 30-day notice must be given to terminate contract. Charges for copying and postage.

NEW AGENT SPOTLIGHT

SARAH NEGO
(CORVISIERO LITERARY)

corvisieroagency.com

@sarahnego

ABOUT SARAH: She divides her time between her own writing and working with amazing authors. Her background is in marketing, and she uses her experience to help authors build their platforms and promote their work.

SHE IS SEEKING: middle grade and young adult fiction manuscripts—open to any genre within those age groups, but prefers speculative fiction. Contemporary is not her favorite, but she will look at it.

HOW TO QUERY: Send your letter, 1-2 page synopsis and the first 5 pages pasted into the body of an e-mail to Query@CorvisieroAgency.com. Please use "Query for Sarah" as your subject line.

TIPS "Put your best foot forward. Contact us when you simply can't make your project any better on your own, and please be sure your work fits with what the agent you're approaching represents. Little things count, so copyedit your work. Join a writing group and attend conferences to get objective and constructive feedback before submitting. Be active about building your platform as an author before, during, and after publication. Remember this is a business and your agent is a business partner."

⊙ NANCY GALLT LITERARY AGENCY

273 Charlton Ave., South Orange NJ 07079. (973)761-6358. **Fax:** (973)761-6318. **E-mail:** submissions@nancygallt.com. **Website:** www.nancygallt.com. **Contact:** Nancy Gallt, Marietta Zacker. Represents 40 clients. 30% of clients are new/unpublished writers. Currently handles: juvenile books 100%.

○ Prior to opening her agency, Ms. Gallt was subsidiary rights director of the children's book division at Morrow, Harper and Viking.

MEMBER AGENTS Nancy Gallt; Marietta Zacker.

REPRESENTS juvenile. **Considers these fiction areas:** juvenile, middle grade, picture books, young adult.

○—π "We only handle children's books." Actively seeking picture books, middle grade, and young adult novels. Does not want to receive rhyming picture book texts.

HOW TO CONTACT Submit through online submission form on agency website. Accepts simultaneous submissions. Obtains most new clients through recommendations from others, solicitations.

TERMS Agent receives 15% commission on domestic sales. Agent receives 20% commission on foreign sales. Offers written contract; 30-day notice must be given to terminate contract.

RECENT SALES Rick Riordan's books (Hyperion); *Something Extraordinary* by Ben Clanton (Simon & Schuster); *The Baby Tree* by Sophie Blackall (Nancy Paulsen Books/Penguin); *Fenway And Hattie* by Victoria J Coe (Putnam/Penguin); *The Meaning Of Maggie* by Megan Jean Sovern (Chronicle); *The Misadventures Of The Family Fletcher* By Dana Alison Levy

(Random House); *Abrakapow!* by Isaiah Campbell (Simon & Schuster); *Subway Love* by Nora Raleigh Baskin (Candlewick).

TIPS "Writing and illustrations stand on their own, so submissions should tell the most compelling stories possible--whether visually, in words, or both."

GELFMAN SCHNEIDER / ICM PARTNERS

850 7th Ave., Suite 903, New York NY 10019. (212)245-1993. **Fax:** (212)245-8678. **E-mail:** mail@gelfman schneider.com. **Website:** www.gelfmanschneider. com. **Contact:** Jane Gelfman, Deborah Schneider. Member of AAR. Represents 300+ clients. 10% of clients are new/unpublished writers.

MEMBER AGENTS Jane Gelfman, Victoria Marini, Heather Mitchell.

REPRESENTS fiction and nonfiction books. **Considers these nonfiction areas:** creative nonfiction, popular culture. **Considers these fiction areas:** historical, literary, mainstream, middle grade, mystery, suspense, women's, young adult.

- Does not want to receive romance, science fiction, westerns, or illustrated children's books.

HOW TO CONTACT Query. Send queries via snail mail only. No unsolicited mss. Please send a query letter, a synopsis, and a SAMPLE CHAPTER ONLY. Consult website for each agent's submission requirements. Responds in 1 month to queries. Responds in 2 months to mss.

TERMS Agent receives 15% commission on domestic sales. Agent receives 20% commission on foreign sales. Agent receives 15% commission on film sales. Offers written contract. Charges clients for photocopying and messengers/couriers.

BARRY GOLDBLATT LITERARY LLC

320 Seventh Ave. #266, Brooklyn NY 11215. (718)832-8787. **E-mail:** query@bgliterary.com. **Website:** www. bgliterary.com/. **Contact:** Barry Goldblatt. Estab. 2000.

MEMBER AGENTS Barry Goldblatt.

REPRESENTS Considers these fiction areas: middle grade, young adult.

- "Please see our website for specific submission guidelines and information on our particular tastes."

HOW TO CONTACT Obtains clients through referrals, queries, and conferences.

TERMS Agent receives 15% commission on domestic sales; 20% on foreign and dramatic sales. Offers written contract. 60 days notice must be given to terminate contract.

RECENT SALES *Read Between the Lines*, by Jo Knowles; *Bright Before Sunrise*, by Tiffany Schmidt; *The Infamous Ratsos*, by Kara LaReau; *Wonders of the Invisible World*, by Christopher Barzak.

TIPS "We're a hands-on agency, focused on building an author's career, not just making an initial sale. We don't care about trends or what's hot; we just want to sign great writers."

IRENE GOODMAN LITERARY AGENCY

27 W. 24th St., Suite 700B, New York NY 10010. **E-mail:** irene.queries@irenegoodman.com. **Website:** www.irenegoodman.com. **Contact:** Irene Goodman, Miriam Kriss. Member of AAR.

MEMBER AGENTS Irene Goodman; Beth Vesel; Miriam Kriss; Barbara Poelle; Rachel Ekstrom.

REPRESENTS nonfiction, novels. **Considers these nonfiction areas:** narrative nonfiction dealing with social, cultural and historical issues; an occasional memoir and current affairs book, parenting, social issues, francophilia, anglophilia, Judaica, lifestyles, cooking, memoir. **Considers these fiction areas:** crime, detective, historical, mystery, romance, thriller, women's, young adult.

- "Specializes in the finest in commercial fiction and nonfiction. We have a strong background in women's voices, including mysteries, romance, women's fiction, thrillers, suspense. Historical fiction is one of Irene's particular passions and Miriam is fanatical about modern urban fantasies. In nonfiction, Irene is looking for topics on narrative history, social issues and trends, education, Judaica, Francophilia, Anglophilia, other cultures, animals, food, crafts, and memoir." Barbara is looking for commercial thrillers with strong female protagonists; Miriam is looking for urban fantasy and edgy sci-fi/young adult. No children's picture books, screenplays, poetry, or inspirational fiction.

HOW TO CONTACT Query. Submit synopsis, first 10 pages. E-mail queries only! See the website submission page. No e-mail attachments. Responds in 2 months to queries. Consult website for each agent's submission guidelines.

PETER KNAPP
(PARK LITERARY GROUP)

parkliterary.com

@petejknapp

ABOUT PETER: Prior to joining Park Literary, he was the story editor at Floren Shieh Productions, where he consulted on book-to-film adaptations for Los Angeles-based film and TV entities. He graduated from New York University with a B.A. in Art History.

HE IS SEEKING: middle grade and young adult fiction, as well as suspense and thrillers for all ages. He does not represent picture books or nonfiction.

HOW TO SUBMIT: queries@parkliterary.com. Put "Query for Peter: [Title]" in the subject line. All materials must be in the body of the e-mail.

RECENT SALES *The Ark*, by Boyd Morrison; *Isolation*, by C.J. Lyons; *The Sleepwalkers*, by Paul Grossman; *Dead Man's Moon*, by Devon Monk; *Becoming Marie Antoinette*, by Juliet Grey; *What's Up Down There*, by Lissa Rankin; *Beg for Mercy*, by Toni Andrews; *The Devil Inside*, by Jenna Black.

TIPS "We are receiving an unprecedented amount of e-mail queries. If you find that the mailbox is full, please try again in two weeks. E-mail queries to our personal addresses will not be answered. E-mails to our personal inboxes will be deleted."

❶ DOUG GRAD LITERARY AGENCY, INC.

68 Jay Street, Suite W11, Brooklyn NY 11201. (718)788-6067. **E-mail:** doug.grad@dgliterary.com. **E-mail:** query@dgliterary.com. **Website:** www.dgliterary.com. **Contact:** Doug Grad. Estab. 2008.

Prior to being an agent, Doug Grad spent the last 22 years as an editor at 4 major publishing houses.

MEMBER AGENTS Doug Grad (narrative nonfiction, military, sports, celebrity memoir, thrillers, mysteries, historical fiction, young adult fiction, romance, music, style, business, home improvement, cookbooks, self-help, science and theater); **George Bick** (science fiction [no fantasy!], narrative nonfiction, business, thrillers, mysteries, military, pop science, pop culture, and travel).

REPRESENTS Considers these nonfiction areas: business, cooking, creative nonfiction, military, music, popular culture, science, self-help, sports, theater, travel. **Considers these fiction areas:** historical, mystery, science fiction, thriller, young adult.

HOW TO CONTACT Query by e-mail first at query@dgliterary.com. No sample material unless requested; no printed submissions by mail.

RECENT SALES *The Earthend Saga*, by Gillian Anderson and Jeff Rovin (Simon451); *Written Off: The Heroic Ordeal of Medal of Honor Nominee Captain William Albracht,* by William Albracht and Marvin Wolf (Berkley/Caliber); *Gordie Howe's Sun: A Hall of Fame Life in the Shadow of Mr. Hockey*, by Mark Howe with Jay Greenberg (HarperCanada/Triumph Books US).

SANFORD J. GREENBURGER ASSOCIATES, INC.

55 Fifth Ave., New York NY 10003. (212)206-5600. **Fax:** (212)463-8718. **Website:** www.greenburger.com. Member of AAR. Represents 500 clients.

MEMBER AGENTS Matt Bialer, LRibar@sjga.com (fantasy, science fiction, thrillers, and mysteries as well as a select group of literary writers, and also loves smart narrative nonfiction including books about current events, popular culture, biography, history, music, race, and sports); **Brenda Bowen**, queryBB@ sjga.com (literary fiction, writers and illustrators of picture books, chapter books, and middle grade and teen fiction); **Lisa Gallagher**, lgsubmissions@sjga. com (accessible literary fiction, quality commercial women's fiction, crime fiction, lively narrative nonfiction); **Faith Hamlin**, fhamlin@sjga.com (receives submissions by referral); **Heide Lange**, queryHL@ sjga.com; **Daniel Mandel**, querydm@sjga.com (literary and commercial fiction, as well as memoirs and nonfiction about business, art, history, politics, sports, and popular culture); **Courtney Miller-Callihan**, cmiller@sjga.com (YA, middle grade, women's fiction, romance, and historical novels, as well as non-fiction projects on unusual topics, humor, pop culture, and lifestyle books); **Nicholas Ellison**, nellison@sjga. com; **Chelsea Lindman**, clindman@sjga.com (playful literary fiction, upmarket crime fiction, and forward thinking or boundary-pushing nonfiction); **Rachael Dillon Fried**, rfried@sjga.com (both fiction and non-fiction authors, with a keen interest in unique literary voices, women's fiction, narrative nonfiction, memoir, and comedy); **Lindsay Ribar**, co-agents with Matt Bailer (young adult and middle grade fiction).

REPRESENTS nonfiction books and novels. **Considers these nonfiction areas:** art, biography, business, creative nonfiction, current affairs, ethnic, history, humor, memoirs, music, popular culture, politics, sports. **Considers these fiction areas:** crime, fantasy, historical, literary, middle grade, mystery, picture books, romance, science fiction, thriller, women's, young adult.

No Westerns. No screenplays.

HOW TO CONTACT E-query. "Please look at each agent's profile page for current information about what each agent is looking for and for the correct e-mail address to use for queries to that agent. Please be sure to use the correct query e-mail address for each agent." Accepts simultaneous submissions. Responds in 2 months to queries and mss. Obtains most new clients through recommendations from others.

TERMS Agent receives 15% commission on domestic sales. Agent receives 20% commission on foreign sales. Charges for photocopying and books for foreign and subsidiary rights submissions.

RECENT SALES *Inferno*, by Dan Brown; *Hidden Order*, by Brad Thor; *The Chalice*, by Nancy Bilveau; *Horns*, by Joe Hill.

THE GREENHOUSE LITERARY AGENCY

11308 Lapham Dr., Oakton VA 22124. **E-mail:** submissions@greenhouseliterary.com. **Website:** www. greenhouseliterary.com. Member of AAR. Other memberships include SCBWI. Represents 20 clients. 100% of clients are new/unpublished writers. Currently handles: juvenile books 100%.

Sarah Davies has had an editorial and management career in children's publishing spanning 25 years; for 5 years prior to launching the Greenhouse she was Publishing Director of Macmillan Children's Books in London, and publishing leading authors from both sides of the Atlantic.

MEMBER AGENTS Sarah Davies, vice president (middle grade and young adult); **John M. Cusick**, agent (picture books, middle grade, YA, and boy books for kids); **Polly Nolan**, agent (fiction by UK, Irish, Commonwealth—including Australia, NZ and India—authors, from picture books to young fiction series, through middle grade and young adult).

REPRESENTS juvenile. **Considers these fiction areas:** juvenile, middle grade, picture books, young adult.

"We exclusively represent authors writing fiction for children and teens. The agency has offices in both the USA and UK, and Sarah Davies (who is British) personally represents authors to both markets. The agency's commission structure reflects this—taking 15% for sales to both US and UK, thus treating both as 'domestic' markets.' " All genres of children's and YA fiction—ages 5+. Does not want to receive nonfiction, poetry, picture books (text or illustration) or work aimed at adults; short stories, educational or religious/inspirational work, pre-school/novelty material, or screenplays.

CLAIRE ANDERSON-WHEELER
(REGAL LITERARY)

regal-literary.com

ABOUT CLAIRE: Claire previously worked at Anderson Literary Management in New York, and at Christine Green Authors' Agent in London, UK. She holds an LLB from Trinity College, Dublin, and a Master's in Creative Writing from the University of East Anglia, UK. Claire is Irish, was born in DC, and grew up in Dublin, Geneva, and Brussels.

SHE IS SEEKING: YA with a strong voice (realistic or high-concept), works of narrative nonfiction and pop culture/pop psychology, literary fiction, and commercial women's fiction driven by strong contemporary issues.

HOW TO QUERY: E-mail your query, attaching a synopsis and the first three chapters as MS Word documents. Send to submissions@regal-literary.com, and put "Query for Claire: [Title]" in the subject line.

HOW TO CONTACT Query one agent only. Put the target agent's name in the subject line. Paste the first 5 pages of your story (or your complete picture book) after the query. Obtains most new clients through recommendations from others, solicitations, conferences.
TERMS Agent receives 15% commission on domestic sales. Agent receives 25% commission on foreign sales. Offers written contract. This agency occasionally charges for submission copies to film agents or foreign publishers.
RECENT SALES *Fracture*, by Megan Miranda (Walker); *Paper Valentine*, by Brenna Yovanff (Razorbill); *Uses for Boys*, by Erica L. Scheidt (St Martin's); *Dark Inside*, by Jeyn Roberts (Simon & Schuster); *Breathe*, by Sarah Crossan (HarperCollins); *After the Snow*, by SD Crockett (Feiwel/Macmillan); *Sean Griswold's Head*, by Lindsey Leavitt (Hyperion).
WRITERS CONFERENCES Bologna Children's Book Fair, ALA and SCBWI conferences, BookExpo America.
TIPS "Before submitting material, authors should read the Greenhouse's 'Top 10 Tips for Authors of Children's Fiction' and carefully follow our submission guidelines which can be found on the website."

◑ KATHRYN GREEN LITERARY AGENCY, LLC

250 West 57th St., Suite 2302, New York NY 10107. (212)245-4225. **Fax:** (212)245-4042. **E-mail:** query@kgreenagency.com. **Contact:** Kathy Green. Memberships include Women's Media Group. Represents approximately 20 clients. 50% of clients are new/unpublished writers. Currently handles: nonfiction books 50%, novels 25%, juvenile books 25%.

◑   Prior to becoming an agent, Ms. Green was a book and magazine editor.

REPRESENTS nonfiction books, novels, short story collections, juvenile, middle grade and young adult only). **Considers these nonfiction areas:** autobiography, biography, business, child guidance, cooking, current affairs, diet/nutrition, economics, education, foods, history, how-to, humor, interior design, investigative, juvenile nonfiction, memoirs, parenting, popular culture, psychology, satire, self-help, sports, true crime, women's issues, women's studies, juvenile. **Considers these fiction areas:** crime, detective, family saga, historical, humor, juvenile, literary, mainstream, middle grade, mystery, police, romance, satire, suspense, thriller, women's, young adult.

☛ Keeping the client list small means that writers receive my full attention throughout the process of getting their project published. Does not want to receive science fiction or fantasy.

HOW TO CONTACT Query to query@kgreenagency.com. Send no samples unless requested. Accepts simultaneous submissions. Responds in 1-2 months to mss. Obtains most new clients through recommendations from others, solicitations, conferences.

TERMS Agent receives 15% commission on domestic sales. Agent receives 20% commission on foreign sales. No written contract.

RECENT SALES *Welcome To The Dark House; Extinct For A Reason; The Arnifour Affair; The Civil War In Color; The Racecar Book.*

TIPS "This agency offers a written agreement."

⦿ JILL GRINBERG LITERARY AGENCY

16 Court St., Suite 3306, Brooklyn NY 11241. (212)620-5883. **Fax:** (212)627-4725. **E-mail:** info@grinberglit erary.com. **Website:** www.jillgrinbergliterary.com. Estab. 1999.

○ Prior to her current position, Ms. Grinberg was at Anderson Grinberg Literary Management.

MEMBER AGENTS Jill Grinberg, jill@jillgrinber gliterary.com; **Cheryl Pientka**, cheryl@jillgrinber gliterary.com; **Katelyn Detweiler**, katelyn@jillgrin bergliterary.com.

REPRESENTS nonfiction books, novels. **Considers these nonfiction areas:** biography, cooking, ethnic, history, science, travel. **Considers these fiction areas:** fantasy, juvenile, literary, mainstream, romance, science fiction, young adult.

HOW TO CONTACT Please send your query letter to info@jillgrinbergliterary.com and attach the first 50 pages (fiction) or proposal (nonfiction) as a Word doc file. All submissions will be read, but electronic mail is preferred.

RECENT SALES *Cinder*, Marissa Meyer; *The Hero's Guide to Saving Your Kingdom*, Christopher Healy; *Kiss and Make Up*, Katie Anderson; i, T.J. Stiles; *Eon and Eona*, Alison Goodman; *American Nations*, Colin Woodard; HALO Trilogy, Alexandra Adornetto; *Babymouse*, Jennifer & Matthew Holm; Uglies/Levia-

than Trilogy, Scott Westerfeld; *Liar*, Justine Larbalestier; *Turtle in Paradise*, Jennifer Holm; *Wisdom's Kiss* and *Dairy Queen*, Catherine Gilbert Murdock.

TIPS "We prefer submissions by mail."

○ HEACOCK HILL LITERARY AGENCY, INC.

West Coast Office, 1020 Hollywood Way, #439, Burbank CA 91505. (818)951-6788. **E-mail:** agent@hea cockhill.com. **Website:** www.heacockhill.com. **Contact:** Catt LeBaigue or Tom Dark. Estab. 2009. Member of AAR. Other memberships include SCBWI.

○ Prior to becoming an agent, Ms. LeBaigue spent 18 years with Sony Pictures and Warner Bros.

MEMBER AGENTS Tom Dark (adult fiction, nonfiction); **Catt LeBaigue** (juvenile fiction, adult nonfiction including arts, crafts, anthropology, astronomy, nature studies, ecology, body/mind/spirit, humanities, self-help).

REPRESENTS nonfiction, fiction. **Considers these nonfiction areas:** art, business, gardening, politics. **Considers these fiction areas:** juvenile, middle grade, picture books, young adult.

☛ Not presently accepting new clients for adult fiction. Please check the website for updates.

HOW TO CONTACT E-mail queries only. No unsolicited manuscripts. No e-mail attachments. Responds in 1 week to queries. Obtains most new clients through recommendations from others, solicitations.

TERMS Offers written contract.

TIPS "Write an informative original e-query expressing your book idea, your qualifications, and short excerpts of the work. No unfinished work, please."

⦿ HERMAN AGENCY

350 Central Park West, New York NY 10025. (212)749-4907. **E-mail:** Ronnie@HermanAgencyInc.com. **Website:** www.hermanagencyinc.com. Estab. 1999. Currently handles: books for young readers.

MEMBER AGENTS Ronnie Ann Herman.

REPRESENTS children's.

HOW TO CONTACT Submit via e-mail to one of our agents. See website for specific agents' specialties.

TIPS "Check our website to see if you belong with our agency."

⦿ HSG AGENCY

287 Spring St., New York NY 10013. **E-mail:** chan nigan@hsgagency.com; jsalky@hsgagency.com; jget zler@hsgagency.com. **Website:** hsgagency.com. **Con-**

NEW AGENT SPOTLIGHT

SHANNON HASSAN
(MARSAL LYON LITERARY AGENCY)

marsallyonliteraryagency.com

@ShannonHassan

ABOUT SHANNON: Based in Boulder, Colorado, she is also eager to hear from authors with a unique perspective on the New West. Previously, Shannon was an agent at the Warner Literary Group, and an acquisitions editor at Fulcrum Publishing. Before entering the publishing world, she was a corporate attorney at Arnold & Porter in New York, and she received her J.D. from Harvard and her B.A. from George Washington University.

SHE IS SEEKING: literary and commercial fiction, young adult fiction, and select nonfiction. For nonfiction: She is interested in memoirists with exceptional stories to tell, as well as authors with a strong platform in current affairs, history, education, or law.

HOW TO QUERY: Shannon@MarsalLyonLiteraryAgency.com and write "Query" in the subject line. In all submissions, please include a contact phone number as well as your e-mail address.

tact: Carrie Hannigan; Jesseca Salky; Josh Getzler. Estab. 2011.

○ Prior to opening HSG Agency, Ms. Hannigan, Ms. Salky and Mr. Getzler were agents at Russell & Volkening.

MEMBER AGENTS Carrie Hannigan, Jesseca Salky, Josh Getzler.

REPRESENTS Considers these nonfiction areas: business, creative nonfiction, current affairs, education, foods, memoirs, photography, politics, psychology, science. **Considers these fiction areas:** commercial, crime, historical, literary, middle grade, mystery, picture books, thriller, women's, young adult.

⚭ Ms. Hannigan is actively seeking both fiction and nonfiction children's books in the picture book and middle grade age range, as well as adult women's fiction and select photography projects that would appeal to a large audience. Ms. Salky is actively seeking literary and commercial fiction that appeals to women and men; "all types of nonfiction, with a particular interest in memoir and narrative nonfiction in the areas of science, pop-psychology, politics, current affairs, business, education, food, and any other topic that is the vehicle for a great story." Mr. Getzler is actively seeking adult historical and crime-related fiction (mystery, thriller), select nonfiction and YA projects (particularly those that fit within historical or crime fiction). He is also interested in smart women's fiction.

HOW TO CONTACT Electronic submission only. Send query letter, first 5 pages of ms within e-mail to appropriate agent. Avoid submitting to multiple agents within the agency. Picture books: include entire ms. Responds in 4-6 weeks.

RECENT SALES *The Beginner's Goodbye*, by Anne Tyler (Knopf); *Blue Sea Burning*, by Geoff Rodkey (Putnam); *The Partner Track*, by Helen Wan (St. Martin's Press); *The Thrill of the Haunt*, by E.J. Copperman (Berkley); *Aces Wild*, by Erica Perl (Knopf Books for Young Readers); *Steve & Wessley: The Sea Monster*, by Jennifer Morris (Scholastic); *Infinite Worlds*, by Michael Soluri (Simon & Schuster).

ⓘ INKWELL MANAGEMENT, LLC

521 Fifth Ave., 26th Floor, New York NY 10175. (212)922-3500. **Fax:** (212)922-0535. **E-mail:** submissions@inkwellmanagement.com. **Website:** www.inkwellmanagement.com. Represents 500 clients.

MEMBER AGENTS Monika Woods (literary and commercial fiction, young adult, memoir, and compelling nonfiction in popular culture, science, and current affairs); **Lauren Smythe** (smart narrative nonfiction [narrative journalism, modern history, biography, cultural criticism, personal essay, humor], personality-driven practical nonfiction [cookbooks, fashion and style], and contemporary literary fiction); **David Hale Smith**; **Hannah Schwartz**; **Eliza Rothstein** (literary and commercial fiction, narrative nonfiction, memoir, popular science, and food writing); **Charlie Olsen** (fiction, children's books, graphic novels and illustrated works, and compelling narrative nonfiction); **Jacqueline Murphy**; **Alyssa Mozdzen**; **Nathaniel Jacks** (memoir, narrative nonfiction, social sciences, health, current affairs, business, religion, and popular history, as well as fiction—literary and commercial, women's, young adult, historical, short story, among others); **Alexis Hurley** (literary and commercial fiction, memoir, narrative nonfiction and more); **Allison Hunter** (literary and commercial fiction [including romance], memoir, narrative nonfiction, cultural studies, pop culture and prescriptive titles, including cookbooks); **David Forrer** (literary, commercial, historical and crime fiction to suspense/thriller, humorous nonfiction and popular history); **Catherine Drayton** (bestselling authors of books for children, young adults and women readers); **William Callahan** (nonfiction of all stripes, especially American history and memoir, pop culture and illustrated books, as well as voice-driven fiction that stands out from the crowd); **Lizz Blaise** (literary fiction, women's and young adult fiction, suspense, and psycho-

logical thriller); **Kimberly Witherspoon**; **Michael V Carlisle**; **Richard Pine**.

REPRESENTS nonfiction books, novels. **Considers these nonfiction areas:** biography, business, cooking, creative nonfiction, current affairs, foods, health, history, humor, memoirs, popular culture, religious, science. **Considers these fiction areas:** commercial, crime, historical, literary, middle grade, picture books, romance, short story collections, suspense, thriller, women's, young adult.

HOW TO CONTACT In the body of your e-mail, please include a query letter and a short writing sample (1-2 chapters). We currently accept submissions in all genres except screenplays. Due to the volume of queries we receive, our response time may take up to two months. Feel free to put "Query for [Agent Name]: [Your Book Title]" in the e-mail subject line. Obtains most new clients through recommendations from others.

TERMS Agent receives 15% commission on domestic sales. Agent receives 20% commission on foreign sales. Offers written contract.

TIPS "We will not read mss before receiving a letter of inquiry."

⊘⊙ ICM PARTNERS

730 Fifth Ave., New York NY 10019. (212)556-5600. **Website:** www.icmtalent.com. **Contact:** Literary Department. Member of AAR. Signatory of WGA.

REPRESENTS nonfiction, fiction, novels, juvenile books.

↤ *We do not accept unsolicited submissions.*

HOW TO CONTACT This agency is generally not open to unsolicited submissions. However, some agents do attend conferences and meet writers then. The agents take referrals, as well. Obtains most new clients through recommendations from others.

TERMS Agent receives 15% commission on domestic sales. Agent receives 20% commission on foreign sales.

ⓘ JABBERWOCKY LITERARY AGENCY

49 West 45th St., New York NY 10036. (718)392-5985. **Website:** www.awfulagent.com. **Contact:** Joshua Bilmes. Memberships include SFWA. Represents 40 clients. 15% of clients are new/unpublished writers. Currently handles: nonfiction books 15%, novels 75%, scholarly books 5%, other 5% other.

MEMBER AGENTS Joshua Bilmes; Eddie Schneider; Lisa Rodgers; Sam Morgan.

REPRESENTS novels. **Considers these nonfiction areas:** autobiography, biography, business, cooking, current affairs, diet/nutrition, economics, film, foods, gay/lesbian, government, health, history, humor, language, law, literature, medicine, money, popular culture, politics, satire, science, sociology, sports, theater, war, women's issues, women's studies, young adult. **Considers these fiction areas:** action, adventure, contemporary issues, crime, detective, ethnic, family saga, fantasy, gay, glitz, historical, horror, humor, lesbian, literary, mainstream, middle grade, police, psychic, regional, satire, science fiction, sports, supernatural, thriller, young adult.

⚷ This agency represents quite a lot of genre fiction and is actively seeking to increase the amount of nonfiction projects. It does not handle children's or picture books. Book-length material only—no poetry, articles, or short fiction.

HOW TO CONTACT "We are currently open to unsolicited queries. No e-mail, phone, or fax queries, please. Query with SASE. Please check our website, as there may be times during the year when we are not accepting queries. Query letter only; no manuscript material unless requested." Accepts simultaneous submissions. Responds in 3 weeks to queries. Obtains most new clients through solicitations, recommendation by current clients.

TERMS Agent receives 15% commission on domestic sales. Agent receives 20% commission on foreign sales. Offers written contract, binding for 1 year. Charges clients for book purchases, photocopying, international book/ms mailing.

RECENT SALES Sold 30 US and 100 foreign titles in the last year. *Dead Ever After*, by Charlaine Harris; *Words of Radiance*, by Brandon Sanderson; *The Daylight War*, by Peter V. Brett; *Limits of Power*, by Elizabeth Moon. Other clients include Tanya Huff, Simon Green, Jack Campbell, Myke Cole, William C. Dietz, and Marie Brennan.

TIPS "In approaching with a query, the most important things to us are your credits and your biographical background to the extent it's relevant to your work. I (and most agents) will ignore the adjectives you may choose to describe your own work."

🌐⊘ JANKLOW & NESBIT ASSOCIATES

445 Park Ave., New York NY 10022. (212)421-1700. **Fax:** (212)980-3671. **E-mail:** submissions@janklow.

com. **Website:** www.janklowandnesbit.com. Estab. 1989.

MEMBER AGENTS Morton L. Janklow; Anne Sibbald; Lynn Nesbit; Luke Janklow; Cullen Stanley; PJ Mark (interests are eclectic, including short stories and literary novels. His nonfiction interests include journalism, popular culture, memoir/narrative, essays and cultural criticism); Richard Morris (books that challenge our common assumptions, be it in the fields of cultural history, business, food, sports, science or faith); Paul Lucas (literary and commercial fiction, focusing on literary thrillers, science fiction and fantasy; also seeks narrative histories of ideas and objects, as well as biographies and popular science); Emma Parry (nonfiction by experts, but will consider outstanding literary fiction and upmarket commercial fiction. I'm not looking for children's books, middle grade, or fantasy); Alexandra Machinist; Kirby Kim (formerly of WME).

REPRESENTS nonfiction, fiction.

⚷ Does not want to receive unsolicited submissions or queries.

HOW TO CONTACT Query via snail mail or e-mail. Include a synopsis and the first 10 pages if sending fiction. For nonfiction, send a query and full outline. Accepts simultaneous submissions. Responds in 8 weeks to queries/mss. Obtains most new clients through recommendations from others.

TIPS "Please send a short query with first 10 pages or artwork."

◉ KIRCHOFF/WOHLBERG, INC.

897 Boston Post Rd., Madison CT 06443. (203)245-7308. **Fax:** (203)245-3218. **Website:** www.kirchoffwohlberg.com. **Contact:** Ronald Zollshan. Memberships include SCBWI, Society of Illustrators, SPAR, Bookbuilders of Boston, New York Bookbinders' Guild, AIGA.

◑ Kirchoff/Wohlberg has been in business for more than 35 years.

REPRESENTS Considers these fiction areas: juvenile, middle grade, picture books, young adult.

⚷ This agency specializes in juvenile fiction and nonfiction through young adult.

HOW TO CONTACT "Submit by mail to address above. We welcome the submission of mss from first-time or established children's book authors. Please enclose an SASE, but note that while we endeavor to read all submissions, we cannot guarantee a reply or their return." Accepts simultaneous submissions.

TERMS Offers written contract, binding for at least 1 year. Agent receives standard commission, depending upon whether it is an author only, illustrator only, or an author/illustrator.

⊘ BARBARA S. KOUTS, LITERARY AGENT

P.O. Box 560, Bellport NY 11713. (631)286-1278. **Fax:** (631) 286-1538. **Contact:** Barbara S. Kouts. Member of AAR. Represents 50 clients. 10% of clients are new/unpublished writers.

REPRESENTS juvenile.

8━▪ This agency specializes in children's books.

HOW TO CONTACT Query with SASE. Accepts queries by mail only. Accepts simultaneous submissions. Responds in 1 week to queries; 2 months to mss. Obtains most new clients through recommendations from others, solicitations, conferences.

TERMS Agent receives 10% commission on domestic sales. Agent receives 20% commission on foreign sales. This agency charges clients for photocopying.

RECENT SALES *Code Talker*, by Joseph Bruchac (Dial); *The Penderwicks*, by Jeanne Birdsall (Knopf); *Froggy's Baby Sister*, by Jonathan London (Viking).

TIPS "Write, do not call. Be professional in your writing."

◑ KT LITERARY, LLC

9249 S. Broadway, #200-543, Highlands Ranch CO 80129. (720)344-4728. **Fax:** (720)344-4728. **E-mail:** queries@ktliterary.com. **Website:** ktliterary.com. **Contact:** Kate Schafer Testerman. Member of AAR. Other memberships include SCBWI. Represents 20 clients. 60% of clients are new/unpublished writers.

◑ Prior to her current position, Ms. Schafer was an agent with Janklow & Nesbit.

MEMBER AGENTS Kate Schafer Testerman, Renee Nyon.

REPRESENTS Considers these fiction areas: middle grade, young adult.

8━▪ "I'm bringing my years of experience in the New York publishing scene, as well as my lifelong love of reading, to a vibrant area for writers, proving that great work can be found, and sold, from anywhere." "We're thrilled to be actively seeking new clients writing brilliant, funny, original middle grade and young adult fiction, both literary and commercial." Does

not want picture books, serious nonfiction, and adult literary fiction.

HOW TO CONTACT "To submit to kt literary, please e-mail us a query letter with the first three pages of your manuscript in the body of the e-mail. The subject line of your e-mail should include the word 'Query' along with the title of your manuscript. Queries should not contain attachments. Attachments will not be read, and queries containing attachments will be deleted unread. We aim to reply to all queries within two weeks of receipt. No snail mail queries." Responds in 2 weeks to queries. Responds in 2 months to mss. Obtains most new clients through recommendations from others, solicitations, conferences.

TERMS Agent receives 15% commission on domestic sales. Agent receives 20% commission on foreign sales. Offers written contract; 30-day notice must be given to terminate contract.

RECENT SALES *Albatross*, by Julie Bloss; *The Last Good Place of Lily Odilon*, by Sara Beitia; *Texting the Underworld*, by Ellen Booraem. A full list of clients is available on the agency website.

WRITERS CONFERENCES Various SCBWI conferences, BookExpo.

TIPS "If we like your query, we'll ask for (more). Continuing advice is offered regularly on my blog 'Ask Daphne,' which can be accessed from my website."

◑ LIPPINCOTT MASSIE MCQUILKIN

27 West 20th Street, Suite 305, New York NY 10011. **Fax:** (212)352-2059. **E-mail:** info@lmqlit.com. **Website:** www.lmqlit.com.

MEMBER AGENTS Shannon O'Neill (writing that informs, intrigues, or inspires: special interests include narrative nonfiction, popular science, current affairs, the history of ideas, and literary and upmarket fiction); **Laney Katz Becker**; **Kent Wolf** (literary fiction, upmarket women's fiction, memoir, pop culture, all types of narrative nonfiction, and select YA); **Ethan Bassoff** (emerging and established writers of literary and crime fiction and narrative nonfiction including history, science, humor, and sports writing); **Jason Anthony** (specializes in young adult and commercial fiction and most areas of nonfiction, including pop culture, memoir, true crime, and general psychology); **Will Lippincott** (politics, current events, narrative nonfiction and history); **Maria Massie** (literary fiction, memoir, and cultural history); **Rob Mc-**

ROZ FOSTER
(SANDRA DIJKSTRA LITERARY AGENCY)

dijkstraagency.com

@RozFoster

ABOUT ROZ: Roz has a B.A. in English Literature from UC San Diego, studied philosophy for a year at the University of Sheffield, UK, and earned her M.A. in English, with an emphasis in Composition & Rhetoric and Creative Writing, from Portland State University. She's been learning French since 2009.

SHE IS SEEKING: Roz is interested in literary and commercial fiction, women's fiction, literary sci-fi, and literary YA. She loves novels that make her feel like the author is tuned into a rising revolution—cultural, political, literary, or what-not—that's about to burst on the scene. Nonfiction: current affairs, design, business, cultural anthropology/social science, politics, psychology and memoir.

HOW TO QUERY: roz@dijkstraagency.com. Please send a query, a 1-page synopsis, a brief bio (including a description of your publishing history), and the first 10-15 pages of your manuscript. Please send all items in the body of the e-mail, not as an attachment.

Quilkin (fiction, memoir, history, sociology, psychology, and graphic works).
REPRESENTS nonfiction books, novels, short story collections, scholarly, graphic novels. **Considers these nonfiction areas**: animals, anthropology, archeology, architecture, art, autobiography, biography, business, child guidance, cultural interests, current affairs, design, economics, ethnic, film, gay/lesbian, government, health, history, inspirational, language, law, literature, medicine, memoirs, military, money, music, parenting, popular culture, politics, psychology, religious, science, self-help, sociology, technology, true crime, women's issues, women's studies, young adult. **Considers these fiction areas**: action, adventure, cartoon, comic books, confession, family saga, feminist, gay, historical, humor, lesbian, literary, mainstream, regional, satire.

"LMQ focuses on bringing new voices in literary and commercial fiction to the market, as well as popularizing the ideas and arguments of scholars in the fields of history, psychology, sociology, political science, and current affairs. Actively seeking fiction writers who already have credits in magazines and quarterlies, as well as nonfiction writers who already have a media platform or some kind of a university affiliation." Does not want to receive romance, genre fiction, or children's material.
HOW TO CONTACT E-query. "Include the word 'Query' as well as the agent you are querying in the subject line of your e-mail (i.e., 'Query for Maria Massie'). If your project is fiction, please also include

the first 5-10 pages pasted into the body of your e-mail. We look forward to reviewing your work." Accepts simultaneous submissions. Obtains most new clients through recommendations from others, solicitations, conferences.

TERMS Agent receives 15% commission on domestic sales. Agent receives 20% commission on foreign sales. Offers written contract; 30-day notice must be given to terminate contract. Only charges for reasonable business expenses upon successful sale.

RECENT SALES Clients include: Peter Ho Davies, Kim Addonizio, Natasha Trethewey, Anne Carson, David Sirota, Katie Crouch, Uwen Akpan, Lydia Millet, Tom Perrotta, Jonathan Lopez, Chris Hayes, Caroline Weber.

○ LOWENSTEIN ASSOCIATES INC.

121 W. 27th St., Suite 501, New York NY 10001. (212)206-1630. **Fax:** (212)727-0280. **E-mail:** assistant@bookhaven.com. **Website:** www.lowensteinassociates.com. **Contact:** Barbara Lowenstein. Member of AAR. Represents 150 clients.

MEMBER AGENTS Barbara Lowenstein, president (nonfiction interests include narrative nonfiction, health, money, finance, travel, multicultural, popular culture, and memoir; fiction interests include literary fiction and women's fiction); Emily Gref (young adult, middle grade, fantasy, science fiction, literary, commercial, various nonfiction).

REPRESENTS nonfiction books, novels. **Considers these nonfiction areas:** creative nonfiction, health, memoirs, money, multicultural, popular culture, travel. **Considers these fiction areas:** commercial, fantasy, literary, middle grade, science fiction, women's, young adult.

⌐ Barbara Lowenstein is currently looking for writers who have a platform and are leading experts in their field, including business, women's issues, psychology, health, science and social issues, and is particularly interested in strong new voices in fiction and narrative nonfiction. Does not want Westerns, textbooks, children's picture books and books in need of translation.

HOW TO CONTACT "For fiction, please send us a one-page query letter, along with the first ten pages pasted in the body of the message by e-mail to assistant@bookhaven.com. If nonfiction, please send a one-page query letter, a table of contents, and,

if available, a proposal pasted into the body of the e-mail to assistant@bookhaven.com. Please put the word QUERY and the title of your project in the subject field of your e-mail and address it to the agent of your choice. Please do not send an attachment as the message will be deleted without being read and no reply will be sent." Accepts simultaneous submissions. Responds in 6 weeks to queries. Obtains most new clients through recommendations from others, solicitations, conferences.

TERMS Agent receives 15% commission on domestic sales. Agent receives 20% commission on foreign sales. Offers written contract. Charges for large photocopy batches, messenger service, international postage.

WRITERS CONFERENCES Malice Domestic.

TIPS "Know the genre you are working in and read! Also, please see our website for details on which agent to query for your project."

○ GINA MACCOBY LITERARY AGENCY

P.O. Box 60, Chappaqua NY 10514. (914)238-5630. **E-mail:** query@maccobylit.com. **Contact:** Gina Maccoby. Member of AAR. AAR Board of Directors; Ethics and Contracts subcommittees; Authors Guild. Represents 25 clients. Currently handles: nonfiction books 33%, novels 33%, juvenile books 33%.

MEMBER AGENTS Gina Maccoby.

REPRESENTS nonfiction books, novels, juvenile. **Considers these nonfiction areas:** autobiography, biography, cultural interests, current affairs, ethnic, history, juvenile nonfiction, popular culture, women's issues, women's studies. **Considers these fiction areas:** juvenile, literary, mainstream, mystery, thriller, young adult.

HOW TO CONTACT Query by e-mail only. Accepts simultaneous submissions. Owing to volume of submissions, may not respond to queries unless interested. Obtains most new clients through recommendations from clients and publishers.

TERMS Agent receives 15% commission on domestic sales. Agent receives 20-25% commission on foreign sales, which includes subagents commissions. Charges clients for photocopying. May recover certain costs, such as legal fees or the cost of shipping books by air to Europe or Japan.

RECENT SALES *The Perfect Ghost*, by Linda Barnes (St. Martin's Minotaur, April 2013); *Supreme City: How Jazz Age Manhattan Gave Birth to Modern America* by Donald L. Miller (Simon & Schuster, May 2014);

Stripes of All Types by Susan Stockdale (Peachtree, April 2013); *You Read to Me, I'll Read to You: Very Short Tall Tales to Read Aloud* by Mary Ann Hoberman (Little Brown, April 2014); *True Colors* by Natalie Kinsey-Warnock (Yearling, November 2013).

◑ MANSION STREET LITERARY MANAGEMENT

E-mail: mansionstreet@gmail.com. **E-mail:** query mansionstreet@gmail.com (Jean); querymichelle@mansionstreet.com. **Website:** mansionstreet.com. **Contact:** Jean Sagendorph; Michelle Witte.
MEMBER AGENTS Jean Sagendorph (pop culture, gift books, cookbooks, general nonfiction, lifestyle, design, brand extensions), **Michelle Witte** (young adult, middle grade, juvenile nonfiction).
REPRESENTS Considers these nonfiction areas: cooking, design, popular culture. **Considers these fiction areas:** juvenile, middle grade, young adult.
HOW TO CONTACT Send a query letter and no more than the first 10 pages of your manuscript in the body of an e-mail. Query one specific agent at this agency. No attachments. You must list the genre in the subject line. If the genre is not in the subject line, your query will be deleted. Responds in up to 6 weeks.
RECENT SALES Authors: Paul Thurlby, Steve Ouch, Steve Seabury, Gina Hyams, Sam Pocker, Kim Siebold, Jean Sagendorph, Heidi Antman, Shannon O'Malley, Meg Bartholomy, Dawn Sokol, Hollister Hovey, Porter Hovey, Robb Pearlman.

⊕ SEAN MCCARTHY LITERARY AGENCY

E-mail: submissions@mccarthylit.com. **Website:** www.mccarthylit.com. **Contact:** Sean McCarthy.
Prior to his current position, Sean McCarthy began his publishing career as an editorial intern at Overlook Press and then moved over to the Sheldon Fogelman Agency.
REPRESENTS Considers these fiction areas: juvenile, middle grade, picture books, young adult.
Sean is drawn to flawed, multifaceted characters with devastatingly concise writing in YA, and boy-friendly mysteries or adventures in MG. In picture books, he looks more for unforgettable characters, off-beat humor, and especially clever endings. He is not currently interested in high fantasy, message-driven stories, or query letters that pose too many questions.

HOW TO CONTACT E-query. "Please include a brief description of your book, your biography, and any literary or relevant professional credits in your query letter. If you are a novelist: Please submit the first three chapters of your manuscript (or roughly 25 pages) and a one page synopsis in the body of the e-mail or as a Word or PDF attachment. If you are a picture book author: Please submit the complete text of your manuscript. We are not currently accepting picture book manuscripts over 1,000 words. If you are an illustrator: Please attach up to 3 JPEGs or PDFs of your work, along with a link to your website."

○ MCINTOSH & OTIS, INC.

353 Lexington Ave., New York NY 10016. (212)687-7400. **Fax:** (212)687-6894. **E-mail:** info@mcintoshandotis.com. **Website:** www.mcintoshandotis.com. **Contact:** Eugene H. Winick, Esq. Estab. 1927. Member of AAR, SCBWI Currently handles: juvenile books.
MEMBER AGENTS Elizabeth Winick Rubinstein, EWRquery@mcintoshandotis.com (literary fiction, women's fiction, historical fiction, and mystery/suspense, along with narrative nonfiction, spiritual/self-help, history and current affairs); **Shira Hoffman**, SHquery@mcintoshandotis.com (young adult, MG, mainstream commercial fiction, mystery, literary fiction, women's fiction, romance, urban fantasy, fantasy, science fiction, horror and dystopian); **Christa Heschke**, CHquery@mcintoshandotis.com (picture books, middle grade, young adult and new adult projects); **Adam Muhlig**, AMquery@mcintoshandotis.com (music—from jazz to classical to punk—popular culture, natural history, travel and adventure, and sports); **Eugene Winick; Ira Winick**.
REPRESENTS Considers these nonfiction areas: creative nonfiction, current affairs, history, popular culture, self-help, spirituality, sports, travel. **Considers these fiction areas:** fantasy, historical, horror, literary, middle grade, mystery, new adult, paranormal, picture books, romance, science fiction, suspense, urban fantasy, women's, young adult.
Actively seeking "books with memorable characters, distinctive voices, and great plots."
HOW TO CONTACT Prefers e-mail submissions. Each agent has their own e-mail address for subs. For fiction: Please send a query letter, synopsis, author bio, and the first three consecutive chapters (no more than 30 pages) of your novel. For nonfiction: Please

send a query letter, proposal, outline, author bio, and three sample chapters (no more than 30 pages) of the manuscript. For children's & young adult: Please send a query letter, synopsis and the first three consecutive chapters (not to exceed 25 pages) of the manuscript. Obtains clients through recommendations from others, editors, conferences and queries.

TERMS Agent receives 15% commission on domestic sales; 20% on foreign sales.

WRITERS CONFERENCES Attends Bologna Book Fair, in Bologna Italy in April; SCBWI Conference in New York in February; and regularly attends other conferences and industry conventions.

O HOWARD MORHAIM LITERARY AGENCY

30 Pierrepont St., Brooklyn NY 11201. (718)222-8400. **Fax:** (718)222-5056. **Website:** www.morhaimliterary.com. Member of AAR.

MEMBER AGENTS Howard Morhaim, Kate McKean; **Paul Lamb** (new as of 2014); **Maria Ribas** (new as of 2014).

REPRESENTS Considers these nonfiction areas: cooking, crafts, creative nonfiction, design, humor, sports. **Considers these fiction areas:** fantasy, historical, literary, middle grade, new adult, romance, science fiction, women's, young adult, LGBTQ young adult, magical realism, fantasy should be high fantasy, historical fiction should be no earlier than the 20th century.

☛ Kate McKean is open to many subgenres and categories of YA and MG fiction. Check the website for the most details. Actively seeking fiction, nonfiction, and young adult novels. Kate does not want "mysteries, thrillers, crime, paranormal romance, or urban fantasy. She is not the best reader of fiction that features: cops/private detectives/FBI/CIA, fairy tale retellings, dragons, werewolves/vampires/zombies etc., satire, spoof, or the picaresque. No novellas."

HOW TO CONTACT Query via e-mail with cover letter and three sample chapters. See each agent's listing for specifics.

① MOVEABLE TYPE MANAGEMENT

244 Madison Ave., Suite 334, New York NY 10016. (646)431-6134. **Website:** www.mtmgmt.net.

MEMBER AGENTS Adam Chromy.

REPRESENTS Considers these nonfiction areas: business, creative nonfiction, history, how-to, humor, memoirs, money, popular culture. **Considers these fiction areas:** commercial, literary, mainstream, romance, women's, young adult.

☛ Mr. Chromy is a generalist, meaning that he accepts fiction submissions of virtually any kind (except juvenile books aimed for middle grade and younger) as well as nonfiction. He has sold books in the following categories: new adult, women's, romance, memoir, pop culture, young adult, lifestyle, horror, how-to, general fiction, and more.

RECENT SALES *The Gin Lovers* by Jamie Brenner (St. Martin's Press); *Miss Chatterley* by Logan Belle (Pocket/S&S); *Sons Of Zeus*, by Noble Smith (Thomas Dunne Books); *World Made By Hand And Too Much Magic* by James Howard Kunstler (Grove/Atlantic Press); *Dirty Rocker Boys* by Bobbie Brown (Gallery/S&S).

⊘ ⊙ ERIN MURPHY LITERARY AGENCY

2700 Woodlands Village, #300-458, Flagstaff AZ 86001. **Fax:** (928)525-2480. **Website:** emliterary.com. **Contact:** Erin Murphy, president; Ammi-Joan Paquette, senior agent; Tricia Lawrence, associate agent. 25% of clients are new/unpublished writers. Currently handles: juvenile books.

REPRESENTS Considers these fiction areas: middle grade, picture books, young adult.

☛ Specializes in children's books only.

TERMS Agent receives 15% commission on domestic sales; 20-30% on foreign sales. Offers written contract. 30 days notice must be given to terminate contract.

O JEAN V. NAGGAR LITERARY AGENCY, INC.

216 E. 75th St., Suite 1E, New York NY 10021. (212)794-1082. **E-mail:** jweltz@jvnla.com; atasman@jvnla.com. **Website:** www.jvnla.com. **Contact:** Jean Naggar. Member of AAR. Other memberships include PEN, Women's Media Group, Women's Forum, SCBWI. Represents 450 clients. 20% of clients are new/unpublished writers.

💬 Ms. Naggar has served as president of AAR.

MEMBER AGENTS Jennifer Weltz (well researched and original historicals, thrillers with a unique voice, wry dark humor, and magical realism; enthralling narrative nonfiction; young adult, middle grade); **Jean Naggar** (taking no new clients); **Alice Tasman**

LAURA ZATS
(RED SOFA LITERARY)

redsofaliterary.com

@LZats

ABOUT LAURA: Laura graduated from Grinnell College with degrees in English and Anthropology. She's been working as an editor for several years and has held positions at companies in both the US and the UK. In her free time, Laura likes to craft, swing dance, bake, and binge on Netflix marathons of "Buffy the Vampire Slayer" and "Doctor Who."

SHE IS SEEKING: young adult and middle grade (especially contemporary for both), romance, new adult, contemporary women's fiction, sci-fi, fantasy, and erotica.

HOW TO QUERY: laura@redsofaliterary.com. Put "Query" in the subject line.

(literary, commercial, YA, middle grade, and nonfiction in the categories of narrative, biography, music or pop culture); **Elizabeth Evans** (narrative nonfiction, memoir, current affairs, pop science, journalism, health and wellness, psychology, history, pop culture, and humor); **Laura Biagi** (literary fiction, magical realism, young adult novels, middle grade novels, and picture books).

REPRESENTS nonfiction books, novels. **Considers these nonfiction areas:** biography, creative nonfiction, current affairs, health, history, humor, memoirs, music, popular culture, psychology, science. **Considers these fiction areas:** commercial, fantasy, literary, middle grade, picture books, thriller, young adult.

☞ This agency specializes in mainstream fiction and nonfiction and literary fiction with commercial potential.

HOW TO CONTACT This agency now has an online submission form on its website. Accepts simultaneous submissions. Obtains most new clients through recommendations from others.

TERMS Agent receives 15% commission on domestic sales. Agent receives 20% commission on foreign sales. Offers written contract. Charges for overseas mailing, messenger services, book purchases, long-distance telephone, photocopying—all deductible from royalties received.

RECENT SALES *Night Navigation*, by Ginnah Howard; *After Hours at the Almost Home*, by Tara Yelen; *An Entirely Synthetic Fish: A Biography of Rainbow Trout*, by Anders Halverson; *The Patron Saint of Butterflies*, by Cecilia Galante; *Wondrous Strange*, by Lesley Livingston; *6 Sick Hipsters*, by Rayo Casablanca; *The Last Bridge*, by Teri Coyne; *Gypsy Goodbye*, by Nancy Springer; *Commuters*, by Emily Tedrowe; *The Language of Secrets*, by Dianne Dixon; *Smiling to Freedom*, by Martin Benoit Stiles; *The Tale of Halcyon Crane*, by Wendy Webb; *Fugitive*, by Phillip Margolin; *BlackBerry Girl*, by Aidan Donnelley Rowley; *Wild Girls*, by Pat Murphy.

WRITERS CONFERENCES Willamette Writers Conference; Pacific Northwest Writers Conference;

Bread Loaf Writers Conference; Marymount Manhattan Writers Conference; SEAK Medical & Legal Fiction Writing Conference.

TIPS "Use a professional presentation. Because of the avalanche of unsolicited queries that flood the agency every week, we have had to modify our policy. We will now only guarantee to read and respond to queries from writers who come recommended by someone we know. Our areas are general fiction and nonfiction—no children's books by unpublished writers, no multimedia, no screenplays, no formula fiction, and no mysteries by unpublished writers. We recommend patience and fortitude: the courage to be true to your own vision, the fortitude to finish a novel and polish it again and again before sending it out, and the patience to accept rejection gracefully and wait for the stars to align themselves appropriately for success."

NELSON LITERARY AGENCY

1732 Wazee St., Suite 207, Denver CO 80202. (303)292-2805. **E-mail:** query@nelsonagency.com. **Website:** www.nelsonagency.com. **Contact:** Kristin Nelson, president and senior literary agent; Sara Megibow, associate literary agent. Estab. 2002. Member of AAR, RWA, SCBWI, SFWA.

○ Prior to opening her own agency, Ms. Nelson worked as a literary scout and subrights agent for agent Jody Rein.

MEMBER AGENTS Kristin Nelson; Sara Megibow.

REPRESENTS Considers these fiction areas: commercial, fantasy, literary, mainstream, middle grade, new adult, romance, science fiction, women's, young adult.

☞ NLA specializes in representing commercial fiction and high-caliber literary fiction. They represent many pop genre categories, including things like historical romance, steampunk, and all subgenres of YA. Does not want short story collections, mysteries, thrillers, Christian, horror, children's picture books, or screenplays.

HOW TO CONTACT Query by e-mail. Put the word "Query" in the e-mail subject line. No attachments. Address your query to Sara or Kristin. Responds within 1 month.

RECENT SALES *Champion*, by Marie Lu (young adult); *Wool*, by Hugh Howey (science fiction); *The Whatnot*, by Stefan Bachmann (middle grade); *Catching Jordan*, by Miranda Kenneally (young adult); *Bro-*

ken Like This, by Monica Trasandes (debut literary fiction); *The Darwin Elevator*, by Jason Hough (debut science fiction). A full list of clients is available online.

NEW LEAF LITERARY & MEDIA, INC.

110 W. 40th St., Suite 410, New York NY 10018. (646)248-7989. **Fax:** (646)861-4654. **E-mail:** query@newleafliterary.com. **Contact:** Joanna Volpe; Kathleen Ortiz; Suzie Townsend; Pouya Shahbazian. Member of AAR.

MEMBER AGENTS Joanna Volpe (women's fiction, thriller, horror, speculative fiction, literary fiction and historical fiction, young adult, middle grade, art-focused picture books); Kathleen Ortiz, director of subsidiary rights (new voices in YA and animator/illustrator talent); Suzie Townsend (new adult, young adult, middle grade, romance [all subgenres], fantasy [urban fantasy, science fiction, steampunk, epic fantasy] and crime fiction [mysteries, thrillers]; Pouya Shahbazian, film and television agent.

REPRESENTS Considers these fiction areas: crime, fantasy, historical, horror, literary, mainstream, middle grade, mystery, new adult, paranormal, picture books, romance, thriller, women's, young adult.

HOW TO CONTACT E-mail queries only. "Put the word QUERY in subject line, plus the agent's name." No attachments. Responds only if interested.

RECENT SALES *Allegiant*, by Veronica Roth; *The Sharpest Blade*, by Sandy Williams (Ace); *Siege and Storm,* by Leigh Bardugo (Henry Holt); *Erased*, by Jennifer Rush (Little Brown Books for Young Readers).

PARK LITERARY GROUP, LLC

270 Lafayette St., Suite 1504, New York NY 10012. (212)691-3500. **Fax:** (212)691-3540. **E-mail:** queries@parkliterary. **Website:** www.parkliterary.com. Estab. 2005.

MEMBER AGENTS Theresa Park (plot-driven fiction and serious nonfiction); Abigail Koons (popular science, history, politics, current affairs and art, and women's fiction); Peter Knapp (middle grade and young adult fiction, as well as suspense and thrillers for all ages).

REPRESENTS nonfiction books, novels. Considers these nonfiction areas: art, current affairs, history, politics, science. Considers these fiction areas: middle grade, suspense, thriller, women's, young adult.

☞ The Park Literary Group represents fiction and nonfiction with a boutique approach: an emphasis on servicing a relatively small number of

LARA PERKINS
(ANDREA BROWN LITERARY AGENCY)

andreabrownlit.com

@lara_perkins

ABOUT LARA: Lara has a B.A. in English and Art History from Amherst College and an M.A. in English Literature from Columbia University, where she studied Victorian Brit Lit. In her pre-publishing life, she trained to be an architect, before deciding that books, not bricks, are her true passion. She spent over a year at the B.J. Robbins Literary Agency in Los Angeles before coming to Andrea Brown Literary Agency.

SHE IS SEEKING: smart and raw young adult fiction, character-driven middle grade fiction with a totally original, hilarious voice, and so-adorable-she-can't-stand-it picture books, preferably with some age-appropriate emotional heft. She's a sucker for a great mystery and is passionate about stories that teach her new things or open up new worlds.

HOW TO QUERY: lara@andreabrownlit.com. ABLA only allows writers to query one agent per agency, so please do not query Lara if you have queried other ABLA agents in the past. There are various submission instructions depending on what you are submitting, and everything is laid out nicely on the agency submission page online.

clients, with the highest professional standards and focused personal attention. Does not want to receive poetry or screenplays.

HOW TO CONTACT Please specify the first and last name of the agent to whom you are submitting in the subject line of the e-mail and send your query letter and accompanying material to queries@parkliterary.com. All materials must be in the body of the e-mail. Responds if interested. For fiction submissions to Abigail Koons or Theresa Park, please include a query letter with short synopsis and the first three chapters of your work. For middle grade and young adult submissions to Peter Knapp, please include a query let-

ter and the first three chapters or up to 10,000 words of your novel (no synopsis necessary). For nonfiction submissions, please send a query letter, proposal, and sample chapter(s).

RECENT SALES This agency's client list is on their website. It includes bestsellers Nicholas Sparks and Debbie Macomber.

⊕ RUBIN PFEFFER CONTENT

648 Hammond St., Chestnut Hill MA 02467. **E-mail:** info@rpcontent.com. **Website:** www.rpcontent.com. **Contact:** Rubin Pfeffer. Rubin Pfeffer Content is a literary agency exclusively representing children's and young adult literature, as well as content that will

serve educational publishers and digital developers. Working closely with authors and illustrators, RPC is devoted to producing long-lasting children's literature: work that exemplifies outstanding writing, innovative creativity, and artistic excellence.

Note: This agent accepts submissions by referral only. Specificy the contact information of your reference when submitting.

RECENT SALES Recent Titles: *Marti Feels Proud*, by Micha Archer; *Burning*, by Elana K. Arnold; *Junkyard*, by Mike Austin; *Little Dog, Lost*, by Marion Dane Bauer; *Not Your Typical Dragon*, by Tim Bowers; *Ghost Hawk*, by Susan Cooper.

HOW TO CONTACT Authors/illustrators should send a query and a 1-3 chapter ms via e-mail (no postal submissions). The query, placed in the body of the e-mail, should include a synopsis of the piece, as well as any relevant information regarding previous publications, referrals, websites, and biographies. The ms may be attached as a .doc or a .pdf file. Specifically for illustrators, attach a PDF of the dummy or artwork to the e-mail.

PIPPIN PROPERTIES, INC.

110 w. 40th Street, Suite 1704, New York NY 10018. (212)338-9310. **Fax:** (212)338-9579. **E-mail:** info@pippinproperties.com. **Website:** www.pippinproperties.com. **Contact:** Holly McGhee. Represents 52 clients. Currently handles: juvenile books 100%.

Prior to becoming an agent, Ms. McGhee was an editor for 7 years and in book marketing for 4 years.

MEMBER AGENTS Holly McGhee, Elena Giovinazzo.

REPRESENTS Juvenile. **Considers these fiction areas:** middle grade, picture books, young adult.

"We are strictly a children's literary agency devoted to the management of authors and artists in all media. We are small and discerning in choosing our clientele." Actively seeking middle grade and young adult novels.

HOW TO CONTACT Query via e-mail. Include a synopsis of the work(s), your background and/or publishing history, and anything else you think is relevant. Accepts simultaneous submissions. Responds in 3 weeks to queries if interested. Responds in 10 weeks to mss. Obtains most new clients through recommendations from others.

TERMS Agent receives 15% commission on domestic sales. Agent receives 25% commission on foreign sales. Offers written contract; 30-day notice must be given to terminate contract. Charges for color copying and UPS/FedEx.

TIPS "Please do not start calling after sending a submission."

PROSPECT AGENCY

551 Valley Road, PMB 377, Upper Montclair NJ 07043. (718)788-3217. **Fax:** (718)360-9582. **Website:** www.prospectagency.com. Estab. 2005. Member of AAR. Currently handles: 60% of material handled is books for young readers.

MEMBER AGENTS Emily Sylvan Kim, esk@prospectagency.com; **Rachel Orr**, rko@prospectagency.com (no new clients); **Becca Stumpf**, becca@prospectagency.com (young adult, middle grade, fantasy, sci-fi, literary mysteries, literary thrillers, spicy romance); **Carrie Pestritto**, carrie@prospectagency.com (narrative nonfiction, general nonfiction, biography, and memoir; commercial fiction with a literary twist, historical fiction, "new adult," YA, and middle grade); **Teresa Kietlinski**, tk@prospectagency.com (picture book artists and illustrators).

REPRESENTS **Considers these nonfiction areas:** biography, memoirs. **Considers these fiction areas:** commercial, historical, juvenile, middle grade, mystery, new adult, picture books, romance, thriller, young adult.

"We're looking for strong, unique voices and unforgettable stories and characters."

HOW TO CONTACT Note that each agent at this agency has a different submission e-mail address and different submission policies. Check the agency website for the latest formal guideline per each agent. Obtains new clients through conferences, recommendations, queries, and some scouting.

TERMS Agent receives 15% on domestic sales, 20% on foreign sales sold directly and 25% on sales using a subagent. Offers written contract.

RECENT SALES Recent sales include: *Ollie and Claire* (Philomel), *Vicious* (Bloomsbury), *Tempest Rising* (Walker Books), *Where Do Diggers Sleep at Night* (Random House Children's), *A DJ Called Tomorrow* (Little, Brown), *The Princesses of Iowa* (Candlewick).

P.S. LITERARY AGENCY

20033 - 520 Kerr St., Oakville ON L6K 3C7 Canada. **E-mail:** query@psliterary.com. **Website:** www.pslit

KATIE REED
(ANDREA HURST & ASSOCIATES)

andreahurst.com

ABOUT KATIE: Katie obtained her Bachelor's in English from California State University, Sacramento. Katie resides in the small town of Durham, California, with her incredible husband, her joyful son, and Snoodles, her loyal cat. Besides her addiction to reading, she is also a die-hard Miami Heat fan and obsessed with all things Disney.

SHE IS SEEKING: all areas of young adult, particularly: commercial (with a compelling hook and a protagonist who battles real-life teen issues), science fiction (soft), and fantasy; commercial and literary adult fiction in the genres of book club women's fiction, science fiction (soft), fantasy, suspense/thriller, and contemporary romance. For nonfiction: memoir/biography with a strong platform, self-help, crafts/how-to, inspirational, parenting.

HOW TO QUERY: Katie@andreahurst.com. Put "Query" in the subject line of your query. No attachments. Do not send proposals, sample chapters or manuscripts unless specifically requested by an agent. Please indicate if you are simultaneously submitting to other agents.

erary.com. **Contact:** Curtis Russell, principal agent; Carly Watters, agent; Maria Vincente, associate agent. Estab. 2005. Currently handles: nonfiction books 50%, novels 50%.
REPRESENTS nonfiction, novels, juvenile books. **Considers these nonfiction areas:** autobiography, biography, business, child guidance, cooking, current affairs, diet/nutrition, economics, environment, foods, government, health, history, how-to, humor, law, memoirs, military, money, parenting, popular culture, politics, science, self-help, sports, technology, true crime, war, women's issues, women's studies. **Considers these fiction areas:** action, adventure, detective, erotica, ethnic, family saga, historical, horror, humor, juvenile, literary, mainstream, middle grade, mystery, new adult, picture books, romance, sports, thriller, women's, young adult, biography/autobiography, business, child guidance/parenting, cooking/food/nutrition, current affairs, government/politics/law, health/medicine, history, how-to, humor, memoirs, military/war, money/finance/economics, nature/environment, popular culture, science/technology, self-help/personal improvement, sports, true crime/investigative, women's issues/women's studies.

⚷➞ "What makes our agency distinct: We take on a small number of clients per year in order to provide focused, hands-on representation. We pride ourselves in providing industry-leading client service." Actively seeking both fiction and nonfiction. Seeking both new and established writers. Does not want to receive poetry or screenplays.

AGENTS AND ART REPS

HOW TO CONTACT Queries by e-mail only. Submit query, and bio. "Please limit your query to one page." Accepts simultaneous submissions. Responds in 4-6 weeks to queries/proposals; mss 4-8 weeks. Obtains most new clients through solicitations.

TERMS Agent receives 15% commission on domestic sales. Agent receives 25% commission on foreign sales. We offer a written contract, with 30-days notice terminate. "This agency charges for postage/messenger services only if a project is sold."

TIPS "Please review our website for the most up-to-date submission guidelines. We do not charge reading fees. We do not offer a critique service."

✪ THE PURCELL AGENCY

E-mail: TPAqueries@gmail.com. **Website:** www.the purcellagency.com. **Contact:** Tina P. Schwartz. Estab. 2012.

REPRESENTS Considers these nonfiction areas: juvenile nonfiction. **Considers these fiction areas:** juvenile, middle grade, young adult.

❦ This agency also takes juvenile nonfiction for MG and YA markets. At this point, the agency is not considering fantasy, science fiction or picture book submissions.

HOW TO Contact E-query. Mention if you are part of SCBWI. For fiction, send a query, the first 3 chapters, and synopsis. No attachments. For nonfiction, send table of contents + intro and sample chapter, author's credentials. Accepts simultaneous submissions. Responds in 1-3 months.

RED FOX LITERARY

129 Morro Ave., Shell Beach CA 93449. **E-mail:** info@ redfoxliterary.com. **Website:** http://redfoxliterary. com/. This agency specializes in books for children, looking for both authors and illustrators.

HOW TO CONTACT With regret, due to the volume of submissions received, Karen Grencik and Abigail Samoun can no longer accept unsolicited queries. Submissions will only be accepted from attendees at conferences at which they present, or through referrals from their clients or from professionals in the industry. As of 2014, writers should check the website for when Danielle is accepting queries. A full list of book sales and clients (and illustrator portfolios) is available on the agency website. (This agency added agent Danielle Smith, who is temporarily open to queries in 2014. Check the website.)

◑ RED SOFA LITERARY

2163 Grand Ave., #2, St. Paul MN 55105. (651)224-6670. **E-mail:** dawn@redsofaliterary.com; jennie@ redsofaliterary.com. **Website:** www.redsofaliterary. com. **Contact:** Dawn Frederick, literary agent and owner; Jennie Goloboy, agent; Laura Zats, associate agent. Red Sofa is a member of the Authors Guild and the MN Publishers Round Table. Represents 20 clients. 80% of clients are new/unpublished writers. Currently handles: nonfiction books 97%, novels 2%, story collections 1%.

○ **Dawn Frederick:** Prior to her current position, Ms. Frederick spent 5 years at Sebastian Literary Agency. In addition, Ms. Frederick worked more than 10 years in indie and chain book stores, and at an independent children's book publisher. Ms. Frederick has a master's degree in library and information sciences from an ALA-accredited institution. **Jennie Goloboy:** In Fall 2011, Jennie Goloboy joined Red Sofa Literary as an associate agent. Jennie Goloboy has a PhD in the History of American Civilization from Harvard. She is also a published author of both history and fiction, and a member of SFWA, RWA, SHEAR, OAH, the AHA, and Codex Writers Group. Her funny, spec-fic short stories appear under her pen name, Nora Fleischer. As of 2014, **Laura Zats** was the newest RS agent.

REPRESENTS nonfiction, fiction, juvenile books. **Considers these nonfiction areas:** animals, anthropology, archeology, crafts, cultural interests, current affairs, gay/lesbian, government, health, history, hobbies, humor, investigative, law, popular culture, politics, satire, sociology, true crime, women's issues, women's studies, extreme sports. **Considers these fiction areas:** erotica, fantasy, middle grade, romance, science fiction, women's, young adult.

HOW TO CONTACT Query by e-mail or mail with SASE. No attachments, please. Submit full proposal plus 3 sample chapters and any other pertinent writing samples. Accepts simultaneous submissions. Responds in 3 weeks to queries; 6 weeks to mss. Obtains most new clients through recommendations from others, solicitations.

TERMS Agent receives 15% commission on domestic sales. Agent receives 20% commission on foreign sales. Offers written contract. May charge a one-time $100 fee for partial reimbursement of postage and phone expenses incurred if the advance is below $15,000.

WRITERS CONFERENCES Madison Writers' Institute; Novel-in-Progress Bookcamp; OWFI Conference; SDSU Writers' Conference; Florida Writer's Association Conference; The Loft Literary Center; DFW Writers' Conference; MN SCBWI Conference, Bloomington Writers' Festival and Book Fair; Women of Words Retreat; ISD 196; First Pages (Hennepin County); Writer's Digest Webinar.

TIPS "Always remember the benefits of building an author platform, and the accessibility of accomplishing this task in today's industry. Most importantly, research the agents queried. Avoid contacting every literary agent about a book idea. Due to the large volume of queries received, the process of reading queries for unrepresented categories (by the agency) becomes quite the arduous task. Investigate online directories, printed guides (like *Writer's Market*), individual agent websites, and more, before beginning the query process. It's good to remember that each agent has a vision of what s/he wants to represent and will communicate this information accordingly. We're simply waiting for those specific book ideas to come in our direction."

RED TREE LITERARY AGENCY

320 7th Ave., #183, Brooklyn NY 11215. **E-mail:** elana@redtreeliterary.com. **Website:** www.redtreeliterary.com. **Contact:** Elana Roth.

○ Elana is a graduate of Barnard College and the Jewish Theological Seminary, where she earned degrees in English literature and Bible.

REPRESENTS Considers these fiction areas: juvenile, middle grade, young adult.

HOW TO CONTACT E-mail only.

RECENT SALES *Doug-Dennis and the Flyaway Fib*, by Darren Farrel; *Juniper Berry*, by M.P. Kozlowsky; *The Selection*, by Kiera Cass; *Unison Spark*, by Andy Marino.

● REGAL LITERARY AGENCY

236 W. 26th St., #801, New York NY 10001. (212)684-7900. **Fax:** (212)684-7906. **E-mail:** info@regal-literary.com. **E-mail:** submissions@regal-literary.com. **Website:** www.regal-literary.com. London Office: 36 Gloucester Ave., Primrose Hill, London NW1 7BB, United Kingdom, uk@regal-literary.com Estab. 2002. Member of AAR. Represents 70 clients. 20% of clients are new/unpublished writers.

MEMBER AGENTS Michelle Andelman; Claire Anderson-Wheeler; Markus Hoffmann; Leigh Huffine; Lauren Pearson; Joseph Regal.

REPRESENTS Considers these nonfiction areas: creative nonfiction, memoirs, psychology, science. **Considers these fiction areas:** literary, middle grade, picture books, thriller, women's, young adult.

⚲ Actively seeking literary fiction and narrative nonfiction. "We do not consider romance, science fiction, poetry, or screenplays."

HOW TO CONTACT "Query with SASE or via e-mail. No phone calls. Submissions should consist of a 1-page query letter detailing the book in question, as well as the qualifications of the author. For fiction, submissions may also include the first 10 pages of the novel or one short story from a collection." Responds if interested. Accepts simultaneous submissions.

TERMS Agent receives 15% commission on domestic sales. Agent receives 20% commission on foreign sales. "We charge no reading fees."

RECENT SALES Audrey Niffenegger's *The Time Traveler's Wife* (Mariner) and *Her Fearful Symmetry* (Scribner), Gregory David Roberts' *Shantaram* (St. Martin's), Josh Bazell's *Beat the Reaper* (Little, Brown), John Twelve Hawks' *The Fourth Realm Trilogy* (Doubleday), James Reston, Jr.'s *The Conviction of Richard Nixon* (Three Rivers) and *Defenders of the Faith* (Penguin), Michael Psilakis' *How to Roast a Lamb: New Greek Classic Cooking* (Little, Brown), Colman Andrews' *Country Cooking of Ireland* (Chronicle) and *Reinventing Food: Ferran Adria and How He Changed the Way We Eat* (Phaidon).

TIPS "We are deeply committed to every aspect of our clients' careers, and are engaged in everything from the editorial work of developing a great book proposal or line editing a fiction manuscript to negotiating state-of-the-art book deals and working to promote and publicize the book when it's published. We are at the forefront of the effort to increase authors' rights in publishing contracts in a rapidly changing commercial environment. We deal directly with co-agents and publishers in every foreign territory and also work directly and with co-agents for feature film and television rights, with extraordinary success in both arenas. Many of our clients' works have sold in dozens of translation markets, and a high proportion of our books have been sold in Hollywood. We have strong relationships with speaking agents, who can assist in arranging author tours and other corporate and college speaking opportunities when appropriate. We also have a staff publicist and marketer to help promote our clients and their work."

RODEEN LITERARY MANAGEMENT

3501 N. Southport #497, Chicago IL 60657. E-mail: submissions@rodeenliterary.com. E-mail: submissions@rodeenliterary.com. Website: www.rodeenliterary.com. Contact: Paul Rodeen. Estab. 2009.

Paul Rodeen established Rodeen Literary Management in 2009 after 7 years of experience with the literary agency Sterling Lord Literistic, Inc.

REPRESENTS nonfiction books, novels, juvenile books, illustrations, graphic novels. Considers these fiction areas: middle grade, picture books, young adult, graphic novels, comics.

Actively seeking "writers and illustrators of all genres of children's literature including picture books, early readers, middle grade fiction and nonfiction, graphic novels and comic books, as well as young adult fiction and nonfiction." This is primarily an agency devoted to children's books.

HOW TO CONTACT Unsolicited submissions are accepted by e-mail only to submissions@rodeenliterary.com. Cover letters with synopsis and contact information should be included in the body of your e-mail. An initial submission of 50 pages from a novel or a longer work of nonfiction will suffice and should be pasted into the body of your e-mail. Electronic portfolios from illustrators are accepted but please keep the images at 72 dpi—a link to your website or blog is also helpful. Electronic picture book dummies and picture book texts are accepted. Graphic novels and comic books are accepted. Accepts simultaneous submissions. Response time varies.

VICTORIA SANDERS & ASSOCIATES

241 Avenue of the Americas, Suite 11 H, New York NY 10014. (212)633-8811. Fax: (212)633-0525. E-mail: queriesvsa@gmail.com. Website: www.victoriasanders.com. Contact: Victoria Sanders. Estab. 1992. Member of AAR. Signatory of WGA. Represents 135 clients. 25% of clients are new/unpublished writers.

MEMBER AGENTS Tanya McKinnon, Victoria Sanders, Chris Kepner, Bernadette Baker-Baughman. REPRESENTS nonfiction books, novels. Considers these nonfiction areas: autobiography, biography, cultural interests, current affairs, ethnic, film, gay/lesbian, government, history, humor, law, literature, music, popular culture, politics, psychology, satire, theater, translation, women's issues, women's studies. Considers these fiction areas: action, adventure, contemporary issues, crime, ethnic, family saga, feminist, lesbian, literary, mainstream, mystery, new adult, picture books, thriller, young adult.

HOW TO CONTACT Query by e-mail only. "We will not respond to e-mails with attachments or attached files."

TERMS Agent receives 15% commission on domestic sales. Agent receives 20% commission on foreign/film sales. Offers written contract. Charges for photocopying, messenger, express mail. If in excess of $100, client approval is required.

RECENT SALES Sold 20+ titles in the last year.

TIPS "Limit query to letter (no calls) and give it your best shot. A good query is going to get a good response."

WENDY SCHMALZ AGENCY

402 Union St., #831, Hudson NY 12534. (518)672-7697. E-mail: wendy@schmalzagency.com. Website: www.schmalzagency.com. Contact: Wendy Schmalz. Estab. 2002. Member of AAR.

REPRESENTS Considers these nonfiction areas: Many nonfiction subjects are of interest to this agency. Considers these fiction areas: literary, mainstream, middle grade, young adult.

Actively seeking young adult novels, middle grade novels. Obtains clients through recommendations from others. Not looking for picture books, science fiction or fantasy.

HOW TO CONTACT Accepts only e-mail queries. Paste all text into the e-mail. Do not attach the ms or sample chapters or synopsis. Replies to queries only if they want to read the ms. (2014: Not currently accepting submissions of genre fiction or children's picture books.) If you do not hear from this agency within 6 weeks, consider that a no. Obtains clients through recommendations from others.

TERMS Agent receives 15% commission on domestic sales; 20% on foreign sales; 25% for Asian sales.

SUSAN SCHULMAN LITERARY AGENCY

454 W. 44th St., New York NY 10036. (212)713-1633. Fax: (212)581-8830. E-mail: schulmanqueries@yahoo.com. Website: www.publishersmarketplace.com/

members/Schulman/. **Contact:** Susan Schulman. Estab. 1980. Member of AAR. Signatory of WGA. Other memberships include Dramatists Guild. 10% of clients are new/unpublished writers. Currently handles: nonfiction books 50%, novels 25%, juvenile books 15%, stage plays 10%.

REPRESENTS Considers these nonfiction areas: biography, business, cooking, ethnic, health, history, money, religious, science, travel, women's issues, women's studies. **Considers these fiction areas:** juvenile, literary, mainstream, women's.

❧ "We specialize in books for, by and about women and women's issues including nonfiction self-help books, fiction and theater projects. We also handle the film, television and allied rights for several agencies as well as foreign rights for several publishing houses." Actively seeking new nonfiction. Considers plays. Does not want to receive poetry, television scripts or concepts for television.

HOW TO CONTACT "For fiction: Query letter with outline and three sample chapters, resume and SASE. For nonfiction: Query letter with complete description of subject, at least one chapter, resume and SASE. Queries may be sent via regular mail or e-mail. Please do not submit queries via UPS or Federal Express. Please do not send attachments with e-mail queries." Accepts simultaneous submissions. Responds in 6 weeks to queries/mss. Obtains most new clients through recommendations from others, solicitations, conferences.

TERMS Agent receives 15% commission on domestic sales. Agent receives 20% commission on foreign sales. Offers written contract; 30-day notice must be given to terminate contract.

RECENT SALES Sold 50 titles in the last year; hundred of subsidiary rights deals.

WRITERS CONFERENCES Geneva Writers' Conference (Switzerland); Columbus Writers' Conference; Skidmore Conference of the Independent Women's Writers Group.

TIPS "Keep writing!" Schulman describes her agency as "professional boutique, long-standing, eclectic."

◑ SERENDIPITY LITERARY AGENCY, LLC
305 Gates Ave., Brooklyn NY 11216. (718)230-7689. **Fax:** (718)230-7829. **E-mail:** rbrooks@serendipitylit. com; info@serendipitylit.com. **Website:** www.seren dipitylit.com; facebook.com/serendipitylit. **Contact:** Regina Brooks. Represents 50 clients. 50% of clients are new/unpublished writers. Currently handles: nonfiction books 50%, other 50% fiction.

○ Prior to becoming an agent, Ms. Brooks was an acquisitions editor for John Wiley & Sons, Inc. and McGraw-Hill Companies.

MEMBER AGENTS Regina Brooks; Dawn Michelle Hardy (sports, pop culture, blog and trend, music, lifestyle and social science); **Karen Thomas** (narrative nonfiction, celebrity, pop culture, memoir, general fiction, women's fiction, romance, mystery, self-help, inspirational, Christian-based fiction and nonfiction including Evangelical); **John Weber** (unique YA and middle grade); **Folade Bell** (literary and commercial women's fiction, YA, literary mysteries & thrillers, historical fiction, African-American issues, gay/lesbian, Christian fiction, humor and books that deeply explore other cultures); **Nadeen Gayle** (romance, memoir, pop culture, inspirational/ religious, women's fiction, parenting young adult, mystery and political thrillers, and all forms of nonfiction); **Chelcee Johns** (narrative nonfiction, investigative journalism, memoir, inspirational self-help, religion/spirituality, international, popular culture, and current affairs as well as literary and commercial fiction).

REPRESENTS nonfiction books, novels, juvenile, scholarly, children's books. **Considers these nonfiction areas:** creative nonfiction, current affairs, humor, inspirational, investigative, memoirs, music, parenting, popular culture, religious, self-help, spirituality, sports. **Considers these fiction areas:** commercial, gay, historical, humor, lesbian, literary, middle grade, mystery, romance, thriller, women's, young adult.

❧ African-American nonfiction, commercial fiction, young adult novels with an urban flair and juvenile books. No stage plays, screenplays or poetry.

HOW TO CONTACT Check the website, as there are online submission forms for fiction, nonfiction and juvenile. Accepts simultaneous submissions. Obtains most new clients through conferences, referrals.

TERMS Agent receives 15% commission on domestic sales. Agent receives 20% commission on foreign sales. Offers written contract; 2-month notice must be given to terminate contract. Charges clients for office fees, which are taken from any advance.

RECENT SALES *Putting Makeup on the Fat Boy*, by Bil Wright; *You Should Really Write a Book: How to Write Sell, and Market Your Memoir*, by Regina

Brooks; *Living Color*, by Nina Jablonski; *Swirling*, by Christelyn D. Kazarin and Janice R. Littlejohn; *Red Thread Sisters*, by Carol Peacock; *Nicki Minaj: Hop Pop Moments 4 Life*, by Isoul Harris; *Forgotten Burial*, by Jodi Foster.

TIPS "See the book *Writing Great Books for Young Adults.*"

◑ THE SEYMOUR AGENCY

475 Miner St., Canton NY 13617. (315)386-1831. **E-mail:** marysue@twcny.rr.com; nicole@theseymouragency.com. **Website:** www.theseymouragency.com. **Contact:** Mary Sue Seymour, Nicole Resciniti. Member of AAR. Signatory of WGA. Other memberships include RWA, Authors Guild. Represents 50 clients. 5% of clients are new/unpublished writers. Currently handles: nonfiction books 50%, other 50% fiction.

◑ Ms. Seymour is a retired New York State certified teacher. Ms. Resciniti was recently named "Agent of the Year" by the ACFW.

MEMBER AGENTS Mary Sue Seymour (accepts queries in Christian, inspirational, romance, and nonfiction); **Nicole Resciniti** (accepts all genres of romance, young adult, middle grade, new adult, suspense, thriller, mystery, sci-fi, fantasy).

REPRESENTS nonfiction books, novels. **Considers these nonfiction areas:** business, health, how-to, self-help, Christian books; cookbooks; any well-written nonfiction that includes a proposal in standard format and 1 sample chapter. **Considers these fiction areas:** action, fantasy, middle grade, mystery, new adult, religious, romance, science fiction, suspense, thriller, young adult.

HOW TO CONTACT For Mary Sue: E-query with synopsis, first 50 pages for romance. Accepts e-mail queries. For Nicole: E-mail the query plus first 5 pages of the manuscript. Accepts simultaneous submissions. Responds in 1 month to queries. Responds in 3 months to mss.

TERMS Agent receives 12-15% commission on domestic sales.

RECENT SALES Sales include: *New York Times* best-selling Author Shelley Shepard Gray 8-book deal to Harper Collins; Jen Turano 3-book deal to Bethany House, Pat Trainum's 4-book deal to Revell; Jennifer Beckstrand's 6- book deal to Kensington Publishing; Amy Lillard's 3-Book Deal To Kensington Publishing; Vannetta Chapman's Multi-Book Deal to Zondervan; Jerry Eicher's 3-book deal to Harvest House; Mary Ellis's 3-Book Deal To Harvest House; NYT bestseller Julie Ann Walker's next four books in her Black Knights Inc series; Melissa Lander's YA sci-fi, *Alienated*, to Disney/Hyperion; and Kate Meader's new contemporary romance series to Pocket/Gallery.

◔ THE SPIELER AGENCY

27 W. 20 St., Suite 305, New York NY 10011. **E-mail:** thespieleragency@gmail.com. **Contact:** Joe Spieler. Represents 160 clients. 2% of clients are new/unpublished writers.

◔ Prior to opening his agency, Mr. Spieler was a magazine editor.

MEMBER AGENTS Eric Myers, eric@TheSpielerAgency.com (pop culture, memoir, history, thrillers, young adult, middle grade, new adult, and picture books (text only); **Victoria Shoemaker**, victoria@TheSpielerAgency.com (environment and natural history, popular culture, memoir, photography and film, literary fiction and poetry, and books on food and cooking); **John Thornton**, john@TheSpielerAgency.com (nonfiction); **Joe Spieler**, joe@TheSpielerAgency.com (nonfiction and fiction and books for children and young adults).

REPRESENTS novels, juvenile books. **Considers these nonfiction areas:** cooking, environment, film, foods, history, memoirs, photography, popular culture. **Considers these fiction areas:** literary, middle grade, New Age, picture books, thriller, young adult.

HOW TO CONTACT Before submitting projects to the Spieler Agency, check the listings of our individual agents and see if any particular agent shows a general interest in your subject (e.g. history, memoir, YA, etc.). Please send all queries either by e-mail or regular mail. If you query us by regular mail, we can only reply to you if you include a self-addressed, stamped envelope. Accepts simultaneous submissions. Cannot guarantee a personal response to all queries. Obtains most new clients through recommendations, listing in *Guide to Literary Agents*.

TERMS Agent receives 15% commission on domestic sales. Charges clients for messenger bills, photocopying, postage.

WRITERS CONFERENCES London Book Fair.

TIPS "Check www.publishersmarketplace.com/members/spielerlit/."

STIMOLA LITERARY STUDIO

308 Livingston Ct., Edgewater NJ 07020. **E-mail:** info@stimolaliterarystudio.com. **Website:** www.stimolaliterarystudio.com. **Contact:** Rosemary B. Stimola. Estab. 1997. Member of AAR. Represents 45 clients. 15% of clients are new/unpublished writers. Currently handles: 10% novels, 90% juvenile books.

○ Agency is owned and operated by a former educator and children's bookseller with a PhD in Linguistics.

MEMBER AGENTS Rosemary B. Stimola.

⚷ Actively seeking remarkable young adult fiction and debut picture book author/illustrators. No institutional books.

HOW TO CONTACT Query via e-mail. "No attachments, please!" Accepts simultaneous submissions. Responds in 3 weeks to queries "we wish to pursue further." Responds in 2 months to requested mss. While unsolicited queries are welcome, most clients come through editor, agent, client referrals.

TERMS Agent receives 15% commission on domestic sales. Agent receives 20% (if subagents are employed) commission on foreign sales. Offers written contract, binding for all children's projects. 60 days notice must be given to terminate contract.

RECENT SALES *The Vanishing Season*, by Jodi Lynn Anderson (Harper Collins); *A Year In The Jungle* by Suzanne Collins and James Proimos; *Hello! Hello!* by Matt Cordell; *Better Off Friends* by Elizabeth Eulberg (Scholastic); *Scare Scape* by Sam Fisher (Scholastic); *The Secret Hum Of A Daisy* by Tracy Holczer (Putnam/Penguin); *Vasya's Noisy Paintbox* by Barb Rosenstock and Mary Grand Pre; *Chengdu Would Not Could Not Fall Asleep* by Barney Saltzberg (Hyperion); *Courage Has No Color* by Tanya Lee Stone.

TIPS Agent is hands-on, no-nonsense. May request revisions. Does not line edit but may offer suggestions for improvement. Well-respected by clients and editors. "A firm but reasonable deal negotiator."

THE STRINGER LITERARY AGENCY, LLC

E-mail: stringerlit@comcast.net. **Website:** www.stringerlit.com. **Contact:** Marlene Stringer.

REPRESENTS Considers these fiction areas: fantasy, middle grade, mystery, romance, thriller, women's, young adult.

⚷ This agency specializes in fiction. This agency is seeking all kinds of romance, except inspirational or erotic. Does not want to receive picture books, plays, short stories, or poetry. The agency is also seeking nonfiction as of this time (2014).

HOW TO CONTACT Electronic submissions through website submission form only. Accepts simultaneous submissions.

RECENT SALES *The Secret History*, by Stephanie Thornton (NAL); The Night Prowlers Series, by J.T. Geissinger (Montlake); *Wisp of a Thing*, by Alex Bledsoe (Tor); *Breath of Frost*, by Alyxandra Harvey (Walker); *Housewitch*, by Katie Schickel (Forge); *The Paper Magician*, by Charlie Holmberg (47 North); *Fly by Night,* by Andrea Thalasinos (Forge); *Duty of Evil*, by April Taylor (Carina).

TIPS "If your ms falls between categories, or you are not sure of the category, query and we'll let you know if we'd like to take a look. We strive to respond as quickly as possible. If you have not received a response in the time period indicated on website, please re-query."

THE STROTHMAN AGENCY, LLC

P.O. Box 231132, Boston MA 02123. **E-mail:** info@strothmanagency.com. **Website:** www.strothmanagency.com. **Contact:** Wendy Strothman, Lauren MacLeod. Member of AAR. Other memberships include Authors' Guild. Represents 50 clients.

○ Prior to becoming an agent, Ms. Strothman was head of Beacon Press (1983-1995) and executive vice president of Houghton Mifflin's Trade & Reference Division (1996-2002).

MEMBER AGENTS Wendy Strothman; Lauren MacLeod.

REPRESENTS novels, juvenile books. **Considers these nonfiction areas:** business, current affairs, environment, government, history, language, law, literature, politics, travel. **Considers these fiction areas:** literary, middle grade, young adult.

⚷ "Because we are highly selective in the clients we represent, we increase the value publishers place on our properties. We specialize in narrative nonfiction, memoir, history, science and nature, arts and culture, literary travel, current affairs, and some business. We have a highly selective practice in literary fiction, young adult and middle grade fiction, and nonfiction. We are now opening our doors to more commercial fiction but from authors who have a platform. If you have a platform, please mention it in your query letter. The Strothman Agency seeks out scholars, journalists, and other acknowledged and emerging experts in their fields. We are now actively looking for authors of well-written young adult fiction and nonfiction. Browse the Latest News to get an idea of the types of books that we represent. For more about what we're looking for, read Pitching an Agent: The Strothman Agency on the publishing website www.strothmanagency.com." Does not want to receive commercial fiction, romance, science fiction or self-help.

HOW TO CONTACT Accepts queries only via e-mail at strothmanagency@gmail.com. See submission guidelines online. Accepts simultaneous submissions. Responds in 4 weeks to queries. Responds in 6 weeks to mss. Obtains most new clients through recommendations from others.

TERMS Agent receives 15% commission on domestic sales. Agent receives 20% commission on foreign sales. Offers written contract; 30-day notice must be given to terminate contract.

◑ TALCOTT NOTCH LITERARY

2 Broad St., Second Floor, Suite 10, Milford CT 06460. (203)876-4959. **Fax:** (203)876-9517. **E-mail:** editori al@talcottnotch.net. **Website:** www.talcottnotch.net. **Contact:** Gina Panettieri, President. Represents 35 clients. 25% of clients are new/unpublished writers.

◑ Prior to becoming an agent, Ms. Panettieri was a freelance writer and editor.

MEMBER AGENTS Gina Panettieri, gpanettieri@talcottnotch.net (history, business, self-help, science, gardening, cookbooks, crafts, parenting, memoir, true crime and travel, women's fiction, paranormal, urban fantasy, horror, science fiction, historical, mystery, thrillers and suspense); **Paula Munier**, pmunier@talcottnotch.net (mystery/thriller, SF/fantasy, romance, YA, memoir, humor, pop culture, health & wellness, cooking, self-help, pop psych, New Age, inspirational, technology, science, and writing); **Rachael Dugas**, rdugas@talcottnotch.net (young adult, middle grade, romance, and women's fiction); **Jessica Negron**, jnegron@talcottnotch.net (commercial fiction, sci fi and fantasy [and all the little subgenres], psychological thrillers, cozy mysteries, romance, erotic romance, YA).

REPRESENTS Considers these nonfiction areas: business, cooking, crafts, gardening, health, history, humor, inspirational, memoirs, parenting, popular culture, psychology, science, self-help, technology, travel, true crime. **Considers these fiction areas:** commercial, fantasy, historical, horror, mainstream, middle grade, mystery, New Age, paranormal, romance, science fiction, suspense, thriller, urban fantasy, women's, young adult.

HOW TO CONTACT Query via e-mail (preferred) with first 10 pages of the ms within the body of the e-mail, not as an attachment. Accepts simultaneous submissions. Responds in 1 week to queries. Responds in 4-6 weeks to mss.

TERMS Agent receives 15% commission on domestic sales. Agent receives 20% commission on foreign sales. Offers written contract, binding for 1 year.

RECENT SALES Sold 36 titles in the last year. *Delivered From Evil*, by Ron Franscell (Fairwinds) and *Sourtoe* (Globe Pequot Press); *Hellforged*, by Nancy Holzner (Berkley Ace Science Fiction); *Welcoming Kitchen*; *200 Allergen- and Gluten-Free Vegan Recipes*, by Kim Lutz and Megan Hart (Sterling); *Dr. Seteh's Love Prescription*, by Dr. Seth Meyers (Adams Media); *The Book of Ancient Bastards,* by Brian Thornton (Adams Media); *Hope in Courage*, by Beth Fehlbaum (Westside Books) and more.

TIPS "Know your market and how to reach them. A strong platform is essential in your book proposal. Can you effectively use social media/Are you a strong networker? Are you familiar with the book bloggers in your genre? Are you involved with the interest-specific groups that can help you? What can you do to break through the 'noise' and help present your book to your readers? Check our website for more tips and information on this topic."

◑◑ TRANSATLANTIC LITERARY AGENCY

2 Bloor St., Suite 3500, Toronto ON M4W 1A8 Canada. (416)488-9214. **E-mail:** info@transatlanticagency.com. **Website:** transatlanticagency.com. Represents 250 clients. 10% of clients are new/unpublished writers.

MEMBER AGENTS Trena White (nonfiction); **Amy Tompkins** (fiction, nonfiction, juvenile); **Stephanie Sinclair** (fiction, nonfiction); **Patricia Ocampo** (juvenile/illustrators); **Fiona Kenshole** (juvenile, illustrators); **Samantha Haywood** (fiction, nonfiction, graphic novels); **Jesse Finkelstein** (nonfiction); **Marie Campbell** (middle grade fiction); **Shaun Bradley**

(referrals only); **Jennifer Starkman; Barb Miller; Lynn Bennett; David Bennett.**

REPRESENTS nonfiction books, novels, juvenile. **Considers these nonfiction areas:** business, creative nonfiction, cultural interests, current affairs, environment, how-to, investigative, memoirs, politics, religious, technology, true crime, women's issues. **Considers these fiction areas:** commercial, historical, juvenile, literary, middle grade, new adult, picture books, romance, women's, young adult.

8→ "In both children's and adult literature, we market directly into the United States, the United Kingdom and Canada." Actively seeking literary children's and adult fiction, nonfiction. Does not want to receive picture books, poetry, screenplays or stage plays.

HOW TO CONTACT Always refer to the website, as guidelines will change, and only various agents are open to new clients at any given time. Obtains most new clients through recommendations from others.

TERMS Agent receives 15% commission on domestic sales. Agent receives 20% commission on foreign sales. Offers written contract; 45-day notice must be given to terminate contract. This agency charges for photocopying and postage when it exceeds $100.

RECENT SALES Sold 250 titles in the last year.

⊘⊙ S©OTT TREIMEL NY

434 Lafayette St., New York NY 10003. (212)505-8353. **E-mail:** general@scotttreimelny.com. **Website:** ScottTreimelNY.blogspot.com; www.ScottTreimelNY.com. Estab. 1995. Member of AAR. Other memberships include Authors Guild, SCBWI. 10% of clients are new/unpublished writers. Currently handles: 100% juvenile/teen books.

⚬ Prior to becoming an agent, Mr. Treimel was an assistant to Marilyn E. Marlow at Curtis Brown, a rights agent for Scholastic, a book packager and rights agent for United Feature Syndicate, a freelance editor, a rights consultant for HarperCollins Children's Books, and the founding director of Warner Bros. Worldwide Publishing.

REPRESENTS nonfiction books, novels, juvenile, children's, picture books, young adult.

8→ This agency specializes in tightly focused segments of the trade and institutional markets.

HOW TO CONTACT No longer accepts simultaneous submissions. Wants queries only from writers he has met at conferences.

TERMS Agent receives 15% commission on domestic sales. Agent receives 20% commission on foreign sales. Offers verbal or written contract. Charges clients for photocopying, express postage, messengers, and books needed to sell foreign, film and other rights.

RECENT SALES *The Hunchback Assignments,* by Arthur Slade (Random House, HarperCollins Canada; HarperCollins Australia); *Shotgun Serenade,* by Gail Giles (Little, Brown); *Laundry Day,* by Maurie Manning (Clarion).

WRITERS CONFERENCES SCBWI NY, NJ, PA, Bologna; The New School; Southwest Writers' Conference; Pikes Peak Writers' Conference.

TIPS "We look for dedicated authors and illustrators able to sustain longtime careers in our increasingly competitive field. I want fresh, not derivative story concepts with overly familiar characters. We look for gripping stories, characters, pacing, and themes. We remain mindful of an authentic (to the age) point-of-view, and look for original voices. We spend significant time hunting for the best new work, and do launch debut talent each year. It is best *not* to send manuscripts with lengthy submission histories already."

◑ TRIDENT MEDIA GROUP

41 Madison Ave., 36th Floor, New York NY 10010. (212)333-1511. **E-mail:** press@tridentmediagroup.com; info@tridentmediagroup.com. **E-mail:** ellen.assistant@tridentmediagroup.com. **Website:** www.tridentmediagroup.com. **Contact:** Ellen Levine. Member of AAR.

MEMBER AGENTS Kimberly Whalen, ws.assistant@tridentmediagroup (commercial fiction and nonfiction, women's fiction, suspense, paranormal, and pop culture); **Scott Miller,** smiller@tridentmediagroup.com (thrillers, crime fiction, women's and book club fiction, and a wide variety of nonfiction, such as military, celebrity and pop culture, narrative, sports, prescriptive, and current events); **Alex Glass,** aglass@tridentmediagroup (literary fiction, crime fiction, pop culture, sports, health and wellness, narrative nonfiction, and children's books); **Melissa Flashman,** mflashman@tridentmediagroup.com (pop culture, memoir, wellness, popular science, business and economics, and technology—also fiction in the genres of mystery, suspense or YA); **Alyssa Eisner Henkin,** ahenkin@tridentmediagroup.com (juvenile, children's, young adult); **Don Fehr,** dfehr@

tridentmediagroup.com (literary and commercial fiction, narrative nonfiction, memoirs, travel, science, and health); **John Silbersack**, silbersack.assistant@tridentmediagroup.com (commercial and literary fiction, science fiction and fantasy, narrative nonfiction, young adult, thrillers); **Erica Spellman-Silverman**; **Ellen Levine**, levine.assistant@tridentmediagroup.com (popular commercial fiction and compelling nonfiction—memoir, popular culture, narrative nonfiction, history, politics, biography, science, and the odd quirky book); **Mark Gottlieb**, mgottlieb@tridentmediagroup.com; **MacKenzie Fraser-Bub**, MFraserBub@tridentmediagroup.com (many genres of fiction—specializing in women's fiction).

REPRESENTS Considers these nonfiction areas: biography, business, creative nonfiction, current affairs, economics, health, history, memoirs, military, popular culture, politics, science, sports, technology, travel. **Considers these fiction areas:** commercial, crime, fantasy, juvenile, literary, middle grade, mystery, paranormal, science fiction, suspense, thriller, women's, young adult.

☞ Actively seeking new or established authors in a variety of fiction and nonfiction genres.

HOW TO CONTACT Preferred method of query is through the online submission form on the agency website. Query only one agent at a time.

RECENT SALES Recent sales include: *Sacred River*, by Syl Cheney-Coker; *Saving Quinton*, by Jessica Sorensen; *The Secret History of Las Vegas*, by Chris Abani; *The Summer Wind*, by Mary Alice Munroe.

TIPS "If you have any questions, please check FAQ page before e-mailing us."

◐ THE UNTER AGENCY

23 W. 73rd St., Suite 100, New York NY 10023. (212)401-4068. **E-mail:** Jennifer@theunteragency.com. **Website:** www.theunteragency.com. **Contact:** Jennifer Unter. Estab. 2008.

◖ Ms. Unter began her book publishing career in the editorial department at Henry Holt & Co. She later worked at the Karpfinger Agency while she attended law school. She then became an associate at the entertainment firm of Cowan, DeBaets, Abrahams & Sheppard LLP where she practiced primarily in the areas of publishing and copyright law.

REPRESENTS Considers these nonfiction areas: biography, environment, foods, health, memoirs, popular culture, politics, travel, true crime, nature subjects. **Considers these fiction areas:** commercial, mainstream, middle grade, picture books, young adult.

☞ This agency specializes in children's and nonfiction, but does take quality fiction.

HOW TO CONTACT Send an e-query. There is also an online submission form. If you do not hear back from this agency within 3 months, consider that a no.

RECENT SALES A full list of recent sales/titles is available on the agency website.

◑ UPSTART CROW LITERARY

244 Fifth Avenue, 11th Floor, New York NY 10001. **E-mail:** danielle.submission@gmail.com; alexandra.submission@gmail.com. **Website:** www.upstartcrowliterary.com. **Contact:** Danielle Chiotti, Alexandra Penfold. Estab. 2009.

MEMBER AGENTS Michael Stearns (not accepting submissions); **Danielle Chiotti** (books ranging from contemporary women's fiction to narrative nonfiction, from romance to relationship stories, humorous tales, and YA fiction); **Ted Malawer** (accepting queries only through conference submissions and client referrals); **Alexandra Penfold** (children's—picture books, middle grade, YA; illustrators and author/illustrators).

REPRESENTS Considers these nonfiction areas: cooking, foods. **Considers these fiction areas:** middle grade, picture books, women's, young adult.

HOW TO CONTACT Upstart Crow agents that are currently accepting submissions are Danielle Chiotti and Alexandra Penfold.

✛◉ WELLS ARMS LITERARY

E-mail: info@wellsarms.com. **Website:** www.wellsarms.com. **Contact:** Victoria Wells Arms. Estab. 2013.

◖ Prior to opening her agency, Victoria was a children's book editor for Dial Books.

REPRESENTS Considers these fiction areas: juvenile, middle grade, picture books, young adult.

☞ We focus on books for readers of all ages, and we particularly love board books, picture books, readers, chapter books, middle grade, and young adult fiction—both authors and illustrators. We do not represent to the textbook, magazine, adult romance or fine art markets.

HOW TO CONTACT E-query. Put "Query" in your e-mail subject line. No attachments.

WERNICK & PRATT AGENCY

E-mail: info@wernickpratt.com. **Website:** www.wernickpratt.com. **Contact:** Marcia Wernick; Linda Pratt. Member of AAR, SCBWI.

Prior to co-founding Wernick & Pratt Agency, Ms. Wernick worked at the Sheldon Fogelman Agency, in subsidiary rights, advancing to director of subsidiary rights; Ms. Pratt also worked at the Sheldon Fogelman Agency.

MEMBER AGENTS Marcia Wernick, Linda Pratt.

"Wernick & Pratt Agency specializes in children's books of all genres, from picture books through young adult literature and everything in between. We represent both authors and illustrators. We do not represent authors of adult books." Wants people who both write and illustrate in the picture book genre; humorous young chapter books with strong voice, and which are unique and compelling; middle grade/YA novels, both literary and commercial. No picture book mss of more than 750 words, or mood pieces; work specifically targeted to the educational market; fiction about the American Revolution, Civil War, or World War II unless it is told from a very unique perspective.

HOW TO CONTACT Submit via e-mail only. "Please indicate to which agent you are submitting." Detailed submission guidelines available on website. Responds in 6 weeks.

WOLF LITERARY SERVICES, LLC

Website: wolflit.com. Estab. 2008.

MEMBER AGENTS Kirsten Wolf (no queries); Adrianna Ranta (all genres for all age groups with a penchant for edgy, dark, quirky voices, unique settings, and everyman stories told with a new spin; she loves gritty, realistic, true-to-life stories with conflicts based in the real world; women's fiction and nonfiction; accessible, pop nonfiction in science, history, and craft; and smart, fresh, genre-bending works for children); Kate Johnson (literary fiction, particularly character-driven stories, psychological investigations, modern-day fables, and the occasional high-concept plot; she also represents memoir, cultural history and narrative nonfiction, and loves working with journalists); Allison Devereux (magical realism, literary fiction, stories featuring picaresque characters, and books on art and design).

REPRESENTS Considers these nonfiction areas: art, crafts, creative nonfiction, history, memoirs, science, women's issues. Considers these fiction areas: literary, women's, young adult, magical realism.

HOW TO CONTACT To submit a project, please send a query letter along with a 50-page writing sample (for fiction) or a detailed proposal (for nonfiction) to queries@wolflit.com. Samples may be submitted as an attachment or embedded in the body of the e-mail. Responds if interested.

RECENT SALES *Hoodoo*, by Ronald Smith (Clarion); *Edible*, by Daniella Martin (Amazon Publishing); *Not a Drop to Drink*, by Mandy McGinnis (Katherine Tegen Books); *The Empire Striketh Back*, by Ian Doescher (Quirk Books).

WRITERS HOUSE

21 W. 26th St., New York NY 10010. (212)685-2400. **Fax:** (212)685-1781. **Website:** www.writershouse.com. **Contact:** Michael Mejias. Estab. 1973. Member of AAR. Represents 440 clients. 50% of clients are new/unpublished writers.

MEMBER AGENTS Amy Berkower; Stephen Barr, sbarr@writershouse.com; Susan Cohen; Dan Conaway; Lisa DiMona; Susan Ginsburg; Leigh Feldman; Merrilee Heifetz; Brianne Johnson; Daniel Lazar; Simon Lipskar; Steven Malk; Jodi Reamer, Esq.; Robin Rue; Rebecca Sherman; Geri Thoma; Albert Zuckerman.

REPRESENTS nonfiction books, novels, juvenile. Considers these nonfiction areas: animals, art, autobiography, biography, business, child guidance, cooking, decorating, diet/nutrition, economics, film, foods, health, history, humor, interior design, juvenile nonfiction, medicine, military, money, music, parenting, psychology, satire, science, self-help, technology, theater, true crime, women's issues, women's studies. Considers these fiction areas: adventure, cartoon, contemporary issues, crime, detective, erotica, ethnic, family saga, fantasy, feminist, frontier, gay, hi-lo, historical, horror, humor, juvenile, literary, mainstream, middle grade, military, multicultural, mystery, New Age, occult, picture books, police, psychic, regional, romance, spiritual, sports, thriller, translation, war, women's, young adult.

This agency specializes in all types of popular fiction and nonfiction. Does not want to receive scholarly, professional, poetry, plays, or screenplays.

HOW TO CONTACT Query with SASE. Do not contact two agents here at the same time. While snail mail is OK for all agents, some agents do accept e-queries. Check the website for individual agent bios. "Please send us a query letter of no more than 2 pages, which includes your credentials, an explanation of what makes your book unique and special, and a synopsis. (If submitting to Steven Malk: Writers House, 7660 Fay Ave., #338H, La Jolla, CA 92037. Note that Malk only accepts queries on an exclusive basis.)" Accepts simultaneous submissions. Obtains most new clients through recommendations from authors and editors.
TERMS Agent receives 15% commission on domestic sales. Agent receives 20% commission on foreign sales. Offers written contract, binding for 1 year. Agency charges fees for copying mss/proposals and overseas airmail of books.
TIPS "Do not send mss. Write a compelling letter. If you do, we'll ask to see your work. Follow submission guidelines and please do not simultaneously submit your work to more than 1 Writers House agent."

ART REPS

CAROL BANCROFT & FRIENDS

P.O. Box 2030, Danbury CT 06813. (203)730-8270 or (800)720-7020. **Fax:** (203)730-8275. **E-mail:** cb_friends8270@sbcglobal.net; cbfriends@sbcglobal.net. **Website:** www.carolbancroft.com. **Contact:** Joy Elton Tricarico, owner; Carol Bancroft, founder. "Internationally known for representing artists who specialize in illustrating art for all aspects of the children's market. We also represent many artists who are well known in other aspects of the field of illustration." Clients include, but not limited to, Scholastic, Houghton Mifflin Harcourt, HarperCollins, Marshall Cavendish, McGraw Hill, Hay House.
REPRESENTS Specializes in illustration for children's publishing-text and trade; any children's-related material.
TERMS Rep receives 25% commission. Advertising costs are split: 75% paid by talent; 25% paid by representative.
HOW TO CONTACT Either e-mail 2-3 samples with your address or mail 6-10 samples, along with a SASE to the P.O. Box address. For promotional purposes, artists must provide "laser copies (not slides), tearsheets,

promo pieces, good color photocopies, etc.; 6 pieces or more is best; narrative scenes and children interacting."
TIPS "We look for artists who can draw animals and people with imagination and energy, depicting engaging characters with action in situational settings."

BOOKMAKERS LTD.

32 Parkview Avenue, Wolfville NS., Canada B4P 2K8. (902)697-2569. **E-mail:** reg@bookmakersltd.com. **Website:** www.bookmakersltd.com
REPRESENTS Over 20 illustrators of children's books.
RECENT SALES Works with "most major book publishers."
HOW TO CONTACT E-mail with inquiries at reg@bookmakersltd.com.

○ CORNELL & MCCARTHY LLC

2-D Cross Highway, Westport CT 06880. (203)454-4210. **Fax:** (203)454-4258. **E-mail:** contact@cmartreps.com. **Website:** www.cmartreps.com. **Contact:** Merial Cornell.
REPRESENTS Specializes in children's books: trade, mass market, educational. Obtains new talent through recommendations, solicitation, conferences.
TERMS Agent receives 25% commission. Advertising costs are split: 75% paid by talent; 25% paid by representative.
HOW TO CONTACT For first contact, send query letter, direct mail flier/brochure, tearsheets, photocopies and SASE or preferably e-mail. For promotional purposes, talent must provide 10-12 strong portfolio pieces relating to children's publishing.

CRAVEN DESIGN, INC.

1202 Lexington Ave., Box 242, New York, NY 10028. (212)288-1022. **Fax:** (212)249-9910 **E-mail:** cravendesign@mac.com. **Website:** www.cravendesignstudios.com. **Contact:** Meryl Jones.
REPRESENTS "We represent more than 20 professional illustrators with experience in a full range of genres, from humorous to realistic, decorative and technical, electronic and traditional, including maps, charts and graphs."
RECENT SALES Specializes in textbook illustration for all ages, juvenile through adult, elementary through secondary school.
HOW TO CONTACT E-mail with any inquiries.

FAMOUS FRAMES

5839 Green Valley Circle, Suite 104, Culver City, CA 90230. (855)530-3375. Additional phone numbers: (212)980-7979 (NY); (310)642-2721 (LA). **Fax:** 310.642.2728 **E-mail:** artincgw@gmail.com. www.fa mousframes.com.

REPRESENTS A "roster of 100+ of the world's top illustrators."

RECENT SALES Sells to a wide client base made up of many commercial organizations and some publishers.

HOW TO CONTACT E-mail portfolio@famous frames.com and include samples/links along with contact information within the body of the e-mail.

FRIEND + JOHNSON

Contact information varies based upon location. East: 37 W 26th St. Suite 313, New York, NY 10010. (212)337-0055. West/Southwest: 870 Market St. Suite 1017, San Francisco, CA 94102. (415)927-4500. **E-mail:** bjohnson@friendandjohnson.com. **Contact:** Beth Johnson. Midwest: 901 W Madison St Suite 918., Chicago, IL 60607. (312)435-0055. **E-mail:** sfriend@ friendandjohnson.com. **Contact:** Simone Friend .**Website:** www.friendandjohnson.com

REPRESENTS A diverse and original group of artists, photographers, designers, illustrators and typographists.

HOW TO CONTACT Please send your inquiry and a link to your website in an e-mail to agent@friendandjohnson.com. Don't contact the agents directly. Will reply only if interested.

HEART ARTIST'S AGENCY

Heart USA Inc., 611 Broadway Suite 734, New York, NY 10012 . (212)995-9386 **Fax:** (212)995-9386. **E-mail:** mail@heartagency.com. **Website:** www.heart agency.com

REPRESENTS Currently open to illustrators seeking representation. Is highly selective.

HOW TO CONTACT Accepts submissions in the form of website links via e-mail to mail@heartagency. com. If no website exists please provide printed samples by post. If you would like your samples returned, please supply a stamped self-addressed-envelope in your package.

SCOTT HULL ASSOCIATES

3875 Ferry Road, Bellbrook, Ohio 45305. (937)433-8383. **Fax:** (937)433-0434 **E-mail:** scott@scotthull. com. **Website:** www.scotthull.com.

REPRESENTS A very large group of illustrators who specialize in a vairety of fields, including publishing.

RECENT SALES Has done business with Scholastic, Harper Collins, Chronicle Books, Crown Publishing, Bantam Books, and many other publishers

HOW TO CONTACT E-mail with inquiries or fill out the form on the website.

ILLUSTRATORSREP.COM

5 W. Fifth Street, Suite 300, Covington, KY 41011. (513)861-1400. **Fax:** (859)980-0820. **E-mail:** bob@il lustratorsrep.com. **Website:** www.illustratorsrep.com.

REPRESENTS Small group of illustrators and photographers.

RECENT SALES "We have serviced such accounts as Disney, Rolling Stone Magazine and Procter & Gamble, just to name a few."

HOW TO CONTACT For information about representation, e-mail samples to info@illustratorsrep.com.

THE JULY GROUP

(212) 932-8583. **Website:** www.thejulygroup.com.

REPRESENTS Currently open to illustrators seeking representation. Their current group of illustrators' and animators' professional skills include: licensed images, children's book illustration, science fiction and fantasy art, graphic novels, CD art, educational illustration, and multimedia animation."

RECENT SALES Works with a variety of clients, including publishers and commercial.

HOW TO CONTACT Work can be submitted via a form on the website.

KID SHANNON

Shannon Associates, 333 West 57th Street, Suite 809, New York, New York 10019. (212)333-2551. **E-mail:** Use e-mail form online. **Website:** www.shan nonassociates.com/kidshannon.

REPRESENTS Very large group of illustrators, some photographers and some authors.

RECENT SALES Sells to many major publishing companies, including Penguin and Random House,

HOW TO CONTACT Fill out the form on the website.

TIPS The website has a "Resources" tab that contains great advice, articles and tips for beginning and/or freelance illustrators

LEMONADE ILLUSTRATION AGENCY

347 Fifth Ave. Suite 1402, New York, NY 10016. **E-mail:** studio@lemonadeillustration.com. **Website:** www.lemonadeillustration.com.

REPRESENTS A wide variety of illustrators, including those for children's books.

RECENT SALES Sells to many major book publishers, including Penguin Books, Pearson, McGraw-Hill, Scholastic, and Random House.

HOW TO CONTACT Only replies to inquiries if interested. "We only accept links to your own website or sample copies via snail mail, addressed to either our NYC office or: Submissions Dept., Lemonade Illustration Agency, Hill House, Suite 231, 210 Upper Richmond Road, London, SW15 6NP."

TIPS "Please try and write a little about yourself and your work in your e-mail. A professional presentation of your illustrations is key."

MARTHA PRODUCTIONS, INC.

7550 West 82nd Street, Playa Del Rey, CA 90293. (310)670-5300. **Fax:** (310) 670-3644. **E-mail:** contact@marthaproductions.com. **Website:** www.marthaproductions.com.

REPRESENTS Wide range of illustration styles, all categorized on website.

HOW TO CONTACT "We always welcome submissions from illustrators considering representation. Please e-mail us a few small digital files of your work or mail us non-returnable samples. We will contact you if we think we would be able to sell your work or if we'd like to see more."

MB ARTISTS

775 Sixth Ave., #6, New York NY 10001. (212)689-7830. **E-mail:** mela@mbartists.com. **Website:** www.mbartists.com. **Contact:** Mela Bolinao.

REPRESENTS Specializes in illustration for juvenile markets. Markets include: advertising agencies; editorial/magazines; publishing/books, board games, stationary, etc.

TERMS Rep receives 25% commission. No geographic restrictions. Advertising costs are split: 75% paid by talent; 25% paid by representative.

HOW TO CONTACT For first contact, send query letter, direct mail flier/brochure, website address, tearsheets, slides, photographs or color copies and SASE or send website link to mela@mbartists.com. Portfolio should include at least 12 images appropriate for the juvenile market.

⊘ MGI KIDS (MORGAN GAYNIN INC.)

149 Madison Avenue, Suite 1140, New York, NY 10016. (212)475-0440. **E-mail:** info@morgangaynin.com. **Website:** www.morgangaynin.com.

REPRESENTS "Select international illustrators." Features many of Morgan Gaynin's illustrators who also specialize in children's illustration.

RECENT SALES Has a wide client base. Artists have won several awards from organizations like American Illustration and Society of Illustrators New York and Los Angles.

HOW TO CONTACT Not accepting submissions at this time.

RED PAINTBOX

676A Ninth Avenue, New York, NY 10036. (212)397-7330. **E-mail:** representation@redpaintbox.com. **Website:** www.redpaintbox.com.

REPRESENTS Represents many illustrators and artists, over 30 of them children's books illustrators.

RECENT SALES Has "world-wide access to clients."

HOW TO CONTACT For representation inquiries, please e-mail one or two jpgs to representation@redpaintbox.com. Will reply only if interested

RILEY ILLUSTRATION

PO Box 92, New Paltz, NY 12561. (845)255-3309. **E-mail:** info@rileyillustration.com. **Website:** www.rileyillustration.com.

REPRESENTS Several award winning illustrators.

RECENT SALES Works with "art directors and designers, publishers, corporations, organizations, architects, and product developers."

HOW TO CONTACT E-mail any inquiries to info@rileyillustration.com.

LIZ SANDERS AGENCY

2415 E. Hangman Creek Ln., Spokane WA 99224-8514. (509)993-6400. **E-mail:** liz@lizsanders.com; artsubmissions@lizsanders.com. **Website:** www.lizsanders.com. **Contact:** Liz Sanders, owner. Commercial illustration representative. Represents Kyle Poling, Amy Ning, Tom Pansini, Sudi McCollum, Suzanne Beaky, Maria Paula Dufour, Lois Rosio Sprague, Thodoris Tibilis and more.

REPRESENTS Markets include publishing, licensed properties, entertainment and advertising. Currently open to illustrators seeking representation. Open to both new and established illustrators.

TERMS Receives 30% commission against pro bono mailing program. Offers written contract.

HOW TO CONTACT For first contact, send tearsheets, direct mail flier/brochure, color copies, non-returnable or e-mail to artsubmissions@lizsanders.com. Obtains new talent through recommendations from industry contacts, conferences and queries/solicitations, Literary Market Place.

RICHARD SOLOMON ARTISTS REPRESENTATIVE, LLC

110E 30th St., Suite 501, New York, NY, 10016. (212)223-9545. **Fax:** (212)223-9633 **E-mail:** richard@richardsolomon.com. **Website:** www.richardsolomon.com.

REPRESENTS "We represent an ever-expanding 'big tent' of award-winning illustrators and fine artists, who work collaboratively with the best art directors and designers throughout the world. Looking for a signature style that shows consistency and a breadth of applications. Contact form on website."

RECENT SALES Has done work with Harper Collins, Random House, Scholastic, and many others

HOW TO CONTACT Send inquiries via e-mail or fill out the submission form on the website.

STORE 44 REPS

PO Box 251, Flagstaff, AZ 86002 . (323)230-0044. **E-mail:** art@store44.com. **Website:** www.store44.com.

REPRESENTS Photopgraphers, fine artists, and illustrators on an international level.

RECENT SALES Works with a wide client base, including Macmillan Publishing Group

HOW TO CONTACT "We consider new artists for representation during our internal quarterly portfolio reviews. We also hold an open annual portfolio review during September. Attach up to 16 JPG images, or a PDF Portfolio. Include your contact info, résumé, client or gallery list, along with links to examples of your work. Use the body of your e-mail to briefly describe why you are seeking representation, and be sure to reference 'Artist Submission' in the subject line. You should also include keywords in your email like 'fashion' and 'photographer.' Please do not attach ZIP files or Word documents."

T2 CHILDREN'S ILLUSTRATORS

2231 Grandview Avenue, Cleveland Heights, OH 44106. (216)707-0854. **E-mail:** nicole@tugeau2.com. **Website:** www.tugeau2.com **Contact:** Nicole Tugeau.

REPRESENTS Currently open to children's illustrators seeking representation.

RECENT SALES Works with a variety of publishers, such as Tricycle (division of Random House), Raven Tree Press, and Piggy Toes Press.

HOW TO CONTACT "To submit your work for consideration, please send Nicole a short e-mail with a link to your personal website and/or five pictures of your best and most recent artwork."

THOROGOOD KIDS/GOOD ILLUSTRATION

11-15 Betterton St., Covent Garden, London WC2H 9BPUnited Kingdom . (347)627-0243. **E-mail:** draw@goodillustration.com. **Website:** www.goodillustration.com. Represents 30 illustrators including: Bill Dare, Kanako and Yuzuru, Shaunna Peterson, Nicola Slater, Dan Hambe, David Bromley, Robin Heighway-Bury, Anja Boretzki, Olivier Latyk, Al Sacui, John Woodcock, Carol Morley, Leo Timmers, Christiane Engel, Anne Yvonne Gilbert, Philip Nicholson, Adria Fruitos, Ester Garcia Cortes, Lisa Zibamanzar, Alessandra Cimatoribus, Marta and Leonor, Iryna Bodnaruk. Open to illustrators seeking representation. Accepting both new and established illustrators.

HOW TO CONTACT "For first contact, send tearsheets, photocopies, SASE, direct mail flyer/brochure. After initial contact, we will contact the illustrator if we want to see the portfolio. Portfolio should include tearsheets, photocopies. Finds illustrators through queries/solicitations, conferences." Accepts illustration, illustration/manuscript packages.

TIPS "Be unique and research your market. Talent will win out!"

GWEN WALTERS ARTIST REPRESENTATIVE

1801 S. Flagler Dr.,#1202, W. Palm Beach FL 33401. (561)805-7739. **E-mail:** artincgw@gmail.com. **Website:** www.gwenwaltersartrep.com. **Contact:** Gwen Walters.

REPRESENTS Currently open to illustrators seeking representation. Looking for established illustrators only.

RECENT SALES Sells to "All major book publishers."

TERMS Receives 30% commission. Artist needs to supply all promo material. Offers written contract.

HOW TO CONTACT For first contact, send e-mail including samples. Finds illustrators through recommendations from others.

TIPS "You need to pound the pavement for a couple of years to get some experience under your belt. Don't forget to sign all artwork. So many artists forget to stamp their samples."

WILKINSON STUDIOS, INC.

1121 E. Main St., Suite 310, St. Charles, IL 06174. (630)549-0504. **Website:** www.wilkinsonstudios.com.

REPRESENTS Represents several professional illustrators, including those specializing in children's illustration. "What sets us apart from the other rep firms is that we also offer art management services for large volume blackline and color illustration programs."

RECENT SALES Works with a wide variety of clients, nationally and internationally.

HOW TO CONTACT Has a contact form online. Accepts appropriate hard copy samples, tear sheets, color copies, or digital print-outs only via mail. Accepts digital submissions from non-US artists only.

CLUBS & ORGANIZATIONS

//

Contacts made through organizations such as the ones listed in this section can be quite beneficial for children's writers and illustrators. Professional organizations provide numerous educational, business, and legal services in the form of newsletters, workshops, or seminars. Organizations can provide tips about how to be a more successful writer or artist, as well as what types of business cards to keep, health and life insurance coverage to carry, and competitions to consider.

An added benefit of belonging to an organization is the opportunity to network with those who have similar interests, creating a support system. As in any business, knowing the right people can often help your career, and important contacts can be made through your peers. Membership in a writer's or artist's organization also shows publishers you're serious about your craft. This provides no guarantee your work will be published, but it gives you an added dimension of credibility and professionalism.

Some of the organizations listed here welcome anyone with an interest, while others are only open to published writers and professional artists. Organizations such as the Society of Children's Book Writers and Illustrators (SCBWI, scbwi.org) have varying levels of membership. SCBWI offers associate membership to those with no publishing credits, and full membership to those who have had work for children published. International organizations such as SCBWI also have regional chapters throughout the U.S. and the world. Write or call for more information regarding any group that interests you, or check the websites of the many organizations that list them. Be sure to get information about local chapters, membership qualifications, and services offered.

AMERICAN ALLIANCE FOR THEATRE & EDUCATION

4908 Auburn Ave., Bethesda MD 20814. (301)200-1944. **Fax:** (301). **E-mail:** info@aate.com. **Website:** www.aate.com. Purpose of organization: to promote standards of excellence in theatre and drama education. "We achieve this by assimilating quality practices in theatre and theatre education, connecting artists, educators, researchers and scholars with each other, and by providing opportunities for our members to learn, exchange and diversify their work, their audiences and their perspectives." Membership cost: retiree rate ($70) is for individuals over 65; international rates vary from $70-95. Rate for Canadians listed is $95. Rate for University changes each year. Holds annual conference (July or August). Contests held for unpublished play reading project and annual awards in various categories. Awards plaque and stickers for published playbooks. Publishes list of unpublished plays deemed worthy of performance and stages readings at conference. Contact national office at number above or see website for contact information for Playwriting Network Chairpersons. **Contact:** Alexis Truitt, operations manager.

AMERICAN SOCIETY OF JOURNALISTS AND AUTHORS

Times Square, 1501 Broadway, Suite 403, New York NY 10036. (212)-997-0947. **Website:** www.asja.org. Qualifications for membership: "Need to be a professional freelance nonfiction writer. Refer to website for further qualifications." Membership cost: Application fee—$50; annual dues—$210. Group sponsors national conferences. Professional seminars online and in person around the country. Workshops/conferences open to nonmembers. Publishes a newsletter for members that provides confidential information for nonfiction writers. **Contact:** Alexandra Owens, executive director. Contact form on website.

⬤ ◐ ⊕ ARIZONA AUTHORS ASSOCIATION

6145 West Echo Lane, Glendale AZ 85302. (623)847-9343. **E-mail:** info@azauthors.com. **Website:** www.azauthors.com. Purpose of organization: to offer professional, educational and social opportunities to writers and authors, and serve as a network. Members must be authors, writers working toward publication, agents, publishers, publicists, printers, illustrators, etc. Membership cost: $45/year writers; $30/year students; $60/year other professionals in publishing industry. Holds regular workshops and meetings. Publishes bimonthly newsletter and *Arizona Literary Magazine*. Sponsors Annual Literary Contest in poetry, essays, short stories, novels, and published books with cash prizes and awards bestowed at a public banquet. Winning entries are also published or advertised in the *Arizona Literary Magazine*. First and second place winners in poetry, essay and short story categories are entered in the Pushcart Prize. Winners in published categories receive free listings by www.fivestarpublications.com. Send SASE or view website for guidelines. **Contact:** Toby Heathcotte, president.

THE AUTHORS GUILD, INC.

31 E. 32nd St., 7th Floor, New York NY 10016. (212)563-5904. **Fax:** (212)563-5904. **E-mail:** staff@authorsguild.org. **Website:** www.authorsguild.org. Purpose of organization: to offer services and materials intended to help authors with the business and legal aspects of their work, including contract problems, copyright matters, freedom of expression and taxation. Guild has 8,000 members. Qualifications for membership: You may qualify as an author published by an established U.S. book publisher, as a freelance writer published by periodicals of general circulation in the U.S., or as a book author or freelance writer earning writing income, which may include income from self-published works, of at least $5,000 in an 18-month period: First year dues $90. Following years, dues based on sliding scale. Associate membership also available. Annual dues: $90. Different levels of membership include: associate membership with all rights except voting available to an author who has a firm contract offer or is currently negotiating a royalty contract from an established American publisher. "The Guild offers free contract reviews to its members. The Guild conducts several symposia each year at which experts provide information, offer advice and answer questions on subjects of interest and concern to authors. Typical subjects have been the rights of privacy and publicity, libel, wills and estates, taxation, copyright, editors and editing, the art of interviewing, standards of criticism and book reviewing. Transcripts of these symposia are published and circulated to members. The *Authors Guild Bulletin*, a quarterly journal, contains articles on matters of interest to writers, reports of Guild activities, contract surveys, advice on problem clauses in contracts,

transcripts of Guild and League symposia and information on a variety of professional topics. Subscription included in the cost of the annual dues." **Contact:** Paul Aiken, executive director.

☺ CANADIAN SOCIETY OF CHILDREN'S AUTHORS, ILLUSTRATORS AND PERFORMERS

720 Bathurst St, Suite 504, Toronto, ON, Canada, M5S 2R. (416)515-1559. **E-mail:** office@canscaip. org. **Website:** www.canscaip.org. Purpose of organization: development of Canadian children's culture and support for authors, illustrators and performers working in this field. Qualifications for membership: Members—professionals who have been published (not self-published) or have paid public performances/records/tapes to their credit. Friends—share interest in field of children's culture. Membership cost: $85 (Members dues), $45 (Friends dues). Sponsors workshops/conferences. Manuscript evaluation services; publishes newsletter: includes profiles of members; news round-up of members' activities countrywide; market news; news on awards, grants, etc; columns related to professional concerns. **Contact:** Jennifer Gordon, administrative director.

LEWIS CARROLL SOCIETY OF NORTH AMERICA

11935 Beltsville Dr., Beltsville MD 20705. **E-mail:** secretary@lewiscarroll.org. **Website:** www.lewiscarroll.org. "We are an organization of Carroll admirers of all ages and interests and a center for Carroll studies." Qualifications for membership: "An interest in Lewis Carroll and a simple love for Alice (or the Snark for that matter)." Membership cost: $35 (regular membership), $50 (foreign membership), $100 (sustaining membership). The Society meets twice a year--in spring and in fall; locations vary. Publishes a semi-annual journal, *Knight Letter*, and maintains an active publishing program. **Contact:** Clare Imholtz, secretary.

FLORIDA FREELANCE WRITERS ASSOCIATION

P.O. Box A, North Stratford NH 03590. (603)922-8338. **E-mail:** FFWA@writers-editors.com. **Website:** www. ffwamembers.com; www.writers-editors.com. Purpose of organization: To provide a link between Florida writers and buyers of the written word; to help writers run more effective editorial businesses. Qualifications for membership: "None. We provide a vari-

ety of services and information, some for beginners and some for established pros." Membership cost: US mailing address members costs $90, Canadian mailing address members costs $98, international mailing address members costs $105, online membership (any address) costs $80. Annual Directory of Florida Markets included in FFWA newsletter section and electronic download. Publishes annual *Guide to CNW/Florida Writers*, which is distributed to editors around the country. Sponsors contest: annual deadline March 15. Guidelines on website. Categories: juvenile, adult nonfiction, adult fiction and poetry. Awards include cash for top prizes, certificate for others. Contest open to nonmembers. **Contact:** Dana K. Cassell, executive director.

GRAPHIC ARTISTS GUILD

32 Broadway, Suite 1114, New York NY 10004. (212)791-3400. **Fax:** 212-791-0333. **E-mail:** admin@gag.org. **Website:** www.graphicartistsguild.org. Purpose of organization: "To promote and protect the economic interests of member artists. It is committed to improving conditions for all creators of graphic arts and raising standards for the entire industry." Qualification for full membership: 50% of income derived from the creation of graphic artwork. Associate members include those in allied fields and students. Initiation fee: $30. Full memberships: $200; student membership: $75/year. Associate membership: $170/year. Publishes *Graphic Artists Guild Handbook*, *Pricing and Ethical Guidelines* (members receive a copy as part of their membership). **Contact:** Patricia McKiernan, executive director.

HORROR WRITERS ASSOCIATION

244 5th Avenue, Suite 2767, New York NY 10001. **E-mail:** hwa@horror.org; membership@horror.org. **Website:** www.horror.org. Purpose of organization: To encourage public interest in horror and dark fantasy and to provide networking and career tools for members. Qualifications for membership: Complete membership rules online at www.horror.org/memrule.htm. At least one low-level sale is required to join as an affiliate. Non-writing professionals who can show income from a horror-related field may join as an associate (booksellers, editors, agents, librarians, etc.). To qualify for full active membership, you must be a published, professional writer of horror. Membership cost: Affiliate, Associate, Academic, and Active members are $69.00 per year. Dues for Support-

ing members $48. Holds annual Stoker Awards Weekend and HWA Business Meeting. Publishes monthly newsletter focusing on market news, industry news, HWA business for members. Sponsors awards. We give the Bram Stoker Awards for superior achievement in horror annually. Awards include a handmade Stoker trophy designed by sculptor Stephen Kirk. Awards open to nonmembers. **Contact:** James Chambers, membership chair. It's best to contact the Horror Writers Association as a whole, not necessarily to contact individuals within the group itself.

INTERNATIONAL READING ASSOCIATION

800 Barksdale Rd., P.O. Box 8139, Newark DE 19714. (800)336-7323 (U.S. and Canada). **Fax:** (302)731-1057. **E-mail:** customerservice@reading.org. **Website:** www.reading.org. Purpose of organization: "The mission of the International Reading Association is to promote reading by continuously advancing the quality of literacy instruction and research worldwide." Membership: "Online membership: $29.00, basic membership: $39.00, student membership: $24.00. Details listed on site." **Open to students.** Sponsors annual convention. Publishes a newsletter called "Reading Today." Sponsors a number of awards and fellowships. Visit the IRA website for more information on membership, conventions and awards.

INTERNATIONAL WOMEN'S WRITING GUILD

The International Women's Writing Guild, 317 Madison Avenue, Suite 1704, New York, NY 10017. (917)720-6959. **E-mail:** iwwgquestions@gmail.com. **Website:** www.iwwg.org. IWWG is "a network for the personal and professional empowerment of women through writing." Qualifications: Open to any woman connected to the written word regardless of professional portfolio. Membership cost: $55 annually. "IWWG sponsors several annual conferences a year in all areas of the U.S. The major conference is a week-long conference attracting 350 women internationally." Also publishes a 32-page newsletter, *Network*, 4 times/year. **Contact:** Hannelore Hahn, founder/executive editor.

☺ LEAGUE OF CANADIAN POETS

312-192 Spadina Ave., Toronto ON M5T 2C2Canada . (416)504-1657. **Fax:** (416)504-0096. **E-mail:** joanna@poets.ca. **Website:** www.poets.ca. The L.C.P. is a national organization of published Canadian poets. Our constitutional objectives are to advance poetry in Canada and to promote the professional interests of the members. Qualifications for membership: full—publication of at least 1 book of poetry by a professional publisher; associate membership—an active interest in poetry, demonstrated by several magazine/periodical publication credits; student—an active interest in poetry, 12 sample poems required; supporting--any friend of poetry. Membership fees: Full membership is now $185 annually.Associate memberships now $70 and open to students in university creative writing programs (a discounted rate). Student membership, $30, is open to secondary school students. Supporting membership is $110. Holds an Annual General Meeting every spring; some events open to nonmembers. "We also organize reading programs in schools and public venues. We publish a newsletter that includes information on poetry/poetics in Canada and beyond. Also publish the books *Poetry Markets for Canadians*; *Who's Who in the League of Canadian Poets*; *Poets in the Classroom* (teaching guide), and online publications. The Gerald Lampert Memorial Award for the best first book of poetry published in Canada in the preceding year and The Pat Lowther Memorial Award for the best book of poetry by a Canadian woman published in the preceding year. Deadline for awards: November 1. Visit www.poets.ca for more details. Sponsors youth poetry competition. Visit www.youngpoets.ca for details. **Contact:** Joanna Poblocka, executive director.

LITERARY MANAGERS AND DRAMATURGS OF THE AMERICAS

P.O. Box 36. 20985 P.A.C.C., New York NY 10129. (800)680-2148. **E-mail:** info@lmda.org. **Website:** www.lmda.org. LMDA is a not-for-profit service organization for the professions of literary management and dramaturgy. Student Membership: $25/year. Open to students in dramaturgy, performing arts and literature programs, or related disciplines. Proof of student status required. Includes national conference, New Dramaturg activities, local symposia, job phone and select membership meetings. Active Membership: $60/year. Open to full-time and part-time professionals working in the fields of literary management and dramaturgy. All privileges and services including voting rights and eligibility for office. Institutional Membership: $200/year. Open to theaters, universities, and other organizations. Includes all privileges and services except voting rights and eligibility for office. Publishes a newsletter featuring articles on literary management, dramaturgy, LMDA program updates and other articles of interest. Spotlight sponsor membership $500/year. Student memberships are $30 and individual memberships are $75. Open to theatres,universities, and other organizations; includes all priviledges for up to six individual members, plus additional promotional benefits.

THE NATIONAL LEAGUE OF AMERICAN PEN WOMEN

Pen Arts Building, 1300 17th St. N.W., Washington D.C. 20036-1973. (202)785-1997. **Fax:** (202)452-8868. **E-mail:** contact@nlapw.org. **Website:** www.americanpenwomen.org. Purpose of organization: to promote professional work in art, letters, and music since 1897. Qualifications for membership: An applicant must show "proof of sale" in each chosen category--art, letters, and music. Levels of membership include: Active, Associate, International Affiliate, Members-at-Large, Honorary Members (in one or more of the following classifications: Art, Letters, and Music). Holds workshops/conferences. Publishes magazine 4 times/year titled *The Pen Woman*. Sponsors various contests in areas of Art, Letters, and Music. Awards made at Biennial Convention. Biannual scholarships awarded to non-Pen Women for mature women. Awards include cash prizes—up to $1,000. Specialized contests open to nonmembers. **Contact:** Nina Brooks, corresponding secretary.

NATIONAL WRITERS ASSOCIATION

National Writers Association, 10940 S. Parker Road, #508, Parker, CO 80134. (303)841-0246. **Fax:** (303)841-2607. **E-mail:** natlwritersassn@hotmail.com. **Website:** www.nationalwriters.com. Purpose of organization: association for freelance writers. Qualifications for membership: associate membership—must be serious about writing; professional membership—must be published and paid writer (cite credentials). Membership cost: $85; $35 for students. Sponsors workshops/conferences: TV/screenwriting workshops, NWAF Annual Conferences, Literary Clearinghouse, editing and critiquing services, local chapters, National Writer's School. Open to non-members. Publishes industry news of interest to freelance writers; how-to articles; market information; member news and networking opportunities. Nonmember subscription: $20. Sponsors poetry contest; short story contest; article contest; novel contest. Awards cash for top 3 winners; books and/or certificates for other

winners; honorable mention certificate places 5-10. Contests open to nonmembers.

NATIONAL WRITERS UNION

256 W. 38th St., Suite 703, New York NY 10018. (212)254-0279. **Fax:** (212)-254-0673. **E-mail:** nwu@nwu.org. **Website:** www.nwu.org. Purpose of organization: Advocacy for freelance writers. Qualifications for membership: "Membership in the NWU is open to all qualified writers, and no one shall be barred or in any manner prejudiced within the Union on account of race, age, sex, sexual orientation, disability, national origin, religion or ideology. You are eligible for membership if you have published a book, a play, three articles, five poems, one short story or an equivalent amount of newsletter, publicity, technical, commercial, government or institutional copy. You are also eligible for membership if you have written an equal amount of unpublished material and you are actively writing and attempting to publish your work." Membership cost: annual writing income less than $5,000-$120/year; $5,001-15,000-$195; $15,001-30,000-$265/year; $30,001-$45,000-$315 a year; $45,001 and up -$340/year. Holds workshops throughout the country. Members only section on website offers rich resources for freelance writers. Skilled contract advice and grievance help for members.

PEN AMERICAN CENTER

588 Broadway, Suite 303, New York NY 10012. (212)334-1660. **Fax:** (212)334-2181. **E-mail:** pen@pen.org. **Website:** www.pen.org. Purpose of organization: "An association of writers working to advance literature, to defend free expression, and to foster international literary fellowship." Qualifications for membership: "The standard qualification for a writer to become a member of PEN is publication of two or more books of a literary character, or one book generally acclaimed to be of exceptional distinction. Also eligible for membership: editors who have demonstrated commitment to excellence in their profession (usually construed as five years' service in book editing); translators who have published at least two book-length literary translations; playwrights whose works have been produced professionally; and literary essayists whose publications are extensive even if they have not yet been issued as a book. Candidates for membership may be nominated by a PEN member or they may nominate themselves with the sup-

port of two references from the literary community or from a current PEN member. Membership dues $125. Associate Membership: $50 ($25 for students) Qualification is having published one or more books. Associate membership is open to anyone who supports PEN's mission. Many PEN members contribute their time by serving on committees, conducting campaigns and writing letters in connection with freedom-of-expression cases, contributing to the PEN journal, participating in PEN public events, helping to bring literature into underserved communities, and judging PEN literary awards. PEN members receive a subscription to the PEN journal, the PEN Annual Report, and have access to medical insurance at group rates. Members living in the New York metropolitan and tri-state area, or near the Branches, are invited to PEN events throughout the year. Membership in PEN American Center includes reciprocal privileges in PEN American Center branches and in foreign PEN Centers for those traveling abroad. Application forms are available on the Web at www.pen.org. Associate Membership is open to everyone who supports PEN's mission, and your annual dues ($40; $20 for students) provides crucial support to PEN's programs. When you join as an Associate Member, not only will you receive a subscription to the *PEN Journal* http://pen.org/page.php/prmID/150 and notices of all PEN events but you are also invited to participate in the work of PEN. PEN American Center is the largest of the 141 centers of PEN International, the world's oldest human rights organization and the oldest international literary organization. PEN International was founded in 1921 to dispel national, ethnic, and racial hatreds and to promote understanding among all countries. PEN American Center, founded a year later, works to advance literature, to defend free expression, and to foster international literary fellowship. The Center has a membership of 3,400 distinguished writers, editors, and translators. In addition to defending writers in prison or in danger of imprisonment for their work, PEN American Center sponsors public literary programs and forums on current issues, sends prominent authors to inner-city schools to encourage reading and writing, administers literary prizes, promotes international literature that might otherwise go unread in the United States, and offers grants and loans to writers facing financial or medical emergencies. In carrying out this work, PEN American Center builds upon the achievements of such dedicated past members as W.H. Auden, James Baldwin, Willa Cather, Robert Frost, Langston Hughes, Thomas Mann, Arthur Miller, Marianne Moore, Susan Sontag, and John Steinbeck. The Children's Book Authors' Committee sponsors annual public events focusing on the art of writing for children and young adults and on the diversity of literature for juvenile readers. The PEN/Phyllis Naylor Working Writer Fellowship was established in 2001 to assist a North American author of fiction for children or young adults (**E-mail:** awards@pen.org). Visit www.pen.org for complete information. Sponsors several competitions per year. Monetary awards range from $2,000-35,000.

PUPPETEERS OF AMERICA, INC.

Puppeteers of America, 310 East 38th Street, Suite 228, Minneapolis, MN 55409. (612)821-2382. **E-mail:** cmaloney@puppeteers.org. **Website:** www.puppeteers.org. Purpose of organization: to promote the art and appreciation of puppetry as a means of communications and as a performing art. The Puppeteers of America boasts an international membership. Qualifications for membership: interest in the art form. Membership cost: single adult, $55; seniors (65+) and youth members, (6-17 years of age), $35; full-time college student, $35; family, $75; couple, $65; senior couple, $55, Company, $90. Membership discounts to festivals and puppetry store purchases, access to the Audio Visual Library & Consultants in many areas of puppetry. The *Puppetry Journal*, a quarterly periodical, provides a color photo gallery, news about puppeteers, puppet theaters, exhibitions, touring companies, technical tips, new products, new books, films, television, and events sponsored by the Chartered Guilds in each of the 8 P of A regions. Includes *Playboard, The P of A Newsletter*; subscription to the *Puppetry Journal* only, $40 (libraries/ institutions only). **Contact:** Cheryl Maloney.

SCIENCE-FICTION AND FANTASY WRITERS OF AMERICA, INC.

P.O. Box 3238, Enfield CT 06083. **Website:** www.sfwa.org. Purpose of organization: to encourage public interest in science fiction literature and provide organization format for writers/editors/artists within the genre. Qualifications for membership: at least 1 professional sale or other professional involvement within the field. Membership cost: annual active dues—$90; affiliate—$70; one-time installation fee of $10; dues year begins July 1. Different levels of membership include: active—requires 3 professional short stories or 1 novel published; associate—requires 1 professional sale; or affiliate—which requires some other professional involvement such as artist, editor, librarian, bookseller, teacher, etc. Workshops/conferences: annual awards banquet, usually in April or May. Open to nonmembers. Publishes quarterly journal, the *SFWA Bulletin*. Nonmember subscription: $32/year in U.S. Sponsors Nebula Awards for best published science fiction or fantasy in the categories of novel, novella, novelette and short story. Awards trophy. Also presents the Damon Knight Memorial Grand Master Award for Lifetime Achievement, and, beginning in 2006, the Andre Norton Award for Outstanding Young Adult Science Fiction or Fantasy Book of the Year.

SOCIETY OF CHILDREN'S BOOK WRITERS AND ILLUSTRATORS

8271 Beverly Blvd., Los Angeles CA 90048. (323)782-1010. **Fax:** (323)782-1892. **E-mail:** scbwi@scbwi.org. **Website:** www.scbwi.org. Purpose of organization: to assist writers and illustrators working or interested in the field. Qualifications for membership: an interest in children's literature and illustration. Membership cost: $95/first year, and $80 in subsequent years. Different levels of membership include: P.A.L. membership—published by publisher listed in SCBWI Market Surveys; full membership—published authors/illustrators (includes self-published); associate membership--unpublished writers/illustrators. Holds 100 events (workshops/conferences) worldwide each year. National Conference open to nonmembers. Publishes bi-monthly magazine on writing and illustrating children's books. Sponsors annual awards and grants for writers and illustrators who are members. **Contact:** Stephen Mooser, president; Lin Oliver, executive director.

SOCIETY OF ILLUSTRATORS

128 E. 63rd St., New York NY 10065. (212)838-2560. **Fax:** (212)838-2561. **E-mail:** info@societyillustrators.org. **Website:** www.societyillustrators.org. "Our mission is to promote the art and appreciation of illustration, its history and evolving nature through exhibitions, lectures and education." Annual dues for nonresident illustrator members (those living more than 125 air miles from SI's headquarters): $300. Dues for resident illustrator members: $500 per year; resident associate members: $500. "Artist members shall

include those who make illustration their profession and earn at least 60% of their income from their illustration. Associate members are those who earn their living in the arts or who have made a substantial contribution to the art of illustration. This includes art directors, art buyers, creative supervisors, instructors, publishers and like categories. The candidate must complete and sign the application form, which requires a brief biography, a listing of schools attended, other training and a résumé of his or her professional career. Candidates for illustrators membership, in addition to the above requirements, must submit examples of their work." **Contact:** Anelle Miller, executive director.

SOCIETY OF MIDLAND AUTHORS

Website: www.midlandauthors.com. Contact form on site. Purpose of organization: create closer association among writers of the Middle West; stimulate creative literary effort; maintain collection of members' works; encourage interest in reading and literature by cooperating with other educational and cultural agencies. Qualifications for membership: membership by invitation only. Must be author or co-author of a book demonstrating literary style and published by a recognized publisher and be identified through residence with Illinois, Indiana, Iowa, Kansas, Michigan, Minnesota, Missouri, Nebraska, North Dakota, Ohio, South Dakota or Wisconsin. **Open to students** (if authors). Membership cost: $35/year dues. Different levels of membership include: regular—published book authors; associate, nonvoting—not published as above but having some connection with literature, such as librarians, teachers, publishers and editors. Program meetings held 5 times a year, featuring authors, publishers, editors or the like individually or on panels. Usually second Tuesday of October, November, February, March and April. Also holds annual awards dinner in May. Publishes a newsletter focusing on news of members and general items of interest to writers. Sponsors contests. "Annual awards in six categories, given at annual dinner in May. Monetary awards for books published that premiered professionally in previous calendar year. Send SASE to contact person for details." Categories include adult fiction, adult nonfiction, juvenile fiction, juvenile nonfiction, poetry, biography. No picture books. Contest open to nonmembers. Deadline for contest: February 1. **Contact:** Meg Tebo, president.

SOCIETY OF SOUTHWESTERN AUTHORS

SSA Membership, PO Box 30355, Tucson, AZ 85751 **Fax:** (520)751-7877. **E-mail:** wporter202@aol.com; contest questions to info@ssa-az.org. **Website:** www. ssa-az.org. Purpose of organization: to promote fellowship among professional and associate members of the writing profession, to recognize members' achievements, to stimulate further achievement, and to assist persons seeking to become professional writers. Qualifications for membership: Professional Membership: proof of publication of a book, articles, TV screenplay, etc. Associate Membership: proof of desire to write, and/or become a professional. Self-published authors may receive status of Professional Membership at the discretion of the board of directors. Membership cost: $30 initiation plus $30/year dues. The Society of Southwestern Authors sponsors an annual 2-day writers conference (all genres) held September 26-27; watch website ssa-az.org. SSA publishes a bimonthly newsletter, *The Write Word*, promoting members' published works, advice to fellow writers, and up-to-the-minute trends in publishing and marketing. Yearly writing contest open to all writers; short story, memoir, poetry, children's stories. Applications available in February—e-mail Mike Rom at Mike_Rom@hotmail.com; Subject Line: SSA Writer's Contest. **Contact:** Penny Porter.

○ TEXT & ACADEMIC AUTHORS ASSOCIATION (TAA)

P.O. Box 56359, St. Petersburg FL 33732. (727)563-0020. **E-mail:** Michael.Spinella@taaonline.net. **Website:** www.taaonline.net. TAA's overall mission is to enhance the quality of textbooks and other academic materials, such as journal articles, monographs and scholarly books, in all fields and disciplines. Qualifications for membership: all authors and prospective authors are welcome. Membership cost: $30 first year; graduated levels for following years. Workshops/conferences: June each year. Newsletter focuses on all areas of interest to textbook and academic authors.

Contact: Michael Spinella, executive director; Kim Pawlick, associate executive director.

THEATRE FOR YOUNG AUDIENCES/USA

Young Audiences/USA, c/o The Theatre School, 2350 N. Racine Ave, Chicago, IL 60614. (773)325-7981. **Fax:** (773)325-7920. **E-mail:** info@tyausa.org. **Website:** www.assitej-usa.org. Purpose of organization: to promote theater for children and young people by linking professional theaters and artists together; sponsoring national, international and regional conferences and providing publications and information. Also serves as U.S. Center for International Association of the Theatre for Children and Young People. Different levels of memberships include: organizations, individuals, students, retirees, libraries. TYA Today includes original articles, reviews and works of criticism and theory, all of interest to theater practitioners (included with membership). Publishes *Marquee*, a directory that focuses on information on members in U.S.

VOLUNTEER LAWYERS FOR THE ARTS

1 E. 53rd St., 6th Floor, New York NY 10022. (212)319-2787, ext. 1. **Fax:** (212)752-6575. **E-mail:** vlany@vlany. org. **Website:** www.vlany.org. Purpose of organization: Volunteer Lawyers for the Arts is dedicated to providing free arts-related legal assistance to low-income artists and not-for-profit arts organizations in all creative fields. Over 1,000 attorneys in the New York area donate their time through VLA to artists and arts organizations unable to afford legal counsel. Everyone is welcome to use VLA's Art Law Line, a legal hotline for any artist or arts organization needing quick answers to arts-related questions. VLA also provides clinics, seminars and publications designed to educate artists on legal issues which affect their careers. Members receive discounts on publications and seminars as well as other benefits. Some of the many publications we carry are *All You Need to Know About the Music Business*; *Business and Legal Forms for Fine Artists, Photographers & Authors & Self-Publishers*; *Contracts for the Film & TV Industry*, plus many more.

CONFERENCES & WORKSHOPS

//

Writers and illustrators eager to expand their knowledge of the children's publishing industry should consider attending one of the many conferences and workshops held each year.
Whether you're a novice or seasoned professional, conferences and workshops are great
places to pick up information on a variety of topics and network with experts in the publishing industry, as well as with your peers.

Listings in this section provide details about what conference and workshop courses
are offered, where and when they are held, and the costs. Some of the national writing and
art organizations also offer regional workshops throughout the year. Write, call or visit
websites for information.

Members of the Society of Children's Book Writers and Illustrators can find information
on conferences in national and local SCBWI newsletters. Nonmembers may attend SCBWI
events as well. (Some SCBWI regional events are listed in this section.) For information on
SCBWI's annual national conferences and all of their regional events, check their website
(scbwi.org) for a complete calendar of conferences and happenings.

⊕ ALASKA WRITERS CONFERENCE

Alaska Writers Guild, PO Box 670014, Chugiak AK 99567. **E-mail:** bahartman@me.com; alaskawriters guild.awg@gmail.com. **Website:** alaskawritersguild. com. **Contact:** Brooke Hartman. Annual event held in the fall—usually September. Duration: 2 days. There are many workshops and instructional tracks of courses. This event sometimes teams up with SCBWI and Alaska Pacific University to offer courses at the event. Several literary agents are in attendance each year to hear pitches and meet writers.

COSTS 2013 costs: Up to $275, though discounts for different memberships brings down that number.

ACCOMMODATIONS Crowne Plaza Hotel in Anchorage. Conference room rates available. Several scholarships are available (see the website).

ASPEN SUMMER WORDS LITERARY FESTIVAL & WRITING RETREAT

Aspen Writers' Foundation, 110 E. Hallam St., #116, Aspen CO 81611. (970)925-3122. **Fax:** (970)925-5700. **E-mail:** info@aspenwriters.org. **Website:** www.as penwriters.org. **Contact:** Natalie Lacy, programs coordinator. Estab. 1976. 2014 dates: June 14-18. ASW is one part laboratory and one part theater. It is comprised of two tracks—the Writing Retreat and the Literary Festival—which approach the written word from different, yet complementary angles. The Retreat features introductory and intensive workshops with some of the nation's most notable writing instructors and includes literature appreciation symposia and professional consultations with literary agents and editors. The Writing Retreat supports writers in developing their craft by providing a winning combination of inspiration, skills, community, and opportunity. The Literary Festival is a booklover's bliss, where the written word takes center stage. Since 2005, each edition of the Festival has celebrated a particular literary heritage and culture by honoring the stories and storytellers of a specific region. Annual conference held the fourth week of June. Conference duration: 5 days. Average attendance: 150 at writing retreat; 300+ at literary festival.

COSTS Check website each year for updates.

ACCOMMODATIONS Discount lodging at the conference site will be available. 2014 rates to be announced (see website). Free shuttle around town.

⊕ ATLANTA WRITERS CONFERENCE

E-mail: awconference@gmail.com. **E-mail:** gjwein stein@yahoo.com. **Website:** atlantawritersconference.

com. **Contact:** George Weinstein. The Atlanta Writers Conference happens twice a year (every 6 months) and invites several agents, editors and authors each time. There are instructional sessions, and time to pitch professionals.

ACCOMMODATIONS Westin Airport Atlanta Hotel

ADDITIONAL INFORMATION There is a free shuttle that runs between the airport and the hotel.

BALTIMORE WRITERS' CONFERENCE

English Department, Liberal Arts Building, Towson University, 8000 York Rd., Towson MD 21252. (410)704-3695. **E-mail:** prwr@towson.edu. **Website:** baltimorewritersconference.org. Estab. 1994. "Annual conference held in November at Towson University. Conference duration: 1 day. Average attendance: 150-200. Covers all areas of writing and getting published. Held at Towson University. Session topics include fiction, nonfiction, poetry, magazine and journals, agents and publishers. Sign up the day of the conference for quick critiques to improve your stories, essays, and poems."

COSTS 2013 costs: $75-95 (includes all-day conference, lunch and reception). Student special rate of $35 before mid-October, $50 thereafter.

ACCOMMODATIONS Hotels are close by, if required.

ADDITIONAL INFORMATION Writers may register through the BWA website. Send inquiries via e-mail.

BAY TO OCEAN WRITERS' CONFERENCE

P.O. Box 544, St. Michaels MD 21663. (443)786-4536. **E-mail:** info@baytoocean.com. **Website:** www.bayto ocean.com. Estab. 1998. Contacts include Diane Marquette, Mala Burt, Judy Reveal (coordinators).

COSTS Adults $155, students $55. A paid manuscript review is also available—details on website. Includes continental breakfast and networking lunch.

ADDITIONAL INFORMATION Mail-in registration form available on website in December prior to the conference. Pre-registration is required, no registration at door. Conference usually sells out one month in advance. Conference is for all levels of writers.

⊕ BIG SUR WRITING WORKSHOP

Henry Miller Library, Highway One, Big Sur CA 93920. (831)667-2574. **Website:** bigsurwriting.word press.com. Annual workshops focusing on children's and young adult writing (picture books, middle grade, and young adult). (2014 dates: both March 7-9 and Dec. 5-7.) Workshop held in Big Sur Lodge in Pfeiffer

State Park. Cost of workshop: $770; included meals, lodging, workshop, Saturday evening reception; $600 if lodging not needed. www.henrymiller.org. This event is helmed by the literary agents of the Andrea Brown Literary Agency, which is the most successful agency nationwide in selling kids books. All attendees meet with at least 2 faculty members, so work is critiqued.

⊕ BOOKS-IN-PROGRESS CONFERENCE

Carnegie Center for Literacy and Learning, 251 West Second Street, Lexington KY 40507. (859)254-4175. **E-mail:** ccll1@carnegiecenterlex.org; lwhitaker@carnegiecenterlex.org. **Website:** carnegiecenterlex.org/events/books-in-progress-conference/. **Contact:** Laura Whitaker. Estab. 2010. This is an annual writing conference at the Carnegie Center for Literacy and Learning in Lexington, KY. "The conference will offer writing and publishing workshops and includes a keynote presentation." Literary agents are flown in to meet with writers and hear pitches. Website is updated several months prior to each annual event.
COSTS As of 2013, costs were $175.
ACCOMMODATIONS Several area hotels are nearby.

BREAD LOAF WRITERS' CONFERENCE

Middlebury College, Middlebury College, Middlebury VT 05753. (802)443-5286. **Fax:** (802)443-2087. **E-mail:** ncargill@middlebury.edu. **E-mail:** blwc@middlebury.edu. **Website:** www.middlebury.edu/blwc. **Contact:** Michael Collier, Director. Estab. 1926. Annual conference held in late August. Conference duration: 10 days. Offers workshops for fiction, nonfiction, and poetry. Agents and editors will be in attendance.
COSTS $2,935 (includes tuition, housing).
ACCOMMODATIONS Bread Loaf Campus in Ripton, Vermont.
ADDITIONAL INFORMATION 2014 Conference Dates: August 13-23. Location: mountain campus of Middlebury College. Average attendance: 230.

🌙 BYRON BAY WRITERS FESTIVAL

Northern Rivers Writers' Centre, P.O. Box 1846, 69 Johnson St., Byron Bay NSW 2481 Australia. 040755-2441. **E-mail:** jeni@nrwc.org.au. **Website:** www.byronbaywritersfestival.com. **Contact:** Jeni Caffin, director. Estab. 1997. Annual festival held the first weekend in August at Byron's Bay Belongil Fields. Festival duration: 3 days. Celebrate and reflect with over 100 of the finest writers from Australia and overseas.

Workshops, panel discussions, and literary breakfasts, lunches, and dinners will also be offered. The Byron Bay Writers Festival is organised by the staff and Committee of the Northern Rivers Writers' Centre, a member based organisation receiving core funding from Arts NSW.
COSTS See costs online under Tickets. Early bird, NRWC members and students, kids.
ADDITIONAL INFORMATION "2014 Festival dates are August 1-3 with workshops beginning July 28 and discounted Early Bird passes are on sale from April 4 at our website or 02 6685 6262. Full program on sale June 9.

CAPE COD WRITERS CENTER ANNUAL CONFERENCE

P.O. Box 408, Osterville MA 02655. **E-mail:** writers@capecodwriterscenter.org. **Website:** www.capecodwriterscenter.org. **Contact:** Nancy Rubin Stuart, executive director. Duration: 3 days; first week in August. Offers workshops in fiction, commercial fiction, nonfiction, poetry, writing for children, memoir, pitching your book, screenwriting, digital communications, getting published, ms evaluation, mentoring sessions with faculty. Held at Resort and Conference Center of Hyannis, Hyannis, MA.
COSTS Vary, depending on the number of courses selected.

CAPON SPRINGS WRITERS' WORKSHOP

2836 Westbrook Drive, Cincinnati OH 45211-0627. (513)481-9884. **E-mail:** beckcomm@fuse.net. Estab. 2000. No conference scheduled for 2014. There is a tentative 2015 event, Check the website often for updates. Conference duration: 3 days. Covers fiction, creative nonfiction, and publishing basics. Conference is held at Capon Springs and Farms Resort, a secluded 5,000-acre mountain resort in West Virginia.
COSTS Check in 2015.
ACCOMMODATIONS Facility has swimming, hiking, fishing, tennis, badminton, volleyball, basketball, ping pong, etc. A 9-hole golf course is available for an additional fee.
ADDITIONAL INFORMATION Brochures available for SASE. Inquire via e-mail.

CELEBRATION OF SOUTHERN LITERATURE

Southern Lit Alliance, 3069 S. Broad St., Suite 2, Chattanooga TN 37408-3056. (423)267-1218. **Fax:** (866)483-6831. **E-mail:** srobinson@southernlital liance.org. **Website:** www.southernlitalliance.org. **Contact:** Susan Robinson. "The Celebration of Southern Literature stands out because of its unique collaboration with the Fellowship of Southern Writers, an organization founded by towering literary figures like Eudora Welty, Cleanth Brooks, Walker Percy, and Robert Penn Warren to recognize and encourage literature in the South. The 2015 celebration marked 26 years since the Fellowship selected Chattanooga for its headquarters and chose to collaborate with the Celebration of Southern Literature. More than 50 members of the Fellowship will participate in the 2015 event, discussing hot topics and reading from their latest works. The Fellowship will also award 11 literary prizes and induct new members, making this event the place to discover up-and-coming voices in Southern literature. The Southern Lit Alliance's Celebration of Southern Literature attracts more than 1,000 readers and writers from all over the U.S. It strives to maintain an informal atmosphere where conversations will thrive, inspired by a common passion for the written word. The Southern Lit Alliance (formerly The Arts & Education Council) started as 1 of 12 pilot agencies founded by a Ford Foundation grant in 1952. The Alliance is the only organization of the 12 still in existence. The Southern Lit Alliance celebrates southern writers and readers through community education and innovative literary arts experiences."

⊕ CHICAGO WRITERS CONFERENCE

E-mail: ines@chicagowritersconference.org; mare@chicagowritersconference.org. **E-mail:** ines@chicagowritersconference.org; mare@chicagowritersconference.org. **Website:** chicagowritersconference.org. **Contact:** Mare Swallow. Estab. 2011. This conference happens every year in the fall. 2014 dates: Oct 24-26. Find them on Twitter at @ChiWritersConf. The conference brings together a variety of publishing professionals (agents, editors, authors) and brings together several Chicago literary, writing, and bookselling groups.

CLARION WEST WRITERS WORKSHOP

P.O. Box 31264, Seattle WA 98103-1264. (206)322-9083. **E-mail:** info@clarionwest.org. **Website:** www.clarionwest.org. "Contact us through our webform." **Contact:** Nelle Graham, workshop director. Clarion West is an intensive 6-week workshop for writers preparing for professional careers in science fiction and fantasy, held annually in Seattle WA. Usually goes from mid-June through end of July. Conference duration: 6 weeks. Average attendance: 18. Held near the University of Washington. Deadline for applications is March 1. Instructors are well-known writers and editors in the field.

COSTS $3,600 (for tuition, housing, most meals). Limited scholarships are available based on financial need.

ACCOMMODATIONS Workshop tuition, dormitory housing and most meals: $3,600. Students stay on-site in workshop housing at one of the University of Washington's sorority houses. "Students write their own stories every week while preparing critiques of all the other students' work for classroom sessions. This gives participants a more focused, professional approach to their writing. The core of the workshop remains speculative fiction, and short stories (not novels) are the focus." Conference information available in Fall. For brochure/guidelines send SASE, visit website, e-mail or call. Accepts inquiries by e-mail, phone, SASE. Limited scholarships are available, based on financial need. Students must submit 20-30 pages of ms with 4-page biography and $40 fee ($30 if received prior to February 10) for applications sent by mail or e-mail to qualify for admission.

ADDITIONAL INFORMATION This is a critique-based workshop. Students are encouraged to write a story every week; the critique of student material produced at the workshop forms the principal activity of the workshop. Students and instructors critique mss as a group. Conference guidelines are available for a SASE. Visit the website for updates and complete details.

CLARKSVILLE WRITERS CONFERENCE

1123 Madison St., Clarksville TN 37040. (931)551-8870. **E-mail:** artsandheritage@cdelightband.net; burawac@apsu.edu. **E-mail:** artsandheritage@cdelightband.net; burawac@apsu.edu. **Website:** www.artsandheritage.us/writers/. **Contact:** Ellen Kanervo. Annual conference held in the summer. The conference features a variety of presentations on fiction, nonfiction and more. Past attendees include: Darnell Arnoult, Earl S. Braggs, Christopher Burawa, Susan Gregg Gilmore, James & Lynda O'Connor, Katharine Sands, George Singleton, Bernis Terhune, p.m. terrell. Our presentations and workshops are valuable to writers and interesting to readers. This fun, affordable, and talent-laden conference is presented at Austin Peay State University and the Clarksville Country Club.

COSTS Costs available online; prices vary depending on how long attendees stay and if they attend the banquet dinner.

ADDITIONAL INFORMATION Multiple literary agents are flown in to the event every year to meet with writers and take pitches.

CONFERENCE FOR WRITERS & ILLUSTRATORS OF CHILDREN'S BOOKS

Book Passage, 51 Tamal Vista Blvd., Corte Madera CA 94925. (415)927-0960, ext. 239. **E-mail:** bpconferences@bookpassage.com. **Website:** www.bookpassage.com. Contact Kathryn Petrocelli, conference coordinator. Writer and illustrator conference geared toward beginner and intermediate levels. Sessions cover such topics as the nuts and bolts of writing and illustrating, publisher's spotlight, market trends, developing characters/finding voice in your writing, and the author/agent relationship. Four-day conference held each summer. Includes opening night dinner, 3 lunches and a closing reception.

CRESTED BUTTE WRITERS CONFERENCE

P.O. Box 1361, Crested Butte CO 81224. **E-mail:** coordinator@conf.crestedbuttewriters.org. **Website:** www.crestedbuttewriters.org/conf.php. **Contact:** Barbara Crawford or Theresa Rizzo, co-coordinators. Estab. 2006.

COSTS $330 nonmembers; $300 members; $297 Early Bird; The Sandy Writing Contest Finalist $280; and groups of 5 or more $280.

ACCOMMODATIONS The conference is held at The Elevation Hotel, located at the Crested Butte Mountain Resort at the base of the ski mountain (Mt. Crested Butte, CO). The quaint historic town lies nestled in a stunning mountain valley 3 short miles from the resort area of Mt. Crested Butte. A free bus runs frequently between the 2 towns. The closest airport is 30 miles away, in Gunnison CO. Our website lists 3 lodging options besides rooms at the Event Facility. All condos, motels and hotel options offer special conference rates. No special travel arrangements are made through the conference; however, information for car rental from Gunnison airport or the Alpine Express shuttle is listed on the conference FAQ page.

ADDITIONAL INFORMATION "Our conference workshops address a wide variety of writing craft and business. Our most popular workshop is Our First Pages Readings—with a twist. Agents and editors read opening pages volunteered by attendees-with a few best-selling authors' openings mixed in. Think the A/E can identify the bestsellers? Not so much. Each year one of our attendees has been mistaken for a bestseller and obviously garnered requests from some on the panel. Agents attending: Carlie Webber—CK Webber Associates and TBDs. The agents will be speaking and available for meetings with attendees through our Pitch and Pages system. Editors attending: Christian Trimmer, senior editor at Disney Hyperion Books, and Jessica Williams of Harper Collins. Award-winning authors: Mark Coker, CEO of Smashwords; Kristen Lamb, social media guru, Kim Killion, book cover designer; Jennifer Jakes; Sandra Kerns; and Annette Elton. Writers may request additional information by e-mail."

⊕ DETROIT WORKING WRITERS ANNUAL WRITERS CONFERENCE

Detroit Working Writers, Box 82395, Rochester MI 48308. **E-mail:** conference@detworkingwriters.org. **Website:** dww-writers-conference.org/. Estab. 1961. 2014 dates: May 17. The theme in 2014 is "A Writer's Worth." Location is the main branch of the Clinton-Macomb Public Library in Clinton Twp, MI. Conference is one day, with breakfast, luncheon and keynote speaker, 4 breakout sessions, and three choices of workshop session. Much more info available online. Detroit Working Writers was founded on June 5, 1900, as the Detroit Press Club, The City of Detroit's first press club. Today, more than a century later, it is a 501 (c)(6) organization, and the State of Michigan's oldest writer's organization. In addition to the Conference, DWW hold quarterly workshops on craft-related topics such as the elements of poetry, finding the perfect agent, and memoir development.

COSTS $60-150, depending on early bird registration and membership status within the organization.

FLATHEAD RIVER WRITERS CONFERENCE

P.O. Box 7711, Kalispeil MT 59904-7711. (406)881-4066. **E-mail:** answers@authorsoftheflathead.org. **Website:** www.authorsoftheflathead.org/conference.asp. Estab. 1990. Two day conference packed with energizing speakers. After a focus on publishing the past two years, this year's focus is on writing, getting your manuscripts honed and ready for your readers. Highlights include two literary agents who will review 12 manuscripts one-on-one with the first 24 paid attendees requesting this opportunity, a synopsis writing workshop, a screenwriting workshop, poetry, and more.

COSTS Check teh website for updated cost information.

ACCOMMODATIONS Rooms are available at a discounted rate.

ADDITIONAL INFORMATION Watch website for additional speakers and other details. Register early as seating is limited.

GREAT LAKES WRITERS FESTIVAL

Lakeland College, P.O. Box 359, Sheboygan WI 53082-0359. **E-mail:** elderk@lakeland.edu. **Website:** www.greatlakeswritersfestival.org. Estab. 1991. Annual. Last conference held November 7-8, 2013. Conference duration: 2 days. "Festival celebrates the writing of poetry, fiction, and creative nonfiction." Site: "Lakeland College is a small, 4-year liberal arts college of 235 acres, a beautiful campus in a rural setting, founded in 1862." No themes or panels; just readings and workshops. 2013 faculty included Nick Lantz and Allyson Goldin Loomis.

COSTS Free and open to the public. Participants may purchase meals and must arrange for their own lodging.

ACCOMMODATIONS Does not offer overnight accommodations. Provides list of area hotels or lodging options.

ADDITIONAL INFORMATION All participants who would like to have their writing considered as an object for discussion during the festival workshops should submit it to Karl Elder electronically by October 15. Participants may submit material for workshops in 1 genre only (poetry, fiction, or creative nonfiction). Sponsors contest. Contest entries must contain the writer's name and address on a separate title page, typed, and be submitted as clear, hard copy on Friday at the festival registration table. Entries may be in each of 3 genres per participant, yet only 1 poem, 1 story, and/or 1 nonfiction piece may be entered. There are 2 categories—high school students on 1 hand, all others on the other—of cash awards for first place in each of the 3 genres. The judges reserve the right to decline to award a prize in 1 or more of the genres. Judges will be the editorial staff of *Seems* (a.k.a. Word of Mouth Books), excluding the festival coordinator,

Karl Elder. Information available in September. For brochure, visit website.

GREEN MOUNTAIN WRITERS CONFERENCE

47 Hazel St., Rutland VT 05701. (802)236-6133. **E-mail:** ydaley@sbcglobal.net. **E-mail:** yvonnedaley@me.com. **Website:** vermontwriters.com. **Contact:** Yvonne Daley, director. Estab. 1999. "Annual conference held in the summer. Covers fiction, creative nonfiction, poetry, journalism, nature writing, essay, memoir, personal narrative, and biography. Held at The Mountain Top Inn and Resort, a beautiful lakeside inn located in Chittenden, VT. Speakers have included Grace Paley, Ruth Stone, Howard Frank Mosher, Chris Bohjalian, Yvonne Daley, David Huddle, David Budbill, Jeffrey Lent, Verandah Porche, Tom Smith, and Chuck Clarino."

COSTS $500 before May 1; $550 and up after May 1. Partial scholarships are available.

ACCOMMODATIONS Dramatically reduced rates at The Mountain Top Inn and Resort for attendees. Close to other area hotels, b&bs in Rutland County.

ADDITIONAL INFORMATION Participants' mss can be read and commented on at a cost. Sponsors contests. Conference publishes a literary magazine featuring work of participants. Brochures available on website or e-mail. "We offer the opportunity to learn from some of the nation's best writers at a small, supportive conference in a lakeside setting that allows one-to-one feedback. Participants often continue to correspond and share work after conferences."

GULF COAST WRITERS CONFERENCE

P.O. Box 35038, Panama City FL 32412. (850)628-6028. **E-mail:** PottersvillePress@mchsi.com. **Website:** www.gulfcoastwritersconference.com/. Estab. 1999. Annual conference held in September in Panama City, Fla. Conference duration: 2 days. Average attendance: 100+. This conference is deliberately small and writer-centric with an affordable attendance price. (The 2013 event was the first time the conference was completely free.) Speakers include writers, editors and agents. Cricket Freeman of the August Agency is often in attendance. A former keynote speaker was mystery writer Michael Connelly.

⊕ HAMPTON ROADS WRITERS CONFERENCE

P.O. Box 56228, Virginia Beach VA 23456. **E-mail:** hrwriters@cox.net. **Website:** hamptonroadswriters.

org. Workshops cover fiction, nonfiction,screenplays, memoir, poetry, and the business of getting published. A bookshop, book signings, and many networking opportunities will be available. Multiple literary agents are in attendance each year to meet with writers. Much more information available on the website.

COSTS Up to $255. Costs vary. There are discounts formembers, for early bird registration, for students and more.

HEDGEBROOK

PO Box 1231, Freeland WA 98249-9911. (360)321-4786. **Fax:** (360)321-2171. **Website:** www.hedgebrook. org. **Contact:** Vito Zingarelli, residency director. Estab. 1988. "Hedgebrook is a retreat for women writers on Whidbey Island on 48 beautiful acres, near Seattle, where writers of diverse cultural backgrounds working in all genres, published or not, come from around the globe to write, rejuvenate, and be in community with each other. Located on beautiful Whidbey Island near Seattle, Hedgebrook offers one of the few residency programs in the world exclusively dedicated to supporting the creative process of women writers, and bringing their work to the world through innovative public programs."

ADDITIONAL INFORMATION Go online for more information.

⊕ HOUSTON WRITERS GUILD CONFERENCE

HOUSTON WRITERS GUILD CONFERENCE 31160, Houston TX 77231. (713)721-4773. **E-mail:** HoustonWritersGuild@Hotmail.com. **E-mail:** HoustonWritersGuild@Hotmail.com. **Website:** houston writersguild.org. 2014 date: Saturday, April 12. This annual conference, organized by the Houston Writers Guild, has concurrent sessions and tracks on the craft and business of writing. Each year, multiple agents are in attendance taking pitches from writers.

COSTS Costs are different for members and non-members. 2014 costs: $100 members, $125 non-members.

ADDITIONAL INFORMATION There is a writing contest at the event. There is also a for-pay pre-conference workshop the day before the conference.

HOW TO BE PUBLISHED WORKSHOPS

P.O. Box 100031, Irondale AL 35210-3006. **E-mail:** mike@writing2sell.com. **Website:** www.writing2sell. com. **Contact:** Michael Garrett. Estab. 1986. Workshops are offered continuously year-round at various locations. Conference duration: 1 session. Average attendance: 10-15. Workshops to "move writers of category fiction closer to publication." Focus is not on how to write, but how to get published. Site: Workshops held at college campuses and universities. Themes include marketing, idea development, characterization, and ms critique. Special critique is offered, but advance submission is not required. Workshop information available on website. Accepts inquiries by e-mail.

COSTS $79-99.

JAMES RIVER WRITERS CONFERENCE

ArtWorks Studios 136, 320 Hull St., #136, Richmond VA 23224. (804)433-3790. **Fax:** (804)291-1466. **E-mail:** info@jamesriverwriters.com; fallconference@james riverwriters.com. **Website:** www.jamesriverwriters. com. **Contact:** Katharine Herndon, exec. director. Estab. 2003.

COSTS In 2013, the cost was up to $240, though less expensive options were available. See the website for all pricing options.

ACCOMMODATIONS Richmond is easily accessibly by air and train. Provides list of area hotels or lodging options. "Each year we arrange for special conference rates at an area hotel."

ADDITIONAL INFORMATION Workshop material is not required, however we have offered an option for submissions: the first pages critique session in which submissions are read before a panel of agents and editors who are seeing them for the first time and are asked to react on the spot. No additional fee. No guarantee that a particular submission will be read. Details posted on the website, www.jamesriverwriters.com. Information available in June. For brochure, visit website. Agents participate in conference. Editors participate in conference. Both meet with writers to take pitches. Previous agents in attendance include April Eberhardt, Deborah Grosvenor, Victoria Skurnick, and Paige Wheeler.

JOURNEY INTO THE IMAGINATION: A FIVE-DAY WRITING RETREAT

995 Chapman Rd., Yorktown NY 10598. (914)962-4432. **E-mail:** emily@emilyhanlon.com. **Website:** www.thefictionwritersjourney.com/Spring_Writing_Retreat.html. **Contact:** Emily Hanlon. PO Box 536 Estab. 2004. Annual. 2014 dates: May 6-11. Average attendance: 8-12. "Purpose of workshop: fiction, memoir, short story, creativity, and the creative process." Site: Pendle Hill Retreat Center in Wallingford, PA

(just north of Philadelphia). "Excellent food and lovely surroundings and accommodations. The core of this weekend's work is welcoming the unknown into your writing. We will go on a magical mystery tour to find and embrace new characters and to deepen our relationship to characters who already may people our stories. Bring something on which you are already working or simply bring along your Inner Writer, pen and a journal, and let the magic unfold!"

COSTS 2014: 5 nights—$1150 if you register before March 1. $1250 after March 1. All rooms are private with shared bath.

ADDITIONAL INFORMATION For brochure, visit website.

⊕ KACHEMAK BAY WRITERS CONFERENCE

Kenai Peninsula College—Kachemak Bay Campus, 533 East Pioneer Ave., Homer AK 99603. **E-mail:** iyconf@uaa.alaska.edu. **Website:** writersconference.uaa.alaska.edu. Annual writers conference held in the summer (usually June). 2014 dates: June 13-17; keynote speaker is Alice Sebold. Sponsored by Kachemak Bay Campus—Kenai Peninsula College / UAA. This nationally recognized writing conference features workshops, readings and panel presentations in fiction, poetry, nonfiction, and the business of writing. There are "open mic" sessions for conference registrants; evening readings open to the public; agent / editor consultations, and more.

COSTS See the website. Some scholarships available; see the website.

ACCOMMODATIONS Homer is 225 miles south of Anchorage, Alaska on the southern tip of the Kenai Peninsula and the shores of Kachemak Bay. There are multiple hotels in the area.

⊕ KENTUCKY WRITERS CONFERENCE

Western Kentucky University and the Southern Kentucky Book Fest, Western Kentucky University Libraries, 1906 College Heights Blvd., Bowling Green KY 42101. (270)745-4502. **E-mail:** kristie.lowry@wku.edu. **Website:** www.sokybookfest.org/KYWritersConf. **Contact:** Kristie Lowry. This event is entirely free to the public. (2014 dates: April 25-26.) Duration: 1 day. Precedes the Southern Kentucky Book Fest the next day. Authors who will be participating in the Book Fest on Saturday will give attendees at the Writers Conference the benefit of their wisdom on Friday. Free workshops on a variety of writing topics will be presented during this day-long event. Sessions run for 75 minutes and the day begins at 9:00am and ends at 3:30pm. The conference is open to anyone who would like to attend including high school students, college students, teachers, and the general public.

KENYON REVIEW WRITERS WORKSHOP

Kenyon College, Gambier OH 43022. (740)427-5207. **Fax:** (740)427-5417. **E-mail:** kenyonreview@kenyon.edu; writers@kenyonreview.org. **Website:** www.kenyonreview.org. **Contact:** Anna Duke Reach, director. Estab. 1990. Annual 8-day workshop held in June. Participants apply in poetry, fiction, creative nonfiction, literary hybrid/book arts or writing online, and then participate in intensive daily workshops which focus on the generation and revision of significant new work. Held on the campus of Kenyon College in the rural village of Gambier, Ohio. Workshop leaders have included David Baker, Ron Carlson, Rebecca McClanahan, Meghan O'Rourke, Linda Gregorson, Dinty Moore, Tara Ison, Jane Hamilton, Lee K. Abbott, and Nancy Zafris.

COSTS $1,995; includes tuition, room and board.

ACCOMMODATIONS The workshop operates a shuttle to and from Gambier and the airport in Columbus, Ohio. Offers overnight accommodations. Participants are housed in Kenyon College student housing. The cost is covered in the tuition.

ADDITIONAL INFORMATION Application includes a writing sample. Admission decisions are made on a rolling basis. Workshop information is available online at www.kenyonreview.org/workshops in November. For brochure send e-mail, visit website, call, fax. Accepts inquiries by SASE, e-mail, phone, fax.

KINDLING WORDS EAST

VT **Website:** www.kindlingwords.org. Annual retreat held in late January near Burlington, Vermont. A retreat with three strands: writer, illustrator and editor; professional level. Intensive workshops for each strand, and an open schedule for conversations and networking. Registration limited to approximately 70. Hosted by the 4-star Inn at Essex (room and board extra). Participants must be published by a CCBC listed publisher, or if in publishing, occupy a professional position. Registration opens August 1 or as posted on the website, and fills quickly. Check website to see if spaces are available, to sign up to be notified when registration opens each year, or for more information.

LA JOLLA WRITERS CONFERENCE

P.O. Box 178122, San Diego CA 92177. (858)467-1978. **E-mail:** akuritz@san.rr.com. **Website:** www.lajolla writersconference.com. **Contact:** Jared Kuritz, director. Estab. 2001. Annual conference held in October/November. Conference duration: 3 days. Average attendance: 200. The LJWC covers all genres and both fiction and nonfiction as well as the business of writing. We take particular pride in educating our attendees on the business aspect of the book industry and have agents, editors, publishers, publicists, and distributors teach classes. There is unprecedented access to faculty at the LJWC. Our conference offers lecture sessions that run for 50 minutes, and workshops that run for 110 minutes. Each block period is dedicated to either workshop or lecture-style classes, with 6-8 classes on various topics available each block. For most workshop classes, you are encouraged to bring written work for review. Literary agents from prestigious agencies such as The Andrea Brown Literary Agency, The Dijkstra Agency, The McBride Agency and Full Circle Literary Group, the Zimmerman Literary Agency, the Van Haitsma Literary Agency, the Farris Literary Agency and more have participated in the past, teaching workshops in which they are familiarized with attendee work. Late night and early bird sessions are also available. The conference creates a strong sense of community, and it has seen many of its attendees successfully published.

COSTS Information available online at website.

LAS VEGAS WRITERS CONFERENCE

Henderson Writers' Group, 614 Mosswood Dr., Henderson NV 89015. (702)564-2488; or, toll-free, (866)869-7842. **E-mail:** marga614@mysticpublish ers.com. **Website:** www.lasvegaswritersconference. com. Annual. Held in April. Conference duration: 3 days. Average attendance: 150 maximum. "Join writing professionals, agents, industry experts, and your colleagues for 3 days in Las Vegas as they share their knowledge on all aspects of the writer's craft. While there are formal pitch sessions, panels, workshops, and seminars, the faculty is also available throughout the conference for informal discussions and advice. Plus, you're bound to meet a few new friends, too. Workshops, seminars, and expert panels will take you through writing in many genres including fiction, creative nonfiction, screenwriting, journalism, and business and technical writing. There will be many

Q&A panels for you to ask the experts all your questions." Site: Sam's Town Hotel and Gambling Hall in Las Vegas.

COSTS $425 until 1/14/14; $475 starting 1/15/14; $500 at door; $300 for one day.

ADDITIONAL INFORMATION Sponsors contest. Agents and editors participate in conference.

LAURA THOMAS JUNIOR WRITERS AUTHORS CONFERENCE

Laura Thomas Communications, Delta British Colombia V6X 2M9 Canada. (604)307-4971. **E-mail:** laura@laurathomascommunications.com. **Website:** laurathomascommunications.com/conference/. **Contact:** Laura Thomas. Estab. 2013. New conference held in the fall and spring each year. Conference duration: 1 day, 9-5. Covers poetry and writing for children and young adults, ages 9-21. Fall 2013 conference held in Richmond at Sandsman Signature Hotel & Resort. Spring 2014 conference held at the Manor House Hotel, Guildford, Surrey, UK, in May. Speakers have included Michelle Barker (author and editor), Deneka Michaud (journalist and communications professional), Lois Peterson (author), Darlene Foster (author), and George Opacic (author and publisher).

COSTS $89 single ticket and $79 sibling rate. Includes workshops and meals, scholarships are available.

ADDITIONAL INFORMATION Writers may request information by e-mail.

MENDOCINO COAST WRITERS CONFERENCE

1211 Del Mar Dr., second address is P.O. Box 2087, Fort Bragg CA 95437. (707)485-4032. **E-mail:** info@ mcwc.org. **Website:** www.mcwc.org. Estab. 1988. Annual conference held in July. Average attendance: 80. Provides workshops for fiction, nonfiction, and poetry. Held at a small community college campus on the northern Pacific Coast. Workshop leaders have included Kim Addonizio, Lynne Barrett, John Dufresne, John Lescroart, Ben Percy, Luis Rodriguez, Peter Orner, Judith Barrington and Ellen Sussman. Agents and publishers will be speaking and available for meetings with attendees.

COSTS $525+ (includes panels, meals, 2 socials with guest readers, 4 public events, 3 morning intensive workshops in 1 of 6 subjects, and a variety of afternoon panels and lectures).

ACCOMMODATIONS Information on overnight accommodations is made available.

ADDITIONAL INFORMATION Emphasis is on writers who are also good teachers. Registration opens March 15. Send inquiries via e-mail.

MIDWEST WRITERS WORKSHOP

Ball State University, Department of Journalism, Muncie IN 47306. (765)282-1055. **E-mail:** midwest writers@yahoo.com. **Website:** www.midwestwriters.org. **Contact:** Jama Kehoe Bigger, director. Annual workshop held in late July in eastern Indiana. Writer workshops geared toward writers of all levels. Topics include most genres. Faculty/speakers have included Joyce Carol Oates, George Plimpton, Clive Cussler, Haven Kimmel, James Alexander Thom, William Zinsser, Phillip Gulley, Lee Martin, and numerous bestselling mystery, literary fiction, young adult, and children's authors. Workshop also includes agent pitch sessions ms evaluation and a writing contest. Registration tentatively limited to 200.
COSTS $150-375. Most meals included.
ADDITIONAL INFORMATION Offers scholarships. See website for more information.

⊕ MISSOURI WRITERS' GUILD CONFERENCE

St. Louis MO **E-mail:** mwgconferenceinfo@gmail.com. **Website:** www.missouriwritersguild.org. **Contact:** Tricia Sanders, vice president/conference chairman. Writer and illustrator workshops geared to all levels. **Open to students.** Annual conference held early April or early May each year. Annual conference "gives writers the opportunity to hear outstanding speakers and to receive information on marketing, research, and writing techniques." Agents, editors, and published authors in attendance.
ACCOMMODATIONS 2014: Ramada Plaza Hotel downtown.
ADDITIONAL INFORMATION The primary contact individual changes every year, because the conference chair changes every year. See the website for contact info.

MONTROSE CHRISTIAN WRITERS' CONFERENCE

218 Locust St., Montrose PA 18801. (570)278-1001 or (800)598-5030. **Fax:** (570)278-3061. **E-mail:** mbc@montrosebible.org. **Website:** montrosebible.org. Estab. 1990. "Annual conference held in July. Offers workshops, editorial appointments, and professional critiques. We try to meet a cross-section of writing needs, for beginners and advanced, covering fiction, poetry, and writing for children. It is small enough to allow personal interaction between attendees and faculty. Speakers have included William Petersen, Mona Hodgson, Jim Fletcher, and Terri Gibbs." Held in Montrose, from July 20-25, 2014.
COSTS Tuition is $180.
ACCOMMODATIONS Will meet planes in Binghamton, NY and Scranton, PA. On-site accommodations: room and board $325-370/conference; $75-80/day including food (2014 rates). RV court available.
ADDITIONAL INFORMATION "Writers can send work ahead of time and have it critiqued for a small fee." The attendees are usually church related. The writing has a Christian emphasis. Conference information available in April. For brochure, visit website, e-mail or call. Accepts inquiries by phone or e-mail.

JENNY MCKEAN MOORE COMMUNITY WORKSHOPS

English Department, George Washingtion University, 801 22nd St. NW, Rome Hall, Suite 760, Washington DC 20052. (202) 994-6180. **Fax:** (202) 994-7915. **E-mail:** lpageinc@aol.com. **Website:** www.gwu.edu/~english/creative_jennymckeanmoore.html. **Contact:** Lisa Page, Acting Director of creative writing. Estab. 1976. Workshop held each semester at the university. Average attendance: 15. Concentration varies depending on professor—usually fiction or poetry. The Creative Writing department brings an established poet or novelist to campus each year to teach a writing workshop for GW students and a free community workshop for adults in the larger Washington community. Details posted on website in June, with an application deadline at the end of August or in early September.
ADDITIONAL INFORMATION Admission is competitive and by ms.

MUSE AND THE MARKETPLACE

Grub Street, 160 Boylston St., 4th Floor, Boston MA 02116. (617)695.0075. **E-mail:** info@grubstreet.org. **Website:** grubstreet.org/. The conferences are held in the late spring, such as early May. (2014 dates are May 2-4.) Conference duration: 3 days. Average attendance: 400. Dozens of agents are in attendance to meet writers and take pitches. Previous keynote speakers include Jonathan Franzen. The conferences has workshops on all aspects of writing.
COSTS Varies, depending on if you're a Member or Non-Member (includes 6 workshop sessions and 2

Hour of Power sessions with options for the Manuscript Mart and a Five-Star lunch with authors, editors and agents). Other passes are available for Saturday-only and Sunday-only guests.

NAPA VALLEY WRITERS' CONFERENCE

Napa Valley College, 1088 College Ave., St. Helena CA 94574. (707)967-2900, x1611. **E-mail:** writecon@napa valley.edu. **Website:** www.napawritersconference.org. **Contact:** John Leggett and Anne Evans, program directors. Estab. 1981. Established 1981. Annual weeklong event, 2014 dates: July 27—Aug. 1. Location: Upper Valley Campus in the historic town of St. Helena, 25 miles north of Napa in the heart of the valley's wine growing community. Excellent cuisine provided by Napa Valley Cooking School. Average attendance: 48 in poetry and 48 in fiction. "Serious writers of all backgrounds and experience are welcome to apply." Offers poets workshops, lectures, faculty readings, ms critiques, and meetings with editors. "Poetry session provides the opportunity to work both on generating new poems and on revising previously written ones." **COSTS** Total participation fee is $900. More cost info (including financial assistance info) is online.

ADDITIONAL INFORMATION The conference is held at the Upper Valley Campus of Napa Valley College, located in the heart of California's Wine Country. During the conference week, attendees' meals are provided by the Napa Valley Cooking School, which offers high quality, intensive training for aspiring chefs. The goal of the program is to provide each student with hands-on, quality, culinary and pastry skills required for a career in a fine-dining establishment. The disciplined and professional learning environment, availability of global externships, low student teacher ratio and focus on sustainability make the Napa Valley Cooking School unique.

NETWO WRITERS CONFERENCE

Northeast Texas Writers Organization, P.O. Box 411, Winfield TX 75493. (469)867-2624 or Paul at (903)573-6084. **E-mail:** jimcallan@winnsboro.com. **Website:** www.netwo.org. Estab. 1987. Annual conference held in April. (2014 dates are April 25-26.) Conference duration: 2 days. Presenters include agents, writers, editors, and publishers. Agents in attendance will take pitches from writers. The conference features a writing contest, pitch sessions, critiques from professionals, as well as dozens of workshops and presentations. **COSTS** $60+ (discount offered for early registration).

ACCOMMODATIONS Online, we have posted information on lodging - motels and hotels. As the conference has moved to the Mount Pleasant Civic Center, we no longer have the "dorm accommodations" available in 2011 and before. The NETWO Writers Conference is at the Mount Pleasant Civic Center, in Mt. Pleasant, Texas. Located on U.S. Business 271 just one block south of Interstate 30, it is easily accessible from north, south, east and west. It offers excellent facilities: climate control, large rooms, excellent sound systems, ability to handle Power Point presentations, ample room for the on-site lunch which is part of the conference, improved restroom facilities, and private rooms for the one-on-one interviews with agents, editor and publisher. There is ample parking available. Several motels are within two blocks.

ADDITIONAL INFORMATION Conference is co-sponsored by the Texas Commission on the Arts. See website for current updates.

NIMROD ANNUAL WRITERS' WORKSHOP

800 S. Tucker Dr., Tulsa OK 74104. (918)631-3080. **E-mail:** nimrod@utulsa.edu. **Website:** www.utulsa.edu/nimrod. **Contact:** Eilis O'Neal, editor-in-chief. Estab. 1978. Annual conference held in October. Conference duration: 1 day. Offers one-on-one editing sessions, readings, panel discussions, and master classes in fiction, poetry, nonfiction, memoir, and fantasy writing. Speakers have included Ted Kooser, Colum McCann, Molly Peacock, Peter S. Beagle, Aimee Nezhukumatathil, Philip Levine, and Linda Pastan. Full conference details are online in August.

COSTS Approximately $50. Lunch provided. Scholarships available for students.

ADDITIONAL INFORMATION *Nimrod International Journal* sponsors *Nimrod* Literary Awards: The Katherine Anne Porter Prize for fiction and The Pablo Neruda Prize for poetry. Poetry and fiction prizes: $2,000 each and publication (1st prize); $1,000 each and publication (2nd prize). Deadline: must be postmarked no later than April 30.

NORTH CAROLINA WRITERS' NETWORK FALL CONFERENCE

P.O. Box 21591, Winston-Salem NC 27120. (336)293-8844. **E-mail:** mail@ncwriters.org. **Website:** www.ncwriters.org. Estab. 1985. Annual conference held in November in different NC venues. Average attendance: 250. This organization hosts 2 conferences: 1 in the spring and 1 in the fall. Each conference is a weekend full of workshops, panels, book signings, and readings (including open mic). There will be a keynote speaker, a variety of sessions on the craft and business of writing, and opportunities to meet with agents and editors.

COSTS Approximately $250 (includes 4 meals).

ACCOMMODATIONS Special rates are usually available at the Conference Hotel, but conferees must make their own reservations.

ADDITIONAL INFORMATION Available at www.ncwriters.org.

NORTHERN COLORADO WRITERS CONFERENCE

108 East Monroe Dr., Fort Collins CO 80525. (970)556-0908. **E-mail:** kerrie@northerncolorado writers.com. **Website:** www.northerncoloradowriters.com. Estab. 2006. Annual conference held in the spring (usually March or April) in Colorado. Conference duration: 2-3 days. The conference features a variety of speakers, agents and editors. There are workshops and presentations on fiction, nonfiction, screenwriting, children's books, staying inspired, and more. Previous agents who have attended and taken pitches from writers include Jessica Regel, Kristen Nelson, Rachelle Gardner, Andrea Brown, Ken Sherman Jessica Faust, Jon Sternfeld, and Jeffrey McGraw. Each conference features more than 30 workshops from which to choose from. Previous keynotes include Chuck Sambuchino. Andrew McCarthy and Stephen J. Cannell.

COSTS $295-445, depending on what package the attendee selects, and whether you're a member or nonmember.

ACCOMMODATIONS The conference is hosted at the Fort Collins Hilton, where rooms are available at a special rate.

OKLAHOMA WRITERS' FEDERATION, INC. ANNUAL CONFERENCE

3800 Bonaire Place, Edmond OK 73013. **Website:** www.owfi.org. **Contact:** Christine Jarmola, president. Annual conference held just outside Oklahoma City. Held first weekend in May each year. Writer workshops geared toward all levels. Oklahoma Writers Federation, Inc. is open and welcoming to writers of all genres and all skill levels. Our goal is to help writers become better and to help beginning writers understand and master the craft of writing.Editorial Comments The theme of our conference is to create

good stories with strong bones. We will be exploring cultural writing and cultural sensitivity in writing. This year we will also be looking at the cutting edge of publishing and the options it is producing.

COSTS $175 before April; $200 after April. Cost includes awards banquet and famous author banquet. Three extra sessions are available for an extra fee. Visit our website for a complete faculty list and conference information

⊕ OREGON CHRISTIAN WRITERS SUMMER CONFERENCE

Red Lion Hotel on the River, 909 N. Hayden Island Dr., Portland OR 97217-8118. **E-mail:** summerconf@oregonchristianwriters.org. **Website:** www.oregonchristianwriters.org. **Contact:** Lindy Jacobs, OCW Summer Conference Director. Estab. 1989. Held annually in August at the Red Lion Hotel on the River, a full-service hotel. Conference duration: 4 days. 2014 dates: August 4-7; 2015 dates: August 10-13. Average attendance: 225 (175 writers, 50 faculty). Top national editors, agents, and authors in the field of Christian publishing teach 12 intensive coaching classes and 30 workshops plus critique sessions. Published authors as well as emerging writers have opportunities to improve their craft, get feedback through manuscript reviews, meet one-on-one with editors and agents, and have half-hour mentoring appointments with published authors. Classes include fiction, nonfiction, memoir, young adult, poetry, magazine articles, devotional writing, children's books, and marketing. Daily general sessions include worship and an inspirational keynote address. Each year contacts made during the OCW summer conference lead to publishing contracts. 2014 conference theme will be "Writing with God: Take Heart," based on Psalm 27:14. 2014 Keynote speakers: Allen Arnold and Dan Walsh. Agents: Chip MacGregor, Mary Sue Seymour, Sue Brower, Bill Jensen, and Sandra Bishop. Other speakers/teachers: Susan May Warren, James Rubart, Randy Ingermanson, Jeff Gerke, Mary DeMuth, Jill Williamson, Leslie Gould, Susan Meissner, Joanna Echols, and Susan King. Past speakers have included: Liz Curtis Higgs, Francine Rivers, Bill Myers, Jeff Gerke, Angella Hunt, James L. Rubart, Susan May Warren, and James Scott Bell.

COSTS $475 for OCW members, $495 for nonmembers. Registration fee includes all classes, workshops, and 2 lunches and 3 dinners. Lodging additional. Full-time registered conferees may also pre-submit three proposals for review by an editor through the conference, plus sign up for a half-hour mentoring appointment with an author.

ACCOMMODATIONS Conference is held at the Red Lion on the River Hotel. Conferees wishing to stay at the hotel must make a reservation through the hotel. Some conferees commute. A block of rooms has been reserved at the hotel at a special rate for conferees and held until mid-July. The hotel reservation link will be posted on the website in late spring. Shuttle bus transportation will be provided by the hotel for conferees from Portland Airport (PDX) to the hotel, which is 20 minutes away.

ADDITIONAL INFORMATION Conference details will be posted online beginning in January. All conferees are welcome to attend the Cascade Awards ceremony, which takes place Wednesday evening during the conference. For more information about the Cascade Writing Contest, please check the website.

OZARK CREATIVE WRITERS, INC. CONFERENCE

P.O. Box 424, Eureka Springs AR 72632. **E-mail:** ozarkcreativewriters@gmail.com. **Website:** www.ozarkcreativewriters.org. Open to professional and amateur writers, workshops are geared to all levels and all forms of the creative process and literary arts. Sessions sometimes include songwriting, with presentations by best-selling authors, editors, and agents. The OCW Conference promotes writing by offering competition in all genres. The annual event is held in October at the Inn of the Ozarks, in the resort town of Eureka Springs, Arkansas. Approximately 200 attend each year; many also enter the creative writing competitions.

PACIFIC COAST CHILDREN'S WRITERS WHOLE-NOVEL WORKSHOP: FOR ADULTS AND TEENS

P.O. Box 244, Aptos CA 95001. (831)684-2042. **Website:** www.childrenswritersworkshop.com. Estab. 2003. 2014 dates: Oct. 17-19. "Our seminar offers semi-advanced through published adult writers an editor and/or agent critique on their full novel or 15-30 page partial. (Mid-book and synopsis critique may be included with the partial.) A concurrent workshop is open to students age 13 and up, who give adults target-reader feedback. Focus on craft as a marketing tool. Team-taught master classes (open clinics for manuscript critiques) explore such topics as "Story Architecture and Arcs." Continuous close contact with faculty, who have included Andrea Brown, agent, and Simon Boughton, VP/executive editor at 3 Macmillan imprints. **Past seminars:** Oct. 10-12, 2013. Registration limited to 16 adults and 10 teens. For the most critique options, submit sample chapters and synopsis with e-application by mid May; open until filled. **Content:** Character-driven novels with protagonists ages 11 and older. Collegial format; 90 percent hands-on. Our pre-workshop anthology of peer manuscripts maximizes learning and networking. Several enrollees have landed contracts as a direct result of our seminar. **Details:** visit our website and e-mail Director Nancy Sondel via the contact form."

PACIFIC NORTHWEST WRITER ASSN. SUMMER WRITER'S CONFERENCE

PMB 2717, 1420 NW Gilman Blvd., Ste. 2, Issaquah WA 98027. (425)673-2665. **E-mail:** pnwa@pnwa.org. **Website:** www.pnwa.org. Writer conference geared toward beginner, intermediate, advanced and professional levels. Meet agents and editors. Learn craft from renowned authors. Uncover new marketing secrets. PNWA's 59th Annual Conference will be held July 17-20, 2014, at the Hilton Seattle Airport & Conference Center, at the Hyatt Regency, Bellevue, WA 98004. This event usually has 10-20 literary agents in attendance taking pitches from writers.

PENNWRITERS CONFERENCE

RR #2, Box 241, Middlebury Center PA 16935. **Website:** www.pennwriters.org/prod/. Estab. 1987. The Mission of Pennwriters Inc. is to help writers of all levels,from the novice to the award-winning and multi-published, improve and succeed in their craft. The annual Pennwriters conference is held every year in May in Pennsylvania, switching between locations -- Lancaster in even years and Pittsburgh in odd years. 2014 event: May 16-18 at Eden Resort in Lancaster.

ACCOMMODATIONS See website for current information.

ADDITIONAL INFORMATION Sponsors contest. Published authors judge fiction in various categories. Agent/editor appointments are available on a first-come, first serve basis.

PHILADELPHIA WRITERS' CONFERENCE

P.O. Box 7171, Elkins Park PA 19027-0171. (215) 619-7422. **E-mail:** info@pwcwriters.org. **E-mail:** info@pwcwriters.org. **Website:** pwcwriters.org. Estab. 1949.

Annual. Conference held in June. Average attendance: 160-200. Conference covers many forms of writing: novel, short story, genre fiction, nonfiction book, magazine writing, blogging, juvenile, poetry.

ACCOMMODATIONS Wyndham Hotel (formerly the Holiday Inn), Independence Mall, Fourth and Arch Streets, Philadelphia, PA 19106-2170. "Hotel offers discount for early registration."

ADDITIONAL INFORMATION Accepts inquiries by e-mail. Agents and editors attend conference. Visit us on the web for further agent and speaker details. Many questions are answered online.

PIKES PEAK WRITERS CONFERENCE

Pikes Peak Writers, PO Box 64273, Colorado Springs CO 80962. (719)244-6220. **E-mail:** info@pikespeak writers.com. **Website:** www.pikespeakwriters.com. Estab. 1993. Annual conference held in April Conference duration: 3 days. Average attendance: 300. Workshops, presentations, and panels focus on writing and publishing mainstream and genre fiction (romance, science fiction/fantasy, suspense/thrillers, action/adventure, mysteries, children's, young adult). Agents and editors are available for meetings with attendees on Saturday.

COSTS $300-500 (includes all meals).

ACCOMMODATIONS Marriott Colorado Springs holds a block of rooms at a special rate for attendees until late March.

ADDITIONAL INFORMATION Readings with critiques are available on Friday afternoon. Also offers a contest for unpublished manuscripts; entrants need not attend the conference. Deadline: November 1. Registration and contest entry forms are online; brochures are available in January. Send inquiries via e-mail.

ROCKY MOUNTAIN FICTION WRITERS COLORADO GOLD

Rocky Mountain Fiction Writers, P.O. Box 735, Confier CO 80433. **E-mail:** conference@rmfw.org. **Website:** www.rmfw.org. Estab. 1982. Annual conference held in September. Conference duration: 3 days. Average attendance: 350. Themes include general novel-length fiction, genre fiction, contemporary romance, mystery, science fiction/fantasy, mainstream, young adult, screenwriting, short stories, and historical fiction. Speakers have included Margaret George, Jodi Thomas, Bernard Cornwell, Terry Brooks, Dorothy Cannell, Patricia Gardner Evans, Diane Mott Da-

vidson, Constance O'Day, Connie Willis, Clarissa Pinkola Estes, Michael Palmer, Jennifer Unter, Margaret Marr, Ashley Krass, and Andren Barzvi. Approximately 8 editors and 5 agents attend annually.

COSTS Available online.

ACCOMMODATIONS Special rates will be available at conference hotel.

ADDITIONAL INFORMATION Editor-conducted workshops are limited to 8 participants for critique, with auditing available. Pitch appointments available at no charge. Friday morning master classes available. Craft workshops include beginner through professional levels. New as of 2013: Writers' retreat available immediately following conference; space is limited.

⊕ SALT CAY WRITERS RETREAT

Salt Cay Bahamas. (732)267-6449. **E-mail:** admin@ saltcaywritersretreat.com. **Website:** www.saltcay writersretreat.com. **Contact:** Karen Dionne and Christopher Graham. 5-day retreat held in the Bahamas in October. "The Salt Cay Writers Retreat is particularly suited for novelists (especially those writing literary, upmarket commercial fiction, or genre novelists wanting to write a break-out book), memoirists and narrative non-fiction writers. However, any author (published or not-yet-published) who wishes to take their writing to the next level is welcome to apply." Speakers have included or will include Editors Chuck Adams (Algonquin Books), Amy Einhorn (Amy Einhorn Books); Agents Jeff Kleinman, Michelle Brower, Erin Niumata, Erin Harris (Folio Literary Management); authors Robert Goolrick, Jacquelyn Mitchard.

COSTS $2,450 through May 1; $2,950 after.

ACCOMMODATIONS Comfort Suites, Paradise Island, Nassau, Bahamas.

SAN DIEGO STATE UNIVERSITY WRITERS' CONFERENCE

SDSU College of Extended Studies, 5250 Campanile Dr., San Diego State University, San Diego CA 92182-1920. (619)594-2517. **Fax:** (619)594-8566. **E-mail:** sd suuwritersconference@mail.sdsu.edu. **Website:** ces. sdsu.edu/writers. Estab. 1984. Annual conference held in January/February. Conference duration: 2.5 days. Average attendance: 350. Covers fiction, nonfiction, scriptwriting and e-books. Held at the Doubletree Hotel in Mission Valley. Each year the conference offers a variety of workshops for the beginner and advanced writers. This conference allows the individual writer to choose which workshop best suits his/her needs. In addition to the workshops, editor reading appointments and agent/editor consultation appointments are provided so attendees may meet with editors and agents one-on-one to discuss specific questions. A reception is offered Saturday immediately following the workshops, offering attendees the opportunity to socialize with the faculty in a relaxed atmosphere. Last year, approximately 60 faculty members attended.

COSTS Approximately $399-435

ACCOMMODATIONS Attendees must make their own travel arrangements. A conference rate for attendees is available at the Doubletree Hotel.

SAN FRANCISCO WRITERS CONFERENCE

1029 Jones St., San Francisco CA 94109. (415)673-0939. **Fax:** (415)673-0367. **E-mail:** Barbara@sfwriters.org. **Website:** sfwriters.org. **Contact:** Barbara Santos, marketing director. Estab. 2003. "Annual conference held President's Day weekend in February. Average attendance: 400+. Top authors, respected literary agents, and major publishing houses are at the event so attendees can make face-to-face contact with all the right people. Writers of nonfiction, fiction, poetry, and specialty writing (children's books, cookbooks, travel, etc.) will all benefit from the event. There are important sessions on marketing, self-publishing, technology, and trends in the publishing industry. Plus, there's an optional 4-hour session called Speed Dating for Agents where attendees can meet with 20+ agents. Speakers have included Jennifer Crusie, Richard Paul Evans, Jamie Raab, Mary Roach, Jane Smiley, Debbie Macomber, Firoozeh Dumas, Zilpha Keatley Snyder, Steve Berry, Jacquelyn Mitchard. More than 20 agents and editors participate each year, many of whom will be available for meetings with attendees."

COSTS Check the website for pricing on later dates. 2014 pricing was $650-795 depending on when you signed up and early bird registration, etc.

ACCOMMODATIONS The Intercontinental Mark Hopkins Hotel is a historic landmark at the top of Nob Hill in San Francisco. The hotel is located so that everyone arriving at the Oakland or San Francisco airport can take BART to either the Embarcadero or Powell Street exits, then walk or take a cable car or taxi directly to the hotel.

ADDITIONAL INFORMATION "Present yourself in a professional manner and the contact you will make will be invaluable to your writing career. Brochures and registration are online."

☼ SASKATCHEWAN FESTIVAL OF WORDS

217 Main St. N., Moose Jaw SK S6J 0W1 Canada. **Website:** www.festivalofwords.com. Estab. 1997. Annual 4-day event, third week of July (2014 dates: July 17-20). Location: Moose Jaw Library/Art Museum complex in Crescent Park. Average attendance: about 4,000 admissions. "Canadian authors up close and personal for readers and writers of all ages in mystery, poetry, memoir, fantasy, graphic novels, history, and novel. Each summer festival includes more than 60 events within 2 blocks of historic Main Street. Audience favorite activities include workshops for writers, audience readings, drama,performance poetry, concerts, panels, and music."

ACCOMMODATIONS Information available at www.templegardens.sk.ca, campgrounds, and bed and breakfast establishments. Complete information about festival presenters, events, costs, and schedule also available on website.

☼ SCBWI--CANADA EAST

Canada. **E-mail:** canadaeast@scbwi.org. **Website:** www.canadaeast.scbwi.org. **Contact:** Lizann Flatt, regional advisor. Writer and illustrator events geared toward all levels. Usually offers one event in spring and another in the fall. Check website Events pages for updated information.

SCBWI COLORADO/WYOMING (ROCKY MOUNTAIN); EVENTS

E-mail: denise@rmcscbwi.org; todd.tuell@rmc scbwi.org. **Website:** www.rmc.scbwi.org. **Contact:** Todd Tuell and Denise Vega, co-regional advisors. SCBWI Rocky Mountain chapter (CO/WY) offers special events, schmoozes, meetings, and conferences throughout the year. Major events: Fall Conference (annually, September); Summer Retreat, "Big Sur in the Rockies" (bi- and triannually). More info on website.

SCBWI--MIDATLANTIC; ANNUAL FALL CONFERENCE

P.O. Box 3215, Reston VA 20195. **E-mail:** teaganek@ hotmail.com; valopttrsn@verizon.net. **Website:** midatlantic.scbwi.org/. **Contact:** Erin Teagan and Valerie Patterson, conference co-chairs; Ellen R. Braff, advisor. For updates and details visit website. Registration limited to 275. Conference fills quickly. Cost: $145 for SCBWI members; $175 for nonmembers. Includes continental breakfast and boxed lunch. Optional craft-focused workshops and individual consultations with conference faculty are available for additional fees.

SCBWI WINTER CONFERENCE ON WRITING AND ILLUSTRATING FOR CHILDREN

8271 Beverly Blvd., Los Angeles CA 90048. (323)782-1010. **Fax:** (323)782-1892. **E-mail:** scbwi@scbwi.org. **Website:** www.scbwi.org. **Contact:** Stephen Mooser. Estab. 2000. (formerly SCBWI Midyear Conference), Society of Children's book Writers and Illustrators. Annual. Conference held in February. Average attendance: 1,000. Conference is to promote writing and illustrating for children: picture books; fiction; nonfiction; middle grade and young adult; network with professionals; financial planning for writers; marketing your book; art exhibition; etc. Site: Manhattan.

COSTS See website for current cost and conference information.

ADDITIONAL INFORMATION SCBWI also holds an annual summer conference in August in Los Angeles. See the listing in the West section or visit website for details.

☺ THE SCHOOL FOR WRITERS FALL WORKSHOP

The Humber School for Writers, Humber Institute of Technology & Advanced Learning, 3199 Lake Shore Blvd. W., Toronto ON M8V 1K8 Canada. (416)675-6622. **E-mail:** antanas.sileika@humber.ca; hilary.higgins@humber.ca. **Website:** www.humber.ca/scapa/programs/school-writers. The School for Writers Workshop has moved to the fall with the International Festival of Authors. The workshop runs during the last week in October. Conference duration: 1 week. Average attendance: 60. New writers from around the world gather to study with faculty members to work on their novels, short stories, poetry, or creative nonfiction. Agents and editors participate in the conference. Include a work-in-progress with your registration. Faculty has included Martin Amis, David Mitchell, Kevin Barry, Rachel Kuschner, Peter Carey, Roddy Doyle, Tim O'Brien, Andrea Levy, Barry Unsworth, Edward Albee, Ha Jin, Julia Glass, Mavis Gallant, Bruce Jay Friedman, Isabel Huggan, Alistair MacLeod, Lisa Moore, Kim Moritsugu, Francine Prose,

Paul Quarrington, Olive Senior, and D.M. Thomas, Annabel Lyon, Mary Gaitskill, M. G. Vassanji.

COSTS around $850 (in 2014). Some limited scholarships are available.

ADDITIONAL INFORMATION Accepts inquiries by e-mail, phone, and fax.

SCHOOL OF THE ARTS AT RHINELANDER UW-MADISON CONTINUING STUDIES

21 N Park St., 7th Floor, Madison WI 53715-1218. (608)262-7389. **E-mail:** lkaufman@dcs.wisc.edu. **Website:** continuingstudies.wisc.edu/lsa/soa/. Estab. 1964. "Each summer for 50 years, more than 250 people gather in northern Wisconsin for a week of study, performance, exhibits, and other creative activities. More than 50 workshops in writing, body/mind/spirit; food and fitness; art and folk art; music; and digital media are offered. Participants can choose from any and all 1-, 2-, 3- and 5-day classes to craft their own mix for creative exploration and renewal." Dates: July 19-23, 2014. Location: James Williams Middle School and Rhinelander High School, Rhinelander, WI. Average attendance: 250.

COSTS Ranges from $20-$300 based on workshops.

ACCOMMODATIONS Informational available from Rhinelander Chamber of Commerce.

SEWANEE WRITERS' CONFERENCE

735 University Ave., 119 Gailor Hall, Stamler Center, Sewanee TN 37383-1000. (931) 598-1654. **E-mail:** al latham@sewanee.edu. **Website:** www.sewaneewriters.org. **Contact:** Adam Latham. Estab. 1990. Annual conference. 2014 dates: July 22 - Aug. 3. Average attendance: 150. "The University of the South will host the 25th session of the Sewanee Writers' Conference. Thanks to the generosity of the Walter E. Dakin Memorial Fund, supported by the estate of the late Tennessee Williams, the Conference will gather a distinguished faculty to provide instruction and criticism through workshops and craft lectures in poetry, fiction, and playwriting. During an intense twelve-day period, participants will read and critique each other's manuscripts under the leadership of some of our country's finest fiction writers, poets, and playwrights. All faculty members and fellows give scheduled readings; senior faculty members offer craft lectures; open-mic readings accommodate many others. Additional writers, along with a host of writing professionals, visit to give readings, participate in panel discussions, and entertain questions from the audience. Recep-

tions and mealtimes offer opportunities for informal exchange. This year's faculty includes fiction writers John Casey, Tony Earley, Adrianne Harun, Randall Kenan, Margot Livesey, Jill McCorkle, Alice McDermott, Christine Schutt, Allen Wier, and Steve Yarbrough; and poets Claudia Emerson, B.H. Fairchild, Debora Greger, William Logan, Maurice Manning, Charles Martin, Mary Jo Salter, and A.E. Stallings. Daisy Foote and Dan O'Brien will lead the playwriting workshop. Diane Johnson and Wyatt Prunty will read from their work. The Conference will offer its customary Walter E. Dakin Fellowships and Tennessee Williams Scholarships, as well as awards in memory of Stanley Elkin, Horton Foote, Barry Hannah, John Hollander, Donald Justice, Romulus Linney, Howard Nemerov, Father William Ralston, Peter Taylor, Mona Van Duyn, and John N. Wall. Additional scholarships have been made possible by Georges and Anne Borchardt and Gail Hochman. Every participant—whether contributor, scholar, or fellow—receives assistance. The Conference fee reflects but two-thirds of the actual cost to attend. Additional funding is awarded to fellows and scholars."

COSTS $1,000 for tuition and $800 for room, board, and activity costs

ACCOMMODATIONS Participants are housed in single rooms in university dormitories. Bathrooms are shared by small groups.

SOCIETY OF CHILDREN'S BOOK WRITERS & ILLUSTRATORS ANNUAL SUMMER CONFERENCE ON WRITING AND ILLUSTRATING FOR CHILDREN

8271 Beverly Blvd., Los Angeles CA 90048-4515. (323)782-1010. **Fax:** (323)782-1892. **E-mail:** scbwi@scbwi.org. **Website:** www.scbwi.org. Estab. 1972. Annual conference held in early August. Conference duration: 4 days. Average attendance: 1,000. Held at the Century Plaza Hotel in Los Angeles. Speakers have included Andrea Brown, Steven Malk, Ashley Bryan, Bruce Coville, Karen Hesse, Harry Mazer, Lucia Monfried, and Russell Freedman. Agents will be speaking and sometimes participate in ms critiques.

COSTS Approximately $450 (does not include hotel room).

ACCOMMODATIONS Information on overnight accommodations is made available.

ADDITIONAL INFORMATION Ms and illustration critiques are available. Brochure/guidelines are available in June online or for SASE.

⊕ SOUTH CAROLINA WRITERS WORKSHOP

4840 Forest Drive, Suite 6B: PMB 189, Columbia SC 29206. **E-mail:** scwwliaison@gmail.com; scww2013@gmail.com. **Website:** www.myscww.org/. Estab. 1991. Conference in October held at the Hilton Myrtle Beach Resort in Myrtle Beach, SC. Held almost every year. (2014 dates: Oct. 24-26.) Conference duration: 3 days. The conference features critique sessions, open mic readings, presentations from agents and editors and more. The conference features more than 50 different workshops for writers to choose from, dealing with all subjects of writing craft, writing business, getting an agent and more. Agents will be in attendance.

ACCOMMODATIONS Hilton Myrtle Beach Resort.

SOUTH COAST WRITERS CONFERENCE

Southwestern Oregon Community College, P.O. Box 590, 29392 Ellensburg Ave., Gold Beach OR 97444. (541)247-2741. **Fax:** (541)247-6247. **E-mail:** scwc@socc.edu. **Website:** www.socc.edu/scwriters. Estab. 1996. Annual conference held Presidents Day weekend in February. Conference duration: 2 days. Covers fiction, poetry, children's, nature, songwriting, and marketing. Melissa Hart is the next scheduled keynote speaker, and presenters include Robert Arellano, Bill Cameron, Tanya Chernov, Heidi Connolly, Kelly Davio, Tawna Fenske, Kim Cooper Findling, Stefanie Freele, and songwriter Chuck Pyle.

ADDITIONAL INFORMATION See website for cost and additional details.

SOUTHEASTERN WRITERS ASSOCIATION--ANNUAL WRITERS WORKSHOP

161 Woodstone, Athens GA 30605. **E-mail:** purple@southeasternwriters.org. **Website:** www.southeasternwriters.com. **Contact:** Amy Munnell & Sheila Hudson, presidents. Estab. 1975. **Open to all writers**. (2014 dates: June 13-17.) Contests with cash prizes. Instruction offered for novel and short fiction, nonfiction, writing for children, humor, inspirational writing, and poetry. Manuscript deadline April 1st, includes free evaluation conference(s) with instructor(s). Agent in residence. Annual 4-day workshop held in June. Cost of workshop: $445 for 4 days or lower prices for daily tuition. (See online.) Accommodations: Offers overnight accommodations on workshop site. Visit website for more information and cost of over-

night accommodations. E-mail or send SASE for brochure.

ACCOMMODATIONS Multiple hotels available in St. Simon's Island, GA.

SPACE COAST WRITERS GUILD ANNUAL CONFERENCE

No public address available, (321)956-7193. **E-mail:** scwg-jm@cfl.rr.com; stilley@scwg.org. **Website:** www.scwg.org/conference.asp. Annual conference held last weekend of January along the east coast of central Florida. Conference duration: 2 days. Average attendance: 150+. This conference is hosted each winter in Florida and features a variety of presenters on all topics writing. Critiques are available for a price, and agents in attendance will take pitches from writers. Previous presenters have included Debra Dixon, Davis Bunn (writer), Ellen Pepus (agent), Jennifer Crusie, Chuck Sambuchino, Madeline Smoot, Mike Resnick, Christina York, Ben Bova, Elizabeth Sinclair.

COSTS $180-220. Agent and editor appointments cost more.

ACCOMMODATIONS The conference is hosted on a beachside hotel, with special room rates available.

ADDITIONAL INFORMATION Agents are in attendance taking pitches every year.

SPACE (SMALL PRESS AND ALTERNATIVE COMICS EXPO)

Back Porch Comics, P.O. Box 20550, Columbus OH 43220. **E-mail:** bpc13@earthlink.net. **Website:** www.backporchcomics.com/space.htm. Next conference/trade show to be held April 12-13, 2014. Conference duration: 2 days. "The Midwest's largest exhibition of small press, alternative, and creator-owned comics." Site: Held at Ramada Plaza Hotel and Conference Center, 4900 Sinclair Rd., Columbus, OH 43229. Over 150 small press artists, writers, and publishers.

COSTS Admission: $5 per day or $8 for weekend.

ADDITIONAL INFORMATION For brochure, visit website. Editors participate in conference.

SQUAW VALLEY COMMUNITY OF WRITERS

P.O. Box 1416, Nevada City CA 95959-1416. (530)470-8440. **E-mail:** info@squawvalleywriters.org. **Website:** www.squawvalleywriters.org. **Contact:** Brett Hall Jones, executive director. Estab. 1969.

COSTS Tuition is $995, which includes 6 dinners.

ACCOMMODATIONS The Community of Writers rents houses and condominiums in the Valley for participants to live in during the week of the conference. Single room (1 participant): $700/week. Double room (twin beds, room shared by conference participant of the same sex): $465/week. Multiple room (bunk beds, room shared with 2 or more participants of the same sex): $295/week. All rooms subject to availability; early requests are recommended. Can arrange airport shuttle pick-ups for a fee.

ADDITIONAL INFORMATION Admissions are based on submitted ms (unpublished fiction, 1 or 2 stories or novel chapters); requires $35 reading fee. Submit ms to Brett Hall Jones, Squaw Valley Community of Writers, P.O. Box 1416, Nevada City, CA 95959. Brochures are available online or for a SASE in February. Send inquiries viae-mail. Accepts inquiries by SASE, e-mail, phone. Agents and editors attend/participate in conferences.

STORY WEAVERS CONFERENCE

Oklahoma Writer's Federation, (405)682-6000. **E-mail:** president@owfi.org. **Website:** www.OWFI.org. **Contact:** Linda Apple, president. Oklahoma Writer's Federation, Inc. is open and welcoming to writers of all genres and all skill levels. Our goal is to help writers become better and to help beginning writers understand and master the craft of writing.

COSTS Cost is $150 before April. $175 after April. Cost includes awards banquet and famous author banquet. Three extra sessions are available for an extra fee: How to Self-Publish Your Novel on Kindle, Nook, and iPad (and make more money than being published by New York), with Dan Case; When Polar Bear Wishes Came True: Understanding and Creating Meaningful Stories, with Jack Dalton; How to Create Three-Dimensional Characters, with Steven James.

ACCOMMODATIONS The site is at the Embassy Suite using their meeting halls. There are very few stairs and the rooms are close together for easy access.

ADDITIONAL INFORMATION "We have 20 speakers, five agents, and nine publisher/editors for a full list and bios; please see website."

SUMMER WRITING PROGRAM

Naropa University, 2130 Arapahoe Ave., Boulder CO 80302. (303)245-4862. **Fax:** (303)546-5287. **E-mail:** swpr@naropa.edu. **Website:** www.naropa.edu/swp. **Contact:** Kyle Pivarnik, special projects manager. Estab. 1974. Annual. 2014 Workshops held June 1-28. Workshop duration: 4 weeks. Average attendance: 250. Offers college credit. Accepts inquiries by e-mail, phone. With 13 workshops to choose from each of the 4 weeks of the program, students may study poetry, prose, hybrid/cross-genre writing, small press printing, or book arts. Site: All workshops, panels, lectures and readings are hosted on the Naropa University main campus. Located in downtown Boulder, the campus is within easy walking distance of restaurants, shopping, and the scenic Pearl Street Mall.

ACCOMMODATIONS Housing is available at Snow Lion Apartments. Additional info is available on the housing website: naropa.edu/student-life/housing/.

ADDITIONAL INFORMATION Writers can elect to take the Summer Writing Program for noncredit, graduate, or undergraduate credit. The registration procedure varies, so consider whether or not you'll be taking the SWP for academic credit. All participants can elect to take any combination of the first, second, third, and/or fourth weeks. To request a catalog of upcoming program or to find additional information, visit naropa.edu/swp. Naropa University als welcomes participants with disabilities. Contact Andrea Rexilius at (303)546-5296 or arexilius@naropa.edu before May 15 to inquire about accessibility and disability accommodations needed to participate fully in this event.

☁ SURREY INTERNATIONAL WRITERS' CONFERENCE

SIWC, P.O. Box 42023 RPO Guildford, Surrey BC V3R 1S5 Canada. **E-mail:** kathychung@siwc.ca. **Website:** www.siwc.ca. **Contact:** Kathy Chung, proposals contact and conference coordinator. Annual writing conference outside Vancouver, CA, held every October. Writing workshops geared toward beginner, intermediate, and advanced levels. More than 70 workshops and panels, on all topics and genres. Blue Pencil and Agent/Editor Pitch sessions included. Different conference price packages available. Check our website for more information. This event has many literary agents in attendance taking pitches.

TAOS SUMMER WRITERS' CONFERENCE

Department of English Language and Literature, MSC 03 2170, 1 University of New Mexico, Albuquerque NM 87131-0001. (505)277-5572. **Fax:** (505)277-2950. **E-mail:** taosconf@unm.edu. **Website:** www.unm.edu/~taosconf. **Contact:** Sharon Oard Warner. Estab. 1999. Annual conference held in July. Offers workshops and master classes in the novel, short story, poetry, creative nonfiction, memoir, prose style,

screenwriting, humor writing, yoga and writing, literary translation, book proposal, the query letter and revision.Participants may also schedule a consultation with a visiting agent/editor.

COSTS Weeklong workshop registration $650, weekend workshop registration $350, master classes between $1,250 and $1,525.

ACCOMMODATIONS Held at the Sagebrush Inn and Conference Center.

⊕ TEXAS WRITING RETREAT

Grimes County TX **E-mail:** PaulTCuclis@gmail.com. **E-mail:** PaulTCuclis@gmail.com. **Website:** www.texaswritingretreat.com. **Contact:** Paul Cuclis, coordinator. Estab. 2013. The Texas Writing Retreat is an intimate event with a limited number of attendees. Held on a private residence ranch an hour outside of Houston, it has an agent and editor in attendance teaching. All attendees get to pitch the attending agent. Meals and excursions and amenities included. This is a unique event that combines craft sessions, business sessions, time for writing, relaxation, and more.

COSTS Costs vary per year. Check the website for latest updates. There are different pricing options for those staying onsite vs. commuters.

ACCOMMODATIONS Private ranch residence in Texas.

TMCC WRITERS' CONFERENCE

Truckee Meadows Community College, 5270 Neil Rd., Reno NV 89502. (775)829-9010. **Fax:** (775)829-9032. **E-mail:** wdce@tmcc.edu. **Website:** wdce.tmcc.edu. Estab. 1991. Annual conference held April 27. Average attendance: 150. Conference focuses on strengthening mainstream/literary fiction and nonfiction works and how to market them to agents and publishers. Site: Truckee Meadows Community College in Reno, Nevada. "There is always an array of speakers and presenters with impressive literary credentials, including agents and editors." Speakers have included Chuck Sambuchino, Sheree Bykofsky, Andrea Brown, Dorothy Allison, Karen Joy Fowler, James D. Houston, James N. Frey, Gary Short, Jane Hirschfield, Dorrianne Laux, and Kim Addonizio

COSTS $119 for a full-day seminar; $32 for a 10-minute one-on-one appointment with an agent or editor.

ACCOMMODATIONS Contact the conference manager to learn about accommodation discounts.

ADDITIONAL INFORMATION "The conference is open to all writers, regardless of their level of experience. Brochures are available online and mailed in January. Send inquiries via e-mail."

UMKC WRITING CONFERENCE

5300 Rockhill Rd., Kansas City MO 64110. (816)235-2736. **Fax:** (816)235-5279. **E-mail:** wittfeldk@umkc.edu. **Website:** www.newletters.org/writers-wanted/nl-weekend-writing-conference. **Contact:** Kathi Wittfeld. New Letters Weekend Writing Conference will be held June 27-29, 2014 at Diastole. New Letters Writer's Conference is geared toward all levels -- beginner, intermediate, advanced and professional levels. Conferenvce open to students and community. Annual workshops. Workshops held in Summer. Cost of workshop varies. Write for more information. Mark Twain Writers Workshop will not be held in 2014.

✛ UNICORN WRITERS CONFERENCE

P.O. Box 176, Redding CT 06876. (203)938-7405. **E-mail:** bookings@unicornwritersconference.com; unicornwritersconference@gmail.com. **E-mail:** bookings@unicornwritersconference.com; unicornwritersconference@gmail.com. **Website:** www.unicornwritersconference.com. This writers conference draws upon its close proximity to New York City and pulls in many literary agents and editors to pitch each year. There are sessions, tracks, pitch gatherings, query/manuscript review sessions, and more.

ACCOMMODATIONS Held at Saint Clements Castle in Connecticut. Directions available on event website.

UNIVERSITY OF NORTH DAKOTA WRITERS CONFERENCE

Department of English, 110 Merrifield Hall, 276 Centennial Drive, Stop 7209, Grand Forks ND 58202. (701)777-2393. **Fax:** (701)777-2373. **E-mail:** crystal.alberts@email.und.edu. **Website:** und.edu/orgs/writers-conference/. **Contact:** Crystal Alberts, director. Estab. 1970. Annual conference. 2014 dates: April 2-4. Offers panels, readings, and films focused around a specific theme. Almost all events take place in the UND Memorial Union, which has a variety of small rooms and a 1,000-seat main hall. Past speakers include Art Spiegelman, Truman Capote, Sir Salman Rushdie, Allen Ginsberg, Alice Walker, and Louise Erdrich.

COSTS All events are free and open to the public. Donations accepted.

ACCOMMODATIONS All events are free and open to the public. Accommodations available at area hotels. Information on overnight accommodations available on website.

ADDITIONAL INFORMATION Schedule and other information available on website.

UW-MADISON WRITERS' INSTITUTE

21 North Park St., Room 7331, Madison WI 53715. (608)265-3972. **Fax:** (608)265-2475. **E-mail:** lscheer@dcs.wisc.edu. **Website:** www.uwwritersinstitute.org. **Contact:** Laurie Scheer. Estab. 1989. Annual. Conference usually held in April. Site: Madison Concourse Hotel, downtown Madison. Average attendance: 350-500. Conference speakers provide workshops and consultations. For information, send e-mail, visit website, call, fax. Accepts inquiries by SASE, e-mail, phone, fax. Agents and editors participate in conference.

COSTS $160-260; includes materials, breaks.

ACCOMMODATIONS Provides a list of area hotels or lodging options.

ADDITIONAL INFORMATION Sponsors contest.

VIRGINIA CENTER FOR THE CREATIVE ARTS

154 San Angelo Dr., Amherst VA 24521. (434)946-7236. **Fax:** (434)946-7239. **E-mail:** vcca@vcca.com. **Website:** www.vcca.com. Estab. 1971. Offers residencies year-round, typical residency lasts 2 weeks to 2 months. Open to originating artists: composers, writers, and visual artists. Accommodates 25 at one time. Personal living quarters include 22 single rooms, 2 double rooms, bathrooms shared with one other person. All meals are served. Kitchens for fellows' use available at studios and residence. The VCCA van goes into town twice a week. Fellows share their work regularly. Four studios have pianos. No transportation costs are covered. "Artists are accepted into the VCCA without regard for their ability to contribute financially to their residency. Daily cost is $180 per fellow. We ask fellows to contribute according to their ability."

COSTS Application fee: $30. Deadline: May 15 for October-January residency; September 15 for February-May residency; January 15 for June-September residency. Send SASE for application form or download from website. Applications are reviewed by panelists.

WESTERN RESERVE WRITERS & FREELANCE CONFERENCE

7700 Clocktower Dr., Kirtland OH 44094. (440) 525-7812. **E-mail:** deencr@aol.com. **Website:** www.deannaadams.com. **Contact:** Deanna Adams, director/conference coordinator. Estab. 1983. Biannual. Last conference held September 28, 2013. Conference duration: 1 day or half-day. Average attendance: 120. "The Western Reserve Writers Conferences are designed for all writers, aspiring and professional, and offer presentations in all genres—nonfiction, fiction, poetry, essays, creative nonfiction, and the business of writing, including Web writing and successful freelance writing." Site: "Located in the main building of Lakeland Community College, the conference is easy to find and just off the I-90 freeway. The Fall 2013 conference featured top-notch presenters from newspapers and magazines, along with published authors, freelance writers, and professional editors. Presentations included developing issues in today's publishing and publishing options, turning writing into a lifelong vocation, as well as workshops on plotting, creating credible characters, writing mysteries, romance writing, and tips on submissions, getting books into stores, and storytelling for both fiction and nonfiction writers. Included throughout the day are one-on-one editing consults, Q&A panel, and book sale/author signings."

COSTS Fall all-day conference includes lunch: $95. Spring half-day conference, no lunch: $69.

ADDITIONAL INFORMATION Brochures for the conferences are available by January (for spring conference) and July (for fall). Also accepts inquiries by e-mail and phone. Check Deanna Adams' website for all updates. Editors and agents often attend the conferences.

WHIDBEY ISLAND WRITERS' CONFERENCE

P.O. Box 1289, Langley WA 98260. **E-mail:** admin@nila.edu; wiwc@nila.edu. **Website:** www.nila.edu/wiwc/. This is an annual writing conference in the Pacific Northwest. There are a variety of sessions on topics such as fiction, craft, poetry, platform, agents, screenwriting, and much more. Topics are varied, and there is something for all writers. Multiple agents and editors are in attendance. The schedule and faculty change every year, and those changes are reflected online.

WILLAMETTE WRITERS CONFERENCE

2108 Buck St., West Linn OR 97068. (503)305-6729. **Fax:** (503)344-6174. **Website:** www.willamettewriters.com/wwc/3/. Estab. 1981. Annual conference held in August. (2014 dates: Aug. 1-3.) Conference duration: 3 days. Average attendance: 600. "Willamette Writers is open to all writers, and we plan our conference accordingly. We offer workshops on all aspects of fiction, nonfiction, marketing, the creative process, screenwriting, etc. Also, we invite top-notch inspirational speakers for keynote addresses. We always include at least 1 agent or editor panel and offer a variety of topics of interest to both fiction and nonfiction writers and screenwriters." Agents will be speaking and available for meetings with attendees.

COSTS Pricing schedule available online.

ACCOMMODATIONS If necessary, arrangements can be made on an individual basis through the conference hotel. Special rates may be available. 2014 location is the Lloyd Center DoubleTree Hotel.

ADDITIONAL INFORMATION Brochure/guidelines are available for a catalog-sized SASE.

⊃ WINCHESTER WRITERS' CONFERENCE, FESTIVAL AND BOOKFAIR, AND IN-DEPTH WRITING WORKSHOPS

University of Winchester, Winchester Hampshire WA SO22 4NR United Kingdom. 44 (0) 1962 827238. **E-mail:** judith.heneghan@winchester.ac.uk. **Website:** www.writersfestival.co.uk. The 34th Winchester Writers' Festival will be held on June 20-22 at the University of Winchester, Winchester, Hampshire SO22 4NR. Joanne Harris, internationally acclaimed author of *Chocolat*, will give the Keynote Address and will lead an outstanding team of 60 best-selling authors, commissioning editors and literary agents offering day-long workshops, 40 short talks and 500 one-to-one appointments to help writers harness their creative ideas, turn them into marketable work and pitch to publishing professionals. Participate by entering some of the 12 writing competitions, even if you can't attend. Over 120 writers have now reported major publishing successes as a direct result of their attendance at past conferences. This leading international literary event offers a magnificent source of support, advice, inspiration and networking opportunities for new and published writers working in all genres. Enjoy a creative writing holiday in Winchester, the oldest city in England and only one hour from London.To view Festival programme, including all the competition details please go to: www.writersfestival.co.uk.

WISCONSIN BOOK FESTIVAL

Madison Public Library, 201 W. Mifflin St., Madison WI 53703. (608)266-6300. **E-mail:** bookfest@mplfoundation.org. **Website:** www.wisconsinbookfestival.org. Estab. 2002. Annual festival held in October. Conference duration: 5 days. The festival features readings, lectures, book discussions, writing workshops, live interviews, children's events, and more. Speakers have included Isabel Allende, Jonathan Alter, Paul Auster, Michael Chabon, Billy Collins, Phillip Gourevitch, Ian Frazier, Tim O'Brien, Elizabeth Strout.

COSTS All festival events are free.

WOMEN WRITERS WINTER RETREAT

Homestead House B&B, 38111 West Spaulding, Willoughby OH 44094. (440)946-1902. **E-mail:** deencr@aol.com. **Website:** www.deannaadams.com. Estab. 2007. Annual—always happens the last weekend in February. Conference duration: 3 days. Average attendance: 35-40. Retreat. "The Women Writers' Winter Retreat was designed for aspiring and professional women writers who cannot seem to find enough time to devote to honing their craft. Each retreat offers class time and workshops facilitated by successful women writers, as well as allows time to do some actual writing, alone or in a group. A Friday night dinner and keynote kick-starts the weekend, followed by Saturday workshops, free time, meals, and an open mic to read your works. Sunday wraps up with 1 more workshop and fellowship. All genres welcome. Choice of overnight stay or commuting." Site: Located in the heart of downtown Willoughby, this warm and attractive bed and breakfast is easy to find, around the corner from the main street, Erie Street, and behind a popular Arabica coffee house. Door prizes and book sale/author signings throughout the weekend.

COSTS Single room: $315; shared room: $235 (includes complete weekend package, with B&B stay and all meals and workshops); weekend commute: $165; Saturday only: $125 (prices include lunch and dinner).

ADDITIONAL INFORMATION Brochures for the writers retreat are available by December. Accepts inquiries and reservations by e-mail or phone. See Deanna's website for additional information and updates.

WORDS & MUSIC

624 Pirate's Alley, New Orleans LA 70116. (504)586-1609. **Fax:** (504)522-9725. **E-mail:** info@wordsandmusic.org. **Website:** www.wordsandmusic.org. Estab. 1997. Annual conference held in November. 2014 conference: 20-24. Conference duration: 5 days. Average attendance: 300. Presenters include authors, agents, editors and publishers. Past speakers included agents Deborah Grosvenor, Judith Weber, Stuart Bernstein, Nat Sobel, Jeff Kleinman, Emma Sweeney, Liza Dawson and Michael Murphy; editors Lauren Marino, Webster Younce, Ann Patty, Will Murphy, Jofie Ferrari-Adler, Elizabeth Stein; critics Marie Arana, Jonathan Yardley, and Michael Dirda; fiction writers Oscar Hijuelos, Robert Olen Butler, Shirley Ann Grau, Mayra Montero, Ana Castillo, H.G. Carrillo. Agents and editors critique manuscripts in advance; meet with them one-on-one during the conference.

COSTS See website for a costs and additional information on accommodations. Website will update closer to date of conference.

ACCOMMODATIONS Hotel Monteleone in New Orleans.

WRITE CANADA

The Word Guild, P.O. Box 1243, Trenton ON K8V 5R9 Canada. **E-mail:** info@thewordguild.com. **E-mail:** writecanada@rogers.com. **Website:** www.writecanada.org. Conference duration: 3 days. Annual conference. 2014 dates: June 12-14 in Guelph, Ontario for writers who are Christian of all types and at all stages. Offers solid instruction, stimulating interaction, exciting challenges, and worshipful community.

WRITER'S DIGEST CONFERENCES

F+W Media, Inc., 10151 Carver Road, Suite 200, Blue Ash OH 45242. **E-mail:** jill.ruesch@fwmedia.com. **E-mail:** phil.sexton@fwmedia.com. **Website:** www.writersdigestconference.com. Estab. 1995. The Writer's Digest conferences feature an amazing line up of speakers to help writers with the craft and business of writing. Each calendar year typically features multiple conferences around the country. In 2014, the New York conference will be Aug. 1-3, while the Los Angeles conference will be Aug. 15-17. The most popular feature of the east coast conference is the agent pitch slam, in which potential authors are given the ability to pitch their books directly to agents. For the 2014 conference, there will be more than 50 agents in attendance. For more details, see the website.

COSTS Cost varies by location and year. There are typically different pricing options for those who wish to stay for the entire event vs. daylong passes.

ACCOMMODATIONS A block of rooms at the event hotel is reserved for guests.

WRITERS' LEAGUE OF TEXAS AGENTS CONFERENCE

Writers' League of Texas, 611 S. Congress Ave., Suite 200 A-3, Austin TX 78704. (512)499-8914. **Fax:** (512)499-0441. **E-mail:** conference@writersleague. org. **E-mail:** jennifer@writersleague.org. **Website:** www.writersleague.org. Estab. 1982. Established in 1981, the Writers' League of Texas is a nonprofit professional organization whose primary purpose is to provide a forum for information, support, and sharing among writers, to help members improve and market their writing skills, and to promote the interests of writers and the writing community. The Writers' League of Texas Agents & Editors Conference is for writers at every stage of their career. Beginners can learn more about this mystifying industry and prepare themselves for the journey ahead. Those with completed manuscripts can pitch to agents and get feedback on their manuscripts from professional editors. Published writers can learn about market trends and network with rising stars in the world of writing. No matter what your market, genre, or level, our conference can benefit you.

COSTS Rates vary based on membership and the date of registration. The starting rate (registration through January 15) is $309 for members and $369 for non-members. Rate increases by through later dates. See website for updates.

ACCOMMODATIONS 2013 event is at the Hyatt Regency Austin, 208 Barton Springs Road, Austin, TX 78704. Check back often for new information.

ADDITIONAL INFORMATION Event held from June 27-29, 2014. Contests and awards programs are offered separately. Brochures are available upon request.

WRITERS WEEKEND AT THE BEACH

P.O. Box 877, Ocean Park WA 98640. (360)262-0160. **E-mail:** pelkeyjc@hotmail.com. **E-mail:** bobtracie@ hotmail.com; pelkeyjc@hotmail.com. **Contact:** John Pelkey. Estab. 1992. Annual conference held in April. Conference duration: 2 days. Average attendance: 45. A retreat for writers with an emphasis on poetry, fiction, and nonfiction. Held at the Ocean Park Meth-

odist Retreat Center & Camp. Speakers have included Miralee Ferrell, Leslie Gould, Linda Clare, Birdie Etchison, Colette Tennant, Gail Dunham, and Marion Duckworth.

COSTS $200 for full registration before March 1 and $215 after March 1.

ACCOMMODATIONS Offers on-site overnight lodging.

THE WRITERS' WORKSHOP

387 Beaucatcher Rd., Asheville NC 28805. (828)254-8111. **E-mail:** writersw@gmail.com. **Website:** www. twwoa.org. Estab. 1984. Biannual writing retreat at Folly Beach, SC. 2014 dates: May 15-18. Kurt Vonnegut said: "God bless The Writers' Workshop of Asheville!" He and Don De Lillo, Peter Matthiessen, E.L. Doctorow, Eudora Welty, John le Carre and many other distinguished authors have given benefit readings for us. We offer classes, contests, retreats, and other events. Workshops in all genres of writing, for beginning or experienced writers, are held in Asheville and Charlotte, NC. Our in-house Renbourne Editorial Agency offers the highest quality editing and revising services for writes of all genres.

COSTS Vary. Financial assistance available to low-income writers. Information on overnight accommodations is made available.

ADDITIONAL INFORMATION We also sponsor these contests, open to all writers: Annual Poetry Contest, Prizes from $100-300 (Deadline: Feb. 28); Hard Times Writing Contest, Prizes from $100-300, (Deadline: May 30); Fiction Contest, Prizes from $150-350 (Deadline: Aug. 30); Annual Memoirs Competition, Prizes from $150-350 (Deadline: Nov. 30). Contests for young writers are posted at our website.

WRITING AND ILLUSTRATING FOR YOUNG READERS CONFERENCE

1480 East 9400 South, Sandy UT 84093. **E-mail:** staff@wifyr.com. **Website:** www.wifyr.com. Estab. 2000. Annual workshop held in June 2014. Conference duration: 5 days. Average attendance: 100+. Learn how to write, illustrate, and publish in the children's and young adult markets. Beginning and advanced writers and illustrators are tutored in a small-group workshop setting by published authors and artists and receive instruction from and network with editors, major publishing house representatives, and literary agents. Afternoon attendees get to hear practical writing and publishing tips from published authors, literary agents, and editors. Held at the Waterford School in Sandy, UT. Speakers have included John Cusick, Stephen Fraser, Alyson Heller, and Ruth Katcher.

COSTS Costs available online.

ACCOMMODATIONS A block of rooms are available at the Best Western Cotton Tree Inn in Sandy, UT at a discounted rate. This rate is good as long as there are available rooms.

⊕ WYOMING WRITERS CONFERENCE

Sheridan WY **E-mail:** pfrolander@rangeweb.net. **Website:** wyowriters.org. **Contact:** Patricia Frolander. This is a statewide writing conference for writers of Wyoming and neighboring states. Next conference: June 6-8, 2014 in Sheridan, WY. Each year, multiple published authors, editors and literary agents are in attendance.

CONTESTS,
AWARDS
& GRANTS

///

Publication is not the only way to get your work recognized. Contests and awards can also be great ways to gain recognition in the industry. Grants, offered by organizations like SCBWI, offer monetary recognition to writers, giving them more financial freedom as they work on projects.

When considering contests or applying for grants, be sure to study guidelines and requirements. Regard entry deadlines as gospel and follow the rules to the letter.

Note that some contests require nominations. For published authors and illustrators, competitions provide an excellent way to promote your work. Your publisher may not be aware of local competitions such as state-sponsored awards—if your book is eligible, have the appropriate person at your publishing company nominate or enter your work for consideration.

To select potential contests and grants, read through the listings that interest you, then send for more information about the types of written or illustrated material considered and other important details. A number of contests offer information through websites given in their listings.

If you are interested in knowing who has received certain awards in the past, check your local library or bookstores or consult *Children's Books: Awards & Honors*, compiled and edited by the Children's Book Council (cbcbooks.org). Many bookstores have special sections for books that are Caldecott and Newbery Medal winners. Visit the American Library Association website, ala.org, for information on the Caldecott, Newbery, Coretta Scott King and Printz Awards. Visit hbook.com for information on The Boston Globe-Horn Book Award. Visit scbwi.org/awards.htm for information on The Golden Kite Award.

JANE ADDAMS CHILDREN'S BOOK AWARDS

Website: www.janeaddamspeace.org. **Contact:** Marianne I. Baker, chair. The Jane Addams Children's Book Awards are given annually to the children's books published the preceding year that effectively promote the cause of peace, social justice, world community, and the equality of the sexes and all races as well as meeting conventional standards for excellence. Books eligible for this award may be fiction, poetry, or nonfiction. Books may be any length. Entries should be suitable for ages 2-12. See website for specific details on guidelines and required book themes. Deadline: December 31. Judged by a national committee of WILPF members concerned with children's books and their social values is responsible for making the changes each year.

☺ ALCUIN CITATION AWARD

P.O. Box 3216, Vancouver BC V6B 3X8 Canada. (604)732-5403. **Fax:** (604)985-1091. **E-mail:** awards@alcuinsociety.com. **Website:** www.alcuinsociety.com. **Contact:** Leah Gordon. Submit previously published material from the year before the award's call for entries. Submissions made by the publisher, author or designer. Alcuin Citations are awarded annually for excellence in Canadian book design. Winners are selected from books designed and published in Canada. Awards are presented annually at appropriate ceremonies held in each year. Winning books are exhibited nationally and internationally at the Tokyo, Frankfurt, and Leipzig Book Fairs, and are Canada's entries in the international competition in Leipzig, "Book Design from all over the World" in the following spring. Deadline: March 15. Prize: Prizes: 1st, 2nd, and 3rd in each category (at the discretion of the judges). Judging by professionals and those experienced in the field of book design.

AMERICA & ME ESSAY CONTEST

P.O. Box 30400, 7373 W. Saginaw Hwy., Lansing MI 48917. **E-mail:** lfedewa@fbinsmi.com. **Website:** https://www.farmbureauinsurance-mi.com/About_Us/Corporate_And_Social_Responsibility/America_And_Me/. Focuses on encouraging students to write about their personal Michigan heroes: someone they know personally who has encouraged them and inspired them to want to live better and achieve more. Open to Michigan eighth graders. Contest rules and entry form available on website. Encourages Michigan youth to explore their roles in America's future. Deadline: November 15. Prize: $1,000, plaque, and medallion for top 10 winners.

AMERICAN ASSOCIATION OF UNIVERSITY WOMEN AWARD IN JUVENILE LITERATURE

4610 Mail Service Center, Raleigh NC 27699-4610. (919)807-7290. **E-mail:** michael.hill@ncdcr.gov. **Contact:** Michael Hill, awards coordinator. Annual award. Book must be published during the year ending June 30. Submissions made by author, author's agent or publisher. SASE for contest rules. Author must have maintained either legal residence or actual physical residence, or a combination of both, in the state of North Carolina for 3 years immediately preceding the close of the contest period. Only published work (books) eligible. Recognizes the year's best work of juvenile literature by a North Carolina resident. Deadline: July 15. Prize: Awards a cup to the winner and winner's name inscribed on a plaque displayed within the North Carolina Office of Archives and History. Judged by three-judge panel.
Ω   Competition receives 10-15 submissions per category.

AMERICAS AWARD

Website: http://claspprograms.org/americasaward. **Contact:** Claire Gonzalez. The Américas Award encourages and commends authors, illustrators, and publishers who produce quality children's and young adult books that portray Latin America the Caribbean, or Latinos in the United States. Up to 2 awards (for primary and secondary reading levels) are given in recognition of US published works of fiction, poetry, folklore, or selected nonfiction (from picture books to works for young adults). The award winners and commended titles are selected for their (1) distinctive literary quality; (2) cultural contextualization; (3) exceptional integration of text, illustration and design; and (4) potential for classroom use. To nominate a copyright title from the previous year, publishers are invited to submit review copies to the committee members listed on the website. Publishers should send 8 copies of the nominated book. Deadline: January 18. Prize: $500, plaque and a formal presentation at the Library of Congress, Washington D.C.

HANS CHRISTIAN ANDERSEN AWARD

Nonnenweg 12, Postfach Ba CH-4003 Switzerland . **E-mail:** liz.page@ibby.org. **E-mail:** ibby@ibby.org. **Web-**

site: www.ibby.org. **Contact:** Liz Page, director. The Hans Christian Andersen Award, awarded every two years by the International Board on Books for Young People (IBBY), is the highest international recognition given to an author and an illustrator of children's books. The Author's Award has been given since 1956, the Illustrator's Award since 1966. Her Majesty Queen Margrethe II of Denmark is the Patron of the Hans Christian Andersen Awards. The awards are presented at the biennial congresses of IBBY. Awarded to an author and to an illustrator, living at the time of the nomination, who by the outstanding value of their work are judged to have made a lasting contribution to literature for children and young people. The complete works of the author and of the illustrator will be taken into consideration in awarding the medal, which will be accompanied by a diploma. Candidates are nominated by National Sections of IBBY in good standing. Prize: Awards medals according to literary and artistic criteria. Judged by the Hans Christian Andersen Jury.

⚙ ATLANTIC WRITING COMPETITION FOR UNPUBLISHED MANUSCRIPTS

1113 Marginal Rd., Halifax NS B3H 4P7. (902)423-8116. **Fax:** (902)422-0881. **E-mail:** programs@writers. ns.ca. **Website:** www.writers.ns.ca. **Contact:** Hillary Titley. Annual program designed to honor work by unpublished writers in all 4 Atlantic Provinces. Entry is open to writers unpublished in the category of writing they wish to enter. Prizes are presented in the fall of each year. Categories include: adult novel, writing for children, poetry, short story, juvenile/young adult novel, creative nonfiction, and play. Judges return written comments when competition is concluded. Page lengths and rules vary based on categories. See website for details. Anyone resident in the Atlantic Provinces since September 1st immediately prior to the deadline date is eligible to enter. Only one entry per category is allowed. Each entry requires its own entry form and registration fee. Deadline: February 3. Prize: Prizes vary based on categories. See website for details.

⚙ MARILYN BAILLIE PICTURE BOOK AWARD

40 Orchard View Blvd., Suite 217, Toronto ON M4R 1B9 Canada. (416)975-0010, ext. 222. **Fax:** (416)975-8970. **E-mail:** meghan@bookcentre.ca. **Website:** www.bookcentre.ca. **Contact:** Meghan Howe. The

Marilyn Baillie Picture Book Award honors excellence in the illustrated picture book format. To be eligible, the book must be an original work in English, aimed at children ages 3-8, written and illustrated by Canadians and first published in Canada. Eligible genres include fiction, nonfiction and poetry. Books must be published between Jan. 1 and Dec. 31 of the previous calendar year. New editions or re-issues of previously published books are not eligible for submission. Deadline: December 20. Prize: $20,000.

MILDRED L. BATCHELDER AWARD

Website: http://www.ala.org/alsc/awardsgrants/bookmedia/batchelderaward. **Contact:** Jean Hatfield, Chair. The Batchelder Award is given to the most outstanding children's book originally published in a language other than English in a country other than the United States, and subsequently translated into English for publication in the US. Visit website for terms and criteria of award. The purpose of the award, a citation to an American publisher, is to encourage international exchange of quality children's books by recognizing US publishers of such books in translation. Deadline: December 31.

JOHN AND PATRICIA BEATTY AWARD

2471 Flores St., San Mateo CA 94403. (650)376-0886. **Fax:** (650)539-2341. **E-mail:** bartlett@scfl.lib.ca.us. **Website:** www.cla-net.org. **Contact:** Diane Bartlett, award chair. The California Library Association's John and Patricia Beatty Award, sponsored by Baker & Taylor, honors the author of a distinguished book for children or young adults that best promotes an awareness of California and its people. Must be a children's or young adult books published in the previous year, set in California, and highlight California's cultural heritage or future. Send title suggestiosn to the committee members. Deadline: January 31. Prize: $500 and an engraved plaque. Judged by a committee of CLA members, who select the winning title from books published in the United States during the preceding year.

⚙ THE GEOFFREY BILSON AWARD FOR HISTORICAL FICTION FOR YOUNG PEOPLE

40 Orchard View Blvd., Suite 217, Toronto ON M4R 1B9 Canada. (416)975-0010, ext. 222. **Fax:** (416)975-8970. **Website:** www.bookcentre.ca. **Contact:** Meghan Howe. Awarded annually to reward excellence in the writing of an outstanding work of historical fiction for

young readers, by a Canadian author, published in the previous calendar year. Open to Canadian citizens and residents of Canada for at least 2 years. Books must be published between January 1 and December 31 of the previous year. Books must be first foreign or first Canadian editions. Autobiographies are not eligible. Jury members will consider the following: historical setting and accuracy, strong character and plot development, well-told, original story, and stability of book for its intended age group. Deadline: December 20. Prize: $5,000.

THE IRMA S. AND JAMES H. BLACK AWARD

Bank Street College of Education, 610 W. 112th St., New York NY 10025-1898. (212)875-4458. **Fax:** (212)875-4558. **E-mail:** kfreda@bankstreet.edu; apryce@bankstreet.edu. **Website:** http://bankstreet.edu/center-childrens-literature/irma-black-award/. **Contact:** Kristin Freda. Award give to an outstanding book for young children—a book in which text and illustrations are inseparable, each enhancing and enlarging on the other to produce a singular whole. Entries must have been published during the previous calendar year. Publishers submit books. Submit only one copy of each book. Does not accept unpublished mss. Deadline: mid-December. Prize: A scroll with the recipient's name and a gold seal designed by Maurice Sendak. Judged by a committee of older children and children's literature professionals. Final judges are first-, second-, and third-grade classes at a number of cooperating schools.

BOSTON GLOBE-HORN BOOK AWARDS

56 Roland St., Suite 200, Boston MA 02129. (617)628-0225. **Fax:** (617)628-0882. **E-mail:** info@hbook.com; khedeen@hbook.com. **Website:** hbook.com/bghb/. **Contact:** Katrina Hedeen. Offered annually for excellence in literature for children and young adults (published June 1-May 31). Categories: picture book, fiction and poetry, nonfiction. Judges may also name up to 2 honor books in each category. Books must be published in the US, but may be written or illustrated by citizens of any country. The Horn Book Magazine publishes speeches given at awards ceremonies. Guidelines for SASE or online. Submit a book directly to each of the judges. See website for details on submitting, as well as contest guidelines. Deadline: May 15. Prize: $500 and an engraved silver bowl; honor book recipients receive an engraved silver plate. Judged by a panel of 3 judges selected each year.

ANN CONNOR BRIMER AWARD

Website: www.nsla.ns.ca/. **Contact:** Heather MacKenzie, award director. In 1990, the Nova Scotia Library Association established the Ann Connor Brimer Award for writers residing in Atlantic Canada who have made an outstanding contribution to children's literature. Author must be alive and residing in Atlantic Canada at time of nomination. Book intended for youth up to the age of 15. Book in print and readily available. Fiction or nonfiction (except textbooks). To recognize excellence in writing. Prize: $2,000.

BUCKEYE CHILDREN'S BOOK AWARD

Website: www.bcbookaward.info. **Contact:** Christine Watters, president. The Buckeye Childeren's Book Award Program is designed to encourage children to read literature critically, to promote teacher and librarian involvement in children's literature programs, and to commend authors of such literature, as well as to promote the use of libraries. Open to Ohio students. Award offered every year. Students may only nominate books published in the previous 2 years (for paperbacks, check the original hardcover publication date), and the book must be originally published in the United States. A book in a series that has previously won the award are not eligible for nonfiction. Deadline: March 15. Nominees submitted by students starting January 1.

RANDOLPH CALDECOTT MEDAL

50 E. Huron, Chicago IL 60611-2795. (312)944-7680. **Fax:** (312)440-9374. **E-mail:** alsc@ala.org; lschulte@ala.org. **Website:** www.ala.org/alsc/caldecott.cfm. The Caldecott Medal was named in honor of nineteenth-century English illustrator Randolph Caldecott. It is awarded annually by the Association for Library Service to Children, a division of the American Library Association, to the artist of the most distinguished American picture book for children. Illustrator must be U.S. citizen or resident. Must be published year preceding award. SASE for award rules. Entries are not returned. Honors the artist of the most outstanding picture book for children published in the U.S. Deadline: December 31.

CALIFORNIA YOUNG PLAYWRIGHTS CONTEST

3675 Ruffin Rd., Suite 330, San Diego CA 92123-1870. (858)384-2970. **Fax:** (858)384-2974. **E-mail:** write@playwrightsproject.org. **Website:** www.playwrightsproject.org. **Contact:** Cecelia Kouma, executive director. Annual contest open to Californians under age 19. Annual contest. "Our organization and the contest is designed to nurture promising young writers. We hope to develop playwrights and audiences for live theater. We also teach playwriting." Submissions are required to be unpublished and not produced professionally. Submissions made by the author. SASE for contest rules and entry form. Scripts must be a minimum of 10 standard typewritten pages; send 2 copies. Scripts will *not* be returned. If requested, entrants receive detailed evaluation letter. Guidelines available online. Deadline: June 1. Prize: Scripts will be produced in spring at a professional theatre in San Diego. Writers submitting scripts of 10 or more pages receive a detailed script evaluation letter upon request. Judged by professionals in the theater community, a committee of 5-7; changes somewhat each year.

CALLIOPE FICTION CONTEST

5975 W. Western Way, PMD 116Y, Tucson AZ 85713. **E-mail:** cynthia@theriver.com. **Website:** www.calliopewriters.org. **Contact:** Cynthia Sabelhaus, General Editor. Annual contest for unpublished work (any genre, but no violence, profanity, or extreme horror). Open to students. Submissions made by author. Winners must retain sufficient rights to have their stories published in the January/February issue, or their entries will be disqualified; one-time rights. Open to all writers. No special considerations—other than following the guidelines. Contest theme, due dates and sometimes entry fees change annually. The purpose of fiction in Calliope is to entertain its readers, most of whom are writers, or trying to be. Calliope is open to any genre of short fiction, including science fiction, fantasy, horror, mystery, and all their sub-genres. Mixed genre stories and experimental forms are also welcome. Mainstream/literary stories will be considered if they are in some way out of the ordinary. Humor and satire are greatly appreciated. Deadline: Changes annually. Prize: Up to $75 for 1st place.

✪ CANADIAN SHORT STORY COMPETITION

Unit #6, 477 Martin St., Penticton BC V2A 5L2 Canada. (778)476-5750. **Fax:** (778)476-5750. **E-mail:** dave@redtuquebooks.ca. **Website:** www.redtuquebooks.ca. **Contact:** David Korinetz, contest director. Offered annually for unpublished works. Purpose of award is to promote Canada and Canadian publishing. Stories require a Canadian element. There are three ways to qualify. They can be written by a Canadian, written about Canadians, or take place somewhere in Canada. Deadline: December 31. Prize: 1st Place: $500; 2nd Place: $150; 3rd Place: $100; and 10 prizes of $25 will be given to honorable mentions. All 13 winners will be published in an anthology. They will each receive a complimentary copy. Judged by Canadian authors in the fantasy/sci-fi/horror field. Acquires first print rights. Contest open to anyone.

CASCADE WRITING CONTEST & AWARDS

1075 Willow Lake Road N., Keizer Oregon 97303. **E-mail:** cascade@oregonchristianwriters.org. **Website:** http://oregonchristianwriters.org/ocw-cascade-writing-contest/. **Contact:** Marilyn Rhoads and Julie McDonald Zander. The Cascade Awards are presented at the annual Oregon Christian Writers Summer Conference (held at the Red Lion on the River in Portland, Oregon each August) attended by national editors, agents, and professional authors. Award given for each of the following categories: Published Fiction Book, Unpublished Fiction Book, Nonfiction/Memoir, Poetry, Devotional Books, Young Adult Novels, Middle Grade Fiction Book and Middle Grade Nonfiction Book, Children's Fiction and Nonfiction Book, and Short Entries, including: Articles, Stories, and Published Blog. Two additional special Cascade Awards are presented each year, the Trailblazer Award to a writer who has distinguished him/herself in the field of Christian writing and a Writer of Promise Award for a writer who demonstrates unusual promise in the field of Christian writing. For a full list of categories, entry rules, and scoring elements, visit website. Guidelines and rules available on the website. Entry forms will be available on the first day for entry. Annual multi-genre competition to encourage both published and emerging writers in the field of Christian writing. Deadline: February 14-March 31. Prize: Award certificate presented at the Cascade Awards ceremony during the Oregon Christian Writers Annual Summer Conference. Finalists are listed in the conference notebook and winners are listed online. Cascade Trophies are awarded to the recipients of the Trailblazer and Writer of Promise Awards. Judged by published authors, editors, librarians, and retail book store owners and employees. Final judging by editors, agents, and published authors from the Christian publishing industry.

CHILDREN'S AFRICANA BOOK AWARD

c/o Rutgers University, 132 George St., New Brunswick NJ 08901. (732)932-8173; (301)585-9136. **Fax:** (732)932-3394. **E-mail:** africaaccess@aol.com. **E-mail:** harrietmcguire@earthlink.net. **Website:** www.africaaccessreview.org. **Contact:** Brenda Randolph, chairperson. The Children's Africana Book Awards are presented annually to the authors and illustrators of the best books on Africa for children and young people published or republished in the U.S. The awards were created by the Outreach Council of the African Studies Association (ASA) to dispel stereotypes and encourage the publication and use of accurate, balanced children's materials about Africa. The awards are presented in 2 categories: Young Children and Older Readers. Entries must have been published in the calendar year previous to the award. Nominated titles are read by committee members and reviewed by external African Studies scholars with specialized academic training.

CHILDREN'S BOOK GUILD AWARD FOR NONFICTION

E-mail: theguild@childrensbookguild.org. **Website:** www.childrensbookguild.org. Annual award. "One doesn't enter. One is selected. Our jury annually selects one author for the award." Honors an author or illustrator whose total work has contributed significantly to the quality of nonfiction for children. Prize: Cash and an engraved crystal paperweight. Judged by a jury of Children's Book Guild specialists, authors, and illustrators.

CHILDREN'S WRITER WRITING CONTESTS

95 Long Ridge Rd., West Redding CT 06896-0811. (203)792-8600. **Fax:** (203)792-8406. **Website:** www.childrenswriter.com. Contest offered twice a year by *Children's Writer*, the monthly newsletter of writing and publishing trends. Each contest has its own theme. Any original unpublished piece, not accepted by any publisher at the time of submission, is eligible. Submissions made by the author. To obtain the rules and theme for the current contest go to the website and click on "Writing Contests," or send a SASE to *Children's Writer* at the above address. Put "Contest Request" in the lower left of your envelope. Open to any writer. Entries are judged on age targeting, originality, quality of writing and, for nonfiction, how well the information is conveyed and accuracy. Promotes higher quality children's literature. Deadline: End of February and October. Prize: 1st place: $250 or $500, a certificate and publication in *Children's Writer*; 2nd place: $100 or $250, and certificate; 3rd-5th places: $50 or $100 and certificates. Judged by a panel of 4 selected from the staff of the Institute of Children's Literature.

CHRISTIAN BOOK AWARDS

9633 S. 48th St., Suite 140, Phoenix AZ 85044. (480)966-3998. **Fax:** (480)966-1944. **E-mail:** info@ecpa.org; mkuyper@ecpa.org. **Website:** www.ecpa.org. **Contact:** Mark W. Kuyper, president and CEO. The Evangelical Christian Publishers Association recognizes quality and encourages excellence by presenting the ECPA Christian Book Awards (formerly known as Gold Medallion) each year. Categories include children, fiction, nonfiction, Bibles, Bible reference, inspiration, and new author. All entries must be evangelical in nature and submitted through an ECPA member publisher. Books must have been published in the calendar year prior to the award. Publishing companies submitting entries must be ECPA members in good standing. See website for details. The Christian Book Awards recognize the highest quality in Christian books and is among the oldest and most prestigious awards program in Christian publishing. Deadline: September 30. Submission period begins September 2.

☺ THE CITY OF VANCOUVER BOOK AWARD

Woodward's Heritage Building, 111 W. Hastings St., Suite 501, Vancouver BC V6B 1H4 Canada. (604)829-2007. **Fax:** (604)871-6005. **E-mail:** marnie.rice@vancouver.ca. **Website:** https://vancouver.ca/people-programs/city-of-vancouver-book-award.aspx. The annual City of Vancouver Book Award recognizes authors of excellence of any genre who contribute to the appreciation and understanding of Vancouver's history, unique character, or the achievements of its residents. The book must not be copyrighted prior to the previous year. Submit four copies of book. See website for details and guidelines. Deadline: May 15. Prize: $2,000. Judged by an independent jury.

COLORADO BOOK AWARDS

(303)894-7951, ext. 21. **Fax:** (303)864-9361. **E-mail:** abu-baker@coloradohumanities.org. **Website:** www.coloradohumanities.org. **Contact:** Reem Abu-Baker. An annual program that celebrates the accomplishments of Colorado's outstanding authors, editors, illustrators, and photographers. Awards are presented in at least ten categories including anthology/collection, biography, children's, creative nonfiction, fiction, history, nonfiction, pictorial, poetry, and young adult. To be eligible for a Colorado Book Award, a primary contributor to the book must be a Colorado writer, editor, illustrator, or photographer. Current Colorado residents are eligible, as are individuals engaged in on-going literary work in the state and authors whose personal history, identity, or literary work reflect a strong Colorado influence. Authors not currently Colorado residents who feel their work is inspired by or connected to Colorado should submit a letter with his/her entry describing the connection. Celebrates books and their creators and promotes them to readers.

CRICKET LEAGUE

P.O. Box 300, Peru IL 61354. **E-mail:** cricket@carus pub.com. **E-mail:** mail@cricketmagkids.com. **Website:** www.cricketmagkids.com. Cricket League contests encourage creativity and give young people an opportunity to express themselves in writing, drawing, painting or photography. There is a contest in each issue. Possible categories include story, poetry, art, or photography. Each contest relates to a specific theme described on each *Cricket* issue's Cricket League page and on the website. Signature verifying originality, age and address of entrant and permission to publish required. Entries which do not relate to the current month's theme cannot be considered. Unpublished submissions only. Cricket League rules, contest theme, and submission deadline information can be found in the current issue of *Cricket* and via website. Deadline: The 25th of each month. Prize: Certificates. Judged by *Cricket* editors.

CWW ANNUAL WISCONSIN WRITERS AWARDS

6973 Heron Way, De Forest WI 53532. **E-mail:** kar lahuston@gmail.com. **Website:** www.wiswriters.org. **Contact:** Geoff Gilpin, president and annual awards co-chair; Karla Huston, secretary and annual awards co-chair; Marilyn L. Taylor, annual awards chair; Alice D'Allesio, annual awards co-chair. Offered annually for work published by Wisconsin writers during the previous calendar year. Nine awards: Major Achievement (presented in alternate years); short fiction; short nonfiction; nonfiction book; poetry book; fiction book; children's literature; Lorine Niedecker Poetry Award; Christopher Latham Sholes Award for

Outstanding Service to Wisconsin Writers p(resented in alternate years); Essay Award for Young Writers. Open to Wisconsin residents. Entries may be submitted via postal mail or e-mail, based on category. See website for guidelines and entry forms. Submissions are accepted between November 1 and January 31. Prize: Prizes: Awards vary based on each category. The Christopher Latham Sholes Award carries a $500 prize; the Major Achievement Award carries a $1,000 prize.

MARGARET A. EDWARDS AWARD

50 East Huron St., Chicago IL 60611-2795. (312)280-4390 or (800)545-2433. **Fax:** (312)280-5276. **E-mail:** yalsa@ala.org; noconnor@ala.org. **Website:** www.ala.org/yalsa/edwards. **Contact:** Nichole O'Connor. Annual award administered by the Young Adult Library Services Association (YALSA) of the American Library Association (ALA) and sponsored by *School Library Journal* magazine. Awarded to an author whose book or books, over a period of time, have been accepted by young adults as an authentic voice that continues to illuminate their experiences and emotions, giving insight into their lives. The book or books should enable them to understand themselves, the world in which they live, and their relationship with others and with society. The book or books must be in print at the time of the nomination. Submissions must be previously published no less than 5 years prior to the first meeting of the current Margaret A. Edwards Award Committee at Midwinter Meeting. Nomination form is available on the YALSA website. Deadline: December 1. Prize: $2,000. Judged by members of the Young Adult Library Services Association.

ERB'S NEW VOICE IN YA

P.O. Box 172873, Tampa FL 33672. **E-mail:** elephant rockbooksya@gmail.com. **Website:** elephantrock books.com/ya.html. **Contact:** Jotham Burrello and Amanda Hurley. Guidelines are available on the website: http://www.elephantrockbooks.com/about. html#submissions. "Elephant Rock Books' new teen imprint is looking for a great story to lead the way. We're after quality stories with heart, guts, and a clear voice. We're especially interested in the quirky, the hopeful, and the real. We are not particularly interested in genre fiction and prefer standalone novels, unless you've got the next *Hunger Games*. We seek writers who believe in the transformative power of a great story, so show us what you've got." Deadline: September 15. Prize: $1,000 as an advance.

FAIRY TALE CASTLE ART CONTEST

E-mail: artcontest@DianaPerryBooks.com. **Website:** dianaperrybooks.com. Purpose: "To give exposure to beginning artists/illustrators trying to break in to the business and get noticed." Deadline: October 31. Prize: 1st Place: $200, trophy, mention on website, t-shirt, press releases in your local newspapers; 2nd Place: $150, trophy, mention on website, t-shirt, press releases in your local newspapers; 3rd Place: $100, trophy, mention on website, t-shirt, press releases in your local newspapers; 4th/5th places: $50/$25, plaque, mention on website, t-shirt, press releases in your local newspapers. "We also list names of next 25 honorable mentions on website. Contest guidelines and entry form on website. CHECK WEBSITE FOR GUEST JUDGES. E-mail your picture via JPG or PDF no later than October 31 with "Fairy Tale Castle Art Contest" as subject. Also write your full name and address in body of text so we can match up with your snail-mail submission. Mail entry form and a $15 money order only to Fairy Tale Castle Art Contest at above address postmarked no later than October 31. Winners announced both on website and via snail mail December 1. Prizes mailed within 10 days of announcement.

FAIRY TALE FICTION CONTEST

E-mail: dianaperry@DianaPerryBooks.com. **Website:** dianaperrybooks.com. **Contact:** Diana Perry. "Write a classic fairy tale befitting Grimm, Hans Christian Anderson, or the bedtime stories you came to love as a child, suitable for emergent readers up to age 8, or for adults reading to smaller children." Rules on website. Length: up to 12 pages or 1,500 words. Purpose: "To give exposure to beginning poets trying to break in to the business and get noticed." Deadline: July 31. Prize: 1st Place: $200, trophy, mention on website, t-shirt, press releases in your local newspapers; 2nd Place: $150, trophy, mention on website, t-shirt, press releases in your local newspapers; 3rd Place: $100, trophy, mention on website, t-shirt, press releases in your local newspapers; 4th/5th places: $50/$25, plaque, mention on website, t-shirt, press releases in your local newspapers. "We also list names of next 25 honorable mentions on website. Contest guidelines and entry form on website. CHECK WEBSITE FOR GUEST JUDGES. Mail entry form, your story, and

a $15 money order only to Fairy Tale Fiction Contest at above address postmarked no later than July 31. Winners announced both on website and via snail mail September 1. Prizes mailed within 10 days of announcement. Judged by Diana Perry and guest judge.

SHUBERT FENDRICH MEMORIAL PLAYWRITING CONTEST

P.O. Box 4267, Englewood CO 80155. (303)779-4035. **Fax:** (303)779-4315. **E-mail:** editors@pioneerdrama.com. **E-mail:** submissions@pioneerdrama.com. **Website:** www.pioneerdrama.com. **Contact:** Lori Conary, submissions editor. Previously unpublished submissions only. Open to all writers not currently published by Pioneer Drama Service. SASE for contest rules and guidelines or view online. No entry fee. Cover letter, SASE for return of ms, and proof of production or staged reading must accompany all submissions. Encourages the development of quality theatrical material for educational and family theater. Deadline: Ongoing contest; a winner is selected by June 1 each year from all submissions received the previous year. Prize: $1,000 royalty advance in addition to publication. Judged by editors.

DOROTHY CANFIELD FISHER CHILDREN'S BOOK AWARD

578 Paine Tpke. N., Berlin VT 05602. (802)828-6954. **E-mail:** grace.greene@state.vt.us. **Website:** www.dcfaward.org. **Contact:** Mary Linney, chair. Annual award to encourage Vermont children to become enthusiastic and discriminating readers by providing them with books of good quality by living American or Canadian authors published in the current year. E-mail for entry rules. Titles must be original work, published in the U.S., and be appropriate to children in grades 4-8. The book must be copyrighted in the current year. It must be written by an American author living in the U.S. or Canada, or a Canadian author living in Canada or the U.S. Deadline: December of year book was published. Prize: Awards a scroll presented to the winning author at an award ceremony. Judged by children, grades 4-8, who vote for their favorite book.

☉ THE NORMA FLECK AWARD FOR CANADIAN CHILDREN'S NONFICTION

40 Orchard View Blvd., Suite 217, Toronto ON M4R 1B9 Canada. (416)975-0010 ext. 222. **Fax:** (416)975-8970. **E-mail:** meghan@bookcentre.ca. **Website:** www.bookcentre.ca. **Contact:** Meghan Howe, library

coordinator. The Norma Fleck Award was established by the Fleck Family Foundation to recognize and raise the profile of exceptional nonfiction books for young people. Offered annually for books published between January 1 and December 31 of the previous calendar year. Open to Canadian citizens or landed immigrants. Books must be first foreign or first Canadian editions. Nonfiction books in the following categories are eligible: culture and the arts, science, biography, history, geography, reference, sports, activities, and pastimes. Deadline: December 20. Prize: $10,000. The award will go to the author unless 40% or more of the text area is composed of original illustrations, in which case the award will be divided equally between author and illustrator. Judged by at least 3 of the following: a teacher, a librarian, a bookseller, and a reviewer. A judge will have a deep understanding of, and some involvement with, Canadian children's books.

FLICKER TALE CHILDREN'S BOOK AWARD

Morton Mandan Public Library, 609 W. Main St., Mandan ND 58554. **E-mail:** laustin@cdln.info. **Website:** www.ndla.info/ftaward.htm. **Contact:** Linda Austin. Award gives children across the state of North Dakota a chance to vote for their book of choice from a nominated list of 20: 4 in the picture book category; 4 in the intermediate category; 4 in the juvenile category (for more advanced readers); 4 in the upper grade level nonfiction category. Also promotes awareness of quality literature for children. Previously published submissions only. Submissions nominated by librarians and teachers across the state of North Dakota. Deadline: April. Prize: A plaque from North Dakota Library Association and banquet dinner. Judged by children in North Dakota.

DON FREEMAN MEMORIAL GRANT-IN-AID

8271 Beverly Blvd., Los Angeles CA 90048. (323)782-1010. **Fax:** (323)782-1892. **E-mail:** scbwi@scbwi.org. **Website:** www.scbwi.org. The grant-in-aid is available to both full and associate members of the SCBWI who, as artists, seriously intend to make picture books their chief contribution to the field of children's literature. Applications and prepared materials are available in October. Grant awarded and announced in August. SASE for award rules and entry forms. SASE for return of entries. Enables picture book artists to further their understanding, training, and work in

the picture book genre. Deadline: February 1-March 1. Prize: Pize: One grant of $1,500 and one runner-up grant of $500.

THEODOR SEUSS GEISEL AWARD

50 E. Huron, Chicago IL 60611. (800)545-2433. **E-mail:** alscawards@ala.org. **Website:** www.ala.org. The Theodor Seuss Geisel Awar, is given annually beginning to the author(s) and illustrator(s) of the most distinguished American book for beginning readers published in English in the United States during the preceding year. The award is to recognize the author(s) and illustrator(s) who demonstrate great creativity and imagination in his/her/their literary and artistic achievements to engage children in reading. Terms and criteria for the award are listed on the website. Entry will not be returned. Deadline: December 31. Prize: Medal, given at awards ceremony during the ALA Annual Conference.

☼ AMELIA FRANCES HOWARD GIBBON ILLUSTRATOR'S AWARD

1150 Morrison Drie, Suite 400, Ottawa ON K 2H859 Canada. (613)232-9625. **Fax:** (613) 563-9895. **E-mail:** lynne@marigold.ab.ca. **Website:** www.cla.ca. Annually awarded to an outstanding illustrator of a children's book published in Canada during the previous calendar year. The award is bestowed upon books that are suitable for children up to and including age 12. To be eligible for the award, an illustrator must be a Canadian citizen or a permanent resident of Canada, and the text of the book must be worthy of the book's illustrations. Prize: A plaque and a check for $1,000 (CAD).

GOLDEN KITE AWARDS

SCBWI Golden Kite Awards, 8271 Beverly Blvd., Los Angeles CA 90048-4515. (323)782-1010. **E-mail:** sara rutenberg@scbwi.org. **Website:** www.scbwi.org. Society of Children's Book Writers and Illustrators, 8271 Beverly Blvd.Los Angeles CA 90048. (323)782-1010. **E-mail:** scbwi@scbwi.org. **Website:** www.scbwi.org. **Contact:** SCBWI Golden Kite Coordinator. Annual award. Estab. 1973. "The works chosen will be those that the judges feel exhibit excellence in writing, and in the case of the picture-illustrated books—in illustration, and genuinely appeal to the interests and concerns of children. For the fiction and nonfiction awards, original works and single-author collections of stories or poems of which at least half are new and never before published in book form are eligible—anthologies and translations are not. For the picture-illustration awards, the art or photographs must be original works (the texts—which may be fiction or nonfiction—may be original, public domain or previously published). Deadline for entries: December 15. SASE for award rules. No entry fee. Awards, in addition to statuettes and plaques, the four winners receive $2,500 cash award plus trip to LA SCBWI Conference. The panel of judges will consist of professional authors, illustrators, editors or agents." Requirements for entrants: "must be a member of SCBWI and books must be published in that year." Winning books will be displayed at national conference in August. Books to be entered, as well as further inquiries, should be submitted to: The Society of Children's Book Writers and Illustrators, above address. Given annually to recognize excellence in children's literature in 4 categories: fiction, nonfiction, picture book text, and picture book illustration. Books submitted must be published in the previous calendar year. Both individuals and publishers may submit. Submit 4 copies of book. Submit to one category only, except in the case of picture books. Deadline: December 1. Prize: One Golden Kite Award Winner and one Honor Book will be chosen per category. Winners and Honorees will receive a commemorative poster also sent to publishers, bookstores, libraries, and schools; a press release; an announcement on the SCBWI website; and on SCBWI Social Networks. Also receive an expense-paid trip to Los Angeles to attend the award ceremony.

☯ GOVERNOR GENERAL'S LITERARY AWARD FOR CHILDREN'S LITERATURE

150 Elgin St., P.O. Box 1047, Ottawa ON K1P 5V8 Canada. (613)566-4414, ext. 5573. **Website:** www.canadacouncil.ca/prizes/ggla. Offered for the best English-language and the best French-language works of children's literature by a Canadian in 2 categories: text and illustration. Publishers submit titles for consideration. Deadline: Depends on the book's publication date. Books in English: March 15, June 1, or August 7. Books in French: March 15 or July 15. Prize: Each laureate receives $25,000; non-winning finalists receive $1,000.

☯ GOVERNOR GENERAL'S LITERARY AWARDS

150 Elgin St., P.O. Box 1047, Ottawa ON K1P 5V8 Canada. (613)566-4414, ext. 5573. **Website:** www.canadacouncil.ca/prizes/ggla. Established by Parliament, the Canada Council for the Arts provides a wide range of grants and services to professional Canadian artists and art organizations in dance, media arts, music, theater, writing, publishing, and the visual arts. Books must be first edition trade books written, translated, or illustrated by Canadian citizens or permanent residents of Canada and published in Canada or abroad in the previous year. Collections of poetry must be at least 48 pages long, and at least half the book must contain work not published previously in book form. In the case of translation, the original work must also be a Canadian-authored title. Books must be submitted by publishers with a Publisher's Registration Form, which is available by request from the Writing and Publishing Section of the Canada Council for the Arts. Guidelines and current deadlines are available on our website, by mail, telephone, fax, or e-mail. The Governor General's Literary Awards are given annually for the best English-language and French-language work in each of 7 categories, including fiction, nonfiction, poetry, drama, children's literature (text), children's literature (illustration), and translation. Deadline: Depends on the book's publication date. Prize: Each GG winner receives $25,000. Non-winning finalists receive $1,000. Judged by fellow authors, translators, and illustrators. For each category, a jury makes the final selection.

HACKNEY LITERARY AWARDS

1305 2nd Ave. N, #103, Birmingham AL 35203. (205)226-4921. **E-mail:** info@hackneyliteraryawards.org. **Website:** www.hackneyliteraryawards.org. **Contact:** Myra Crawford, PhD, executive director. Offered annually for unpublished novels, short stories (maximum 5,000 words) and poetry (50 line limit). Guidelines on website. Deadline: September 30 (novels), November 30 (short stories and poetry). Prize: $5,000 in annual prizes for poetry and short fiction ($2,500 national and $2,500 state level). 1st Place: $600; 2nd Place: $400; 3rd Place: $250); plus $5,000 for an unpublished novel. Competition winners will be announced on the website each March.

THE MARILYN HALL AWARDS FOR YOUTH THEATRE

P.O. Box 148, Beverly Hills CA 90213. **Website:** www.beverlyhillstheatreguild.com. **Contact:** Candace Coster, competition coordinator. The Marilyn Hall Awards consist of 2 monetary prizes for plays suitable for grades 6-8 (middle school) or for plays suitable for grades 9-12 (high school). The 2 prizes will be awarded on the merits of the play scripts, which includes its suitability for the intended audience. The plays should be approximately 45-75 minutes in length. There is no production connected to any of the prizes, though a staged reading is optional at the discretion of the BHTG. Unpublished submissions only. Authors must be U.S. citizens or legal residents and must sign entry form personally. **Deadline:** Postmarked between January 15 and the last day of February. **Prize:** 1st Prize: $700; 2nd Prize: $300.

HIGHLIGHTS FOR CHILDREN FICTION CONTEST

803 Church St., Honesdale PA 18431-1824. (570)253-1080. **Fax:** (570)251-7847. **E-mail:** eds@highlights-corp.com. **Website:** www.highlights.com. **Contact:** Christine French Cully, fiction contest editor. Unpublished submissions only. Open to any writer 16 years of age or older. Winners announced in May. Length up to 800 words. Stories for beginning readers should not exceed 500 words. Stories should be consistent with Highlights editorial requirements. No violence, crime or derogatory humor. Send SASE or visit website for guidelines and current theme. Stimulates interest in writing for children and rewards and recognizes excellence. **Deadline:** January 31. Submission period begins January 1. **Prize:** Three prizes of $1,000 or tuition for any Highlights Foundation Founders Workshop.

MARILYN HOLINSHEAD VISITING SCHOLARS FELLOWSHIP

113 Anderson Library, 222 21st Ave. South, Minneapolis MN 55455. **Website:** http://www.lib.umn.edu/clrc/awards-grants-and-fellowships. Marilyn Hollinshead Visiting Scholars Fund for Travel to the Kerlan Collection will be available for research study in 2014. Applicants may request up to $1,500. Send a letter with the proposed purpose and plan to use specific research materials (manuscripts and art), dates, and budget (including airfare and per diem). Travel and a written report on the project must be completed and submitted in 2014. **Deadline:** January 30.

THE JULIA WARD HOWE/BOSTON AUTHORS AWARD

15 Claremont St., Newton MA 02458-1925. (617)244-0646. **E-mail:** bostonauthors@aol.com; leev@bc.edu. **Website:** www.bostonauthorsclub.org. **Contact:** Vera Lee. This annual award honors Julia Ward Howe and her literary friends who founded the Boston Authors Club in 1900. It also honors the membership over 110 years, consisting of novelists, biographers, historians, governors, senators, philosophers, poets, playwrights, and other luminaries. There are 2 categories: trade books and books for young readers (beginning with chapter books through young adult books). Works of fiction, nonfiction, memoir, poetry, and biography published in 2010 are eligible. Authors must live or have lived (college counts) within a 100-mile radius of Boston within the last 5 years. Subsidized books, cook books and picture books are not eligible.

HRC SHOWCASE THEATRE PLAYWRITING CONTEST

P.O. Box 940, Hudson NY 12534. (518)851-7244. **Website:** www.hrc-showcasetheatre.com. **Contact:** Jesse Waldinger, chair. HRC Showcase Theatre invites submissions of full-length plays to its annual contest from new, aspiring, or established playwrights. Each submitted play should be previously unpublished, run no more than 90 minutes, require no more than 6 actors, and be suitable for presentated as a staged reading by Equity actors. **Deadline:** March 1. **Prize:** $500. Four runner-ups will receive $100 each.

CAROL OTIS HURST CHILDREN'S BOOK PRIZE

Westfield Athenaeum, 6 Elm St., Westfield MA 01085. (413)568-7833. **Website:** www.westath.org. The Carol Otis Hurst Children's Book Prize honors outstanding works of fiction and nonfiction written for children and young adults through the age of 18. For a work to be considered, the writer must either be a native or a current resident of New England. While the prize is presented annually to an author whose work best exemplifies the highest standards of writing for this age group regardless of genre or topic or geographical setting, the prize committee is especially interested in those books that treat life in the region. Further, entries will be judged on how well they succeed in portraying one or more of the following elements: childhood, adolescence, family life, schooling, social and political developments, fine and performing artistic expression, domestic arts, environmental issues, transportation and communication, changing technology, military experience at home and abroad, business and manufacturing, workers and the labor movement, agriculture and its transformation, racial and ethnic diversity, religious life and institutions, immigration and adjustment, sports at all levels, and the evolution of popular entertainment. Books must have been copyrighted in their original format during the calendar year, January 1 to December 31, of the year preceding the year in which the prize is awarded. Any individual, publisher, or organization may nominate a book. See website for details and guidelines. Prize: $500.

INSIGHT WRITING CONTEST

Fax: (301)393-4055. **E-mail:** insight@rhpa.org. **Website:** www.insightmagazine.org. **Contact:** Omar Miranda, editor. Annual contest for writers in the categories of student short story, general short story, and student poetry. Unpublished submissions only. General category is open to all writers; student categories must be age 22 and younger. Deadline: July 31. Prize: Prizes: Student Short and General Short Story: 1st Prize: $250; 2nd Prize: $200; 3rd Prize: $150. Student Poetry: 1st Prize: $100; 2nd Prize: $75; 3rd Prize: $50.

INTERNATIONAL READING ASSOCIATION CHILDREN'S AND YOUNG ADULTS BOOK AWARDS

P.O. Box 8139, 800 Barksdale Rd., Newark DE 19714-8139. (302)731-1600, ext. 221. **E-mail:** exec@reading.org. **E-mail:** committees@reading.org. **Website:** reading.org. **Contact:** Kathy Baughman. Children's and Young Adults Book Awards is intended for newly published authors who show unusual promise in the children's and young adults' book field. Awards are given for fiction and nonfiction in each of three categories: primary, intermediate, and young adult. Books from all countries and published in English for the first time during the previous calendar year will be considered. See website for eligibility and criteria information. Entry should be the author's first or second book. Deadline: November 1. Prize: $1,000.

IRA SHORT STORY AWARD

International Reading Association, 800 Barksdale Rd., PO Box 8139, Newark DE 19714-8139. (302)731-1600. **Fax:** (302)731-1057. **E-mail:** committees@reading.org. **Website:** www.reading.org. Offered to reward author of an original short story published for the first time in a periodical for children. (Periodicals should generally be aimed at readers around age 12.) Write for guidelines or download from website. Both fiction and nonfiction stories are eligible; each will be rated according to the characteristics that are appropriate for the genre. The story should: create a believable world for the readers, be truthful and authentic in its

presentation of information, serve as a reading and literary standard by which readers can measure other writing, and encourage young readers by providing them with an enjoyable reading experience. Deadline: November 15. Prize: $1,000 stipend.

JUVENILE ADVENTURE FICTION CONTEST

E-mail: dianaperry@DianaPerryBooks.com. **Website:** dianaperrybooks.com. **Contact:** Diana Perry. "Tell an adventurous tale with an 8-year-old to 12-year-old protagonist; refer to Robert Louis Stevenson or Mark Twain stories. Nothing too dangerous, but very exciting, bigger than life. Must be suitable for juvenile readers." Rules on website. Length: up to 20 pages or 5,000 words. Purpose: "To give exposure to beginning poets trying to break in to the business and get noticed." Deadline: May 31. Prize: 1st Place: $300, trophy, mention on website, t-shirt, press releases in your local newspapers; 2nd Place: $200, trophy, mention on website, t-shirt, press releases in your local newspapers; 3rd Place: $100, trophy, mention on website, t-shirt, press releases in your local newspapers; 4th/5th places: $50/$25, plaque, mention on website, t-shirt, press releases in your local newspapers. "We also list names of next 25 honorable mentions on website. Contest guidelines and entry form on website. CHECK WEBSITE FOR GUEST JUDGES. Mail entry form, your story, and a $15 money order only to Juvenile Adventure Fiction Contest at above address postmarked no later than May 31. Winners announced both on website and via snail mail July 1. Prizes mailed within 10 days of announcement. Judged by Diana Perry and guest judge.

EZRA JACK KEATS/KERLAN MEMORIAL FELLOWSHIP

113 Elmer L. Andersen Library, 222 21st Ave. S., University of Minnesota, Minneapolis MN 55455. **E-mail:** clrc@umn.edu. **Website:** https://www.lib.umn.edu/clrc/awards-grants-and-fellowships. **Contact:** Lisa Von Drasek, curator. This fellowship from the Ezra Jack Keats Foundation will provide $1,500 to a talented writer and/or illustrator of children's books who wishes to use the Kerlan Collection for the furtherance of his or her artistic development. Special consideration will be given to someone who would find it difficult to finance a visit to the Kerlan Collection. The Ezra Jack Keats Fellowship recipient will receive transportation costs and a per diem allotment.

See website for application deadline and for digital application materials. Winner will be notified in February. Study and written report must be completed within the calendar year. Deadline: January 30.

THE EZRA JACK KEATS NEW WRITER AND NEW ILLUSTRATOR AWARDS

450 14th St., Brooklyn NY 11215. **E-mail:** jchang@nypl.org. **Website:** www.ezra-jack-keats.org. **Contact:** Julia Chang, program coordinator. Annual award to recognize and encourage new authors and illustrators starting out in the field of children's books. Many past winners of the Ezra Jack Keats Book Award have gone on to distinguished careers, creating books beloved by parents, children, librarians, and teachers around the world. Writers and illustrators must have had no more than 3 books previously published. Prize: $1,000 honorarium for each winner. Judged by a distinguished selection committee of early childhood education specialists, librarians, illustrators and experts in children's literature.

KENTUCKY BLUEGRASS AWARD

Northern Kentucky University, 405 Steely Library, Nunn Drive, Highland Heights KY 41099. (859)572-6620. **E-mail:** smithjen@nku.edu. **Website:** kba.nku.edu. The Kentucky Bluegrass Award is a student choice program. The KBA promotes and encourages Kentucky students in kindergarten through grade 12 to read a variety of quality literature. Each year, a KBA committee for each grade category chooses the books for the four Master Lists (K-2, 3-5, 6-8 and 9-12). All Kentucky public and private schools, as well as public libraries, are welcome to participate in the program. To nominate a book, see the website for form and details. Deadline: March 1. Judged by students who read books and choose their favorite.

CORETTA SCOTT KING BOOK AWARDS

50 E. Huron St., Chicago IL 60611. (800)545-2433. **Website:** www.ala.org/csk. The Coretta Scott King Book Awards are given annually to outstanding African American authors and illustrators of books for children and young adults that demonstrate an appreciation of African American culture and universal human values. This award commemorates the life and work of Dr. Martin Luther King, Jr., and honors his wife, Mrs. Coretta Scott King, for her courage and determination to continue the work for peace and world brotherhood. Must be written for a youth audience in one of three categories: preschool-4th grade; 5th-8th grade; or 9th-12th grade. Book must be published in the year preceding the year the award is given, evidenced by the copyright date in the book. See website for full details, criteria, and eligibility concerns. Deadline: December 1.

LEAGUE OF UTAH WRITERS CONTEST

(435)755-7609. **E-mail:** luwcontest@gmail.com. **Website:** www.luwriters.org. **Contact:** Tim Keller, Contest Chair. Open to any writer, the LUW Contest provides authors an opportunity to get their work read and critiqued. Multiple categories are offered; see webpage for details. Entries must be the original and unpublished work of the author. Winners are announced at the Annual Writers Round-Up in September. Those not present will be notified by e-mail. Submission Period: March 15-June 15. Prize: Cash prizes are awarded. Judged by professional authors and editors from outside the League.

MCLAREN MEMORIAL COMEDY PLAY WRITING COMPETITION

2000 W. Wadley, Midland TX 79705. (432)682-2544. **Fax:** (432)682-6136. **Website:** www.mctmidland.org. The McLaren Memorial Comedy Play Writing Competition was established to honor long-time MCT volunteer Mike McLaren who loved a good comedy, whether he was on stage or in the front row. Open to students. Annual contest. Unpublished submissions only. Submissions made by author. SASE for contest rules and entry forms. Rights to winning material acquired or purchased. First right of production or refusal is acquired by MCT. The contest is open to any playwright, but the play submitted must be unpublished and never produced in a for-profit setting. One previous production in a nonprofit theatre is acceptable. "Readings" do not count as productions. Deadline: February 28. Prize: $400 for full-length winner and $200 for one-act winner as well as staged readings for 3 finalists in each category. Judged by the audience present at the McLaren festival when the staged readings are performed.

☁ THE VICKY METCALF AWARD FOR CHILDREN'S LITERATURE

460 Richmond St. W., Suite 600, Toronto ON M5V 1Y1 Canada. (416)504-8222. **E-mail:** info@writerstrust.com. **Website:** www.writerstrust.com. **Contact:** Amanda Hopkins. The Metcalf Award is presented to a Canadian writer for a body of work in children's literature at The Writers' Trust Awards event held in

Toronto each Fall. Open to Canadian citizens and permanent residents only.

MILKWEED NATIONAL FICTION PRIZE

1011 Washington Ave. S., Suite 300, Minneapolis MN 55415. (612)332-3192. **Fax:** (612)215-2550. **E-mail:** editor@milkweed.org. **Website:** www.milkweed.org. **Contact:** Daniel Slager, award director. The Milkweed National Fiction Prize is awarded to a writer not previously published by the press. Mss should be one of the following: a novel, a collection of short stories, one or more novellas, or a combination of short stories and one or more novellas. Work previously published as a book in the US is not eligible, but individual stories or novellas previously published in magazines or anthologies are eligible. Milkweed Editions reserves the right not to award the prize for any given year. Unpublished submissions only "in book form." Send SASE or visit website for award guidelines. The prize is awarded to the best work for children ages 8-13 that Milkweed agrees to publish in a calendar year. Recognizes an outstanding literary novel for readers ages 8-13 and encourage writers to turn their attention to readers in this age group. Prize: $5,000 advance against royalties agreed to at the time of acceptance. Judged by the editors of Milkweed Editions.

MINNESOTA BOOK AWARDS

325 Cedar Street, Suite 555, St. Paul MN 55101. **E-mail:** mnbookawards@thefriends.org; friends@thefriends.org; info@thefriends.org. **Website:** www.thefriends.org. Annual award. Recognizes and honors achievement by members of Minnesota's book community. All books must be the work of a Minnesota author or primary artistic creator (current Minnesota resident who maintains a year-round residence in Minnesota). All books must be published within the calendar year of the competition.

☯ MUNICIPAL CHAPTER OF TORONTO IODE JEAN THROOP BOOK AWARD

40 Orchard View Blvd., Suite 219, Toronto ON M4R 1B9 Canada. (416)925-5078. **Fax:** (416)925-5127. **E-mail:** ioedtoronto@bellnet.ca. **Website:** www.bookcentre.ca/awards/iode_book_award_municipal_chapter_toronto. **Contact:** Jennifer Werry, contest director. Each year, the Municipal Chapter of Toronto IODE presents an award intended to encourage the publication of books for children between the ages of 6-12 years. The award-winner must be a Canadian citizen, resident in Toronto or the surrounding area,

and the book must be published in Canada. Deadline: November 1. Prize: Award and cash prize of $2,000. Judged by a selected committee.

NATIONAL BOOK AWARDS

The National Book Foundation, 90 Broad St., Suite 604, New York NY 10004. (212)685-0261. **E-mail:** nationalbook@nationalbook.org. **Website:** www.nationalbook.org. The National Book Foundation and the National Book Awards celebrate the best of American literature, expand its audience, and enhance the cultural value of great writing in America. The contest offers prizes in 4 categories: fiction, nonfiction, poetry, and young people's literature. Books should be published between December 1 and November 30 of the past year. Submissions must be previously published and must be entered by the publisher. General guidelines available on website. Interested publishes should phone or e-mail the Foundation. Deadline: Entry form and payment by May 15; a copy of the book by July 1. Prize: $10,000 in each category. Finalists will each receive a prize of $1,000. Judged by a category specific panel of 5 judges for each category.

NATIONAL OUTDOOR BOOK AWARDS

(208)282-3912. **E-mail:** wattron@isu.edu. **Website:** www.noba-web.org. **Contact:** Ron Watters. Nine categories: History/biography, outdoor literature, instructional texts, outdoor adventure guides, nature guides, children's books, design/artistic merit, natural history literature, and nature and the environment. Additionally, a special award, the Outdoor Classic Award, is given annually to books which, over a period of time, have proven to be exceptionally valuable works in the outdoor field. Application forms and eligibilty requirements are available online. Applications for the Awards program become available in early June. Deadline: September 1. Prize: Winning books are promoted nationally and are entitled to display the National Outdoor Book Award (NOBA) medallion.

NATIONAL PEACE ESSAY CONTEST

United States Institute of Peace, 2301 Constitution Avenue, NW, Washington DC 20037. (202)457-1700. **Fax:** (202)429-6063. **E-mail:** essaycontest@usip.org. **Website:** www.usip.org. The Academy for International Conflict Management and Peacebuilding is the education and training arm of the United States Institute of Peace and runs the National Peace Essay Contest based on the belief that questions about peace, justice, freedom, and security are vital to civic education. Each year over 1,100 students submit entries to the essay contest while thousands more participate in related writing and other classroom exercises in high schools around the country. Promotes serious discussion among high school students, teachers, and national leaders about international peace and conflict resolution today and in the future; complements existing curricula and other scholastic activities; strengthens students' research, writing, and reasoning skills; and meets National Contents Standards. **Deadline:** February 10. **Prize:** First-place state winners receive scholarships and are invited to Washington for a five-day awards program. The Institute pays for expenses related to the program, including travel, lodging, meals and entertainment. This unique five-day program promotes an understanding of the nature and process of international peacemaking by focusing on a region and/or theme related to the current essay contest.

NATIONAL WRITERS ASSOCIATION NONFICTION CONTEST

10940 S. Parker Rd., #508, Parker CO 80134. (303)841-0246. **E-mail:** natlwritersassn@hotmail.com. **Website:** www.nationalwriters.com. Only unpublished works may be submitted. Judging of entries will not begin until the contest ends. Nonfiction in the following areas will be accepted: articles—submission should include query letter, 1st page of manuscript, separate sheet citing 5 possible markets; essay—the complete essay and 5 possible markets on separate sheet; nonfiction book proposal including query letter, chapter by chapter outline, first chapter, bio and market analysis. Those unsure of proper manuscript format should request Research Report #35. The purpose of the National Writers Association Nonfiction Contest is to encourage the writing of nonfiction and recognize those who excel in this field. **Deadline:** December 31. **Prize:** 1st - 5th place awards will be presented at the NWAF Conference. Other winners will be notified by March 31st. 1st Prize: $200 and Clearinghouse representation if winner is book proposal; 2nd Prize: $100; 3rd Prize: $50; 4th - 10th places will receive a book. Honorable Mentions receive a certificate. Judging will be based on originality, marketability, research, and reader interest. Copies of the judges evaluation sheets will be sent to entrants furnishing an SASE with their entry.

NATIONAL WRITERS ASSOCIATION SHORT STORY CONTEST

10940 S. Parker Rd., #508, Parker CO 80134. (303)841-0246. **E-mail:** natlwritersassn@hotmail.com. **Website:** www.nationalwriters.com. Opens April 1. Any genre of short story manuscript may be entered. All entries must be postmarked by July 1. Only unpublished works may be submitted. All manuscripts must be typed, double-spaced, in the English language. Maximum length is 5,000 words. Those unsure of proper manuscript format should request Research Report #35. The entry must be accompanied by an entry form (photocopies are acceptable) and return SASE if you wish the material and rating sheets returned. Submissions will be destroyed, otherwise. The U.S. Postal Service will not allow us to use your metered postage unless it is undated. Receipt of entry will not be acknowledged without a return postcard. Author's name and address must appear on the first page. Entries remain the property of the author and may be submitted during the contest as long as they are not published before the final notification of winners. Final prizes will be awarded at the NWAF Workshop in June. The purpose of the National Writers Assn. Short Story Contest is to encourage the development of creative skills, recognize and reward outstanding ability in the area of short story writing. **Prize:** 1st - 5th place awards will be presented at the NWAF Conference. 1st Prize: $250; 2nd Prize: $100; 3rd Prize: $50; 4th - 10th places will receive a book. 1st - 3rd place winners may be asked to grant one-time rights for publication in *Authorship* magazine. Honorable Mentions receive a certificate. Judging will be based on originality, marketability, research, and reader interest. Copies of the judges evaluation sheets will be sent to entrants furnishing an SASE with their entry.

JOHN NEWBERY MEDAL

50 E. Huron, Chicago IL 60611. (800)545-2433, ext. 2153. **Fax:** (312)280-5271. **E-mail:** alscawards@ala.org. **Website:** www.ala.org. The Newbery Medal is awarded annually by the American Library Association for the most distinguished American children's book published the previous year. Previously published submissions only; must be published prior to year award is given. SASE for award rules. Entries not returned. Medal awarded at Caldecott/Newbery banquet during ALA annual conference. Deadline:

December 31. Judged by Newbery Award Selection Committee.

NEW ENGLAND BOOK AWARDS

1955 Massachusetts Ave., #2, Cambridge MA 02140. (617)547-3642. **Fax:** (617)547-3759. **E-mail:** nan@neba.org. **Website:** http://www.newenglandbooks.org/BookAwards. **Contact:** Nan Sorenson, assistant executive director. Annual award. Previously published submissions only. Submissions made by New England booksellers; publishers. Submit written nominations only; actual books should not be sent. Member bookstores receive materials to display winners' books. Award is given to a specific title, fiction, nonfiction, children's. The titles must be either about New England, set in New England or by an author residing in the New England. The titles must be hardcover, paperback orginal or reissue that was published between September 1 and August 31. Entries must be still in print and available. Deadline: June 13. Judged by NEIBA membership.

NEW VOICES AWARD

Website: www.leeandlow.com. Open to students. Annual award. Lee & Low Books is one of the few minority-owned publishing companies in the country and has published more than 90 first-time writers and illustrators. Winning titles include *The Blue Roses*, winner of a Patterson Prize for Books for Young People; *Janna and the Kings*, an IRA Children's Book Award Notable; and *Sixteen Years in Sixteen Seconds*, selected for the Texas Bluebonnet Award Masterlist. Submissions made by author. SASE for contest rules or visit website. Restrictions of media for illustrators: The author must be a writer of color who is a resident of the U.S. and who has not previously published a children's picture book. For additional information, send SASE or visit Lee & Low's website. Encourages writers of color to enter the world of children's books. Deadline: September 30. Prize: New Voices Award: $1,000 prize and standard publication contract (regardless of whether or not writer has an agent) along with an advance against royalties; New Voices Honor Award: $500 prize. Judged by Lee & Low editors.

NORTH AMERICAN INTERNATIONAL AUTO SHOW HIGH SCHOOL POSTER CONTEST

1900 W. Big Beaver Rd., Troy MI 48084-3531. (248)643-0250. **Fax:** (248)283-5148. **E-mail:** sherp@dada.org. **Website:** www.naias.com. Open to students. Annual contest. Submissions made by the author and illustrator. Entrants must be Michigan high school students enrolled in grades 10-12. Winning posters may be displayed at the NAIAS 2012 and reproduced in the official NAIAS program, which is available to the public, international media, corporate executives and automotive suppliers. Winning posters may also be displayed on the official NAIAS website at the sole discretion of the NAIAS. Contact Detroit Auto Dealers Association (DADA) for contest rules and entry forms or retrieve rules from website. Prize: Chairman's Award: $1,000; State Farm Insurance Award: $1,000; Designer's Best of Show (Digital and Traditional): $500; Best Theme: $250; Best Use of Color: $250; Most Creative: $250. A winner will be chosen in each category from grades 10, 11 and 12. Prizes: 1st place in 10, 11, 12: $500; 2nd place: $250; 3rd place: $100. Judged by an independent panel of recognized representatives of the art community.

NORTHERN CALIFORNIA BOOK AWARDS

c/o Poetry Flash, 1450 Fourth St. #4, Berkeley CA 94710. (510)525-5476. **E-mail:** ncbr@poetryflash.org; editor@poetryflash.org. **Website:** www.poetryflash.org. **Contact:** Joyce Jenkins, executive director. Annual Northern California Book Award for outstanding book in literature, open to books published in the current calendar year by Northern California authors. Annual award. NCBR presents annual awards to Bay Area (northern California) authors annually in fiction, nonfiction, poetry and children's literature. Previously published books only. Must be published the calendar year prior to spring awards ceremony. Submissions nominated by publishers; author or agent could also nominate published work. Send 3 copies of the book to attention: NCBR. Encourages writers and stimulates interest in books and reading. Deadline: December 28. Prize: $100 honorarium and award certificate. Judging by voting members of the Northern California Book Reviewers.

OHIOANA BOOK AWARDS

274 E. First Ave., Suite 300, Columbus OH 43201-3673. (614)466-3831. **Fax:** (614)728-6974. **E-mail:** ohioana@ohioana.org. **Website:** www.ohioana.org. **Contact:** David Weaver, executive director. Writers must have been born in Ohio or lived in Ohio for at least 5 years, but books about Ohio or an Ohioan need not be written by an Ohioan. Results announced in August or September. Winners notified by mail in early sum-

mer. Offered annually to bring national attention to Ohio authors and their books, published in the last year. (Books can only be considered once.) Categories: Fiction, nonfiction, juvenile, poetry, and books about Ohio or an Ohioan. Deadline: December 31. Prize: Certificate and glass sculpture. Judged by a jury selected by librarians, book reviewers, writers and other knowledgeable people.

OKLAHOMA BOOK AWARDS

200 NE 18th St., Oklahoma City OK 73105. (405)521-2502. **Fax:** (405)525-7804. **E-mail:** carmstrong@oltn.odl.state.ok.us. **Website:** www.odl.state.ok.us/ocb. **Contact:** Connie Armstrong, executive director. This award honors Oklahoma writers and books about Oklahoma. Awards are presented to best books in fiction, nonfiction, children's, design and illustration, and poetry books about Oklahoma or books written by an author who was born, is living or has lived in Oklahoma. SASE for award rules and entry forms. Winner will be announced at banquet in Oklahoma City. The Arrell Gibson Lifetime Achievement Award is also presented each year for a body of work. Previously published submissions only. Submissions made by the author, author's agent, or entered by a person or group of people, including the publisher. Must be published during the calendar year preceding the award. Deadline: January 10. Prize: Awards a medal. Judging by a panel of 5 people for each category, generally a librarian, a working writer in the genre, booksellers, editors, etc.

ONCE UPON A WORLD CHILDREN'S BOOK AWARD

1399 S. Roxbury Dr., Los Angeles CA 90035-4709. (310)772-7605. **Fax:** (310)772-7628. **E-mail:** bookaward@wiesenthal.net. **Website:** www.museumoftolerance.com. **Contact:** Adaire J. Klein, award director. The Simon Wiesenthal Center/Museum of Tolerance welcomes submissions for the Once Upon a World Children's Book Award. Book publishers and members of the public are invited to nominate children's books that meet the following criteria: young readers' books for ages 6-8 that promote the themes of tolerance, diversity, and social justice; older readers' books for ages 9-12 that promote the themes of tolerance, diversity, respect, and social justice. Books may be a picture book, fiction, nonfiction, or poetry. Deadline: February 28. Prize: $1,000 award in each category.

ORBIS PICTUS AWARD FOR OUTSTANDING NONFICTION FOR CHILDREN

1111 W. Kenyon Rd., Urbana IL 61801-1096. (217)328-3870. **Fax:** (217)328-0977. **Website:** www.ncte.org/awards/orbispictus. The NCTE Orbis Pictus Award promotes and recognizes excellence in the writing of nonfiction for children. Orbis Pictus commemorates the work of Johannes Amos Comenius, *Orbis Pictus—The World in Pictures* (1657), considered to be the first book actually planned for children. Submissions should be made by an author, the author's agent, or by a person or group of people. Must be published in the calendar year of the competition. Deadline: December 31. Prize: A plaque given at the NCTE Elementary Section Luncheon at the NCTE Annual Convention in November. Up to 5 honor books awarded. Judged by members of the Orbis Pictus Committee.

OREGON BOOK AWARDS

925 SW Washington St., Portland OR 97205. (503)227-2583. **Fax:** (503)241-4256. **E-mail:** la@literary-arts.org. **Website:** www.literary-arts.org. **Contact:** Susan Denning. The annual Oregon Book Awards celebrate Oregon authors in the areas of poetry, fiction, nonfiction, drama and young readers' literature published between August 1 and July 31 of the previous calendar year. Awards are available for every category. See website for details. Entry fee determined by initial print run; see website for details. Entries must be previously published. Oregon residents only. Accepts inquiries by phone and e-mail. Finalists announced in January. Winners announced at an awards ceremony in November. List of winners available in April. Deadline: August 29. Prize: Grant of $2,500. (Grant money could vary.). Judged by writers who are selected from outside Oregon for their expertise in a genre. Past judges include Mark Doty, Colson Whitehead and Kim Barnes.

OREGON LITERARY FELLOWSHIPS

925 S.W. Washington, Portland OR 97205. (503)227-2583. **E-mail:** susan@literary-arts.org. **Website:** www.literary-arts.org. **Contact:** Susan Denning, director of programs and events. Annual fellowships for writers of fiction, poetry, literary nonfiction, young readers and drama. Guidelines available in February for SASE. Accepts inquiries by e-mail, phone. Oregon residents only. Recipients announced in January. Deadline: Last Friday in June. Prize: $2,500 minimum award, for ap-

proximately 10 writers and 2 publishers. Judged by out-of-state writers

THE ORIGINAL ART

128 E. 63rd St., New York NY 10065. (212)838-2560. **Fax:** (212)838-2561. **E-mail:** kim@societyillustrators.org; info@societyillustrators.org. **Website:** www.societyillustrators.org. **Contact:** Kate Feirtag, exhibition director. The Original Art is an annual exhibit created to showcase illustrations from the year's best children's books published in the US. For editors and art directors, it's an inspiration and a treasure trove of talent to draw upon. Previously published submissions only. Request "call for entries" to receive contest rules and entry forms. Works will be displayed at the Society of Illustrators Museum of American Illustration in New York City October-November annually. Deadline: July 18. Judged by 7 professional artists and editors.

HELEN KEATING OTT AWARD FOR OUTSTANDING CONTRIBUTION TO CHILDREN'S LITERATURE

10157 SW Barbur Blvd. #102C, Portland OR 97219. (503)244-6919. **Fax:** (503)977-3734. **E-mail:** csla@worldaccessnet.com. **Website:** www.cslainfo.org. **Contact:** Glenda Strombom; Judy Janzen, administrator of CSLA. Annual award given to a person or organization that has made a significant contribution to promoting high moral and ethical values through children's literature. Recipient is honored in July during the conference. Awards certificate of recognition, the awards banquet, and one-night's stay in the hotel. A nomination for an award may be made by anyone. An application form is available by contacting Judy Janzen. Elements of creativity and innovation will be given high priority by the judges. A detailed description of the reasons for the nomination should be given, accompanied by documentary evidence of accomplishment. The nominator should give his or her name, address, telephone number, e-mail address, and a brief explanation of his or her knowledge of the individual's efforts. Elements of creativity and innovation will be given high priority. Applications should include at least 2 examples of your work (published or unpublished, 30 pages maximum) and a short biographical note including a description of your current and anticipated work. Also, indicate what you will work on while attending the Blue Mountain residency. Send three copies of these writing samples. Samples will not be returned.

PATERSON PRIZE FOR BOOKS FOR YOUNG PEOPLE

One College Blvd., Paterson NJ 07505. (973)684-6555. **Fax:** (973)523-6085. **E-mail:** mgillan@pccc.edu. **Website:** www.pccc.edu/poetry. **Contact:** Maria Mazziotti Gillan, executive director. Award for a book published in the previous year in each age category (Pre-K-Grade 3, Grades 4-6, Grades 7-12). Deadline: March 15. Prize: $500.

THE KATHERINE PATERSON PRIZE FOR YOUNG ADULT AND CHILDREN'S WRITING

Vermont College of Fine Arts, 36 College St., Montpelier VT 05602. (802)828-8517. **E-mail:** hungermtn@vcfa.edu. **Website:** www.hungermtn.org. **Contact:** Miciah Bay Gault, editor. The annual Katherine Paterson Prize for Young Adult and Children's Writing honors the best in young adult and children's literature. Submit young adult or middle grade mss, and writing for younger children, short stories, picture books, or novel excerpts, under 10,000 words. Guidelines available on website. Deadline: June 30. Prize: $1,000 and publication for the first place winner; $100 each and publication for the three category winners. Judged by a guest judge every year. The 2014 judge is Katherine Applegate, the Newbery Award-winning author of *The One and Only Ivan*.

PENNSYLVANIA YOUNG READERS' CHOICE AWARDS PROGRAM

148 S. Bethelehem Pike, Ambler PA 19002-5822. (215)643-5048. **E-mail:** bellavance@verizon.net. **Website:** www.psla.org. **Contact:** Jean B. Bellavance, coordinator. Submissions nominated by a person or group. Must be published within 5 years of the award—for example, books published in 2010 to present are eligible for the 2014-2015 award. SASE for contest rules and entry forms or check the Program wiki at pyrca.wikispaces.com. View information at the Pennsylvania School Librarians' website or the Program wiki. Must be currently living in North America. The purpose of the Pennsylvania Young Reader's Choice Awards Program is to promote the reading of quality books by young people in the Commonwealth of Pennsylvania, to encourage teacher and librarian collaboration and involvement in children's literature, and to honor authors whose works have been recognized by the students of Pennsylvania. Deadline: September 1. Prize: Framed certificate to winning au-

thors. Four awards are given, one for each of the following grade level divisions: K-3, 3-6, 6-8, YA. Judged by children of Pennsylvania (they vote).

PEN/PHYLLIS NAYLOR WORKING WRITER FELLOWSHIP

PEN American Center, 588 Broadway, Suite 303, New York NY 10012. **E-mail:** awards@pen.org. **Website:** www.pen.org. **Contact:** Nick Burd, awards program director. Offered annually to an author of children's or young adult fiction. The Fellowship has been developed to help writers whose work is of high literary caliber but who have not yet attracted a broad readership. The Fellowship is designed to assist a writer at a crucial moment in his or her career to complete a book-length work-in-progress. Candidates have published at least two novels for children or young adults which have been received warmly by literary critics, but have not generated suficient income to support the author. Writers must be nominated by an editor or fellow author. See website for eligibility and nomination guidelines. Deadline: February 15. Prize: $5,000.

PLEASE TOUCH MUSEUM BOOK AWARD

Memorial Hall in Fairmount Park, 4231 Avenue of the Republic, Philadelphia PA 19131. (215)578-5153. **Fax:** (215)578-5171. **E-mail:** hboyd@pleasetouchmuseum. org. **Website:** www.pleasetouchmuseum.org. **Contact:** Heather Boyd. This prestigious award has recognized and encouraged the publication of high quality books for young children. The award is given to books that are imaginative, exceptionally illustrated and help foster a child's life-long love of reading. To be eligible for consideration, a book must: (1) Be distinguished in text, illustration, and ability to explore and clarify an idea for young children (ages 7 and under); (2) be published within the last year by an American publisher; and (3) be by an American author and/or illustrator. Deadline: October 1. Judged by a panel of volunteer educators, artists, booksellers and librarians in conjunction with museum staff.

PNWA LITERARY CONTEST

(452)673-2665. **E-mail:** pnwa@pnwa.org. **Website:** www.pnwa.org. Annual literary contest with 12 different categories. See website for details and specific guidelines. Each entry receives 2 critiques. Winners announced at the PNWA Summer Conference, held annually in mid-July. Deadline: February 21. Prize: 1st Place: $700; 2nd Place: $300. Judged by an agent or editor attending the conference.

POCKETS FICTION-WRITING CONTEST

P.O. Box 340004, Nashville TN 37203-0004. (615)340-7333. **Fax:** (615)340-7267. **E-mail:** pockets@upper room.org. **Website:** www.pockets.upperroom.org. **Contact:** Lynn W. Gilliam, senior editor. Designed for 6- to 12-year-olds, *Pockets* magazine offers wholesome devotional readings that teach about God's love and presence in life. The content includes fiction, scripture stories, puzzles and games, poems, recipes, colorful pictures, activities, and scripture readings. Freelance submissions of stories, poems, recipes, puzzles and games, and activities are welcome. Stories should be 750-1,000 words. Multiple submissions are permitted. Past winners are ineligible. The primary purpose of *Pockets* is to help children grow in their relationship with God and to claim the good news of the gospel of Jesus Christ by applying it to their daily lives. *Pockets* espouses respect for all human beings and for God's creation. It regards a child's faith journey as an integral part of all of life and sees prayer as undergirding that journey. Deadline: Entries are received beginning March 1 and must be postmarked no later than August 15. Prize: $500 and publication in magazine.

EDGAR ALLAN POE AWARD

1140 Broadway, Suite 1507, New York NY 10001. (212)888-8171. **Fax:** (212)888-8107. **E-mail:** mwa@ mysterywriters.org. **Website:** www.mysterywriters. org. Mystery Writers of America is the leading association for professional crime writers in the United States. Members of MWA include most major writers of crime fiction and nonfiction, as well as screenwriters, dramatists, editors, publishers, and other professionals in the field. Purpose of the award: Honor authors of distinguished works in the mystery field. Previously published submissions only. Submissions made by the author, author's agent; "normally by the publisher." Work must be published/produced the year of the contest. Deadline: November 30. Prize: Awards ceramic bust of "Edgar" for winner; scrolls for all nominees. Judged by professional members of Mystery Writers of America (writers).

MICHAEL L. PRINTZ AWARD

50 E. Huron, Chicago IL 60611. **Fax:** (312)280-5276. **E-mail:** yalsa@ala.org; ala@ala.org. **Website:** www.ala. org/yalsa/printz. The Michael L. Printz Award annually honors the best book written for teens, based entirely on its literary merit, each year. In addition, the

Printz Committee names up to 4 honor books, which also represent the best writing in young adult literature. The award-winning book can be fiction, nonfiction, poetry or an anthology, and can be a work of joint authorship or editorship. The books must be published between January 1 and December 31 of the preceding year and be designated by its publisher as being either a young adult book or one published for the age range that YALSA defines as young adult, e.g. ages 12 through 18. Deadline: December 1. Judged by an award committee.

PURPLE DRAGONFLY BOOK AWARDS

4696 W. Tyson St., Chandler AZ 85226-2903. (480)940-8182. **Fax:** (480)940-8787. **E-mail:** cristy@fivestarpublications.com. **Website:** www.purpledragonflybookawards.com; www.fivestarpublications.com; www.fivestarbookawards.com. **Contact:** Cristy Bertini, contest coordinator. Five Star Publications presents the Purple Dragonfly Book Awards, which were conceived and designed with children in mind. "Not only do we want to recognize and honor accomplished authors in the field of children's literature, but we also want to highlight and reward up-and-coming, newly published authors and younger published writers." The Purple Dragonfly Book Awards are divided into 3 distinct subject categories, ranging from books on the environment and cooking to sports and family issues. (Click on the "Categories" tab on the website for a complete list.) The Purple Dragonfly Book Awards are geared toward stories that appeal to children of all ages. Looking for stories that inspire, inform, teach or entertain. "A Purple Dragonfly seal on your book's cover tells parents, grandparents, educators and caregivers they are giving children the very best in reading excellence." Being honored with a Purple Dragonfly Award confers credibility upon the winner, as well as provides positive publicity to further their success. The goal of these awards is to give published authors the recognition they deserve and provide a helping hand to further their careers. The awards are open to books published in any calendar year and in any country that are available for purchase. Books entered must be printed in English. Traditionally published, partnership published and self-published books are permitted, as long as they fit the above criteria. Deadline: May 1 (postmarked). Submissions postmarked March 1 or earlier that meet all submission requirements are eligible for the Early

Bird reward: A free copy of *The Economical Guide to Self-Publishing* or *Promote Like a Pro: Small Budget, Big Show*. Prize: Grand Prize winner will receive a $300 cash prize, 100 foil award seals (more can be ordered for an extra charge), 1 hour of marketing consultation from Five Star Publications, and $100 worth of Five Star Publications' titles, as well as publicity on Five Star Publications' websites and inclusion in a winners' news release sent to a comprehensive list of media outlets. The Grand Prize winner will also be placed in the Five Star Dragonfly Book Awards virtual bookstore with a thumbnail of the book's cover, price, 1-sentence description and link to Amazon.com for purchasing purposes, if applicable. 1st Place: All first-place winners of categories will be put into a drawing for a $100 prize. In addition, each first-place winner in each category receives a certificate commemorating their accomplishment, 25 foil award seals (more can be ordered for an extra charge) and mention on Five Star Publications' websites. Judged by industry experts with specific knowledge about the categories over which they preside.

QUILL AND SCROLL INTERNATIONAL WRITING AND PHOTO CONTEST, AND BLOGGING COMPETITION

School of Journalism, Univ. of Iowa, 100 Adler Journalism Bldg., Iowa City IA 52242-2004. (319)335-3457. **Fax:** (319)335-3989. **E-mail:** quill-scroll@uiowa.edu. **E-mail:** vanessa-shelton@uiowa.edu. **Website:** quillandscroll.org. **Contact:** Vanessa Shelton, contest director. Entries must have been published in a high school or profesional newspaper or website during the previous year, and must be the work of a currently enrolled high school student, when published. Open to students. Annual contest. Previously published submissions only. Submissions made by the author or school media adviser. Deadline: February 5. Prize: Winners will receive *Quill and Scroll*'s National Award Gold Key and, if seniors, are eligible to apply for one of the scholarships offered by *Quill and Scroll*. All winning entries are automatically eligible for the International Writing and Photo Sweepstakes Awards. Engraved plaque awarded to sweepstakes winners.

◎ REGINA BOOK AWARD

P.O. Box 20025, Regina SK S4P 4J7 Canada. (306)569-1585. **E-mail:** director@bookawards.sk.ca. **Website:** www.bookawards.sk.ca. **Contact:** Joanne Skidmore, SBA Board Chair. Offered annually. In recognition of the vitality of the literary community in Regina, this award is presented to a Regina author for the best book, judged on the quality of writing. Books from the following categories will be considered: Children's; drama; fiction (short fiction by a single author, novellas, novels); nonfiction (all categories of nonfiction writing except cookbooks, directories, how-to books, or bibliographies of minimal critical content); poetry. Deadline: November 1. Prize: $2,000 (CAD).

TOMÁS RIVERA MEXICAN AMERICAN CHILDREN'S BOOK AWARD

Dr. Jesse Gainer, Texas State University, 601 University Drive, San Marcos TX 78666-4613. (512)245-2357. **Website:** riverabookaward.org. **Contact:** Dr. Jesse Gainer, award director. Texas State University College of Education developed the Tomas Rivera Mexican American Children's Book Award to honor authors and illustrators who create literature that depicts the Mexican American experience. The award was established in 1995 and was named in honor of Dr. Tomas Rivera, a distinguished alumnus of Texas State University. The book will be written for children and young adults (0-16 years). The text and illustrations will be of highest quality. The portrayal/representations of Mexican Americans will be accurate and engaging, avoid stereotypes, and reflect rich characterization. The book may be fiction or non-fiction. See website for more details and directions. Deadline: November 1.

◎ ROCKY MOUNTAIN BOOK AWARD: ALBERTA CHILDREN'S CHOICE BOOK AWARD

Box 42, Lethbridge AB T1J 3Y3 Canada. (403)381-0855. **Website:** http://rmba.lethsd.ab.ca/. **Contact:** Michelle Dimnik, contest director. Annual contest open to Alberta students. No entry fee. Awards: Gold medal and author tour of selected Alberta schools. Judging by students. Canadian authors and/or illustrators only. Previously unpublished submissions only. Submissions made by author's agent or nominated by a person or group. Must be published within the 3 years prior to that year's award. Register before January 15th to take part in the Rocky Mountain Book Award. SASE for contest rules and entry forms. Purpose of contest: "Reading motivation for students, promotion of Canadian authors, illustrators and publishers."

ROYAL DRAGONFLY BOOK AWARDS

4696 W. Tyson St., Chandler AZ 85226. (480)940-8182. **Fax:** (480)940-8787. **E-mail:** cristy@fivestarpublications.com. **Website:** www.fivestarpublications.com; www.fivestarbookawards.com; www.royaldragonflybookawards.com. **Contact:** Cristy Bertini. Offered annually for any previously published work to honor authors for writing excellence of all types of literature—fiction and nonfiction—in 52 categories, appealing to a wide range of ages and comprehensive list of genres. Open to any title published in English. Entry forms are downloadable at www.royaldragonflybookawards.com. Prize: Grand Prize winner receives $300, while another entrant will be the lucky winner of a $100 drawing. All first-place winners receive foil award seals and are included in a publicity campaign announcing winners. All first- and second-place winners and honorable mentions receive certificates.

◎ SASKATCHEWAN CHILDREN'S LITERATURE AWARD

Box 20025, Regina SK S4P 4J7 Canada. (306)569-1585. **Fax:** (306)569-4187. **E-mail:** director@bookawards.sk.ca. **E-mail:** info@bookawards.sk.ca. **Website:** www.bookawards.sk.ca. **Contact:** Joanne Skidmore, SBA Board Chair. Offered annually. This award is presented to a Saskatchewan author or pair of authors, or to Saskatchewan author and a Saskatchewan illustrator, for the best book of children's literature, for ages 0-11, judged on the quality of the writing and illustration. Deadline: November 1. Prize: $2,000 (CAD).

◎ SASKATCHEWAN FIRST BOOK AWARD

P.O. Box 20025, Regina SK S4P 4J7 Canada. (306)569-1585. **E-mail:** director@bookawards.sk.ca. **Website:** www.bookawards.sk.ca. **Contact:** Joanne Skidmore, SBA Board Chair. Offered annually. This award is presented to a Saskatchewan author for the best first book, judged on the quality of writing. Books from the following categories will be considered: Children's; drama; fiction (short fiction by a single author, novellas, novels); nonfiction (all categories of nonfiction writing except cookbooks, directories, how-to books, or bibliographies of minimal critical content); and poetry. Deadline: November 1. Prize: $2,000 (CAD).

SCBWI MAGAZINE MERIT AWARDS

8271 Beverly Blvd., Los Angeles CA 90048. **Website:** www.scbwi.org. **Contact:** Stephanie Gordon, award coordinator. The SCBWI is a professional organization of writers and illustrators and others interested in children's literature. Membership is open to the general public at large. All magazine work for young people by an SCBWI member—writer, artist or photographer—is eligible during the year of original publication. In the case of co-authored work, both authors must be SCBWI members. Members must submit their own work. Requirements for entrants: 4 copies each of the published work and proof of publication (may be contents page) showing the name of the magazine and the date of issue.Previously published submissions only. For rules and procedures see website. Must be a SCBWI member. Recognizes outstanding original magazine work for young people published during that year, and having been written or illustrated by members of SCBWI. Deadline: January 1-December 15 of the year of publication. Prize: Awards plaques and honor certificates for each of 4 categories (fiction, nonfiction, illustration and poetry). Judged by a magazine editor and two "full" SCBWI members.

SCBWI WORK-IN-PROGRESS GRANTS

Website: www.scbwi.org. The SCBWI Work-in-Progress Grants have been established to assist children's book writers in the completion of a specific project. Four categories: (1) General Work-in-Progress Grant. (2) Grant for a Contemporary Novel for Young People. (3) Nonfiction Research Grant. (4) Grant for a Work Whose Author Has Never Had a Book Published. SASE for applications for grants. In any year, an applicant may apply for any of the grants except the one awarded for a work whose author has never had a book published. The recipient of this grant will be chosen from entries in all categories. The grants are available to both full and associate members of the SCBWI. They are not available for projects on which there are already contracts. Previous recipients not eligible to apply. Deadline: February 1-April 1. Requests for applications may be made beginning October 1. Prize: 5 grants of $1,500; runner-up grants of $500 (one in each category).

SHABO AWARD FOR CHILDREN'S PICTURE BOOK WRITERS

The Loft Literary Center, 1011 Washington Ave. S., Suite 200, Open Book Minneapolis MN 55415. (612)215-2575. **Fax:** (612)215-2576. **E-mail:** loft@loft.org. **Website:** www.loft.org. **Contact:** Jerod Santek. The Shabo Award is offered to children's picture book writers to develop "nearly there" mss into publish-

able pieces. Up to 8 advanced writers will be chosen annually. Participants should have few, or no, publications to date. Guidelines available online in April. Deadline: August 10.

SKIPPING STONES BOOK AWARDS

Website: www.skippingstones.org. Open to published books, publications/magazines, educational videos, and DVDs. Annual awards. Submissions made by the author or publishers and/or producers. Send request for contest rules and entry forms or visit website. Many educational publications announce the winners of our book awards. The reviews of winning books and educational videos/DVDs are published in the May-August issue of *Skipping Stones* and/or on the website. *Skipping Stones* multicultural magazine has been published for over 25 years. Recognizes exceptional, literary and artistic contributions to juvenile/children's literature, as well as teaching resources and educational audio/video resources in the areas of multicultural awareness, nature and ecology, social issues, peac,e and nonviolence. Deadline: February 1. Prize: Winners receive gold honor award seals, attractive honor certificates and publicity via multiple outlets. Judged by an honor roll of about 20 to 25 books and A/V with teaching resources are selected by a multicultural selection committee of editors, students, parents, teachers, and librarians.

SKIPPING STONES YOUTH HONOR AWARDS

P.O. Box 3939, Eugene OR 97403-0939. (541)342-4956. **E-mail:** editor@SkippingStones.org. **Website:** www.SkippingStones.org. Now celebrating its 26th year, *Skipping Stones* is a winner of N.A.M.E.EDPRESS, Newsstand Resources and Parent's Choice Awards. Open to students. Annual awards. Submissions made by the author. The winners are published in the September-October issue of *Skipping Stones*. Everyone who enters the contest receives the September-October issue featuring Youth Awards. SASE for contest rules or download from website. Entries must include certificate of originality by a parent and/or teacher and a cover letter that included cultural background information on the author. Submissions can either be mailed or e-mailed. Up to ten awards are given in three categories: (1) Compositions (essays, poems, short stories, songs, travelogues, etc.): Entries should be typed (double-spaced) or neatly handwritten. Fiction or nonfiction should be limited to 1,000 words; poems to 30 lines. Non-English writings are also welcome. (2) Artwork (drawings, cartoons, paintings or photo essays with captions): Entries should have the artist's name, age and address on the back of each page. Send the originals with SASE. Black & white photos are especially welcome. Limit: 8 pieces. (3) Youth Organizations: Describe how your club or group works to: (a) preserve the nature and ecology in your area, (b) enhance the quality of life for low-income, minority or disabled or (c) improve racial or cultural harmony in your school or community. Use the same format as for compositions. Recognizes youth, 7 to 17, for their contributions to multicultural awareness, nature and ecology, social issues, peace and nonviolence. Also promotes creativity, self-esteem and writing skills and to recognize important work being done by youth organizations. Deadline: May 25. Judged by *Skipping Stones* staff.

KAY SNOW WRITING CONTEST

Willamette Writers, 2108 Buck St., West Linn OR 97068. (503)305-6729. **Fax:** (503)344-6174. **E-mail:** wilwrite@willamettewriters.com. **Website:** www.willamettewriters.com. **Contact:** Lizzy Shannon, contest director. Willamette Writers is the largest writers' organization in Oregon and one of the largest writers' organizations in the United States. It is a non-profit, tax-exempt Oregon corporation led by volunteers. Elected officials and directors administer an active program of monthly meetings, special seminars, workshops and annual writing conference. Continuing with established programs and starting new ones is only made possible by strong volunteer support. See website for specific details and rules. There are fivedifferent categories writers can enter: Adult Fiction, Adult Nonfiction, Poetry, Juvenile Short Story, and Student Writer. The purpose of this annual writing contest, named in honor of Willamette Writer's founder, Kay Snow, is to help writers reach professional goals in writing in a broad array of categories and to encourage student writers. Deadline: April 23. Prize: One first prize of $300, one second place prize of $150, and a third place prize of $50 per winning entry in each of the six categories.

SOCIETY OF MIDLAND AUTHORS AWARD

Society of Midland Authors, P.O. Box 10419, Chicago IL 60610-0419. **E-mail:** loerzel@comcast.net. **Website:** www.midlandauthors.com. **Contact:** Meg Tebo, President. Since 1957, the Society has presented an-nual awards for the best books written by Midwestern authors. The contest is open to any title published within the year prior to the contest year. Open to authors or poets who reside in, were born in, or have strong ties to a Midland state, which includes Illinois, Indiana, Iowa, Kansas, Michigan, Minnesota, Missouri, Nebraska, North Dakota, South Dakota, Ohio and Wisconsin. The Society of Midland Authors (SMA) Award is presented to one title in each of six categories: adult nonfiction, adult fiction, adult biography and memoir, children's nonfiction, children's fiction, and poetry. Deadline: February 1. Prize: cash prize of $500 and a plaque that is awarded at the SMA banquet in May in Chicago.

SOUTHWEST WRITERS

3200 Carlisle Blvd., NE Suite #114, Albuquerque NM 87110. (505)830-6034. **E-mail:** swwriters@juno.com. **Website:** www.southwestwriters.com. The South-West Writers Writing Contest encourages and honors excellence in writing. In addition to competing for cash prizes and the coveted Storyteller Award, contest entrants may receive an optional written critique of their entry from a qualified contest critiquer. Non-profit organization dedicated to helping members of all levels in their writing. Members enjoy perks such as networking with professional and aspiring writers; substantial discounts on mini-conferences, workshops, writing classes, and annual and quarterly SWW writing contest; monthly newsletter; two writing programs per month; critique groups, critique service (also for nonmembers); discounts at bookstores and other businesses; and website linking. Deadline: May 1 (up to May 15 with a late fee). Submissions begin March 1. Prize: A 1st, 2nd, and 3rd place winner will be judged in each of the 12 categories. 1st place: $200; 2nd place: $150; 3rd place: $100. $1,500 for the Storyteller Award, the entry judged the best of all entries in all categories. Judged by a panel; the top 10 in each category will be sent to appropriate editors or literary agents to determine the final top 3 places.

SOUTHWEST WRITERS ANNUAL CONTEST

3200 Carlisle Blvd. NE, Suite 114, Albuquerque NM 87110. (505)830-6034. **E-mail:** swwcontest@gmail.com. **Website:** www.southwestwriters.com; www.swwcontest.com. Open to adults and students. Annual contest to encourage writers of all genres. Also offers mini-conferences, critique service—for $60/year, offers 2 monthly programs, monthly newsletter, annual writing and bi-monthly writing contests, other workshops, various discount perks, website linking, e-mail addresses, classes and critique service (open to nonmembers). See website for more information or call or write. Deadline: Entries are open from March 1 to May 1 and may be submitted after May 1 until May 15 with payment of a late fee.

SYDNEY TAYLOR BOOK AWARD

P.O. Box 1118, Teaneck NJ 07666. (212)725-5359. **E-mail:** chair@sydneytaylorbookaward.org; heidi@ cbiboca.org. **Website:** www.sydneytaylorbookaward. org. **Contact:** Barbara Bietz, chair. The Sydney Taylor Book Award is presented annually to outstanding books for children and teens that authentically portray the Jewish experience. December 31, "but we cannot guarantee that books received after December 1 will be considered.". Prize: Gold medals are presented in 3 categories: younger readers, older readers, and teen readers. Honor books are awarded in silver medals, and notable books are named in each category.

SYDNEY TAYLOR MANUSCRIPT COMPETITION

Sydney Taylor Manuscript Award Competition, 204 Park St., Montclair NJ 07042-2903. **E-mail:** stma cajl@aol.com. **Website:** www.jewishlibraries.org/ main/Awards/SydneyTaylorManuscriptAward.aspx. **Contact:** Aileen Grossberg. This competition is for unpublished writers of fiction. Material should be for readers ages 8-13, with universal appeal that will serve to deepen the understanding of Judaism for all children, revealing positive aspects of Jewish life. Download rules and forms from website. Must be an unpublished fiction writer or a student; also, books must range from 64-200 pages in length. "AJL assumes no responsibility for publication, but hopes this cash incentive will serve to encourage new writers of children's stories with Jewish themes for all children." Deadline: September 30. Prize: $1,000. Judging by qualified judges from within the Association of Jewish Libraries.

○ TD CANADIAN CHILDREN'S LITERATURE AWARD

40 Orchard View Blvd., Suite 217, Toronto ON M4R 1B9 Canada. (416)975-0010, ext. 222. **Fax:** (416)975-8970. **Website:** www.bookcentre.ca. **Contact:** Meghan Howe. The TD Canadian Children's Literature Award is for the most distinguished book of the

year. All books, in any genre, written and illustrated by Canadians and for children ages 1-12 are eligible. Only books first published in Canada are eligible for submission. Books must be published between January 1 and December 31 of the previous calendar year. Open to Canadian citizens and/or permanent residents of Canada. Submission deadline: December 20. Prize: Prizes: Two prizes of $30,000, 1 for English, 1 for French. $10,000 will be divided among the Honour Book English titles and Honour Book French titles, to a maximum of 4; $2,500 shall go to each of the publishers of the English and French grand-prize winning books for promotion and publicity.

TEEN HAUNTED HOUSE ART CONTEST

E-mail: artcontest@DianaPerryBooks.com. **Website:** dianaperrybooks.com. "Create the inside of a haunted house with exploring teens inside. Be creative. Rules on website." One page, any media. Purpose: "To give exposure to beginning artists/illustrators trying to break in to the business and get noticed." Deadline: April 30. Prize: 1st Place: $200, trophy, mention on website, t-shirt, press releases in your local newspapers; 2nd Place: $150, trophy, mention on website, t-shirt, press releases in your local newspapers; 3rd Place: $100, trophy, mention on website, t-shirt, press releases in your local newspapers; 4th/5th places: $50/$25, plaque, mention on website, t-shirt, press releases in your local newspapers. "We also list names of next 25 honorable mentions on website. Contest guidelines and entry form on website. CHECK WEBSITE FOR GUEST JUDGES. E-mail your picture via JPG or PDF no later than April 30 with "Teen Haunted House Art Contest"as subject. Also write your full name and address in body of text so we can match up with your snail-mail submission. Mail entry form and a $15 money order only to Teen Haunted House Art Contest at above address postmarked no later than April 30. Winners announced both on website and via snail mail June 1. Prizes mailed within 10 days of announcement. Judged by guest judge.

TEEN MYSTERY FICTION CONTEST

E-mail: dianaperry@DianaPerryBooks.com. **Website:** dianaperrybooks.com. **Contact:** Diana Perry. "Hit the ground running with an exciting, fast-paced mystery with lots of action. Cast of 6-8 teens ages 13-18." Rules on website. Length: up to 20 pages or 5,000 words. Purpose: "To give exposure to beginning poets trying to break in to the business and get noticed." Deadline: January 31. Prize: 1st Place: $300, trophy, mention on website, t-shirt, press releases in your local newspapers; 2nd Place: $200, trophy, mention on website, t-shirt, press releases in your local newspapers; 3rd Place: $100, trophy, mention on website, t-shirt, press releases in your local newspapers; 4th/5th places: $50/$25, plaque, mention on website, t-shirt, press releases in your local newspapers. "We also list names of next 25 honorable mentions on website. Contest guidelines and entry form on website. CHECK WEBSITE FOR GUEST JUDGES. Mail entry form, your story, and a $15 money order only to Teen Mystery Fiction Contest at above address postmarked no later than January 31. Winners announced both on website and via snail mail March 1. Prizes mailed within 10 days of announcement. Judged by Diana Perry and guest judge.

☯ TORONTO BOOK AWARDS

100 Queen St. W., City Clerk's Office, 2nd floor, West Tower, Toronto ON M5H 2N2 Canada. **E-mail:** pro tocol@toronto.ca. **Website:** www.toronto.ca/book_ awards. The Toronto Book Awards honour authors of books of literary or artistic merit that are evocative of Toronto. To be eligible, books must be published between January 1 and December 31 of previous year. Deadline: March 28. Prize: Each finalist receives $1,000 and the winning author receives the remaining prize money ($15,000 total in prize money available).

VEGETARIAN ESSAY CONTEST

P.O. Box 1463, Baltimore MD 21203. (410)366-VEGE. **Fax:** (410)366-8804. **E-mail:** vrg@vrg.org. **Website:** www.vrg.org. A 2-3 page essay on any aspect of vegetarianism. Entrants should base their paper on interviewing, research, and/or personal opinon. You need not be a vegetarian to enter. Three different entry categories: age 14-18; age 9-13; and age 8 and under. Prize: $50.

VFW VOICE OF DEMOCRACY

406 W. 34th St., Kansas City MO 64111. (816)968-1117. **E-mail:** kharmer@vfw.org. **Website:** http://www.vfw. org/Community/Voice-of-Democracy/. The Voice of Democracy Program is open to students in grades 9-12 (on the Nov. 1 deadline), who are enrolled in a public, private or parochial high school or home study program in the United States and its territories. Contact your local VFW Post to enter (entry must not be mailed to the VFW National Headquarters, only to a local, participating VFW Post. Purpose is to give high

school students the opportunity to voice their opinions about their responsibility to our country and to convey those opinions via the broadcast media to all of America. Deadline: November 1. Prize: Winners receive awards ranging from $1,000-30,000.

WESTERN HERITAGE AWARDS

1700 NE 63rd St., Oklahoma City OK 73111-7997. (405)478-2250. **Fax:** (405)478-4714. **E-mail:** ssimp son@nationalcowboymuseum.org. **Website:** www. nationalcowboymuseum.org. **Contact:** Shayla Simpson, PR director. The National Cowboy & Western Heritage Museum Western Heritage Awards were established to honor and encourage the legacy of those whose works in literature, music, film, and television reflect the significant stories of the American West. Accepted categories for literary entries: western novel, nonfiction book, art book, photography book, juvenile book, magazine article, or poetry book. Previously published submissions only; must be published the calendar year before the awards are presented. Requirements for entrants: The material must pertain to the development or preservation of the West, either from a historical or contemporary viewpoint. Literary entries must have been published between December 1 and November 30 of calendar year. Five copies of each published work must be furnished for judging with each entry, along with the completed entry form. Works recognized during special awards ceremonies held annually at the museum. There is an autograph party preceding the awards. Awards ceremonies are sometimes broadcast. The WHA are presented annually to encourage the accurate and artistic telling of great stories of the West through 16 categories of western literature, television, film and music; including fiction, nonfiction, children's books and poetry. Deadline: November 30. Prize: Awards a Wrangler bronze sculpture designed by famed western artist, John Free. Judged by a panel of judges selected each year with distinction in various fields of western art and heritage.

WESTERN WRITERS OF AMERICA

271CR 219, Encampment WY 82325. (307)329-8942. **Fax:** (307)327-5465 (call first). **E-mail:** wwa. moulton@gmail.com. **Website:** www.westernwriters. org. **Contact:** Candy Moulton, executive director. 17 Spur Award categories in various aspects of the American West. Send entry form with your published work. Accepts multiple submissions, each with its own entry form. The nonprofit Western Writers of America has promoted and honored the best in Western literature with the annual Spur Awards, selected by panels of judges. Awards, for material published last year, are given for works whose inspirations, image and literary excellence best represent the reality and spirit of the American West.

LAURA INGALLS WILDER MEDAL

50 E. Huron, Chicago IL 60611. (800)545-2433. **E-mail:** alsc@ala.org; ala@ala.org. **Website:** www.ala. org/alsc. Award offered every 2 years. The Wilder Award honors an author or illustrator whose books, published in the US, have made, over a period of years, a substantial and lasting contribution to literature for children. The candidates must be nominated by ALSC members. Medal presented at Newbery/Caldecott banquet during annual conference. Judging by Wilder Award Selection Committee.

WILLA LITERARY AWARD

E-mail: pamtartaglio@yahoo.com. **Website:** www. womenwritingthewest.org. **Contact:** Pam Tartaglio. The WILLA Literary Award honors the best in literature featuring women's or girls' stories set in the West published each year. Women Writing the West (WWW), a nonprofit association of writers and other professionals writing and promoting the Women's West, underwrites and presents the nationally recognized award annually (for work published between January 1 and December 31). The award is named in honor of Pulitzer Prize winner Willa Cather, one of the country's foremost novelists. The award is given in 7 categories: Historical fiction, contemporary fiction, original softcover fiction, creative nonfiction, scholarly nonfiction, poetry, and children's/young adult fiction/nonfiction. Deadline: November 1-February 1. Prize: $100 and a trophy. Finalist receives a plaque. Both receive digital and sticker award emblems for book covers. Winning and finalist titles mailed to more than 4,000 booksellers, libraries, and others. Award announcement is in early August, and awards are presented to the winners and finalists at the annual WWW Fall Conference. Judged by professional librarians not affiliated with WWW.

RITA WILLIAMS YOUNG ADULT PROSE PRIZE CATEGORY

E-mail: pennobhill@aol.com. **Website:** www.soul makingcontest.us. **Contact:** Eileen Malone. Grades 9-12 or equivalent age. Up to 3,000 words in story,

essay, journal entry, creative nonfiction or memoir. Complete rules and guidelines available online. Deadline: November 30 (postmarked). Prize: $100 for first place; $50 for second place; $25 for third place. Judged by Rita Wiliams, an Emmy-award winning investigative reporter with KTVU-TV in Oakland, California.

WRITE A STORY FOR CHILDREN COMPETITION

(44)(148)783-2752. **Fax:** (44)(148)783-2752. **E-mail:** enquiries@childrens-writers.co.uk. **Website:** www. childrens-writers.co.uk. **Contact:** Contest director. Annual contest for the best unpublished short story writer for children. Guidelines and entry forms online or send SAE/IRC. Open to any unpublished writer over the age of 18. Mss must not exceed 2,000 words in length. It may be a short story or the first 2,000 words of a novel/longer story. Deadline: April 30. Prize: 1st Place: £2,000; 2nd Place: £300; 3rd Place: £200. Judged by a panel appointed by the Academy of Children's Writers. Judges will be looking for such qualities as originality, imagination, and flair.

WRITE NOW

Indiana Repertory Theatre, 140 W. Washington St., Indianapolis IN 46204. 480-921-5770. **E-mail:** info@ writenow.co. **Website:** www.writenow.co. The purpose of this biennial workshop is to encourage writers to create strikingly original scripts for young audiences. It provides a forum through which each playwright receives constructive criticism and the support of a development team consisting of a professional director and dramaturg. Finalists will spend approximately one week in workshop with their development team. At the end of the week, each play will be read as a part of the Write Now convening. Guidelines available online. Deadline: July 31.

WRITER'S DIGEST SELF-PUBLISHED BOOK AWARDS

10151 Carver Road, Suite #200, Blue Ash OH 45242. (715)445-4612, ext. 13430. **E-mail:** WritersDigest SelfPublishingCompetition@fwmedia.com. **Website:** www.writersdigest.com. **Contact:** Nicole Howard. Contest open to all English-language, self-published books for which the authors have paid the full cost of publication, or the cost of printing has been paid for by a grant or as part of a prize. Categories include: Mainstream/Literary Fiction, Genre Fiction, Nonfiction, Inspirational (spiritual/new age), Life Stories (biographies/autobiographies/family histories/

memoirs), Children's Books, Reference Books (directories/encyclopedias/guide books), Poetry, and Middle grade/Young Adult Books. Judges reserve the right to re-categorize entries. Judges reserve the right to withhold prizes in any category. All winners will be notifed by October 17. Entrants must send a printed and bound book. Entries will be evaluated on content, writing quality, and overall quality of production and appearance. No handwritten books are accepted. Books must have been published within the past 5 years from the competition deadline. Books which have previously won awards from *Writer's Digest* are not eligible. Early bird deadline: April 1; Deadline: May 1. Prize: Prizes: Grand Prize: $3,000, a trip to the Writer's Digest Conference, promotion in *Writer's Digest* and *Publisher's Weekly*, and 10 copies of the book will be sent to major review houses with a guaranteed review in *Midwest Book Review*; 1st Place (9 winners): $1,000 and promotion in *Writer's Digest*; Honorable Mentions:$50 worth of Writer's Digest Books and promotion on writersdigest.com. All entrants will receive a brief commentary from one of the judges.

WRITERS-EDITORS NETWORK ANNUAL INTERNATIONAL WRITING COMPETITION

E-mail: contest@writers-editors.com. **E-mail:** info@writers-editors.com. **Website:** www.writers-editors.com. **Contact:** Dana K. Cassell, executive director. Annual award to recognize publishable talent. Categories: Nonfiction (previously published article/essay/column/nonfiction book chapter; unpublished or self-published article/essay/column/nonfiction book chapter); fiction (unpublished or self-published short story or novel chapter); children's literature (unpublished or self-published short story/nonfiction article/book chapter/poem); poetry (unpublished or self-published free verse/traditional). Guidelines available online. Open to any writer. Accepts inquiries by e-mail, phone and mail. Entry form online. Results announced May 31. Winners notified by mail and posted on website. Results available for SASE or visit website. Deadline: March 15. Prize: 1st Place: $100; 2nd Place: $75; 3rd Place: $50. All winners and Honorable Mentions will receive certificates as warranted. Judged by editors, librarians, and writers.

✪ WRITERS GUILD OF ALBERTA AWARDS

Percy Page Centre, 11759 Groat Rd., Edmonton AB T5M 3K6 Canada. (780)422-8174. **Fax:** (780)422-2663.

E-mail: mail@writersguild.ab.ca. **Website:** www.writersguild.ab.ca. **Contact:** Executive Director. Offers the following awards: Wilfrid Eggleston Award for Nonfiction; Georges Bugnet Award for Fiction; Howard O'Hagan Award for Short Story; Stephan G. Stephansson Award for Poetry; R. Ross Annett Award for Children's Literature; Gwen Pharis Ringwood Award for Drama; Jon Whyte Memorial Essay Prize; James H. Gray Award for Short Nonfiction; Amber Bowerman Memorial Travel Writing Award. Eligible entries will have been published anywhere in the world between January 1 and December 31 of the current year. The authors must have been residents of Alberta for at least 12 of the 18 months prior to December 31. Unpublished mss, except in the drama, essay, and short nonfiction categories, are not eligible. Anthologies are not eligible. Works may be submitted by authors, publishers, or any interested parties. Deadline: December 31. Prize: Winning authors receive $1,500; essay prize winners receive $700.

WRITERS' LEAGUE OF TEXAS BOOK AWARDS

611 S. Congress Ave., Suite 505, Austin TX 78704. (512)499-8914. **Fax:** (512)499-0441. **E-mail:** wlt@writersleague.org. **E-mail:** sara@writersleague.org. **Website:** www.writersleague.org. Open to Texas authors of books published the previous two years. Authors are required to show proof of Texas residency, but are not required to be members of the Writers' League of Texas. Deadline: Open to submissions from January 1 to April 30. Prize: $750, a commemorative award, and an appearance at a WLT Third Thursday panel at BookPeople in Austin, TX.

WRITING CONFERENCE WRITING CONTESTS

P.O. Box 664, Ottawa KS 66067-0664. (785)242-1995. **Fax:** (785)242-1995. **E-mail:** jbushman@writingconference.com. **E-mail:** support@studentq.com. **Website:** www.writingconference.com. **Contact:** John H. Bushman, contest director. Unpublished submissions only. Submissions made by the author or teacher. Purpose of contest: To further writing by students with awards for narration, exposition and poetry at the elementary, middle school and high school levels. Deadline: January 8. Prize: Awards plaque and publication of winning entry in The Writers' Slate online, April issue. Judged by a panel of teachers.

YEARBOOK EXCELLENCE CONTEST

100 Adler Journalism Building, Iowa City IA 52242-2004. (319)335-3457. **Fax:** (319)335-3989. **E-mail:** quill-scroll@uiowa.edu. **Website:** www.quilland scroll.org. **Contact:** Vanessa Shelton, executive director. High school students who are contributors to or staff members of a student yearbook at any public or private high school are invited to enter the competition. Awards will be made in each of the 18 divisions. There are two enrollment categories: Class A: more than 750 students; Class B: 749 or less. Winners will receive Quill and Scroll's National Award Gold Key and, if seniors, are eligible to apply for one of the Edward J. Nell Memorial or George and Ophelia Gallup scholarships. Open to students whose schools have Quill and Scroll charters. Previously published submissions only. Submissions made by the author or school yearbook adviser. Must be published in the 12-month span prior to contest deadline. Visit website for list of current and previous winners. Purpose is to recognize and reward student journalists for their work in yearbooks and to provide student winners an opportunity to apply for a scholarship to be used freshman year in college for students planning to major in journalism. Deadline: November 1.

☺ YOUNG ADULT CANADIAN BOOK AWARD

1150 Morrison Dr.,, Suite 400, Ottawa ON K2H 8S9 Canada. (613)232-9625. **Fax:** (613)563-9895. **E-mail:** khebig@wheatland.sk.ca. **Website:** www.cla.ca. **Contact:** Kim Hebig, Wheatland Regional Library Chair. This award recognizes an author of an outstanding English language Canadian book which appeals to young adults between the ages of 13 and 18. To be eligible for consideration, the following must apply: it must be a work of fiction (novel, collection of short stories, or graphic novel), the title must be a Canadian publication in either hardcover or paperback, and the author must be a Canadian citizen or landed immigrant. The award is given annually, when merited, at the Canadian Library Association's annual conference. Deadline: December 1. Prize: $1,000.

THE YOUTH HONOR AWARD PROGRAM

Skipping Stones Magazine, P.O. Box 3939, Eugene OR 97403. (541)342-4956. **E-mail:** info@skippingstones. org. **E-mail:** editor@skippingstones.org. **Website:** www.skippingstones.org. **Contact:** Arun N. Toke, Editor and Publisher. Original writing and art from youth, ages 7 to 17, should be typed or neatly handwritten. The entries should be appropriate for ages 7 to 17. Prose under 1,000 words; poems under 30 lines. Non-English and bilingual writings are welcome. To promote multicultural, international and nature awareness. Deadline: May 25. Prize: An Honor Award Certificate, a subscription to Skipping Stones and five nature and/or multicultural books. They are also invited to join the Student Review Board. Everyone who enters the contest receives the autumn issue featuring the 10 winners.

ANNA ZORNIO MEMORIAL CHILDREN'S THEATRE PLAYWRITING COMPETITION

Department of Theatre and Dance, PCAC, 30 Academic Way, Durham NH 03824. (603)862-3038. **Fax:** (603)862-0298. **E-mail:** mike.wood@unh.edu. **Website:** http://cola.unh.edu/theatre-dance/resource/zor nio. **Contact:** Michael Wood. Offered every 4 years for unpublished well-written plays or musicals appropriate for young audiences with a maximum length of 60 minutes. May submit more than 1 play, but not more than 3. Honors the late Anna Zornio, an alumna of The University of New Hampshire, for dedication to and inspiration of playwriting for young people, K-12th grade. Deadline: March of 2016. Prize: $500.

SUBJECT INDEX

ACTIVITY BOOKS
Chicago Review Press 211
Child's Play (International) Ltd. 256
Concordia Publishing House 213
Farrar, Straus & Giroux for Young Readers 219
Fulcrum Publishing 221
Gibbs Smith 221
Godine, Publisher, David R. 221
Jewish Lights Publishing 225
Kar-Ben Publishing 227
Kids Can Press 259
Legacy Press 228
Magination Press 229
Master Books 230
Meriwether Publishing Ltd. 231
Nomad Press 233
Rainbow Publishers 240
Sasquatch Books 242
Sterling Publishing Co., Inc. 246
Williamson Books 250

ADVENTURE
Advocate, PKA's Publication 267
Amulet Books 204
Azro Press 205
Boys' Quest 270
Bread for God's Children 271
Cadet Quest Magazine 272
Calliope 272
Child's Play (International) Ltd. 256
Cicada Magazine 274
Creative Company 214
Cricket Books 214
Davey and Goliath's Devotions 276
Dial Books for Young Readers 215

Disney Hyperion Books for Children 215
Dutton Children's Books 216
Eerdmans Books for Young Readers 217
Faces 278
Farrar, Straus & Giroux for Young Readers 219
Fickling Books, David 257
Flux 220
Freestone/Peachtree, Jr. 220
Fun for Kidz 279
Godine, Publisher, David R. 221
Highlights for Children 281
Hopscotch 282
Horsepower 282
Jack and Jill 284
JourneyForth 225
Kar-Ben Publishing 227
Kids Can Press 259
Ladybug 285
Little, Brown and Co. Books for Young Readers 229
Milkweed Editions 231
New Moon Girls 288
OnStage Publishing 233
Orca Book Publishers 260
Pockets 288
Random House Children's Books 260
Roaring Brook Press 241
Sasquatch Books 242
Seedling Continental Press 244
SHINE brightly 290
Simon & Schuster Books for Young Readers 244
Sleeping Bear Press 245
Sparkle 291
Spider 292
Tanglewood Books 247
TC Magazine (Teenage Christian) 293

Thistledown Press Ltd. 262
Tor Books 248
Tradewind Books 262
Tyndale House Publishers, Inc. 249
Usborne Publishing 263
Viking Children's Books 249
Whitman, Albert & Company 250
Wiseman Books, Paula 251
Young Rider 294

ANIMAL (FICTION)
Advocate, PKA's Publication 267
Aquila 268
Azro Press 205
Boys' Quest 270
Candlewick Press 209
Child's Play (International) Ltd. 256
Cicada Magazine 274
Creative Company 214
Cricket Books 214
Dial Books for Young Readers 215
Disney Hyperion Books for Children 215
Dutton Children's Books 216
Eerdmans Books for Young Readers 217
Farrar, Straus & Giroux for Young Readers 219
Fickling Books, David 257
Freestone/Peachtree, Jr. 220
Fun for Kidz 279
Godine, Publisher, David R. 221
Highlights for Children 281
Hopscotch 282
Ideals Children's Books and Candycane Press 224
JourneyForth 225
Kids Can Press 259
Ladybug 285
Little, Brown and Co. Books for Young Readers 229
Little Tiger Press 259
New Moon Girls 288
Orca Book Publishers 260
Orchard Books 234
Piccadilly Press 260
Pineapple Press, Inc. 238
Random House Children's Books 260
Renaissance House 241
Roaring Brook Press 241
Sasquatch Books 242
Seedling Continental Press 244
SHINE brightly 290
Simon & Schuster Books for Young Readers 244
Sleeping Bear Press 245
Sparkle 291
Tafelberg Publishers 262
Tanglewood Books 247
Tor Books 248
Tradewind Books 262
Viking Children's Books 249
Wiseman Books, Paula 251
Young Rider 294

ANIMAL (NONFICTION)
Advocate, PKA's Publication 267
Aquila 268
ASK 269
Azro Press 205
Boys' Quest 270
Child's Play (International) Ltd. 256
Creative Company 214
Faces 278
Farrar, Straus & Giroux for Young Readers 219
Freestone/Peachtree, Jr. 220
Fun for Kidz 279
Godine, Publisher, David R. 221
Guide 280
Highlights for Children 281
Hopscotch 282
Jack and Jill 284
Kids Can Press 259
Ladybug 285
Master Books 230
Muse 287
National Geographic Kids 287
New Moon Girls 288
Owen, Richard C., Publishers, Inc. 235
Pineapple Press, Inc. 238
Ronsdale Press 261
Sasquatch Books 242
Scholastic Library Publishing 243
Seedling Continental Press 244
SHINE brightly 290
Skipping Stones 290
Sparkle 291
Spider 292
Viking Children's Books 249
Weigl Publishers Inc. 249
Whitman, Albert & Company 250
Williamson Books 250
Wiseman Books, Paula 251
World Book, Inc. 252
Young Rider 294

ANTHOLOGY
Child's Play (International) Ltd. 256
Creative Company 214
Disney Hyperion Books for Children 215
Farrar, Straus & Giroux for Young Readers 219
Fickling Books, David 257
Lee & Low Books 228
Meriwether Publishing Ltd. 231
Random House Children's Books 260
Renaissance House 241
Tafelberg Publishers 262
Thistledown Press Ltd. 262
Tor Books 248
Wiseman Books, Paula 251

ARTS/CRAFTS
Advocate, PKA's Publication 267
Aquila 268

ASK 269
Boys' Quest 270
Bright Ring Publishing, Inc. 208
Brilliant Star 271
Cadet Quest Magazine 272
Calliope 272
Carolrhoda Books, Inc. 209
Chicago Review Press 211
Cobblestone 275
Concordia Publishing House 213
Creative Company 214
Dramatics Magazine 277
Faces 278
Farrar, Straus & Giroux for Young Readers 219
Fun for Kidz 279
Gibbs Smith 221
Girls' Life 280
Highlights for Children 281
Hopscotch 282
Horsepower 282
Jack and Jill 284
Kar-Ben Publishing 227
Kids Can Press 259
Ladybug 285
Legacy Press 228
Little, Brown and Co. Books for Young Readers 229
National Geographic Kids 287
New Moon Girls 288
Rainbow Publishers 240
Scholastic Library Publishing 243
Seedling Continental Press 244
SHINE brightly 290
Sparkle 291
Spider 292
Sterling Publishing Co., Inc. 246
Whitman, Albert & Company 250
Williamson Books 250
World Book, Inc. 252

BIOGRAPHY
Advocate, PKA's Publication 267
American Cheerleader 268
ASK 269
Calliope 272
Candlewick Press 209
Carolrhoda Books, Inc. 209
ChemMatters 274
Cicada Magazine 274
Cobblestone 275
Creative Company 214
Cricket 276
Dial Books for Young Readers 215
Dig 277
Faces 278
Farrar, Straus & Giroux for Young Readers 219
Godine, Publisher, David R. 221
Highlights for Children 281
Hopscotch 282

Horsepower 282
JourneyForth 225
Kamehameha Publishing 226
Kar-Ben Publishing 227
Kids Can Press 259
Lee & Low Books 228
Master Books 230
Mitchell Lane Publishers, Inc. 232
Muse 287
National Geographic Kids 287
New Moon Girls 288
Paulist Press 236
Pelican Publishing Company 236
Pineapple Press, Inc. 238
Puffin Books 239
Ronsdale Press 261
Scholastic Library Publishing 243
Second Story Press 262
Seedling Continental Press 244
Simon & Schuster Books for Young Readers 244
Skipping Stones 290
Sparkle 291
TC Magazine (Teenage Christian) 293
Viking Children's Books 249
Weigl Publishers Inc. 249
Williamson Books 250
Wiseman Books, Paula 251

CAREERS
Advocate, PKA's Publication 267
American Cheerleader 268
ASK 269
CollegeXpress Magazine 276
Creative Company 214
Dramatics Magazine 277
Farrar, Straus & Giroux for Young Readers 219
Highlights for Children 281
Horsepower 282
Kar-Ben Publishing 227
Kids Can Press 259
New Moon Girls 288
Owen, Richard C., Publishers, Inc. 235
Scholastic Library Publishing 243
Seedling Continental Press 244
Seventeen Magazine 289
SHINE brightly 290
Sparkle 291
TC Magazine (Teenage Christian) 293
Weigl Publishers Inc. 249
Williamson Books 250
World Book, Inc. 252
Young Rider 294

CONCEPT (FICTION)
Candlewick Press 209
Child's Play (International) Ltd. 256
Eerdmans Books for Young Readers 217
Farrar, Straus & Giroux for Young Readers 219
Fickling Books, David 257

Ideals Children's Books and Candycane Press 224
Kar-Ben Publishing 227
Kids Can Press 259
Lee & Low Books 228
Little Tiger Press 259
Sasquatch Books 242
Sleeping Bear Press 245
Tanglewood Books 247
Tor Books 248
Whitman, Albert & Company 250
Wiseman Books, Paula 251

CONCEPT (NONFICTION)

Advocate, PKA's Publication 267
Aquila 268
Candlewick Press 209
Child's Play (International) Ltd. 256
Concordia Publishing House 213
Farrar, Straus & Giroux for Young Readers 219
Kar-Ben Publishing 227
Kids Can Press 259
Ladybug 285
Lee & Low Books 228
Paulist Press 236
Puffin Books 239
Sasquatch Books 242
Scholastic Library Publishing 243
Seedling Continental Press 244
Simon & Schuster Books for Young Readers 244
Sparkle 291
TC Magazine (Teenage Christian) 293
Viking Children's Books 249
Wiseman Books, Paula 251
World Book, Inc. 252

CONTEMPORARY

Advocate, PKA's Publication 267
Amulet Books 204
Aquila 268
Brilliant Star 271
Candlewick Press 209
Child's Play (International) Ltd. 256
Cicada Magazine 274
Creative Company 214
Cricket 276
Cricket Books 214
Davey and Goliath's Devotions 276
Disney Hyperion Books for Children 215
Dutton Children's Books 216
Eerdmans Books for Young Readers 217
Farrar, Straus & Giroux for Young Readers 219
Fickling Books, David 257
Flux 220
Freestone/Peachtree, Jr. 220
Godine, Publisher, David R. 221
Highlights for Children 281
Jack and Jill 284
JourneyForth 225

Kids Can Press 259
Lee & Low Books 228
Little, Brown and Co. Books for Young Readers 229
Little Tiger Press 259
Meriwether Publishing Ltd. 231
Milkweed Editions 231
New Moon Girls 288
OnStage Publishing 233
Orca Book Publishers 260
Orchard Books 234
Piccadilly Press 260
Pockets 288
PUSH 239
Random House Children's Books 260
Roaring Brook Press 241
Sasquatch Books 242
SHINE brightly 290
Simon & Schuster Books for Young Readers 244
Skipping Stones 290
Sparkle 291
Spider 292
Tafelberg Publishers 262
Tanglewood Books 247
TC Magazine (Teenage Christian) 293
Thistledown Press Ltd. 262
Tor Books 248
Usborne Publishing 263
Viking Children's Books 249
Wiseman Books, Paula 251

COOKING

Advocate, PKA's Publication 267
Aquila 268
Boys' Quest 270
Calliope 272
Faces 278
Farrar, Straus & Giroux for Young Readers 219
Fun for Kidz 279
Gibbs Smith 221
Hopscotch 282
Jack and Jill 284
Kar-Ben Publishing 227
Kids Can Press 259
Ladybug 285
National Geographic Kids 287
New Moon Girls 288
Pockets 288
Seventeen Magazine 289
SHINE brightly 290
Skipping Stones 290
Sparkle 291
Spider 292
Sterling Publishing Co., Inc. 246

FANTASY

Advocate, PKA's Publication 267
Amulet Books 204
Aquila 268

Atheneum Books for Young Readers 205
Brilliant Star 271
Candlewick Press 209
Carolrhoda Books, Inc. 209
Cicada Magazine 274
Creative Company 214
Cricket 276
Cricket Books 214
Dial Books for Young Readers 215
Disney Hyperion Books for Children 215
Dutton Children's Books 216
Farrar, Straus & Giroux for Young Readers 219
Fickling Books, David 257
Flux 220
Highlights for Children 281
JourneyForth 225
Kids Can Press 259
Ladybug 285
Leading Edge 286
Milkweed Editions 231
New Moon Girls 288
OnStage Publishing 233
Orca Book Publishers 260
Piccadilly Press 260
Random House Children's Books 260
Roaring Brook Press 241
Simon & Schuster Books for Young Readers 244
Spider 292
Tafelberg Publishers 262
Tanglewood Books 247
Thistledown Press Ltd. 262
Tor Books 248
Usborne Publishing 263
Viking Children's Books 249
Whitman, Albert & Company 250
Wiseman Books, Paula 251

FASHION

Advocate, PKA's Publication 267
American Cheerleader 268
Faces 278
Girls' Life 280
Horsepower 282
SHINE brightly 290
Sparkle 291

FOLKTALES

Advocate, PKA's Publication 267
Aquila 268
Brilliant Star 271
Calliope 272
Child's Play (International) Ltd. 256
Cobblestone 275
Creative Company 214
Cricket 276
Davey and Goliath's Devotions 276
Dial Books for Young Readers 215
Disney Hyperion Books for Children 215

Eerdmans Books for Young Readers 217
Faces 278
Farrar, Straus & Giroux for Young Readers 219
Fickling Books, David 257
Freestone/Peachtree, Jr. 220
Godine, Publisher, David R. 221
Highlights for Children 281
Jack and Jill 284
JourneyForth 225
Kar-Ben Publishing 227
Kids Can Press 259
Ladybug 285
Little, Brown and Co. Books for Young Readers 229
New Moon Girls 288
Owen, Richard C., Publishers, Inc. 235
Piano Press 237
Pineapple Press, Inc. 238
Pockets 288
Random House Children's Books 260
Renaissance House 241
Seedling Continental Press 244
Skipping Stones 290
Sleeping Bear Press 245
Spider 292
Tafelberg Publishers 262
Tradewind Books 262
Wiseman Books, Paula 251

GAMES/PUZZLES

Advocate, PKA's Publication 267
Aquila 268
ASK 269
Boys' Quest 270
Brilliant Star 271
Cadet Quest Magazine 272
Calliope 272
Cricket 276
Dig 277
Faces 278
Fun for Kidz 279
Guide 280
Hopscotch 282
Horsepower 282
Jack and Jill 284
National Geographic Kids 287
New Moon Girls 288
Pockets 288
SHINE brightly 290
Skipping Stones 290
Sparkle 291
Spider 292
TC Magazine (Teenage Christian) 293

GEOGRAPHY

Advocate, PKA's Publication 267
ASK 269
Azro Press 205
Brilliant Star 271

Candlewick Press 209
Carolrhoda Books, Inc. 209
Cobblestone 275
Creative Company 214
Cricket 276
Faces 278
Farrar, Straus & Giroux for Young Readers 219
Highlights for Children 281
Hopscotch 282
National Geographic Kids 287
Owen, Richard C., Publishers, Inc. 235
Pineapple Press, Inc. 238
Scholastic Library Publishing 243
Sparkle 291
Spider 292
Tor Books 248
Viking Children's Books 249
Weigl Publishers Inc. 249
Williamson Books 250
World Book, Inc. 252

HEALTH (FICTION)
Advocate, PKA's Publication 267
Aquila 268
Farrar, Straus & Giroux for Young Readers 219
Fickling Books, David 257
Flux 220
Freestone/Peachtree, Jr. 220
Horsepower 282
Jack and Jill 284
Magination Press 229
SHINE brightly 290
Sparkle 291
TC Magazine (Teenage Christian) 293
Wiseman Books, Paula 251

HEALTH (NONFICTION)
American Cheerleader 268
Aquila 268
ASK 269
Catholic Forester 273
ChemMatters 274
CollegeXpress Magazine 276
Creative Company 214
Farrar, Straus & Giroux for Young Readers 219
Freestone/Peachtree, Jr. 220
Highlights for Children 281
Horsepower 282
Kids Can Press 259
Magination Press 229
National Geographic Kids 287
New Moon Girls 288
Scholastic Library Publishing 243
SHINE brightly 290
Sparkle 291
TC Magazine (Teenage Christian) 293
Whitman, Albert & Company 250
Williamson Books 250

World Book, Inc. 252
Young Rider 294

HI-LO (FICTION)
Azro Press 205
Farrar, Straus & Giroux for Young Readers 219
Fickling Books, David 257
Orca Book Publishers 260
Tafelberg Publishers 262
Viking Children's Books 249
Wiseman Books, Paula 251

HI-LO (NONFICTION)
Azro Press 205
Farrar, Straus & Giroux for Young Readers 219
Owen, Richard C., Publishers, Inc. 235
Viking Children's Books 249

HISTORY (FICTION)
Amulet Books 204
Aquila 268
Azro Press 205
Boys' Quest 270
Calkins Creek 208
Calliope 272
Candlewick Press 209
Cicada Magazine 274
Cobblestone 275
Creative Company 214
Cricket 276
Cricket Books 214
Dial Books for Young Readers 215
Disney Hyperion Books for Children 215
Dutton Children's Books 216
Eerdmans Books for Young Readers 217
Faces 278
Farrar, Straus & Giroux for Young Readers 219
Fickling Books, David 257
Flux 220
Freestone/Peachtree, Jr. 220
Fun for Kidz 279
Godine, Publisher, David R. 221
Highlights for Children 281
Hopscotch 282
Horsepower 282
Ideals Children's Books and Candycane Press 224
Jack and Jill 284
JourneyForth 225
Kar-Ben Publishing 227
Kids Can Press 259
Lee & Low Books 228
Little, Brown and Co. Books for Young Readers 229
New Moon Girls 288
OnStage Publishing 233
Orca Book Publishers 260
Orchard Books 234
Pelican Publishing Company 236
Pineapple Press, Inc. 238

Roaring Brook Press 241
Ronsdale Press 261
Second Story Press 262
SHINE brightly 290
Simon & Schuster Books for Young Readers 244
Sleeping Bear Press 245
Tor Books 248
Usborne Publishing 263
Viking Children's Books 249
White Mane Kids 250
Whitman, Albert & Company 250
Wiseman Books, Paula 251

HISTORY (NONFICTION)

Advocate, PKA's Publication 267
Aquila 268
ASK 269
Azro Press 205
Boys' Quest 270
Calkins Creek 208
Calliope 272
Carolrhoda Books, Inc. 209
ChemMatters 274
Chicago Review Press 211
Cobblestone 275
Creative Company 214
Cricket 276
Dial Books for Young Readers 215
Dig 277
Eerdmans Books for Young Readers 217
Faces 278
Farrar, Straus & Giroux for Young Readers 219
Freestone/Peachtree, Jr. 220
Friend Magazine, The 279
Fun for Kidz 279
Godine, Publisher, David R. 221
Greenhaven Press 222
Highlights for Children 281
Horsepower 282
Jack and Jill 284
Kamehameha Publishing 226
Kar-Ben Publishing 227
Kids Can Press 259
Lee & Low Books 228
Little, Brown and Co. Books for Young Readers 229
Muse 287
National Geographic Kids 287
New Moon Girls 288
Nomad Press 233
Owen, Richard C., Publishers, Inc. 235
Pelican Publishing Company 236
Pineapple Press, Inc. 238
Puffin Books 239
Ronsdale Press 261
Scholastic Library Publishing 243
Simon & Schuster Books for Young Readers 244
Skipping Stones 290

Sparkle 291
Spider 292
Tor Books 248
Viking Children's Books 249
Weigl Publishers Inc. 249
White Mane Kids 250
Whitman, Albert & Company 250
Williamson Books 250
Wiseman Books, Paula 251
World Book, Inc. 252

HOBBIES

Advocate, PKA's Publication 267
Boys' Quest 270
Cadet Quest Magazine 272
Creative Company 214
Farrar, Straus & Giroux for Young Readers 219
Fun for Kidz 279
Girls' Life 280
Highlights for Children 281
Hopscotch 282
Horsepower 282
Jack and Jill 284
Kids Can Press 259
National Geographic Kids 287
New Moon Girls 288
Scholastic Library Publishing 243
Seventeen Magazine 289
SHINE brightly 290
Sparkle 291
Sterling Publishing Co., Inc. 246
TC Magazine (Teenage Christian) 293
Whitman, Albert & Company 250
Williamson Books 250
World Book, Inc. 252

HOW-TO

Advocate, PKA's Publication 267
American Cheerleader 268
Aquila 268
Boys' Quest 270
Bread for God's Children 271
Bright Ring Publishing, Inc. 208
Brilliant Star 271
Cadet Quest Magazine 272
CollegeXpress Magazine 276
Dramatics Magazine 277
Faces 278
Farrar, Straus & Giroux for Young Readers 219
Fun for Kidz 279
Gibbs Smith 221
Highlights for Children 281
Hopscotch 282
Horsepower 282
Jack and Jill 284
Kar-Ben Publishing 227
Kids Can Press 259
Legacy Press 228

Meriwether Publishing Ltd. 231
Owen, Richard C., Publishers, Inc. 235
Rainbow Publishers 240
Scholastic Library Publishing 243
Seventeen Magazine 289
SHINE brightly 290
Sparkle 291
Sterling Publishing Co., Inc. 246
TC Magazine (Teenage Christian) 293
Tor Books 248
Williamson Books 250
World Book, Inc. 252

HUMOR (FICTION)
Advocate, PKA's Publication 267
Aquila 268
Azro Press 205
Boys' Quest 270
Cadet Quest Magazine 272
Candlewick Press 209
Catholic Forester 273
Child's Play (International) Ltd. 256
Cicada Magazine 274
Cricket 276
Cricket Books 214
Dial Books for Young Readers 215
Disney Hyperion Books for Children 215
Dutton Children's Books 216
Eerdmans Books for Young Readers 217
Farrar, Straus & Giroux for Young Readers 219
Fickling Books, David 257
Flux 220
Freestone/Peachtree, Jr. 220
Fun for Kidz 279
Highlights for Children 281
Hopscotch 282
Horsepower 282
Jack and Jill 284
JourneyForth 225
Kar-Ben Publishing 227
Kids Can Press 259
Ladybug 285
Little, Brown and Co. Books for Young Readers 229
Little Tiger Press 259
Meriwether Publishing Ltd. 231
New Moon Girls 288
OnStage Publishing 233
Orchard Books 234
Piccadilly Press 260
Price Stern Sloan, Inc. 239
Random House Children's Books 260
Roaring Brook Press 241
Sasquatch Books 242
Seedling Continental Press 244
SHINE brightly 290
Simon & Schuster Books for Young Readers 244
Skipping Stones 290
Sleeping Bear Press 245

Sparkle 291
Tafelberg Publishers 262
Tanglewood Books 247
TC Magazine (Teenage Christian) 293
Thistledown Press Ltd. 262
Tor Books 248
Usborne Publishing 263
Viking Children's Books 249
Whitman, Albert & Company 250
Wiseman Books, Paula 251

HUMOR (NONFICTION)
Advocate, PKA's Publication 267
ASK 269
Boys' Quest 270
Brilliant Star 271
Cadet Quest Magazine 272
CollegeXpress Magazine 276
Faces 278
Friend Magazine, The 279
Fun for Kidz 279
Guide 280
Hopscotch 282
Horsepower 282
Jack and Jill 284
Ladybug 285
New Moon Girls 288
Seventeen Magazine 289
SHINE brightly 290
Skipping Stones 290
TC Magazine (Teenage Christian) 293

INTERVIEW/PROFILE
Advocate, PKA's Publication 267
American Cheerleader 268
Aquila 268
ASK 269
Cadet Quest Magazine 272
CollegeXpress Magazine 276
Dramatics Magazine 277
Faces 278
Girls' Life 280
Highlights for Children 281
Horsepower 282
Jack and Jill 284
Muse 287
National Geographic Kids 287
New Moon Girls 288
Seventeen Magazine 289
Skipping Stones 290
Sparkle 291
TC Magazine (Teenage Christian) 293

MATH
Aquila 268
ASK 269
Boys' Quest 270
Hopscotch 282
Ladybug 285

Muse 287
New Moon Girls 288
Science Weekly 289
Sparkle 291
Spider 292

MULTICULTURAL (FICTION)

Aquila 268
Boys' Quest 270
Brilliant Star 271
Cadet Quest Magazine 272
Candlewick Press 209
Child's Play (International) Ltd. 256
Cicada Magazine 274
Cobblestone 275
Cricket Books 214
Dial Books for Young Readers 215
Disney Hyperion Books for Children 215
Dutton Children's Books 216
Eerdmans Books for Young Readers 217
Faces 278
Farrar, Straus & Giroux for Young Readers 219
Fickling Books, David 257
Flux 220
Freestone/Peachtree, Jr. 220
Fun for Kidz 279
Highlights for Children 281
JourneyForth 225
Kar-Ben Publishing 227
Kids Can Press 259
Ladybug 285
Lee & Low Books 228
Little, Brown and Co. Books for Young Readers 229
Magination Press 229
Milkweed Editions 231
New Moon Girls 288
Orca Book Publishers 260
Orchard Books 234
Pelican Publishing Company 236
Piano Press 237
Piñata Books 238
Pockets 288
PUSH 239
Random House Children's Books 260
Renaissance House 241
Roaring Brook Press 241
Seedling Continental Press 244
SHINE brightly 290
Skipping Stones 290
Sleeping Bear Press 245
Sparkle 291
Tafelberg Publishers 262
Tilbury House 247
Tor Books 248
Tradewind Books 262
Usborne Publishing 263
Viking Children's Books 249
Whitman, Albert & Company 250

Wiseman Books, Paula 251

MULTICULTURAL (NONFICTION)

ASK 269
Brilliant Star 271
Chicago Review Press 211
Child's Play (International) Ltd. 256
Cobblestone 275
Creative Company 214
Cricket 276
Dramatics Magazine 277
Eerdmans Books for Young Readers 217
Farrar, Straus & Giroux for Young Readers 219
Freestone/Peachtree, Jr. 220
Fulcrum Publishing 221
Guide 280
Highlights for Children 281
Kamehameha Publishing 226
Kar-Ben Publishing 227
Kids Can Press 259
Lee & Low Books 228
Little, Brown and Co. Books for Young Readers 229
Mitchell Lane Publishers, Inc. 232
Muse 287
National Geographic Kids 287
New Moon Girls 288
Owen, Richard C., Publishers, Inc. 235
Pelican Publishing Company 236
Piano Press 237
Piñata Books 238
Pockets 288
Ronsdale Press 261
Scholastic Library Publishing 243
Seedling Continental Press 244
Seventeen Magazine 289
SHINE brightly 290
Skipping Stones 290
Sparkle 291
Spider 292
Tilbury House 247
Tor Books 248
Viking Children's Books 249
Weigl Publishers Inc. 249
Whitman, Albert & Company 250
Williamson Books 250
Wiseman Books, Paula 251

MUSIC/DANCE

Child's Play (International) Ltd. 256
Creative Company 214
Farrar, Straus & Giroux for Young Readers 219
Godine, Publisher, David R. 221
Kids Can Press 259
Owen, Richard C., Publishers, Inc. 235
Piano Press 237
Viking Children's Books 249
Whitman, Albert & Company 250
Williamson Books 250

NATURE/ENVIRONMENT (FICTION)

Advocate, PKA's Publication 267
Aquila 268
Azro Press 205
Boys' Quest 270
Brilliant Star 271
Candlewick Press 209
Child's Play (International) Ltd. 256
Cicada Magazine 274
Creative Company 214
Davey and Goliath's Devotions 276
Dutton Children's Books 216
Eerdmans Books for Young Readers 217
Farrar, Straus & Giroux for Young Readers 219
Fickling Books, David 257
Freestone/Peachtree, Jr. 220
Fun for Kidz 279
Godine, Publisher, David R. 221
Hopscotch 282
Ideals Children's Books and Candycane Press 224
Jack and Jill 284
JourneyForth 225
Kids Can Press 259
Ladybug 285
Lee & Low Books 228
Little, Brown and Co. Books for Young Readers 229
Milkweed Editions 231
New Moon Girls 288
OnStage Publishing 233
Orca Book Publishers 260
Piccadilly Press 260
Pineapple Press, Inc. 238
Pockets 288
Random House Children's Books 260
Renaissance House 241
Roaring Brook Press 241
Sasquatch Books 242
Seedling Continental Press 244
SHINE brightly 290
Skipping Stones 290
Sleeping Bear Press 245
Sparkle 291
Tafelberg Publishers 262
Tilbury House 247
Tor Books 248
Usborne Publishing 263
Viking Children's Books 249
Wiseman Books, Paula 251

NATURE/ENVIRONMENT (NONFICTION)

Advocate, PKA's Publication 267
Aquila 268
ASK 269
Brilliant Star 271
Candlewick Press 209
Carolrhoda Books, Inc. 209
ChemMatters 274
Chicago Review Press 211

Child's Play (International) Ltd. 256
Creative Company 214
Davey and Goliath's Devotions 276
Eerdmans Books for Young Readers 217
Faces 278
Farrar, Straus & Giroux for Young Readers 219
Freestone/Peachtree, Jr. 220
Friend Magazine, The 279
Fulcrum Publishing 221
Gibbs Smith 221
Godine, Publisher, David R. 221
Grosset & Dunlap Publishers 222
Highlights for Children 281
Hopscotch 282
Jack and Jill 284
Ladybug 285
Little, Brown and Co. Books for Young Readers 229
Master Books 230
Muse 287
National Geographic Kids 287
New Moon Girls 288
Owen, Richard C., Publishers, Inc. 235
Pineapple Press, Inc. 238
Sasquatch Books 242
Seedling Continental Press 244
SHINE brightly 290
Skipping Stones 290
Sparkle 291
Spider 292
Tilbury House 247
Tor Books 248
Viking Children's Books 249
Weigl Publishers Inc. 249
Whitman, Albert & Company 250
Williamson Books 250
Wiseman Books, Paula 251
World Book, Inc. 252

POETRY

Advocate, PKA's Publication 267
Babybug 269
Boys' Quest 270
Brilliant Star 271
Calliope 272
Candlewick Press 209
Child's Play (International) Ltd. 256
Cicada Magazine 274
Cobblestone 275
Creative Company 214
Cricket 276
Dial Books for Young Readers 215
Disney Hyperion Books for Children 215
Dutton Children's Books 216
Eerdmans Books for Young Readers 217
Faces 278
Farrar, Straus & Giroux for Young Readers 219
Fickling Books, David 257
Friend Magazine, The 279

Fun for Kidz 279
Godine, Publisher, David R. 221
Hopscotch 282
Jack and Jill 284
Kids Can Press 259
Ladybug 285
Lee & Low Books 228
Orchard Books 234
Piano Press 237
PUSH 239
Random House Children's Books 260
Roaring Brook Press 241
Spider 292
TC Magazine (Teenage Christian) 293
Thistledown Press Ltd. 262
Viking Children's Books 249
Wiseman Books, Paula 251

PROBLEM-SOLVING (FICTION)
Advocate, PKA's Publication 267
Aquila 268
Boys' Quest 270
Bread for God's Children 271
Brilliant Star 271
Cadet Quest Magazine 272
Clarion Books 213
Davey and Goliath's Devotions 276
Fun for Kidz 279
Highlights for Children 281
Horsepower 282
Ladybug 285
New Moon Girls 288
Pockets 288
SHINE brightly 290
Sparkle 291
TC Magazine (Teenage Christian) 293

PROBLEM-SOLVING (NONFICTION)
Advocate, PKA's Publication 267
American Cheerleader 268
ASK 269
Boys' Quest 270
Cadet Quest Magazine 272
ChemMatters 274
CollegeXpress Magazine 276
Davey and Goliath's Devotions 276
Fun for Kidz 279
Guide 280
Highlights for Children 281
Horsepower 282
Ladybug 285
Muse 287
New Moon Girls 288
Science Weekly 289
SHINE brightly 290
Skipping Stones 290
Sparkle 291
Spider 292

TC Magazine (Teenage Christian) 293

REFERENCE
Farrar, Straus & Giroux for Young Readers 219
Legacy Press 228
Rainbow Publishers 240
Tor Books 248
World Book, Inc. 252

RELIGIOUS
Aquila 268
Behrman House Inc. 206
Bread for God's Children 271
Brilliant Star 271
Cadet Quest Magazine 272
Catholic Forester 273
Concordia Publishing House 213
Creative Company 214
Davey and Goliath's Devotions 276
Eerdmans Books for Young Readers 217
Faces 278
Farrar, Straus & Giroux for Young Readers 219
FCA Magazine 279
Fickling Books, David 257
Flux 220
Friend Magazine, The 279
Guide 280
Ideals Children's Books and Candycane Press 224
Jewish Lights Publishing 225
Kar-Ben Publishing 227
Keys for Kids 285
Legacy Press 228
Meriwether Publishing Ltd. 231
New Moon Girls 288
Our Sunday Visitor, Inc. 234
Pauline Books & Media 235
Paulist Press 236
Pockets 288
Rainbow Publishers 240
Roaring Brook Press 241
SHINE brightly 290
Skipping Stones 290
Sleeping Bear Press 245
Sparkle 291
Standard Publishing 246
TC Magazine (Teenage Christian) 293
Tyndale House Publishers, Inc. 249
URJ Press 249
Viking Children's Books 249
Wiseman Books, Paula 251

ROMANCE
Advocate, PKA's Publication 267
Cicada Magazine 274

SCIENCE
Advocate, PKA's Publication 267
Aquila 268
ASK 269
Cadet Quest Magazine 272

ChemMatters 274
Chicago Review Press 211
Child's Play (International) Ltd. 256
Creative Company 214
Cricket 276
Dig 277
Eerdmans Books for Young Readers 217
Farrar, Straus & Giroux for Young Readers 219
Freestone/Peachtree, Jr. 220
Gibbs Smith 221
Grosset & Dunlap Publishers 222
Highlights for Children 281
Hopscotch 282
Jack and Jill 284
Kids Can Press 259
Ladybug 285
Leading Edge 286
Lee & Low Books 228
Little, Brown and Co. Books for Young Readers 229
Master Books 230
Muse 287
National Geographic Kids 287
New Moon Girls 288
Nomad Press 233
Owen, Richard C., Publishers, Inc. 235
Pineapple Press, Inc. 238
Scholastic Library Publishing 243
Science Weekly 289
Seedling Continental Press 244
Sparkle 291
Spider 292
Sterling Publishing Co., Inc. 246
Tor Books 248
Viking Children's Books 249
Weigl Publishers Inc. 249
Whitman, Albert & Company 250
Williamson Books 250
World Book, Inc. 252

SCIENCE FICTION
Advocate, PKA's Publication 267
Amulet Books 204
Aquila 268
Atheneum Books for Young Readers 205
Candlewick Press 209
Carolrhoda Books, Inc. 209
Cicada Magazine 274
Cricket 276
Cricket Books 214
Dial Books for Young Readers 215
Disney Hyperion Books for Children 215
Farrar, Straus & Giroux for Young Readers 219
Fickling Books, David 257
Flux 220
Ladybug 285
Leading Edge 286
New Moon Girls 288
OnStage Publishing 233

Random House Children's Books 260
Roaring Brook Press 241
Spider 292
Tafelberg Publishers 262
Thistledown Press Ltd. 262
Tor Books 248
Usborne Publishing 263
Viking Children's Books 249
Wiseman Books, Paula 251

SELF HELP
Farrar, Straus & Giroux for Young Readers 219
Free Spirit Publishing, Inc. 220
Impact Publishers, Inc. 225
Little, Brown and Co. Books for Young Readers 229
Magination Press 229
Piccadilly Press 260

SOCIAL ISSUES
Advocate, PKA's Publication 267
ASK 269
Brilliant Star 271
Cobblestone 275
CollegeXpress Magazine 276
Cricket 276
Davey and Goliath's Devotions 276
Faces 278
Girls' Life 280
Muse 287
National Geographic Kids 287
New Moon Girls 288
Seventeen Magazine 289
SHINE brightly 290
Skipping Stones 290
Sparkle 291
TC Magazine (Teenage Christian) 293

SPECIAL NEEDS (NONFICTION)
Creative Company 214
Farrar, Straus & Giroux for Young Readers 219
Free Spirit Publishing, Inc. 220
Freestone/Peachtree, Jr. 220
Kar-Ben Publishing 227
Kids Can Press 259
Magination Press 229
Scholastic Library Publishing 243
Whitman, Albert & Company 250

SPORTS (FICTION)
Amulet Books 204
Aquila 268
Boys' Quest 270
Bread for God's Children 271
Cadet Quest Magazine 272
Candlewick Press 209
Cicada Magazine 274
Creative Company 214
Cricket Books 214
Dial Books for Young Readers 215
Disney Hyperion Books for Children 215

Eerdmans Books for Young Readers 217
Farrar, Straus & Giroux for Young Readers 219
Fickling Books, David 257
Flux 220
Freestone/Peachtree, Jr. 220
Fun for Kidz 279
Highlights for Children 281
Hopscotch 282
Jack and Jill 284
Kids Can Press 259
Ladybug 285
Lee & Low Books 228
New Moon Girls 288
Random House Children's Books 260
Roaring Brook Press 241
SHINE brightly 290
Sleeping Bear Press 245
Sparkle 291
Tafelberg Publishers 262
TC Magazine (Teenage Christian) 293
Viking Children's Books 249
Wiseman Books, Paula 251

SPORTS (NONFICTION)
Advocate, PKA's Publication 267
American Cheerleader 268
Aquila 268
ASK 269
Boys' Quest 270
Cadet Quest Magazine 272
Carolrhoda Books, Inc. 209
CollegeXpress Magazine 276
Creative Company 214
Cricket 276
Dial Books for Young Readers 215
Farrar, Straus & Giroux for Young Readers 219
FCA Magazine 279
Freestone/Peachtree, Jr. 220
Fun for Kidz 279
Girls' Life 280
Highlights for Children 281
Jack and Jill 284
Kids Can Press 259
Lee & Low Books 228
Little, Brown and Co. Books for Young Readers 229
National Geographic Kids 287
New Moon Girls 288
Owen, Richard C., Publishers, Inc. 235
Scholastic Library Publishing 243
SHINE brightly 290
Skipping Stones 290
Sparkle 291
TC Magazine (Teenage Christian) 293
Viking Children's Books 249
Weigl Publishers Inc. 249
Whitman, Albert & Company 250
Wiseman Books, Paula 251
Young Rider 294

SUSPENSE/MYSTERY
Advocate, PKA's Publication 267
Amulet Books 204
Aquila 268
Candlewick Press 209
Cicada Magazine 274
Cricket 276
Cricket Books 214
Disney Hyperion Books for Children 215
Eerdmans Books for Young Readers 217
Farrar, Straus & Giroux for Young Readers 219
Fickling Books, David 257
Flux 220
Freestone/Peachtree, Jr. 220
Godine, Publisher, David R. 221
Highlights for Children 281
Hopscotch 282
JourneyForth 225
Kids Can Press 259
Ladybug 285
Little, Brown and Co. Books for Young Readers 229
Milkweed Editions 231
New Moon Girls 288
OnStage Publishing 233
Orca Book Publishers 260
Random House Children's Books 260
Roaring Brook Press 241
Simon & Schuster Books for Young Readers 244
Sparkle 291
Tafelberg Publishers 262
Thistledown Press Ltd. 262
Tor Books 248
Tyndale House Publishers, Inc. 249
Usborne Publishing 263
Viking Children's Books 249
Whitman, Albert & Company 250
Wiseman Books, Paula 251

TEXTBOOKS
Behrman House Inc. 206
Farrar, Straus & Giroux for Young Readers 219
Gryphon House, Inc. 222
Meriwether Publishing Ltd. 231

TRAVEL
Advocate, PKA's Publication 267
CollegeXpress Magazine 276
Cricket 276
Faces 278
Girls' Life 280
Horsepower 282
National Geographic Kids 287
New Moon Girls 288
SHINE Brightly 290
Skipping Stones 290
Sparkle 291
TC Magazine (Teenage Christian) 293

EDITOR AND AGENT NAMES INDEX

Abbey, Caroline (Golden Books for Young Readers Group) 221

Abkemeier, Laurie (Defiore & Co.) 304

Abou, Stéphanie (Foundry Literary + Media) 311

Abramo, Lauren E. (Dystel & Goderich Literary Management) 306

Adams, Tracy (Adams Literary) 297

Adams, Josh (Adams Literary) 297

Adams, Wesley (Farrar, Straus & Giroux for Young Readers) 219

Anderson-Wheeler, Claire (Regal Literary) 317

Andelman, Michelle (Regal Literary Agency) 333

Anthony, Jason (Lippincott Massie McQuilkin) 322

Arms, Victoria Wells (Wells Arms Literary) 340

Arroyo, Erika (Facts on File, Inc) 218

Axford, Elizabeth C. (Piano Press) 237

Bailey, Raquel D. (Lyrical Passion Poetry E-Zine) 286

Baker-Baughman, Bernadette (Victoria Sanders & Associates) 334

Baker, Charles (Calliope) 272

Baker, Rosalie (Dig Magazine) 277

Baker, Sue (Child's Play (International) Ltd.) 256

Baker, T. (Fulcrum Publishing) 221

Balmuth, Deborah (Storey Publishing) 246

Balzer, Alessandra (Balzer & Bray) 206

Bancroft, Carol (Carol Bancroft & Friends) 342

Barbara, Stephen (Foundry Literary + Media) 311

Barney, Stacey (G.P. Putnam's Sons Hardcover) 240

Barr, Stephen (Writers House) 341

Bassoff, Ethan (Lippincott Massie McQuilkin) 322

Beck, Suzanne (Spider) 292

Becker, Laney Katz (Lippincott Massie McQuilkin) 322

Beckerman, Chad (Abrams Books for Young Readers) 204

Beecher, Jim (Junior Baseball) 284

Bell, Folade (Serendipity Literary Agency, LLC) 335

Belton, Neil (Faber & Faber Ltd) 257

Bender, Faye (Faye Bender Literary Agency) 297

Bennet, David (Transatlantic Literary Agency) 338

Bennet, Lynn (Transatlantic Literary Agency) 338

Bergonzi, Megan (Seedling Continental Press) 244

Berkower, Amy (Writers House) 341

Berry, Jackie (Aquila) 268

Besser, Jennifer (G.P. Putnam's Sons Hardcover) 240

Bewley, Elizabeth (Little Brown and Co. Books for Young Readers) 229

Biagi, Laura (Jean V. Naggar Literary Agency, Inc.) 326

Bialer, Matt (Sanford J. Greenburger Associates, Inc.) 316

Bick, George (Doug Grad Literary Agency, Inc.) 315

Bilmes, Joshua (Jabberwocky Literary Agency) 320

Blaise, Lizz (Inkwell Management, LLC) 320

Blasdell, Caitlin (Liza Dawson Associates) 303

Bobco, Ann (Margaret K. McElderry Books) 230

Bolinau, Mela (MB Artists) 344

Bourret, Michael (Dystel & Goderich Literary Management) 306

Bowen, Brenda (Sanford J. Greenburger Associates, Inc.) 316

Bowie, Liz (Edupress, Inc.) 217

Bowles, Brandi (Foundry Literary Media) 311

Bowman, Hannah (Liza Dawson Associates) 303

Brackstone, Lee (Faber & Faber Ltd) 257

Bradley, Shaun (Transatlantic Literary Agency) 338

Bradford, Laura (Bradford Literary Agency) 298

Bray, Donna (Balzer & Bray) 206

Brazis, Tamar (Amulet Books) 204

Brill, Calista (First Second) 219

Broene, G. Richard (Cadet Quest Magazine) 272

Brooks, Regina (Serendipity Literary Agency, LLC) 335

Brower, Michelle (Folio Literary Management, LLC) 310

Brown, Andrea (Andrea Brown Literary Agency, Inc.) 298

Brown, Gayle (Eerdmans Books for Young Readers) 217

Bryan, Jeffrey (Whitecap Books, Ltd.) 263

Buck, Bethany (Aladdin) 204

Buckley, Susan (Appleseeds) 268

Buffington, Peter (Peace Hill Press) 236

Burde, Neil (Child's Play (International, Ltd.) 256

Callahan, William (Inkwell Management, LLC) 320

Cameron, Kimberley (Kimberley Cameron & Associates) 300

Campbell, Marie (Transatlantic Literary Agency) 338

Caplan, Dave (Little Brown and Co. Books for Young Readers) 229

Caplan, Deborah (RazorBill) 241

Capron, Elise (Sandra Dijkstra Literary Agency) 305

Cardon, Diane (Leading Edge) 286

Cargill, Angus (Faber & Faber Ltd) 257

Carlisle, Michael V (Inkwell Management, LLC) 320

Carlson, Jennifer (Dunow, Carlson & Lerner Agency) 306

Carus, Marianne (Spider) 292

Cascardi, Andrea (Egmont USA) 218

Casella, Maura Kye (Don Congdon Associates Inc.) 300

Cash, Mary (Holiday House, Inc.) 224

Casner, Matheau (FCA Magazine) 279

Cavnar, Cindy (Our Sunday Visitor, Inc.) 234

Charner, Kathy (Gryphon House, Inc.) 222

Chambers, James (Facts on File, Inc) 218

Chanda, Justin (Atheneum Books for Young Readers) 205

Chanda, Justin (Margaret K. McElderry Books) 230

Chenes, Betz Des (GreenHaven Press) 222

Chiotti, Danielle (Upstart Crow Literary) 340

Chilton, Jamie Weiss (Andrea Brown Literary Agency, Inc.) 298

Chromy, Adam (Howard Morhaim Literary Agency) 326

Ciovacco, Justine (Facts on File, Inc) 218

Clark, Ginger (Curtis Brown, Ltd.) 301

Cloughley, Amy (Kimberley Cameron & Associates) 300

Clement, Emily (Arthur A. Levine Books) 228

Clementson, Elizabet (Lizzie Skurnick Books) 245

Cohen, Susan (Writers House) 341

Collier, Harold (White Mane Kids) 250

Collins, Amy (Orca Book Publishers) 260

Concepcion, Cristina (Don Congdon Associates Inc.) 300

Congdon, Michael (Don Congdon Associates Inc.) 300

Conaway, Dan (Writers House) 341

Corathers, Don (Dramatics Magazine) 277

Corcoran, Jill (Jill Corcoran Literary Agency) 301

Cornell, Merial (Cornell & McCarthy LLC) 342

Corvisiero, Marisa A. (Corvisiero Literary Agency) 301

Counihan, Claire (Holiday House, Inc.) 224

Cross, Claudia (Folio Literary Management, LLC) 310

Cully, Christine French (Highlights for Children) 281

Cusick, John M. (The Greenhouse Literary Agency) 316

Cussen, June (Pinapple Press, Inc.) 238

Dark, Tom (Heacock Hill Literary Agency, Inc.) 318

Davie, Mike (Manor House Publishing, Inc) 259

Davies, Sarah (The Greenhouse Literary Agency) 316

Dawson, Havis (Liza Dawson Associates) 303

Dawson, Kathy (Kathy Dawson Books) 214

Dawson, Kathy (Dial Books for Young Readers) 215

Dawson, Liza (Liza Dawson Associates) 303

Deason, Jennifer (HarperTeen) 223

DeChiara, Jennifer (The Jennifer DeChiara Literary Agency) 304

DeFiore, Brian (Defiore & Co.) 304

Depkin, Kristen (Golden Books for Young Readers Group) 221

Detweiler, Katelyn (Jill Grinberg Literary Agency) 318

Devereux, Allison (Wolf Literary Services, LLC) 341

Dickinson, Philippa (Random House Children's Books) 260

Diforio, Bob (D4EO Literary Agency) 302

Dighton, Samantha (D4EO Literary Agency) 302

Dijkstra, Sandra (Sandra Dijkstra Literary Agency) 305

Dillon, Ann (Calliope) 272

Dillon, Ann (Dig) 277

DiMona, Lisa (Writers House) 341

Dlouhy, Caitlyn (Atheneum Books for Young Readers) 205

Dominguez, Adriana (Full Circle Literary, LLC) 312

Donahue, Walter (Faber & Faber Ltd) 257

Drayton, Catherine (Inkwell Management, LLC) 320

Driskell, Kathleen (The Louisville Review) 286

Dugas, Rachael (Talcott Notch Literary) 338

Duncan, Virgina (GreenWillow Books) 222

Dunham, Jennie (Dunham Literary, Inc.) 305

Dunow, Henry (Dunow, Carlson & Lerner Agency) 306

Dystel, Jane (Dystel & Goderich Literary Management) 306

Dziena, David (Our Sunday Visitor, Inc.) 234

Eason, Amanda (Ledge Hill Publishing) 227

Eaton, Jonathan (Tilbury House) 247

Edwards, Marilyn (Boys' Quest) 270

Edwards, Marilyn (Fun For Kidz) 279

Edwards, Marilyn (Hopscotch) 282

Eisenhardt, Gae (Azro Press) 205

Ekstrom, Rachel (Irene Goodman Literary Agency) 314

Elblonk, Matthew (Defiore & Co.) 304

Ellenberg, Ethan (Ethan Ellenberg Literary Agency) 309

Ellison, Nicholas (Sanford J. Greenbruger Associates, Inc.) 316

Ellwood, Nancy (DK Publishing) 216

Enderle, Kristine (Imagination Press) 229

Enete, Shannon (Enete Enterprises) 218

Engbring, Kate (HarperCollins Children's Books/ HarperCollins Publishers) 223

Engle, Susan (Brilliant Star) 271

English, Elaine (The Elaine P. English Literary Agency) 309

Epstein, Linds (The Jennifer DeChiara Literary Agency) 304

Ertle, Jenny (Ransom Publishing) 261

Evans, Elizabeth (Jean V. Naggar Literary Agency, Inc.) 326

Fabre, Emily (Margaret K. McElderry Books) 230

Faktorovich, Anna (Anaphora Literary Press) 204

Farrey, Brian (Flux) 220

Fausset, Katherine (Curtis Brown, Ltd.) 301

Featherstone, Hannah (David Fickling Books) 257

Fehr, Don (Trident Media Group) 339

Feiwel, Jean (Feiwel and Friends) 219

Feldman, Leigh (Writers House) 341

Feresten, Nancy (National Geographic Children's Books) 233

Ferguson, Greg (Egmont USA) 218

Ferguson, Margaret (Farrar, Straus & Giroux for Young Readers) 219

Ferguson, T.S. (Harlequin Teen) 223

Finkelstein, Jesse (Transatlantic Literary Agency) 338

Fishel, Randy (Guide) 280

Fisk, Karen (Tilbury House) 247

Fitzhenry, Sharon (Fitzhenry & Whiteside Ltd.) 257

Flannery, Jennifer (Flannery Literary) 310

Flashman, Melissa (Trident Media Group) 339

Forrer, David (Inkwell Management, LLC) 320

Forrie, Allan (Thistledown Press Ltd.) 262

Foster, Frances (Farrar, Straus & Giroux for Young Readers) 219

Foster, Roz (Sandra Dijkstra Literary Agency) 305

Fran, Carol (Tradewind Books) 262

Frank, Catherine (Viking Children's Books) 249

Frank, Sylvie (Paula Wiseman Books) 251

Fraser, Stephen (The Jennifer DeChiara Literary Agency) 304

Fraser-Bub, MacKenzie (Trident Media Group) 339

Frederick, Dawn (Red Sofa Literary) 332

Frederick, Holly (Curtis Brown, Ltd.) 301

Fried, Rachael Dillon (Sanford J. Greenbruger Associates, Inc.) 316

Friedman, Phil (Scholastic Library Publishing) 243

Friend, Simone (Friend + Johnson) 343

Frisch, Aaron (Creative Company) 214

Fritts, Dana (HarperCollins Children's Books/ HarperCollins Publishers) 223

Froman, Craig (Master Books) 230

Fumich, Jita (Folio Literary Management, LLC) 310

Gabel, Claudia (Katherine Tegen Books) 247

Gahan, Tom (First Edition Design Publishing) 219

Gallagher, Lisa (Sanford J. Greenburger Associates, Inc.) 316

Gallt, Nancy (Nancy Gallt Literary Agency) 313

Garrick, Kate (Defiore & Co.) 304

Garrison, Jessica (Dial Books for Young Readers) 215

Gaticia, Shersta (Cedar Fort, Inc) 210

Gaudet, Mary-Kate (Little Brown and Co. Books for Young Readers) 229

Gayle, Nadeen (Serendipity Literary Agency, LLC) 335

Gaynin, Morgan (MGI Kids (Morgan Gaynin Inc.) 344

Geist, Ken (Orchard Books) 234

Gelbman, Leslie (Berkley Books) 207

Gelfman, Jane (Gelfman Schneider / ICM Partners) 314

Gendell, Yfat Reiss (Foundry Literary Media) 311

German, Donna (Arbordale Publishing) 205

Getzler, Josh (HSG Agency) 318

Ghahremani, Lily (Full Circle Literary, LLC) 312

Ghezzi, Bert (Our Sunday Visitor, Inc.) 234

Gholson, Kris (Eakin Press) 216

Gibbs, Judith M. (Bread for God's Children) 271

Gilliam, Lynn W. (Pockets) 288

Gillner, Tim (Boyds Mills Press) 208

Gilmore, Kelli (Shine Brightly) 290

Gilmore, Kelli (Sparkle) 291

Gilson, Kristin (Puffin Books) 239

Ginsberg, Peter (Curtis Brown, Ltd.) 301

Ginsberg, Susan (Writers House) 341

Giovinazzo, Elena (Pippin Properties, Inc.) 330

Glass, Alex (Trident Media Group) 339

Glick, Molly (Foundry Literary Media) 311

Glick, Stacey Kendall (Dystel & Goderich Literary Management) 306

Goderich, Miriam (Dystel & Goderich Literary Management) 306

Goldberg, Michael H. (URJ Press) 249

Goldblatt, Barry (Barry Goldblatt Literary LLC) 314

Goldman, Michael (Boys' Life) 270

Goldsmith, Connor (Foreword Literary) 310

Goldstein, Debra (Defiore & Co.) 304

Goloby, Jennie (Red Sofa Literary) 332

Goodman, Irene (Irene Goodman Literary Agency) 314

Gordon, Deborah E. (First Edition Design Publishing) 219

Gordon, Hannah Brown (Foundry Literary Media) 311

Gordon, Russell (Aladdin) 204

Gottlieb, Mark (Trident Media Group) 339

Gourley, Robbin (Boyds Mills Press) 208

Gourley, Robbin (Farrar, Straus & Giroux for Young Readers) 219

Grad, Doug (Doug Grad Literary Agency, Inc.) 315

Grant, Tim (Green Teacher) 280

Green, Kathy, (Kathryn Green Literary Agency, LLC) 317

Green, Michael (Philomel Books) 237

Greene, Jennifer (Clarion Books) 213

Gref, Emily (Lowenstein Associates Inc.) 324

Gregory, Evan (Ethen Ellenberg Literary Agency) 309

Gregory, John, (Legacy Press) 228

Grencik, Karen (Red Fox Literary) 332

Griffin, Regina (Egmont USA) 218

Griffiths, Hanna (Faber & Faber Ltd) 257

Grillone, Jennifer (Gibbs Smith) 221

Grimm, Katie (Don Congdon Associates Inc.) 300

Grinberg, Jill (Jill Grinberg Literary Agency) 318

Gruber, Pamela (Little Brown and Co. Books for Young Readers) 229

Grzeslo, Barbara (Boyds Mills Press) 208

Hall, Katie (Arbordale Publishing) 205

Ham, Julie (Charlesbridge Publishing) 210

Hamlin, Faith (Sanford J. Greenbruger Associates, Inc.) 316

Hamlin, Kairi (Tanglewood Books) 247

Hamilton, Dianne (Onstage Publishing) 233

Hannigan, Carrie (HSG Agency) 318

Hardy, Dawn Michelle (Serendipity Literary Agency, LLC) 335

Harkin, Christie (Fitzhenry & Whiteside Ltd.) 257

Harriot, Michael (Folio Literary Management, LLC) 310

Harris, Erin (Folio Literary Management, LLC) 310

Harris, Patti Ann (Little Brown and Co. Books for Young Readers) 229

Harriss, Helen (Freestone/PeachTree, Jr.) 220

Harriss, Helen (PeachTree Children's Books) 236

Harding, Elizabeth (Curtis Brown, Ltd.) 301

Harvey, Ellery (Rain Town Press) 240

Harvey, Sarah (Orca Book Publishers) 260

Harris, Cornithia (Chemmaters) 274

Harrison, Kate (Dial Books for Young Readers) 215

Hart, Cate (Corvisiero Literary Agency) 301

Hassan, Shannon (Mayrsal Lyon Literary Agency) 319

Hatch, Ronald B. (Ronsdale Press) 261

Hatch, Veronica (Ronsdale Press) 261

Haywood, Samantha (Transatlantic Literary Agency) 338

Hazelton, Marilyn (Red Lights) 289

Heifetz, Merrilee (Writers House) 341

Henkin, Eisner (Trident Media Group) 339

Herman, Ronnie Ann (Herman Agency) 318

Hernandez, Saritza (Corvisiero Literary Agency) 301

Herschke, Christa (Mcintosh & Otis, Inc.) 325

Hillman, Dennis R. (Kregel Publications) 227

Hinz, Carol (The MillBrook Press) 232

Hirsch, Gretchen (Margaret K. McElderry Books) 230

Hodgkins, Fran (Tilbury House) 247

Hoffman, Marcus (Regal Literary Agency) 333

Hoffman, Scott (Folio Literary Management, LLC) 310

Hoffman, Shira (Mcintosh & Otis, Inc.) 325

Holland, Joyce (D4EO Literary Agency) 302

Holtz, Tim (Jewish Lights Publishing) 225

Hoppe, Anne (Clarion Books) 213

Hornik, Lauri (Dial Books for Young Readers) 215

Hosier, Erin (Dunow, Carlson & Lerner Agency) 306

Howick, Jr., E. Keith (WindRiver Publishing, Inc.) 251

Howick, Gail (WindRiver Publishing, Inc.) 251

Hsu, Connie (Little Brown and Co. Books for Young Readers) 229

Hubbard, Mandy (D4EO Literary Agency) 302

Huffine, Leigh (Regal Literary Agency) 333

Hughes, Amy (Dunow, Carlson & Lerner Agency) 306

Hughes, Catherine (National Geographic Kids) 287

Hughes, Heather (Sleeping Bear Press) 245

Hull, Scott (Scott Hull Associates) 343

Hurley, Alexis (Inkwell Management, LLC) 320

Hunt, Jennifer Bailey (Little Brown and Co. Books for Young Readers) 229

Hunter, Allison (Inkwell Management, LLC) 320

Hunter, Lisa (Sparkle) 291

Huyck, Liz (Ask) 269

Iverson, Talinda (Tyndale House Publishers, Inc.) 249

Ives, Melanie McMahon (Freestone/PeachTree, Jr.) 220

Jacks, Nathaniel (Inkwell Management, LLC) 320

Jackson, Eleanor (Dunow, Carlson & Lerner Agency) 306

Jaffa, Molly (Folio Literary Management, LLC) 310

Jameson, Amy (A+B Works) 297

Jameson, Brandon (A+B Works) 297

Janklow, Luke (Janklow & Nesbit Associates) 321

Janklow, Morton I. Janklow (Janklow & Nesbit Associates) 321

Janus, Mark-David (Paulist Press) 236

Jenvy, Suzy (Faber & Faber Ltd) 257

Johns, Chelcee (Serendipity Literary Agency, LLC) 335

Johnson, Beth (Friend + Johnson) 343

Johnson, Brianne (Writers House) 341

Johnson, Kate (Wolf Literary Services, LLC) 341

Jones, Chris (Australasian Journal of Early Childhood) 269

Jones, Meryl (Craven Design, Inc.) 342

Joyner, Loraine (Freestone/PeachTree, Jr.) 220

Kaffel, Meredith (Defiore & Co.) 304

Kahan, Alex (Nomad Press) 233

Kaiser, Cecily (Amulet Books) 204

Kanabel, Jerry (American Careers) 267

Kanellos, Nicolas (Piñata Books) 238

Karmatz-Rudy, Caryn (Defiore & Co.) 304

Karre, Andrew (Carolrhoda Lab) 209

Karsbaek, Jen (Foreword Literary) 310

Kasdin, Steve (Curtis Brown, Ltd.) 301

Katcher, Ruth (Egmont USA) 218

Katz, Michael (Tradewind Books) 262

Keegan, Paul (Faber & Faber Ltd) 257

Keller, Patricia (Advocate, PKA's Publication) 267

Kenny, Julia (Dunow, Carlson & Lerner Agency) 306

Kenshole, Fiona (Transatlantic Literary Agency) 338

Kepner, Chris (Victoria Sanders & Associates) 334

Kettner, Christine (Clarion Books) 213

Keyes, Emily (Foreword Literary) 310

Kietlinski, Teresa (Prospect Agency) 330

Kim, Chun (Girls' Life) 280

Kim, Emily Sylvan (Prospect Agency) 330

Kim, Kirby (Janklow & Nesbit Associates) 321

Kissock, Heather (Weigl Publishers Inc.) 249

Klein, Cherly (Arthur A. Levine Books) 228

Kleinman, Jeff (Folio Literary Management, LLC) 310

Knapp, Peter (Park Literary Group) 315

Knowlton, Ginger (Curtis Brown, Ltd.) 301

Knowlton, Timothy (Curtis Brown, Ltd.) 301

Kobasa, Paul A. (World Book, Inc.) 252

Kohl, Mary-Anne (Bright Ring Publishing, Inc.) 208

Kolakowski, Ann (Turn The Page Publishing LLC) 248

Kooij, Nina (Pelican Publishing Company) 236

Koons, Abigail (Park Literary Group, LLC) 328

Kotchmant, Katie (Don Congdon Associates Inc.) 300

Kouts, Barbara S. (Barbara S. Kouts, Literary Agent) 322

Kracht, Elizabeth (Kimberley Cameron & Associates) 300

Kriss, Miriam (Irene Goodman Literary Agency) 314

Lakosil, Natalie (Bradford Literary Agency) 298

Lamb, Paul (Howard Morhaim Literary Agency) 326

Lamba, Marie (The Jennifer DeChiara Literary Agency) 304

Lancer, Owen (Facts on File, Inc) 218

Lange, Heidi (Sanford J. Greenbruger Associates, Inc.) 316

LaPolla, Sarah (Bradford Literary Agency) 298

Larson, Ellen (The Poisoned Pencil) 239

Lasner, Robert (Lizzie Skurnick Books) 245

Latshaw, Katherine (Folio Literary Management, LLC) 310

Laughran, Jennifer (Andrea Brown Literary Agency, Inc.) 298

Lawrence, Tricia (Erin Murphy Literary Agency) 326

Lazar, Daniel (Writers House) 341

LeBaigue, Catt (Heacock Hill Literary Agency, Inc.) 318

Lee, Thau (Sandra Dijkstra Literary Agency) 305

Lee, Quinlan (Adams Literary) 297

Lentin, Roseann (Turn The Page Publishing LLC) 248

Lenze, Heidi (Sasquatch Books) 242

Lerner, Betsy (Dunow, Carlson & Lerner Agency) 306

Letko, Ken (The Kerf) 285

Levine, Arthur A. (Arthur A. Levine Books) 228

Lewis, Kevin (Disney Hyperion Books for Children) 215

Lewin, Arianne (G.P. Putnam's Sons Hardcover) 240

Levine, Ellen (Trident Media Group) 339

Levinson, Gillian (RazorBill) 241

Likoff, Laurie (Facts on File, Inc) 218

Linder, B. (Educational Design Services LLC) 308

Lindman, Chelsea (Sanford J. Greenbruger Associates, Inc.) 316

Lindsey, Jacquelyn (Our Sunday Visitor, Inc.) 234

Ling, Alvina (Little Brown and Co. Books for Young Readers) 229

Lippincott, Will (Lippincott Massie McQuilkin) 322

Lipskar, Simon (Writers House) 341

Little, Denise (Ethan Ellenberg Literary Agency) 309

Lohr, Nancy (JourneyForth) 225

Loose, Julian (Faber & Faber Ltd) 257

Louise, Steyn (Tafelberg Publishers) 262

Lowenstein, Barbara (Lowenstein Associates Inc.) 324

Lucas, Paul (Janklow & Nesbit Associates) 321

Luke, Gary (Sasquatch Books) 242

Lurie, Stephanie Owens (Disney Hyperion Books for Children) 215

Lyons, Jonathan (Curtis Brown, Ltd.) 301

MacCarone, Grace (Holiday House, Inc.) 224

Machinist, Alexandra (Janklow & Nesbit Associates) 321

Mackenzie, Catherine (Christian Focus Publications) 256

MacLeod, Lauren (The Strothman Agency, LLC) 337

MacMillan, Colleen (Annick Press, Ltd.) 253

Maccoby, Gina (Gina Maccoby Literary Agency) 324

Maikels, Terence (Sasquatch Books) 242

Malawer, Ted (Upstart Crow Literary) 340

Malcolm, Lily (Dial Books for Young Readers) 215

Malk, Steven (Writers House) 341

Mandel, Daniel (Sanford J. Greenbruger Associates, Inc.) 316

Marcus, Kendra (Bookstop Literary Agency) 297

Marett Hazel (Keys for Kids) 285

Marini, Victoria (Gelfman Schneider / ICM Partners) 314

Mark, PJ (Janklow & Nesbit Associates) 321

Marr, Jill (Sandra Dijkstra Literary Agency) 305

Martin, Betsy (Skinner House Books) 245

Martindale, Taylor (Full Circle Literary, LLC) 312

Massie, Maria (Lippincott Massie McQuilkin) 322

Mattero, Anthony (Foundry Literary Media) 311

Matthews, Belinda (Faber & Faber Ltd) 257

Mattson, Jennifer (Andrea Brown Literary Agency, Inc.) 298

May, Louise (Lee & Low Books) 228

Mayberry, Dr. Claude (Science Weekly) 289

McCarthy, Jim (Dystel & Goderich Literary Management) 306

McCarthy, Sean (Sean McCarthy Literary Agency) 325

McDonald, Doreen (Corvisiero Literary Agency) 301

McGhee, Holly (Pippin Properties, Inc.) 330

McGuigan, Peter (Foundry Literary Media) 311

McKean, Kate (Howard Morhaim Literary Agency) 326

McKinnon, Tanya (Victoria Sanders & Associates) 334

McLean, Laurie (Foreword Literary) 310

McIntyre, Casey (RazorBill) 241

McQuilkin, Rob (Lippincott Massie McQuilkin) 322

Meehan, Emily (Disney Hyperion Books for Children) 215

Megan, Tingley (Little Brown and Co. Books for Young Readers) 229

Megged, Semadar (Philomel Books) 237

Megibow, Sara (Nelson Literary Agency) 328

Mejisas, Michael (Writers House) 341

Melton, Dnise (Martin Sisters Publishing, LLC) 230

Mendel, Ms. Gerry (Stone Soup) 293

Menon, Pooja (Kimberley Cameron & Associates) 300

Meyer, Clay (FCA Magazine) 279

Miller, Barb (Transatlantic Literary Agency) 338

Miller-Callihan, Courtney (Sanford J. Greenbruger Associates, Inc.) 316

Miller, Kathryn (Shine Brightly) 290

Miller, Scott (Trident Media Group) 339

Miller-Vincent, Kristin (D4EO Literary Agency) 302

Mitchard, Jacquelyn (Merit Press) 231

Mitchell, Barbara (Mitchell Lane Publishers, Inc.) 232

Mitchell, Heather (Gelfman Schneider / ICM Partners) 314

Morgan, Sam (Jabberwocky Literary Agency) 320

Morhaim, Howard (Howard Morhaim Literary Agency) 326

Moore, Mary C. (Kimberley Cameron & Associates) 300

Morris, Richard (Janklow & Nesbit Associates) 321

Moscovich, Rotem (Disney Hyperion Books for Children) 215

Mozdzen, Alyssa (Inkwell Management, LLC) 320

Munier, Paula (Talcott Notch Literary) 338

Muhlig, Adam (Mcintosh & Otis, Inc.) 325

Mulligan, Brianne (RazorBill) 241

Murphy, Erin (Erin Murphy Literary Agency) 326

Murphy, Jacqueline (Inkwell Management, LLC) 320

Murphy, Paula (Boys' Life) 270

Myers, Eric (The Spieler Agency) 336

Nagel, Karen (Aladdin) 204

Naggar, Jean (Jean V. Naggar Literary Agency, Inc.) 326

Nagler, Michelle (Golden Books for Young Readers Group) 221

Nego, Sarah (Corvisiero Literary) 313

Negovetich, Sarah (Corvisiero Literary Agency) 301

Negron, Jessica (Talcott Notch Literary) 311

Nelson, Kristin (Nelson Literary Agency) 328

Nesbit, Lynn (Janklow & Nesbit Associates) 321

Neuhaus, Kirsten (Foundry Literary Media) 311

Newman, Melissa (Martin Sisters Publishing, LLC) 230

Niehaus, Alisha (Dial Books for Young Readers) 215

Niumata, Erin (Folio Literary Management, LLC) 310

Nobles, Kristin (Candlewick Press) 209

Nolan, Polly (The Greenhouse Literary Agency) 316

Ocampo, Patricia (Transatlantic Literary Agency) 338

Odom, Monica (Liza Dawson Associates) 303

Odgen, Bree (D4EO Literary Agency) 302

Olsen, Charlie (Inkwell Management, LLC) 320

Olswanger, Anna (Liza Dawson Associates) 303

O'Malley, Janine (Farrar, Straus & Giroux for Young Readers) 219

O'Neil, Shannon (Lippincott Massie McQuilkin) 322

Orr, Rachel (Prospect Agency) 330

Ortiz, Kathleen (New Leaf Literary & Media, Inc) 328

O'Sullivan, Kate (Houghton Mifflin Harcourt Books for Children) 224

Ottinger, Tyler (Our Sunday Visitor, Inc.) 234

Owen, J.D. (Boys' Life) 270

Owen, Richerd (Richard C. Owen Publisher, Inc.) 235

Pages, Patrice (Chemmaters) 274

Panettieri, Gina (Talcott Notch Literary) 338

Papin, Jessica (Dystel & Goderich Literary Management) 306

Paprocki, Karin (Aladdin) 204

Paquette, Ammi-Joan (Erin Murphy Literary Agency) 326

Parel-Sewell, Amethel (Brilliant Star) 271

Park, Chris (Foundry Literary Media) 311

Park, Theresa (Park Literary Group, LLC) 328

Parry, Emma (Janklow & Nesbit Associates) 321

Patterson, David (Foundry Literary Media) 311

Patton, Katara Washington (Tyndale House Publishers, Inc.) 249

Paulsen, Nancy (G.P. Putnam's Sons Hardcover) 240

Pearson, Lauren (Regal Literary Agency) 333

Pederson, Juliet (Tor Books) 248

Pelletier, Sharon (Dystel & Goderich Literary Management) 306

Penfold, Alexandra (Upstart Crow Literary) 340

Perkins, Lara (Andrea Brown Literary Agency, Inc.) 298

Peskin, Joy (Farrar, Straus & Giroux for Young Readers) 219

Pestritto, Carrie (Prospect Agency) 330

Peterson, Laura Blake (Curtis Brown, Ltd.) 301

Pfeffer, Rubin (Rubin Pfeffer Content) 329

Phelan, Beth (Bent Literary) 307

Pientka Cheryl (Jill Grinberg Literary Agency) 318

Pieper, Paul B. (The Friend Magazine) 279

Pitchford, Mary (American Careers) 267

Pine, Richard (Inkwell Management, LLC) 320

Podos, Rebecca (Rees Literary Agency) 299

Poelle, Barbara (Irene Goodman Literary Agency) 314

Pohlen, Jerome (Chicago Review Press) 211

Polvino, Lynne (Clarion Books) 213

Pomerance, Ruth (Folio Literary Management, LLC) 310

Porter, Deb (Click) 274

Porter, Freeman (Impact Publishers, Inc.) 225

Posner, Marcy (Folio Literary Management, LLC) 310

Pratt, Linda (Wernick & Pratt Agency) 341

Pusey, Alyssa (Charlesbridge Publishing) 210

Quay, Corus (Kids Can Press) 259

Quigley, Brandon (Green Teacher) 280

Radke, Linda F. (Five Star Publications, Inc) 219

Ramer, Susan (Don Congdon Associates Inc.) 300

Ranta, Adrianna (Wolf Literary Services, LLC) 341

Raymo, Margaret (Houghton Mifflin Harcourt Books for Children) 224

Reamer, Jodi (Writers House) 341

Reardon, Lisa (Chicago Review Press) 211

Reed, Katie (Andrea Hurst & Associates) 331

Reese, Brandon (Guide) 280

Regal, Joseph (Regal Literary Agency) 333

Regel, Jessica (Foundry Literary Media) 311

Reil, Douglas (North Atlantic Books) 233

Rennert, Laura (Andrea Brown Literary Agency, Inc.) 298

Resciniti, Nicole (The Seymour Agency) 336

Reynolds, Sara (Dutton Children's Books) 216

Ribas, Maria (Howard Morhaim Literary Agency) 326

Ribar, Lindsay (Sanford J. Greenbruger Associates, Inc.) 316

Rider, Anne (Houghton Mifflin Harcourt Books for Children) 224

Rissi, Anica Mrose (Katherine Tegen Books) 247

Robin, Rue (Writers House) 341

Robison, Mark W. (The Friend Magazine) 279

Rodeen, Paul (Rodeen Literary Management) 334

Rodgers, Lisa (Jabberwocky Literary Agency) 320

Rofé, Jennifer (Andrea Brown Literary Agency, Inc.) 298

Rose, Adrienne (Zumaya Publications, LLC) 252

Roth, Elana (Red Tree Literary Agency) 333

Rothenberg, Jessica (RazorBill) 241

Rothstein (Inkwell Management, LLC) 320

Rubinstein, Elizabeth Winick (Mcintosh & Otis, Inc.) 325

Rudolph, John (Dystel & Goderich Literary Management) 306

Russel, Curtis (P.S. Literary Agency) 330

Sagendorph, Jean (Mansion Street Literary Management) 325

Salky, Jesseca (HSG Agency) 318

Samoun, Abigail (Red Fox Literary) 332

Sanders, Liz (Liz Sanders Agency) 344

Sanders, Victoria (Victoria Sanders & Associates) 334

Sandford, John (Cricket Books) 214

Sandusky, Cathy (Fitzhenry & Whiteside Ltd.) 257

Saylor, David (Scholastic Press) 243

Schear, Adam (Defiore & Co.) 304

Schmalz, Wendy (Wendy Schmalz Agency) 334

Schneider, Deborah (Gelfman Schneider / ICM Partners) 314

Schneider, Eddie (Jabberwocky Literary Agency) 320

Schroder, Heather (Compass Talent) 300

Schulman, Susan (Susan Schulman Literary Agency) 334

Schwartz, Anne (Schwartz & Wade Books) 244

Schwartz, Hannah (Inkwell Management, LLC) 320

Schwartz, Tina P. (The Purcell Agency) 332

Sciuto, Sara (Foreword Literary) 310

Scott, Yolanda (Charlesbridge Publishing) 210

Searcy, John (DK Publishing) 216

Sedita, Francesco (Grosset & Dunlap Publisher) 222

Sedita, Francesco (Price Stern Sloan, Inc.) 239

Seidman, Yishai (Dunow, Carlson & Lerner Agency) 306

Seigel, Mark (First Second) 219

Seymour, Mary Sue (The Seymour Agency) 336

Shahbazian, Pouya (New Leaf Literary & Media, Inc) 328

Shank, Kevin (Nature Friend Magazine) 287

Shapiro, Sheryl (Annick Press, Ltd.) 253
Sherman, Rebecca (Writers House) 341
Sherman, Susan (Charlesbridge Publishing) 210
Sherry, Cynthia (Chicago Review Press) 211
Shoemaker, Victoria (The Spieler Agency) 336
Sibbald, Anne (Janklow & Nesbit Associates) 321
Silbersack, John (Trident Media Group) 339
Silen, Andrea (National Geographic Kids) 287
Simas, Rebecca (Corvisiero Literary Agency) 301
Simonsen, Reka (Atheneum Books for Young
    Readers) 205
Simpson, Fiona (Aladdin) 204
Sinclair, Stephanie (Transatlantic Literary Agency)
    338
Skouras, Lindsey (The Elaine P. English Literary
    Agency) 309
Skurnick, Lizzie (Lizzie Skurnick Books) 245
Smith, Danielle (Red Fox Literary) 332
Smith, David Hale (Inkwell Management, LLC) 320
Smoot, Madeline (Children's Brains Are Yummy
    Books) 211
Smythe, Lauren (Inkwell Management, LLC) 320
Solomon, Richard (Richard Solomon Artists
    Representative, LLC) 344
Soloway, Jeff (Facts on File, Inc) 218
Spellman-Silverman, Erica (Trident Media Group)
    339
Spieler, Joe (The Spieler Agency) 336
Spooner, Andrea (Little Brown and Co. Books for
    Young Readers) 229
Stafford, Susan (Horsepower) 282
Stanley, Cullen (Janklow & Nesbit Associates) 321
Staples, Debra (SynergeBooks) 247
Starkman, Jennifer (Transatlantic Literary Agency)
    338
Stearns, Michael (Upstart Crow Literary) 340
Steele, Emily (Medallion Media Group) 230
Steiner, Sarah (Concordia Publishing House) 213
Stephens, R. David (Tradewind Books) 262
Stevenson, Dina (Clarion Books) 213
Stimola, Rosemary B. (Stimola Literary Studio) 337
Stone, Annie (Harlequin Teen) 223
Stout, Rachel (Dystel & Goderich Literary
    Management) 306
Strauss, Rebecca (Defiore & Co.) 304
Strauss-Gabel, Julie (Dutton Children's Books) 216
Stringer, Marlene (The Stringer Literary Agency,
    LLC) 337
Strothman, Wendy (The Strothman Agency, LLC)
    337
Stumpf, Becca (Prospect Agency) 330
Sumner, Jay (National Geographic Kids) 287
Szabla, Liz (Feiwel and Friends) 219
Tao, Amy (Click) 274
Tasman, Alice (Jean V. Naggar Literary Agency, Inc.)
    326

Taylor, Suzanne (Gibbs Smith) 221
Taylor, Yuval (Chicago Review Press) 211
Tegen, Katherine (Katherine Tegen Books) 247
Teitelbaum, Maura (Folio Literary Management,
    LLC) 310
Testerman, Kate Schafer (KT Literary, LLC) 322
Thoma, Geri (Writers House) 341
Thomas, Karen (Serendipity Literary Agency, LLC)
    335
Thomas, Patrick (Milkweed Editions) 231
Thompson, Ruth (Illumination Arts) 225
Thornton, John (The Spieler Agency) 336
Tierney, Peggy (Tanglewood Books) 247
Toké, Arun (Skipping Stones: A Multicultural
    Literary Magazine) 290
Tompkins, Amy (Transatlantic Literary Agency) 338
Townsend, Suzie (New Leaf Literary & Media, Inc)
    328
Treimel, Scott (S©ott Treimel NY) 339
Tricarico, Joy Elton (Carol Bancroft & Friends) 342
Tripathi, Namrata (Dial Books for Young Readers)
    215
Troha, Steve (Folio Literary Management, LLC) 310
Tugeau, Nicole (T2 children's Illustrators) 345
Turner, Mary Jane (Kids Life Magazine) 285
Tyrell, Bob (Orca Book Publishers) 260
Unter, Jennifer (The Unter Agency) 340
Ursell, Geoffry (Coteau Books) 256
Usborne Publishing, 262
Van Beek, Emily (Folio Literary Management, LLC)
    310
Van Doren, Elizabeth, (Boyds Mills Press) 208
Van Hylckama Vlieg, Pam (Foreword Literary) 310
Van Romburgh, Danita (Tafelberg Publishers) 262
Van Straaten, Daniel (Christian Focus Publications)
    256
Venable, Colleen (First Second) 219
Vesel, Beth (Irene Goodman Literary Agency) 314
Vincente, Maria (P.S. Literary Agency) 330
V'Marie Misty (Rain Town Press) 240
Voges, Liza (Eden Street Literary) 308
Volpe, Joanna (New Leaf Literary & Media, Inc) 328
Von Borstel, Stefanie (Full Circle Literary, LLC) 312
Wade, Lee (Schwartz & Wade Books) 244
Walker, Marisa (American Cheerleader) 268
Wallace, Beth (Rainbow Rumpus) 289
Waller, Jessica D'Argenio (Girls' Life) 280
Walters, Gwen (Gwen Walters Artist Representative)
    345
Walters, Maureen (Curtis Brown, Ltd.) 301
Waniewski, Liz (Dial Books for Young Readers) 215
Ward, Lesley (Young Rider) 294
Warnock, Gordon (Foreword Literary) 310
Warren, Deborah (East/West Literary Agency, LLC.)
    308
Waryncia, Lou (Calliope) 272

Waryncia, Lou (Dig) 277

Waters, Mitchell (Curtis Brown, Ltd.) 301

Watters, Carly (P.S. Literary Agency) 330

Watterson, Jessica (Sandra Dijkstra Literary Agency) 305

Watts, Franklin (Children's Press/ Franklin Watts) 212

Weber, John (Serendipity Literary Agency, LLC) 335

Weimann, Frank (Folio Literary Management, LLC) 310

Weiss, Alison (Egmont USA) 218

Wells, Julia (Faber & Faber Ltd) 257

Wells, Roseanne (The Jennifer DeChiara Literary Agency) 304

Weltz, Jennifer (Jean V. Naggar Literary Agency, Inc.) 326

Wernick, Marcia Wells, Victoria (Wells Arms Literary) 340

Whalen, Kimberly (Trident Media Group) 339

Wheeler, Paige (Folio Literary Management, LLC) 310

White, Melissa Sarver (Folio Literary Management, LLC) 310

White, Trena (Transatlantic Literary Agency) 338

Whitman, Albert (Albet Whitman & Company) 250

Whitman, Stacy (Tu Books) 248

Wiegand, Erin (North Atlantic Books) 233

Wilks, Rick (Annick Press, Ltd.) 253

Wilson, Natashya (Harlequin Teen) 223

Wingertzahn, Jennifer (Clarion Books) 213

Winick, Eugene (Mcintosh & Otis, Inc.) 325

Winick, Ira (Mcintosh & Otis, Inc.) 325

Wiseman, Caryn (Andrea Brown Literary Agency, Inc.) 298

Wiseman, Paula (Paula Wiseman Books) 251

Witherspoon, Kimberly (Inkwell Management, LLC) 320

Witte, Michelle (Mansion Street Literary Management) 325

Wojtyla, Karen (Margaret K. McElderry Books) 230

Wolf, Kent (KT Literacy, LLC) 322

Wolf, Kirsten (Wolf Literary Services, LLC) 341

Wood, Dinah (Faber & Faber Ltd) 257

Woods, Monica (Inkwell Management, LLC) 320

Woolridge, Andrew (Orca Book Publishers) 260

Wray, Rhonda (Mreiwether Publishing LTD.) 231

Yoder, Carolyn (Calkins Creek) 208

Yung, Cecilia (G.P. Putnam's Sons Hardcover) 240

Zacker, Marietta (Nancy Gallt Literary Agency) 313

Zakris, Paul (GreenWillow Books) 222

Zapel, Ted (Mreiwether Publishing LTD.) 231

Zappy, Erica (Houghton Mifflin Harcourt Books for Children) 224

Zats, Laura (Red Sofa Literary) 327

Zefian, Anne (Atheneum Books for Young Readers) 205

Zollshan, Ronald (Kirchoff/Wohlberg, Inc.) 321

Zuckerman, Albert (Writers House) 341

AGE-LEVEL INDEX

MIDDLE READERS

ASK 269
Brilliant Star 271
Capstone Press 209
Grosset & Dunlap Publishers 222
Junior Baseball 284
Kathy Dawson Books 214
Kerf, The 285
Keys for Kids 285
Little, Brown and Co. Books for Young Readers 229
Milkweed Editions 231
Mitchell Lane Publishers, Inc. 232
National Geographic Children's Books 233
Owen, Richard C., Publishers, Inc. 235
PageSpring Publishing 235
Pelican Publishing Company 236
Rainbow Rumpus 289
Rain Town Press 234, 240
Rosen Publishing 242
Schwartz & Wade Books 244
Stone Soup 293
Tanglewood Books 247
Tu Books 248
URJ Press 249

PICTURE BOOKS

Anaphora Literary Press 204
Atheneum Books for Young Readers 205
Babybug 269
Bailiwick Press 206
Candlewick Press 209
Capstone Press 209
Children's Brains are Yummy (CBAY) Books 211
Dial Books for Young Readers 215

Grosset & Dunlap Publishers 222
Gryphon House, Inc. 222
JourneyForth 225
McElderry Books, Margaret K. 230
Mitchell Lane Publishers, Inc. 232
National Geographic Children's Books 233
Nature Friend Magazine 287
Owen, Richard C., Publishers, Inc. 235
Pauline Books & Media 235
Paulist Press 236
Piñata Books 238
Puffin Books 239
Renaissance House 241
Schwartz & Wade Books 244
Tanglewood Books 247
URJ Press 249

YOUNG ADULT

Anaphora Literary Press 204
ASK 269
Atheneum Books for Young Readers 205
Bailiwick Press 206
Candlewick Press 209
ChemMatters 274
Children's Brains are Yummy (CBAY) Books 211
Dial Books for Young Readers 215
Harlequin Teen 223
JourneyForth 225
Junior Baseball 284
Kathy Dawson Books 214
Kerf, The 285
Lizzie Skurnick Books 245
McElderry Books, Margaret K. 230
PageSpring Publishing 235

Pauline Books & Media 235
Paulist Press 236
Pelican Publishing Company 236
Piñata Books 238
POISONED PENCIL, THE 239
Puffin Books 239
Rainbow Rumpus 289
Rain Town Press 234, 240
Renaissance House 241
Tu Books 248

YOUNG READERS
Anaphora Literary Press 204
Atheneum Books for Young Readers 205
Bailiwick Press 206
Candlewick Press 209
Capstone Press 209
Children's Brains are Yummy (CBAY) Books 211
Davey and Goliath's Devotions 276
Dial Books for Young Readers 215
Grosset & Dunlap Publishers 222

Jack and Jill 284
JourneyForth 225
Junior Baseball 284
Kerf, The 285
Keys for Kids 285
Little, Brown and Co. Books for Young Readers 229
McElderry Books, Margaret K. 230
National Geographic Children's Books 233
Nature Friend Magazine 287
Pauline Books & Media 235
Paulist Press 236
Piñata Books 238
Puffin Books 239
Renaissance House 241
Rosen Publishing 242
Schwartz & Wade Books 244
Stone Soup 293
Tanglewood Books 247
Tu Books 248
URJ Press 249

PHOTOGRAPHY INDEX

Abbeville Family, 204
Aladdin, 204
Amulet Books, 204
Balzer & Bray, 206
Behrman House Inc. 206
Calkins Creek, 208
Chicago Review Press, 211
Children's Brains Are Yummy Books, 211
Christian Focus Publications, 256
Creative Company, 214
David Fickling Books, 257
Disney Hyperion Books for Children, 215
Edupress, Inc. 217
Fitzhenry & Whiteside Ltd. 257
Five Star Publications, Inc. 219
Frances Lincoln Children's Books, 258
Free Spirit Publishing, Inc. 220
Fulcrum Publishing, 221
Gryphon House Inc. 222
Lee & Low Books, 228
Little Brown and Co. Books for Young Readers, 229
Mitchell Lane Publishers, Inc. 232
Piano Press, 237
Puffin Books, 239
Rain Town Press, 240
Random House Children's Books, 260
Seedling Continental Press, 244
Skinner House Books, 245
Sterling Publishing Co., Inc. 246
Tilbury House, 247
Tyndale House Publishers, Inc. 249
URJ Press, 249
Usborne Publishing, 262
Weigl Publishers Inc. 249

Whitecap Books, Ltd. 263
White Mane Kids, 250
Williamson Books, 250
Wordsong, 251
World Book, Inc. 252

MAGAZINES
Advocate, PKA's Publication, 267
American Careers, 267
American Cheerleader, 268
Ask, 269
Babybug, 269
Boys' Life, 270
Boys' Quest, 270
Brilliant Star, 271
Cadet Quest Magazine, 272
Calliope, 272
Catholic Forester, 273
Chemmaters, 274
Cicada Magazine, 274
Cobblestone, 275
Dig, 277
Dig Magazine, 277
Dramatics Magazine, 277
Faces, 278
FCA Magazine, 279
Fun For Kidz, 279
Girls' Life, 280
Green Teacher, 280
Highlights for Children, 281
Hopscotch, 282
Horsepower, 282
Hunger Mountain, 283
Insight, 283

Junior Baseball, 284
National Geographic Kids, 287
Nature Friend Magazine, 287
New Moon Girls, 288
Pockets, 288
Seventeen Magazine, 289

Shine Brightly, 290
Skipping Stones: A Multicultural Magazine, 290
Sparkle, 291
Spider, 292
TC Magazine (Teenage Christian), 293
Young Rider, 294

ILLUSTRATION INDEX

Abbeville Family, 204
Abrams Books for Young Readers, 204
Aladdin, 204
Amulet Books, 204
Arbordale Publishing, 205
Azro Press, 205
Ballwick Press, 206
Balzer & Bray, 206
Behrman House Inc. 206
Boyd Mills Press, 208
Calkins Creek, 208
Candlewick Press, 209
Capstone Press, 209
Chicago Review Press, 211
Child's Play (International) Ltd. 256
Children's Brains Are Yummy Books, 211
Christian Focus Publications, 256
Chronicle Books for Children, 212
Clarion Books, 213
Concordia Publishing House, 213
David Fickling Books, 257
Dial Books for Young Readers, 215
Disney Hyperion Books for Children, 215
Edupress, Inc. 217
Eerdmans Books for Young Readers, 217
Egmont USA, 218
Facts on File, Inc. 218
Farrar, Straus & Giroux for young Readers 219
Fitzhenry & Whiteside Ltd. 257
Five Star Publications, Inc 219
Frances Lincoln Children's Books, 258
Free Spirit Publishing, Inc. 220
Freestone/PeachTree, Jr. 220
Gibbs Smith, 221

David R. Godine, Publisher, 221
Gryphon House, Inc. 222
Holiday House, Inc. 224
Impact Publishers, Inc. 225
JourneyForth, 225
Kamehameha Publishing, 226
Kids Can Press, 259
Lee & Low Books, 228
Little Brown and Co. Books for Young Readers, 229
Little Tiger Press, 259
Magination Press, 229
Meriwether Publishing Ltd. 231
Mitchell Lane Publishers, Inc. 232
Onstage Publishing, 233
Orca Book Publishers, 260
Random House Children's Books, 260
Richard C. Owen Publishers, Inc. 235
Pauline Books & Media, 235
Pelican Publishing Company, 236
Philomel Books, 237
Piano Press, 237
Piccadilly Press, 260
Piñata Books, 238
Pineapple Press, Inc. 238
Puffin Books, 239
Rainbow Publishers, 240
Rain Town Press, 240
Renaissance House, 241
Ronsdale Press, 261
Sasquatch Books, 242
Scholastic Library Publishing, 243
Scholastic Press, 243
Seedling Continental Press, 244
Simon & Schuster Books for Young Readers, 244

Skinner House Books, 245
Spinner Books, 245
Sterling Publishing Co., Inc. 246
Tafelberg Publishers, 262
Tanglewood Books, 247
Tilbury House, 247
Thistledown Press Ltd. 262
Tradewind Books, 262
Tu Books, 248
Tyndale House Publishers, Inc. 249
URJ Press, 249
Viking Children's Books, 249
Weigl Publishers Inc.) 249
Whitecap Books, Ltd. 263
White Mane Kids, 250
Williamson Books, 250
Paula Wiseman Books, 251
Wordsong, 251
World Book, Inc. 252

MAGAZINES

Advocate, PKA's Publication, 267
American Cheerleader, 268
Appleseeds, 268
Aquila, 268
Ask, 269
Babybug, 269
Boys' Life, 270
Boys' Quest, 270
Bread for God's Children, 271
Brilliant Star, 271

Cadet Quest Magazine, 272
Catholic Forester, 273
Chemmaters, 274
Cicada Magazine, 274
Click, 274
Cobblestone, 275
Collegexpress Magazine, 276
Cricket, 276
Dig, 277
Dramatics Magazine, 277
Faces, 278
The Friend Magazine, 279
Fun For Kidz, 279
Green Teacher, 280
Hopscotch, 282
Horsepower, 282
Jack and Jill, 284
Ladybug, 285
Leading Edge, 286
Muse, 287
New Moon Girls, 288
Rainbow Rumpus, 289
Seventeen Magazine, 289
Shine Brightly, 290
Skipping Stones: A Multicultural Magazine, 290
Sparkle, 291
Spider, 292
TC Magazine (Teenage Christian), 293

Young Rider, 294

GENERAL INDEX

Abbeville Family 204
Abrams Books for Young Readers 204
A+B Works 297
Adams Literary 297
Addams Children's Book Awards, Jane 380
Advocate, PKA's Publication 267
Aladdin 204
Alaska Writers Conference 356
Alcuin Citation Award 380
America & Me Essay Contest 380
American Alliance for Theatre & Education 348
American Association of University Women Award in
    Juvenile Literature 380
American Careers 267
American Cheerleader 268
American Society of Journalists and Authors 348
Américas Award 380
Amulet Books 204
Anaphora Literary Press 204
Andersen Award, Hans Christian 380
Annick Press, Ltd. 255
AppleSeeds 268
Aquila 268
Arbordale Publishing 205
Arizona Authors Association 348
ASK 269
Aspen Summer Words Literary Festival & Writing
    Retreat 356
Atheneum Books for Young Readers 205
Atlanta Writers Conference 356
Atlantic Writing Competition for Unpublished
    Manuscripts 381
Australasian Journal of Early Childhood 269
Authors Guild, Inc., The 348

Azro Press 205
Babybug 269
Bailiwick Press 206
Baillie Picture Book Award, Marilyn 381
Baltimore Writers' Conference 356
Balzer & Bray 206
Bancroft, Carol & Friends 342
Bantam Books 206
Batchelder Award, Mildred L. 381
Bay to Ocean Writers' Conference 356
Beatty Award, John and Patricia 381
Behrman House Inc. 206
Bender Literary Agency, Faye 297
Berkley Books 207
Bethany House Publishers 207
Big Sur Writing Workshop 356
Bilson Award for Historical Fiction for Young People,
    The Geoffrey 381
Black Award, The Irma S. and James H. 382
Bloomsbury Children's Books 207
Books-in-Progress Conference 357
Bookstop Literary Agency 297
Borealis Press, Ltd. 255
Boston Globe-Horn Book Awards 382
Boyds Mills Press 208
Boys' Life 270
Boys' Quest 270
Bradford Literary Agency 298
Bread for God's Children 271
Bread Loaf Writers' Conference 357
Bright Ring Publishing, Inc. 208
Brilliant Star 271
Brimer Award, Ann Connor 382
Brown Literary Agency, Inc., Andrea 298

Brown, Ltd., Curtis 301
Brucedale Press, The 255
Buckeye Children's Book Award 382
Buster Books 255
Byron Bay Writers Festival 357
Cadet Quest Magazine 272
Caldecott Medal, Randolph 382
California Young Playwrights Contest 382
Calkins Creek 208
Calliope 272
Calliope Fiction Contest 383
Cameron & Associates, Kimberley 300
Canadian Short Story Competition 383
Canadian Society of Children's Authors, Illustrators
    and Performers (CANSCAIP) 349
Candlewick Press 209
Cape Cod Writers Center Annual Conference 357
Capon Springs Writers' Workshop 357
Capstone Press 209
Carolrhoda Books, Inc. 209
Carroll Society of North America, Lewis 349
Cartwheel Books 210
Carus Publishing Company 273
Cascade Writing Contest & Awards 383
Catholic Forester 273
Cedar Fort, Inc. 210
Celebration of Southern Literature 357
Charlesbridge Publishing 210
ChemMatters 274
Chicago Review Press 211
Chicago Writers Conference 358
Children's Africana Book Award 384
Children's Book Guild Award for Nonfiction 384
Children's Brains are Yummy (CBAY) Books 211
Children's Press/Franklin Watts 212
Children's Writer Writing Contests 384
Child's Play (International) Ltd. 256
Child Welfare League Of America 212
Christian Book Awards 384
Christian Focus Publications 256
Chronicle Books for Children 212
Cicada Magazine 274
City of Vancouver Book Award, The 384
Clarion Books 213
Clarion West Writers Workshop 358
Clarksville Writers Conference 358
Click 274
Cobblestone 275
CollegeXpress Magazine 276
Colorado Book Awards 384
Compass Talent 300
Concordia Publishing House 213
Conference for Writers & Illustrators of Children's
    Books 359
Congdon Associates Inc., Don 300
Cornell & McCarthy LLC 342

Corvisiero Literary Agency 301
Coteau Books 256
Craigmore Creations 213
Creative Company 214
Crested Butte Writers Conference 359
Cricket 276
Cricket Books 214
Cricket League 385
CWW Annual Wisconsin Writers Awards 385
D4EO Literary Agency 302
Davey and Goliath's Devotions 276
Dawson Associates, Liza 303
DeChiara Literary Agency, The Jennifer 304
DeFiore & Co. 304
Delacorte Press 214
Detroit Working Writers Annual Writers Conference
    359
Dial Books for Young Readers 215
Dig 277
Dig Magazine 277
Dijkstra Literary Agency, Sandra 305
Disney Hyperion Books for Children 215
Diversion Press 215
DK Publishing 216
DNA Press and Nartea Publishing 216
Dramatics Magazine 277
Dundurn Press, Ltd. 257
Dunham Literary, Inc. 305
Dunow, Carlson, & Lerner Agency 306
Dutton Children's Books 216
Dystel & Goderich Literary Management 306
Eakin Press 216
East/West Literary Agency, LLC 308
Eden Street Literary 308
Educational Design Services LLC 308
Edupress, Inc. 217
Edwards Award, Margaret A. 385
Eerdmans Books for Young Readers 217
Egmont USA 218
Ellenberg Literary Agency, Ethan 309
Enete Enterprises 218
English Literary Agency, The Elaine P. 309
ERB's New Voice in YA 385
Faber & Faber Ltd 257
Faces 278
Facts On File, Inc. 218
Fairy Tale Castle Art Contest 386
Fairy Tale Fiction Contest 386
Farrar, Straus & Giroux for Young Readers 219
FCA Magazine 279
Feiwel and Friends 219
Fendrich Memorial Playwriting Contest, Shubert
    386
Fickling Books, David 257
First Edition Design Publishing 219
First Second 219

Fisher Children's Book Award, Dorothy Canfield 386
Fitzhenry & Whiteside Ltd. 257
Five Star Publications, Inc. 219
Flannery Literary 310
Flathead River Writers Conference 359
Fleck Award for Canadian Children's Nonfiction, The Norma 386
Flicker Tale Children's Book Award 387
Florida Freelance Writers Association 349
Flux 220
Folio Literary Management, LLC 310
Foreword Literary 310
Foundry Literary + Media 311
Frances Lincoln Children's Books 258
Franklin Watts 258
Freeman Memorial Grant-In-Aid, Don 387
Free Spirit Publishing, Inc. 220
Freestone/Peachtree, Jr. 220
Friend Magazine, The 279
Fulcrum Publishing 221
Full Circle Literary, LLC 312
Fun for Kidz 279
Gallt Literary Agency, Nancy 313
Geisel Award, Theodor Seuss 387
Gelfman Schneider Literary Agents, Inc. 314
Gibbon Illustrator's Award, Amelia Frances Howard 387
Gibbs Smith 221
Girls' Life 280
Godine, Publisher, David R. 221
Goldblatt Literary LLC, Barry 314
Golden Books for Young Readers Group 221
Golden Kite Awards 387
Goodman Literary Agency, Irene 314
Governor General's Literary Award for Children's Literature 388
Governor General's Literary Awards 388
Grad Literary Agency, Inc., Doug 315
Graphic Artists Guild 349
Great Lakes Writers Festival 360
Greenburger Associates, Inc., Sanford J. 316
Greenhaven Press 222
Greenhouse Literary Agency, The 316
Green Literary Agency, LLC, Kathryn 317
Green Mountain Writers Conference 360
Green Teacher 280
Greenwillow Books 222
Grinberg Literary Agency, Jill 318
Grosset & Dunlap Publishers 222
Groundwood Books 258
Gryphon House, Inc. 222
Guide 280
Gulf Coast Writers Conference 360
Hackney Literary Awards 388
Hall Awards for Youth Theatre, The Marilyn 388
Hampton Roads Writers Conference 360

Harlequin Teen 223
HarperCollins Children's Books/HarperCollins Publishers 223
HarperTeen 223
Heacock Hill Literary Agency, Inc. 318
Hedgebrook 361
Herman Agency3 318
Highlights for Children 281
Highlights for Children Fiction Contest 389
Holiday House, Inc. 224
Holinshead Visiting Scholars Fellowship, Marilyn 389
Hopscotch 282
Horror Writers Association 349
Horsepower 282
Houghton Mifflin Harcourt Books for Children 224
Houston Writers Guild Conference 361
Howe/Boston Authors Award, The Julia Ward 389
How to Be Published Workshops 361
HRC Showcase Theatre Playwriting Contest 389
HSG Agency 318
Hunger Mountain 283
Hurst Children's Book Prize, Carol Otis 389
ICM Partners 320
Ideals Children's Books and Candycane Press 224
Ideals Publications, Inc. 224
Illumination Arts 225
Impact Publishers, Inc. 225
InkWell Management, LLC 320
Insight 283
Insight Writing Contest 390
International Reading Association 350
International Reading Association Children's and Young Adults Book Awards 390
International Women's Writing Guild 350
IRA Short Story Award 390
Jabberwocky Literary Agency 320
Jack and Jill 284
James River Writers Conference 361
Janklow & Nesbit Associates 321
Jewish Lights Publishing 225
Jill Corcoran Literary Agency 301
JourneyForth 225
Journey Into the Imagination 361
Junior Baseball 284
Juvenile Adventure Fiction Contest 390
Kachemak Bay Writers Conference 362
Kamehameha Publishing 226
Kane/Miller Book Publishers 226
Kar-Ben Publishing 227
Katherine Tegen Books 247
Kathy Dawson Books 214
Keats/Kerlan Memorial Fellowship, Ezra Jack 390
Keats New Writer and New Illustrator Awards, The Ezra Jack 391
Kentucky Bluegrass Award 391

Kentucky Writers Conference 362
Kenyon Review Writers Workshop 362
Kerf, The 285
Keys for Kids 285
Kids Can Press 259
Kids Life Magazine 285
Kindling Words East 362
King Book Awards, Coretta Scott 391
Kirchoff/Wohlberg, Inc. 321
Kouts, Literary Agent, Barbara S. 322
Kregel Publications 227
KT Literary, LLC 322
Ladybug 285
LaJolla Writers Conference 363
Las Vegas Writers Conference 363
Leading Edge 286
League of Canadian Poets 350
League of Utah Writers Contest 391
Ledge Hill Publishing 227
Lee & Low Books 228
Legacy Press 228
Levine Books, Arthur A. 228
Lippincott Massie McQuilkin 322
Literary Managers and Dramaturgs of the Americas 350
Little, Brown and Co. Books for Young Readers 229
Little Tiger Press 259
Lizzie Skurnick Books 245
Louisville Review, The 286
Lowenstein Associates Inc. 324
Lucky Marble Books 229
Lyrical Passion Poetry E-Zine 286
Maccoby Literary Agency, Gina 324
Magination Press 229
Manor House Publishing, Inc. 259
Mansion Street Literary Management 325
Martin Sisters Publishing, LLC 230
Master Books 230
MB Artists 344
McCarthy Literary Agency, Sean 325
McElderry Books, Margaret K. 230
McIntosh & Otis, Inc. 325
McLaren Memorial Comedy Play Writing Competition 391
Medallion Media Group 230
Mendocino Coast Writers Conference 363
Meriwether Publishing Ltd. 231
Metcalf Award for Children's Literature, The Vicky 391
Midwest Writers Workshop 364
Milkweed Editions 231
Milkweed National Fiction Prize 392
Millbrook Press, The 232
Minnesota Book Awards 392
Missouri Writers' Guild Conference 364
Mitchell Lane Publishers, Inc. 232

Montrose Christian Writers' Conference 364
Moody Publishers 232
Moore Community Workshops, Jenny McKean 364
Morhaim Literary Agency, Howard 326
Moveable Type Management 326
Municipal Chapter of Toronto IODE Book Award 392
Murphy Literary Agency, Erin 326
Muse 287
Muse and the Marketplace 364
Naggar Literary Agency, Inc., Jean V. 326
Napa Valley Writers' Conference 365
National Book Awards 392
National Geographic Children's Books 233
National Geographic Kids 287
National League of American Pen Women, The 351
National Outdoor Book Awards 392
National Peace Essay Contest 392
National Writers Association 351
National Writers Association Nonfiction Contest 393
National Writers Association Short Story Contest 393
National Writers Union 351
Nature Friend Magazine 287
Nelson Literary Agency 328
NETWO Writers Conference 365
Newbery Medal, John 393
New England Book Awards 394
New Leaf Literary & Media, Inc. 328
New Moon Girls 288
New Voices Award 394
Nimrod Annual Writers' Workshop 365
Nomad Press 233
North American International Auto Show High School Poster Contest 394
North Atlantic Books 233
North Carolina Writers' Network Fall Conference 365
Northern California Book Awards 394
Northern Colorado Writers Conference 366
Ohioana Book Awards 394
Oklahoma Book Awards 395
Oklahoma Writers' Federation, Inc. Annual Conference 366
Once Upon a World Children's Book Award 395
OnStage Publishing 233
Orbis Pictus Award for Outstanding Nonfiction for Children 395
Orca Book Publishers 260
Orchard Books 234
Oregon Book Awards 395
Oregon Christian Writers Summer Conference 366
Oregon Literary Fellowships 395
Original Art, The 396
Ott Award for Outstanding Contribution to Children's Literature, Helen Keating 396

Our Sunday Visitor, Inc. 234
Owen, Richard C., Publishers, Inc. 235
Ozark Creative Writers, Inc. Conference 367
Pacific Coast Children's Writers Whole-Novel
    Workshop 367
Pacific Northwest Writers Assn. Summer Writer's
    Conference 367
PageSpring Publishing 235
Park Literary Group, LLC 328
Paterson Prize for Books for Young People 396
Paterson Prize for Young Adult and Children's
    Writing, The Katherine 396
Pauline Books & Media 235
Paulist Press 236
Peace Hill Press 236
Peachtree Children's Books 236
Pelican Publishing Company 236
PEN American Center 351
Pennsylvania Young Readers' Choice Awards
    Program 396
Pennwriters Conference 367
PEN/Phyllis Naylor Working Writer Fellowship 397
Pfeffer Content, Rubin 329
Philadelphia Writers' Conference 367
Philomel Books 237
Piano Press 237
Piccadilly Press 260
Pikes Peak Writers Conference 368
Piñata Books 238
Pineapple Press, Inc. 238
Pippin Properties, Inc. 330
Please Touch Museum Book Award 397
PNWA Literary Contest 397
Pockets 288
POCKETS Fiction-Writing Contest 397
Poe Award, Edgar Allan 397
POISONED PENCIL, THE 239
Price Stern Sloan, Inc. 239
Printz Award, Michael L. 397
Prospect Agency 330
P.S Literary Agency 330
Puffin Books 239
Puppeteers of America, Inc. 352
Purcell Agency, The 332
Purple Dragonfly Book Awards 398
PUSH 239
Putnam's Sons Hardcover, GP 240
Quill and Scroll International Writing and Photo
    Contest, and Blogging Competition 398
Rainbow Publishers 240
Rainbow Rumpus 289
Raincoast Book Distribution, Ltd. 260
Rain Town Press 234, 240
Random House Children's Books 260
Ransom Publishing 261
Razorbill 241

RED FOX LITERARY 332
red lights 289
Red Sofa Literary 332
Red Tree Literary Agency 333
Regal Literary Agency 333
Regina Book Award 398
Renaissance House 241
Ripple Grove Press 241
Rivera Mexican American Children's Book Award,
    Tomás 399
Roaring Brook Press 241
Rocky Mountain Book Award 399
Rocky Mountain Fiction Writers Colorado Gold 368
Rodeen Literary Management 334
Ronsdale Press 261
Rosen Publishing 242
Royal Dragonfly Book Awards 399
Salt Cay Writers Retreat 368
Sanders & Associates, Victoria 334
Sanders, Liz, Agency 344
San Diego State University Writers' Conference 368
San Francisco Writers Conference 369
Saskatchewan Children's Literature Award 399
Saskatchewan Festival of Words 369
Saskatchewan First Book Award 399
Sasquatch Books 242
Scarletta Press 243
SCBWI--Canada East 369
SCBWI Colorado/Wyoming (Rocky Mountain);
    Events 369
SCBWI Magazine Merit Awards 399
SCBWI--Midatlantic; Annual Fall Conference 369
SCBWI Winter Conference on Writing and
    Illustrating for Children 370
SCBWI Work-in-Progress Grants 400
Schmalz Agency, Wendy 334
Scholastic Library Publishing 243
Scholastic Press 243
School for Writers Fall Workshop, The 370
School of The Arts at Rhinelander UW-Madison
    Continuing Studies 370
Schulman Literary Agency, Susan 334
Schwartz & Wade Books 244
Science-Fiction and Fantasy Writers of America,
    Inc. 352
Science Weekly 289
Second Story Press 262
Seedling Continental Press 244
Serendipity Literary Agency, LLC 335
Seventeen Magazine 289
Sewanee Writers' Conference 370
Seymour Agency, The 336
Shabo Award for Children's Picture Book Writers
    400
SHINE brightly 290
Simon & Schuster Books for Young Readers 244

Skinner House Books 245
Skipping Stones 290
Skipping Stones Book Awards 400
Skipping Stones Youth Honor Awards 400
Sleeping Bear Press 245
Snow Writing Contest, Kay 401
Society of Children's Book Writers and Illustrators
    (SCBWI) 353
Society of Children's Book Writers & Illustrators
    Annual Summer Conference on Writing and
    Illustrating for Children 371
Society of Illustrators 353
Society of Midland Authors 353
Society of Midland Authors Award 401
Society of Southwestern Authors 354
South Carolina Writers Workshop 371
South Coast Writers Conference 371
Southeastern Writers Association--Annual Writers
    Workshop 371
Southwest Writers 401
Southwest Writers Annual Contest 401
Space Coast Writers Guild Annual Conference 372
SPACE (Small Press and Alternative Comics Expo)
    372
Sparkle 291
Spider 292
Spieler Agency, The 336
Spinner Books 245
Squaw Valley Community of Writers 372
Standard Publishing 246
Sterling Publishing Co., Inc. 246
Stimola Literary Studio 337
Stone Soup 293
Storey Publishing 246
Story Weavers Conference 372
Stringer Literary Agency, LLC, The 337
Strothman Agency, LLC, The 337
Summer Writing Program 372
Surrey International Writers' Conference 373
SynergEbooks 247
Tafelberg Publishers 262
Talcott Notch Literary 338
Tanglewood Books 247
Taos Summer Writers' Conference 373
Taylor Book Award, Sydney 402
Taylor Manuscript Competition, Sydney 402
TC Magazine (Teenage Christian) 293
TD Canadian Children's Literature Award 402
Teen Haunted House Art Contest 402
Teen Mystery Fiction Contest 402
Texas Writing Retreat 373
Text & Academic Authors Association (TAA) 354
Theatre For Young Audiences/USA 354
Thistledown Press Ltd. 262
Thomas Junior Writers Authors Conference, Laura
    363

Thorogood Kids/Good Illustration 345
Tilbury House 247
TMCC Writers' Conference 373
Tor Books 248
Toronto Book Awards 403
Tradewind Books 262
Transatlantic Literary Agency 338
Treimel NY, S©ott 339
Trident Media Group 339
Tu Books 248
Turn the Page Publishing LLC 248
Turtle Magazine for Preschool Kids 293
Tyndale House Publishers, Inc. 249
UMKC Writing Conference 374
Unicorn Writers Conference 374
University of North Dakota Writers Conference 374
Unter Agency, The 340
Upstart Crow Literary 340
URJ Press 249
Usborne Publishing 263
UV-Madison Writers' Institute 374
Vegetarian Essay Contest 403
VFW Voice of Democracy 403
Viking Children's Books 249
Virginia Center for the Creative Arts 374
Volunteer Lawyers for the Arts 354
Walters, Gwen, Artist Representative 345
Weigl Educational Publishers, Ltd. 263
Weigl Publishers Inc. 249
Wells Arms Literary 340
Wernick & Pratt Agency 341
Western Heritage Awards 403
Western Reserve Writers & Freelance Conference
    375
Western Writers of America 403
Whidbey Island Writers' Conference 375
Whitecap Books, Ltd. 263
White Mane Kids 250
Whitman, Albert & Company 250
Wilder Medal, Laura Ingalls 404
WILLA Literary Award 404
Willamette Writers Conference 375
Williamson Books 250
Williams Young Adult Prose Prize Category, Rita 404
Winchester Writer's Conference, Festival and
    Bookfair, and In-Depth Writing Workshops 375
WindRiver Publishing, Inc. 251
Wisconsin Book Festival 376
Wiseman Books, Paula 251
Wolf Literary Services, LLC 341
Women Writers Winter Retreat 376
Words & Music 376
Wordsong 251
World Book, Inc. 252
Write A Story for Children Competition 404
Write Canada 376

Write Now 404

Writer's Digest Conferences 376

Writer's Digest Self-Published Book Awards 404

Writers-Editors Network Annual International Writing Competition 405

Writers Guild of Alberta Awards 405

Writers House 341

Writers' League of Texas Agents Conference 377

Writers' League of Texas Book Awards 405

Writers Weekend at the Beach 377

Writers' Workshop, The 377

Writing and Illustrating for Young Readers Conference 377

Writing Conference Writing Contests 405

Wyoming Writers Conference 378

Yearbook Excellence Contest 406

Young Adult Canadian Book Award 406

Young Rider 294

Youth Honor Award Program, The 406

Zornio Memorial Children's Theatre Playwriting Competition, Anna 406

Zumaya Publications, LLC 252